THE ICSA HEALTH SERVICE GOVERNANCE HANDBOOK

THE ICSA

HEALTH SERVICE GOVERNANCE HANDBOOK

Claire Lea

icsa
Trust through governance

First published 2015

ICSA Publishing
Saffron House
6–10 Kirby Street
London EC1N 8TS

Designed and typeset by Paul Barrett Book Production, Cambridge
Printed by Hobbs the Printers Ltd, Totten Hampshire

British Cataloguing in Publication Data
A catalogue record for this book is available from the British Library.

ISBN 978 1 860726514

Contents

Dedication

The new [Narnia] was a deeper country: every rock and flower and blade of grass looked like it meant more. I can't describe it any better than that: if you ever get there you will know what I mean. It was the unicorn who summed up what everyone was feeling. He stamped his right fore-hoof on the ground and neighed, and then cried:
"I have come home at last! This is my real country! I belong here."

The Last Battle, CS Lewis

Preface

This is the first edition of the ICSA Health Service Governance Handbook, which has been compiled to replace the ICSA Health Service Governance Study Text. The rationale behind this is to create a user-friendly publication for all those involved in the delivery of governance within the NHS, whether students or experienced practitioners. There have been numerous changes and updates in both legislation and guidance since the first study text was published in 201s; this serves to demonstrate the sheer pace of change both within the field of governance itself as well as within the NHS.

This pace of change, combined with the occasional duplication of regulatory requirements, results in a field of professional practice that requires both students and experienced practitioners to constantly add new compliance requirements to their checklists. However, there is some comfort in that the underlying principles remain constant – namely, ensuring that the appropriate checks and balances continue to be rigorous and adaptive, so those who have been entrusted with high levels of decision-making powers do so in the best interests of patients and the general public.

The debates that continue in the corporate sector following the shockwaves of the banking crisis of 2007–2009, the more recent governance scandals at the Co-operative Group and the shareholder spring of 2014 – which saw significant shareholder revolts over pay for senior executives – will continue to cast their shadow over health service governance. In addition, the tragedies of poor care at NHS trusts such as Mid Staffs and Morecambe Bay, and the failure of the authorities in Rotherham to act effectively against child sexual abuse, demonstrate more clearly than ever the impact of poor governance.

This context only serves to prove more powerfully than ever the vital role played by governance practitioners within the NHS. I hope that this handbook will help to empower and equip you in this critical role. By studying and debating the issues raised in this handbook, NHS bodies can move away from a checklist approach to governance and begin to embody good governance as 'the way we do things round here'.

Thank you to the ICSA who have supported the production of this work. The ICSA is the chartered membership and qualifying body for people working in governance, risk and compliance, including company secretaries. With over 120 years' experience of the skills, knowledge and experience required for governance professionals, the ICSA is the home of good governance!

Thank you also to the NHS Providers who have also supported the development of the Health Service Governance module and who have continued to work with me to ensure that this handbook is as accurate as it can be at the time of publication.

Thank you also to the many colleagues, both NHS and otherwise, who have shared their stories and experiences with me. Sometimes we may be tearing our hair out to encourage and foster best practice but it's great to know there are others out there who 'get it'.

Finally, thank you to my family. They are unbelievably patient about the long hours this work takes and on a day-to-day basis have to live with someone who loves systems and processes. Thank you!

Claire Lea
Director, Charis Consultants Limited
October 2014

Endorsements

GGI have always supported the ICSA Health Service Governance qualification and were instrumental in its establishment in 2006. At the time we were struggling with borrowed codes and financial models from industry but with this publication the programme has come of age truly reflecting public service values and demands. GGI fully endorse this guidance as an essential addition to good governance knowledge, thinking and practice.

Over the coming years the NHS must find some £20bn of additional expenditure to meet growing demand and expectations. To justify and account for this additional investment from government, users and staff we must demonstrate good governance focused on purpose, clarity of role and competence to deliver. Claire Lea and ICSA have done much here to support that requirement; the rest is up to those of us who sit on Boards or support those who do.

Dr John Bullivant, Chair
Good Governance Institute

Good governance provides ambitious, effective, prudent direction that helps deliver success over time. In delivering good corporate governance boards depend on the skills, knowledge and practical know-how of company secretaries. In the NHS chairs, chief executives and board directors, particularly non-executive directors, are finding an increasing need to turn individuals within their own organisation who are able to provide reliable corporate governance advice and to provide significant personal support in implementing it. That is most often the company secretary, so it is vital that company secretaries not only have the skills and knowledge required to deliver, but also access to up to date information on the nuts and bolts of corporate governance.

The ICSA Health Service Governance Handbook provides comprehensive guidance on governance in the NHS. It combines clarity and nuance and provides accurate coverage of the many complexities of today's NHS. Clearly it will be a significant source text those seeking to become qualified company secretaries, but just as importantly it is also a first rate point of reference for all of us who work in the field of governance in the NHS. We are delighted to endorse it.

NHS Providers

Acronyms and abbreviations

ABI	Association of British Insurers
ACCA	Association of Chartered Certified Accountants
AEF	Assurance and Escalation Framework
AfC	Agenda for Change
AGM	annual general meeting
AGS	annual governance statement
AHA	area health authority
ALB	arm's-length body
AO	accounting officer/accountable officer
APR	annual plan review
BAF	board assurance framework
C&AG	Comptroller and Auditor General
CACG	Commonwealth Association for Corporate Governance
CBC	Community Based Care organisation
CCA	Civil Contingencies Act 2004
CEO	Chief executive officer
CCG	Clinical Commissioning Group
CCG ARM	Clinical Commissioning Group Annual Reporting Manual
CFO	chief financial officer
CFSMS	Counter Fraud and Security Management Service – now called NHS Protect
CHAI	Commission for Healthcare Audit and Inspection
CHI	Commission for Health Improvement
CIMA	Chartered Institute of Management Accountants
CIP	cost improvement plan
CIPFA	Chartered Institute of Public Finance and Accountancy
CMA	Competitions and Markets Authority
COSO	committee of Sponsoring Organizations
CoSRR	continuity of services risk rating
CQC	Care Quality Commission
CQUINs	Commissioning for Quality Improvement
CRO	chief risk officer
CRS	commissioner requested services
CSR	corporate social responsibility
CSU	commissioning support unit
DCLG	Department for Communities and Local Government
DDD	Director of Delivery & Development

DoF	director of finance
DH	Department of Health
DHA	district health authority
DTR	Disclosure and Transparency Rules
ED	executive director
EIR	Environmental Information Regulation
ENDPB	executive non-departmental public body
EPLO	Emergency Planning Liaison Officer
ERRA	Enterprise and Regulatory Reform Act 2013
EU	European Union
FCA	Financial Conduct Authority
FOIA	Freedom of Information Act
FPC	family practitioner committee
FRAB	Financial Reporting Advisory Board
FRC	Financial Reporting Council
FReM	Financial Reporting Manual
FT	foundation trust
FT ARM	Foundation Trust Annual Reporting Manual
FTC	foundation trust consolidation schedule
FTGA	Foundation Trust Governors Association
FTN	NHS Providers
GGI	Good Governance Institute
GMC	General Medical Council
GMS	general medical services
GP	general practitioner
GRR	governance risk rating
HEE	Health Education England
HFEA	Human Fertilisation and Embryology Authority
HFMA	Heathcare Financial Management Association
HMRC	Her Majesty's Revenue and Customs
HOSC	Health Oversight and Scrutiny Committee
HPA	Health Protection Agency
HRA	Health Research Authority
HRO	high reliability organisation
HSC	Health and Social Care
HSCA 2012	Health and Social Care Act 2012
HSE	Health and Safety Executive
IBE	Institute of Business Ethics
ICAEW	Institute of Chartered Accountants in England and Wales
ICGN	International Corporate Governance Network
IFAC	International Federation of Accountants
IIA	Chartered Institute of Internal Auditors
IIRC	International Integrated Reporting Council

IMCA	Independent Mental Advocate Service
JSNA	Joint Strategic Needs Assessment
JHWS	Joint Health and Wellbeing Strategy
KPI	key performance indicator
LINks	Local Involvement Networks
LLA	liability limitation agreement
MSFT	Mid Staffordshire NHS Foundation Trust
NAO	National Audit Office
NAPF	National Association of Pension Funds
NCVO	National Council of Voluntary Organisations
NDPBs	non-departmental public bodies
NED	non-executive director
NHS	National Health Service
NHSCB	NHS Commissioning Board
NHS FT ARM	NHS Foundation Trust Annual Reporting Manual
NHS TDA	NHS Trust Development Authority
NICE	National Institute of Clinical Excellence
NMC	Nursing and Midwifery Council
NSFs	National Service Frameworks
NYSE	New York Stock Exchange
OECD	Organisation for Economic Co-operation and Development
OF	Operating Framework
OPM	Office for Public Management
OSC	Overview and Scrutiny Committee
PCT	Primary Care Trust
PFI	Private Finance Initiative
PHE	Public Health England
PHSO	Parliamentary and Health Service Ombudsman
PIDA	Public Interest Disclosure Act
PPI	Patient and Public Involvement
PROMs	patient reported outcome measures
QIPP	Quality, Innovation, Productivity and Prevention
QGF	Quality Governance Framework
RAF	Risk Assessment Framework
RCGP	Royal College of General Practitioners
RHA	Regional Health Authority
SEC	Securities and Exchange Commission
SHAs	Strategic Health Authorities
SIC	Statement on Internal Control
SID	senior independent director
SLHT	South London Healthcare NHS Trust
SOCA	Serious Organised Crime Agency
Solace	Society of Local Authority Chief Executives

SOX	Sarbanes-Oxley Act
TITO	time in/time out sessions
TSA	Trust Special Administrator
TSR	total shareholder return
VFM	value for money
VSM	Very Senior Managers

PART ONE

The governance landscape

finitions and issues
governance

■ Defining governance

'Governance' refers to the way in which something is governed and to the function of governing. However, the term is so commonly used that it is often hard to define exactly what it means and its objectives. The governance of a country, for example, refers to the powers and actions of the legislative assembly, the executive government and the judiciary.

Governance is not an easy concept to understand. In the case of governing a country, it would be concerned with who has the power to rule and what the governors of the country should be trying to achieve. The government of a democratic country sets itself the objective of protecting its people and acting in their best interests, whatever these might be. Powers are shared between the legislative, executive and judiciary, but it is a matter of debate how these powers should be shared and exercised. In the UK, for example, there is healthy political debate about the respective powers of Parliament, the Prime Minister and the Cabinet, the UK law courts, and the powers of the government bodies and courts of the EU. In the case of governing an organisation, NHS or otherwise, governance would be concerned with how powers are shared and exercised by the directors, and how the holders of power in the organisation should be held accountable for what they do.

For the purposes of this handbook, specific definitions have been used to offer clarity about what is being referred to. These definitions may be used interchangeably in practice, but adhering to these definitions within the handbook will enable the reader to distinguish between different landscapes in which governance needs to be understood. The defined meanings are as follows.

- **Governance:** the concepts of governance which are generally applicable regardless of landscape.
- **Corporate governance:** the governance applied to the corporate commercial business world, including public and private companies.
- **Health service governance:** the governance applied to NHS organisations.
- **Public sector governance:** the governance applied across the wider public sector including the NHS.

Health service governance operates on two levels:

1. the manner in which the government department (DH) is held to account by the electorate for the way in which it manages the provision of healthcare
2. the way in which individual parts of the NHS are governed and to what purpose.

This handbook will focus on the aspects of health service governance concerned with the practices and procedures for governing the individual parts of the NHS. Such practices seek to ensure that these individual parts are run in such a way that they achieve their objectives and are in line with public sector values such as value for money (VFM) and providing universal and free healthcare benefits to all those in need.

Membership and the balance of power

Companies and NHS organisations alike are legal entities or 'legal persons' established according to statutory obligations such as the Companies Act or Health and Social Care Act legislation. As legal persons, they can enter into contracts and make business transactions. They can own assets and owe money to others, and they can sue and be sued in law. However, decisions about what the company or organisation should do are taken by individuals in the company or organisation's name. There is a gap, therefore, between the legal entity and its owners (members). This gap is 'bridged' by the individuals who act on the entity's behalf. Governance is the foundation of that 'bridge'.

- The citizens of a country, even in a democracy, have relatively few powers. Power is in the hands of the legislative (Parliament) and the executive (the government). Similarly, shareholders have relatively few powers, and these are restricted mainly to certain voting rights. Power is in the hands of the board of directors, or perhaps just one or two individual directors on the board.
- Just as a country has citizens, a company has members. The members of a company are its owners, the 'equity' shareholders. The membership of large companies changes constantly, as investors buy and sell the company's shares.
- For large companies, the main issue with corporate governance is the relationship between the board of directors and the shareholders, and the way in which the board exercises its powers. The relationship between the shareholders and the board can be described as a 'principal–agent' relationship. In some companies other stakeholders may have significant influence.
- For NHS organisations, the members are a wide and diverse range of stakeholders. Health service governance is concerned with how powers are shared and exercised by different groups to ensure that the objectives of health provision for the general public, the political direction being given by the DH, and other interest groups such as employees, suppliers and the local community are balanced and managed.

In health service governance, the idea of membership is more complex because of the range and diversity of stakeholders. Whilst a foundation trust (FT) will have a clear membership structure, the members are not, strictly speaking, the owners of the trust. Instead, they are the recipients of the health services provided, who might be seen as 'proxy shareholders' on behalf of the general public. Further complications arise as the FT is still required to consider the views of the community it serves, regardless of whether they are members, and is also required to consider the views of its other stakeholders such as employees, trade unions, local authorities, clinical commissioning groups, and NHS England.

Clinical commissioning groups (CCGs) also have a membership structure, comprising all of the general practices in their constituency. Even so, CCGs are also required to consider the wider views of its other stakeholders, including those organisations which provide the services they commission. For other parts of the NHS structure (e.g. non-FTs) there is no established membership structure but there is an equivalent variety of stakeholders. It is this variety of stakeholders and the different levels of influence that they are able to exercise within the NHS that makes health service governance an interesting and challenging subject.

The study of governance within the NHS is complicated by the overuse of the term 'governance'. The role of the governance practitioner or NHS company secretary is also made more complex (and potentially more interesting) by the way in which the term 'governance' is used so widely. In the NHS there is quality governance, information governance, governance risk ratings for FTs and board governance – to name just a few.

At times this handbook will refer to these other areas of governance to ensure that the breadth of the role of the NHS governance practitioner or company secretary is fully considered. Such references will specifically highlight the type of governance that is being referred to, e.g. quality governance.

The interests of stakeholders

Health service governance as set out by this handbook is defined as the process, practices and procedures by which power is shared and exercised by the board of directors (and the council of governors in FTs or governing body in a Clinical Commissioning Group), and how the holders of power in the organisation should be held accountable for what they do.

Guidelines and constraints in both the public and private sector include behaving in an ethical way and in compliance with laws and regulations. This framework of law, regulation and guidance puts in place boundaries for those who exercise this power and authority to run the organisation on behalf of stakeholders. These are the groups with an interest in how an organisation acts; they include the communities in which the organisation operates, customers, the DH, employees, the general public, patients, sector regulators and suppliers. The aim of health service governance should be to monitor and control management to ensure that it runs the organisation in the interests of these stakeholders.

Health service governance can therefore be defined as a process for monitoring and control to ensure that management runs the organisation in the interests of stakeholders. The numerous stakeholders and the variety of their roles will be explored in Chapter 2.

Corporate comparisons

Companies in the private sector – which are mostly governed in accordance with the interests of the shareholders – provide a useful comparison with healthcare organisations. Primarily, the objective of a company in the private sector is maximising the wealth of its owners (the shareholders), subject to various guidelines and constraints. But it can be argued that they should also be governed in the interests of all its major stakeholders, not just its owners. This argument is particularly relevant to large companies whose activities have a big impact on the economy and society where regard must be given to other groups or individuals with an interest in what the company does.

Principles of corporate governance are, therefore, based on the view that a company should be governed in the interests of the shareholders, and possibly also in the interests of other stakeholder groups. The board ought to use its powers in an appropriate and responsible way, and should be accountable in some ways to the shareholders (and perhaps other stakeholders).

The work of Lord Hutton and the Ownership Commission, set out in its March 2012 *Report on Plurality, Stewardship and Engagement*, raises interesting questions about the responsibilities of companies to consider the interests of a wider group of stakeholders. The Commission was established following the recent banking crisis and the expenses scandal in government where the balancing of interests has proven to be a key factor. Another recent example was that of the successful takeover of Cadbury by Kraft.

CASE STUDY: Kraft

Kraft, the world's second-largest food maker with annual revenues of $42 billion, appealed directly to Cadbury's shareholders after the Cadbury's board rejected its proposal. Kraft stressed it was committed to working towards a recommended transaction and to maintaining a constructive dialogue. Cadbury put out a statement, confirming it had received an 'unsolicited' proposal from Kraft that was conditional on financing and due diligence.

'The board of Cadbury reviewed the proposal with its advisers and rejected it,' it said. 'The board is confident in Cadbury's standalone strategy and growth prospects as a result of its strong brands, unique category and geographic scope and the continued successful delivery of its Vision into Action plan. The board believes that the proposal fundamentally undervalues the group and its prospects.'

Shareholder vs. Stakeholder interests

> However, the final offer proved to be too attractive for the shareholders and the board was required to act in their best interests even though it did not believe the takeover was in the interests of a wider group of stakeholders.

The relationship between the board of directors and its variety of stakeholders, and the way in which the board exercises its powers, are significant distinctions between corporate governance and health service governance. Health service governance principles are based on the view that the organisation should be governed in such a way that balances the requirements of a wide variety of stakeholders. The board is required to use its powers in an appropriate and responsible way, and is accountable in different ways to each of the stakeholders.

Why is governance important?

Regardless of sector, governance is a key issue as it regulates the power and decision-making of a small group of people who have been given a large responsibility for the stewardship of the assets of a third party.

In the context of the NHS, this stewardship involves both public assets and healthcare services. The outcome of decisions really can be a matter of life and death, as well as a matter of severe financial loss. As a result, NHS organisations have clear aims that have been set out in the NHS Constitution. They should be governed in such a way that they move towards the achievement of these aims.

Although NHS organisations and companies exist as legal persons, in reality each organisation is the organised, collective effort of many different individuals. They are controlled by boards of directors or governing bodies in the interests of their stakeholders. The interests of the board and the stakeholders ought to coincide, but in practice they may be in conflict with each other. The challenge of good health service governance is to find a way in which the interests of a wide variety of stakeholders and the directors can all be sufficiently satisfied. This is also a challenge for companies, but the major concern rests largely on balancing the interests of the board of directors and the shareholders.

Governance and management

It is important to recognise the difference between the governance of any organisation and its management.

Powers to manage the affairs of an NHS organisation are given to the board of directors or to the governing body in the case of a CCG. The term 'board' or 'board of directors' will be used for both, with the distinguishing aspects of the governance of a CCG highlighted (see Chapter 12 for more on CCGs).

Most powers are delegated to a chief executive officer (CEO) or managing director, and further delegated to executive directors (EDs) and executive managers. The board of directors should retain some powers and responsibilities with certain matters reserved for board decision-making rather than delegated to the management team (see Chapter 4).

The board of directors should be responsible for monitoring the performance of the management team. However, the board of directors itself is not responsible for day-to-day management. It is responsible for governing the organisation. Responsibilities for governance go beyond management, and governance should not be confused with management. Even so, it is probably true to say that when a senior executive manager is 'promoted' to the board, he or she may consider the position of an ED to be recognition of his senior executive position. However, the promotion of an executive manager to the board creates new responsibilities for governance that are not related to management. The ED ought to think as a member of the board in performing his duties as a director, rather than as a senior executive.

unitary boards This structure – where there is an effective single board that is collectively responsible for controlling the organisation or company, with no one individual having unfettered powers of decision-making – is known as the unitary board. When an ED becomes a board member, they take on part of the collective responsibility for ensuring the achievement of corporate aims and objectives, and must not solely contribute to discussions and decisions in the light of their particular executive function.

It is important to note that CCGs have not been established on the basis of a unity board. Instead, the *Good Governance Standard for Public Services* (2004), upon which CCG governance is based, presupposes a form of leadership that is not based on the principle of a unitary board. This is in stark contrast to most other NHS organisations (e.g. FTs) for whom the unitary board is a core principle of governance.

The purpose of the unitary board principle is to ensure that the interests of all stakeholders are properly considered and balanced. This is explored in more detail in Chapter 4.

■ Principles of good corporate governance

Several concepts apply to sound corporate governance in all countries where international investors invest their money. Many of these are ethical in nature and the King III Code (see Chapter 3) describes them as the 'overarching corporate governance principles'. These are:

■ fairness
■ accountability
■ responsibility
■ transparency.

These principles are directly applicable to an understanding of health service governance and are set out here with examples from both corporate and health service governance.

Fairness

Fairness refers to the principle that all shareholders should receive equal consid- *UK* eration. For example, minority shareholders should be treated in the same way *company* as majority shareholders. This concept might seem straightforward in the UK, *law* where the rights of minority shareholders are protected to a large extent by company law. In some countries, however, larger shareholders and the board of directors often disregard minority shareholder rights. There should also be fairness in the treatment of stakeholders other than shareholders.

The NHS Constitution sets out a number of rights and pledges that underpin the principle of fairness such as:

- the right to access
- the right to drugs
- the right to complain
- staff rights.

Accountability

Decision-makers who act on behalf of an organisation should be accountable for the decisions they make and the actions they take. In a company, the board of directors should be accountable to the shareholders (the company's owners). Shareholders should be able to assess the actions of the board of directors and the committees of the board, and have the opportunity to query and challenge them. In an NHS organisation, a variety of stakeholders provide that level of accountability.

One problem with accountability is deciding how the board of directors should be accountable, and in particular over what period of time. According to the financial theory for companies, if the objective of a company is to maximise the wealth of its shareholders, this will be achieved by maximising the financial returns to shareholders through increases in profits, dividends, prospects for profit growth and an increasing share price. It might therefore follow that directors should be held accountable to shareholders on the basis of the returns on shareholder capital that the company has achieved. However, there is little consensus about the period over which returns to shareholders and increases in share value should be measured. Performance can be measured over a short term of one year, over a longer period of five or ten years, or even longer.

In practice, it is usual to measure returns over the short term and assess performance in terms of profitability over a 12-month period. In the short term, however, a company's share price may be affected by influences unrelated to the company's underlying performance, such as excessive optimism or pessimism in the stock markets. In the short term, it is also easier to soothe investors with promises for the future, even though current performance is not good. It is only when a company fails consistently to deliver on its promises that investor confidence ebbs away.

If company performance were to be solely judged by the return to shareholders over a 12-month period, the directors would focus on short-term results and short-term movements in the stock market price. Short-termism is easy to criticise, but difficult to disregard in practice if performance targets ignore the long term. Directors should really be looking after the underlying business of the company and its profitability over the longer term.

The problem of accountability remains, however. Even if it is accepted that company performance should not be judged by short-term financial results and share price movements, how can the board be made accountable for its contribution to longer-term success?

By way of contrast, accountability for an NHS organisation can be measured in a number of ways. These include:

- Regulators: Care Quality Commission (CQC), Monitor.
- Commissioners: NHS England, Clinical Commissioning Groups, GPs.
- Political scrutiny: DH, overview and scrutiny committees, Health and Wellbeing boards, Healthwatch.
- Public opinion: Friends and Family Test, patient surveys, Patient Choice agenda, national staff surveys.

Short-termism is also an issue for NHS organisations, as changes in government policy often drives the form of accountability practiced by the regulators, commissioners and political scrutineers. The views expressed by public opinion can also focus on very local issues that need to be balanced against wider healthcare changes for the public benefit.

The NHS Constitution sets out that the NHS is accountable to the public, communities and patients that it serves. The government ensures that there is always a clear and up-to-date statement of NHS accountability for this purpose (see Chapter 2).

Responsibility

The board of directors is given authority to act on behalf of the company. A further principle of corporate governance is that the board should accept full responsibility for the powers that it is given and the authority that it exercises. A board of directors should understand what its responsibilities are, and should carry them out to the best of its abilities.

Accountability goes hand-in-hand with responsibility. The board of directors should be made accountable to the shareholders for the way in which it has carried out its responsibilities. Similarly, executive management should be responsible for the exercise of powers delegated to them by the board of directors, and should be made accountable to the board for their achievements and performance.

Within the NHS there are a number of mechanisms for delegating responsibility, such as the scheme of delegation and standing financial instructions. The role of the board committees is to oversee and scrutinise these delegated powers, and to provide assurance to the board that responsibility is being taken appropriately by the EDs.

Transparency

Transparency means openness. In the context of corporate governance, this is a willingness by the company to provide clear information to shareholders and other stakeholders about what the company has done and hopes to achieve, without giving away commercially sensitive information. It might be useful to think of openness in terms of its opposite; being a 'closed book' and refusing to divulge any information whatsoever.

Transparency should not be confused with 'understandability'. Information should be communicated in a way that is understandable, but transparency is concerned more with the content of the information that is communicated. A principle of good governance is that stakeholders should be informed about what an organisation is doing and plans to do in the future, and about the risks involved in its business strategies.

Transparency in NHS organisations is set out by the requirements of the Freedom of Information Act (FOIA) 2000 and the requirements of openness set out in the Nolan Standards in Public Life. The NHS Constitution requires that the system of responsibility and accountability for making decisions in the NHS should be transparent and clear to the public, patients and staff. The development of a 'duty of candour' is the most recent development in the NHS which underpins the principle of transparency (see Chapter 3).

■ Key issues in governance

Good governance should promote the best long-term interests of the organisation. It requires an effective board of directors, with an appropriate balance of skills and experience, and well-motivated individuals as directors. The composition of the board, its functions and responsibilities, and its effectiveness, are therefore core issues in governance.

At the heart of the debate about corporate governance lie conflicts of interest (and potential conflicts of interest) between shareholders, the board of directors as a whole, individual board members, and possibly also a number of other stakeholder groups. Directors may be tempted to take risks and make decisions aimed at boosting short-term performance. Many shareholders are more concerned with long-term performance, the continuing survival of their company and the value of their investment. If a company gets into financial difficulties, professional managers can move on to another company to start again, whereas shareholders suffer a financial loss.

Similar conflicts of interest arise in health service governance, such as pressure to conceal financial or performance information, inadequate risk management processes and poor communication with key stakeholders. For example, one stakeholder group may have a particular focus on an area of service delivery while directors have to manage the wider provision of healthcare services. Directors often have to manage the competing interests of patient groups and the financial decisions contained within government policy. Directors also have to consider their own careers within the NHS, managing the performance requirements of the regulators and any consideration of a longer-term strategy for the particular body for whom they are responsible.

Transparent reporting and auditing

The board of directors or EDs may try to disguise the true performance of the organisation by giving less than honest statements or 'dressing up' publicly available information on performance, quality, safety and finances. 'Window-dressed' information makes it difficult for stakeholders to reach a reasoned judgment about the performance of an organisation, and subsequently assess whether public funding is being correctly managed and expended on key areas of service delivery.

Concerns about misleading published accounts in the corporate commercial world in the 1980s and early 1990s provided an impetus to the movement for better corporate governance in the UK. Accounting irregularities in a number of companies led to a tightening of accounting standards, although the problems of window dressing are unlikely ever to disappear completely. Concerns about financial reporting in the USA emerged with the collapse of Enron in 2001, which filed for bankruptcy after 'adjusting' its accounts. This was followed by similar problems at other US companies, including telecommunications group WorldCom (which admitted to fraud in its accounting), Global Crossing and Rank Xerox. It was also suggested that incomprehensible or misleading accounts contributed to the global banking crisis, with banks such as Lehman Brothers (which collapsed in 2008) possibly using questionable accounting practices to disguise the true state of their financial position.

Throughout the peak of the banking crisis of 2007–2009, when Britain's financial system looked at its most vulnerable, the Co-operative Bank portrayed itself as a cut above the rest, offering ethical values untouched by the bonus culture for EDs and the high levels of debt that infected so many other banks. Yet, in 2013, the Co-operative Group hit the headlines when its governance shortfalls became public leading to significant losses resulting from a capital shortfall and controversy about its former chair Paul Flowers.

More recently, Tesco's overstatement of its expected first-half profits by £250 million in September 2014, resulting in Tesco's share value falling to its lowest level in a decade, demonstrates that corporate governance issues continue to undermine confidence in national companies. Tesco's auditor, PricewaterhouseCoopers (PwC) may also face tough questions over its performance.

The governance issue at stake in these examples is the extent to which the directors in each case were aware of these situations, and if they knew about the problems why shareholders were not informed much sooner. It is now widely accepted that the directors of a company should be responsible for giving an assurance to their shareholders that they consider their company to be a going concern that will not collapse within the next 12 months.

When the annual financial statements of a company prove to have been misleading, questions are inevitably raised about the effectiveness of the external auditors. There are two main issues relating to the external audit of a company:

- whether it should be the job of the auditors to discover financial fraud and material errors; and
- the problem of the relationship between a client company and its auditors, and the extent to which the auditors are independent and free from the influence of the company's management.

CASE STUDY: Enron

Enron was founded in 1985 with the merger of two US natural gas pipelines. In the 1990s it diversified into selling electricity and other activities; by 2000 it was one of the world's largest companies when measured by reported annual revenue. Both its board of directors and its audit committee appeared to be highly competent.

However, although investors and regulators were not aware of it at the time, the rapid growth in the reported assets and profits of Enron was attributable largely to misleading accounting practices. It inflated the value of its reported assets (sometimes recording expenses as assets) and it kept liabilities off its balance sheet by establishing 'special purpose entities'. It also anticipated profits by becoming the first non-financial services company to adopt 'mark to market' accounting techniques. This enabled it to earn profits on long-term contracts 'up front' as soon as the contract started. In one case it claimed a large profit on a 20-year contract agreed with Blockbuster Video in 2000, and continued to claim the profit even after the project failed and Blockbuster pulled out of the deal.

Senior management were rewarded on the basis of annual earnings and were highly motivated to continue reporting large increases in profits, regardless of the longer-term consequences. Investors began to have doubts about the reliability of Enron's reported profits in 2001. A 'whistleblower' (see Chapter 15) reported her concerns to the chief executive officer, but her allegations of dubious accounting practices were ignored. However, in October 2001 Enron was eventually forced to announce that it would be re-stating its accounts for 1997–2000 to correct accounting violations. The US Securities and Exchange Commission (SEC) announced an investigation into the company and the stock price collapsed. There were also doubts about whether Enron had sufficient liquidity (cash) to remain in business for long. Its debt was downgraded to junk bond status and in December 2001 the company filed for bankruptcy.

The company's auditors were Arthur Andersen, one of the 'big five' global accounting firms. The firm – in particular its Houston office – took extraordinary measures to protect its client. When the SEC investigation was announced in 2001, Andersen staff attempted to cover up evidence of negligence in its audit work by destroying several tonnes of documents, as well as many e-mails and computer files. The firm, especially the Houston office, was accused of losing its independence from Enron and over-relying on income from the non-audit work that it did for the company. Arthur Andersen was charged with obstructing the course of justice by shredding the documents and destroying the files. Although a guilty verdict was subsequently overturned by the Supreme Court, this was too late to save the firm from the loss of its major clients and collapse.

Several Enron employees were brought to trial for financial crimes. Andrew Fastow, a former chief financial officer (CFO) of Enron, was found guilty of crimes including fraud, money laundering, insider trading and conspiracy. Two former chief executive officers, Kenneth Lay and Jeffrey Skilling, were charged with a range of financial crimes and brought to trial in 2006. Both were found guilty: Skilling was imprisoned and Lay died before sentence was passed.

Transparent reporting and auditing is vital for NHS organisations and it is subject to a high level of scrutiny. It must be remembered that the financial position of an NHS organisation is closely linked to its performance targets and its level of activity. While there is some guidance on how targets should be measured so correct financial data can be collated, the pressure to reach performance targets can lead to irregularities in the measurement of target data.

CASE STUDY: whistleblowing

An NHS finance director took a leading teaching hospital to an employment tribunal over claims he was sacked for 'whistleblowing' over fiddled statistics for cancelled operations.

The director queried why a senior executive had instructed a junior member of staff to record the number of weekly cancelled operations as zero, instead of the recorded number, in a form sent to the DH to help determine the hospital's performance rating. It emerged that the figure zero had been entered for a number of weeks, during which time a number of operations were believed to have been cancelled on the day of the operation for non-clinical reasons – though no such cancellations were ever recorded.

The hospital had been under pressure because of its poor record on cancelled operations, and evidence of improvement would have gained it a greater share of a large performance fund made available by the DH.

> ### CASE STUDY: monitoring arrangements
>
> A trust's financial position deteriorated significantly over a three-month period, so that instead of a modest surplus the trust was forecasting a significant deficit. When the deterioration became apparent, the trust failed to raise the matter promptly or notify Monitor, the regulator, of risks associated with its recovery plan. The Compliance Framework requires trusts to report any material, actual or prospective changes that may affect their ability to comply with any aspect of their authorisation.
>
> The trust submitted a re-forecast plan to Monitor, setting out a recovery in the following quarter. This largely relied on a significant reduction in staff costs. However, given the record of the trust in consistently overspending on pay, Monitor was not convinced that the recovery plan would be delivered.
>
> Furthermore, the re-forecast showed a significant liquidity risk in the medium term that the board had neither put in place contingencies against nor taken any steps to mitigate. Overspend on pay had been reported to every board meeting over a protracted period, but plans to deal with the overspend were not due to take effect until the following financial year and the trust failed to identify that the situation would not be remedied in the short term.
>
> There was no evidence that the level of challenge in the boardroom on financial issues was sufficient in the light of the level of financial deterioration. Despite the urgent need to improve the financial situation, Monitor noted that evidence suggested that the board was not sufficiently engaged in holding the executive to account for delivery of improvements and had tolerated slippage in delivery and extended timelines. The trust remained under enhanced monitoring arrangements until it was deemed to no longer be in breach of its terms of authorisation.

Exercise of board-level power

Most decision-making powers in an organisation are held by the board of directors. The governance debate continues to be about the extent to which professional managers, acting as board directors, exercise those powers in the interests of their principal stakeholders (and any other organisational stakeholders), and whether the powers of directors should be restricted.

Key issues include:

- the structure of the board of directors
- the role of independent non-executive directors (NEDs)
- the responsibilities of the board of directors
- the duties of directors.

Risk management

In the corporate world, investors typically expect higher rewards to compensate them for taking higher business risks. If a company makes decisions that increase the scale of the risks it faces, profits and dividends are usually expected to increase. A further issue in corporate governance is that the directors might take decisions intended to increase profits without giving due regard to the risks. In some cases, companies may continue to operate without regard to the changing risk profile of their existing businesses. When investors buy shares in a company, they have an idea of the type of company they are buying into, the nature of its business, the probable returns it will provide for shareholders and the nature of its business and financial risks. Directors, on the other hand, are rewarded on the basis of the returns the company achieves – profits or dividend growth – and their remuneration is not linked in any direct way to the risk aspects of their business. Some companies are also guilty of poor procedures and systems, so that the risk of breakdowns, errors and fraud can be high.

Good governance therefore requires an organisation to control its 'business risk' by having effective internal controls for managing operational risks. As a result, risk management is now recognised as a key ingredient of sound corporate governance.

Risk management is just as crucial in health service governance. Not only does it set out to protect public assets and the use of taxpayers' money, it also protects the quality of the healthcare services being delivered.

Risk is managed at two levels: at a strategic/management level and at a day-to-day operational level. The focus of risk management is on the management of business risks associated with running an NHS organisation – which include financial, IT and ethical risks –while managing the clinical risks involved in the delivery of healthcare services. A mixture of legislation, regulation and voluntary guidance governs risk management in healthcare. Operational issues that may lead to a significant risk of poor care or fraud should be brought to an NHS organisation board's attention.

When referring to 'risk management' in health service governance, the issues mainly relate to 'internal control' and quality performance. Public sector organisations in general have had a long history of errors, fraud, inefficiency and poorly controlled spending. NHS organisations, along with other local government bodies, are now required by law to publish an annual governance statement (AGS) each year to provide a more coherent and consistent reporting mechanism. These draw together position statements and evidence on governance, risk management and control.

Stakeholder engagement

Another issue in corporate governance is communication between the board of directors and the company's shareholders. Shareholders, particularly those with a large financial interest in a company, should be able to voice their concerns to the directors and expect to have their opinions heard. Small shareholders should at least be informed about the company, its financial position and its plans for the future – even if their opinions carry comparatively little weight.

In health service governance it is an explicit aspect of government policy that stakeholders are to be involved in the design and delivery of their own healthcare. Therefore, it is vital that NHS organisations provide public information about their services and future plans. Providing opportunities for the views and opinions of stakeholders to be heard is a key driver within health service governance. Better-informed boards of directors will make better healthcare decisions. In addition, the increased focus on patient choice results from research in the UK and overseas that treatments are more effective if patients choose, understand and control their own care. Patient choices now include the right to choose a GP, which hospital to go to and the right to be involved in decisions about their own healthcare.

This right to choose, combined with the introduction of 'internal market' or 'quasi-market' policies, has led to a greater degree of information about the performance of individual GPs, consultants and hospitals. This has introduced the commercial concepts of marketing and market share, and a much greater awareness of costs, efficiency and accountability.

Further, the introduction of the FOIA 2000 provided a clear procedure for all public bodies to respond to requests for information about their organisations. In addition, the requirements to make NHS annual accounts, reports from regulators (such as Monitor and the CQC), national NHS surveys (staff and patient surveys) and the introduction of Quality Accounts for all providers of healthcare services, all serve to ensure a greater transparency in the relationships with NHS stakeholders.

Corporate social responsibility and the NHS

Ethical conduct is a major governance issue. There is a growing recognition that organisations need to consider social and environmental issues for commercial and governance reasons, as well as purely ethical reasons. Stakeholders expect organisations to have regard to social and environmental issues, while the financial risks from government regulation to protect the environment continue to grow. A sustainable healthcare system is achieved by delivering high quality care and improved public health without exhausting natural resources or causing severe ecological damage.

In the NHS, sustainable development is often referred to as good corporate citizenship. This means using NHS organisations' corporate powers and resources in ways that benefit, rather than damage, the social, economic, and physical environment. How the NHS itself behaves can impact on people's health and to the wellbeing of society, the economy and the environment. Behaving as a good corporate citizen can save money, benefit population health and can help reduce health inequalities. Many measures that improve health also contribute to sustainable development and vice versa.

Sustainability reporting is increasingly required within NHS organisations' annual reports and Quality Accounts.

■ A brief history of corporate governance

To best understand the principles of health service governance it is important to understood the developments in corporate governance over time. These developments now underpin much of what currently exists in health service governance.

What seems clear from each development is that processes and systems only go so far. References are repeatedly made to behaviour and culture as the foundation stones of good governance.

While concerns about corporate governance had been growing for some time during the late twentieth century, the main impetus for better practices in corporate governance began in the UK in the late 1980s and early 1990s.

The Cadbury Code

The *Report of the Committee on the Financial Aspects of Corporate Governance* was published in 1992, and was described as 'a landmark in thinking on corporate governance'. The report included a Code of Best Practice (the Cadbury Code), and UK listed companies came under pressure from City institutions to comply with the requirements of the code.

Whilst the terms of reference for the Committee were primarily focused on financial governance, concerns about the principles and values behind good corporate governance also meant that its findings went further than just financial governance. The Code also made recommendations relating to the structure and effectiveness of boards, internal controls and accountability to shareholders. Sir Adrian Cadbury's statement, following the review, makes interesting reading for health service governance practitioners:

> 'Corporate governance is concerned with holding the balance between economic and social goals and between individual and communal goals. The governance framework is there to encourage the efficient use of resources and equally to require accountability for the stewardship of those resources. The aim is to align as nearly as possible the interests of individuals, corporations and society.'

The significant legacies of the Cadbury Code include a voluntary system of good practice with the principles of openness, integrity and accountability at its heart and self-regulation based on 'comply or explain'.

The Greenbury Report

On the recommendation of the Cadbury Committee, a second committee was set up to review progress on corporate governance in UK listed companies. This committee issued the Greenbury Report in 1995, which focused mainly on directors' remuneration. At the time, the UK press was condemning 'fat cat' directors, particularly those in newly privatised companies.

The Greenbury Report issued a Code of Best Practice covering directors' remuneration. Its major recommendations included:

- the remuneration committee should be made up of entirely NEDs
- there should be an annual remuneration report for shareholders included within the annual report and accounts
- remuneration (and any other benefits) should be linked to performance (both by the company and the individual director).

The Combined Code

A further committee on corporate governance, chaired by Sir Ronald Hampel, was set up in 1995 to review the recommendations of the Cadbury and Greenbury Committees. Its final report was published in 1998. The report covered a number of governance issues, such as:

- the composition of the board and role of directors
- directors' remuneration
- the role of shareholders (particularly institutional shareholders)
- communications between the company and its shareholders
- financial reporting, auditing and internal controls.

The Hampel Report also suggested that its recommendations should be combined with those of the Cadbury and Greenbury Committees into a single code of corporate governance. This suggestion led to the publication of the original 1998 Combined Code on Corporate Governance (Combined Code), which applied to all UK listed companies. Interestingly, the Hampel report makes it clear that:

'Good corporate governance is not just a matter of prescribing particular corporate structures and complying with a number of hard and fast rules. There is a need for broad principles. All concerned should then apply these flexibly and with common sense to the varying circumstances of individual companies.'

The Combined Code was updated in 2003 to take account of the Higgs and Smith reports (see below), as well as in 2006 and 2008. It became the UK Corporate Governance Code in 2010.

The Turnbull Guidance

A committee was set up in 1998 to provide guidance on the board's responsibilities for internal control and risk management. This committee produced the Turnbull Report. This was revised and re-named *Internal Control: Guidance to Directors* (2005) by the Financial Reporting Council (FRC) in 2005, then amalgamated with the 2009 Going Concern guidance notes into the *Guidance on Risk Management and Internal Control and Related Financial and Business Reporting* in 2014.

The Turnbull Report defined an internal control system as 'the policies, processes, tasks, behaviours and other aspects of an organisation' that, taken together:

- help it to operate effectively and efficiently: these operational controls should allow the organisation to respond in an appropriate way to significant risks to achieving the organisation's objectives (this includes the safeguarding of assets from inappropriate use or from loss and fraud and ensuring that liabilities are identified and managed)
- help it to ensure the quality of external and internal financial reporting (financial controls)
- help to ensure compliance with applicable laws and regulations, and also with internal policies for the conduct of business (compliance controls).

The Higgs Report and *Improving Board Effectiveness*
Corporate governance issues remained in the spotlight in the UK in 2003 with two influential reports published in that year.

The Higgs Report, commissioned by the government, considered the role and effectiveness of the chair and independent NEDs. This was updated in 2010 following a review on behalf of the FRC by ICSA. Amended guidance was issued with the title *Improving Board Effectiveness*. In a similar vein to Cadbury and Hampel, Higgs was at pains to point out that people, behaviour and culture were the key to good governance, not a process of box-ticking exercises.

The Smith Report and the *FRC Guidance on Audit Committees*
Further work and more detailed guidance on the role of the audit committee was commissioned by the FRC in 2003. The ensuing report was originally called the Smith Report (after the name of the committee chair) but is now called the *FRC Guidance on Audit Committees*. It was revised in 2005, 2008 and 2012.

The Walker Report
The global financial markets and world economy were badly damaged by the banking crisis that emerged in 2007 and 2008. In the US, Lehman Brothers collapsed and other banks and brokerage firms were taken over to prevent their collapse. In the UK, the Northern Rock bank collapsed in 2007 while Royal Bank of Scotland was virtually nationalised in 2008. At the same time, the government acquired a major stake in Lloyds TSB Bank after Lloyds had agreed to take over another ailing bank, HBOS.

Recognition of governance problems in UK banks led to a review by Sir David Walker. Some recommendations of the Walker Report were included by the FRC in the 2010 UK Corporate Governance Code.

The Davies Report

In 2010, Lord Davies of Abersoch initiated a review into boardroom diversity at the request of the UK Government, publishing a report entitled *Women on Boards* in 2011.

The review rejected the imposition of a mandatory quota system, instead recommending voluntary targets and reporting requirements. In May 2011, the FRC began consulting on possible amendments to the UK Corporate Governance Code that would require companies to publish their policy on boardroom diver- E + D sity, report against it annually and to consider the board's diversity when assessing its effectiveness (among other factors). These were added to the Code in 2012.

The UK Corporate Governance Code

The FRC has reviewed and amended the Combined Code regularly, and in June 2010 issued a significantly revised version under the new name of the UK Corporate Governance Code.

In September 2011, the FRC announced that it intended to consult on proposed further changes to the code in relation to audit committees and audit retendering. In October 2011, the FRC announced that changes resulting from the Davies Report would also be implemented in a revised version of the code. This revised version was issued in 2012 and applied to financial years beginning on or after 1 October 2012. The 2012 revision also took account of the findings of the Walker Report.

The most recent update to the code was in September 2014. This included a number of significant changes.

Going concern, risk management and internal control

- a statement on the going concern basis of accounting
- assessment of the principal risks and how they are being managed or mitigated;
- statement on whether a company believes they will be able to continue in operation and meet its liabilities taking account of its current position and principal risks, and specify the period covered by the statement and why it is appropriate
- monitoring of risk management and internal control systems and an annual review of their effectiveness, published in the annual report.

Remuneration

- Greater emphasis was placed on ensuring that remuneration policies are designed with the long-term success of the company in mind, and that the lead responsibility for doing so rests with the remuneration committee and
- Companies should put in place arrangements that will enable them to recover or withhold variable pay when appropriate to do so, and should consider appropriate vesting and holding periods for deferred remuneration.

Shareholder engagement
- Companies should explain when publishing general meeting results how they intend to engage with shareholders when a significant percentage of them have voted against any resolution.

Other issues

The FRC also highlighted the importance of the board's role in establishing the 'tone from the top' of the company in terms of its culture and values. The directors should lead by example in order to encourage good behaviours throughout the organisation. In addition, the FRC emphasised that key to the effective functioning of any board is dialogue, which is both constructive and challenging.

Such debate can be encouraged through having sufficient diversity on the board, including gender and race and in difference of approach and experience. The FRC has agreed to consider this as part of its review of board succession planning for the next update to the Code (due in 2016).

Alongside the updated Code, the FRC issued three related documents:

- the *Guidance on Risk Management and Internal Control and Related Financial and Business Reporting*;
- the *Guidance for Directors of Banks on Solvency and Liquidity Risk Management*; and
- the *Going Concern Basis of Accounting and the Revised Auditing Standards* which requires auditors to consider and report on narrative disclosures (including risks), the going concern basis of accounting (and material uncertainties relating thereto) and the longer term viability statement and the risk management disclosure.

The UK Stewardship Code

The UK Stewardship Code was published in 2010 and subsequently reviewed in 2012.

Whereas the UK Corporate Governance Code is concerned with governance by companies, the Stewardship Code is for institutional investors that are share owners or that manage shareholdings for other financial institutions such as pension funds. The Stewardship Code is the responsibility of the FRC and it aims to enhance the quality of engagement between institutional investors and companies, so that institutional shareholders contribute positively to the governance of the companies in which they invest.

The Kay Report

Following the banking crisis and the Walker Report, confidence continued to fall in the way that organisations were run with long-term objectives as short-termism seemed to prevail. Professor John Kay was therefore commissioned to review the UK equity markets. His 2012 report recommended that there should be a much-needed shift in the culture of the stock market which included restoring relationships built on long-term trust and confidence, and realigning incentives across the investment chain. His specific recommendations related to:

- collective engagement
- executive remuneration and reward structures
- narrative reporting
- shareholder consultation
- stewardship.

Governance and UK law

The Companies Act 2006 introduced statutory duties of directors (similar to the duties that existed previously in common law and equity), and contained a requirement for quoted companies to be more accountable to shareholders by publishing a strategic business review (known as a business review until 2013) in narrative form each year. In 2012, the UK Government also began consulting on proposed changes to the rules on directors' remuneration.

Some aspects of corporate governance have also been transposed into UK law from the European Union (EU) Directives.

Amendments to the Fourth and Seventh EU Company Law Directives approved in 2006 included a requirement for quoted companies to include a corporate governance statement in their annual reports, and amendments to the Eighth Company Law Directive in 2008 requires 'public interest entities' (including listed companies) to have an audit committee consisting of independent NEDs and to publish an annual corporate governance statement.

Corporate governance in other countries

The UK is seen as a leading country in the development of a corporate governance framework, but there have been similar developments in many other countries. For many countries, particularly developing countries, good corporate governance is seen as an essential basic requirement for attracting foreign investment capital.

In South Africa, the King Committee developed a code of corporate governance. This was revised and strengthened in 2002 and again in 2009 (King III, see Chapter 3). On an international basis, recommended principles on corporate governance have been published by the Organization for Economic Co-operation and Development (OECD).

Although the US appeared to show little concern for better corporate governance throughout the 1990s, the situation changed dramatically with the collapse of Enron and other major companies in 2001. The New York Stock Exchange (NYSE) proposed recommendations for change, and statutory provisions on corporate governance were introduced in 2002 with the Sarbanes-Oxley Act (SOX). However, the adequacy of corporate governance provisions in the USA (and the UK) continues to be questioned following the banking crisis in 2007–2009.

■ Governance in the public and voluntary sectors

The public sector includes central government, state government (in some countries) and local government, state-run health and education services and many other regulatory and advisory bodies. While many of the principles of good corporate governance can be applied to the governing bodies of the public sector, there are also significant differences. For example, public bodies are not profit-making and are not accountable to shareholders.

The public sector has therefore adapted principles of good governance to its own specific circumstances, and to some extent the definition of 'governance' for the public sector differs in some ways from 'governance' of companies.

In the UK, the Chartered Institute of Public Finance and Accountancy (CIPFA) and Solace (the Society of Local Authority Chief Executives) published a governance framework in 2007 aimed at local government bodies called *Delivering Good Governance in Local Government*. This sets out principles of governance that local government bodies are encouraged to adopt and apply to their own particular circumstances. The framework defines governance as:

> '[H]ow local government bodies ensure that they are doing the right things, in the right way, for the right people, in a timely, inclusive, open, honest and accountable manner. It comprises systems and processes, and cultures and values, by which local government bodies are directed and controlled and through which they account to, and engage with, and, where appropriate, lead their communities.'

Nolan's Principles of Public Life

A key development for the governance of the UK public sector was the Nolan Committee on Standards in Public Life. The Committee was set up in 1995 in response to concerns that the conduct of some politicians was unethical – in particular, allegations over MPs taking cash for putting questions to Parliament.

While the Committee focused on MPs, its terms of reference also covered government departments and non-departmental public bodies (NDPBs). The Principles were originally intended as guidelines for individuals who were involved in public affairs and public bodies, whether as paid employees or as non-paid members of governing bodies. They are now considered to have much wider relevance and have formed the basis in the UK for developing governance guidelines for both the public sector and the voluntary sector.

The Committee of Standards in Public Life recently undertook a review of best practice in promoting good behaviour in public life, and in January 2013 it

published its 14th *Report of the Committee on Standards in Public Life: A review* *further*
of best practice in promoting good behaviour in public life. The report amended *reading*
the definitions of the seven Nolan principles as shown in Table 1.1. Public sector
boards and their members should adhere to these seven principles of public life.

Table 1.1: The Principles of Public Life

Selflessness	Holders of public office should act solely in terms of the public interest.
Integrity:	Holders of public office must avoid placing themselves under any obligation to people or organisations that might try inappropriately to influence them in their work. They should not act or take decisions in order to gain financial or other material benefits for themselves, their family, or their friends. They must declare and resolve any interests and relationships.
Objectivity	Holders of public office must act and take decisions impartially, fairly and on merit, using the best evidence and without discrimination or bias.
Accountability	Holders of public office are accountable to the public for their decisions and actions and must submit themselves to the scrutiny necessary to ensure this.
Openness	Holders of public office should act and take decisions in an open and transparent manner. Information should not be withheld from the public unless there are clear and lawful reasons for so doing.
Honesty	Holders of public office should be truthful.
Leadership	Holders of public office should exhibit these principles in their own behaviour. They should actively promote and robustly support the principles and be willing to challenge poor behaviour wherever it occurs.

The standards for NHS board members

In July 2011, the Council for Healthcare Regulatory Excellence was commissioned to advise the Secretary of State for Health on standards of personal behaviour, technical competence and business practices for members of NHS boards and CCG governing bodies in England. These standards were issued by the Professional Standards Authority in November 2012.

The standards include implementing a transparent and explicit approach to the declaration and handling of conflicts of interest, with good practice requiring the maintenance and publication of a register of interest for all board members. Board meeting agendas should include an opportunity to declare any conflicts at the start of the meeting.

There is a distinct similarity between the Nolan Principles and the NHS board standards, as seen in Table 1.2.

Table 1.2 The Principles of Public Life and NHS board standards

The Seven Principles of Public Life	Standards for NHS Board Members
Selflessness	Responsibility
Integrity	Integrity
Objectivity	Respect
Accountability	Professionalism
Openness	Openness
Honesty	Honesty
Leadership	Leadership

further reading ## The Good Governance Standard for Public Services

The Independent Commission for Good Governance in Public Service was established by the Office for Public Management (OPM) and CIPFA in partnership with the Joseph Rowntree Foundation.

The role of the Commission was to develop a common code and set of principles for good governance across all public services in the UK. In 2004 it published the *Good Governance Standard for Public Services*; a guide for everyone concerned with governance in the public services that applies to all organisations that work for the public using public money. Its application therefore extends from public sector bodies to all private sector organisations that use public money to work for the public. NHS England has advocated adherence with the *Good Governance Standard* as the guidance for health service governance for CCGs.

In justifying the need for the application of good governance principles and practice in the public service sector, the Commission has commented that good governance encourages public trust and participation, whereas bad governance fosters low morale and adversarial relationships.

The *Good Governance Standard* builds on Nolan's Principles and consists of six main principles, each with supporting principles, together with guidelines on how these might be applied in practice. It is useful to look at these and compare them with the principles that apply to good governance in the commercial sector. There are many similarities between these principles and those that should apply in corporate governance to companies (as described earlier in this chapter).

The six main principles and their supporting principles are as follows:

L61

1. Focusing on the organisation's purpose and on its outcome for citizens and users of the organisation's services.

■ Being clear about the purpose of the organisation and its intended outcomes for citizens and service users. It is suggested that the concept of 'public value' may be useful in helping organisations to identify their purpose and intended outcomes.

■ Making sure that users receive a high-quality service.

■ Making sure that taxpayers receive VFM.

2. Performing effectively in clearly defined functions and roles.

■ Being clear about the functions of the organisation's governing body. It is recommended that the governing body should describe in a published document its approach to achieving each of its stated functions. This document can then be used as a basis for measuring actual performance and achievements by the governing body. Functions could include, for example, 'scrutinising the activities and performance of the executive management' and 'making sure that the voice of the public is heard in discussions and decision-making'.

■ Being clear about the responsibilities of the non-executive and the executive governors; these will differ. Many governing bodies consist of both executives and non-executive members (who may be unpaid for their services). However, they should have equal status in discussions on policy and strategy. The framework recommends that the roles of CEO and chair of the governing body should not be held by the same individual.

■ Making sure that these responsibilities are properly carried out.

■ Being clear about the relationship between the governors and the public, so that both sides in this relationship know what to expect from the other.

3. Promoting values for the whole organisation and demonstrating good governance through behaviour.

■ Putting the values of the organisation into practice. The governing body should take the lead in doing this.

■ Individual governors behaving in ways that uphold and exemplify effective governance.

4. Taking informed and transparent decisions and managing risk.

■ Being rigorous and transparent about how decisions are taken by the governing body. There should be clearly defined levels of delegation within the organisation. The governing body should not be concerned with matters that are more properly delegated to management. It should also be clear about what the objectives of its own decisions are.

■ Using good quality information, advice and support.

■ Making sure that an effective risk management system is in operation.

5. *Developing the capacity and capability of the governing body to be effective.*

- Making sure that governors have the skills, knowledge and experience to perform well.
- Developing the capabilities of individuals with governance responsibilities.
- Striking a balance in the membership of the governing body between continuity and renewal.
- The creation and refreshing of a governing body is similar in many respects to similar guidelines in corporate governance, although in the public sector, some governors may be elected representatives.

6. *Engaging stakeholders and making accountability real.*

- Understanding formal and informal accountability relationships.
- Taking an active and planned approach to dialogue with and accountability to the public.
- Taking an effective and planned approach to accountability to staff.
- Engaging effectively with institutional stakeholders. Institutional stakeholders in the public sector are very different from institutional shareholders in the corporate world. In local government, for example, institutional stakeholders include bodies representing local people. Engagement with stakeholders should help to improve the accountability of the public sector body to the public.

These are general principles, and individual public sector bodies can develop their own codes of governance that are consistent with and based on these principles.

Good Governance: a code for the voluntary and community sector

The development of codes and rules for corporate governance and public sector governance has also influenced the voluntary sector. For example, the National Council of Voluntary Organisations (NCVO) adapted Nolan's seven Principles of Public Life into a code of conduct for charity trustee. In addition, the Charity Commission's Statement of Recommended Practice requires larger charities to include a statement on risks in their annual report.

Awareness of the need for good governance has also developed in the voluntary sector response to sector-specific issues, including:

- the increase in size and importance of the voluntary sector, particularly as a result of the contracting out of public services to voluntary organisations;
- a perception of a decline in public confidence in charities – charities and other bodies have tried to improve their standards of governance as a way of retaining public confidence in what they are doing;
- greater competition for funding – charities with better standards of governance may succeed better in attracting funds from government and the public;

- a lack of clarity about the duties of voluntary board members, and in particular concerns about the liabilities of charity trustees – these concerns are similar to those in corporate governance, about the responsibilities of the board, the duties of directors and the potential liability of directors;
- a growing demand for accountability to users and beneficiaries of the services provided by charities; and
- demands for greater transparency on how charities spend their donated income, and in particular the proportion spent ('wasted') on administration.

Good Governance: a code for the voluntary and community sector was published in October 2010. This was the second edition of the Code, the previous version of which was published in 2005. The code sets out best practice for governing a voluntary or community organisation. It is not a mandatory code, but organisations that comply with the code are invited to state this in their annual report and other relevant published material, as well as pledge their support for the code by signing up to the online charter.

The code focuses on six key principles that trustees and board members should follow and provides clear information about what those principles imply in practice.

Arguments for and against governance regimes

There are differences of opinion about the benefits of governance, and whether these justify the costs of compliance with governance regulations. It is therefore useful to consider just what the benefits of good governance might be, and what the arguments are against having laws or codes of governance practice.

The main arguments in favour of having a strong governance regime are as follows.

- Good governance will eliminate the risk of misleading or false reporting, and will prevent organisations from being dominated by CEOs or chairs.
- Stakeholders will be better protected by reducing the risks of scandals, and promoting fairness, accountability, responsibility and transparency in organisations.
- Organisations that comply with best practice in governance are more likely to achieve success. Good governance and good leadership and management often go hand-in-hand. Badly governed organisations may be very successful, and well-governed organisations may fail; however, the probability is greater that badly governed organisations will be less successful and more likely to fail than well-governed ones.
- Well-governed organisations will often develop a strong reputation and so will be less exposed to reputation risk (see Chapter 13) than organisations that are

not so well governed. Reputation risk can have an adverse impact on stake-holders such as employees, patients and suppliers.

■ Good corporate governance encourages a longer-term view of success and enables longer-term planning.

The main arguments against having a strong governance regime for organisations focus on costs, benefits and value.

■ For many organisations, compliance with a code of governance is a box-ticking exercise as they adopt the required procedures and systems without considering what the potential benefits might be. The only requirement is to comply with the 'rules' and put a tick in a box when this is done. Governance requirements therefore create a time- and resource-consuming bureaucracy of governance practitioners, and divert the attention of the board of directors from more important matters.

■ Good governance is likely to reduce the risk of scandals and unexpected organisational failures. However, it could be argued that the current regulations or best practice guidelines are far too extensive and burdensome.

■ When regulations and recommended practice become burdensome, there is an inevitable cost, in terms of both time and money, in achieving compliance. It could be argued that less regulation is better regulation. However there has not yet been an authoritative assessment of the costs of governance compliance with the benefits of better governance systems.

■ Organisations that are obliged to comply with governance regulations or best practice are at a competitive disadvantage to rival organisations from countries or regimes where governance regulation is weaker. This is one of the criticisms of widening the number of providers of healthcare beyond that of NHS organisations. If they are not subject to the same level of scrutiny and regulation then the playing field is not level.

■ The connection between good governance and good performance (due to good leadership and management) has not yet been proven or demonstrated.

■ Summary

Governance is a wide-ranging and far-reaching subject. To be a well-versed health service governance practitioner requires an understanding of history, law, specific technical knowledge, politics, health policy and a robust understanding of human behaviour. This diversity and complexity makes for a fascinating area of work despite its connotations of checklists and tick-box exercises. It offers an intriguing insight into how an organisation can plan for its long-term success and then takes steps to deliver that success in a fast-paced changing external environment.

Any type of effective consideration of a subject benefits from clarity around the scope of the subject matter and governance – specifically health service governance – is no different. This handbook aims to provide that clarity and then to offer practical guidance on the practice of governance – enabling practitioners to 'walk the talk'. As a consequence, the following chapters will set out the rules and practices relevant to the chapter heading and also offer insights to what this means in practice. Since much of the basis for health service governance result from guidance from outside of the NHS, this will also be made clear so that the reader can differentiate between various sources.

2

Definitions and issues in health service governance

■ The NHS

Health service governance is the governance that is applied to NHS organisations. Therefore, it is useful to clarify the structure and guiding principles of the NHS.

The NHS is the shared name of three of the four publicly funded healthcare systems in the United Kingdom. They provide a comprehensive range of health services, the vast majority of which are free at the point of use to residents of the United Kingdom.

The NHS in England was created by the NHS Act 1948, which created an NHS for both England and Wales. Responsibility for the NHS in Wales was passed to the Secretary of State for Wales in 1969, leaving the Secretary of State for Social Services solely responsible for the NHS in England.

The English NHS is the only system officially called the NHS, the others being NHS Scotland and NHS Wales. The Northern Irish equivalent to the NHS is called Health and Social Care (HSC). Each system operates independently and is politically accountable to the relevant government: the Scottish Government, the Welsh Government, the Northern Ireland Executive or the UK Government (for the English NHS).

Despite their separate funding and administration, there is no discrimination when a resident of one country of the United Kingdom requires treatment in another – although a patient will often be returned to their home area when they are fit to be moved. The financial and administrative consequences are dealt with by the organisations involved and no personal involvement by the patient is required.

The NHS in England has agreed a formal constitution, which lays down in one document the objectives of the NHS, the rights and responsibilities of the various parties involved in healthcare in England (patients, staff and trust boards) and the guiding principles that govern the service. It was first published on 21 January 2009 as part of a ten-year plan to provide the highest quality of care and service for patients in England. Previously, these rights and responsibilities had evolved in common law or through UK or European Union (EU) law, or were policy pledges by the NHS and government. These have now been written into the Constitution.

In summary, the guiding principles of the NHS are as follows.

- The NHS provides a comprehensive service, available to all irrespective of gender, race, disability, age, sexual orientation, religion, belief, gender reassignment, pregnancy and maternity or marital or civil partnership status.
- Access to NHS services is based on clinical need, not an individual's ability to pay (except in exceptional circumstances sanctioned by Parliament).
- The NHS aspires to the highest standards of excellence and professionalism to provide high-quality care that is safe, effective and focused on the patient experience.
- The NHS aspires to put patients at the heart of everything it does.
- The NHS works across organisational boundaries and in partnership with other organisations in the interest of patients, local communities and the wider population. The NHS is an integrated system of organisations and services bound together by the principles and values reflected in the Constitution.
- The NHS is committed to providing best value for taxpayers' money and the most effective, fair and sustainable use of finite resources.
- The NHS is accountable to the public, communities and patients that it serves.

The DH is the government department responsible for policy in health and social care matters. It is responsible for the NHS in England, along with a few elements of the same matters that are not otherwise devolved to the Scottish, Welsh or Northern Irish governments. The DH then delegates powers to the various authorities and boards established to oversee and scrutinise the provision of healthcare. This structure was altered radically in 2013 by the Health & Social *further* Care Act 2012 (HSCA 2012). *leading*

■ Consequences of poor health service governance

The importance of good governance is often only highlighted in circumstances where an organisation has failed or is in crisis. It tends to be seen in organisations where the separation between stakeholder interests and management is wider. This is a significant risk for NHS organisations; government spending on healthcare for 2014/2015 is budgeted at £113 billion and yet the recipients of the healthcare provided are often very distant from the holders of the healthcare budget. Health service governance in NHS organisations therefore must be resilient enough to hold NHS organisations to account for the responsibility of managing this expenditure. The separation between NHS stakeholders and Parliament is vast, and it is only through the health service governance regimes of the individual parts of the NHS that NHS stakeholders can exercise the relatively limited powers they have to hold the boards of directors to account.

The consequences for the NHS when health service governance goes wrong are often catastrophic for the patients and families involved, as well as very public. Sadly, there have been a number of cases where the poor health service governance has led to tragedy, most recently, at the Mid Staffordshire NHS Foundation Trust.

CASE STUDY: Bristol Royal Infirmary

In the early 1990s, it became clear to the parents of very sick children who had been treated at Bristol Royal Infirmary between 1984 and 1995 that the rate of death or brain damage in or after heart surgery was abnormally high. In 1998 – following an earlier, separate enquiry by the General Medical Council – the health secretary Frank Dobson announced a public inquiry into events at Bristol under the chair of Sir Ian Kennedy. The inquiry, which reported back in 2001, found a number of significant governance failings including:

- unsafe arrangements for caring for the children
- no requirement for consultants to keep their skills and knowledge up to date
- no agreed standards of care
- no openness about clinical performance
- no systematic mechanism for monitoring the clinical performance of healthcare professionals or hospitals.

CASE STUDY: Dr Harold Shipman

Dr Harold Shipman, a GP in Hyde (near Manchester), was convicted at Preston Crown Court on 31 January 2000 of the murder of 15 of his patients and of one count of forging a will. He was sentenced to life imprisonment. Following the trial, a public inquiry was set up that reported over the next five years.

The inquiry identified a number of significant gaps in governance processes that enabled Dr Shipman to continue to murder his patients over a long period of time without detection. Among other issues, these included the need to share information about complaints and concerns raised, the requirement to investigate them systematically, and the importance of establishing strong governance processes and culture.

The Mid Staffordshire NHS Foundation Trust scandal and public inquiry

Mid Staffordshire NHS Foundation Trust was at the centre of one the largest healthcare scandals in recent times.

The scandal came to light because of an investigation by the Healthcare Commission into the operation of Stafford Hospital. The Commission had been first alerted by the high mortality rates in patients admitted as emergencies. When the FT failed to provide what the Commission considered to be an adequate explanation, a full-scale investigation was carried out between March and October 2008.

The Commission's report was released in March 2009. It detailed appalling conditions and inadequacies at the hospital and severely criticised the FT's management. Press reports suggested that between 400 and 1,200 patients died in 2005–2008 because of the sub-standard care compared to what would be normally expected for the type of hospital, although such 'excess free' death statistics did not appear in the final Healthcare Commission report.

As a result, the trust's chief executive, Martin Yeates, was suspended while its chair Toni Brisby resigned. In July 2009, the then-Secretary of State for Health Andrew Burnham announced a further independent inquiry, by Robert Francis QC, into the care provided by the trust. The generally critical inquiry report was published on 24 February 2010. The report made 18 local and national recommendations, including that the regulator Monitor de-authorise the FT. Compensation payments averaging £11,000 were paid to some of the families involved. Robert Francis QC commented:

> 'Whilst the executive and non-executive board members recognised the problems, the action taken by the board was inadequate and lacked an appropriate sense of urgency. The trust's board was found to be disconnected from what was actually happening in the hospital and chose to rely on apparently favourable performance reports by outside bodies such as the Healthcare Commission, rather than effective internal assessment and feedback from staff and patients. The trust failed to listen to patients' concerns, the board did not review the substance of complaints and incident reports were not given the necessary attention.'

In June 2010, the new government announced that a full public inquiry would be held. The inquiry, also chaired by Robert Francis QC, began on 8 November 2010. The final report was published on 6 February 2013, making 290 recommendations and calling for a 'fundamental culture change' across the health and social care system to put patients first at all times. It called for action across six core themes:

- culture
- compassionate care
- leadership
- standards
- information
- openness, transparency and candour.

The government's initial response in March 2013, entitled *Patients First and Foremost*, set out a radical plan to prioritise care, improve transparency and to ensure clear action and clear accountability where poor care was detected. The government instigated a number of immediate significant changes after the publication of the inquiry report to improve inspection, increase transparency, emphasise compassion, standards and safety, increase accountability for failure, and build capability. These changes included the following:

- The Care Quality Commission appointed three Chief Inspectors of hospitals, adult social care and primary care.
- The Chief Inspector of Hospitals began a first wave of inspections of 18 trusts.
- The Care Quality Commission consulted on a new system of ratings with patient care and safety at its heart and on a new set of fundamental standards that must underpin all care in the future: the inviolable principles of safe, effective and compassionate care.
- Legislation to introduce a responsive and effective failure regime looking at quality as well as finance is progressing through Parliament.
- NHS England published guidance to commissioners, *Transforming Participation in Health and Care*, on involving patients and the public in decisions about their care and their services.
- For the first time, NHS England published clinical outcomes by consultants for ten medical specialties and has also begun to publish data on the Friends and Family Test.
- New nurse and midwifery leadership programmes were developed from which 10,000 nurses and midwives will have benefitted by April 2015.
- A new fast-track leadership programme was launched to recruit clinicians and external talent to the top jobs in the NHS in England, including time spent at a world-leading academic institution.
- By the end of 2014, 96% of senior leaders and all ministers at the DH were to have gained frontline experience in health and care settings.

A further paper, *Hard Truths – The Journey to Putting Patients First* was published in January 2014 and provided a detailed response to the 290 recommendations the inquiry made across every level of the system. It also responded to six independent reviews that the government had commissioned to consider some of the key issues identified by the Inquiry:

- *The Review into the Quality of Care and Treatment Provided by 14 Hospital Trusts in England*, led by the NHS Medical Director in NHS England, Professor Sir Bruce Keogh. Expert inspections of hospitals with the highest mortality rates revealed unacceptable standards of care. Eleven hospitals were placed into 'special measures' to put them back on a path to recovery and then to excellence.
- *The Cavendish Review: An Independent Review into Healthcare Assistants and Support Workers in the NHS and Social Care Settings* by Camilla

Cavendish set out how the training and support of healthcare and care assistants could be improved so that patients receive compassionate care in both NHS and social settings.

■ *A Promise to Learn – A Commitment to Act: Improving the Safety of Patients in England* by Professor Don Berwick described a partial loss of focus on quality and safety as primary aims, inadequate openness to the voices of patients and carers, insufficient skills in safety and improvement, inadequate staffing for patients' needs, and a very unhelpful complexity and lack of clarity and cooperation amongst regulatory agencies.

■ *A Review of the NHS Hospitals Complaints System: Putting Patients Back in the Picture* by Rt Hon Ann Clwyd MP and Professor Tricia Hart focused on four areas for improvement, namely the quality of care; the way complaints were handled; independence in the complaints procedures; and whistle-blowing.

■ *Challenging Bureaucracy* led by the NHS Confederation.

■ The report by the Children and Young People's Health Outcomes Forum, co-chaired by Professor Ian Lewis and Christine Lenehan.

Hard Truths also set out how the whole health and care system would prioritise and build on the initial actions taken by the government, including major new action on several vital areas. These were as follows.

■ Transparent monthly reporting of ward-by-ward staffing levels and other safety measures.

■ All hospitals to clearly set out how patients and their families can raise concerns or complain, with independent support available from local Healthwatch or alternative organisations.

■ Trusts to report on complaints data and lessons learned quarterly, with the Ombudsman to significantly increase the number of cases she considers.

■ A statutory duty of candour on providers which was introduced in the Care Act 2014, along with a professional duty of candour on individuals through changes to professional guidance and codes.

■ The government will consult on proposals about whether trusts should reimburse a proportion or all of the NHS Litigation Authority's compensation costs when they have not been open about a safety incident.

■ Clauses to be added to the Criminal Justice and Courts Bill for wilful neglect, so that those responsible for the worst failures in care are held accountable. The new offences will come into effect in 2015, subject to Parliamentary approval.

■ A new fit and proper person's test which will act as a barring scheme which was introduced in the Care Act 2014.

■ All arm's-length bodies and the DH were to sign a protocol to minimise bureaucratic burdens on trusts.

- A new Care Certificate was introduced, ensuring that healthcare assistants and social care support workers have appropriate fundamental training and skills to give personal care to patients and service users.
- The Care Act 2014 introduced a new criminal offence applicable to care providers that supply or publish certain types of false or misleading information where that information is required to comply with a statutory or other legal obligation.

As set out below, the government also published a revised NHS Constitution as a result of the Francis Report.

While poor governance within the NHS is unlikely to lead to its complete disappearance (unlike a corporate body), it is likely to lead to the continual pressure to move towards greater centralisation of control by the government. Political opinions will differ as to whether this is in the best interests of the recipients of a publicly funded healthcare system. Lessons in good practice have generally resulted from such misconduct and poor decision-making. However, it is the reputation of the NHS that repeatedly suffers as a consequence in the meantime.

Common themes in poor governance

Aspects of poor governance include:

- a board of directors that fails to perform its duties properly, perhaps because it is dominated by one or more individuals, or because it fails to carry out its appointed tasks;
- a poor relationship between the board and the main stakeholders;
- failure to deliver the appropriate returns or services required by either statute or by regulators;
- ineffective systems of risk management, and exposure to errors and fraud due to inadequate internal control systems;
- inappropriate remuneration and reward systems for directors and senior executives;
- misleading performance reporting to regulators and stakeholders; and
- unethical business practices.

Therefore, a key issue in governance continues to be the relationship between the board of directors, its main stakeholders (such as patients, staff, and the DH) and other important stakeholders. The following quote from the NHS Providers and Beachcroft LLP publication *The foundations of good governance: a compendium of best practice* is illuminating:

> 'Good governance should not be an end in itself and should not be the preserve of 'governance specialists'. Effective governance is not about processes. It is about successful leadership and making manifest the values of the organisation. It is sometimes regarded as an obscure subject, not necessarily visible in its own right, but it becomes a high profile reputation issue when it is found lacking.'

Defining health service governance

It is essential that there is a good understanding of what health service governance is, and what it is intended to achieve.

The NHS often faces times of uncertainty with short- and long-term policy competing for attention. This is particularly true with the significant changes introduced by the HSCA 2012. Good governance is vital for NHS organisations as they face another series of major changes and will be key to ensuring that there is effective leadership, responsible stewardship of public assets and services and public accountability.

Health service governance is not a product in itself. Instead, it is foundational to the delivery of 'high quality for all' as envisaged in 2008's Darzi report (covered in more detail later).

Health service governance – a definition

There have been numerous attempts to define corporate governance. The classic definition has been provided by the UK Corporate Governance Code and it can be adapted for health service governance as follows:

'Health service governance is the system by which NHS organisations are directed and controlled. Boards of directors or governing bodies are responsible for the governance of their organisations. The stakeholders' role in governance is to appoint the directors and the auditors and to satisfy themselves that an appropriate governance structure is in place. The responsibilities of the board or governing body include setting the organisation's strategic aims, providing the leadership to put them into effect, supervising the management of the business and reporting to stakeholders on their stewardship. The actions of the board or governing body are subject to laws, regulations and the stakeholders in general meeting.'

Governance can, therefore, be defined as a system that allows organisations to be effective in the delivery of their strategic aims. The strategic aims for the NHS are set out in the NHS Constitution, which attempts to clarify the expectations of the taxpayer into rights, and pledges that should be delivered. As a consequence, health service governance has to create a system that enables effective delivery of those healthcare rights and pledges, tailored for the local communities in which it is delivered by the individual parts of the NHS. The Constitution provides an overriding strategy that is then underpinned at a local level by each NHS organisation as it actively considers its own specific local strategy.

The NHS Constitution

The *NHS Constitution for England* is a formal constitution which lays down in one document the objectives of the NHS, the rights and responsibilities of the various parties involved in healthcare in England and the guiding principles that govern the service.

The following are required by law to take account of the NHS Constitution in their decisions and actions:

- the Secretary of State for Health
- all NHS bodies, including, clinical commissioning groups, NHS trusts and NHS FTs
- all private and voluntary sector providers supplying NHS services
- local authorities in the exercise of their public health functions.

The Constitution was first published on 21 January 2009 and was one of a number of recommendations in Lord Darzi's report *High Quality Care for All*. This set out a ten-year plan to provide the highest quality of care and service for patients in England. These rights and responsibilities had previously evolved in common law, through UK or EU law, or were policy pledges by the NHS and government. They have now been written into the Constitution. Under the Health Act 2009, all providers and commissioners of NHS care are under a legal obligation to have regard to the NHS Constitution in all their decisions and actions. The first report on the effect of the NHS Constitution was published in July 2012. This report showed that three years on from the launch of the Constitution, the NHS remained true to the fundamental principles and values as expressed in the Constitution. Those principles and values were as relevant now as they were when the NHS was founded, and it continued to enjoy strong support from the public. The Constitution remains a focal point for what the health service is all about.

There are legally binding requirements for revising and updating the Constitution which guarantee that the principles and values that underpin the NHS are subject to regular review and recommitment. These also mandate that any government which seeks to alter the principles or values of the NHS – or the rights, pledges, duties and responsibilities set out in the Constitution – has to engage in a full and transparent debate with the public, patients and staff. Three public consultations have taken place since the Constitution's publication in 2009 that have proposed adding new patient and staff rights and staff duties. There have been three revisions of the NHS Constitution in light of these consultations. These are as follows.

The first revision

In March 2010, the NHS Constitution was updated to add new patient rights, including:

- a new right for patients to start consultant-led non-emergency treatment within a maximum of 18 weeks of a GP referral and for the NHS to take all reasonable steps to offer a range of alternatives if this is not possible; and

- a new right to be seen by a specialist within a maximum of two weeks from GP referral for urgent referrals where cancer is suspected.

The second revision

In March 2012, the Constitution was updated as part of a series of measures intended to highlight the importance of whistleblowing in the NHS. The update added:

- an expectation that staff should raise concerns at the earliest opportunity;
- a pledge that NHS organisations should support staff when raising concerns; and
- clarity around the existing legal right for staff to raise concerns about safety, malpractice or other wrong doing without suffering any detriment.

The third revision

In April 2013, the Constitution was further updated in relation to a number of key areas such as:

- complaints
- dignity, respect and compassion
- duty of candour
- end of life care
- feedback
- integrated care
- patient information
- patient involvement
- responsibilities and commitments
- staff rights.

Furthermore, as part of the government's initial response to the report into the failings at Mid Staffordshire NHS Foundation Trust by Robert Francis QC, the DH changed the Constitution to reflect that the NHS's most important value is for patients to be at the heart of everything the NHS does. The Francis report emphasises the role of the NHS Constitution in helping to create a positive and caring culture within the NHS. Technical amendments to the Constitution were also made in April 2013 to ensure that the Constitution reflected the changes made by the HSCA 2012.

To accompany the updated NHS Constitution, the DH also published:

- a revised Handbook to the NHS Constitution, which explained the rights, pledges and responsibilities set out in the NHS Constitution in more detail;
- the Government's response to the consultation on the NHS Constitution, which set out the changes made;
- a public health supplement to the NHS Constitution (a joint document from the DH, Public Health England and the Local Government Association),

explaining how the NHS Constitution applies to local authorities in the exercise of their public health functions from 1 April 2013; and

- a guide to the healthcare system in England, including a Statement of NHS Accountability summarising who is accountable for planning, delivering and assuring NHS services in the light of the changes introduced by HSCA 2012.

The Constitution also grants patients rights that are intended to be legally enforceable, as well as making other non-binding 'pledges'. These cover:

- access;
- access to nationally approved treatments, drugs and programmes;
- complaints and redress;
- informed choice;
- involvement in healthcare and the NHS;
- quality of care and environment; and
- respect, consent and confidentiality.

The Constitution also sets out the rights of NHS staff and makes other non-binding pledges to staff, recognising that high quality care requires high quality workplaces.

Principles of the NHS

The NHS provides a comprehensive service, available to all irrespective of gender, race, disability, age, sexual orientation, religion, belief, gender reassignment, pregnancy and maternity or marital or civil partnership status. The service is designed to diagnose, treat and improve both physical and mental health. It has a duty to each and every individual that it serves and must respect their human rights. At the same time, it has a wider social duty to promote equality through the services it provides and to pay particular attention to groups or sections of society where improvements in health and life expectancy are not keeping pace with the rest of the population.

Access to NHS services is based on clinical need, not an individual's ability to pay. NHS services are free of charge, except in limited circumstances sanctioned by Parliament.

The NHS aspires to the highest standards of excellence and professionalism in the following:

- the provision of high-quality care that is safe, effective and focused on patient experience;
- the people it employs and in the support, education, training and development they receive;
- the leadership and management of its organisations; and

- its commitment to innovation and to the promotion, conduct and use of research to improve the current and future health and care of the population.

Respect, dignity, compassion and care should be at the core of how patients and staff are treated not only because it is the right thing to do, but because patient safety, experience and outcomes are all improved when staff are valued, empowered and supported.

The NHS aspires to put patients at the heart of everything it does. It should support individuals to promote and manage their own health. NHS services must reflect, and should be coordinated around and tailored to, the needs and preferences of patients, their families and their carers. Patients, with their families and carers, where appropriate, will be involved in and consulted on all decisions about their care and treatment. The NHS will actively encourage feedback from the public, patients and staff, welcome it and use it to improve its services.

The NHS works across organisational boundaries and in partnership with *p' ship* other organisations in the interest of patients, local communities and the wider *working* population. The NHS is an integrated system of organisations and services bound together by the principles and values now reflected in the Constitution. The NHS is committed to working jointly with other local authorities, other public sector organisations and a wide range of other private, and voluntary sector organisations to provide and deliver improvements in health and wellbeing.

The NHS is committed to providing best value for taxpayers' money and the *VFM* most effective, fair and sustainable use of finite resources. Public funds for healthcare will be devoted solely to the benefit of the people that the NHS serves.

The NHS is accountable to the public, communities and patients that it *Accoun-* serves. The NHS is a national service funded through national taxation, and it is *tability* the government that sets the framework for the NHS and which is accountable to Parliament for its operation. However, most decisions in the NHS, especially those about the treatment of individuals and the detailed organisation of services, are rightly taken by the local NHS body and by patients with their clinicians. The system of responsibility and accountability for taking decisions in the NHS should be transparent and clear to the public, patients and staff. The government will ensure that there is always a clear and up-to-date statement of NHS accountability for this purpose.

Values of the NHS

These values have been developed with patients, public and staff with the intention that they should inspire passion in the NHS and that should underpin everything it does. Individual NHS organisations are expected to develop and build upon these values, tailoring them to their local needs, however, these NHS values provide common ground for co-operation to achieve shared aspirations at all levels of the NHS.

Working together for patients
Patients come first in everything we do. We fully involve patients, staff, families, carers, communities, and professionals inside and outside the NHS. We put the needs of patients and communities before organisational boundaries. We speak up when things go wrong.

Respect and dignity
We value each person – whether patient, their families or carers, or staff – as an individual, respect their aspirations and commitments in life, and seek to understand their priorities, needs, abilities and limits. We take what others have to say seriously. We are honest and open about our point of view and what we can and cannot do.

Commitment to quality of care
We earn the trust placed in us by insisting on quality and striving to get the basics of quality of care – safety, effectiveness and patient experience right every time:. We encourage and welcome feedback from patients, families, carers, staff and the public. We use this to improve the care we provide. and build on our successes.

Compassion
We ensure that compassion is central to the care we provide and respond with humanity and kindness to each person's pain, distress, anxiety or need. We search for the things we can do, however small, to give comfort and relieve suffering. We find time for patients, their families and carers, as well as those we work alongside. We do not wait to be asked, because we care.

Improving lives
We strive to improve health and wellbeing and people's experiences of the NHS. We value excellence and professionalism wherever we find it – in the everyday things that make people's lives better as much as in clinical practice, service improvements and innovation. We recognise that all have a part to play in making ourselves, patients and our communities healthier.

Everyone counts
We maximise our resources for the benefit of the whole community, and make sure nobody is excluded, discriminated against or left behind. We accept that some people need more help, that difficult decisions have to be taken – and that when we waste resources we waste others' opportunities.

Patient rights and pledges provided by the Constitution

The Constitution grants patients 'rights', which are intended to be legally enforceable and also makes other non-binding 'pledges'. These are set out in Table 2.1.

Table 2.1 Patient rights and pledges

Access to healthcare	
Rights	**Pledges**
Free of charge. Non-discriminatory. Never refused on unreasonable grounds. Obtainable from any UK NHS provider or with pre-approval from any European Economic Area or Swiss public provider. Assessed by the local NHS to meet locally assessed needs. Within maximum waiting times, or for the NHS to take all reasonable steps to offer a range of suitable alternative providers if this is not possible.	Access to healthcare will be convenient and easy to access within defined waiting times. Make decisions in a clear and transparent way, so that patients and the public can understand how services are planned and delivered. Transfers from one provider to another will be as smooth as possible and that patients will be involved in all relevant discussions.

Quality of care and environment	
Rights	**Pledges**
Treatment with a professional standard of care, by appropriately qualified and experienced staff and an organisation that meets required levels of safety and quality. Patients can expect NHS organisations to monitor, and make efforts to improve, the quality of healthcare they commission or provide.	Services will be provided in a clean and safe environment that is fit for purpose and based on national best practice. Identify and share best practice in quality of care and treatments. If admitted to hospital, patients will not have to share sleeping accommodation with patients of the opposite sex, except where appropriate, in line with details set out in the Handbook to the NHS Constitution.

Approved treatments, drugs and programmes	
Rights	**Pledges**
Treatment with a professional standard of care, by drugs and treatments that have been recommended by the National Institute for Health and Clinical Excellence (NICE) for use in the NHS, if their doctor says they are clinically appropriate for them.	To provide screening programmes as recommended by the UK National Screening Committee.

Expect local decisions on funding of other drugs and treatments to be made rationally following a proper consideration of the evidence. If the local NHS decides not to fund a drug or treatment that you and your doctor feel would be right for you, the local NHS must explain that decision. Receive the approved vaccinations under an NHS-provided national immunisation programme.	

Respect, consent and confidentiality	
Rights	**Pledges**
To be treated with dignity and respect in accordance with your human rights. Able to accept or refuse treatment that is offered, and not to be given any physical examination or treatment without valid consent. To be given information about the test and treatment options available, what they involve and their risks and benefits. To privacy and confidentiality and to expect the NHS to keep confidential information safe and secure and to be informed about how the information is used. To request that confidential information is not used beyond their own care and treatment and to have their objections considered, and where their wishes cannot be followed, to be told the reasons including the legal basis. Access to their own health records, which will always be used to manage treatment in the patient's best interests.	To ensure those involved in a patient's care and treatment have access to their health information so they can care for them safely and effectively. To anonymise the information collected during the course of treatment and use it to support research and improve care for others. Where identifiable information has to be used, to give patients the chance to object wherever possible. To inform patients of research studies in which they may be eligible to participate. To share with them any correspondence sent between clinicians about their care.

Informed choice	
Rights	**Pledges**
Choose their own GP practice, and to be accepted by that practice unless there are reasonable grounds to refuse.	To inform patients about the healthcare services available locally and nationally.

Express a preference for using a particular doctor within their GP practice, and for the practice to try to comply. Make choices about their NHS care and to information to support these choices.	To offer easily accessible, reliable and relevant information to enable patients to participate fully in their own healthcare decisions and to support them in making choices. This includes information on the quality of clinical services where there is robust and accurate information available.

Involvement in one's own healthcare and in the NHS

Rights	Pledges
To be involved in discussions and decisions about one's own health and care, including your end of life care, and to be given information to enable one to do this. To be involved, directly or through representatives, in the planning of healthcare services, the development and consideration of proposals for changes in the way those services are provided, and in decisions to be made affecting the operation of those services.	To provide the information needed for the people to influence and scrutinise the planning and delivery of NHS services. To work in partnership with patients, their family, carers and their representatives. To involve patients in discussions about planning their care and to offer them a written record of what is agreed if they want one. To encourage and welcome feedback on a patient's health and care experiences and use this to improve services.

Complaint and redress

Rights	Pledges
To have any complaint made about NHS services acknowledged within three working days and to have it properly investigated. To discuss the manner in which the complaint is to be handled, and to know the period within which the investigation is likely to be completed and the response sent. To be kept informed of progress and to know the outcome of any investigation into a complaint, including an explanation of the conclusions and confirmation that any action needed in consequence of the complaint has been taken or is proposed to be taken.	To ensure patients are treated with courtesy and receive appropriate support throughout the handling of a complaint, and the fact that they have made a complaint will not adversely affect their future treatment. To ensure that when mistakes happen or if a patient is harmed while receiving health care they receive an appropriate explanation and apology, delivered with sensitivity and recognition of the trauma experienced, and know that lessons will be learned to help avoid a similar incident occurring again. That the organisation will learn lessons from complaints and claims and will use them to improve NHS services.

To take a complaint to the independent Health Service Ombudsman, if they are not satisfied with the way their complaint was dealt with by the NHS.	
To make a claim for judicial review if they think they have been directly affected by an unlawful act or decision of an NHS body.	
To compensation where they have been harmed by negligent treatment.	

Patient and public responsibilities

The NHS Constitution recognises that patients can make a significant contribution to their own, and their family's, good health and wellbeing, and take personal responsibility for it. The Constitution sets out key responsibilities as follows:

- register with a GP practice – the main point of access to NHS care as commissioned by NHS bodies;
- treat NHS staff and other patients with respect and recognise that violence, or the causing of nuisance or disturbance on NHS premises, could result in prosecution. Abusive and violent behaviour could result in a patient being refused access to NHS services;
- provide accurate information about health, condition and status;
- keep appointments or cancel within reasonable time. Receiving treatment within the maximum waiting times may be compromised otherwise;
- follow the course of treatment agreed upon, and talk to the clinician if this is difficult;
- participate in important public health programmes such as vaccination;
- ensure that those closest to a patient are aware of their wishes about organ donation; and
- give feedback – both positive and negative – about their experiences and the treatment and care received, including any adverse reactions. Feedback will help to improve NHS services for all.

Staff responsibilities

The Constitution applies to all staff doing clinical or non-clinical NHS work – including public health – and their employers. It covers staff wherever they are working, whether in public, private or voluntary sector organisations. Staff have extensive legal rights, embodied in general employment and discrimination law. These are summarised in the Handbook to the NHS Constitution. In addition, individual contracts of employment contain terms and conditions giving staff further rights.

In addition to these legal rights, there are a number of pledges that the NHS is committed to achieve. Pledges go above and beyond the legal rights. They are not legally binding but represent a commitment by the NHS to provide high-quality working environments for staff. The Constitution also sets out the key responsibilities for NHS staff. These duties are:

- to accept professional accountability and maintain the standards of professional practice as set by the appropriate regulatory body applicable to the profession or role;
- to take reasonable care of health and safety at work for themselves, their team and others, and to co-operate with employers to ensure compliance with health and safety requirements;
- to act in accordance with the express and implied terms of the contract of employment;
- not to discriminate against patients or staff and to adhere to equal opportunities and equality and human rights legislation;
- to protect the confidentiality of personal information that they hold; and
- to be honest and truthful in applying for a job and in carrying out that job.

The Constitution also includes expectations that reflect how staff should play their part in ensuring the success of the NHS and delivering high-quality care.

■ The Statement of Accountability

The Statement of Accountability describes how the NHS in England currently works and who is responsible for its different parts. It is required by the NHS Constitution. In May 2013, a revised Statement of NHS Accountability for England was published in *A Guide to the Healthcare System in England,* to bring it into line with the revisions made to the NHS Constitution in April 2013.

The NHS is a system of organisations responsible for organising and providing a comprehensive health service. The funding for running the NHS is granted to the DH by Parliament out of national taxation. There is therefore a continuous thread of accountability to the government running throughout the NHS.

The Secretary of State for Health is accountable to Parliament, and through Parliament to the voters, for the promotion of a comprehensive health service and for the use of public money. Any decision taken by ministers about health policy can be scrutinised by Members of Parliament. The Health Select Committee and the Public Accounts Committee provide a scrutiny function holding the government to account for the delivery of health policy and effective use of resources. Other Select Committees perform similar functions in other policy areas. It is the role of the DH to support the Secretary of State in discharging their duties.

The Secretary of State for Health is a politician, and is the Cabinet minister responsible for health in England. They have a duty to promote a comprehensive health service in England and ministerial responsibility to Parliament for the provision of the health service. The Secretary of State has a number of further legal duties, particularly in relation to improving the quality of services and reducing health inequalities. They must also keep the performance of the health service under review and lay before Parliament a published report on this performance annually. They are responsible to Parliament for the provision of the health service and they work through the DH to provide strategic direction for the NHS (as well as the wider health and care system), and holds all of the national bodies to account for their operational and financial performance, thereby ensuring that the different parts of the system work properly together. They take decisions on national health, public health and social care policy, advised by the civil servants who make up the DH.

The DH's purpose is to help people live better for longer. It leads, shapes and funds health and care in England, making sure people have the support, care and treatment they need, with the compassion and dignity they deserve. The DH, on behalf of the Secretary of State, acts as 'system steward' – it is the only body with oversight over the whole health and care system, and it works to ensure the system operates effectively to meet the needs of people and their communities. This stewardship role has several main aspects. These are as follows.

- Setting national priorities which reflect what patients, service users and the public value. The DH sets ambitions and priorities for the NHS and health care system, through the outcomes frameworks and the Mandate (explained later). It also supports the delivery of ministerial ambitions, priorities and policies; and does this through obtaining information and intelligence, and appropriate monitoring.
- Securing and allocating resources to meet priorities and deliver services. The DH secures and distributes resources for the NHS, and the health and care system, by securing public funding for the NHS, public health and social care from HM Treasury through the Spending Review process. It is an important stakeholder and shareholder in NHS provider organisations, and is a key source of funding for capital investment. It can also secure additional sources of funding, for example through existing prescription and dental charges, and directly allocates resources to local authorities for public health.
- Sponsoring national health and care system bodies by supporting them and holding them to account for the delivery of their role. 'Sponsorship' means the DH ensuring organisations are delivering their functions, meeting their statutory duties, and using public money efficiently and effectively. The specifics of the relationships between the DH and its sponsored bodies are set down in 'framework agreements'.
- Fostering relationships, collaborating with patient organisations, and ensuring the system works well together. This involves ensuring all health and care bodies, and other bodies, work effectively together and with common purpose,

whilst recognising their own unique roles and autonomy in deciding how to carry out their defined functions. The DH also works with other government departments on health matters.

■ Creating and updating the policy and legislative frameworks within which the health and care system operates. It oversees an effective regulatory framework that ensures all organisations and professionals meet essential standards of quality and safety.

■ Accounting to Parliament and the public for the effectiveness of the health and care system. This includes supporting ministerial accountability to Parliament and the public for the effectiveness of the health and care systems, the effective use of resources voted by Parliament, and the discharge of Secretary of State's legal duties. Ultimately, the Secretary of State has powers to remove the chairs of the major national health bodies from office and (in the case of significant failure to exercise their functions properly) powers of direction, which could force an organisation to undertake or cease a particular course of action. Failure to comply with such a direction could result in the function being carried out by another body. The DH is accountable to Parliament and the public. It does not lead on the day-to-day running and organisation of health services.

Whilst the DH remains responsible for the health and care legislative framework and ministers continue to be ultimately accountable, most day-to-day operational management in the NHS takes place at arm's length from the DH since HSCA 2012. With the exception of the remaining special health authorities, all organisations in the NHS have their own statutory functions conferred by legislation, rather than delegated to them by the Secretary of State.

Figure 2.1 shows the main organisations that now make up the healthcare system in England.

As Figure 1 demonstrates, there are a number of areas of focus within the NHS structure, namely:

■ providing care
■ commissioning care
■ improving public health
■ empowering people and local communities
■ supporting the health and care system
■ education and training
■ safeguarding patients' health.

Figure 2.1: The health and care system from April 2013

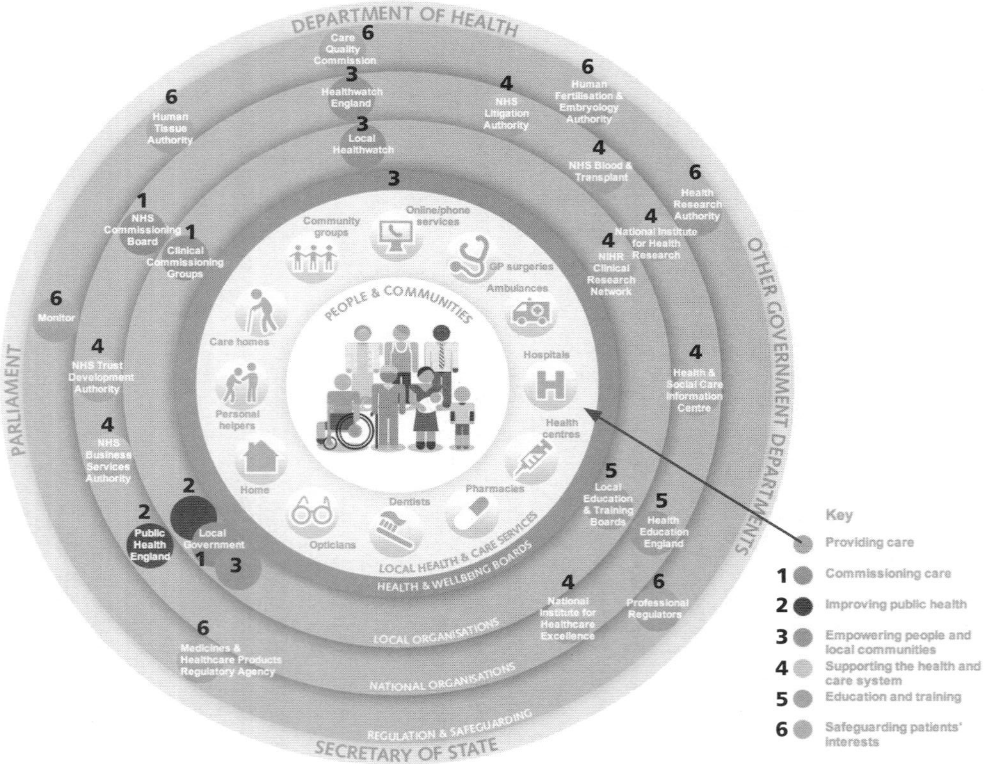

Source: www.gov.uk/government/publications/the-health-and-care-system-explained/the-health-and-care-system-explained

■ Providing care

The provision of healthcare by NHS is divided into two sections: primary and secondary care.

Primary care

Providers of 'primary care' are the first point of contact for physical and mental health and wellbeing concerns in non-urgent cases. These include general practitioners (GPs), dentists, opticians, and pharmacists (for medicines and medical advice). For urgent cases, patients can visit a provider of urgent care, such as an accident and emergency department. Health care professionals within GP practices aim to resolve problems locally, including through services provided by the practice. If a condition requires more specialised treatment, or further investigation, patients may be referred to another healthcare provider. These could be based in a hospital, or in the community. Patients are entitled (where possible) to choose between different types of care and providers of their care. They should be supported to make the choice that is best for them

Community-based care is becoming the preferred means of providing care for the majority of longer-term and mild to moderate conditions. This enables people to keep their normal routine, staying close to family and friends. Hospital services remain a key part of the NHS, such as for specialised, surgical or emergency care.

Secondary care

Providers of secondary care are those bodies that provide acute healthcare. This can be either elective care or emergency care. Elective care means planned specialist medical care or surgery, usually following referral from a primary or community health professional such as a GP. Most of these services are provided by 'NHS bodies', which are part of the public sector.

There are, however, also many other types of organisation involved in providing NHS care, including providers from the independent sector or voluntary sector. For example, pharmacies tend to be independent sector organisations, and most GPs and dentists have traditionally worked as contractors for the NHS, either individually or in partnerships. The third sector includes organisations such as local community groups, voluntary groups, registered charities, social enterprises and co-operatives. All organisations contracted to provide NHS services must meet the NHS's required levels of care. Not all provider organisations, however, will have a board as such; for example, GP practices are unlikely to have boards. Every organisation, however, will have a person or people who are legally accountable for the service they are providing.

The majority of NHS services, such as hospitals, belong to either an NHS trust or NHS FT. It is the government's ambition that all NHS trusts will ultimately become NHS FTs. Each trust can have multiple sites, meaning one or more hospitals often belong to a single trust.

Foundation trusts

In NHS FTs, the board of directors is directly accountable to their local population through their membership and council of governors. The public, patients, service users, their families and carers, and staff can join their local FT as members. Members elect governors to represent them. In an FT, the council of governors oversees the organisation's board, holding the board to account for the performance of their organisation. These are covered in more detail in Chapter 11.

CASE STUDY: a foundation trust

Heart of England NHS Foundation Trust provides over 40 different health-care services and is based across four sites: Birmingham Heartlands Hospital; Solihull Hospital; Good Hope Hospital; and Birmingham Chest Clinic. The services provided by the trust include: general medical, surgical and accident and emergency services, as well as specialist services, such as cardiology, dermatology, orthodontics, paediatrics, radiology, and speech and language therapy.

NHS trusts

In NHS trusts the board is accountable to the Secretary of State for Health via the NHS Trust Development Authority (NHS TDA). The government intends that services and hospitals that are currently part of NHS trusts will become part of NHS FTs (or another type of organisation).

As of November 2014, there were 149 FTs and 96 NHS trusts. It is Monitor's role to 'authorise' new FTs. In order to become an FT, NHS trusts must demonstrate to Monitor that they are well led and able to provide good quality services for patients on a sustainable basis. A key part of the formal assessment process is a comprehensive inspection of the trust by the Chief Inspector of Hospitals. Aspirant trusts will be inspected alongside other organisations as part of the Chief Inspector of Hospital's routine programme. An overall rating of 'Good' or 'Outstanding' will be required to pass to the next stage of the assessment process. Not all NHS trusts will be able to achieve NHS FT status in their current configuration. These trusts may become part of an FT or a different type of organisation. It is the role of NHS TDA to support NHS trusts them to improve the quality and sustainability of their services for patients. In some cases, securing these improvements will mean helping trusts to achieve FT status in their current form.

■ Commissioning care

The NHS is funded by taxation with a fixed budget available to spend on services for the whole population. The challenge faced by the NHS is how to spend that budget in a way that results in the best possible outcomes for individual patients and delivers value for money for the public. This planning and purchasing of NHS services is undertaken by organisations (or individuals) known as commissioners. They are responsible for assessing the reasonable needs of their populations and using their buying power as purchasers to secure services that are affordable and of the highest quality. They can buy services from any provider that meets NHS standards of care and prices. As part of their role, commissioners have to work together with providers to determine the services needed for local areas.

Clinical commissioning groups

Given the complexity and scale of the healthcare system, it is more efficient to plan and commission healthcare at a population level, such as for a town and its surroundings or a metropolitan borough. All GP practices are required to be a member of a clinical commissioning group (CCG). In order to plan their commissioning decisions, local authorities and CCGs (coming together through health and wellbeing boards) use Joint Strategic Needs Assessments (JSNAs), and Joint Health and Wellbeing Strategies (JHWSs) to agree local priorities for local health and care commissioning.

Further detail on the structure and governance arrangements for CCG's can be found in Chapter 12.

NHS England

It is not appropriate to commission some services locally, NHS England ((known in HSCA 2012 as the NHS Commissioning Board) commissions these services, which are more appropriate to commission at a national level. These include specialised services (such as those for rare diseases), offender healthcare and some services for members of the armed forces. NHS England is also responsible for commissioning primary care, including GP services.

In addition to commissioning services itself, NHS England also has responsibility for ensuring the overall system of commissioning NHS-funded services works well. This involves working on plans to improve commissioning for specific conditions (such as dementia) or patient groups (such as children's services). NHS England provides information and resources for CCGs, and holds them to account for how they carry out their commissioning activities and improve the health care outcomes that matter locally.

NHS England is an executive non-departmental public body. It works under its mandate from the Government to improve the quality of NHS care and health outcomes, reduce health inequalities, empower patients and the public and promote innovation. Its key responsibilities include:

- authorisation and oversight of CCGs and support for their on-going development;
- the direct commissioning of primary care, specialised health services, prison healthcare and some public health services (including, for a transitional period, health visiting and family nurse partnerships); and

- developing and sustaining effective partnerships across the health and care system.

NHS England has 27 area teams but is one single organisation with senior clinical leadership at all levels operating to a common model. It has one board, composed of the following:

- the chair of the board (appointed by the Secretary of State);
- at least five other members (appointed by the Secretary of State) who, together with the chair, are the non-executive members of the board; and
- the chief executive and other executive members (the number of executive members shall be less than the number of non-executive members).

NHS England has been set the objective of ensuring that any proposals for major service change meet four tests:

- strong public and patient engagement;
- consistency with current and prospective need for patient choice;
- a clear clinical evidence base; and
- support for proposals from clinical commissioners.

If the relevant local authority does not consider the proposed changes to be in the best interests of the local population, they can refer the matter to the Secretary of State.

NHS England is operationally independent from the DH, with the Secretary of State setting out what the government expects from NHS England in the Mandate. The Mandate highlights the areas of health and care where the government expects to see improvements in the NHS and contains a number of objectives which NHS England must seek to achieve. The Mandate is intended to provide the NHS with stability to plan ahead; it is set for a number of years at a time. The Secretary of State refreshes it every year, albeit not during the year without the agreement of NHS England (except in exceptional circumstances or after a General Election). It is the main way in which the Secretary of State holds NHS England to account for the NHS commissioning system.

The Mandate sets an overarching objective for NHS England to improve outcomes for people using the NHS, in particular to improve against all indicators (or measures) in the NHS Outcomes Framework. The NHS Outcomes Framework sets out the outcomes and corresponding indicators used to hold NHS England to account for improvements in quality. It was developed in partnership between clinicians and stakeholders. Indicators from the NHS Outcomes Framework are also used in the CCG Outcomes Indicator Set, which measures the success of services commissioned by CCGs. This allows the public, and CCGs themselves, to compare performance of different CCGs.

The Mandate, NHS Outcomes Framework and CCG Outcomes Indicator Set cover the same five areas (called 'domains') that are the over-arching priorities for the NHS in England (see Figure 2.2):

Figure 2.2: The five domains

Domain 1	Preventing people from dying prematurely;
Domain 2	Enhancing quality of life for people with long-term conditions;
Domain 3	Helping people to recover from episodes of ill health or following injury;
Domain 4	Ensuring that people have a positive experience of care; and
Domain 5	Treating and caring for people in a safe environment and protecting them from avoidable harm.

Source: ©Nuffield Trust www.gov.uk/government/uploads/system/uploads/attachment_data/file/256456/NHS_outcomes.pdf

Commissioning support units

Commissioning support units (CSUs) provide commissioning support services to NHS commissioners, including local clinical commissioning groups (CCGs), NHS England, acute trusts and local government.

Commissioning support is NHS money spent on non-clinical services. While CSUs do not provide direct patient care or treatment, the 18 CSUs across England play a key role in helping commissioners to improve patient care and achieve savings, releasing resources for reinvestment in frontline clinical services. The units are designed to provide commissioning support services that enable clinical commissioners to maximise resources and focus their clinical expertise and leadership on securing the best outcomes for patients and driving up quality of NHS patient services.

CSU specialist support services include:

- contract management
- business intelligence
- information governance
- financial management
- HR, estates and IT
- clinical procurement
- non-clinical purchasing
- communications and patient engagement
- bespoke services such as individual funding request management, infection prevention, governance and quality

CSUs are not geographically defined. In some cases, customers are local or regional clinical commissioners, and in others they include clinical commissioning groups in other parts of England. Some CSUs also provide services to NHS England, local government, and acute trusts. In addition to specialist business support services, CSUs work in partnership with NHS England, commissioners, acute and community health and social care providers to develop new services and improve existing services through innovation in technology, data intelligence, clinical pathway design, patient experience initiatives and patient information campaigns.

Currently governed by NHS England, CSUs will become autonomous organisations in 2016 and will be fully established, self-sustaining entities in a competitive market.

Local authorities

Local authorities (or councils) have a wide range of duties and responsibilities regarding the health of their populations. These extend beyond the NHS into both public health and social care. Since 1 April 2013, local government has led the public health system at local level. The changes under the HSCA 2012 also mean that local authorities in England have a statutory duty to take steps to improve the health of the people in their area as well as other public health functions and in order to improve their work, CCGs and local authorities have, for example, the freedom to commission services together. The relevant local authorities are:

- county councils
- unitary authorities, including metropolitan district councils
- London boroughs and the Common Council of the City of London
- the Council of the Isles of Scilly.

With these new functions comes the responsibility for a range of services that were previously commissioned and provided by NHS bodies. This does not mean that local authorities are now NHS bodies. However, when they are undertaking their public health functions, they are an important part of the comprehensive health service and, like NHS bodies, must have regard to the NHS Constitution.

Local authorities also commission social care for their local populations based on local criteria and national minimum standards. Unlike NHS care, state-funded social care is means-tested. The DH has responsibility for national adult social care policy, and has committed to changing how care is paid for (subject to legislation) with the overall aim of a sustainable and fair partnership between the government and individual for care costs. The Adult Social Care Outcomes Framework defines national priorities for the social care sector, and includes indicators that enable the public and other stakeholders to assess the performance of services. The Department for Education has responsibility for national children's social care policy.

Upper tier and unitary local authorities in England have, by law, powers to review and scrutinise any matter relating to the planning, provision and operation of the health service (including public health) in its area. This enables scrutiny of the quality of services provided locally and proposals put forward for significant changes to those services, such as re-organising stroke care in an area. An important feature of local authority decision-making has been the Health Overview and Scrutiny Committee (HOSC) which has held NHS bodies to account for the quality of their services through powers to obtain information, ask questions in public and make recommendations for improvements that have to be considered. Proposals for major changes to health services were at times referred to the Secretary of State for determination if they were not considered to be in the interests of local health services. Local authorities are no longer required to have such committees as the means by which they discharge their scrutiny function, although in practice most have retained them.

If there is a HOSC, then it should be involved early on in discussions about any reconfiguration of health services and should take a view about whether changes are in the interests of local health services. For example, it can examines the proposal in light of councillors' knowledge of their local area and make recommendations about how the people who use services, particularly vulnerable groups, can be informed about changes to services. It should also assess the impact of such changes after implementation.

The health and wellbeing boards created by HSCA 2012 operate differently from these existing local authority scrutiny committees because, for the first time, officers (such as the director of adult social services, the director of children's services and the director of public health), clinical commissioning groups and the local Healthwatch will have the same statutory status as councillors.

Figure 2.3: The NHS commissioning structure

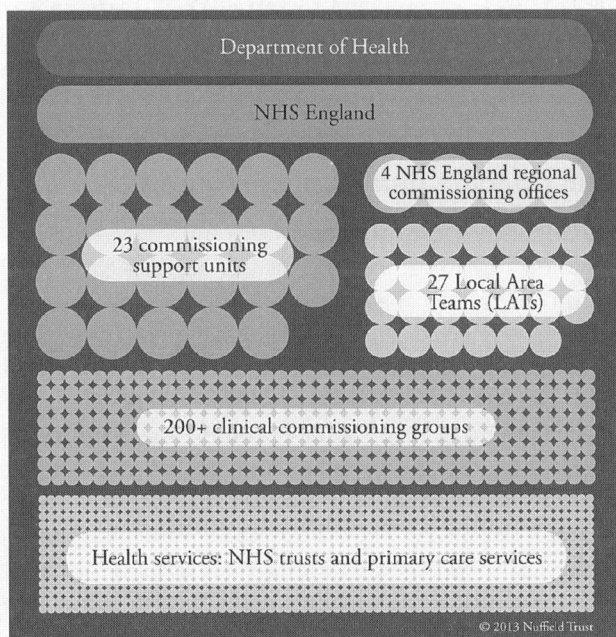

Source: © Nuffield Trust

Every upper tier and unitary local authority area in England also has arrangements with a Local Healthwatch organisation to support patient and public involvement activities in its area.

Local authorities also have the responsibility for improving the public health of the people in their area. This includes the planning and provision of public health services, such as smoking cessation, and considering the public health effects through the planning of other linked services, such as education, housing, social care and transport. Local authorities are supported in this work by Public Health England.

Figure 2.3 sets outs the commissioning structure within the NHS.

■ Improving public health

Whilst responsibilities for improving health lie with both providers and commissioners, Public Health England (PHE) has a key responsibility in this area with regard to local authorities.

Public Health England

PHE is an operationally independent executive agency of the DH, which supports local authorities in their duty to improve public health and has national responsibility for protecting the public against major health risks. NHS England also commissions some national public health services. PHE makes comparative data available to help drive improvements and reports annually on progress against the public health outcomes set out in the Public Health Outcomes Framework.

■ Empowering people and local communities

Overview and Scrutiny Committees

The public's opinion can influence local health services through the overview and scrutiny committees of local authorities. Overview and scrutiny committees (OSCs) are made up of elected local councillors, supported by council officials. They allow democratically elected community leaders to voice the views of their constituents and require local NHS bodies to listen and respond.

OSCs have the power to scrutinise the operation and planning of local health services. All councillors, except for leaders and cabinet members, are able to be members of overview and scrutiny committees. They review the policies made by the council and its partners. They can refer decisions back to the cabinet or decision-maker for reconsideration if they have concerns. This power to scrutiny includes the right to scrutinise and make reports to NHS bodies, require officers of NHS bodies to attend scrutiny committee meetings when requested, ask for information about the planning and provision of services from NHS bodies and require them to respond to their recommendations. Where scrutiny committees have concerns about substantial changes being proposed by NHS bodies, they can refer decisions back to the NHS. If these are not satisfactorily resolved, they can be referred to the Secretary of State.

Under HSCA 2012, local authorities are no longer required to have overview and scrutiny committees to discharge health scrutiny functions, but continue to have such functions, which they are able to discharge in various ways. For example, local authorities may choose to continue to operate their prior health overview and scrutiny committees, or may choose to put in place other arrangements such as appointing committees involving members of the public. HSCA 2012 also provided that the requirements for an NHS body to consult the local authority overview and scrutiny committee and to require officers of NHS bodies to attend before the committee to answer questions will also potentially include CCGs, NHS England and other providers of health services, including independent sector providers.

Health and wellbeing boards

The health and wellbeing board encourages work to improve local health and wellbeing outcomes, including (where appropriate) more joined-up working across the NHS, public health, social care and other services. The core membership of a health and wellbeing board includes commissioners from across the local authority, such as the director of public health, the director of adult social services, the director of children's services and representatives of all CCGs in the health and wellbeing board's area. The local Healthwatch organisation also has a seat on the health and wellbeing board, as well as at least one elected local authority member. Local boards will be free to expand their membership to include a wide range of perspectives and expertise, such as representatives from the charity or voluntary sectors.

Health and wellbeing boards assess the current and future health and social care needs of the local community through JSNAs. JSNAs are based on a principle of analysing the available evidence on the local community's health and social care needs. This includes engaging and working with a wide range of local stakeholders such as patient groups, voluntary organisations and the public. Using the JSNA, health and wellbeing boards jointly agree strategic priorities for local health and social care services in Joint Health and Wellbeing Strategies (JHWSs). Taken together, JSNAs and JHWSs are intended to form the basis of commissioning plans across local health and care services (including public health and children's services) for CCGs, NHS England and local authorities. Boards are under a statutory duty to involve local people in the preparation of Joint Strategic Needs Assessments and the development of joint health and wellbeing strategies.

Guidance has been published to support health and wellbeing boards, including:

- *New Partnerships, New Opportunities:* a resource to assist setting up and running health and wellbeing boards; and
- *Operating Principles for Health and Wellbeing Boards*: a resource to help board members consider how to create really effective partnerships across local government and the NHS.

A progress report published in June 2013, *Making a local difference: state of play and challenges ahead for health and wellbeing boards*, sets out five key lessons which will help health and wellbeing boards meet the challenges they are likely to face in the early stages of their operation as fully fledged statutory bodies. These are as follows.

- The health and wellbeing boards that work best have built good relationships between the local authority and CCGs. Where relationships are most advanced, clinical commissioners are not only at the heart of discussions to develop Joint Strategic Needs Assessments and Joint Health and Wellbeing Strategies, but are reflecting these in their own commissioning plans.
- The key to progress is to be clear and focused about the board's strategic role, and to have the right membership to deliver this. Boards working faster and better strategically have taken the lead in shaping transformational change across the whole system, focusing on a small number of higher-impact, 'big' themes that attempt to add value to 'what would have happened anyway'.
- More progress towards integration is being achieved where boards attempt to understand and influence the delivery as well as commissioning of services. A cooperative relationship between commissioners and providers is beneficial, with providers actively involved in design and development, working closely with commissioners to get the outcomes needed.
- An effective board needs to look outwards to engage with service users, patients, the public, and local communities, not inwards to its members and their organisations alone.
- 'Task and finish' sub-groups help boards drive actions between board meetings and maintain momentum for change. Meeting only infrequently, boards cannot rely solely on members to deliver their duties and goals.

As well as identifying lessons, the report identifies nine key challenges health and wellbeing boards face, it also includes examples of relevant guidance, as well as good practice, from boards across England already addressing them, including establishing ways of leading locally through influence rather than authority in order to effect change

Health and wellbeing boards in their entirety are accountable to communities, service users and overview and scrutiny committees. All board members also have incentives to deliver on shared objectives to improve efficiency.

The Parliamentary and Health Service Ombudsman

The Parliamentary and Health Service Ombudsman (the Ombudsman) is an independent crown servant appointed by the Queen. The Ombudsman's role is to independently investigate complaints that individuals have been treated unfairly or have received poor service from government departments and other public organisations and the NHS in England. Although the service has separate parliamentary and health functions, both come under the same Ombudsman. The Ombudsman can look at complaints about the actions of providers of NHS care, as well as commissioners. The Ombudsman can also look at complaints about the DH, NHS England, the CQC and Monitor.

The Ombudsman is accountable to Parliament through the Public Administration Select Committee. In January 2013, the Ombudsman established a unitary board which combined and replaced the previous executive and advisory boards. The board is chaired by the Ombudsman and is the top-level decision-making body in the organisation. In addition, an executive team has been established which is responsible for day-to-day management of PHSO and is accountable to the board for implementing its decisions. The executive team is chaired by the managing director. The Ombudsman has the right to disagree with the board's decisions – reflecting her statutory accountability – but will do so only as a last resort and will put her reasons in writing to the board. The Ombudsman is independent of the NHS.

For local authority services and for services paid for by local authorities, patients can take their cases to the Local Government Ombudsman. The DH established an independent review in 2013 to consider the handling of concerns and complaints; this recommended legislative changes to provide for a single local government ombudsman in England, presiding over an integrated process for handling complaints against bodies within the jurisdiction of the Local Government Ombudsman Service.

The Ombudsman had already set out principles which were intended to promote a shared understanding of what is meant by good complaint handling and to help public bodies in the Parliamentary and Health Service Ombudsman's jurisdiction deliver first-class complaint handling to all their customers. The Francis report prompted the Prime Minister and the Secretary of State for Health to commission a review of NHS hospital complaints handling, co-chaired by the Rt. Hon Ann Clwyd and Professor Tricia Hart, which endorsed these principles.

Following the publication of this review, the PHSO suggested that NHS organisations use the option of self-referral for the most serious cases to the PHSO for independent investigation. This allows the PHSO to play its part in delivering justice, discovering what went wrong and ultimately helping the NHS to restore public trust in what is such a key public service.

Figure 2.4 sets out how members of the public can influence their health and social care services

Figure 2.4: Ways the public can influence health and social care services

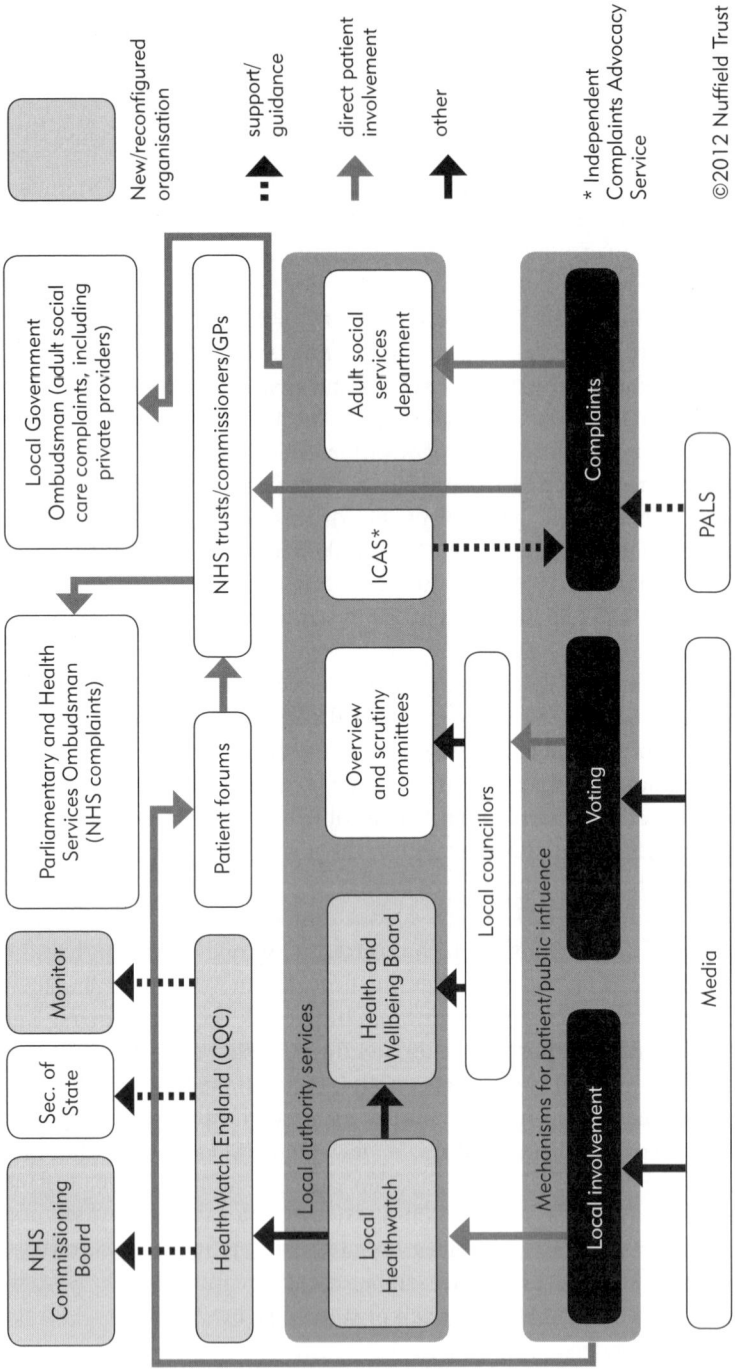

Legend:
- New/reconfigured organisation
- support/guidance
- direct patient involvement
- other
- * Independent Complaints Advocacy Service

©2012 Nuffield Trust

Source: © Nuffield Trust

HealthWatch England and Local HealthWatch

The Healthwatch network consists of two connected levels:

- Healthwatch England works at the national level and supports local Healthwatch organisations. It takes local experiences of health and care and uses them to influence national policy with CQC, NHS England, Monitor and local authorities.
- a local Healthwatch organisation covers every local authority area in England. They take the experiences that people have of local care and use them to help shape local services.

Healthwatch England is the new consumer champion for both health and social care, and has a role in gathering people's views on their local health and care services. It is a committee of the CQC that acts with operational independence in the interests of patients, social care service users and the public providing national leadership, support and advice to local Healthwatch organisations. It ensures that the collective voice of patients has a direct route into the CQC's decision-making processes operating independently from the CQC NHS England can escalate concerns about health and social care services raised by local Healthwatch, users of services and members of the public to the CQC. Healthwatch England is also able to provide advice and information (which could include making recommendations and reports) to the Secretary of State, NHS England, Monitor and local authorities. The recipients of Healthwatch England's advice are required in law to respond to Healthwatch England in writing.

The aim of local Healthwatch is to give citizens and communities a stronger voice to influence and challenge how health and social care services are provided within their area. They enable people to share their views and concerns about their local health and social care services to help build a picture of where services are doing well and where they can be improved. Local Healthwatch can also alert Healthwatch England to concerns about specific health and care providers, as well as provide people with information about their choices and what to do when things go wrong – including supporting people who want to complain about NHS services.

Local Healthwatch organisations are able to enter and view certain health and social care premises, produce reports and make recommendations that influence the way services are designed and delivered. Local Healthwatch organisations provide information and advice to the public about local services, and pass on views to Healthwatch England. They can also make recommendations to Healthwatch England and the Care Quality Commission. If a local Healthwatch organisation sends a report or recommendation to a specified provider or commissioner of a local health or social care service, the provider or commissioner is legally obliged to respond to the local Healthwatch organisation in writing.

The LGA and the DH jointly published a document in 2013 to help local Healthwatch audiences understand the legal requirements that have been set out in regulations. *Local Healthwatch Regulations Explained* aims to explain and provide clarity in relation to the following issues:

- lay person and volunteer involvement in local Healthwatch
- restrictions on activities of a political nature.

◼ Supporting the health and care system

Special health authorities

Special health authorities are health authorities that provide a health service to the whole of England, not just to a local community. They have been set up to provide a national service to the NHS or the public under section 9 of the NHS Act 1977. They are independent, but can be subject to ministerial direction in the same way as other NHS bodies.

NHS Trust Development Agency

The NHS TDA was established as a special health authority in June 2012. Its role is to:

- performance manage NHS trusts;
- manage the FT pipeline;
- gain assurance of clinical quality, governance and risk in NHS trusts; and
- appoint NHS trusts chairs and non-executive members, and trustees for NHS charities where the Secretary of State has a power to appoint.

The NHS TDA has the power to direct NHS trusts over any aspect of their function of providing NHS services, and has a range of intervention powers including appointing and removing chairs and NEDs.

NHS Litigation Authority

The NHS Litigation Authority was established in 1995 as a special health authority as a not-for-profit part of the NHS. It provides indemnity cover for legal claims against the NHS, assists the NHS with risk management, shares lessons from claims and provides other legal and professional services for its members.

The NHS Blood and Transplant Authority

The NHS Blood and Transplant Authority is responsible for the supply of blood, organs, plasma and tissues across the NHS.

National bodies

There are a number of other bodies or authorities involved in the provision or organisation of NHS services. They have responsibility for things that are most effectively carried out or coordinated at the national level. Some examples are as follows.

The National Institute for Health and Care Excellence (NICE) is the main source of evidence-based guidance and advice for health and social care practitioners, patients, service users and the public on the most effective way to prevent, diagnose and treat disease and ill health. NICE produces quality standards – concise sets of statements that describe what high quality care looks like for a particular condition or patient group – which are used to drive up the quality of health and care services. In April 2013 it was established in primary legislation, becoming an executive non-departmental public body (ENDPB) as set out in HSCA 2012. At this time it also took on responsibility for developing guidance and quality standards in social care.

The Medicines and Healthcare Products Regulatory Agency is responsible for ensuring that medicines and medical devices work and are acceptably safe. It was created by Parliament as an executive agency of the DH and is overseen by non-executive members who are appointed by the Secretary of State.

The Human Fertilisation and Embryology Authority (HFEA) is the UK's independent regulator of treatment using eggs and sperm and of treatment and research involving human embryos. They set standards and issue licences to fertility clinics. It is an ENDPB, operating under the provisions in the Human Fertilisation and Embryology Act 1990, as amended. Under the 1990 Act, the HFEA is statutorily independent of government but works in partnership with the DH. It is led by a board made up of a non-executive chair appointed by the Secretary of State for Health; a deputy chair and 10 authority members, also appointed by the Secretary of State. The board appoints the chief executive, who is not a member of the board.

▦ Education and training

Health Education England

A special health authority called Health Education England (HEE) is responsible for promoting high-quality training and education, undertaking national planning and leadership, allocating financial resources, monitoring outcomes and securing the required supply of qualified staff. Long-term national planning is needed because a medical student graduating today will still be providing care in 2050. The DH sets the HEE's direction and its expectations for the whole education and training system through a document called the Education Outcomes Framework. The DH holds the operationally independent HEE board of directors to account for HEE's performance through a document specific to HEE called the 'HEE Mandate'.

Clinical senates

Clinical senates are advisory groups of experts from across health and social care. They are non-statutory bodies and do not have a legal duty to commission health services. There are 12 senates covering areas across England providing strategic clinical advice and leadership across a broad geographical area to CCGs, health and wellbeing boards and NHS England. Senates are formed by clinical leaders from across the healthcare system, as well as those from social care and public health. Patients and members of the public will also be involved. They work with strategic clinical networks, academic health science networks, local education and training boards and research networks to develop an alignment of these organisations to support improvements in quality

LETBS

▪ Safeguarding patients' interests

Organisations providing NHS services are regulated to ensure they meet essential standards. The boards of organisations providing NHS care have the primary responsibility to ensure the care they provide is safe and high quality. Regulators exist to ensure providers are fulfilling their obligations to patients and the public.

The system of regulation is independent from the government and from the NHS itself. It exists to ensure that the care patients receive is safe and of acceptable quality. The regulators also make sure the bodies or healthcare professionals they regulate are sound and fit for purpose.

The 2013 Francis Report identified a lack of clarity about the roles of NHS regulatory organisations. In response, the government announced that the Care Quality Commission (CQC) would focus on assessing the level of quality of care for NHS FTs and NHS trusts. Meanwhile, Monitor and the NHS TDA would focus on using their powers, where necessary, to intervene to resolve quality failings.

Care Quality Commission check devts.

From April 2009, the safety and quality regulator for all health services has been the CQC, which is also responsible for the regulation of adult social care services. The CQC is responsible for assessing and making judgments as to the level of safety and quality of care provided by providers of health and social care. To make these assessments, CQC can look at information received from the provider itself, its patients, staff, and from other organisations, and also conducts its own inspections. Information is published on the CQC website.

Providers of healthcare (including hospitals, care homes, care delivered in the home, dentists, GPs, mental health and other specialist services such as hospices) must register with CQC in order to be able to carry on regulated activities, which include the provision of NHS-funded health services.

The CQC is a non-departmental public body within the DH. The CQC board is the senior decision-making structure and it is accountable to the public, Parliament and the Secretary of State for Health. The board is made up of CQC's chair and commissioners, including the chief executive and the three chief inspectors (namely, Hospitals, Adult Social Care and General Practice).

The CQC's principal function in relation to healthcare is to:

- register healthcare providers (whether or not they provide services for the NHS);
- monitor compliance with registration requirements and, if necessary, use its enforcement powers to ensure all service providers meet those requirements;
- review and publish comparative information on organisations providing and commissioning healthcare, and undertake reviews or studies of particular types of care; and
- monitor the operation of the Mental Health Act and Mental Capacity Act.

The CQC carries out a mixture of announced and unannounced inspections that aim to 'get to the heart' of patients' experiences. The inspections look at the quality and safety of the care provided based on five key areas:

- safety
- effectiveness
- care
- responsiveness to people's need
- well-led.

The inspection teams are led by an experienced CQC manager and chaired by a senior NHS clinician or executive. They always include professional and clinical staff, Experts by Experience and patients. Quality summits are then held with the trust, its local partners and local Healthwatch, which provide an opportunity to hear about the findings of the inspection and to focus on the next steps needed if the trust needs to improve.

If a provider of NHS-funded services is failing to meet required levels of quality, the primary responsibility for resolving these failings sits with the board of the provider, working with their local commissioners. At present, if this action is insufficient, further action can be taken by interventions from the CQC. Additional action can be taken by Monitor (for NHS FTs) and by the NHS TDA (for NHS trusts).

The CQC publishes independent assessments of how organisations are performing by drawing on a range of sources of information, including what patients and the public tell them. It also reports annually to Parliament on how the health and social care systems are working overall. The CQC has the power to inspect all registered healthcare providers and to suspend services, impose fines, prosecute or de-register organisations if it has evidence that suggests a serious problem that may be putting patients at risk.

Revised healthcare inspection regimes for acute hospital providers, community health services, mental health services and GP practices have been piloted and since October 2014 have been rolled out nationally. Under the new inspection regimes CQC will rate services on a four-point scale of:

- Outstanding
- Good
- Requires Improvement
- Inadequate.

Ratings will also be given for each of the five key questions as shown in Figure 2.5.

From April 2015, this will involve meeting a set of essential quality and safety standards known as the fundamental standards. These are 11 new regulations (see below) that set out the fundamental standards of quality and safety, which set out the standards below which care should never fall. These are:

- cleanliness, safety and suitability of premises and equipment
- dignity and respect
- fit and proper persons employed
- good governance
- meeting nutritional needs
- need for consent
- person-centred care
- safe care and treatment
- receiving and acting on complaints
- safeguarding service users from abuse
- staffing.

In addition, the HSCA (Regulated Activities) Regulations 2014 – which came into force into October 2014 – set out the 'fit and proper person' requirement for directors and the statutory duty of candour. Following the final report of the Mid Staffordshire NHS Foundation Trust Public Inquiry, which was published in February 2013, the government made a commitment to implement a statutory duty of candour. The contractual duty of candour had already been included in the NHS Standard Contract 2013/14 for all providers to be open and honest with patients when things go wrong. A current contractual duty of candour imposes an obligation to report some adverse incidents, in restricted circumstances, to some patients and their families. It applied only to contracts for NHS and non-NHS providers of services to NHS patients. As with all duties which apply on a contractual basis, its terms were limited to those who sign the agreement. It did not apply to services commissioned under primary care contracts or to many private providers.

The August 2013 Berwick Review, entitled *A promise to learn – a commitment to act: improving the safety of patients in England*, recommended that, for serious incidents, CQC regulations should require that the patient or carer affected by a safety incident is notified and supported. However, the Berwick Review did not subscribe to an 'automatic' duty of candour, where patients were told about every error or near miss, as it was thought that this would lead to defensive documentation and large bureaucratic overheads that detracted from patient care.

Figure 2.5: The CQC rating framework

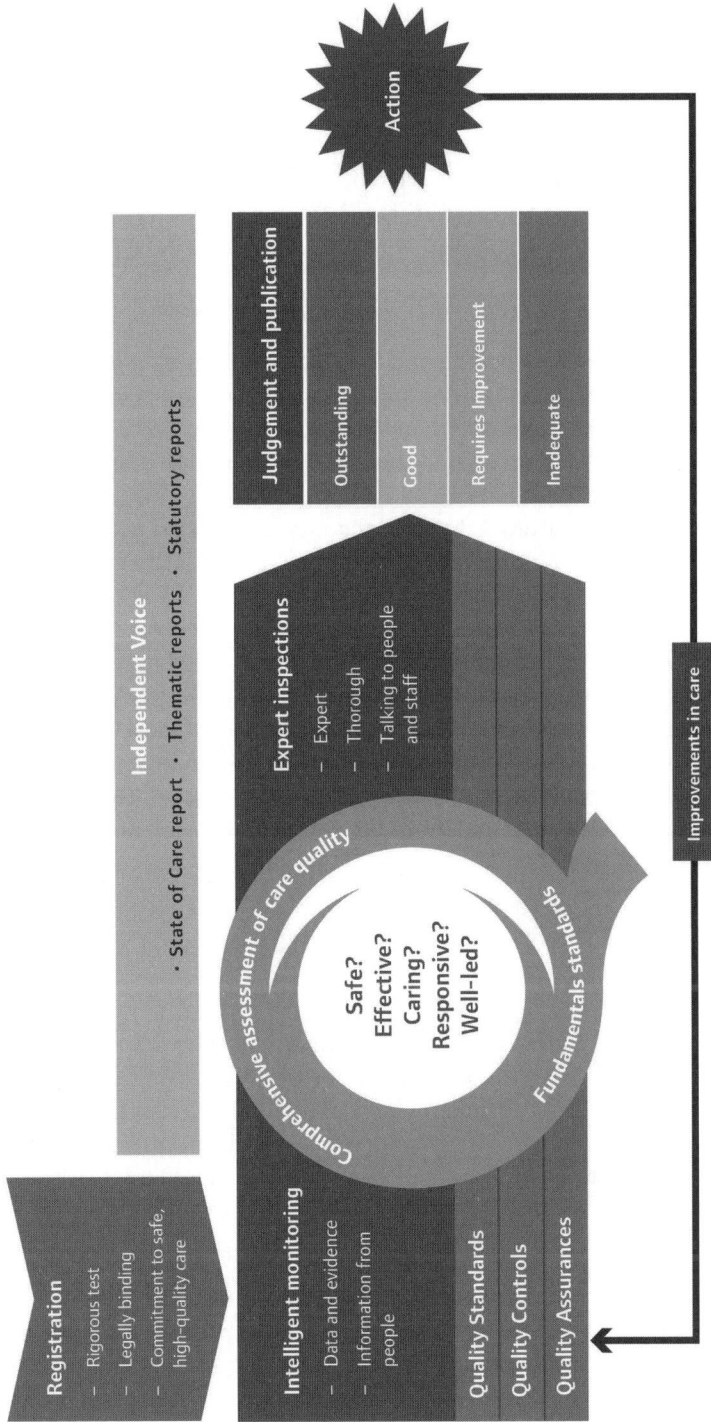

Registration
- Rigorous test
- Legally binding
- Commitment to safe, high-quality care

Independent Voice
- State of Care report • Thematic reports • Statutory reports

Intelligent monitoring
- Data and evidence
- Information from people

Comprehensive assessment of care quality

Safe?
Effective?
Caring?
Responsive?
Well-led?

Fundamentals standards

Quality Standards
Quality Controls
Quality Assurances

Expert inspections
- Expert
- Thorough
- Talking to people and staff

Judgement and publication

Outstanding

Good

Requires Improvement

Inadequate

Action

Improvements in care

Source: © The Care Quality Commission 2015

In March 2014, the Care Quality Commission set out a consultation document entitled *Introducing the Statutory Duty of Candour,* in which the new duty would place a requirement on providers of health and adult social care to be open with patients when things go wrong. Providers would establish the duty throughout their organisations, ensuring that honesty and transparency are the norm in every organisation registered by the CQC. As well as implementing the new duty, the revised registration requirements, as set out above, demonstrate the clear outcomes that providers must meet, which will be core to good service provision.

The duty of candour that can be summarised as follows.

- Healthcare providers will be under a statutory duty of candour to inform the patient, or other duly authorised person as soon as practicable, when they believe or suspect that treatment or care it provided has caused death or serious injury to that patient, and thereafter provide such information and explanation as the patient reasonably may request.

- There will be a statutory duty of candour on registered healthcare professionals to inform their employer where they believe or suspect that treatment has caused death or serious injury.

- It will be a criminal offence for any registered medical practitioner, or nurse or allied health professional or director of an authorised or registered healthcare organisation to knowingly obstruct another in the performance of these statutory duties, provide information to a patient or nearest relative with the intent to mislead them about such an incident or dishonestly make an untruthful statement to a commissioner or regulator, knowing or believing that they are likely to rely on the statement in the performance of their duties.

The harm threshold for healthcare is set to include 'moderate' harm. This means that all harm that is classified as moderate or severe or where 'prolonged psychological harm' has arisen will give rise to a duty of candour to the service user, or a person lawfully acting on their behalf. The duty will also apply in cases of death, if the death relates to the incident of harm rather than to the natural course of the service user's illness or underlying condition. The advantage of using this threshold is that it is the same as the harm threshold used in the contractual duty of candour in the NHS Standard Contract (with the exception of the inclusion of 'prolonged psychological harm). For adult social care providers, the duty will apply to death, serious injury, some moderate harm and prolonged psychological harm, broadly consistent with the application in the NHS.

Where the harm threshold has been breached, specific reporting requirements need to be followed. In summary, the service provider will need to:

- notify the service user (which includes someone lawfully acting on their behalf where necessary) that the incident has occurred. This notification will include an apology;

- advise and if possible agree with the service user what further enquiries are appropriate;
- provide all information directly relevant to the incident;
- provide reasonable support to the service user;
- inform the service user in writing of the original notification and the results of any further enquiries.

The new duty of candour outlines what services must do to make sure they are open and honest with people when something goes wrong with their care and treatment. This is an important step towards ensuring services have the open, honest and positive culture that Sir Robert Francis found was lacking in his inquiry into care at Mid Staffordshire NHS Foundation Trust. When a healthcare service is meeting the duty of candour it will provide:

- a culture within the service that is open and honest at all levels;
- information in a timely manner when moderate and serious incidents, as defined in the national reporting and learning system for safety incidents certain safety incidents, have happened;
- a written and truthful account of the incident and an explanation about any enquiries and investigations that the service will make;
- an apology in writing; and
- reasonable support if there was a direct impact by the incident.

If the service fails to do any of these things, CQC can take immediate legal action against that provider.

The 'fit and proper person' requirement for directors is also introduced by the 2014 regulations and makes it clear that directors and people in 'equivalent' positions of authority are personally responsible for the overall quality and safety of care. When a service is meeting the 'fit and proper person' requirement, its directors will be:

- of good character;
- with the necessary qualifications, skills and experience to be able to perform the role that they are appointed to;
- will supply information, such as certain checks and a full employment history; and
- will never have been responsible for, or involved in, any serious misconduct or mismanagement relating to any office or employment with a service provider.

More detail on this is provided in Chapter 5.

Monitor — NHSI

Under the 2012 Act, Monitor became the sector regulator for health and adult social care. Monitor has a main duty to protect and promote patients' interests by ensuring that health care services are provided effectively, efficiently and economically, while the quality of services is maintained or improved.

Monitor has functions which apply to all providers of NHS-funded care, as well as certain additional functions which apply only to NHS FTs. In the medium term, it will also have a continuing role in assessing NHS trusts for FT status, and for ensuring that FTs are financially viable and well led in terms of both quality and finances. In carrying out its sector regulator role, Monitor licenses providers of NHS services in England, thus requiring any organisation wishing to provide NHS-funded services to be jointly licensed by Monitor and the CQC. The licence sets out the way providers would have to operate, while licensing would enable Monitor to carry out its other roles in three key areas:

- regulating prices: Monitor is responsible for designing a pricing methodology and calculating the efficiency requirements for the sector. This will then be used to set prices in agreement with the NHS England;
- enabling integrated care and preventing anti-competitive behaviour: Monitor's role as the sector regulator will be to work with others, particularly commissioners, to remove any barriers and consider how to enable integrated care provision where this is in the interests of patients; and
- supporting service continuity: Monitor will take on a new role in supporting commissioners to ensure that, in the rare event of the failure of a healthcare provider, patients could continue to access the care that they need.

Monitor is accountable to Parliament but independent of the Secretary of State. It is an executive non-departmental public body of the DH and its board consists of a chair, the chief executive, two EDs and four NEDs who are appointed by the Secretary of State.

Since April 2014, all providers of NHS-funded care (except those exempt in legislation) have been required to hold a provider licence from Monitor in order to operate. This came into effect for NHS FTs from April 2013. NHS trusts have to apply to become NHS FTs and Monitor carries out a robust and challenging process to assess trusts applying for NHS FT status. It examines governance arrangements, financial viability, local accountability and performance against national standards and targets. Further detail on this can be found in Chapter 11.

The licence specifies standards and behaviours that providers must follow or face action from Monitor. Potential action could range from requiring a provider to take a certain course of action, fining a provider or revoking their licence altogether – temporarily or permanently stopping the provider from providing NHS-funded services.

One part of the licence ensures NHS-funded services are priced fairly, with providers properly reimbursed for their work. Monitor is working with NHS England to create a list of prices for NHS services, called the National Tariff. NHS England leads on which services should be included, and Monitor leads on what the prices should be.

Monitor also has a responsibility to investigate if commissioners or providers behave in ways that make competition between different providers unfair where that could act against patients' interests. Other parts of the licence discourage providers from doing things that could prevent healthcare being more joined-up around patients' needs. Choice and competition have existed within the NHS for many years and are now governed by specific rules laid down by Parliament, such as the Competition Act 1998 and the Procurement, Choice and Competition Regulations 2013. It is up to commissioners to decide if, and when, to use competition. However, Monitor polices the rules and makes sure that choice and competition operate in the best interests of patients. In particular, it acts to prevent anti-competitive behaviour by commissioners or providers where it is against patients' interests.

To enable Monitor to carry out this role, it has established a co-operation and competition directorate which can:

- apply and enforce sections of the provider licence related to integrated care and choice and competition;
- apply and enforce the Procurement, Patient Choice and Competition Regulations and relevant sections of the Responsibilities and Standing Rules;
- apply and enforce provisions of the Competition Act 1998 and the Treaty on the Functioning of the European Union that prohibit anti-competitive behaviour; and
- make market investigation references under Part 4 of the Enterprise Act 2002 to the Competition Commission.

Monitor provide the Office of Fair Trading with advice on matters relating to mergers involving FTs.

Monitor has also developed and adopted a common definition for person-centred, coordinated care. To help maintain momentum and accelerate the adoption of new models of coordinated care across the country, Monitor has helped to select 14 local areas to be 'integrated care pioneers' to act as exemplars, demonstrating the use of ambitious and innovative approaches to efficiently deliver integrated care and addressing local barriers.

If providers of NHS-funded services face serious difficulties, ensuring essential services for patients continue is ultimately the responsibility of commissioners, however, Monitor can step in and help ensure that services continue to be delivered so that patients of struggling healthcare providers can be sure of having continued access to critical services if their provider fails. For example, an order confirming the transfer of patients and allowing for the future dissolution of the Mid Staffordshire NHS Foundation Trust was laid in Parliament in October 2014. Patients will be treated by neighbouring NHS trusts following the formal transfer of services, which took place on 1 November 2014.

The provider licence also contains additional extra conditions for NHS FTs. Monitor regulates FTs to ensure that they focus on good leadership and remain financially robust, and holds their boards to account for the early identification and effective resolution of problems. It has powers to intervene in the running of an NHS FT to safeguard NHS patients and services.

Monitor also has a quality governance framework which measures the structures and processes in place to ensure effective, trust-wide, oversight and management of quality performance. More detail on this is set out in Chapter 14.

Since 2008, approximately one in four NHS FTs have been subject to formal regulatory action by Monitor on at least one occasion, with poor governance a contributing factor in almost all of these cases. Monitor maintains that the majority of issues leading to regulatory action occur at least two years post-authorisation. As a consequence Monitor published a paper entitled *Well-led framework for governance reviews: guidance for NHS foundation trusts* in October 2014. This describes the action each FT needs to take to meet the Risk Assessment Framework requirement that FTs carry out an external review of their governance every three years. More detail on this can be found in Chapter 6.

More detail on Monitor's role in relation to FTs is contained in Chapter 11.

Special measures

Following the publication of the Francis Report, Sir Bruce Keogh led a review of 14 trusts (nine NHS FTs and five NHS trusts) that had high mortality rates. The Keogh Review identified significant problems relating to quality and safety and/or leadership in all 14 trusts. In July 2013, 11 of the 14 trusts were put into 'special measures'. This regime was new to the NHS and was set out in the *Guide to Special Measures* published jointly by the CQC, Monitor and NHS TDA.

Special measures apply to NHS trusts and FTs that have serious failures in quality of care and where there are concerns that existing management cannot make the necessary improvements without support. Special measures consist of a set of specific interventions designed to improve the quality of care within a reasonable time.

CQC, through the Chief Inspector of Hospitals, will normally recommend that a trust is placed in special measures when an NHS trust or FT is rated 'inadequate' in the well-led domain (i.e. there are concerns that the organisation's leadership is unable to make sufficient improvements in a reasonable timeframe without extra support) and 'inadequate' in one or more of the other domains (safe, caring, responsive and effective).

When the NHS TDA or Monitor receives a recommendation from the Chief Inspector to place an NHS trust or FT in special measures, the NHS TDA or Monitor will consider the evidence that CQC provides to them alongside other relevant evidence. On the basis of the full range of information, the NHS TDA or Monitor will make a decision whether the trust or FT will be placed in special measures.

The NHS TDA or Monitor may also place a trust or FT into special measures without receiving a recommendation from the Chief Inspector, based on its own evidence. In these circumstances, the NHS TDA or Monitor will always seek advice from CQC. An NHS trust or FT will not enter special measures until the NHS TDA or Monitor formally makes that decision.

The NHS TDA or Monitor will communicate its decision to the trust and then make a formal public announcement through a press release. The period of special measures begins when the NHS TDA or Monitor formally and publicly announces that a trust is in special measures. It is intended that the usual period of time a trust remains in special measures will be a maximum of 12 months, although this may be extended in some circumstances.

The CQC will focus on identifying failures in the quality of care and judging whether improvements have been made. The NHS TDA and Monitor will use their respective powers to support improvement in the quality of care provided.

Typically, providers will be subject to the following interventions, although their detailed application will vary according to the specific circumstances of the organisation.

■ The NHS TDA or Monitor will appoint an improvement director who will act on their behalf to provide assurance of the trust's approach to improving performance.
■ In most cases, the NHS TDA or Monitor will also appoint one or more appropriate partner organisations to provide support in improvement. Partner organisations are selected for their strength in the areas of weakness at the trust in special measures. The nature and amount of support from the partner will be tailored to the trust's requirements but will focus on addressing quality issues identified in the trust's action plan. Arrangements for this appointment will be set out in a memorandum of understanding between the NHS TDA or Monitor and the partner ('buddy') organisation. Partner organisations will be reimbursed by Monitor or the NHS TDA for reasonable expenses and may receive an incentive payment.
■ The NHS TDA or Monitor will review the capability of the trust's leadership. If needed, this may lead to changes to the management of the organisation to make sure that the board and executive team can make the required improvements.
■ The NHS TDA or Monitor will require trusts in special measures to publish their progress against action plans every month on the NHS Choices and their own website, and to participate as required in national and local press conferences.

The CQC reassessed all 14 trusts in the early part of 2014, using its new approach to comprehensive inspections. The Chief Inspector concluded that significant progress had been made at 10 of the 11 trusts. Two had made exceptional progress and were rated 'good' overall. A further three had made good progress and although they still required further improvement, they exited special measures with ongoing support. For a five further trusts, the Chief Inspector recommended a further period in special measures, with a further inspection after six months to ensure that they were continuing to make progress. One trust failed to make significant overall progress and Monitor and CQC agreed to take further urgent action to ensure the quality of care provided to the local population improved as rapidly as possible.

A trust will only come out of special measures if it has made the required improvements. This is usually expected to take place within one year. At the end of the year, the relevant Chief Inspector will inspect the trust and judge whether improvements have been made and if it is delivering good enough care to exit special measures. The NHS TDA or Monitor will only take a trust out of special measures after a trust has been re-inspected, is no longer rated as 'inadequate' in the 'well-led' domain and has made progress across the other four CQC domains. The NHS TDA or Monitor must also be confident that improvements will be sustained.

An inspection and recommendation from the CQC Chief Inspector may result in a range of outcomes for a trust in special measures that includes:

- exit from special measures
- exit after an extension period
- continuing in special measures where Monitor or the NHS TDA has concerns that the trust may not be able to sustain improvements without special measures in place. In this instance, special measures may run in parallel to processes which will consider longer-term solutions, such as a transaction such an acquisition or merger.

In some circumstances, a transaction may be the best means of securing longer-term improvements in the quality of care. In these circumstances, the resulting organisation (whether an acquiring parent organisation, new entity formed by merger, and so on) itself would not automatically be placed into special measures at the point of transaction. The resulting organisation would be assessed on its own merits and regulated accordingly by the CQC, the NHS TDA and Monitor, which would take full account of the nature of the quality problems being taken on within the resulting organisation and how it, as a whole, was seeking to address them.

The Human Tissue Authority

The Human Tissue Authority is an independent watchdog set up in 2005 following events in the 1990s that revealed a culture in hospitals of removing and retaining human organs and tissue without consent. The legislation that established the Authority not only addressed this issue but also updated and brought together other laws that related to human tissue and organs. It protects the public's interest by licensing and inspecting organisations that store and use human tissues and organs for purposes such as research, patient treatment, transplantation, post- mortem examination, teaching and public exhibitions. It was created by Parliament as an executive agency of the DH and is overseen by lay and professional members appointed by the Government.

Professional regulators

There are a number of regulatory bodies that are responsible for the regulation of healthcare professionals. An example is the General Medical Council (GMC), which regulates doctors, and the Nursing and Midwifery Council (NMC), which regulates nurses and midwives.

The professional regulators are independent bodies responsible to Parliament that register and regulate the training and practice of health professionals. They safeguard the safety and the quality of the care that patients receive from health professionals. This includes dealing with concerns about misconduct raised by patients, their families or other professionals. Professional regulators certify new practitioners and ensure that they maintain standards and remain fit to practice.

Health professionals can be reported to the relevant professional regulator and guidance is available on the website of the Council for Healthcare Regulatory Excellence, which provides an oversight role on professional regulation.

Other examples include:

- doctors (the GMC);
- nurses and midwives (Nursing and Midwifery Council);
- dental teams (General Dental Council);
- optical professionals (General Optical Council)
- pharmacists (General Pharmaceutical Council);
- chiropractors (General Chiropractic Council);
- osteopaths (General Osteopathic Council); and
- health, psychological and social work professionals (Health and Care Professions Council).

Figure 2.6 illustrates the regulatory relationships within the NHS

■ Summary

This chapter has included a number of figures in an attempt to demonstrate the inter-relationships that exist within the NHS landscape. Every single part of the structure is bound by health service governance guidance – sometimes in a very direct and explicit way and at other times less so.

All healthcare bodies are bound to act within the constraints of best practice – both in the process, practices and procedures by which power is shared and exercised by those who make up the controlling mind of the organisation – and in how the holders of power in the organisation should be held accountable for what they do. Health service governance is key to ensuring that there is effective leadership, responsible stewardship of public assets and services and public accountability.

Whether you credit the phrase 'with great power comes great responsibility' to Voltaire in nineteenth century France, Franklin D Roosevelt in 1945 or to the uncle of the comic book character Spider-Man, the intention remains the same. Those who exercise power are required to be held to account for the decisions they make. Health service governance provides a framework of law, regulation and guidance to put in place boundaries for those who exercise this power and authority with regard to the world's largest publicly funded health service.

Figure 2.6: NHS regulatory relationships

Regulating and monitoring the quality of services

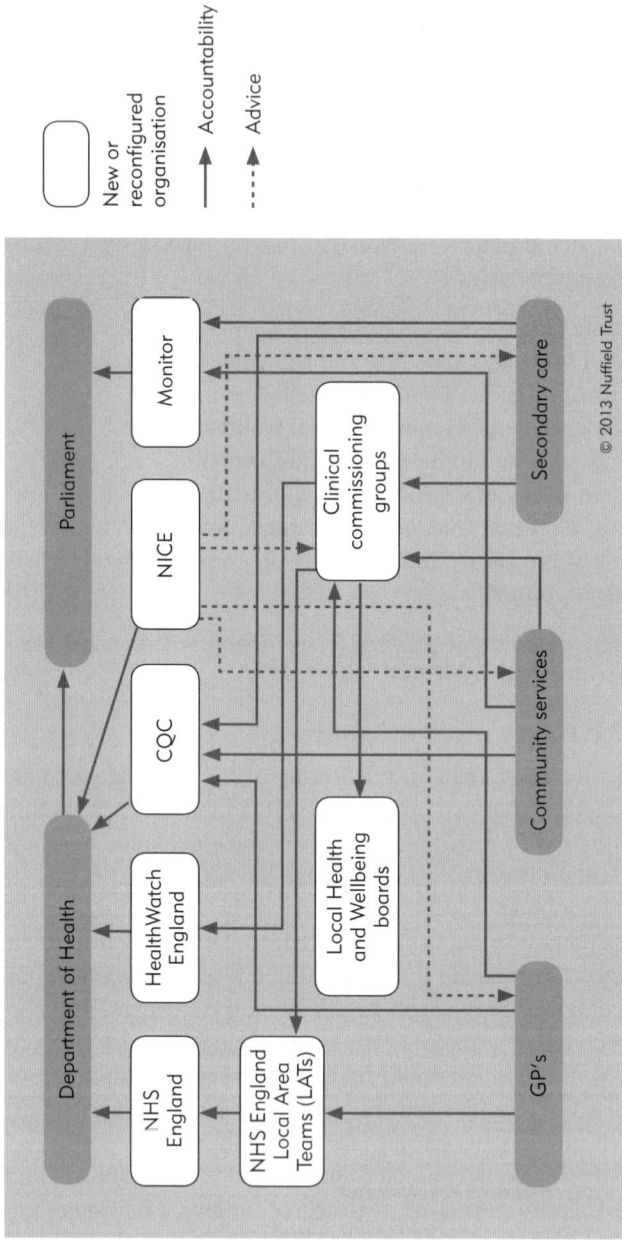

Legend:
- New or reconfigured organisation
- Accountability
- Advice

Organisations shown: Parliament, Department of Health, Monitor, NICE, CQC, HealthWatch England, NHS England, NHS England Local Area Teams (LATs), Clinical commissioning groups, Local Health and Wellbeing boards, Secondary care, Community services, GP's

© 2013 Nuffield Trust

Source: © Nuffield Trust

The law and other regulatory frameworks

To a certain extent, best practice in both health service governance and corporate governance is imposed on organisations by the law or other regulations. There are two different approaches to establishing a system of best practice in governance. One approach is to establish voluntary principles and guidelines, and invite (or expect) organisations to comply with them.

A second approach is to establish laws and other regulations for governance that organisations must obey. In practice, many countries combine both of these approaches by establishing legal and regulatory requirements alongside voluntary principles and codes of conduct.

■ Governance and the law

There is no corporate governance law in any country: rather, some aspects of corporate governance are regulated by sections of different laws. Other aspects of governance are not regulated by law at all, or are regulated only partially. Even in the United States, where there is greater emphasis on regulation of corporate governance, many elements of 'best practice' in corporate governance are voluntary.

Similarly, there is no health service governance law for the NHS. Different aspects of public law and national legislation regulate some aspects of health service governance; there is also a raft of guidance and voluntary codes that have been established for use within the NHS.

It is inevitable that some aspects of health service governance practice are regulated by law, and that organisations should be required to comply with 'best practice'. Regulations on health service governance may be found in:

- healthcare law
- laws on patient and public involvement
- laws on transparency of information, mental capacity, human rights, bribery, corporate manslaughter etc.
- company law.

■ Healthcare law

The *National Health Service Act 1948* established the NHS in 1948. Since that time, there have been significant amendments and additions to the legislation, which has resulted in a fragmented and piecemeal approach to NHS healthcare law. Rather than list each amendment and addition since 1948 this section sets out the main items of legislation that result in the current form and structure of the NHS.

The *NHS Reorganisation Act 1973* provided for lines of authority from NHS providers up to the Secretary of State through the creation of 90 area health authorities (AHAs), which managed both hospitals and community health services. The AHAs were also given joint planning responsibilities with the local authorities. Beneath the AHAs were District Management Teams, which managed hospitals and family practitioner committees (FPCs) that took responsibility for administering contracts for GPs, dentists, pharmacists and opticians. The AHAs were under the supervision of 14 regional health authorities (RHAs), which operated from 1974 to 1996.

The *National Health Service Act 1977* set out the obligations of the Secretary of State to promote a comprehensive health service. The Secretary of State's national responsibilities were delegated to special heath authorities such as the National Blood Authority and NICE, whilst their local responsibilities were delegated to AHAs. Regional health authorities on behalf of the Secretary of State carried out the management of these functions.

The *Health Services Act 1980* abolished the AHAs and District Management Teams and replaced them with district health authorities (DHAs) in 1982.

The *National Health Service and Community Care Act 1990* set out how the NHS should assess and provide for patients based on their needs, requirements and circumstances. It established the split between 'purchasers' (health authorities and some family doctors, under the GP fundholding scheme), who were given budgets to commission healthcare, and 'providers' (acute hospitals, organisations providing care for the mentally ill, people with learning disabilities and the elderly, and ambulance services). The Act introduced the concept of the internal market and established the relationship between the purchasers and the providers as a contractual one. These contractual relationships operated at a common law level but were not judicially enforceable. As a result of the internal market, the state became an 'enabler' rather than a supplier of health and social care provision. The functions of NHS trusts (the 'providers') were partly determined by the 1990 Act and partly through each individual trust's establishment order. The Act also set out key statutory financial obligations such as the obligation to break even, to carry out functions effectively, efficiently and economically, and to hold a public meeting at which the annual report and audited accounts were presented.

The *NHS Trusts (Membership and Procedures) Regulations 1990* set out the composition of the board for NHS trusts, the criteria for appointment and tenure of the chair and NEDs. It sets out the rules regarding the meetings and proceedings of NHS trusts and the appointment procedures for EDs.

The *Health Authorities Act 1995* abolished regional health authorities, district health authorities and family health services authorities and established a single tier of health authorities.

The *Health Act 1999* abolished GP fund-holding in England, Wales and Scotland. The Act amended the National Health Service Act 1977 to make provision for the establishment of new statutory bodies in England and Wales, to be known as primary care trusts (PCTs), and provided for NHS trusts in Scotland to take on additional functions.

The *Health and Social Care (HSC) Act 2001* was designed to deliver many of the aspects of the NHS Plan 2000 that required changes to primary legislation. The Act provided for a new form of trust, care trusts, to provide closer integration of health and social services. It outlined a new delivery system for the NHS, which provided for the commissioning of health and social care by care trusts under partnership arrangements. It also strengthened the arrangements for public and patient involvement in the NHS by providing for local authority OSCs, [oversight committees] whose role was to scrutinise the NHS and to represent local views on the development of local health services. It also created a duty on NHS organisations to have arrangements for involving patients and the public in decision-making about the operation of the NHS. In addition, it legislated for:

■ the establishment of the Healthcare Commission;
■ regulations to be made about complaints procedures in both health and social services; and
■ the Health Service Ombudsman to consider complaints about the handling of NHS complaints by any person or NHS body.

The *National Health Service Reform and Health Care Professions Act 2002* provided for amendment of the structural framework of the NHS. The Act renamed health authorities as statutory health authorities (SHAs) and conferred most of their functions onto PCTs. NHS resources were to be allocated directly to the PCTs by the Secretary of State. Service planning would be undertaken by the PCTs, with the SHAs providing the performance management function for the health services provided within their boundaries. The Act also provided for the creation of an independent 'Patients' Forum' for every NHS trust and PCT in England, to perform an inspection, monitoring and representation role on behalf of patients and the public. The National Commission for Patient and Public Involvement in Health was created to oversee this.

The *Health and Social Care (Community Health and Standards) Act 2003* provided for the establishment of NHS FTs that have the right to enter into legally enforceable contracts. The Act also established a new regulatory body for healthcare – the Commission for Healthcare Audit and Inspection (CHAI).

The *Directions to NHS bodies on Counter Fraud Measures 2004* set out that each NHS organisation must take all necessary steps to counter fraud in the NHS in accordance with the Directions and according to:

- the NHS Counter Fraud and Corruption Manual;
- the policy statement 'Applying appropriate sanctions consistently' published by the Counter Fraud and Security Management Service (CFSMS), now known as NHS Protect; and
- having regard to guidance or advice issued by NHS Protect.

Each NHS organisation must require its chief executive and director of finance to monitor and ensure compliance with these Directions and must cooperate with NHS Protect to enable the CFSMS efficiently and effectively to carry out its counter-fraud functions. Each NHS organisation must also designate a person to undertake specific responsibility for the promotion of counter fraud measures; in the case of an NHS trust this is to be one of the trust's NEDs and in the case of an NHS body other than an NHS trust, it must be one of that organisation's non-officer members.

The *National Health Service Act 2006* redefined the structure of the NHS in England by consolidating much of the existing legislation concerning the health service. The consolidation repealed and re-enacted in its entirety the National Health Service Act 1977, which was itself a consolidation. It also incorporated provisions from:

- the National Health Service and Community Care Act 1990;
- the Health Authorities Act 1995;
- the Primary Care Act 1997;
- the Health Act 1999;
- the Health and Social Care Act 2001;
- the National Health Service Reform and Health Care Professions Act 2002;
- the Health and Social Care (Community Health and Standards) Act 2003; and
- the Health Act 2006.

The *Local Government and Public Involvement in Health Act 2007* reformed the existing arrangements (Patients Forums) for patient and public involvement in the provision of health and social care services with the creation of Local Involvement Networks (LINks).

The *Health and Social Care Act 2008* established the CQC, a single, integrated regulator for health and adult social care to replace the Healthcare Commission (health and adult social care regulator in England), the Commission for Social Care Inspection (social care regulator) and the Mental Health Act Commission (monitoring of Mental Health Act 1983).

The *Health Act 2009* set out the framework for how the NHS Constitution would operate, including a new legal duty on providers of NHS services in England and other relevant bodies to have regard to the Constitution; and a duty on the Secretary of State to consult on, review and re-publish the Constitution at least every ten years, and to report on its impact. The Act also placed a duty on NHS providers to produce Quality Accounts and gave the Secretary of State power to set out in regulations the content (including locally agreed elements), format and timing of Quality Accounts (see Chapter 14).

The Health Act 2009 also amended Chapter 5A of the National Health Service Act 2006 to introduce a special administration process. This made provision for the appointment of a Trust Special Administrator (TSA) over an NHS trust, where the Secretary of State considered it in the interests of the health service.

The key objective of a TSA appointed to an NHS trust is to develop and consult locally on a draft report and make recommendations to the Secretary of State in a final report about what should happen to the trust and the services it provides to ensure the continued provision of key services (location specific services). The legal framework sets out a maximum period of 120 working days for completion of the process (unless extended by order of the Secretary of State), by which time the Secretary of State must make a final decision on the future of the NHS trust following the TSA's recommendations.

With many hospitals facing significant financial difficulties as a result of a variety of complex factors, it is vital, both politically and socially, that NHS services are maintained. The DH assesses NHS trusts according to their performance against a set of financial and quality indicators. If clinical or financial performance is below the required standard and does not improve then the Regime for Unsustainable Providers could be triggered under Chapter 5A of the National Health Service Act 2006 as the only way in which the DH can take decisive action to deal with NHS trusts that are either unsustainable in their current form or significantly failing to make progress towards attaining FT status.

The *Health and Social Care Act 2012* extended this regime to include FTs. It enables Monitor to appoint a TSA where the FT is, or is likely to become, unable to pay its debts. The legal framework applicable to FTs is very similar to NHS trusts, although the timetable is longer to enable Monitor to be consulted (a period of 150 days, unless extended). The framework is different from an ordinary administration under general insolvency legislation in that its main objective is to protect patients and staff from failing services and secure the continued provision of patient services.

Since its inception the regime has been used only twice – in relation to South London Healthcare NHS Trust (SLHT) and Mid Staffordshire NHS Foundation Trust (MSFT).

CASE STUDY: South London Healthcare NHS Trust

SLHT was formed on 1 April 2009 by merging three hospitals. At the time of the merger, these hospitals had a combined deficit of £21.3m.

Following the merger, SLHT ran up debts of more than £150m to become the most financially challenged trust in the NHS. As well as inheriting the financial difficulties of its three predecessor hospitals, six private finance initiative (PFI) schemes operated across the three main sites, adding to its deficit. As a result, SLHT was judged by the Department of Health to be 'not financially viable in its current form' and the first ever TSA was appointed on 16 July 2012.

In accordance with the statutory timetable, on 1 February 2013 the Secretary of State for Health, Jeremy Hunt, made the final decision on the future of SLHT (following on from the recommendations made by the TSA). Ultimately, it was decided that:

- SLHT should be dissolved and its services transferred to other providers, including King's College Hospital NHS Foundation Trust, Lewisham and Greenwich NHS Trust and Oxleas NHS Foundation Trust;
- all vacant or poorly utilised premises should be vacated and sold where possible; and
- the DH should pay the excess costs of the PFI buildings at the Queen Elizabeth and Princess Royal Hospitals, and write off the accumulated debt of SLHT so that the other providers were not saddled with historic debts. The DH also agreed to negotiate an appropriate level of transitional funding to cover implementation.

Importantly, it was also decided that services at Lewisham hospital would be downgraded. This was significant because Lewisham hospital was part of the neighbouring Lewisham Healthcare NHS Trust and did not fall within the remit of SLHT.

The London Borough of Lewisham and a local campaign group called Save Lewisham Hospital applied for judicial review of the TSA's recommendations to scale back services offered at their local hospital and of the Secretary of State's decision to accept those recommendations. The judicial review application was brought on the basis that each NHS trust is a separate legal entity and that the Secretary of State had appointed the TSA only in relation to SLHT.

Both the High Court and the Court of Appeal held that the powers of a TSA appointed over an NHS trust were confined to that particular trust. The TSA's final report and the Secretary of State's decision were held to be *ultra vires* to the extent that they made recommendations about or affected the services provided by Lewisham Healthcare NHS trust at Lewisham hospital.

> In his leading judgment, Lord Justice Sullivan held that: 'If Parliament wishes a TSA appointed in respect of a particular trust to make recommendations for action, not merely in relation to that Trust, but in relation to any trust within all or part of the region in which the trust is located, then it must expressly say so.'
>
> As a result of the judicial review proceedings, amendments to Chapter 5A of the National Health Service Act 2006 were proposed in the passage of the Care Act 2014.

The Health and Social Care Act (HSCA) 2012 introduced significant reforms, which are covered in detail in Chapter 2. It was brought into force by commencement orders. A commencement order is a Statutory Instrument which is designed to bring into force the whole or part of an Act of Parliament. Different parts of an Act may be brought into force at different times.

The *Care Act 2014* sets out a new framework of local authority duties in relation to the arrangement and funding of social care, along with a number of changes to the regulation of social care providers. Whilst primarily aimed at local authorities, the Act has some key implications for NHS organisations due to the growing integration of health and social care.

In particular, the 2014 Act places a specific duty of candour on health and social care providers registered with the CQC (see Chapter 2). A statutory duty of candour must always be one of the registration requirements placed on CQC-registered providers. The duty of candour itself, along with the fit and proper persons test are set out in the Health and Social Care Act 2008 (Regulated Activities) Regulations 2014.

The 2014 Act also reforms the law relating to care and support for adults and the law relating to support for carers. It will make provision about safeguarding adults from abuse or neglect, about care standards, and will establish and make provisions for Health Education England (HEE) and the Health Research Authority (HRA).

The 2014 Act has also introduced extensions to the special administration timetable to give greater time for the TSA to publish their draft report, extend the consultation period and create an obligation for the TSA to consult:

- other NHS trusts and NHS FTs affected by wider recommendations, their staff and their commissioners;
- any local authority in whose area the trust in administration and other affected trusts are located; and
- any Local Healthwatch organisation in the area of any local authority.

The CQC gained a greater role in dealing with quality and safety failure in FTs by requiring also that Monitor appoint a TSA where the CQC is satisfied that there is a serious failure by an NHS FT to provide services that are of sufficient quality. It also requires Monitor to consult more widely with the CQC in various situations, such as before publishing guidance. In addition, TSAs must may not provide draft reports to Monitor without obtaining a statement from the CQC stating that it considers that the recommendations would achieve the sufficient safety and quality of the services

Laws on patient and public involvement

The Health and Social Care Act 2012 introduced significant amendments to the NHS Act 2006, especially with regard to how NHS commissioners will function. These amendments included two complementary duties for CCGs with respect to patient and public participation.

The first duty requires CCGs and NHS England to promote the involvement of patients and carers in decisions which relate to their care or treatment. It requires CCGs to ensure that they commission services which promote involvement of patients across the full spectrum of prevention or diagnosis, care planning, treatment and care management.

The second duty places a requirement on CCGs and NHS England to ensure public involvement and consultation in commissioning processes and decisions. A description of these arrangements must be included in a CCG's constitution. It requires the involvement of the public, patients and carers in:

■ the planning of commissioning arrangements, which might include consideration of allocation of resources, needs assessment and service specification
■ any proposed changes to services which may impact on patients.

CCGs are governed by section 14Z2 of the National Health Service Act 2006, which states:

(1) This section applies in relation to any health services which are, or are to be, provided pursuant to arrangements made by a clinical commissioning group in the exercise of its functions ('commissioning arrangements').

(2) The clinical commissioning group must make arrangements to secure that individuals to whom the services are being or may be provided are involved (whether by being consulted or provided with information or in other ways):

    a) in the planning of the commissioning arrangements by the group,

    b) in the development and consideration of proposals by the group for changes in the commissioning arrangements where the implementation of the proposals would have an impact on the manner in which the services are delivered to the individuals or the range of health services available to them, and

    c) in decisions of the group affecting the operation of the commissioning arrangements where the implementation of the decisions would (if made) have such an impact.

There are two other relevant aspects to section 14Z2. Subsection 3 requires all CCGs to include in their constitution a description of their public engagement arrangements and a statement of the principles that they will follow in when implementing them. Subsection 4 empowers NHS England to publish guidance on compliance with this section, which CCGs must have regard to.

The most recent such guidance on consultations for the NHS was published in September 2013, and is called *Transforming Participation in Health and Care*.

Section 13Q of the Act applies to NHS England and contains effectively identical provisions to section 14Z2. Section 242 of the Act contains the same obligations with regard to patient and public involvement for NHS trusts and FTs. Any NHS body considering a change of the services it commissions or provides must be aware of these obligations.

Section 242(1B) of the National Health Service Act 2006, as amended by the Local Government and Public Involvement in Health Act 2007, provides as follows:

'Each relevant English body must make arrangements, as respects health services for which it is responsible, which secure that users of those services, whether directly or through representatives, are involved (whether by being consulted or provided with information, or in other ways) in –

a) the planning of the provision of those services

b) the development and consideration of proposals for changes in the way those services are provided, and

c) decisions to be made by that body affecting the operation of those services.'

The application of subsections (b) and (c) are only relevant if the proposals under consideration would have an impact on the manner in which the services are delivered to users of those services or the range of health services available to those users.

In summary, any significant commissioning decision or reconfiguration of provision will be caught by these statutory requirements. Whilst the statute does not insist on 'consultation', it seeks to make sure that service users are 'involved'. In practice, some form of consultation exercise will be required for any significant proposed change to services to comply with this duty.

The guidance *Transforming Participation in Health and Care* includes a number of specific tools designed to aid commissioners in their consultation, including the 'Ladder of Engagement and Participation'. This sets out different levels of participation which may be appropriate when involving the public in decisions about healthcare. In addition, an 'Engagement Cycle' sets out key points in the commissioning cycle for public participation.

The guidance also sets out a number of suggested features of public participation. The information provided should be of good quality, and in a number of different formats to ensure that it reaches the intended target. There should be a range of opportunities for participation, which could include online surveys and dedicated local events, as well as work through voluntary and community sector organisations. Patients and the public should be involved from the initial planning stages of service redesign, and special efforts should be made to reach out to diverse communities.

The guidance goes on to suggest the ideal steps which should be taken in order to involve patients and the public. These include:

- identifying expertise in participation within the organisation itself and making best use of it;
- working with health and wellbeing boards on shared approaches with communities; and
- developing a joint approach with local authorities, local Healthwatch, voluntary groups and other organisations with existing relationships with the local community.

It also suggests that commissioners seek feedback through the CCG assurance process as to what is working well and areas of improvement to ensure public participation.

Transforming Participation does not expressly replace the 2008 Department of Health document, *Real Involvement: working with people to improve services*, but commissioners should clearly focus on it as the most recent guidance and the document that they have a statutory responsibility to take into account.

Even so, the 2008 document contains some useful principles on patient and public involvement. According to *Real Involvement*, good involvement

- happens early and continues throughout the process
- is inclusive
- is informed
- is fit for purpose
- is transparent
- is influential – it makes a difference
- is reciprocal – includes feedback
- is proportionate to the issue.

The Cabinet Office's latest statement of 'Consultation Principles' states:

'Timeframes for consultation should be proportionate and realistic to allow stakeholders sufficient time to provide a considered response, and where the consultation spans all or part of a holiday period policy makers should consider what if any impact there may be and take appropriate mitigating action. The amount of time required will depend on the nature and impact of the proposal (for example, the diversity of interested parties or the complexity of the issue, or even external events), and might typically vary between two and 12 weeks. The timing and length of a consultation should be decided on a case-by-case basis; there is no set formula for establishing the right length. In some cases there will be no requirement for consultation, depending on the issue and whether interested groups have already been engaged in the policy making process. For a new and contentious policy, 12 weeks or more may still be appropriate. When deciding on the timescale for a given consultation the capacity of the groups being consulted to respond should be taken into consideration.'

A public body that fails to involve patients and the public leaves itself open to a challenge by way of judicial review. It may not lawfully be able to take decisions and thus implement the changes until consultation has occurred. The courts may also award legal costs against the NHS body.

Judicial review is a process by which a decision of the Secretary of State or an NHS body can be challenged, on the basis that it is unlawful. This right is derived from administrative law and does not just apply to the failure to involve. It is not a right of appeal and is concerned primarily with how decisions are made, rather than the merits of the decision itself. A decision might be unlawful if:

- the decision-maker does not have power to make the decision, or is using their power improperly;
- the decision is irrational;
- the procedure followed by the decision-maker was unfair or biased;
- the decision was in breach of the Human Rights Act; or
- the decision breaches EU law.

If an application for judicial review is successful, the court has six possible remedies:

- Quashing orders: the original decision is struck down and the public body has to take the decision again.
- Prohibiting orders: the public body is forbidden from doing something unlawful in the future.
- Mandatory orders: the public body is ordered to do something specific which it has a duty to do.
- A declaration: on the way to interpret the law in future, for example.
- An injunction: this is usually a temporary remedy until the full application for judicial review is heard.
- Damages: whilst rare, this may be available for example, where there has been a breach of an individual's rights under the Human Rights Act.

The duty to involve arises whether the changes in health service provision are required in response to financial pressures, clinical requirements or other reasons, or a combination of two or more factors. Changes made to comply with DH policy decisions are also subject to the duty to consult. The legal duty to consult both patients and the wider public falls both on the commissioner of health services and on to those providing services. The courts have ruled that, even where a commissioner was simply implementing DH policy, the provision of services was still the commissioner's responsibility and therefore it had an obligation to consult.

Finally, the *Local Authority (Public Health, Health and Wellbeing Boards and Health Scrutiny) Regulations 2013* remove the requirement for local authorities to have a Health Overview and Scrutiny Committee as the means by which they discharge their scrutiny function – although most have retained them. Even so, under Regulation 23, NHS England, CCGs, and public and independent sector providers of NHS services must consult with the local authority about any proposals for a 'substantial' development or variation of the health service in the authority's area. Whilst substantial is not defined, it would be advisable for an NHS body to tell the local authority when it is proposing to consult. If the local authority ultimately disagrees with the decision of the NHS body, it is entitled to refer the matter up to the Secretary of State for a final decision.

CASE STUDY: Save our Surgery

The case of *R (on the application of Save our Surgery Ltd) v Joint Committee of Primary Care Trusts* [2013], related to specialist centres for paediatric cardiac surgery.

It was held that lawful consultation requires that:

- it is undertaken at a time when proposals are still at a formative stage;
- it must include sufficient reasons for particular proposals to allow those consulted to give intelligent consideration and an intelligent response;
- adequate time must be given for this purpose;
- the product of the consultation must be conscientiously taken into account when the ultimate decision is taken.

Healthwatch England is a key player for patient and public involvement under HSCA 2012, not least in its role as the independent consumer champion that gathers and represents the views of the public about health and social care services in England. Local Healthwatch organisations were established in April 2013 and have taken over the work previously done by the LINks, but with additional functions (see Chapter 2).

Local Healthwatch has to be representative of its local community as laid out in HSCA 2012. This includes ethnic groups, different users of services and carers.

Other UK law

There are several other specific pieces of UK legislation with a wide remit that are directly applicable to the NHS.

The *Employment Rights Act 1996* protected employees from detriment if the reason for the employee's action arises from certain cases of whistleblowing – informing on improper practices of employers – where this amounts to a protected disclosure. The whistleblowing legislation is complex. The main principles are as follows:

- a dismissal is automatically unfair if the reason for it is that the employee made a protected disclosure;
- the Employment Rights Act 1996 sets the parameters of what constitutes a protected disclosure, as well as the manner of the permissible disclosure by the worker; and
- different degrees of protection apply depending upon whether the disclosure was made internally within the employer's organisation, or externally to a third party.

A protected disclosure includes the disclosure of any information by a worker that in their reasonable belief tends to show that:

- a criminal offence has been, is about to be or is likely to be committed;
- a person has failed or is about to fail, to comply with a legal obligation imposed upon them, including an obligation imposed upon them by a contract of employment;
- the health and safety of any person has been or is being or is likely to be endangered;
- a miscarriage of justice has occurred, is occurring or is likely to occur;
- the environment has been or is being or is likely to be damaged; or
- information tending to show that one of the above matters has been, or is likely to be, deliberately concealed.

It is not necessary for the worker to show that the act concerned has or will occur. A reasonable belief is sufficient. It is immaterial whether the act has taken place in the UK or elsewhere. The Court determines the state of the employee's disclosure by reference to the date of his or her dismissal or detriment, not the date on which the disclosure was made.

Where a worker is victimised by the employer as a result of making a protected disclosure, a claim can be brought to an employment tribunal. Dismissals or selection for redundancy for making a protected disclosure are automatically unfair. The worker does not have to have been employed for a minimum period of time to make a claim. There is no limit on the compensation that can be awarded. Employment tribunals can award interim relief in unfair dismissal claims.

The *Public Interest Disclosure Act (PIDA) 1998* protects the public by protecting individuals from workplace reprisals for raising a genuine concern, whether a risk to patients or other wrongdoing. The Act's tiered disclosure regime – promoting internal and regulatory disclosures – encourages workplace accountability and self-regulation.

PIDA protects the public by providing a remedy for individuals who suffer a detriment by any act or any deliberate failure to act by their employer for raising a genuine concern, whether it be a risk to patients, financial malpractice, or other wrongdoing. The Act's tiered disclosure regime promotes internal and regulatory disclosures, and encourages workplace accountability and self-regulation.

Under PIDA, workers who act honestly and reasonably are given automatic protection for raising a matter internally. In the NHS an internal disclosure can go up to the highest level and includes going to the responsible Minister at the DH. Protection is also readily available to individuals who make disclosures to prescribed regulators, such as CQC and Monitor.

In certain circumstances, wider disclosures (for example, to an MP or the media) may also be protected. A number of additional tests apply when going wider, including:

- whether it is an exceptionally serious concern
- whether the matter has already been raised
- whether there is good reason to believe that the individual will be subject to a detriment by his employer if the matter were raised internally or with the appropriate regulator
- whether disclosure was reasonable given all the circumstances.

The Act covers all workers, including temporary agency staff, persons on training courses and self-employed staff who are working for and supervised by the NHS. It does not cover volunteers. PIDA also makes it clear that any clause in a contract that purports to gag an individual from raising a concern that would have been protected under the Act is void. Where an individual is subjected to a detriment by their employer for raising a concern or is dismissed in breach of PIDA, they can bring a claim for compensation under PIDA in an employment tribunal. Awards are uncapped and based on the losses suffered.

The *Human Rights Act 2000* came into force in the UK in October 2000. All public bodies (such as courts, police, local governments, hospitals, publicly funded schools, and others) and other bodies carrying out public functions have to comply with the Convention rights. The Act sets out the fundamental rights and freedoms that individuals in the UK have access to.

The *Freedom of Information Act* (FOIA) 2000 created a public 'right of access' to information held by public authorities. The full provisions of the Act came into force on 1 January 2005. The Act led to the renaming of the Data Protection Commissioner (set up to administer the Data Protection Act 1998), who is now known as the Information Commissioner. The Office of the Information Commissioner oversees the operation of the Act. It requires public authorities to have an approved publication scheme, which is a means of providing access to information that an authority proactively publishes. The Information Commissioner's Office has developed and approved a model publication scheme that all public authorities must adopt.

The scheme:

- sets out the types of information that must be routinely published;
- explains the way the information is provided;
- states what charges can be made for providing information; and
- commits the authority to providing and maintaining a guide to the information provided, how it is provided and any charges.

All public authorities should have adopted the model publication scheme and produced a guide to information using either definition documents or template guides to information provided by the Information Commissioner's Office.

The definition documents for the main public sectors give sector-specific guidance on the type of information that authorities are expected to publish and list in their guide to information. The template guides to information are for smaller authorities and are downloadable guides that can be printed off, completed and used without further modification. They have been produced for local councils, schools and NHS practitioners.

The FOIA means that public authorities must disclose official information when people ask for it (unless there is a good legal reason not to), and they must reply within 20 working days.

This model publication scheme for NHS organisations gives examples of the kinds of information that they are expected to provide to meet their commitments under the model publication scheme. They are required to make the information available unless:

- they do not hold the information;
- the information is exempt under one of the FOI exemptions or Environmental Information Regulations (EIRs) exceptions, or its release is prohibited under another statute;
- the information is archived, out of date or otherwise inaccessible; or
- it would be impractical or resource-intensive to prepare the material for routine release.

Freedom of Information requests may be refused if:

- it would cost too much to comply;
- the request is vexatious or repeated; or
- the information is exempt from disclosure under one of the exemptions in the Act.

If any of these criteria apply then the requester must be sent a written refusal notice.

The Act also recognises that there may be valid reasons for withholding information by setting out a number of exemptions from the right to know, some of which are subject to a public interest test. There are 23 exemptions in the FOIA, divided as follows:

- Those that apply to a whole category (or class) of information, for example:
  - information about investigations and proceedings conducted by public authorities
  - court records
  - trade secrets.
- Those that are subject to a 'prejudice' test, where disclosure would, or would be likely to, prejudice, for example:
  - the interests of the United Kingdom abroad
  - the prevention or detection of crime
  - the activity or interest described in the exemption.

Information covered by one or more of the exemptions does not have to be disclosed. However, the decision has to be made as to whether the information should nevertheless be released in the public interest. This is called the 'public interest test' and involves considering the circumstances of each case with the exemption that covers the information. The information must be released unless the public interest in maintaining the exemption outweighs the public interest in releasing it.

Under the FOIA, an authority must apply the public interest test separately to each exemption. When the test does apply, these are called qualified exemptions. Those to which the test does not apply are called absolute exemptions.

There are also exemptions for personal information.

- If personal information relates to the applicant, the request must be dealt with as a 'subject access request' made under the Data Protection Act 1998.
- If the information requested relates to a third party, a decision on whether to release it must be based on whether releasing it would contravene the Data Protection Act.

When refusing a request for information, it is not possible to withhold an entire document because some of the information contained within it is exempt. A redacted version of the document must be provided along with a refusal notice stating why some of the information cannot be released. When refusing an information request the exemption or exemptions applied must be set out, why they have been applied and, where appropriate, the public interest factors for and against disclosure fully explained.

CASE STUDY: Model Publication Scheme for NHS organisations

Who we are and what we do

- Organisational information, structures, locations and contacts
- How we fit into the NHS structure
- Organisational structure
- Lists of and information relating to organisations with which the authority works in partnership
- Senior staff and management board members
- Location and contact details for all public-facing departments

What we spend and how we spend it

- Financial information relating to projected and actual income and expenditure, procurement, contracts and financial audit.
- Annual statement of accounts
- Budgets and variance reports
- Financial audit reports
- Standing financial instructions
- Capital programme
- Staff and board members' allowances and expenses
- Staff pay and grading structures
- Funding (including endowment funds)
- Procurement and tendering procedures
- Details of contracts currently being tendered
- List and value of contracts awarded and their value
- What are our priorities and how are we doing

Strategies and plans, performance indicators, audits, inspections and reviews.

- Annual Report
- Annual business plan
- Targets, aims and objectives
- Strategic Direction document (five year)
- Performance against targets (KPI)/performance
- Clinical
- CQC reviews
- Audit reports
- Service user surveys

How we make decisions

- Decision-making processes and records of decisions for at least the current and previous three years.

- Board papers – agenda, supporting papers and minutes
- Patient and public involvement (PPI) strategy
- Public consultations (for example, concerning closures/variations of services)
- Internal communications guidance and criteria used for decision-making (i.e. process systems and key personnel)

Our policies and procedures

- Current written protocols, policies and procedures for delivering services and responsibilities.
- Policies and procedures relating to the conduct of business and the provision of services
- Policies and procedures relating to human resources (including Race, Disability, Age and Gender, Equal Opportunities)
- Policies and procedures relating to recruitment and employment
- Standing financial procedures
- Standing orders
- Complaints and other customer service policies and procedures
- Data protection/information governance/Caldicott Guardian
- Estate management
- Charging regimes and policies

List and registers

- Any information currently required by law to be held in publicly available registers.
- List of main contractors/suppliers
- Assets registers and Information Asset Register
- Any register of interests kept in the authority
- Register of Gifts and Hospitality provided to board members and senior personnel
- Disclosure Log

The services offered

- Information about the services offered, including leaflets, guidance and newsletters.
- Clinical services provided and/or commissioned
- Non-clinical services
- Services for which the authority is entitled to recover a fee together with those fees
- Patient information leaflets and other booklets and newsletters
- PALS
- Advice and guidance

The *Equality Act 2010* legally protects people from discrimination in the workplace and in wider society. It replaced previous anti-discrimination laws with a single Act, making the law easier to understand and strengthening protection in some situations. It sets out the different ways in which it is unlawful to treat someone. The intention of the general equality duty is to ensure that a public authority must, in the exercise of its functions, have due regard to three main aims:

- eliminating discrimination, harassment, victimisation and any other conduct that is prohibited by or under the Equality Act;
- advancing equality of opportunity between persons who share a relevant protected characteristic and persons who do not share it; and
- fostering good relations between persons who share a relevant protected characteristic and persons who do not share it.

The *Mental Capacity Act 2005* gained Royal Assent in April 2005 and was fully implemented in October 2007. It provides a clear legal framework for people who lack capacity, and their family and carers, to be involved as far as possible in decisions about their care. It sets out five key principles, as well as procedures and safeguards, which are:

- a person must be assumed to have capacity unless it is established that he lacks capacity;
- a person is not to be treated as unable to make a decision unless all practicable steps to help him to do so have been taken without success;
- a person is not to be treated as unable to make a decision merely because he makes an unwise decision;
- an act done, or decision made, under this Act for or on behalf of a person who lacks capacity must be done, or made, in his best interests; and
- before the act is done, or the decision is made, regard must be had to whether the purpose for which it is needed can be as effectively achieved in a way that is less restrictive of the person's rights and freedom of action.

These principles of the Mental Capacity Act apply whether the decisions are life-changing or everyday matters. The underlying philosophy is to ensure that individuals are empowered to make decisions where possible and where this is not possible, that any decision made or action taken is made in their best interests. The Mental Capacity Act Code of Practice also describes the role of the Independent Mental Advocate Service (IMCA) set up under the Act. This service provides support for those particularly vulnerable individuals who lack capacity and have no family or friends so that their views are represented to those working out their best interests.

The *Corporate Manslaughter and Corporate Homicide Act 2007* came into effect on 6 April 2008 and disposed of the need the need to identify a single individual as the 'controlling mind'. This means a trust can be prosecuted as a corporate body.

Section 1 of the *Bribery Act 2010* makes it an offence for a person to offer, promise or give a financial or other advantage to another person in one of two cases:

1. where the intention is to bring about the improper performance by another person of a relevant function or activity or to reward such improper performance.
2. where the intention is that the acceptance of the advantage offered, promised or given in itself constitutes the improper performance of a relevant function or activity.

Section 7 of the Bribery Act also creates a new offence which can be committed by commercial organisations that fail to prevent persons associated with them from bribing another person on their behalf. An organisation that can prove it has adequate procedures in place to prevent persons associated with it from committing bribery will have a defence to the section 7 offence. A 'relevant commercial organisation' is defined at section 7(5) as a body or partnership incorporated or formed in the UK irrespective of where it carries on a business, or an incorporated body or partnership that carries on a business or part of a business in the UK irrespective of the place of incorporation or formation. The key concept here is that of an organisation that 'carries on a business' and so is directly applicable to NHS organisations.

NHS organisations also have statutory responsibilities under the *Health and Safety at Work Act 1974*, the *Management of Health and Safety at Work Regulations 1999* and a number of other health & safety regulations (e.g. *Reporting of Injuries, Diseases and Dangerous Occurrences Regulations 1995, Noise at Work Regulations 1989, Manual Handling Operations Regulations 1992* and the *Control of Substances Hazardous to Health Regulations 2002*).

There have also been a number of EU Directives relating to the NHS. For example, the *EU Clinical Trials Directive 2001* authorised and regulated the conduct of clinical trials, as trials are often conducted in multiple sites across a number of European countries. A revision of this Directive during 2014 introduced changes to speed up the process for authorising new clinical trials and reduce the administrative burden associated with the conduct of these studies. The new EU Directive takes the form of a Regulation, meaning that it will apply directly in each member state of the EU without the need to be transposed into national law, and thereby will ensure the rules are consistent throughout the EU The new EU Regulation is expected to apply from 2016.

Company law and other legislation

While the NHS is not governed by UK company legislation, it provides a useful backdrop for understanding health service governance. In the UK, the main item of company legislation is the *Companies Act 2006*. This includes regulations relating to:

- a the preparation and auditing of annual financial statements, for approval by the shareholders;
- b the powers and duties of directors;
- c other disclosures to shareholders, such as the requirement for companies to publish an annual business review;
- d the disclosure of information about directors' remuneration;
- e general meetings of companies, and shareholder rights to call a general meeting; and
- f shareholder voting rights at general meetings, including the right to re-elect directors.

The impact of this legislation has been felt in health service governance and is covered in the throughout this handbook.

A number of EU company law directives also have relevance for the NHS. ⒺⓊ A proposal for a new or amended EU Directive is initiated by the European Commission in Brussels. Legislation is then agreed by the European Council and the European Parliament in a process known as the 'co-decision procedure'. When a directive has been agreed, its contents must be implemented by all EU member states within a stated timeframe, either in a law or other regulation, if suitable legislation does not already exist. EU Directives on company law have included a requirement for companies to publish an annual business review. Several directives have also been passed affecting companies whose shares are traded on a regulated exchange, including:

- a directive relating to shareholder rights;
- requirements to publish an annual corporate governance statement;
- requirements to have an audit committee;
- requirements to introduce measures that provide for the independence and ethical conduct of their external auditors.

Companies become insolvent for reasons unconnected with corporate governance. Occasionally, however, the directors of a company may allow it to continue in business when they are aware that it is insolvent and will be unable to pay its creditors or employees. In the UK, the Companies Act 2006 includes provisions that make fraudulent trading a criminal offence; in addition, the *Insolvency Act 1986* makes wrongful trading a civil offence.

As discussed earlier, the insolvency framework for NHS organisations is different from an ordinary administration under general insolvency legislation in that its main objective is to protect patients and staff from failing services and secure the continued provision of patient services. The NHS statutory provisions also provide an alternative corporate insolvency procedure for companies to ensure that patients receive uninterrupted services if a provider becomes insolvent.

Money laundering regulations are also in place to protect the UK financial system. Money laundering is the process of disguising the source of money that has been obtained from serious crime or terrorism, so that it appears to come from a legitimate source. Companies are often used for the purpose of money laundering, which is a criminal offence in most countries, and the owners or directors of the companies concerned are often involved in the money laundering activity themselves. If an organisation is covered by the regulations, it must put in place certain controls to prevent it being used for money laundering by criminals and terrorists. These include:

- appointing a 'nominated officer';
- checking the identity of customers;
- keeping all relevant documents; and
- report any suspicious activity to the Serious Organised Crime Agency (SOCA).

Whilst NHS organisations are not specifically covered by the regulations, a number of its suppliers will be such as external and internal audit, counter fraud, and law firms.

■ Compulsory regulation and voluntary best practice

There are aspects of organisations where laws are essential to protect the interests of stakeholders such as employees or shareholders. For example, employment laws are needed to give protection to employees against unfair treatment by employers. Legal requirements for organisations to prepare annual financial statements and have them audited, and the duties of directors are in place to to protect stakeholders. There may be different views about the extent of regulation that is required; however, the need for some regulation seems unquestionable.

Best practice in health service governance has some connection with ethical business practice. Some aspects of behaviour may be considered unethical but legal. Laws are required to prevent or punish activities that are considered so unethical that they should be illegal. Bribery is an example of behaviour that has been tolerated in the past but which is now accepted as illegal by most countries.

Regulation may be needed to address public concerns and maintain public confidence in the governance system. This has probably been most evident in the US. The Sarbanes-Oxley Act of 2002 was a response to public outrage against the many corporate scandals that emerged after the collapse of Enron. Public fury against the banks following the financial crisis in 2007–2008 continues to prompt demands for legislative action that would affect the governance of banks.

Advantages of voluntary regulation of governance issues

It is difficult to devise a set of rules that should apply to all organisations in all circumstances. Rules that are appropriate for one organisation might not be appropriate for another whose circumstances are very different. Although a voluntary system of governance (such as the corporate governance system in the UK) places an expectation on organisations to comply with the guidelines, it also allows them to breach the guidelines if it seems appropriate and sensible to do so.

As a general rule, governance issues become greater as an organisation gets bigger. A voluntary code of best practice in governance can be targeted at the largest organisations; smaller organisations can then choose whether they want to model their own governance systems on parts of the code for the larger organisations. Governance practices can therefore be adapted to the circumstances of the organisation.

In corporate governance, however, there may be a risk that companies will migrate to those countries where the rules are less onerous if different countries have their own corporate governance regulations. Indeed, governments may compete to offer a corporate governance regime that is more attractive in their country than in other countries in order to attract foreign companies. Excessive regulations may deter companies from becoming a listed company, particularly if the rules for listed companies are stricter than the rules for private companies.

In practice, good governance is a combination of regulation and voluntary best practice. In some countries there is more emphasis on regulation and in others there is greater reliance on voluntary codes of practice for large organisations. However, unless law regulates governance, it is probable that standards of governance will vary substantially between organisations.

Voluntary governance frameworks

A voluntary code of governance is issued by an authoritative national or international body and contains principles or best practice in governance that major companies (listed companies) or organisations are encouraged to adopt and apply.

The principles may consist of main principles with associated supporting principles, and for each principle, there may also be provisions or recommendations about how the principle should be applied in practice. Voluntary codes of corporate governance have been adopted in many countries (e.g. in all the countries of the Commonwealth and all the countries of the EU).

There is no statutory requirement for organisations to apply the principles or provisions of a voluntary code. However, a well-established code should attract the support of the significant organisations in that sector, and this develops an expectation that others should adopt the code unless their circumstances are such that non-compliance with some of the code's provisions is a more sensible option.

Although voluntary, organisations may be required to adopt the code of governance, or to explain their non-compliance with any aspect of the code and their reasons for non-compliance in their annual report and accounts. For example, NHS England advocates that CCGs adhere to the *Good Governance Standard for Public Services 2004*. This requirement, common in many countries, is known as 'comply or explain'.

The purpose of a voluntary code is to raise standards of governance. It is principles-based, because there is a recognition that the same set of rules is not necessarily appropriate in every way for all organisations, and that there will be situations where:

- non-compliance with provisions in the code is desirable, given the circumstances that the organisation faces;
- implementing a principle of best practice is not always best achieved by following the detailed provisions or recommendations in the code, and some flexibility should be allowed.

It is also recognised that a code cannot provide detailed guidelines for every situation and circumstance. The preface to the *UK Corporate Governance Code* in 2010 points out:

'It seems that there is almost a belief that complying with the Code in itself constitutes good governance. The Code, however, is of necessity limited to being a guide only in general terms to principles, structure and processes. It cannot guarantee effective board behaviour because the range of situations in which it is applicable is much too great for it to attempt to mandate behaviour more specifically than it does.'

'Comply or explain' and 'apply or explain'

The UK Corporate Governance Code explains:

'The "comply or explain" approach is the trademark of corporate governance in the UK. It has been in operation since the Code's beginnings and is the foundation of its flexibility. It is strongly supported by both companies and shareholders and has been widely admired and imitated internationally. The Code is not a rigid set of rules. It consists of principles (main and supporting) and provisions.'

The UK Code recognises that an alternative to following a provision may be justified in particular circumstances if good governance can be achieved by other means. A condition of doing so is that the reasons for it should be explained clearly and carefully to shareholders, who may wish to discuss the position with the company and whose voting intentions may be influenced as a result.

In providing an explanation, the company should aim to illustrate how its practices:

- are consistent with the principle to which the particular provision relates;
- contribute to good governance; and
- promote delivery of business objectives.

It should set out the background, provide a clear rationale for the action it is taking, and describe any mitigating actions taken to address any additional risk and maintain conformity with the relevant principle. Where deviation from a particular provision is intended to be limited in time, the explanation should indicate when the company expects to conform with the provision.

The UK Code makes it clear that satisfactory engagement between company boards and investors is crucial to the health of the UK's corporate governance regime. In this way both companies and shareholders have responsibility for ensuring that 'comply or explain' remains an effective alternative to a rules-based system. It recognises that there are practical and administrative steps to be taken to improve interaction between boards and shareholders, but it also makes it clear that there is scope for an increase in trust, which could generate a virtuous upward spiral in attitudes to the Code and in its constructive use.

A similar approach has been taken with some voluntary codes in the NHS. Monitor requires FTs to comply with the *NHS FT Code of Governance* or to explain any non-compliance. The same is true of the UK Listing Rules, which require listed companies to comply with the UK Corporate Governance Code.

There is a view that the word 'comply' encourages organisations to follow the provisions of a code in all its details without considering the principles that underpin the code. This may encourage a box-ticking approach, and a view that the detailed provisions must be followed without considering whether the provisions might be appropriate or finding a suitable way of applying the governance principles in the actual circumstances.

For this reason, some countries have adopted governance codes that espouse an 'apply or explain' approach. One such example is the third iteration of *King Code*, the governance code for South Africa. The introduction to King III explains the intention of this approach is to:

> 'show an appreciation for the fact that it is often not a case of whether to comply or not, but rather to consider how the principles and recommendations can be applied. Explaining how the principles and recommendations were applied, or if not applied, results in compliance.'

In an 'apply or explain' approach, following the principles overrides following specific recommended practices. This allows for the explanation to set out how the principle is being followed rather than demonstrating compliance with a recommended practice, which may not be in the best interests of the organisation. King III makes it clear that, under 'apply or explain', that it is the 'board's duty to override a recommended practice if it believes it to be in the best interests of the company. It must then explain why the chosen practice was applied and give the reasons for not applying the recommended practice.

Under King III, entities (whether they be public, private or not-for-profit) are required to make a statement as to whether or not they apply the principles and then explain their practices. The implication of this is that South African entities will have to consider the recommended principles set out in King III, state what their principles are, and explain if and why they differ from the King III recommendations. This is a softer and more flexible approach to governance disclosure, but may lead to abuse if entities fail to justify their deviations from the King III Report's recommended principles.

The UK Corporate Governance Code recognises the dangers of a 'box-ticking' mentality with 'comply or explain' and stresses that it is not intended to be a set of rules:

> 'The Code is not a rigid set of rules ... It is recognised that [non-compliance with a provision] may be justified in particular circumstances if good governance can be achieved by other means.'

Likewise, the introduction to *NHS FT Code of Governance* for FTs makes it clear some FTs may decide that the provisions are disproportionate or less relevant in their case. Therefore, they should actively consider how to adopt the approach in the code in their particular circumstances.

It should be noted that some principles and recommendations have become legislation (such as with Bribery Act 2010) and the practices required by the legislation then become mandatory.

■ Codes for health service governance

Governance in the public sector, and specifically in the NHS, is the subject of several reports. Some of the more prominent reports are as follows.

- *The Nolan Principles on Public Life* (1995): covered in detail the standards of behaviour and principles in public life with particular focus on appointment on merit, with an independent element on all selection panels recommended as the way forward for public bodies (see Chapter 1).
- *The Intelligent Board* (2006): looked at board level information needs and information flow.
- *The Integrated Governance Handbook* (2006): looked in detail at the processes and information requirements of sound governance.
- *Taking it on Trust* (2009): examined how the boards of NHS trusts and FTs in England assure themselves that internal controls are in place and operating effectively.
- *The Healthy NHS Board: principles for good governance* (2013): set out the principles of high-quality governance, and is supported by a regularly updated digital compendium, which puts the principles in an operational context.
- *The NHS Foundation Trust Code of Governance* (2014): set out the governance arrangements for FTs.
- *Well-led framework for Foundation Trusts* (2014): the purpose of this framework is to support NHS FTs in gaining assurance that they are well led.
- *UK Corporate Governance Code*: a corporate framework of governance that underpins much of healthcare governance.
- *FRC Guidance for Boards and Committees*: practical guidance for effective meetings.

The Intelligent Board

This report set out a set of principles and model framework for structuring information to support strategy development and oversight of business delivery and effectiveness. It also suggests practical ways in which boards might use the framework proposed.

The report outlines:

- the information challenge, including discussion of the growing pressure on boards to raise their game and the need to improve the information they receive and how they use it;
- intelligent information for the board, including some key principles that should govern information for the board, together with a proposed framework and minimum data set for reviewing trust performance, supporting decision-making and considering strategy; and
- putting the framework into practice by improving the structure of agendas for the board, developing a 'dashboard' of routine performance indicators and informing the annual cycle of board meetings.

The report was followed by the Intelligent Board series of publications, which includes guidance for mental health trusts, ambulance trusts and clinical commissioners, outlines practical, focused advice for NHS board members on the kind of information they should be using to understand and oversee their organisations' performance.

All the reports in the series are based on the following Intelligent Board principles.

- All information should cover locally defined priorities as well as national 'must do' requirements.
- All information should focus on outcomes, not systems and processes.
- All information should be available in a timely and understandable format.
- All information should be clearly and simply presented.
- All information should be forward-looking, presenting trends and anticipating future issues.
- All information should allow internal comparison between services and make use of external benchmarks.
- All information should provide interpretation and analysis as well as information.
- All information should provide a level of detail that is appropriate to the board's governance role.

The Integrated Governance Handbook

The idea of integrated governance was developed by Professor Michael Deighan and Dr Roger Moore with support from Sir William Wells, Professor Sir Ian Kennedy and Bill Moyes. It was first introduced to the NHS in a paper entitled

'Developing Integrated Governance', published by the NHS Confederation in May 2004.

The handbook was published in 2006 by the DH to ensure that the basic building blocks of integrated governance were in place, with rollout and implementation planned over the following two years. The chief concern that the integrated governance sought to address was the risk of boards governing in silos (e.g. clinical governance, research governance, quality governance, information governance) by moving to an integrated agenda that would enable boards to meet their responsibilities.

Integrated governance is defined as: 'systems, processes and behaviours by which trusts lead, direct and control their functions to achieve organisational objectives, safety and quality of service and in which they relate to patients and carers, the wider community and partner organisations.'

The NHS chief executive at the time, Sir Nigel Crisp, said in issue 245 of the *Chief Executive Bulletin*:

> 'Integrated governance provides the umbrella for all NHS governance approaches. It combines the principles of corporate/financial accountability and it moves towards a single risk sensitivity process which covers all the trust's objectives, supported by a coordinated source of collecting information and subject to coordinated inspection.'

Integrated governance emphasises the critical importance of the board defining, within the overall goals established for the NHS, its own purpose and strategic direction, with clarity of purpose, objective setting and planning of the board's annual cycle of business. The handbook also focused on quality as the driver of change, examined the critical role of clinical governance at the heart of the integrated governance agenda, and covered the legal implications for boards and what they should to do to plan the journey towards good governance.

Integrated governance required an examination of a number of key areas:

- the need for boards to take account of a wide range of NHS requirements in determining overall priorities and drawing up annual operational plans;
- a review of assurance arrangements, with particular reference to the Standards for Better Health (now superseded by the CQC);
- the 'intelligent' information required by boards integrating a wide range of perspectives, including finance, human resources, information systems, research and, most importantly, clinical governance;
- the key role of the Board Assurance Framework, which should complement the strategic priorities identified during the annual business planning cycle; and
- the simplification of committee structures and supports in order to ensure they had clear terms of reference and understood the actions and behaviours expected of them.

It was envisaged that the board would take corporate responsibility for all aspects of strategy setting, performance management and quality assurance, as a result of being assured that the appropriate systems were in place to manage the identified risks.

In particular, the handbook suggested a consideration of the 'company secretary' role within health organisations and a development of the role of the audit committee to scrutinise and streamline committee structures and agendas, ensuring all risks (activity, quality and resources) were anticipated, aligned and integrated.

The key task for integration was an examination of the role of the audit committee to ensure that it scrutinised all the sub-committees reporting to the board. At the time, some boards had more than 40 committees (some, of course, were sub-committees) but they reported either through the audit committee or directly to the board. This was unworkable and did not allow non-executives to fulfil their strategic role. The handbook proposed a phased transition to the following structure:

The handbook recommended that boards should be served by the following main standing committees:

■ audit
■ remuneration and review
■ appointments.

Other committees that boards might find useful included:

■ risk compliance and assurance
■ clinical governance
■ health and safety.

This required a change in board meeting reporting structure to ensure that agendas were robust enough to deal adequately with the business from many of the committees that no longer existed. It also relied upon the strengthened audit committee clarifying much of the work prior to it being placed on the board's agenda.

The handbook set out a direction of travel for health service governance, which was subsequently updated and revised by a further publication entitled *Integrated Governance: a guide to risk and joining up the NHS reforms* in 2011. This outlined a governance development programme that clarifies:

■ the purpose and behaviours of the board;
■ the board structures and systems; and
■ the review and improvement process;

It also set out a number of exercises for board development.

Taking it on Trust

The Audit Commission report *Taking it on Trust* was published in April 2009. It examined the rigour with which NHS trust boards operated the processes available to them and obtained the assurance they need.

The report highlighted discrepancies between trust declarations of compliance with Standards for Better Health (now superseded by the CQC) and subsequent Healthcare Commission inspections; differences between the Statement on Internal Controls (now known as the Annual Governance Statement (AGS)) and core standards declarations; and some major failures in patient care, such as that at Maidstone and Tunbridge Wells NHS Trust and Mid Staffordshire NHS Foundation Trust. There were significant gaps between the processes on paper and the rigour with which they were applied.

The report said that the introduction of FTs had generally reinvigorated governance process. It resulted in the recruitment of non-executives with a greater knowledge of effective risk management and board challenge, drawn from private sector experience. However, the report was critical of assurance processes that had become 'a paper chase' rather than a critical examination of the effectiveness of the trust's internal controls and risk management arrangements.

The report recommended that NHS trusts should:

- ensure that their strategic aims and objectives are clearly defined and few in number so they can be widely understood and clearly cascaded throughout the organisation, and that their strategic risks are identified and aligned to their strategic objectives;
- review their risk management arrangements – including the way in which risks are reported to the board and consider how best to promote and demonstrate the value of risk management work to staff;
- ensure they have systems in place to comply with all statutory, regulatory, clinical and contractual requirements;
- consider cascading the Statement of Internal Control (now the AGS) through the organisation by sub-certification by managers, allied with a more effective compliance function, performance information and performance management;
- review how they identify and then prove assurances on the operation of controls and how these are then evaluated;
- review and increase the assurances they receive from sources other than internal audit, including clinical audit, and in doing so, ensure that their full portfolio of risk is covered;
- maximise the assurance obtained from internal audit by reviewing the scope of internal audit plans and improving its commissioning;
- better align clinical audit programmes to key strategic and operational risks to maximise the assurance provided by the clinical audit function;
- strengthen their compliance mechanisms and distinguish them more clearly from internal audit, which should review the effectiveness of the compliance framework;
- ensure they have robust arrangements for assuring the quality of their data and by developing systematic and formalised review programmes for their data, including checking accuracy back to records; and

- develop policies and guidance on data quality and assurance processes, including defining and allocating responsibility for data quality, to promote consistency and improve awareness of board members.

CASE STUDY: Maidstone and Tunbridge Wells NHS Trust

In the autumn of 2005, Maidstone and Tunbridge Wells NHS Trust suffered a significant outbreak (150 cases) of Clostridium difficile (C. difficile) infection, although it went unrecognised at the time. In April 2006 a second outbreak (258 cases) occurred and was recognised and reported to the SHA (NHS South East Coast) and the Health Protection Agency (HPA). The SHA arranged for an investigation by the Healthcare Commission.

The Commission's report was published in October 2007. As well as analysing the problem and the management of C. difficile specifically, the report also made general comments and criticisms about the leadership and governance of the trust.

One of the central issues was the role of the chair and the NEDs, and their ability to govern. The non-executive board members had struggled to gain a true understanding of what was going on in the organisation, and had also struggled to hold the chief executive and senior managers and clinicians of the trust to account in the period covered by the report. The report stated that the board could have been in a position to ensure the trust managed emergent control of infection issues better than they did if the non-executives had been better advised.

Other issues included the board not providing clear leadership to the organisation as a whole, in its culture and approach to its core business. Board members were reported as being remote and preoccupied with finance and targets.

It was also clear that the board was given information, rather than asking for it. Most information came with a recommendation only that it be noted. The reports to the board on nursing and cleanliness issues were long, academic and did not make clear the success or otherwise of the solutions relied on, such as the nursing quality assurance framework. There was no lack of information or data, but there was an apparent lack of analysis about what it showed. All information appeared to have been given the same weight.

The trust had an assurance framework throughout, but it was mostly not serviceable and not capable of identifying the primary risks at board level. There was no evidence in the minutes that the chair and non-executives made sufficient attempts to clarify what they were being told, to consider the implications, or to identify the decisions that may be required of them.

The Commission estimated that about 90 patients 'definitely or probably' died as a result of the infection.

The Healthy NHS Board: principles for good governance

This 2013 guidance is a refreshed edition of the original guidance, published in 2010. The 2013 guidance was influenced by the Francis Report, and starts from the premise that there is a strong relationship between leadership capability and performance, which is well demonstrated by evidence. It sets out that good leadership leads to a good organisational climate; in turn, good organisational climates lead to sustainable, high-performing organisations via improved staff satisfaction and loyalty.

The report sets out the principles that will allow NHS board members to understand the:

■ collective role of the board including effective governance in relation to the wider health and social care system
■ activities and approaches that are most likely to improve board effectiveness
■ contribution expected of them as individual board members.

The guidance is primarily intended for boards of NHS trusts and FTs, but with some interpretation it is also relevant for organisations operating at a national level. While CCGs, as membership organisations, have developed very specific governance arrangements and are not therefore the primary focus of this guidance, the general principles outlined are relevant to them. It offers a framework that will help them to place reliance on the effective governance of provider organisations.

The guidance sets the three key roles of an effective board as:

■ formulating strategy for the organisation;
■ ensuring accountability by holding the organisation to account for the delivery of the strategy; being accountable for ensuring the organisation operates effectively, with openness, transparency and candour, and by seeking assurance that systems of control are robust and reliable; and
■ shaping a positive culture for the board and the organisation.

These are underpinned by three building blocks that allow boards to exercise their role – namely, that boards:

■ are informed by the external context within which they must operate;
■ are informed by, and shape, the intelligence that provides trend and comparative information on how the organisation is performing together with an understanding of local people's needs, market and stakeholder analyses; and
■ prioritise engagement with key stakeholders and opinion formers within and beyond the organisation. The emphasis here is on building a healthy dialogue with, and being accountable to patients, the public, and staff, governors and members, commissioners and regulators.

The three roles of the board and the three building blocks all interconnect and influence one another. The guidance also sets out clear boundaries for the various roles within the board and outlines an established role for a company secretary.

CASE STUDY: Barking, Havering and Redbridge University Hospitals NHS Trust

The trust had experienced frequent changes to its board. A new chief executive had been in place since February 2011, followed by a medical director (following a number of years where non-permanent staff had provided this function). A number of new NEDs had also been appointed and an interim chair had been in place since 2010.

At the time of CQC registration, the trust had a high number of 'conditions' placed on it to require improvements in care. A series of unannounced inspections in 2010/2011 resulted in some of these being lifted, but also resulted in warning notices being issued to the trust (in March, June and July 2011) on staffing levels and maternity care.

CQC concluded its investigation into the quality and safety of care at the trust. One of the findings of that investigation was that trust governance systems were weak and health service governance was underdeveloped. Governance systems had recently changed, but lines of communication in the new structure were unclear and there was a risk of duplication or issues being missed. The trust was reliant on external reviews to identify issues, and while it held extensive performance information, this was not used to drive change. There was a lack of learning from incidents, with investigations identifying recurring themes.

NHS Foundation Trust Code of Governance

The NHS Foundation Trust Code of Governance (the Monitor Code) was first published in 2006 and was revised in 2010. It was updated again in December 2013, following the significant regulatory change as a result of HSCA 2012. The code builds on the approach, principles and provisions of the UK Corporate Governance Code (and the Combined Codes before it) to bring best practice from the private sector to the NHS.

Monitor, the regulator of FTs, describes the legal framework for NHS FTs as being closer to that of a commercial company than that of other trusts. As such, it adopts a much more 'commercial' approach to their regulation. NHS FTs must comply with Monitor's NHS provider licence, reporting requirements and the Audit Code used by Monitor. Each NHS FT needs to develop individual standing orders, giving authority to each organisation's standing financial instructions, schemes of delegation and matters reserved for the board.

NHS FTs are created as legal entities as public benefit corporations by the National Health Service Act 2006. The legislation constitutes NHS FTs with a new governance regime that is fundamentally different from NHS trusts. NHS FT boards of directors have more autonomy to make financial and strategic decisions. They also have a framework of local accountability through members and a council of governors, which has attempted to central control from the Secretary of State.

NHS FT directors are ultimately and collectively responsible as a board for all aspects of the performance of the FT. Therefore, they need to be able to deliver more focused strategic leadership and more effective scrutiny of the trust's operations. The provisions of the Monitor Code, as best practice advice, do not represent mandatory guidance and accordingly non-compliance is not in itself a breach of NHS Foundation Trust Condition 4 of the NHS provider licence (also known as the 'governance condition'). However, trusts should note the relevant statutory requirements that have been highlighted within the Monitor Code.

The Monitor Code sets out best practice principles and structures and processes (through its provisions), but also makes clear that ultimately only directors and governors can demonstrate and promote the effective board behaviour that is needed to guarantee good corporate governance in practice. The emphasis on governance can be demonstrated from the example of Derbyshire Healthcare NHS Foundation Trust, which was authorised in 2011 after having been unsuccessful in two earlier assessments.

CASE STUDY: Derbyshire Healthcare NHS Foundation Trust

The trust first came to Monitor in 2007 and subsequently requested a deferral, which was agreed and imposed a number of conditions that would need to be resolved before assessment could recommence. These included concerns about the board's capacity to deliver the business plan, and a less than satisfactory working capital report. When assessed again in 2008, Monitor were still not satisfied that the trust's board was able to deliver the business plan, or that the trust was financially viable in the medium term.

Monitor recommended that, among other actions, the trust re-examine the skill mix of the NEDs and how any gaps on the board could be addressed. The trust returned to Monitor for assessment in September 2010.

The actions the trust had taken in the intervening period, following Monitor's recommendations, were evident. A new chair had been appointed, along with four new NEDs. A new finance director had been recruited from an existing FT, and a director of business strategy role had been created. The appointee brought in-depth knowledge of commissioning and an effective working relationship with the local PCT.

Significant time had been committed to board development activities, focusing heavily on the principles of good governance and the characteristics of high performing boards. Monitor observed board meetings and held individual meetings at the trust, and the board was clearly very capable. The executive and non-executive teams worked effectively together, which was apparent throughout the assessment process, and from the outset the integrated business plan had been developed and owned jointly. The trust also demonstrated that it was very focused on quality.

Mike Shewan, Chief Executive of Derbyshire Healthcare NHS Foundation Trust said: 'From day one, Monitor's assessment team was very clear about their expectations and gave us every opportunity to provide the evidence they were looking for. We had learned a lot about the process from our previous assessments and had developed a keen awareness of what Monitor would be looking for. We knew that we needed to be operating as a FT board before we became a FT, and so spent a lot of time developing our board and a strong governance structure. We knew that a high performing unitary board was key to our success, not only in order to achieve FT status, but to continue to deliver in the future.'

The trust's commitment to improving the board and strengthening organisational capacity, based on feedback from Monitor's assessment process, meant that it was authorised as a FT on 1 February 2011.

Source: Monitor Annual Report and Accounts, 2010/2011

The Monitor Code explains that satisfactory engagement between the board of directors, the council of governors, members and patients is crucial to the effectiveness of NHS FTs' corporate governance approach. It outlines that both directors and governors have a responsibility for ensuring that 'comply or explain' remains an effective alternative to a rules-based system and a key aspect of this is ensuring improved interaction between directors, governors, members and – crucially – patients, communities and the public.

The Monitor Code does impose some specific disclosure requirements upon NHS FTs, which are similar to the requirements set out by the UK Listing Authority for listed companies. To meet the requirements of 'comply or explain' each trust must comply with each of the provisions of the Code (which in some cases will require a statement or information to be required in the annual report) or, where appropriate, explain in each case why the trust has departed from the Code.

In addition, and perhaps in light of the comments made in the South African King III corporate governance code, the Monitor Code also requires a trust, when it opts not to comply with a provision, to explain how its approach still reflects the principles of the Monitor Code relating to that provision. The form and content of this part of the statement are not prescribed, the intention being that trusts should have a free hand to explain their governance policies in the light of the principles, including any special circumstances applying to them which have led to a particular approach.

Although compliance with the provisions in the Monitor Code is on a 'comply or explain' basis, it also clearly identifies any relevant statutory requirements that fit closely with the Code. In the first instance, boards, directors and governors should ensure they are meeting the specific governance requirements described in HSCA 2012, which have been subsequently set out in another Monitor publication, *The New NHS Provider Licence and Risk Assessment Framework* (see Chapter 11).

Key aspects of the Monitor Code are set out in more detail in Chapter 11. In essence, the Code adopts a similar structure to the UK Corporate Governance Code with a series of Main Principles, supported by a series of supporting principles, under the following broad headings:

Section A: Leadership
A.1 The role of the board of directors
A.2 Division of responsibilities
A.3 The chair
A.4 Non-executive directors
A.5 Governors

Section B: Effectiveness
B.1 The composition of the board
B.2 Appointments to the board
B.3 Commitment
B.4 Development
B.5 Information and support
B.6 Evaluation
B.7 Re-appointment of directors and re-election of governors
B.8 Resignation of directors

Section C. Accountability
C.1 Financial, quality and operational reporting
C.2 Risk management and internal control
C.3 Audit committee and auditors

Section D. Remuneration
D.1 The level and components of remuneration
D.2 Procedure

Section E. Relations with stakeholders
E.1 Dialogue with members, patients and the local community
E.2 Co-operation with third parties with roles in relation to NHS FTs

The Well-Led Framework
Under Monitor's risk assessment framework and in line with the NHS FT Code of Governance, Monitor expects that NHS FTs carry out an external review of their governance every three years. Monitor give four reasons for requiring such a review.

- Good governance is essential in addressing the challenges the sector faces.
- Oversight of governance systems is the responsibility of NHS FT boards.
- Governance issues are increasing across the sector.
- Regular reviews can provide assurance that governance systems are fit for purpose.

The framework is built along the lines of the existing Quality Governance Framework, with four domains, ten high level questions and a body of 'good practice' outcomes and evidence base that organisations and reviewers can use to assess governance. The four domains are as follows.

1. Strategy and planning: how well is the board setting direction for the organisation?
2. Capability and culture: is the board taking steps to ensure it has the appropriate experience and ability, now and into the future, and can it positively shape the organisation's culture to deliver care in a safe and sustainable way?
3. Process and structures: do reporting lines and accountabilities support the effective oversight of the organisation?
4. Measurement: does the board receive appropriate, robust and timely information and does this support the leadership of the trust?

The evidence base is not intended to be a 'box-ticking' exercise, and should be used to guide trusts' and assessors' views in considering whether the processes and overall organisational culture in these areas are fit for purpose. The framework also sets out the suggested review process and what to take into account when choosing an external reviewer.

Whilst this currently only applies to FTs, Monitor, the CQC and the NHS TDA have committed to developing an aligned framework for making judgements about how well led all NHS providers are. This will mean a reassessment of the Board Governance Assurance Framework currently in place for aspirant FTs.

'Well led' means that the leadership, management and governance of the organisation assure the delivery of high-quality care for patients, support learning and innovation and promote an open and fair culture. The *Well-Led Framework for Governance Reviews* is intended to support the NHS system response to the Francis Report. As part of its 'ward to board' inspection regime, the CQC will ask NHS FTs how they have assured their governance arrangements. This may include asking for information about any independent reviews and how they have been acted on.

Trusts are free to schedule when the reviews take place within the three-year window – there is no mandatory timetable within the three years, as long as the gap between governance reviews is not longer than three years. Trusts are required to inform their Monitor relationship manager of the review and the organisation chosen to carry it out.

In order to gain maximum benefits and assurance from the reviews, Monitor recommends that independent reviewers should be used to ensure objectivity. Generally, Monitor considers reviewers should not have carried out audit or governance-related work for the trust during the previous three years.

■ The UK Corporate Governance Code

The first version of the UK Corporate Governance Code (the Code) was produced in 1992 by the Cadbury Committee. It is a particularly relevant document for FTs, as a significant similarity exists between the Monitor Code of Governance and the UK Corporate Governance Code.

Even so, paragraph 2.5 is still the classic definition of the context of the Code:

'Corporate governance is the system by which companies are directed and controlled. Boards of directors are responsible for the governance of their companies. The shareholders' role in governance is to appoint the directors and the auditors and to satisfy themselves that an appropriate governance structure is in place. The responsibilities of the board include setting the company's strategic aims, providing the leadership to put them into effect, supervising the management of the business and reporting to shareholders on their stewardship. The board's actions are subject to laws, regulations and the shareholders in general meeting.'

Corporate governance is, therefore, about what the board of a company does and how it sets the values of the company. It is to be distinguished from the day-to-day operational management of the company by full-time executives. The Code has been updated regularly and the most recent version was published in September 2014.

The Main Principles of the Code (September 2014 version) can be summarised as follows:

Section A: Leadership
- Every company should be headed by an effective board, which is collectively responsible for the long-term success of the company.
- There should be a clear division of responsibilities at the head of the company between the running of the board and the executive responsibility for the running of the company's business. No one individual should have unfettered powers of decision.
- The chair is responsible for leadership of the board and ensuring its effectiveness on all aspects of its role.
- As part of their role as members of a unitary board, NEDs should constructively challenge and help develop proposals on strategy.

Section B: Effectiveness

- The board and its committees should have the appropriate balance of skills, experience, independence and knowledge of the company to enable them to discharge their respective duties and responsibilities effectively.
- There should be a formal, rigorous and transparent procedure for the appointment of new directors to the board.
- All directors should be able to allocate sufficient time to the company to discharge their responsibilities effectively.
- All directors should receive induction on joining the board and should regularly update and refresh their skills and knowledge.
- The board should be supplied in a timely manner with information in a form and of a quality appropriate to enable it to discharge its duties.
- The board should undertake a formal and rigorous annual evaluation of its own performance and that of its committees and individual directors.
- All directors should be submitted for re-election at regular intervals, subject to continued satisfactory performance.

Section C: Accountability

- The board should present a fair, balanced and understandable assessment of the company's position and prospects.
- The board is responsible for determining the nature and extent of the principal risks it is willing to take in achieving its strategic objectives. The board should maintain sound risk management and internal control systems.
- The board should establish formal and transparent arrangements for considering how they should apply the corporate reporting, risk management and internal control principles and for maintaining an appropriate relationship with the company's auditors.

Section D: Remuneration

- Executive directors' remuneration should be designed to promote the long-term success of the company. Performance-related elements should be transparent, stretching and rigorously applied.
- There should be a formal and transparent procedure for developing policy on executive remuneration and for fixing the remuneration packages of individual directors. No director should be involved in deciding his or her own remuneration.

Section E: Relations with shareholders

- There should be a dialogue with shareholders based on the mutual understanding of objectives. The board as a whole has responsibility for ensuring that a satisfactory dialogue with shareholders takes place.

■ The board should use general meetings to communicate with investors and to encourage their participation.

The Code's function should be to help boards discharge their duties in the best interests of their companies. In recent reviews of the Code, the FRC has focused on changing the 'tone' of the Code by making limited but significant changes to signal the importance of the general principles which should guide board behaviours.

The Combined Code, which was replaced by the UK Corporate Governance Code in 2010, used to have a section that was addressed specifically to institutional shareholders, and dealt with the responsibilities of institutional investors for good corporate governance. This has now been replaced by a separate UK Stewardship Code.

FRC Guidance for Boards and Board Committees

The FRC issues guidance and other publications to assist boards and board committees in considering how to apply the UK Corporate Governance Code to their particular circumstances. These publications cover:

■ board effectiveness
■ the role of audit committees
■ risk management, internal control and related financial and business reporting
■ audit tendering

This guidance is explored in greater detail in Chapters 2 and 4, as it are key to an understanding of board and committees effectiveness.

■ Other codes

The OECD Corporate Governance Principles

In 1999, the OECD issued a number of non-binding principles on corporate governance, which were reviewed and amended in 2004.

The OECD Principles are intended to serve as a reference point for countries to use when evaluating their legal, institutional and regulatory provisions for corporate governance. They offer guidance and suggestions for stock exchanges, investors, companies and other bodies involved in developing good corporate governance practices.

Unlike national codes of corporate governance, the OECD Principles do not contain any detailed provisions about how the principles should be applied in practice. They are simply a set of main principles and supporting principles, with some additional explanations or 'annotations'. The principles deal with six aspects of governance:

■ ensuring the basics for an effective corporate governance framework
■ the rights of shareholders and key ownership functions
■ the equitable treatment of shareholders

- the role of stakeholders in corporate governance
- disclosure and transparency
- the responsibilities of the board.

The OECD Principles begin with a statement that the corporate governance framework should:

- promote transparent and efficient markets
- be consistent with the rule of law
- clearly articulate the division of responsibilities among different supervisory, regulatory and enforcement authorities.

In the UK these basics are probably accepted as 'normal' for public companies, but it is a useful reminder that this is not necessarily the case at all times or in all countries.

The King III Code

The 2009 King III Code is the corporate governance code for South Africa. It is distinctive because it adopts a 'stakeholder inclusive' approach to corporate governance. In taking this approach, King III includes some aspects of governance that are not found in other voluntary codes such as the UK Code.

The introduction to King III states that the 'philosophy of the (Code) revolves around leadership, sustainability and corporate citizenship'. These are described as follows.

- Leadership: companies should be given effective leadership, which should be characterised by the ethical governance values of fairness, accountability, responsibility and transparency.
- Sustainability: the ability of a company to operate its business without compromising the needs of future generations, such as through excessive consumption of natural resources or irreversible environmental damage. King III refers to sustainability as a 'primary moral and economic imperative'.
- Corporate citizenship: a company is a person and like other people it should be aware of its role in society and the need to act as a good citizen. Companies should therefore consider social and environmental (sustainability) issues in the decisions that they make.

Another feature of the King Code is its requirement for 'integrated reporting'. This is reporting that integrates financial aspects of performance with sustainability aspects. It also recommends forward-looking elements to reporting as well as reporting of historical performance.

The King II Code (2004) recommended that companies should produce annual sustainability reports, in addition to their financial statements. King III goes further by calling for an integrated report that combines financial and sustainability issues.

An additional unique feature of King III is that it states specifically that, unlike its predecessor King II, it applies to all entities regardless of the form of their establishment or incorporation. This means that the code applies not only to companies, but also to public sector and not-for-profit organisations.

The code itself has nine sections. Some of these deal with the same issues as the UK Code, whereas others are different (possibly unique).

- Ethical leadership and corporate citizenship: King III places more emphasis on ethical behaviour when compared with the UK Code.
- Boards and directors.
- Audit committees.
- The governance of risk.
- IT governance: this was not included in the earlier King II Code. However, it was considered that directors should be made aware of their responsibilities for IT governance, including the formulation of IT strategy (having due regard for IT risk) and the need for a robust framework for internal control of IT systems.
- Compliance with laws, rules, codes and standards: King III states specifically that compliance risk (see Chapter 11) should be an integral part of the risk management process.
- Internal audit: King III states that there should be an effective risk-based internal audit, and an internal audit function.
- Governing stakeholder relationships: by taking an 'inclusive stakeholder' approach to governance, the board of directors should manage the 'gap' between the expectations of stakeholders and company performance. Relations with stakeholder groups should be managed, and decisions should be taken by the board in the best interests of the company, which means taking into account the legitimate interests and expectations of stakeholders.
- Integrated reporting: as stated earlier, companies should provide integrated annual reports, combining financial and sustainability aspects of performance.

Good Governance: a practical guide for trustees, chairs and CEOs

The National Council of Voluntary Organisations (NCVO) published *Good Governance: a practical guide for trustees, chairs and CEOs* in September 2011. The Code was formulated to help and support board members in the important and rewarding work that they carry out.

The principles set out good practice, but these are closely linked with the responsibilities of charity trustees and other legal requirements that may be imposed on board members. The Code sets out best practice in trusteeship and while it is not mandatory, organisations that comply with it are invited to state this in their annual report.

■ Summary

Best practice in both health service governance and corporate governance is found in the combination of legal and regulatory requirements alongside voluntary principles and codes of conduct. The key issue at stake here is to prevent the tsunami-like wave of regulations, codes and guidance from obliterating the core principles of good governance.

To paraphrase the UK Corporate Governance Code, such frameworks are limited to being a general guide to principles, structure and processes. They cannot guarantee effective board behaviour because the range of situations in which they apply are too great for them to attempt to more specifically mandate behaviour.

PART TWO

The board's role and directors' responsibilities

The board's structure and its committees

An efficient and effective board is a key requirement of good governance. The board should have a clear idea of its responsibilities, and should fulfil these to the best of its abilities. There should be a suitable balance of skills, experience and power on the board. As a consequence, the role and composition of a board, and the duties and responsibilities of directors and committees, will be important. The ability to identify the characteristics of an effective board, and compare these with the actual practice of boards, is also important..

This chapter concentrates on the structures and processes of the board, while boardroom behaviours and practice will be covered in more detail in Part 3. For the purposes of this chapter, reference to the board should be taken to include a CCG's governing body unless expressly set out otherwise.

The board is sometimes referred to as the 'controlling mind' of an organisation or as its 'head'. Though an organisation is not a person in the human sense, it does have characteristics which support the use of these terms, such as entering into contractually binding arrangements. As the head of the organisation, the board has governance responsibilities to control and lead, while being held to account for delivering the organisation's strategic objectives.

Another way of looking at this is to say that the board acts as the agent for the *Summ-* organisation and exercises powers on its behalf. These powers are delegated to the *any* board under the constitutional documents that establish the organisation, such as statutory instruments, core constitutions or standing orders. Underpinning all of this is the expectation that the board is collectively responsible for its actions, and that the individual members of the board make their decisions in the best interests of the organisation.

■ Governance responsibilities of the board

Responsibilities set out in NHS regulation or guidance

It is important to distinguish between the different organisations as there are different guidelines set out for each. These are as follows.

Foundation trusts

According to paragraph 18A of Schedule 7 to the National Health Service Act 2006 (as inserted by HSCA 2012) the duty of the board, and of each director individually, is to act with a view to promoting the success of the corporation so as to maximise the benefits for the members of the corporation as a whole and for the public. This mirrors the duty as set out in the Companies Act 2006 for companies. This is also set out in the Monitor Code, which goes on to say that 'every NHS FT should be headed by an effective board of directors. The board is collectively responsible for the performance of the NHS FT'.

Clinical commissioning groups

The duty of the governing body is to ensure that the CCG has made appropriate arrangements for ensuring that the CCG complies with its obligations to exercise its functions effectively, efficiently and economically. It also has a duty to ensure that it complies with relevant generally accepted principles of good governance. Section 14L of NHS Act 2006, as inserted by section 25 of the HSCA 2012, sets out the duties of the governing bodies of CCGs:

- promoting the NHS Constitution in the securing of health services;
- securing continuous improvement in the quality and safety of health services and in the quality of the experience undergone by patients;
- securing continuous improvement in quality of primary medical services;
- reducing inequalities between patients with respect to their ability to access health services, and with respect to the outcomes achieved for them;
- promoting the involvement of patients, their carers and representatives in relation to their health service;
- enabling patients to make choices with respect to aspects of health services provided to them;
- obtaining appropriate professional health service advice to enable it effectively to discharge its functions;
- promoting innovation in the provision of health services;
- promoting research on matters relevant to health services;
- promoting education and training for the persons connected with the provision of health services; and
- securing health services that are provided in an integrated way to improve quality, reduce inequalities of access or outcome.

NHS trust boards

According to the DH, NHS trust boards have six key functions. They are held accountable for these by the DH on behalf of the Secretary of State. These are:

- to set the strategic direction of the organisation within the overall policies and priorities of the government and the NHS, define its annual and longer-term objectives and agree plans to achieve them;

- to oversee the delivery of planned results by monitoring performance against objectives and ensuring corrective action is taken when necessary;
- to ensure effective financial stewardship through value for money, financial control and financial planning and strategy;
- to ensure that high standards of health service governance and personal behaviour are maintained in the conduct of the business of the whole organisation;
- to appoint, appraise and remunerate senior executives; and
- to ensure that there is effective dialogue between the organisation and the local community on its plans and performance and that these are responsive to the community's needs.

The *Healthy NHS Board* (see Chapter 3) states that 'the purpose of NHS boards is to govern effectively and in doing so build patient, public and stakeholder confidence that their health and healthcare is in safe hands'. *neat summary*

It goes on to say that 'in unitary NHS boards, all directors are collectively and corporately accountable for organisational performance'.

Responsibilities according to the UK Code   *(NHS)? comparison*

The board of directors is the key decision-making body in an organisation. Therefore, an organisation should have an effective board of directors dedicated to ensuring that the organisation achieves its objectives. The UK Code states as *UK* one of its main principles 'every company should be headed by an effective board, *principle* which is collectively responsible for the long-term success of the organisation'.

The introduction of the phrase 'long term' into this principle in 2010 recognised that the board should not focus on short-term achievements, if these are inconsistent with longer-term success.

The UK Code also states that the role of the board should be to:

- provide entrepreneurial leadership for the company within a framework of prudent and effective risk management;
- set the company's strategic aims;
- make sure that the necessary financial and human resources are in place for the company to meet its objectives;
- review management performance;
- set the company's values and standards; and
- make sure that the company's obligations to its shareholders are understood and met.

The board should not get involved with operational matters (except in its monitoring role), with the responsibility delegated to executive management. The UK Code also states that all directors must act in what they consider to be the best interests of the company, without specifying what those 'best interests' are or might be.

The South African King III corporate governance code identifies other responsibilities for the board, including responsibility for:

- ethical conduct and sustainability of the business
- compliance with laws, regulations and codes
- governing the relationships between the company and its stakeholders.

Responsibilities according to the FRC *Guidance on Board Effectiveness*

This FRC *Guidance on Board Effectiveness* states that an effective board is one that:

- provides direction for management;
- demonstrates ethical leadership, displaying and promoting throughout the company behaviours consistent with the culture and values it has defined for the organisation;
- creates a performance culture that drives value creation without exposing the company to excessive risk of value destruction;
- makes well informed and high-quality decisions based on a clear line of sight into the business;
- creates the right framework for helping directors meet their statutory duties under the Companies Act 2006, and/or other relevant statutory and regulatory regimes;
- is accountable, particularly to those that provide the company's capital; and
- thinks carefully about its governance arrangements and embraces evaluation of their effectiveness.

The guidance adds that a board that demonstrates that it has suitable governance policies and systems in place is much more likely to generate trust and support among its shareholders and other stakeholders. It also goes on to look at effective decision-making in boards, as this is an important board activity. The guidance sets out that the board should have clear policies about what matters need a board decision or approval, and the processes required for each type of decision. Good decision-making can be improved by giving directors sufficient time to prepare for meetings, allowing sufficient time for issues to be discussed at board meetings, and making clear to executives what action they must take to implement board decisions.

The guidance also recognises that, even with suitable policies and procedures, the quality of decision-making by the board can be impaired by:

- a dominant personality or group of directors on the board, which can inhibit contributions from other directors;
- insufficient attention to risk along with treating risk as a compliance issue rather than as part of the decision-making process;
- failure to recognise the value implications of running the business on the basis of self interest and other poor ethical standards;
- a reluctance to involve NEDs, or of matters being brought to the board for sign-off rather than debate;

- complacent or intransigent attitudes;
- a weak organisational culture; and
- inadequate information or analysis.

The guidance suggests that boards may wish to consider extra measures to reduce the risk of flawed decisions, such as describing in board papers the process that has been used to arrive at and challenge proposals prior to presenting them to the board. This allows directors not involved in the project to assess the appropriateness of the process as a precursor to assessing the merits of the project itself. It might also be appropriate to put in place additional safeguards to reduce the risk of distorted judgments by:

- commissioning an independent report;
- seeking advice from an expert;
- introducing a 'devil's advocate' to provide challenge;
- establishing a sole purpose sub-committee; or
- convening additional meetings.

The guidance notes that some boards favour separate discussions for important decisions; for example, separating discussions about concepts, proposals for discussion and proposals for decision. This gives EDs more opportunity to put their case at the earlier stages, and all directors the opportunity to share concerns or challenge assumptions well in advance of the point of decision.

Board structures

Unitary boards Like Aunty Bee b!

Organisations are based around a unitary board structure in many countries. The unitary board consists of both executive directors (EDs) and non-executive directors (NEDs) under the leadership of the chair. A unitary board makes collective decisions and is accountable to the shareholders or major stakeholders. It is commonly accepted governance practice that the NEDs in a listed organisation should be independent, although this is not a legal requirement.

In the NHS, the concept of a unitary board has not always been well understood or implemented. In 2006, the *Integrated Governance Handbook* illustrates several dangers of not using a unitary board structure:

'To date, NHS boards have performed in a diverse manner by separating out the roles of the various directors, i.e. finance, medical, nursing etc, and the non-executive director/lay individual input. The result of this is that, if the board takes a decision, it is often deemed to be the decision of, say, the finance director or HR director, rather than being a corporate decision. Board corporacy is paramount. Each decision or agreement entered into in the boardroom is a fully accepted corporate decision. If a decision around finance is taken and the information brought to the board clarifies the debate, if there are implications say, one month after the decision, the responsibility is of the corporate whole, rather than just the finance director.'

There is a clear move away from the unitary board structure for the newly established CCGs. NHS England advocates adherence with the Good Governance Standard for Public Services (2004) as the guidance for best practice in governance, which presupposes a form of leadership not based on the principle of a unitary board. This is in stark contrast to most other NHS organisations (such as FTs) for whom the unitary board is a core principle of governance.

The purpose of the unitary board principle was to ensure that the interests of all stakeholders were properly considered and balanced. As such, CCGs are unlikely to operate in a way that is entirely consistent with the major codes of practice that set out best practice in corporate governance for the NHS – including the UK Corporate Governance Code, King III, the Higgs Report and the Monitor Code.

The concept of the unitary board is reinforced within the governance structure of the NHS FT, even though there may appear to be a two-tier board structure with a council of governors and a board of directors. The Monitor Core Constitution and the Monitor Code make it clear that the concept of the unitary board refers to the fact that NEDs and EDs share the same liability within the board of directors. All directors, executive and non-executive, have the responsibility to constructively challenge the decisions of the board and help develop proposals on priorities, risk mitigation, values, standards and strategy.

The *Healthy NHS Board* adds:

> A key strength of unitary boards is the opportunity provided for the exchange of views between executives and NEDs, drawing on and pooling their experience and capabilities. Boards are "social systems". The most effective boards invest time and energy in the development of mature relationships and ways of working.'

One of the threats to the principle of the unitary board is the increasing emphasis on the role of the NED. The role of independent scrutiny and constructive challenge undertaken by the NED role can create a tension with their responsibility to provide a strategic oversight and to act collectively alongside the executive board members.

For example, it has been seen as good practice for NEDs to meet (at least) annually as a group without the chair or executives present, and also for board committees to be made up solely of NEDs; if not managed correctly, this can divide a unitary board. There is also a further threat, particularly rife in the NHS, which is the increasing requirement for NEDs to be 'champions' for specific areas of management concern. This blurs the boundary between governance and management, and between the roles of the NED and the executive board member.

Having said all that, the concept of a unitary board is still common practice within the NHS and continues to be the subject of a considerable amount of board development.

Two-tier boards

Some countries, including Germany and Austria, have two-tier boards. A two-tier structure usually consists of a supervisory board and a management board.

The management board is responsible for managing the organisation. It is led *Mgt* by the chair of the management board, normally the CEO, and its members are *board* appointed by the supervisory board. The management board consists entirely of EDs. It develops strategy for the organisation in cooperation with the supervisory board, and is responsible for implementing the agreed strategy. It also has responsibility for risk management and for the preparation of the annual financial statements (which are examined by the auditors and the supervisory board). The chair of the management board reports to the supervisory board chair.

The supervisory board is responsible for general oversight of the organisation *Sup* and of the management board. Members are normally elected by shareholders, *board* except in public companies with more than 500 employees where a minimum proportion of the supervisory board must consist of employee representatives. The supervisory board consists entirely of NEDs. The chair leads the supervisory board, which advises the management board and must be involved in decision-making on all fundamental matters affecting the organisation. These include 'decisions or measures which fundamentally change the asset, financial or earnings situations of the enterprise' (German Corporate Governance Code). The audit committee consists entirely of supervisory board members. In Germany, supervisory board members include:

- representatives of trade unions and/or the organisation's employees
- representatives of major shareholders
- former executives of the organisation.

Supervisory board NEDs are therefore not necessarily independent, particularly *Issues* employee representatives. It can therefore be difficult to reconcile the differing views of employee representatives and representatives of major shareholders without antagonising the executives on the management board.

On the other hand, if there are a large number of former executives on the supervisory board, there is a risk that the supervisory board could take a lenient view of management activities. In addition, some independent supervisory board directors might well be senior managers of other companies, where they are management board members. These individuals might therefore sympathise with the views of the management board.

The success of corporate governance in a two-tier structure depends on a functional relationship between the supervisory board and the management board. The chair of the supervisory board plays a key role. They are responsible for making sure that the two boards work well together. The most powerful individuals in the organisation are the chair of the supervisory board and the CEO. If the relationship between these two works well, the chair will effectively speak for the management at meetings of the supervisory board.

The German Corporate Governance Code states that 'the management board and supervisory board co-operate closely to the benefit of the enterprise' and the management board should discuss the implementation of strategy regularly with the supervisory board.

Criticisms of the two-tier board structure

The main concerns are as follows.

- Supervisory boards are too big, having up to 20 members. German supervisory boards include a large number of employee representatives, and large numbers can result in inefficient meetings.
- It has been common to appoint retired former managers of the organisation to the supervisory board, and these individuals might be tempted to retain some influence over the actions and operational decisions of their successors. This is not the purpose of a supervisory board. On the other hand, if former managers are appointed to the supervisory board, the supervisory board will benefit from their knowledge and experience of the business. In Germany former managers are now prohibited from 'moving upstairs' to the supervisory board for at least two years, unless the move receives the support of at least 25% of shareholders, because it is thought a former executive will not be sufficiently independent immediately after retiring.
- Companies with more than 500 employees are required to have workers' or trade union representatives on the supervisory board. Companies with more than 2,000 employees are required to have an even greater percentage of employee representatives on the supervisory board. This requirement is an enforcement of the principle of 'co-determination', embodied in German law, that the workers as well as the management and owners should determine the future of their companies. Unfortunately, workers' representatives can lack the competence to consider strategic issues or are not independent from the organisation. In some instances, worker members of a supervisory board opposing planned initiatives by the organisation have been accused of leaking confidential information to the press.
- Concerns about information leaks can damage communications between supervisory and management boards.

The German Corporate Governance Code suggests that, the unitary board system and two-tier board system are becoming similar in practice because of intensive interaction between the management and supervisory boards. The German Code also suggests that the two types of board structure are equally successful. Developments in some German companies in recent years also suggest that the supervisory boards of large German companies are becoming more responsive to the interests of their shareholders.

The 2009 Walker Report on UK bank corporate governance in considered whether unitary boards contributed to the scale of the financial crisis in 2007–2009, and whether a two-tier board structure might be more suitable for large banks. Its conclusions were fairly critical of the two-tier structure:

'In practice, two-tier structures do not appear to assure members of the supervisory board of access to the quality and timeliness of management information flow that would generally be regarded as essential for non-executives on a unitary board. Moreover, since, in a two-tier structure, members of the supervisory and executive boards meet separately and do not share the same responsibilities, the two-tier model would not provide opportunity for the interactive exchange of views between executives and NEDs, drawing on and pooling their respective experience and capabilities in the way that takes place in a well-functioning unitary board.'

■ Matters reserved for the board

Regardless of structure, the board of directors should meet sufficiently regularly to discharge its duties effectively and have a formal schedule of matters specifically reserved for decision by the board of directors.

The main decision-making powers belong to the board of directors. Although the board delegates many of the operational decision-making responsibilities to executive management, it should retain the most significant decisions and monitor the performance of the executive management. A key aspect of governance is therefore the nature of the decisions the board reserves for itself (rather than delegating them to executive management).

The UK Code does not specify which matters should be reserved by the board, but states simply in a provision that 'there should be a formal schedule of matters reserved for its decision'. It then states that the annual report should include a statement of how the board operates, a high-level statement of the types of decision that it reserves for its own decisions and the types of decision that it delegates to executive management.

ICSA's Guidance Note on matters that should be reserved for the board is consistent with the provisions of the UK Code. The list of items in the Guidance Note includes decisions relating to matters such as:

■ approval of annual operating and capital expenditure budgets;
■ approval of the annual report and accounts;
■ approval of formal communications with shareholders;
■ approval of major contracts and investments;
■ approval of policies on matters such as health and safety, CSR and the environment approval of strategy;

- changes in corporate or capital structure;
- compliance with legal and regulatory requirements;
- oversight of operations (including accounting, planning and internal control systems); and
- performance review.

The company secretary may be given the task of preparing and maintaining the list of matters to be reserved for the board (for board approval), and reminding the board whenever necessary that certain decisions should not be delegated.

Although this guidance is not specifically aimed at NHS boards, it contains best practice which NHS boards should actively consider. Though the formal powers of an NHS organisation are vested in its board, the NHS Code of Accountability allows the board to delegate some of its business to board committees and to the executive.

The board approach to delegation should be consistently set out in:

- its standing orders, which specify how the organisation conducts its business;
- its standing financial instructions, which detail the financial responsibilities, policies and procedures adopted; and
- its scheme of reservation and delegation. This sets out which responsibilities and accountabilities remain at board level and which have been delegated to committees and to the executive, together with the appropriate reporting arrangements that ensure the board has oversight.

A thorough understanding of the matters reserved for the board must underpin a board's approach to delegation. Its schemes of delegation must be subject to regular board review to ensure that the distribution of functions and accountabilities is accurately and appropriately described, and remains appropriate despite changes in the organisation.

■ Size and composition of the board

The effectiveness of a board of directors depends on its size and composition.

Size

The typical size of a board of directors varies with the size of the organisation and/ or the industry or business sector in which it operates. In addition, the average size of boards in listed companies varies between different countries.

A board should not be any larger than it needs to be. Large boards are more difficult to manage, because there are more individuals involved, and board meetings can be very long and time consuming. On the other hand, a board should be large enough for its members to collectively have the knowledge, skills and experience to make effective decisions.

The UK Code suggests that the board should be sufficiently large to avoid a situation in which it becomes over-reliant on one or two individuals, for example as chairmen of board committees (nominations, remuneration, audit and risk committees). It states:

> 'The board should be of sufficient size that the requirements of the business can be met and that changes to the board's composition and that of its committees can be managed without disruption, and should not be so large as to be unwieldy.'

The Walker Review identified that where board membership exceeded 8–12 directors, the risk known as group-think – the phenomenon of a group exhibiting thought processes whereby they seek to minimise conflict and reach consensus without critically testing, analysing and evaluating ideas – increases.

The *Healthy NHS Board* suggests that:

> 'NHS boards should not be so large as to be unwieldy, but must be large enough to provide the balance of skills and experience that is appropriate for the organisation. The number of directors is defined in the trust's establishment order, or in a FT's constitution. The composition of the board should achieve a balance between continuity and renewal. Chairs and non-executive directors (NEDs) of NHS trusts serve a maximum of 10 years in the same NHS post (or two three-year terms for FTs) to ensure this balance. Within this period, any second reappointment must be through open competition. The composition of the board should achieve a balance between continuity and renewal.'

Composition

The composition of a board of directors depends partly on its size. In the UK, the board of a large public company commonly consists of a:

- chair
- possibly a deputy chair
- the CEO
- the senior independent director (SID, who may also be the deputy chair)
- EDs
- NEDs.

Collectively, the members of the board should have sufficient skills and experience to provide effective leadership for the organisation. This suggests that they should have a variety of different backgrounds and expertise.

There should also be a suitable balance of power on the board so that one individual or a small group of individuals is unable to dominate the board and its decision-making. In countries such as the UK, it is considered appropriate to appoint independent NEDs to a board, because they act as a counter-balance to EDs who may give priority to their own interests above those of the shareholders (and other stakeholders). They also have skills and experience that EDs do not have, because they come from a different background and so are able to contribute different ideas and views to board discussions and decision-making. As they do not have a strong personal financial interest in the organisation, NEDs are more easily able to represent the interests of the major stakeholders (typically shareholders) and to act (where required) as a restraint on executive management.

These principles relating to board composition are set out in the UK Code as follows:

'The board and its committees should have the appropriate balance of skills, experience, independence and knowledge of the company to enable them to discharge their respective duties and responsibilities effectively.'

'The board should include an appropriate combination of executive and non-EDs (and in particular independent non-executive directors) such that no individual or small group of individuals can dominate the board's decision-taking.'

The UK Code sets out different requirements for large listed companies – where at least one half of the board, excluding the chair, should be independent NEDs – and for smaller companies (those outside the FTSE 350). Smaller companies should appoint at least two independent NEDs.

Guidelines about the composition of a unitary board differ between countries. The King III Code, for example, recommends that the majority of directors should be NEDs and the majority of NEDs should be independent, but also adds that there should be at least two executive directors on the board – the CEO and chief finance officer (finance director).

NHS board composition

The principle that there should be sufficient independent NEDs to create a suitable balance of power is also reflected in the Monitor Code. However there is a distinction between NEDs and the role of Lay Members on a CCG governing body which is explored in Chapter 12.

In the NHS, the composition of the board is clearly dictated either by:

- the Trust Membership and Procedure Regulations (SI 1990/2024);
- in FTs, by Schedule 7 of the NHS Act 2006; or
- in CCGs by section 14L of the NHS Act 2006 as inserted by section 25 of the HSCA 2012.

The detail of the composition for FTs and CCGs are set out in Chapters 11 and 12 respectively.

The composition for NHS Trusts is as follows.

- The maximum number of directors of an NHS trust shall be 11 and the minimum not less than eight.
- The EDs of an NHS trust shall include the chief officer of the trust; the chief finance officer of the trust; a medical or dental practitioner and a registered nurse or registered midwife.

- There will be a trust chair (appointed by NHS TDA), up to five non-executive directors (appointed by the NHS TDA), and up to five EDs (but not exceeding the number of non-officer members) including the chief executive and the director of finance.

■ Board committees

One aspect of best practice in governance is that the board should decide that the EDs be excluded from the decision-making or monitoring responsibilities for some issues.

This is achieved by delegating certain responsibilities to committees of the board. A board committee might consist entirely or mostly of NEDs, and have the responsibility for dealing with particular issues and making recommendations to the full board. The full board is then usually expected to accept and endorse the recommendations of the relevant board committee. Despite this, the committees only have delegated authority from the board; they do not have the capacity to act independently of board.

According to the Walker Review, the optimum size for a sub-committee is *key back up* between five and nine members. It states 'at five a group becomes more of a team, at seven thinking is optimised; above nine the ability of the cognitive limit of the group is exceeded'.

Three standing committees are recommended by the UK Code:

- an audit committee (1)
- a nomination committee (2)
- a remuneration committee (3)

Guidance for the NHS can be found in the DH publication *The Intelligent Board*, (FTs) which recommended that all NHS trusts should have an audit committee, a nomination committee and a remuneration (and terms of service) committee as part of their governance arrangements. All report to the board of directors.

Nowadays, the model standing orders for NHS Trusts requires an audit committee as well as a remuneration and terms of service committee. In line with its role as a corporate trustee, the board should also establish a charitable funds committee. This enables it to administer any funds held in trust either as charitable or non-charitable funds, in accordance with any statutory/legal requirements or best practice required by the Charity Commission. *charitable aspects of Trust?*

The Monitor core constitution for FTs requires the board to establish:

- a committee consisting of the trust chair, the chief executive and the other non-EDs to appoint or remove the other EDs (nomination committee); and
- a committee of NEDs to decide the remuneration and allowances, and the other terms and conditions of office, of the chief executive and other EDs (remuneration committee).

According to the Monitor Code, FTs may choose to have two nomination committees, one dealing with NEDs and one dealing with EDs. Where an NHS FT has two nomination committees, the nomination committee responsible for the appointment of NEDs should consist of a majority of governors. If only one nominations committee exists, when nominations for non-executives are being discussed – including the appointment of a chair or a deputy chair – there should be a majority of governors on the committee and also a majority of governors on the interview panel. The core constitution also requires the trust to establish an NED committee as an audit committee to perform monitoring, reviewing and other functions. It also requires the council of governors to approve the appointment of all NEDs, including the trust chair.

CCGs are required by statute to appoint an audit committee and the remuneration (see section 14M(1) of the NHS Act 2006, as inserted by section 25 of HSCA 2012). The NHS England guidance *Towards establishment: Creating responsive and accountable clinical commissioning groups* also recommends that CCGs consider the establishment of a quality committee to:

- provide assurance on the quality of services commissioned; and
- to promote a culture of continuous improvement and innovation with respect to safety of services, clinical effectiveness and patient experience.

Some boards might establish other committees. For example, an organisation might have an environment committee if its business activities are likely to have important consequences for the environment – especially if it involves an exposure to government regulation, the law and public opinion. The Walker Review recommended that all banks and life assurance companies establish a risk committee with responsibility for 'oversight and advice to the board on the current risk exposures to the entity and future risk strategy'. In practice, most NHS organisations also have a board committee, which covers quality assurance, governance and/or risk.

Boards should ensure that they delegate authority to committees in line with their constitutional documents, set out clear terms of reference for them – including the composition and quoracy requirements – and provide a clear statement of the remit of the committee. These committees do not absolve the board of its responsibility in their respective areas of scrutiny: rather, they should support the board in carrying out its responsibilities of strategic leadership and holding to account.

The three main committees (audit, nomination and remuneration) are set out in detail in later chapters. Here is a brief summary of their functions.

The audit committee

The FRC *Guidance on Audit Committees* states that the 'audit committee has a particular role, acting independently from the executive, to ensure that the interests of shareholders are properly protected in relation to financial reporting and internal control'. The guidance adds:

'A frank, open working relationship and a high level of mutual respect are essential, particularly between the audit committee chair and the board chair, the chief executive and the finance director. The audit committee must be prepared to take a robust stand, and all parties must be prepared to make information freely available to the audit committee, to listen to their views and to talk through the issues openly.'

At times, it may be necessary for the committee to challenge the position of the external auditors or other professional advisers. The committee should comprise a minimum of three independent NEDS and have clear terms of reference. The chair of the board may they be a member of the committee only in smaller companies, and even then may not chair the committee. These principles are reflected in the *NHS Audit Committee Handbook*, published by the Healthcare Financial Management Association (HFMA). The HFMA handbook says the audit committee plays a key role by:

'critically reviewing and reporting on the relevance and robustness of the governance structures and assurance processes on which the board places reliance. In particular, this requires the committee to understand and scrutinise the organisations overarching framework of governance, risk and control'.

The HFMA handbook stipulates that the chair of the board should not chair the audit committee or be a member of the committee. It also specifies that there at least one member of the committee should have 'recent and relevant financial experience' (in line with the FRC guidance mentioned above).

The audit committee should summarise its work during the year, submitting an annual report to the board promptly after the year-end but before it considers the organisation's annual report and statutory declarations. The UK Code also provides that a separate section of the annual report should describe the work of the committee. This deliberately puts the spotlight on the audit committee and gives it an authority that it might otherwise lack.

The nomination committee

This committee gained a higher profile after the publication of the Higgs Report, which resulted in the UK Code recommending that all listed companies should establish a nomination committee. Its remit covers the review of the structure, size and composition of the board, including:

- the oversight of the board's succession planning requirements for both EDs and NEDs (and the company secretary);
- the identification and assessment of potential board candidates; and
- making nominations to the board for its approval as appropriate.

The committee should comprise the chair, the CEO and the NEDs, all appointed by the board. The majority of its members must be independent NEDs. The chair of the board should chair the committee, except when it is dealing with the appointment of a successor chair: the SID should chair the committee in this instance.

These guidelines are largely followed by NHS organisations in their standing orders or constitutional documents.

The remuneration committee

This committee has received an increased profile in recent times following the publication of the Kay Review and the stirrings of the 'Shareholder Spring' in 2012. Investors have refused to back multi-million pound bonuses for executives when coupled with extremely poor corporate performance.

There has been a greater emphasis on public disclosure of executive remuneration, and a culture change of shareholders refusing to accept severance pay arrangements. The Enterprise and Regulatory Reform Act 2013 underlines the importance of boards and investors engaging on directors' remuneration. The UK Code recommends that the committee determine an appropriate balance between fixed and performance-related, and immediate and deferred, remuneration; that performance conditions should be relevant, stretching and designed to promote the long-term success of the company; and that incentives should be compatible with risk policies and systems. The committee should also consider whether the directors should be eligible for annual bonuses and/or benefits under long-term incentive schemes.

The UK Code states that the committee should comprise at least three independent NEDs (although two is permissible for smaller companies). In addition to the independent NEDs, the chair of the board may also be a member of the committee if they were considered independent on appointment as chair, but may not chair the committee. The ICSA's model terms of reference for the remuneration committee states that it is good practice for the company secretary to act as secretary to the committee, although this is not a provision in the UK Code.

Under the UK Code, companies are required to publish a remuneration report which includes three sections:

■ a statement from the chair of the remuneration committee covering key decisions and changes made to remuneration in the year;
■ a forward-looking remuneration policy report; and
■ an annual report on remuneration which includes both how the policy has been implemented in the year under review and how it will be implemented in the forthcoming year.

Shareholders also have a binding vote on the policy report at least every three years, or whenever any changes are made in addition to an annual advisory vote on the annual remuneration report. HM Treasury also requires NHS organisations to provide a remuneration report in a prescribed format within their annual report and accounts.

Table 4.1: Summary of the UK Code's recommendations regarding membership of board committees key

Nominations committee	Audit committee	Remuneration committee
Chair should be the chair of the board	Chair should be an independent NED	Chair should be an independent NED
Majority of members should be independent NEDs	All independent NEDs – in large companies, at least three, in smaller companies two	All independent NEDs – in large companies, at least three, in smaller companies two
If the board chair is the company chair, he should not act as chair when the committee is considering a successor for the chair	In smaller companies, the chair of the board may also be a member of the audit committee (but not chair of the committee), in addition to the independent NEDs – but only if he was independent on appointment to the chair	The chair of the board may be a member of the committee if they were considered independent on appointment as chair, but may not chair the committee
	At least one member of the committee should have 'recent and relevant financial experience'	

Protecting the independence and effectiveness of board committees

As a way of protecting the independence and improving the effectiveness of board committees, the UK Code recommends that consideration should be given to the benefits of ensuring that committee membership is refreshed that when deciding the chairship and membership of board committees (membership rotation). It adds that undue reliance should not be placed on particular individuals.

In addition, the only individuals who are entitled to attend meetings of the nomination, remuneration and audit committees are the chair and members of the committee, although other individuals may attend at the invitation of the committee.

Governance Checklist

✓ Does the board act as the controlling mind of the organisation?
✓ Does it provide strategic and entrepreneurial leadership?
✓ Are there prudent and effective controls to manage the principal risks faced by the organisation?
✓ Do EDs and NEDs fulfil their roles individually and collectively within a unitary board structure?
✓ Are the statutory board committees properly constituted?
✓ Do they provide effective oversight in their respective areas?
✓ How does assurance flow from committee to board and between committees?
✓ Are the board committees properly constituted with delegated powers and clear terms of reference?
✓ Does the board make the appropriate public disclosures about its work and the work of its committees?

■ Summary

The unitary nature of the board is a key issue in understanding the governance arrangements for the board. The distinct roles for EDs and NEDs must be recognised, though at the same time maintaining the collective responsibility of the board. The board acts as the 'controlling mind' or head of the organisation: checks and balances need to be in place to make sure that it is held fully to account by stakeholders for the decisions that it takes.

In order to further understand the dynamics of the board the following chapters will explore the individual duties and powers of directors and the specific roles played by board members.

Directors' duties and liabilities

It is an accepted governance tenet that boards have a collective responsibility for the way they act and make decisions. However, the individual directors who make up the board also have key duties and responsibilities as a consequence of their roles – and they will be liable for certain outcomes that result from the actions and decisions of the board. There is extensive legal precedent on this subject which cannot be covered in detail in this handbook. However, the information collected here will form the basis of a good understanding for those individuals who take on a director role within an NHS organisation.

As set out in Chapter 4, the directors act as agents of the organisation, binding the organisation in its relationships with a number of third parties. They can do this with 'actual authority' or 'apparent authority' (the directors represented to the third party that they had the authority to act on behalf of the organisation).

This power to act is constrained by the duties that are expected of those directors. These duties stem from two sources – common law and statute. The duties enshrined in common law should be considered for directors of NHS organisations. As far as the legislation is concerned, a 'company' means a company formed and registered under the companies' legislation. NHS organisations that are organisations created by statutory instrument – not registered companies – are not bound by this legislation. Even so, it is good practice to have understanding of the general principles of the companies' legislation and the nature of the original common law duties.

A distinction should be made between the powers and duties of EDs as board members and their responsibilities as managers of the organisation. Managers have neither powers nor duties to bind the organisation. The relationship they have with the organisation (including their authority and responsibilities) is established by their contract of employment and by the law of agency.

■ Who can be a director?

Anyone can become a director under companies legislation, with a few exceptions. The following cannot be a company director.

- someone who is disqualified by the company's own articles of association (the rules relating to the running of the company);
- an undischarged bankrupt;
- someone disqualified by a court order; and
- the company's auditor.

If someone effectively acts as a director, even without the title, they may still legally be seen as a director. The law on a director's duties and liabilities also specifically includes a person who is classed as a 'shadow director'; this is anyone who, despite not officially being a 'director', regularly attends board and strategy meetings and upon whose advice the directors are accustomed to act. This could apply to a lawyer or accountant who advises a company's directors and whose guidance the directors usually take.

■ NHS directors

The 'fit and proper persons' test for NHS directors was introduced under the Health and Social Care Act 2008 (Regulated Activities) Regulations 2014. This means the CQC will assess whether directors are:

- of good character;
- have the necessary qualifications, skills and experience;
- are able to perform the work that they are employed for; and
- can supply information, such as certain checks and a full employment history.

The fit and proper person requirement for directors will have a wider impact, in both the scope of its application and the nature of the test. It makes it clear that individuals who have authority in organisations that deliver care are responsible for the overall quality and safety of that care and, as such, can be held accountable if standards of care do not meet legal requirements.

It will apply to all directors and 'equivalents'. This will include EDs and NEDs of NHS trusts and FTs and members of CCG governing bodies. It will be the responsibility of the healthcare provider and, in the case of FTs and CCGs, the chair, to ensure that all directors meet the fitness test and do not meet any of the 'unfit' criteria. For NHS trusts the NHS TDA is responsible for ensuring NEDs meet the criteria.

In addition to the usual requirements of good character, health, qualifications, skills and experience, the regulation bars individuals who are prevented from holding the office of director (for example, under a directors disqualification order). It also excludes from office people who:

> 'have been responsible for, been privy to, contributed to or facilitated any serious misconduct or mismanagement (whether unlawful or not) in the course of carrying on a regulated activity, or discharging any functions relating to any office or employment with a service provider.'

In addition a director will fail the 'fit and proper person' test if:

- they are an undischarged bankrupt;
- are the subject of a bankruptcy order or an interim bankruptcy order; or
- have an undischarged arrangement with creditors.

Directors will also be unfit if they are included on any barring list preventing them from working with children or vulnerable adults, or are prohibited from holding the position under any other law. This means that a person subject to a disqualification order under the Company Directors' Disqualification Act 1986 or under the Charities Act would not meet the fit and proper person requirement in relation to a registered provider that was a company or charity respectively.

The CQC will require the chair of the board or the NHS TOA to confirm that the fitness of all new directors has been assessed in line with the regulations and to declare to the CQC in writing that they are satisfied that they are fit and proper individuals for that role.

The standing orders of an NHS organisation may also include grounds upon which a person is disqualified from office. These include:

- people who have received a prison sentence or suspended sentence of three months or more in the last five years;
- people who are the subject of a bankruptcy restriction order or interim order;
- anyone who has been dismissed (except by redundancy) by any NHS body;
- in certain circumstances, those who have had an earlier term of appointment terminated; ·
- anyone who is under a disqualification order under the Company Directors' Disqualification Act 1986;
- anyone who has been removed from trusteeship of a charity; ·
- in most circumstances, civil servants within the DH, or members/employees of the Care Quality Commission;
- a member of the council of governors or a chair or member of the governing body of a clinical commissioning group – or an employee of such group or a member of the local authority's overview and scrutiny committee;
- a person who is the spouse, partner, parent or child of a member of the board of directors (including the chair) of the trust;
- a person whose tenure of office as a chair or as an officer or director of a health service body has been terminated on the grounds that their appointment is not in the interests of the health service, for non-attendance at meetings, or for non-disclosure of a pecuniary interest;
- a person who has had their name removed or been suspended from any list prepared under the NHS Act 2006 act who has otherwise been suspended or disqualified from any healthcare profession, and has not had the suspension lifted or qualification reinstated;

■ anyone who has previously been or is currently subject to a sex offender order and/or required to register under the Sexual Offences Act 2003, or has committed a sexual offence prior to the requirement to register under current legislation.

■ The powers of directors

The powers of the board of directors are set out in an organisation's constitution. In UK companies, formed under the UK Companies Act, this means the articles of association. These are similar to, for example, a CCG's constitution or FTs and standing orders. Article 3 of the model articles of association states: 'Subject to the articles, the directors are responsible for the management of the company's business, for which purpose they may exercise all the powers of the company.' The shareholders may instruct the directors what they should do (or should not do) but only by passing a special resolution in general meeting. A special resolution of the shareholders cannot invalidate what the directors have already done. Article 5 allows the directors to delegate any of the powers conferred on them under the articles to any person (such as the CEO) or committee (such as to an audit committee) as they think fit.

In health service governance, the powers of the board of directors are set out in their governing document. For example, FTs have a written constitution, which has to be approved by Monitor. This is then further defined by:

■ the schedule of matters reserved for the board
■ the scheme of delegation
■ standing orders
■ standing financial instructions.

These will be covered in more detail later in this chapter.

■ The duties of directors to their organisation

Directors act as agents of their organisation. They have certain duties which are to the organisation itself – not to its shareholders, its employees or any person external to the organisation, such as the general public. Although an organisation is a legal person in law, it is not human. Since the relationship between directors and the organisation is by its very nature impersonal, it might be wondered just what 'duty' means.

The concept of duty is not easy to understand, and it is helpful to make a comparison with the duties owed by other individuals or groups.

Examples of individuals owing a duty to something inanimate are uncommon, although personnel in the armed forces have a duty to their country. It is more usual to show loyalty to something inanimate than to have a duty. For example, individuals might be expected to show loyalty to their country, and they might voluntarily show loyalty to their sports team, group of friends or work colleagues. Arguably, solicitors have a duty to their profession to act ethically, although the solicitors' practice rules in the UK specify that solicitors owe a duty of care to their clients. Similarly, doctors have a duty to act ethically, but their duty is to their patients. Duty is normally owed to individuals or a group of people. It might therefore be supposed that directors should owe a duty to their shareholders and possibly to the organisation's employees, but this is not the case.

- Accountability and responsibility should not be confused with duty.
- Directors have a responsibility to use their powers in ways that seem best for the organisation and its shareholders or major stakeholders.
- They should be accountable to the 'owners' of the organisation, for the ways in which they have exercised their powers and/or the performance of the organisation.
- They have duties to the organisation.

If a person is guilty of a breach of duty, there should be a process for calling them to account. There might be an established disciplinary procedure, for example, in a court or before a judicial panel, with a recognised set of punishments for misbehaviour.

The common law duties of directors

Until the Companies Act 2006 came into force, the main legal duties of directors to their organisation were duties in common law – a fiduciary duty and duty of skill and care to the organisation.

The Companies Act 2006 has now written the common law duties of directors into statute law. It states that these general duties 'are based on certain common law rules and equitable principles as they apply to directors, and have effect in place of those rules and principles as regards the duties owed to an organisation by a director' (Companies Act 2006, section 170). The Act goes on to state that the statutory general duties should be interpreted in the same way as the common law rules and equitable principles.

Fiduciary duty of directors

'Fiduciary' means given in trust, and the concept of a trustee (as established in US and UK law) is applicable. The directors hold a position of trust because they make contracts on behalf of the organisation and also control the organisation's property. Since this is similar being a trustee of the organisation, a director has a fiduciary duty to the organisation (not its shareholders).

If a director were to act in breach of his fiduciary duty, legal action could be brought against them by the organisation. In such a situation, 'the organisation' might be represented by a majority of the board of directors, or a majority of the shareholders, or a single controlling shareholder.

A director would be in breach of his fiduciary duty in carrying out a particular transaction or series of transactions in any of the following circumstances:

- The transaction is not in any way incidental to the business of the organisation. For example, the CEO of a building construction organisation might decide to trade in diamonds and lose large amounts of money in these diamond trading transactions.
- The transaction is not carried out *bona fide* (in good faith), with honesty and sincerity.
- The transaction has not been made for the benefit of the organisation but for the personal benefit of the director or an associate. A director has a fiduciary duty to avoid a conflict of interest between him or herself personally and the organisation, and must not obtain any personal benefit or profit from a transaction without the consent of the organisation. In other words, it would be a breach of fiduciary duty for a director to make a secret profit from a transaction by the organisation in which he has a personal interest.

CASE STUDY: fiduciary duty

An organisation wishes to buy some land and has identified a property for which it would be prepared to pay a large sum of money. The CEO secretly sets up a private organisation of his own to buy the property, and then sells this on to the organisation of which he is CEO, making a large profit in the process.

The actions of the CEO are breach of fiduciary duty, because his actions have not been *bona fide* and he has made a secret profit at the expense of the organisation. Under the Companies Act 2006, these actions would be a breach of statutory duty.

Director's duty of skill and care

Directors are also subject to a duty of skill and care to the organisation. A director should not act negligently in carrying out his duties, and could be personally liable for losses suffered by the organisation as a consequence of such negligence.

The standard of skill and care expected of a director is the higher of the skill that he has or the skill that would objectively be expected of a director of the particular organisation. In the case *Re D'Jan of London* [1993] (covered later in this chapter), the judge ruled that the common law duty of care was the equivalent to the statutory test applied by section 214 of the Insolvency Act 1986. This statutory test refers to what would be expected of 'a reasonably diligent person having both:

- the general knowledge, skill and experience that may reasonably be expected of a person carrying out the same functions as are carried out by that director in relation to the organisation; and
- the general knowledge, skill and experience that that director has.

A director is expected to show the technical skills that would reasonably be expected from someone of his experience and expertise. If the finance director of a scientific research organisation is a qualified accountant, he would not be expected to possess the technical skills of a scientist, but would be expected to possess some technical skill as an accountant.

However, the duty of skill and care does not extend to spending time in the organisation. A director should attend board meetings if possible, but at other times is not required to be concerned with the affairs of the organisation. This requirement is perhaps best understood with NEDs, who might visit the organisation only for board or committee meetings. The duties of a director are intermittent in nature and arise from time to time only, such as when the board meets. If a director holds an executive position in the organisation, a different situation arises, because he is an employee of the organisation with a contract of service. This contract might call for full-time attendance at the organisation or on its business. However, this requirement arises out of his job as a manager, not out of his position as a director.

It is also not a part of the duty of skill and care to watch closely over the activities of the organisation's management. Unless there are particular grounds for suspecting dishonesty or incompetence, a director is entitled to leave the routine conduct of the organisation's affairs to the management. If the management appears honest, the directors may rely on the information they provide. It is not part of their duty of skill and care to question whether the information is reliable, or whether important information is being withheld.

A board of directors might make a decision that appears ill-judged or careless. However, the courts in the UK are generally reluctant to condemn business decisions made by the board that appear, in hindsight, to show errors of judgement. Directors can exercise reasonable skill and care, but still make bad decisions.

For a legal action against a director to succeed, an organisation would have to prove that serious negligence had occurred. It would not be enough to demonstrate that some loss could have been avoided if the director had been a bit more careful.

CASE STUDY: Dorchester Finance Co Ltd v Stebbing [1989]

In the UK legal case *Dorchester Finance Co Ltd v Stebbing* [1989], a company brought an action against its three directors for alleged negligence and misappropriation of the company's property. The company (Dorchester Finance) was in the money-lending business and it had three directors, S, H and P. Only S was involved with the company full-time; H and P were non-executives who made only rare appearances. There were no board meetings. S and P were qualified accountants and H, although not an accountant, had considerable accountancy experience. S arranged for the company to make some loans to persons with whom he appears to have had dealings. In the loan-making process he had persuaded P and H to sign blank cheques that were subsequently used to make the loans. The loans did not comply with the Moneylenders Acts and they were inadequately secured. When the loans turned out to be irrecoverable, the company brought its action against the directors.

It was held that all three directors were liable to damages. S, as an ED, was held to be grossly negligent. P and H, as non-executives, were held to have failed to show the necessary level of skill and care in performing their duties as non-executives, even though it was accepted that they had acted in good faith at all times.

Wrongful trading and the standard of duty and care

The standard of duty and care required from a director has been partly defined in a number of UK legal cases relating to wrongful trading. Under the Insolvency Act 1986, directors may be liable for wrongful trading by the organisation when they allowed the organisation to continue trading but knew (or should have known) that it would be unable to avoid an insolvent liquidation. When such a situation arises and an organisation goes into liquidation, the liquidator can apply to the court for the director to be held personally liable for negligence. The duty of a director under the Insolvency Act was used in the case of *Re D'Jan of London [1993]* to illustrate a director's general duty of skill and care.

CASE STUDY: Re D'Jan of London [1993]
An insurance broker completed a fire insurance proposal form with an incorrect answer, but a director of the company (Re D'Jan) applying for the insurance policy signed the form. The company premises burned down, and the insurance company, on discovering the mistake on the proposal form, repudiated all liability under the policy. The company went into insolvent liquidation. The liquidator brought an action against the director who had signed the proposal form, alleging a failure to exercise reasonable care to the company. The court found that although it would be unreasonable to expect a director to read every word of every document that he signed, in this case the form consisted of a few simple questions that the director was the best person to answer. The director was therefore guilty of a breach of duty of care, although, in this particular case, the director was exonerated on other grounds.

When there is a question about the extent of the director's duties and responsibilities, a significant factor could be the level of reward that the director was entitled to receive from the company. *Prima facie*, the higher the rewards, the greater the responsibilities should be expected.

The statutory duties of directors

NHS organisations are not registered companies but organisations created by statutory instrument. As such, they are not bound by the Companies Act 2006. Good practice, however, would require an understanding of the general principles of the Act, which are set out here.

The duties of directors were introduced into UK statute law by the Companies Act 2006 (sections 171–177). These consist of a duty to:

- act within powers
- promote the success of the organisation
- exercise independent judgement
- exercise reasonable care, skill and diligence
- avoid conflicts of interest
- not to accept benefits from third parties
- declare any interest in a proposed transaction or arrangement.

Duty to act within powers

A director must act within his powers in accordance with the organisation's constitution, and should only exercise these powers for the purpose for which they were granted. If a director acts outside his powers to make a contractual agreement with a third party, the organisation is still liable for any obligation to the third party, provided that the third party has acted in good faith.

Directors should also ensure that they comply with the organisation's constitution. For example, when a group of directors meets, it must be clear whether the meeting is a full board meeting, a meeting of a board committee or an unofficial meeting of directors. Unless the meeting is a formal board meeting, the directors would be acting outside their powers if they took a decision on a matter that is reserved for decision-making by the board.

Duty to promote the success of the organisation

A director must act, in good faith, in the way he considers would be most likely to 'promote the success of the organisation for the benefit of its members as a whole'. The Act does not define 'success', but the term is likely to be interpreted as meaning 'increasing value for shareholders'. However, in doing so, a director must also have regard, among other matters, to the:

- likely long-term consequences of any decision;
- interests of the organisation's employees;
- need to foster the organisation's relationships with its customers, suppliers and others;
- impact of the organisation's operations on the community and the environment;

- desirability of the organisation maintaining its reputation for high standards of business conduct; and
- need to act fairly as between members of the organisation.

The Act does not create a duty of directors to any stakeholders other than the shareholders (members), but it requires directors to consider the interests of other stakeholders in reaching their decisions. The Act specifically mentions employees, customers, suppliers and the community.

Foundation trust directors now have the same responsibility to promote the success of the corporation so this particular duty is directly applicable to FTs.

Duty to exercise independent judgment

A director must exercise independent judgment. However, this requirement does not prevent a director from acting in a way authorised by the organisation's constitution (such as accepting resolutions passed by the shareholders in general meeting) or from acting in accordance with an agreement already entered into by the organisation that prevents the director from using discretion. The requirement for independent judgment does not prevent a director from taking advice and acting on it.

The ICSA Guidance on *Directors' General Duties* comments as follows on this duty.

- A director must not allow personal interests to affect their independent judgement. This means that if the board is considering a contract in which a director has a personal interest ideally they should leave the meeting while the matter is being discussed (this is also relevant to the duty of directors to avoid any conflict of interest with the organisation).
- An ED should not attend a board meeting to 'promote a collective executive line'. They should attend the board meeting in their own right and give the board the benefit of their independent opinion.
- Similarly, directors representing a particular interest should 'set any representative function aside and make final decisions on their own merits'. For example, a director who is a representative of a family interest in the organisation 'may consult their family but be clear that he will make the final decision'.

Duty to exercise reasonable care, skill and diligence
This is similar to the common law duty of care.

Duty to avoid conflicts of interest
A director has a duty to avoid conflicts of interest with the interests of the organisation. However, this duty is not breached if the director declares to the board their interest in a transaction and the interest is authorised/approved by the board.

In the commercial world, it is inevitable that many directors will have a potential conflict of interest with their organisation (whether direct or indirect). For example, an organisation might be planning to trade with another organisation in which one of its directors is a shareholder. In such a situation, the director concerned is required to declare their interest in the proposed contract and must not make a secret profit.

A director or a connected person might have a material interest in a transaction undertaken by the organisation. For example, the organisation might award a contract to a firm of building contractors to rebuild or develop a property owned by the organisation, and the director or their spouse might own the building organisation.

A director might also have a direct or indirect interest in a contract (or proposed contract) with the organisation. For example, the director might be a member of another organisation with which the organisation is planning to sign a business contract. Such a contract is not illegal, although the organisation can choose to rescind it should it wish to do so.

If a director has an interest in a contract with the organisation and has failed to disclose it, and has received a payment under the contract, they will be regarded as holding the money in the capacity of constructive trustee for the organisation (and so is bound to repay the money).

The 2006 Act recognises three situations in which an actual or potential conflict of interests may arise.

- A conflict of interest may arise in a situation where the organisation is not a party to an arrangement or transaction, but where the director might be able to gain personally from 'the exploitation of any property, information or opportunity'. For example, a director might pursue an opportunity for their personal benefit that the organisation might have pursued itself.

- A conflict of interest may arise about a proposed transaction or arrangement to which the organisation will be a party. If a director has a direct or indirect personal interest in any such transaction or arrangement, they must disclose their interest to the board of directors before it is entered into by the organisation. An example would be a proposal to acquire a target company in which a director owns shares.

- A third type of conflict of interest arises with existing transactions or arrangements in which the organisation is already a party. It can be a criminal offence for a director not to make or update their declaration of interest in an arrangement or transaction to which the organisation is a party.

This is key principle for NHS directors. There are specific guidelines for NHS directors to follow with regard to conflicts of interest, in line with the Nolan principles, which are set out in the NHS Code of Conduct and Accountability (covered later in this chapter)

Duty not to accept benefits from third parties

A director must not accept benefits from a third party unless they have been authorised by the shareholders or cannot reasonably be regarded as creating a potential conflict of their interest. Clearly, accepting a bribe from a supplier in return for awarding a supply contract would be a breach of this duty. It would also be illegal to accept lunch or dinner from the same supplier or customer every week, accepting an all-expenses paid holiday or accepting frequent invitations to 'hospitality' events. On the other hand, it should be within the law to accept an invitation to a day out to tennis at Wimbledon, or an invitation to dinner to celebrate the successful completion of a project.

Many listed companies already have strict policies on the acceptance of gifts and corporate hospitality, especially from other companies that are or might be about to tender for business with the organisation. A policy might include a requirement for a director to obtain clearance from another director before accepting any such benefits, and for all instances of gifts or hospitality to be recorded in a register.

The Bribery Act 2010 sets out that an organisation may be liable for failing to prevent a person from bribing on its behalf, but only if that person performs business services for the organisation. It contains a full defence for an organisation that show it had adequate procedures in place to prevent bribery. It is important to note that guidance on the Act sets out specifically that while hospitality is not prohibited by the Act, facilitation payments are classed as bribes under the Act.

The Bribery Act is applicable to NHS organisations and there are a number of steps that NHS organisations can consider. These include:

- carrying out a bribery and corruption risk assessment;
- putting in place anti-bribery procedures that are proportionate to the identified risks;
- ensuring that when proportionate anti-bribery procedures are put in place, the principles outlined in the guidance are taken into account (top-level commitment, due diligence, communication and training, and monitoring and review);
- being clear that NHS organisations and their employees, contractors and agents are covered by corporate liability for bribery;
- taking steps to make their trust employees and contractors aware of the standards of conduct expected of them, particularly in known risk areas such as procurement; and
- recording any steps taken, as they provide the defence against corporate liability under the Act.

Duty to declare interests in proposed transactions with the organisation

This duty is linked to the duty relating to conflicts of interest. A director must declare the nature and extent of their interest to the other directors, who may then authorise it. The NHS Code of Conduct and Accountability also covers this for NHS directors.

A director may have a personal interest in a proposed transaction with the organisation. For example, a director may own a building that the organisation wants to buy or rent; or a director may be a major shareholder in another organisation that is hoping to become a supplier or customer. Proposed transactions do not necessarily create a conflict of interest, but they must nevertheless be declared and subject to approval by the rest of the board. If a conflict of interest would arise from the proposed transaction, the director must take measures to ensure that the conflict is avoided.

■ Other statutory duties

Directors' responsibilities to third parties

Although the duty of directors is to their organisation, a breach of that duty could also affect outsiders. When the directors make a contract with an outsider, the contract is binding on the organisation when it is made according to its constitutional documents. However, the directors might exceed their powers in making the contract, for example, because they should have obtained stakeholder approval first, but failed to do so. Contracts entered into without proper authority are known as 'irregular contracts', and might seem to be void.

The main provision of UK company law is that an irregular contract is binding on an organisation when an outsider, acting in good faith, enters into the contract and the board of directors has approved the contract. The directors will be liable to the organisation for any loss suffered. This rule means that irregular contracts do not affect third parties (outsiders). Instead, when they occur, they would be a corporate governance problem.

Related party transactions and the UK Disclosure and Transparency Rules for listed companies

In listed companies, the requirements of UK law are reinforced by the UK Disclosure and Transparency Rules, which include a section on related party transactions. In broad terms, a related party means a substantial shareholder of the organisation, a director of the organisation, a member of a director's family or an organisation in which a director or family member holds 30% or more of the shares. A related party transaction is a transaction between an organisation and a related party, other than in the normal course of business and results in a disclosure being made to the stock market and the shareholders. The effect of the rules should be to prevent directors or major shareholders of UK listed companies from obtaining a personal benefit from any non-business transaction with their organisation, unless the shareholders have given their approval.

The NHS Code of Conduct and Accountability covers this for directors and stakeholders of NHS organisations.

Borrowing powers of directors

In the UK, there is no restriction in law on how much the directors can borrow on behalf of their organisation unless the constitutional documents include a specific restriction. As far as the law is concerned, the borrowing powers of companies are limited only by what lenders are prepared to make available to them. Conceivably, the directors could therefore put the investment of their shareholders at risk by borrowing more than the organisation can safely afford.

Foundation trusts are also free to borrow from banks and other private sector lenders to improve the facilities and equipment available to patients. They are, however, subject to statutory controls – unlike voluntary or private providers of healthcare – which give Monitor powers to set limits on the amount they can borrow.

Duty to break even

Although the break-even duty is a statutory requirement for non-foundation NHS trusts, all NHS bodies are expected to operate a balanced budget ensuring that total expenditure does not exceed total income.

Paragraph 2(1) of Schedule 5 to the National Health Service Act 2006 states: 'Each NHS trust must ensure that its revenue is not less than sufficient, taking one financial year with another, to meet outgoings properly chargeable to revenue account.' This is known as the breakeven duty. NHS Trusts and CCGs should normally plan to meet this duty by achieving a balanced position on their income and expenditure accounts each and every year. The breakeven duty includes the phrase 'taking one financial year with another'. This provides some flexibility on the time-scale for matching income with those costs whose incidence is uneven and when managing the recovery of an NHS Trust with serious financial difficulties.

An agreement was reached in 1997 with the Treasury and the Audit Commission that the duty will be assumed to have been met if expenditure is covered by income over a rolling three-year period. Exceptionally, the breakeven duty is assumed to be met if the cumulative deficit being recovered is covered by subsequent surpluses over a four- or five-year period.

2013/14 saw a threefold increase in the number of NHS organisations being reported to the Secretary of State for Health for failing to meet their statutory break-even duty, with 20 trusts failing (compared with only five trusts for 2012/13). In addition, 24 CCGs – 11% of all CCGs – were also referred to the Secretary of State as a result of financial concerns in that period.

Where an NHS Trust or CCG is recovering a cumulative deficit position, the organisation would be required to produce and agree a robust recovery plan with either the NHS TDA or the NHS England.

■ Liability of directors

The starting point for considering the liabilities of individual directors is to understand the role of the board and the corporate nature of the specific NHS organisation (NHS trust, CCG or FT). Any such organisation will be a corporate entity in its own right and will take decisions as such. As noted earlier, this has implications for the role of directors, who are collectively responsible for all decisions.

The corporate nature of the organisation will mean that, in most instances, even if a decision is open to criticism, individual directors will not be legally liable. There are also specific statutory protections where they are acting in good faith (see section. 265 of the Public Health Act 1875). This section covers the circumstances where such personal liability can arise.

Criminal liability

An individual who, in the course of their activities as a director, commits a criminal offence will carry personal responsibility and liability. Perhaps more significantly, a director can be held to have committed a criminal offence where the offence arises under statute that includes explicit provision to hold a director liable. Examples are the Health and Safety at Work Act, the Environmental Protection Act and the Data Protection Act.

Prior to the Corporate Manslaughter Act 2007 coming into force, it was possible for a corporate entity, such as a company, to be prosecuted for a wide range of criminal offences, including the common law offence of gross negligence manslaughter. However, in order for the corporate entity to be guilty of the offence, it was also necessary for a senior individual who could be said to embody the company (also known as a 'controlling mind') to be guilty of the offence. The new law was wider, meaning a corporate entity can be convicted if it can be proven that there was a gross breach of duty of care by senior management, instead of just one individual.

Civil liability to third parties

Civil liability, which generally relates to the payment of compensation, can arise in either contract or tort. Liability in contract will only occur if the contract is entered into in the personal name of the director rather than that of the trust, or where a contract entered into by the trust is found to be *ultra vires* and the director has given a personal warranty or representation that the trust has appropriate powers. Directors therefore need to be careful about what assurances they give about the powers of the organisation.

The more usual risks are for the individual to have a claim in tort made against them, most commonly in relation to either negligence or defamation. A tort can be defined as a wrongful act resulting in injury to another's person, property, or reputation, for which the injured party is entitled to seek compensation where there has been no contractual relationship. Negligence arises where an individual acts without due care towards a person to whom they owe a duty of care, and causes foreseeable loss. Usually, as with clinical negligence claims, the claim is pursued against the trust, not the individual, and the NHS Litigation Authority will provide cover. Indeed, the Liabilities to Third Parties Scheme includes cover for directors similar to that available in the commercial market by way of directors' and officers' liability insurance.

Defamation is a potential risk, and while some degree of protection is afforded where public officers are acting honestly and in the course of their business, there are risks if they step outside the strict parameters of the role.

A potential threat is misfeasance in public office. In practice this is very rare and requires the establishment of deliberate malice, targeting the individual or a limited class of people who has/have suffered loss.

Claims by the NHS organisation

A final area of risk is that of claims by the NHS organisation itself. All directors owe a duty of care and skill to the NHS organisation, and breaches could give rise to claims. There is a material difference in this matter between the position of EDs and NEDs (or Lay Members). The latter are protected by the terms of the standard HM Treasury indemnity, unless they have been reckless. However, EDs could in theory be the subject of claims, even if they have only been negligent.

Although there are some high profile corporate cases, such as Equitable Life, in practice claims against the directors for negligently carrying out their duties are rare. It does, however, underline the need for directors to use care and skills in carrying out their role. Where a matter is outside their competence, they may want to consider whether they need independent advice.

A further area of claim by an NHS organisation would be for breach of fiduciary duty or for repayment of benefits improperly received. This can arise in two main ways. The first is where a director abuses their position to make private gain. This could occur where a director arranged for a contract with a company in which they had an interest, without declaring the relevant interest. In such circumstances the trust can call for an account of the proceeds.

Secondly, and perhaps more commonly, situations may arise where the auditors call into question officers' severance or retirement packages. Irrespective of the propriety of the individual's conduct, if the award of the package was outside the powers of the NHS organisation, or decided upon improperly, it can be clawed back.

Indemnity

As indicated above, directors have a degree of protection against claims. Non-executives will typically have the benefit of the Treasury approved wording (HSG 1999/104):

'A chair or non-executive member or director who has acted honestly and in good faith will not have to meet out of his or her own personal resources any personal civil liability that is incurred in the execution or purported execution of his or her board function. Save where the person has acted recklessly.'

This indemnity may be extended to members of those committees that have delegated powers to make decisions or take actions on behalf of NHS boards. This covers the director for acts carried out in good faith in the execution or purported execution of the functions of the trust, short of recklessness. It does not cover criminal liability, and no indemnity could do so.

There is some doubt about the position where the director is in fact acting outside the powers of the organisation, particularly where to enforce the indemnity would be to allow a collateral enforcement of an *ultra vires* obligation against the trust.

Executive directors will generally be indemnified in relation to claims against them arising from third parties, but difficult issues can arise when staff make allegations of harassment, and trusts will need to tread carefully in such cases.

■ NHS Code of Conduct and Accountability

Unsurprisingly, the duty to avoid conflicts of interest, not to accept benefits from third parties and to declare any interest in a proposed transaction or arrangement are very clearly set out in the Code of Conduct and Accountability for NHS organisations. Given the scale and magnitude of the procurement of contracts and services within the NHS, there is clearly a significant need to regulate the behaviour of both the board and NHS staff in regard to managing conflicts of interests.

The NHS Code of Conduct and Accountability (third revision, April 2013) is quite clear in that NHS boards should act in a way that protects the interest of the NHS in the way they undertake their business.

- Accountability: Everything done by those who work in the NHS must be able to stand the test of parliamentary scrutiny, public judgments on propriety and professional codes of conduct.
- Probity: There should be an absolute standard of honesty in dealing with the assets of the NHS: integrity should be the hallmark of all personal conduct in decisions affecting patients, staff, and suppliers, and in the use of information acquired in the course of NHS duties.
- Openness: There should be sufficient transparency about NHS activities to promote confidence between the NHS organisation and its staff, patients and the public.

Public service values matter in the NHS. Those who work in it have a duty to conduct NHS business with probity. They have a responsibility to respond to staff, patients and suppliers impartially, to achieve value for money from the public funds with which they are entrusted and to demonstrate high ethical standards of personal conduct. The Code makes it clear that chairs and board directors should act impartially and should not be influenced by social or business relationships. Where there is a potential for private interests to be material and relevant to NHS business, the relevant interests should be declared and recorded in the board minutes, and entered into a register which is available to the public. When a conflict of interest is established, the board director should withdraw and play no part in the relevant discussion or decision.

It is vital that NHS board directors should set an example to their organisation in the use of public funds and the need for good value in incurring public expenditure. The use of NHS monies for hospitality and entertainment, including hospitality at conferences or seminars, should be carefully considered. All expenditure on these items should be capable of justification as reasonable in the light of the general practice in the public sector. NHS boards should be aware that expenditure on hospitality or entertainment is the responsibility of management and is open to be challenged by the internal and external auditors and that ill-considered actions can damage respect for the NHS in the eyes of the community.

NHS boards should also have an explicit procedure for the declaration of hospitality and sponsorship offered by, for example, suppliers. Their authorisation should be carefully considered and the decision should be recorded. NHS boards should be aware of the risks in incurring obligations to suppliers at any stage of a contracting relationship.

NHS boards should ensure that staff have a proper and widely publicised procedure for voicing complaints or concerns about maladministration, malpractice, breaches of this code and other concerns of an ethical nature. This has been developed further in whistleblowing procedures, which are set out in more detail in Chapter 15.

The Healthy NHS Board also reinforces the importance of NHS boards acting, and being seen to act, with integrity and in the best interests of the organisation:

> Probity requires that the board maintains an up-to-date register of board members' interests. Board agendas should include an opportunity for board members to declare conflicts of interests that may relate to specific agenda items so that they can be managed appropriately.'

For NHS FTs, there is also a requirement for the board of directors to adopt appropriate standards of conduct and to be open and transparent in their decision-making and the manner in which conflicts of interest are managed. This was clarified further in section 152 of HSCA 2012 as follows:

'The duties that a director of a public benefit corporation has by virtue of being a director include in particular
a) a duty to avoid a situation in which the director has (or can have) a direct or indirect interest that conflicts (or possibly may conflict) with the interests of the corporation;

b) a duty not to accept a benefit from a third party by reason of being a director or doing (or not doing) anything in that capacity.

This duty is not infringed if the situation cannot reasonably be regarded as likely to give rise to a conflict of interest, or the matter has been authorised in accordance with the constitution, or if acceptance of the benefit cannot reasonably be regarded as likely to give rise to a conflict of interest.

If a director of a public benefit corporation has in any way a direct or indirect interest in a proposed transaction or arrangement with the corporation, the director must declare the nature and extent of that interest to the other directors. And if a declaration under this section proves to be, or becomes, inaccurate or incomplete, a further declaration must be made. Any declaration required by this section must be made before the corporation enters into the transaction or arrangement. The section did not require a declaration of an interest of which the director was not aware or where the director was not aware of the transaction or arrangement in question.'

Conflicts of interest are a major governance issue for CCGs. NHS England provided guidance for CCGs in *Managing Conflicts of Interest: Guidance for Clinical Commissioning groups* (2013). This will be covered in more detail in Chapter 12. However, the core of the issue is neatly summarised in the below quote from the September 2011 briefing paper on managing conflicts of interest by the Royal College of General Practitioners (RCGP) and NHS Confederation.

'It is crucial that an interest and involvement in the local healthcare system does not also involve a vested interest in terms of financial or professional bias toward or against particular solutions or decisions. The fact that, in their provider and gatekeeper roles, GPs and their colleagues could potentially profit personally (financially or otherwise) from the decisions of a commissioning group of which they are also members, means that questions about their role in the governance of NHS commissioning bodies are legitimate. Failure to acknowledge, identify and address them could result in poor decision making, legal challenge and reputational damage.'

CCGs need to provide clear guidance to their members and employees on what might constitute a conflict of interest, providing examples that are likely to arise. They should also highlight the following points to members and employees:

- a perception of wrongdoing, impaired judgment or undue influence can be as detrimental as any of them actually occurring;
- if in doubt, it is better to assume a conflict of interest and manage it appropriately rather than ignore it;
- financial gain is not necessary for a conflict to exist.

Governance Checklist

✓ Are the directors aware of the extent of their authority and powers and the purposes for which they have been granted?

✓ Are directors aware of the boundaries set out in the matters reserved for the board and in the standing orders/standing financial instructions?

✓ Are directors aware of the implications of the common law and statutory duties that could be the benchmark their actions are judged against?

✓ Are board members provided with sufficient and accurate information and advice for them to exercise reasonable care, skill and diligence?

✓ Does that information enable them to make decisions which will fulfil their function – for example, promoting the success of the corporation in a FT?

✓ Are the directors confident in identifying potential conflicts of interest, how to declare them and how to manage them?

■ Summary

This chapter makes it clear that the individual directors who compose the board have key duties and responsibilities as a consequence of the role. Consequently, they will be liable for certain outcomes that result from the actions and decisions of the board. Directors need to have a clear understanding of these duties and liabilities: this should form a key part of their induction and ongoing development as board members.

PART THREE

The effective board and its officers

Maintaining an effective board

This chapter deals with governance issues relating to the effectiveness of the board (and again this should be taken to include the governing body of a CCG). Board performance and operation has been highlighted in a number of NHS publications but the key guidance can be found in *The Healthy NHS Board* (2013). (FR)

This area has also been subject to intense scrutiny following the Francis Inquiry Report of February 2013, the subsequent government responses and independent reviews. In line with this trend, Monitor has produced the Well-Led Framework in September 2014. This is intended to support NHS FT boards in gaining assurance on their effectiveness in carrying out their role of setting strategy, leading the organisation and overseeing operations, and being accountable to stakeholders in an open and effective manner. It is likely that this will become the benchmark for assessing effectiveness for NHS trusts and CCGs as well.

Though such guidance is helpful in setting out clear processes and procedures, it is important to recognise the vital interplay of the different roles, personalities and relationships around the board table. Defining an effective board merely in LOY terms of its processes and procedures, without recognising that behaviours and culture are the essential ingredients, is a recipe for poor governance and failing organisations. The role of the nomination committee in recruitment and appointment, as well as ongoing high-quality board development and regular evaluation, are crucial for the life of the effective board.

■ Good boardroom practice

Boardroom practice describes the way in which a board conducts its procedures and reaches its decisions. (FR)

The FRC *Guidance on Board Effectiveness*, issued in 2011, states:

'An effective board develops and promotes its collective vision of the company's purpose, its culture, its values and the behaviours it wishes to promote in conducting its business. In particular it:
- provides direction for management;
- demonstrates ethical leadership, displaying – and promoting throughout the company – behaviours consistent with the culture and values it has defined for the organisation;

- creates a performance culture that drives value creation without exposing the company to excessive risk of value destruction;
- makes well informed and high-quality decisions based on a clear line of sight into the business;
- creates the right framework for helping directors to meet their statutory duties under the Companies Act 2006, and/or other relevant statutory and regulatory regimes;
- is accountable, particularly to those that provide the company's capital; and
- thinks carefully about its governance arrangements and embraces evaluation of their effectiveness.'

The guidance continues to say:

'An effective board should not necessarily be a comfortable place. Challenge, as well as teamwork, is an essential feature. Diversity in board composition is an important driver of a board's effectiveness, creating a breadth of perspective among directors, and breaking down a tendency towards "group think".'

The role of the chair

The Association of British Insurers (ABI) *Report on Board Effectiveness* 2012 makes it quite clear that the chair has a key role to play in the effective board. While the report found no 'one size fits all' approach to the role, with different chairs having different approaches based on what is best for the individual company and board, it did find a significant amount of consensus about the role and responsibilities of the chair.

The report emphasised a number of aspects to the role of the chair on the following five themes:

- creating the right board dynamic and having the right people around the boardroom table;
- helping to set the board agenda, ensuring the board has the right information and is debating the right issues;
- managing the board's relationship with the executives and in particular the chief executive;
- being an ambassador for the company; and
- being fully engaged in the business and understanding what is happening on the ground.

The role of the chair is covered in more detail in Chapter 7.

Board meetings

A basic requirement of an effective board is that there should be regular board meetings. The UK states simply that the board should meet sufficiently regularly to discharge its duties effectively, and there should be a formal schedule of matters reserved for the board. Po∫ℕⲦ

The agenda for board meetings is a governance issue in the sense that the chair decides what the board will discuss when they set the agenda. Although directors can raise matters as 'any other business', most of the time at board meetings is spent in discussion of the items listed on the agenda. It is therefore important that the agenda should include all matters reserved for board decision, whenever they arise. The company secretary can assist the chair by providing advice and reminders.

To contribute effectively to board discussions, directors must be provided with relevant information. They should receive relevant documents in advance of a board meeting, so that they have time to read them and think about the issues they deal with. The UK Code states that 'the board should be supplied in a timely manner with information in a form and of a quality sufficient to enable it to discharge its duties.'

The chair has the responsibility for ensuring that directors receive the information that they need in sufficient time. The UK Code states that management has an obligation to provide the required information, but that the directors should ask for clarification or additional information if required.

The *Intelligent Board* report states that 'every member of the board needs sufficient information at a high enough level to be confident that the organisation is well run, but not so much information that it becomes difficult to tell what is important' and that 'good governance is underpinned by intelligent information'.

Such information enables the board to:

- set an appropriately challenging, but achievable, strategic direction;
- identify the strategic issues that require discussion or decision, and distinguish these issues from operational detail;
- provide constructive challenge;
- ensure taxpayers are receiving VFM;
- identify trends in performance;
- enable comparisons with the performance of similar organisations;
- understand the needs, views and experiences of users and non-users from all backgrounds and communities;
- ensure users are receiving a high-quality service;
- anticipate the potential impact of key policy, technological and socioeconomic developments; and
- assure themselves that the organisation is complying with standards and other regulatory requirements.

All information should:

- be clearly and simply presented, including graphic overviews as well as brief commentary;
- be updated in a timely manner;
- direct the board's attention to significant risks, issues and exceptions; and

- provide a level of detail appropriate to the board's role.

Information flows should be both formal and informal. Information is provided formally in documents or files, but this is supplemented by informal communication by e-mail, telephone or face-to-face conversation. Whether providing information formally or informally, the company secretary should ensure that there are good information flows between the board and its committees, between committees, and between EDs and NEDs.

Decision-making

One critical requirement for an effective board is well-informed and high-quality decision-making. This does not happen by accident. Boards can minimise the risk of poor decisions by investing time in the design of their decision-making policies and processes, including the contribution of committees.

The FRC guidance outlines that 'good decision-making capability can be facilitated by:

- high quality board documentation;
- obtaining expert opinions when necessary;
- allowing time for debate and challenge, especially for complex, contentious or business critical issues;
- achieving timely closure; and
- providing clarity on the actions required, and timescales and responsibilities.'

Boards should be aware of factors, which can limit effective decision-making, such as:

- a dominant personality or group of directors on the board, which can inhibit contribution from other directors;
- insufficient attention to risk, and treating risk as a compliance issue rather than as part of the decision-making process, especially in cases where the level of risk involved in a project could endanger the stability and sustainability of the business itself;
- failure to recognise the value implications of running the business on the basis of self-interest and other poor ethical standards;
- a reluctance to involve NEDs, or of matters being brought to the board for sign-off rather than debate;
- complacent or intransigent attitudes;
- a weak organisational culture; or
- inadequate information or analysis.

Most complex decisions depend on judgment, but the judgment of even the most well-intentioned and experienced leaders can, in certain circumstances, be distorted. Some factors known to distort judgment in decision-making are conflicts of interest, emotional attachments, and inappropriate reliance on previous experience and previous decisions. For significant decisions, therefore, a board may wish to consider extra steps, for example:

- describing in board papers the process that has been used to arrive at and challenge the proposal prior to presenting it to the board, thereby allowing directors not involved in the project to assess the appropriateness of the process as a precursor to assessing the merits of the project itself; or
- where appropriate, putting in place additional safeguards to reduce the risk of distorted judgments by, for example, commissioning an independent report, seeking advice from an expert, introducing a devil's advocate to provide challenge, establishing a sole purpose sub-committee, or convening additional meetings. Some chairs favour separate discussions for important decisions (e.g. concept, proposal for discussion, proposal for decision). This gives EDs more opportunity to put the case at the earlier stages, and all directors the opportunity to share concerns or challenge assumptions well in advance of the point of decision.

Boards can benefit from reviewing past decisions, particularly those with poor outcomes. A review should not focus just on the merits of the decision itself but also on the decision-making process.

Support

As well as receiving relevant and timely information, directors should be given access to independent professional advice, at the organisation's expense, when they consider this necessary in order to fulfil their duties as director. For example, a director might ask to consult a lawyer for advice on a matter where the legal position is not clear.

NEDs and possibly also EDs may also need administrative support or advice on routine matters. Board committees should be provided with sufficient resources to carry out their duties, and all directors should have access to the advice and assistance of the company secretary.

■ Board behaviour

There is a general consensus among recently published reports and reviews in both corporate and health service sectors that the quality of governance depends ultimately on the culture and behaviour of individuals, and consequently the ability of procedures and regulation to provide good governance is limited.

The Walker Report argued that both character and culture of the board members are important for an effective board. It commented that:

'Board conformity with laid-down procedures ... will not alone provide better corporate governance overall if the chair is weak, if the composition and dynamic of the board is inadequate and if there is unsatisfactory ... engagement with its owners.'

The report went on to argue that the main weaknesses in the boards of banks had been caused by behavioural factors and a failure to challenge.

'The sequence in board discussion on major issues should be: presentation by the executive, a disciplined process of challenge, decision on the policy or strategy to be adopted and then full empowerment of the executive to implement. The essential "challenge" step in the sequence appears to have been missed in many board situations and needs to be ... clearly recognised and embedded for the future.'

Back in 2004, the NHS Confederation published *Effective Boards in the NHS*, which identified the behaviour and culture of a board as key determinants of the board's performance. From the interviews, the research identified four characteristics of effective boards:

- a focus on strategic decision-making
- board members who trust each other and act cohesively/behave corporately
- constructive challenge by board members of each other
- effective chairs who ensure meetings have clear and effective processes.

Some boards appeared to be too trusting, with little constructive challenge or debate about strategic issues. Reasons for this lack of challenge included the desire to present a united public face in public meetings. The report recommended that the perceived differences between non-executive and executive roles needed to be addressed, as challenge should not be seen as the preserve of non-executives scrutinising the executive team. The report concluded that a culture that enables board business to be conducted in a sharp and focused manner was required at board level, making clear what decisions are required of the board and what action will follow as a result of the decisions.

As far back as 2002, Jeffrey Sonnenfeld argued that the behaviour of individual board members rather than the structures of the board were key determinants of organisational performance ('What makes boards great', *Harvard Business Review*, September 2002). Sonnenfeld argued that good board governance cannot be legislated but can be built over time. This is supported in the 2012 article by John Deffenbuaugh, 'It's the people in the boardroom' in the *British Journal of Healthcare Management*:

'The current economic and geopolitical environment means that board effectiveness must be increased. This will not be tackled by further structural and process improvement in board operations, but rather by addressing the key relationship issues that underpin decision-making ... First, there is the range of "hats" that board members wear. There are three of these: the individual; the expert; the corporate player ... the second dimension explores the relationship among the "groups" within the board ... the chair, chief executive, non-executives and EDs.'

Building on this analysis The *Healthy NHS Board* identified boards as 'social systems'. It summarised the techniques and practices that support and hinder the effectiveness of these social systems (see Table 6.1).

Table 6.1 – Techniques and practices that support and hinder boards

Ways of working that support good social processes	Ways of working that obstruct good social processes
Building a crystal clear understanding of the roles of the board and individual board members	Board members behaving in a way that suggests a 'master-servant' relationship between non-executive and executive
Actively working to develop and protect a climate of trust and candour	Executive directors only contributing in their functional leadership area rather than actively participating across the breadth of the board agenda
Building cohesion by taking steps to know and understand each other's backgrounds, skills and perspectives	Demonstrating an unwillingness to consider points of view that are different from individual directors' starting positions
Encouraging all board members to offer constructive challenges	Challenge primarily coming from non-executive directors, rather than all directors feeling empowered to challenge one another in board meetings
Sharing corporate responsibility and collective decision-making	Challenging in a way that is unnecessarily antagonistic and not appropriately balanced with appreciation, encouragement and support
Ensuring that neither chair nor chief executive power and dominance act to stifle appropriate participation in board debate	Working in ways that don't demonstrate overall confidence in the executive and that feed individual anxiety and insecurity about capability

In 2009, ICSA submitted a report, entitled *Boardroom Behaviours,* to Sir David Walker, who was reviewing the corporate governance issues that contributed to the 2007–2009 banking crisis in the UK.

The ICSA report suggested that the corporate governance problem was partly attributable to inappropriate 'boardroom behaviours'. Behavioural problems were only a part of the problem of ineffective governance, the report suggested. However, insufficient attention had been given to the problem and there should be better guidance to directors on how to improve board behaviours.

The report suggested that best practice in boardroom behaviour is characterised by:

- a clear understanding of the role of the board
- the appropriate deployment of knowledge, skills, experience and judgement
- independent thinking
- the questioning of assumptions and established orthodoxy
- challenge, which is constructive, confident, principled and proportionate
- rigorous debate
- a supportive decision-making environment
- a common vision
- the achievement of closure on individual items of board business.

The report commented that:

> 'Despite the importance of these ... considerations, it is remarkable that there is practically no guidance in the Code on the main drivers of, and factors affecting, boardroom behaviours ... To improve on existing standards of behaviour in the boardroom, directors need to develop a greater awareness of, and commitment to, "fit for purpose" governance as the means by which the board can collectively agree the business objectives of the company and a strategy for their implementation by executive management.'

Boardroom Behaviours also provided an outline of the guidance that might be useful to directors about boardroom behaviours:

- All directors, including EDs, need to improve their performance in these important areas of boardroom behaviours. The process of achieving this for NEDs can be made more effective by giving them greater exposure to the organisation's operations.
- A knowledgeable board is a function of board balance, and there may be insufficient balance if the board is shrunk to just two EDs (CEO and finance director) in order to achieve a majority of NEDs without making the board too big.
- Diversity of board membership is necessary to provide sufficient independent challenge.
- High standards of performance evaluation are needed to increase the effectiveness of a board.
- At the moment the remuneration of EDs appears to focus on maximising short-term 'value' rather than pursuing the goal of a sustainable business. Remuneration arrangements should give more emphasis to the behaviours of directors in the boardroom, working in the long-term interests of the organisation.
- In terms of developing a wider perspective of the business, directors should look 'forward and out, as well as backwards and in'.
- The board should lead by example, 'evidenced by high levels of visibility and integrity, strong communications, and demanding expectations'.
- Practical issues, such as the timely circulation of board papers, 'can have a disproportionate effect on the quality of decision-making'.

The ICSA research project *Mapping the Gap: highlighting the disconnect between governance best practice and reality in the NHS* (July 2011) was initiated to examine the degree to which trust boards in the NHS understood issues of governance, and the extent to which actual boardroom behaviour reflected guidance on best practice.

The resulting report stated that respondents rated constructive challenge in the top three contributors to sound decision-making, but that the boardroom behaviours observed suggests that more challenge was required to improve discussions and decisions. The project further identified that, on average, respondents saw board trust and collective behaviours as a minimal contributory factor in an effective board. However, in the meetings observed there were a number of behaviours that did not suggest that all board members were fully engaging with the business to be transacted. Examples of poor boardroom behaviour included:

- using electronic devices
- conversing with colleagues
- interrupting
- reading non-board papers
- arriving late, fidgeting
- exchanging knowing looks/raising eyebrows/rolling eyes.

Directors need to see best practice in governance as a 'business facilitator' and not a 'business killer'. The pursuit of best practice in governance should be seen as a way of achieving competitive advantage, because it strengthens the process and quality of decision-making by the board. Directors also need to be aware that failure to perform at a satisfactory level can have negative consequences, and directors need to be aware of their duties and potential liabilities. Failure to provide best practice in governance, and failure to perform at a satisfactory level, creates a risk to the reputation of boards of directors and individual directors.

■ Appointments to the board

The appointment of the chair and NEDs for NHS trusts is overseen by the NHS TDA.

Foundation trust chairs and NEDs are appointed by the council of governors, and will be covered in Chapter 11. The appointment processes for CCGs will be covered in Chapter 12 as they are quite distinct to the procedures illustrated here.

The NHS TDA is responsible for around 650 chair and non-executive appointments to NHS trusts and around 60 NHS charitable trustees. The Secretary of State for Health has the power to make these appointments but has delegated this to the NHS TDA.

The main functions of the NHS TDA in this regard are to:

- appoint, re-appoint and, where necessary, to terminate the appointment of chairs and non-executives of NHS trusts
- ensure chairs and non-executives receive relevant and appropriate training
- ensure through annual performance review that chairs and non-executives are supported and developed in their role and feel valued
- ensure chairs and non-executives receive all necessary support through mentoring programmes
- ensure that overall NHS boards add value to the NHS locally and more widely.

The NHS TDA follows the Commissioner for *Public Appointment's Code of Practice* (August 2009). This guarantees that NHS and other regulated public appointments follow a fair, open and transparent appointments process, which commands public confidence, with appointment based on the principle of merit. The Code of Practice, which is mandatory, sets out the regulatory framework for public appointments processes within the Commissioner's remit.

The Code sets out the following principles.

- **Merit:** All public appointments must be governed by the overriding principle of selection based on merit, by the well-informed choice of individuals who through their abilities, experience and qualities match the need of the public body in question.
- **Independent scrutiny:** No appointment must take place without first being scrutinised by an independent panel or by a group including membership independent of the department filling the post.
- **Equal opportunities:** Departments should sustain programmes to deliver equal opportunities principles.
- **Probity:** Members of public bodies must be committed to the principles and values of public service and perform their duties with integrity.
- **Openness and transparency:** The principles of open government must be applied to the appointments process, its working must be transparent and information provided about the appointments made.
- **Proportionality:** The appointments procedures should be subject to the principle of proportionality, that is, they should be appropriate for the nature of the post and the size and weight of its responsibilities.

NEDs hold a statutory office under the National Health Service Act 2006 and their appointment does not create any contract of service or contract for services between the individual and the NHS trust. Chairs and non-executives are not employees. Her Majesty's Revenue and Customs (HMRC) has determined that the nature of the appointment means that the status of chairs and non-executives is 'employment-like' and that as such they are liable to income tax on their remuneration under Schedule E and Class 1 National Insurance Contributions (NIC). As a result, any tax liability and NIC will be deducted at source under the PAYE scheme. The legislation governing the payment of chairs and non-executives of boards means that they can only be paid remuneration at the levels determined by the Secretary of State. This includes any work on any of the organisation's committees.

At present, the NHS TDA engages and supports NHS trusts throughout the entire recruitment and selection process. It works with the trust's nomination committee (covered later in this chapter) to conduct a full recruitment campaign, including developing a job description and person specification, advertising the post and supporting the interview process. The NHS TDA's Appointments Committee makes the final appointment decision based on the recommendation of the selection panel that assesses the merit of each application received.

The NHS TDA rules state that, in most circumstances, civil servants within eligibility the DH, members/employees of the Care Quality Commission, chairs and mem- criteria bers of the governing body of a clinical commissioning group, and employees of such a group are ineligible as an NED of an NHS trust. The National Health Service Trusts (Membership And Procedure) Amendment Regulations 2014 removed the disqualification which prevents a person being appointed as chair or NED of an NHS trust where they are (a) a chair, NED or member of certain health service bodies, (b) providers or performers of primary health services or (c) an employee of such health service bodies or of such performers or providers.

Suspension or removal from office

The NHS TDA has produced a policy which sets out the principles and processes that the it will use to establish whether and how a chair or NED of an NHS trust should be suspended or removed from office. The policy incorporates three separate but interconnected pathways:

- seeking resignation
- suspending the office holder
- terminating the appointment.

Where there is clear evidence supporting the removal of an NED from office, the individual may choose to resign or a resignation may be actively sought. This is the preferred course of action in most cases.

As these posts are public appointments, information about those appointed and removed is in the public domain. Resignation enables the person to be removed from office with dignity and in a managed way that normally meets the needs of both the individual and the organisation. However, there are circumstances when this would not be appropriate or in the public interest.

If the circumstances associated with an appointee's removal from office are actually or potentially so damaging that it would not be in the public interest for them to be able to take up another non-executive role in the NHS, it might be more appropriate to pursue the suspension and/or termination of appointment procedures.

If the office holder submits their resignation during the course of a suspension or termination procedure, the NHS TDA reserves the right to continue with the procedure. This includes completing any investigation until a conclusion is reached, which may then form part of the person's formal appointment record.

When an appointment to an NHS trust is terminated, an automatic disqualification period lasting two years applies. The NHS TDA may specify a longer period, such as potentially indefinitely in serious cases. The appointee may apply to the NHS TDA to reduce the period of disqualification.

Appointments in the corporate sector

Corporate governance is less prescriptive than health service governance when it comes to appointments, although it is an accepted principle of good corporate governance that the power over board appointments should rest with the whole board. Under UK corporate governance, new appointments can be made to the board at any time during the year, but each newly appointed director must offer themselves for re-election at the next AGM. The company chair and the board committees chairs are appointed by the board. These appointments are not subject to shareholder approval at the next AGM.

Recommendations about new appointments should not belong exclusively to the chair and/or the CEO. Appointments should be made on merit and against objective criteria; however, in practice, criticism has been expressed about the way in which most appointments are made, particularly appointments of NEDs. This criticism centres on the fact that most NED appointments come from a fairly small circle of successful businessmen, many of whom know each other, whereas the net should be cast much wider and individuals from more diverse backgrounds should be chosen.

The UK Code states that there should be 'a formal, rigorous and transparent procedure for the appointment of new directors to the board'. The procedure of identifying candidates for a directorship should be rigorous, and candidates should be investigated thoroughly before the directorship is offered. It goes on to say that appointments should be made on 'merit' and 'against objective criteria'. However, it does not specify what these 'objective criteria' should be.

The procedure should be transparent so that shareholders and other stakeholders are able to see what is happening (what type of person the company is looking for and why a particular individual has been appointed). A formal procedure involves the nomination committee.

The Davies Review

Perhaps somewhat controversially, the UK Code also states that appointments to the board should be made 'with due regard to the benefits of diversity on the board, including gender'. This reflects the widely expressed concern that the boards of major UK companies are dominated by middle-aged to older white males with a commercial or financial background, and that there are not enough directors with different attributes, talents and experience to provide boards with an appropriate balance. The relative shortage of female board directors has been well-publicised in the Davies Review, *Women on Boards* (February 2011).

The review made a strong case for greater diversity on boards, recommending in particular that there should be a greater proportion of women on the boards of FTSE 350 companies. Its general argument in favour of greater diversity was that diverse and balanced boards: 'are more likely to be effective boards, better able to understand their customers and stakeholders, and to benefit fresh per-spectives, vigorous challenge and broad experience. These in turn lead to better decision-making.'

The report rejected the view, for example, that directors (and particularly NEDs) should have had experience of financial responsibilities before their appointment: 'although there is a real need for financial literacy, financial respon-sibility ... can be taught and should not be a pre-requisite for appointments'.

The report recommended a voluntary business-led strategy to bring about a culture change at the heart of business. In a 2013 review, Lord Davies was able to report that progress had been good. Women accounted for 17.3%1 of FTSE 100 and 13.2% of FTSE 250 board directors (as at 1 March 2013), up from 12.5% and 7.8% respectively in February 2011 – an increase of nearly 40%. The FRC has also amended the UK Code to require companies to report on their diversity policies and a voluntary code of conduct for executive search firms is also now in place.

■ Nomination committees

The role of the nomination committee in FTs and CCGs will be covered in Chapters 11 and 12 (respectively), as they are quite distinct to the procedures that follow here. However, best practice as to composition and process should be used as a useful benchmark as far as possible.

Chapter 4 has already set out the background for the nomination commit-tee, along with its basic role and composition. The committee membership is appointed by the board and is usually made up of at least three members, includ-ing the chair and a majority of independent NEDs, and is free of any conflict of interest. The chair of the committee should be the chair or vice-chair of the board of directors or an independent NED. Members conflicted on any aspect of an agenda presented to the committee are required to declare their conflict and with-draw from discussions. The committee makes its recommendations on board appointments and succession planning issues to the whole board.

It is important to note that a nomination committee does not have the author-ity to make new appointments; it simply carries out the search and makes the recommendation. Appointing new directors is a matter for the board, and the whole board should therefore make decisions.

It is also important to note that the need for a new board appointment, or a replacement for an existing board member (succession planning), is not necessarily decided by the nomination committee. The chair has responsibility for ensuring that the composition of the board is appropriate. The need for a new NED may also emerge from the annual review of board performance, if an existing NED has not been performing as well as expected, or if a gap is identified in the range of skills and experience that the board needs. The chair is also responsible for ensuring that there is succession planning for board positions, and may therefore ask the nomination committee to identify potential successors.

If the chair of the board is the chair of the nomination committee, they should not chair the committee when it is dealing with the succession to the role of chair.

The existence of a majority of NEDs should ensure that the chair and CEO do not dominate the appointments process. The committee should consider new appointments to the board and make recommendations to the full board. The full board should then reach a decision about offering a position to the individual concerned so that final responsibility for board appointments remains with the board as a whole.

The main duties of the nomination committee

For NHS trusts, the work of the nomination committee in the appointment of NEDs is supported and underpinned by the NHS TDA. In general though, the main role of the nomination committee is to:

- regularly review the structure, size and composition (including the skills, knowledge and experience) required of the board compared to its current position, and make recommendations to the board with regard to any changes;
- give full consideration to succession planning for all board members in the course of its work, taking into account the challenges and opportunities facing the trust, and what skills and expertise are therefore needed on the board of directors in the future;
- before any appointment is made by the board of directors, evaluate the balance of skills, knowledge and experience on the board, and, in the light of this evaluation prepare a description of the role and capabilities required for a particular appointment. In identifying suitable candidates the committee shall:
  - use open advertising or the services of external advisers to facilitate the search
  - consider candidates from a wide range of backgrounds
  - consider candidates on merit and against objective criteria, taking care that appointees have enough time available to devote to the position;
- review the job descriptions of the director role as required;
- keep under review the leadership needs of the organisation, with a view to ensuring the continued ability of the organisation to deliver services effectively;
- keep up to date and fully informed about strategic issues and commercial changes affecting the trust and the environment in which it operates; and

■ review annually the performance evaluation process for EDs ensuring it is fit for purpose.

The committee shall also make recommendations to the board of directors concerning:

■ formulating plans for succession for EDs
■ membership of the audit and remuneration committees, in consultation with the chairs of those committees
■ any matters relating to the continuation in office of any ED at any time including the suspension or termination of service.

The committee also ensures that the full range of eligibility checks have been performed and references taken and found to be satisfactory.

This is based on the principal duties of the nomination committee which were summarised in the suggestions for good practice in the Higgs Report. These have been adopted in the NHS; a further useful document is the ICSA guidance note *NHS Foundation Trust Non-Executive Directors Nomination Committee*.

The UK Code requires that a separate section of the annual report should describe the work of the nomination committee, including the process it used in relation to appointments that were made during the year. An explanation should be given if neither the services of an external search consultancy ('headhunters') nor advertising were used in making the appointment of chair or NED. If the vacancy was not advertised nor a headhunter used, this would suggest that the appointment was made of a person that the nomination committee already knew or who was recommended privately: this would be contrary to the requirement for a formal, rigorous and transparent appointment procedure. Executive directors may be appointed from within the organisation, so the requirement applies only to the appointment of a chair or NED.

Criteria for appointment

The UK Code includes several provisions about criteria for appointment to the board that are reflected in health service governance for NHS organisations.

■ The search for board candidates should be conducted, and appointments made on merit, against objective criteria and with due regard for the benefits of diversity on the board, including gender.
■ The nomination committee should evaluate the balance of skills, experience, independence and knowledge on the board and, in the light of this evaluation, prepare a description of the role and capabilities required for a particular appointment.
■ On initial appointment, the chair should meet the criteria for independence.
■ For the appointment of a chair, the nomination committee should prepare a job specification, including an assessment of the time required and recognising the need for the chair's availability in times of crisis.

- The departing chair should not chair the nomination committee when it is meeting to consider the appointment of the successor to the role of chair.
- A proposed new chair's other significant commitments should be disclosed to the board before an appointment is made, and included in the annual report (subsequent changes should also be disclosed and reported).

In the NHS, the requirement to openly advertise all NED appointments under the auspices of the NHS TDA has gone some way to addressing issues of ethnicity and gender. The Equality Act 2010 also imposes a duty on public bodies to achieve equal opportunities in the workplace and in wider society. The Act is supported by specific duties, which require public bodies to publish relevant, proportionate information demonstrating their compliance with the equality duty and to set themselves specific, measurable equality objectives. NHS trusts must set objectives that eliminate unlawful discrimination, harassment and victimisation, advance equality of opportunity and foster good relations.

Practical aspects of board appointments: time commitment

In practice, a nomination committee is likely to carry out its responsibilities by:

- using a firm of headhunters to find individuals outside the firm who might be suitable for appointment (as NED, CEO, finance director, and so on)
- vetting the candidates put forward by the headhunters
- making a selection and recommendation to the full board.

When an individual is appointed to the company board, the appointment may be for a fixed term. This is usually the case with NEDs: in the UK, NEDs are typically appointed on a fixed three-year contract, which may then be renewed at the end of each term. Executive directors are commonly appointed for an indeterminate length of time, subject to a minimum notice period (typically six months in the NHS). At present, the more usual term of office being offered to NEDs by the NHS TDA is two years (four years for chairs), due to the uncertainty about the trajectory to attain FT status.

The UK Code states that 'all directors must be able to allocate sufficient time to the company to discharge their responsibilities effectively'. Executive directors are full-time appointments, so the problem of time commitment is not usually significant for them (unless the executive is also appointed as NED for another organisation). The main problem is ensuring that the chair and NEDs give sufficient time to the company. More time will probably be required from the chair than from a NED, and some NEDs (such as the chair of the audit committee) will be expected to commit more time than others.

When the nomination committee prepares a job description for the position, this should include an estimate of the time commitment expected. A NED should undertake that they will have sufficient time to meet what is expected of them. This undertaking could be written into the NED's letter of appointment.

Governing the NHS (June 2003) had this to say about likely time commitments.

'In our view a [NHS] non-executive serving on a board, which is properly focused on its governance responsibilities and which is properly supported by papers and information from the executive team, should be able to fulfil the role in 2.5 days per month. This may be regarded as the minimum acceptable commitment. Clearly some individuals will be able to give more time to the organisation and where this is helpful we are not suggesting that it should be discouraged. However, these additional duties should not be regarded as an extension or part of their board role or cross the boundaries set out above.'

NED posts currently being advertised on the NHS TDA website still show a minimum time commitment of 2.5 days per month. The commitment for an NHS chair is commonly advertised as 2-3 days per week. If an individual who is proposed to the board as chair or NED has significant time commitments outside the organisation, this should be disclosed to the board before the appointment is made.

An organisation should also protect itself against the risk that an ED is unable to commit sufficient time to the organisation because of NED appointments with other organisations. The UK Code states that the board should not allow one of its own EDs to take on more than one NED post in a FTSE 100 company, or the chair of a FTSE 100 company.

Accepting an offer of appointment as an NED

The formal procedures for appointing a new NED are the same for the appointment of an ED, with the exception of the close involvement of the NHS TDA. In addition, a newly appointed NED is likely to be less familiar with the organisation than a senior executive manager and they should not accept an appointment unless they are satisfied that there are no matters of concern.

An individual should only be willing to accept an appointment as NED if:

- the organisation does not use unethical business practices and has a good reputation
- the organisation is a going concern and is not in financial difficulties
- they can commit to the role the time that the organisation expects
- the individual believes that they can contribute positively to the effectiveness of the board
- there is no risk that the directors of the organisation could be held liable for any breach of duty, or that there is sufficient directors' and officers' liability insurance as protection against this risk
- the fee that the organisation has offered is adequate.

As ICSA has commented: 'by making the right enquiries, asking the right questions and taking care to understand the replies, a prospective director can reduce the risk of nasty surprises and dramatically increase the likelihood of success.'

Guidance from ICSA on the due diligence that a prospective NED should undertake recommends asking questions about:

- the business, e.g. its nature and size, and the organisation's market share, financial performance and financial position;
- governance and stakeholder relations – who the major stakeholders are, and about the structure of the board of directors and its committees;
- the role that the NED would be expected to perform, including membership of board committees. The prospective NED should be satisfied that they have the necessary qualities or experience to make an effective contribution to the work of the organisation's board;
- the organisation's risk management systems and controls; and
- ethical issues, and whether there are any ethical matters that might give cause for concern.

NHS NEDs may also want to ask questions about the impact of any health reform legislation.

Answers to many of these questions can be obtained from published documents that are available to the general public, in paper form or on a website. These include the annual report and accounts of the organisation, the organisation's constitution, standing orders, any quality accounts, sustainability report or social and environmental report that the organisation publishes, regulator inspection reports or reviews and press reports about the organisation.

Terms of engagement

If a prospective NED decides to accept the offer of the appointment, terms of engagement should be agreed with the organisation (either with the board as a whole or its nomination committee). The terms that must be agreed are as follows.

- The initial period of tenure in office.
- Time commitment: the organisation must indicate how much time the NED is expected to commit to the organisation, and the NED should make this commitment. This should be included in the formal letter of appointment. Typically, NEDs of listed companies are expected to commit between 15 and 30 days each year, and possibly more for a committee chair. NHS NEDs are expected to commit a minimum of 30 days each year, with more for a committee chair.
- Remuneration: the annual remuneration of the NED should be agreed. This is usually a fixed annual fee. It is generally considered inappropriate for NEDs, including the chair, to be remunerated on the basis of incentive schemes linked to organisation performance, because this would undermine their independence.

The terms of engagement should be set out in a formal letter of appointment. As well as including details of the role that the NED will be required to perform (including initial membership of board committees), the expected time commitment, the tenure and the remuneration, the letter of engagement should also:

- specify that the NED should treat all information received as a director as confidential to the company
- indicate the arrangements for induction
- give details of directors' and officers' liability insurance that will be available
- indicate the need for an annual performance review process for directors
- state what organisation resources will be made available to the NED (e.g. desk, computer terminal and telephone).

A sample letter of appointment for a NED can be found on the ICSA website (www.icsa.org.uk).

■ Succession planning

The key positions on the board of directors are the chair of the board and the CEO. The individuals holding these positions will retire or resign at some time, perhaps because the individual has reached retirement age or has come to the end of a fixed-term contract.

The board of directors should try to ensure a smooth succession, with a replacement lined up to take the place of the departing individual. In the case of a departing CEO, the successor might be an existing executive manager who has been groomed for the role. In the case of a departing chair, the successor might be an external appointment. A smooth succession is desirable to avoid disruptions to the organisation's decision-making processes or changes in policy or direction. The succession can also be planned well in advance, so that the newly appointed individuals will have an opportunity to learn about their new role before the actual succession occurs.

The FRC *Guidance on Board Effectiveness* states that while 'EDs may be recruited from external sources, companies should also develop internal talent and capability'. Initiatives might include middle management development programmes, facilitating engagement from time to time with NEDs, and partnering and mentoring schemes.

The positions of chair and CEO (and director of finance or CFO) are important. It is undesirable to have vacancies in these positions for more than a short period. Ideally, the successor should be in place for immediate appointment. This is why succession planning should be carried out in advance.

Succession planning should be delegated to the nomination committee. If the board of a listed company intends to breach the governance code by appointing the current CEO as the next chair, it would be advisable for a suitable representative of the board (such as the chair of the nomination committee or the SID) to discuss the reasons for their choice with major shareholders and representative bodies of the institutional shareholders. These discussions should take place well in advance of any final decision about the appointment.

There should also be succession planning for NEDs. As stated above, NEDs are typically appointed in the UK for a fixed period of three years, but it is now a requirement of the UK Code that directors of FTSE 350 companies should stand for re-election annually. The three-year contract may be extended at the end of that time for another three years and so on. Over time, however, a NED will lose some of their independence as they become more engaged with the organisation. Chapter 9 sets out that a NED is generally considered 'not independent' under the UK Code if they have been with the organisation for nine years or more. The Monitor Code stipulates six years as the threshold. Interestingly, the NHS TDA is currently having to consider terms of office beyond six years. It is re-appointing existing office holders as it is proving increasingly difficult to attract new candidates for the some of the more challenged NHS trusts under their care.

The Monitor Code and the UK Code both include a provision that any term beyond six years for a NED should be subject to particularly rigorous review. The board should be continually refreshed, and this is achieved by appointing a new NED when the three-year term of an existing NED reaches its end. In the case of a FTSE 350 company where a NED has performed poorly, this may be achieved by not supporting his or her annual re-election.

The nominations committee may recommend the re-appointment of a NED at the end of his first year term, but should be more inclined to terminate the appointment after six years, when the second three-year term ends. Any term of office beyond six years should be subject to annual review.

■ Refreshing board membership

The Monitor Code and the UK Code state that there should be 'progressive refreshing of the board'. Succession planning as outlined above, in terms of horizon scanning for the right skills and experience to manage the future challenges the board will face, is one way of refreshing the board. However, the nomination committee should also be aware of when a vacancy is expected to arise and should plan in advance to appoint the type of person it considers would improve the balance of skills and experience on the board. In addition, there has been increasing pressure for board appointments to be regularly reviewed under a process of annual re-election.

The financial crisis in banking between 2007 and 2009 led to a re-assessment of the UK Code, when it was argued that some or all of the board should be subject to annual re-election. Annual re-election increases the accountability of the directors to the shareholders and also gives more power to the shareholders, who are able to threaten to vote against a director at the next AGM (instead of possibly having to wait up to three years before having the opportunity).

After extensive consultation. the UK Code now requires:

- annual re-election of directors of FTSE 350 companies
- annual re-election of all NEDs who have served longer than nine years on the board
- the same recommendations as before for directors of other companies subject to the UK Code: all other directors to be subject to re-election at the first AGM following their appointment and re-election subsequently at intervals of no more than three years.

The UK Code also requires that, when the board proposes a NED for election at an AGM, they should present reasons why the directors believe that the individual should be appointed. When a director is proposed for re-election, the chair should confirm to the shareholders that following a formal performance evaluation of the individual, they have concluded that the individual's performance continues to be effective and the individual remains committed to the role.

The requirement for the board to ensure planned and progressive refreshing means that re-election of current directors, particularly NEDs, should not be an automatic process. As indicated earlier, plans to refresh the board with new NEDs should be a part of succession planning.

Induction and training of directors

Induction of new directors

The induction of directors is a process by which new directors familiarise themselves with the business, its services and how it operates. New directors need induction in order to become effective contributors to the board decision-making process. The need for induction is more important for NEDs than for EDs, particularly internally appointed EDs, who should be familiar with much of the business before their appointment to the board. However, newly appointed EDs may not be familiar with all the responsibilities and duties of being a director, and may also need induction to make them more aware of what will be expected of them in their new role.

In the NHS, the HFMA provides a structured induction for new chairs, NEDs and CCG lay members around key issues. It includes:

- an introduction to NHS board roles
- sessions on structures, roles, patient safety and individual liabilities
- an introduction to their governance responsibilities; including risk assurance, financial obligations and the board role in delivering a safe and high-quality service.

The UK Code states that all directors should receive an induction on joining the board and that 'to function effectively, all directors need appropriate knowledge of the organisation and access to its operations and staff'.

The chair is responsible for ensuring that new directors receive 'full, formal and tailored' induction. Although there is no specific reference to the company secretary, the chair will probably ask the company secretary to arrange for each director to receive a personalised induction programme. The aim should be to make the director an effective member of the board quickly. An induction programme may therefore focus initially on providing essential information and familiarity with the organisation, such as visits to key sites, meetings with senior management and staff and providing copies of previous board meetings and copies of any current strategy documents. Over time, further induction may then be provided.

Reading is an effective way for an individual to absorb new information quickly, and the company secretary might therefore wish to give a new director a selection of documents as an induction pack.

Training and professional development

Directors should keep their knowledge and skills up to date so they can continue to perform effectively. The organisation should ensure this is provided. The appropriate training and personal development for each individual director will depend on the director's personal situation. All directors may need training or updating when there is a change in an important aspect of the law or when new regulations are introduced that affect the organisation's operations or its governance. Members of board committees may need to be updated or may need to acquire greater in-depth knowledge of matters affecting the work of their committee. Directors may need to be informed about an important new service or product or an important new acquisition for the organisation.

Reflecting as it does the UK Code, the Monitor Code states that:

'The chair should ensure that the directors continually update their skills and the knowledge and familiarity with the organisation required to fulfil their role both on the board and on board committees. The organisation should provide the necessary resources for developing and updating its directors' knowledge and capabilities.'

Meanwhile, the FRC *Guidance on Board Effectiveness* states:

'Non-executive directors should devote time to developing and refreshing their knowledge and skills, including those of communication, to ensure that they continue to make a positive contribution to the board. Being well-informed about the company, and having a strong command of the issues relevant to the business, will generate the respect of the other directors.'

The chair, as part of their annual appraisal, should assess the particular training and development needs for each individual director. Each director should also be able to make suggestions about the type of training or development that might be suitable for them personally. The UK Code includes a provision that the chair should agree a personalised approach to training and development with each director. This should be reviewed regularly. The obvious time to do this is during the annual performance review of the director.

■ Performance evaluation of the board, its committees and individual directors

Requirement for annual evaluation

A possibly contentious issue in both corporate and health service governance is the extent to which the performance of directors should be monitored and assessed, and what form such assessments should take.

In the UK, a requirement for company directors to undergo formal performance appraisals each year was introduced into the UK Code in 2003. Both the Monitor Code and the UK Code state as a main principle that the board should undertake a formal and rigorous annual evaluation of its own performance and that of its committees and individual directors'. The evaluation should consider the 'balance of skills, experience, independence and knowledge of the organisation on the board, its diversity, including gender, how the board works together as a unit, and other factors relevant to its effectiveness'.

Evaluation of individual directors should aim to show whether each director continues to contribute effectively and demonstrates commitment to the role (such as in terms of time spent carrying out director's duties, attendance at board and committee meetings, and on other duties). The evaluation of performance is particularly important for NEDs. Executive directors commit all or most of their time to the organisation and should be fully familiar with the business and the organisation's operations. In contrast, NEDs spend only a part of their time with the organisation, even though they make up the membership of key committees of the board – the audit and remuneration committees in particular. There is a possibility that NEDs will lose some of their enthusiasm for the organisation, and may get into a habit of missing meetings and spending less time with the organisation as expected. In some cases, a director may fail to keep up to date with an important area of his supposed expertise.

The FRC *Guidance on Board Effectiveness* states that 'evaluation should be bespoke in its formulation and delivery' and provides a non-exhaustive list of areas that might be considered, such as:

- the mix of skills, experience, knowledge and diversity on the board, in the context of the challenges facing the organisation;
- clarity of, and leadership given to, the purpose, direction and values of the organisation;
- succession and development plans;
- how the board works together as a unit, and the tone set by the chair and the CEO;

- key board relationships, particularly chair/CEO, chair/senior independent director (SID), chair/company secretary and executive/non-executive;
- effectiveness of individual NEDs and EDs;
- clarity of the senior independent director's role;
- effectiveness of board committees, and how they are connected with the main board;
- quality of the general information provided on the organisation and its performance;
- quality of papers and presentations to the board;
- quality of discussions around individual proposals;
- process the chair uses to ensure sufficient debate for major decisions or contentious issues;
- effectiveness of the secretariat;
- clarity of the decision processes and authorities;
- processes for identifying and reviewing risks; and
- how the board communicates with, and listens and responds to, stakeholders.

Originally, the UK Code did not make any recommendation about how the performance evaluation of the board, its committees and individual directors should be carried out, or who should do it. It became established practice, however, that (except for the performance review of the chair themselves) the chair should organise the performance review process and should be closely involved in it.

One approach is for the chair to carry out the reviews personally, possibly with advice and assistance from the company secretary. Alternatively, the chair may be responsible for deciding on the process that should be used for the performance review, and should act on the findings of the review, but may hand the responsibility for conducting the review to the SID. Organisations may also use the services of specialist external consultants.

The respective chapters for the chair, EDs and NEDS set out the performance evaluation process for each role respectively. In addition, the processes for these roles in FTs and CCGs are set out in Chapters 11 and 12 respectively.

The Monitor Code and the UK Code requires that the board should state in the organisation's annual report how the performance evaluation of the board, its committees and individual directors has been carried out. In addition, the Monitor Code requires the outcomes of the evaluation of the EDs to be reported to the board of directors, and for the chief executive to take the lead on the evaluation of the EDs.

Board evaluation

In the UK, the potential value of external consultants has been recognised, and the UK Code now states that for the evaluation of the board as a whole, the evaluation of the board of FTSE companies should be 'externally facilitated' at least every three years. In other words, the company should use specialist external consultants at least once every three years, and where the company uses external consultants, it should make a statement of whether the consultants have any other connection with the company.

This is echoed in the Monitor Code. It has been formalised in Monitor's Risk Assessment Framework, which requires NHS FTs to carry out an external review of their governance every three years. *Albs = triennial review*

The framework for this evaluation has been published in *The Well-Led Framework for Governance Reviews: Guidance for NHS Foundation Trusts* (May 2014). Though this is specifically aimed at FTs, it is included in this section as there is a firm commitment by Monitor, the CQC and NHS TDA to develop an aligned framework by early 2015 for making judgments about how well led NHS providers are.

By 'well led' they mean that the leadership, management and governance of the organisation assure the delivery of high quality care for patients, support learning and innovation and promote an open and fair culture. The guidance in the framework is, therefore, likely to be rolled out across the sector. The specific detail of the framework for FTs is set out in Chapter 11, however, the aligned framework will set out a clear expectation of what 'good' looks like for a well-led organisation. It will also benefit providers in a number of ways.

- Firstly, the framework should help organisations to improve as it will clearly outline expectations and allow them to benchmark themselves against a common expectation of what good looks like. It is, after all, primarily providers themselves who are responsible for ensuring that they are well led.
- Secondly, it will mean that NHS providers can be confident that Monitor, TDA and CQC all have a consistent view which will form the basis of regulatory judgments on well led. As a regulatory tool it will allow an independent check of how an organisation is performing and facilitate the development action plans to turn around performance.
- Finally, having a joined-up approach should ensure regulatory coordination and a streamlined approach for NHS providers.

It would make sense for an NHS organisation to commission an external review in one year, and then use the lessons obtained from the consultants to carry out an internal performance evaluation for the next two years. In year four, external consultants might be used again as a way of learning new lessons or checking the quality of the internal evaluation process. Other methods of internal evaluation might include self-assessment questionnaires to be completed by board members or documented feedback from internal and external audit, regulators or partners in the local health economy.

The possible reasons for an ineffective board may be any of the following.

- Insufficient information provided to the directors to enable them to make properly considered decisions.

- Directors not given sufficient time before a board meeting to read relevant papers, and so arrive at the meeting not properly briefed.
- Directors not bothering to take time before a board meeting to read relevant papers, and so arrive at the meeting not properly briefed.
- Individual directors failing to attend meetings of the board or meetings of board committees.
- Individual directors not being given enough opportunity to contribute to discussions in board meetings (this would arguably be a failing of the chair rather than an indication of an ineffective board).
- The board failing to carry out its responsibilities in full.
- The board failing to take its annual performance evaluation seriously enough.
- The board making ill-considered (bad) strategic decisions.

To assess the performance of the board, a comparison should be made between what the board should be expected to achieve, and what it has actually achieved. One way of doing this may be to provide answers to a set of questions about performance, possibly through discussions at a special board meeting.

Questions that may provide a useful basis for assessment of board performance are set out below:

- Does the board have any specific performance objectives (e.g. in terms of business performance or quality measures)? How well has the board performed against any such targets?
- What has the board contributed to the development of strategy and what has it done to oversee the implementation of strategy and achievement of strategy targets?
- What has the board contributed to ensuring that the organisation has a robust and effective risk management system?
- Is the board concerning itself with the appropriate issues? Is the list of matters reserved for the board suitable or should it be amended?
- Is the board an appropriate size and is the mix of members suitable (in terms of spread of experience, knowledge, skills and/or background)? Are changes needed?
- How well does the board communicate with patients, the public, management, employees and other stakeholders?

Questions may also be asked about the effectiveness of boardroom practice:

- Do board members receive relevant and clear information in good time for board meetings and decision-making? Is the amount and quality of this information adequate?
- Have there been sufficient board meetings in the past year?
- Are the board meetings too short to be effective or too long?

Evaluation of board committees

Board committees should be evaluated in a similar way to the board as a whole. For each committee, there should be a comparison between what the committee is responsible for doing and what it has actually done. For example:

- Has the nomination committee been successful in identifying suitable individuals for board appointments?
- Have any individuals been appointed to the board who, in retrospect, were not as good as originally thought?
- Has the nomination committee done any succession planning and if so, how good have its plans been?
- Has the committee made clear recommendations to the board, and has the board acted on its recommendations?
- Is the committee an appropriate size and is the mix of members suitable? Are changes needed?
- Have there been enough committee meetings during the past year?

Similar questions can be asked about the remuneration and audit committees as well as any other committees established by the board.

Using the results of a performance review

To obtain practical value from an annual evaluation of the board, its committees and its individual directors, the board should be prepared to act on its findings whenever performance is not considered to be as good as it should be. The chair has the responsibility for acting to deal with poor performance.

The UK Code makes the following provisions for how the performance review should be used:

> 'The chair should act on the results of the performance evaluation by recognising both the strengths and weaknesses of the board and, where appropriate, proposing new members to be appointed to the board or seeking the resignation of directors.'

In the preface to the 2010 UK Code, the chair of the FRC stated: 'Chairs are encouraged to report personally in their annual statements how the principles relating to the role and effectiveness of the board have been applied.' The recommendation is that the chair of an organisation should recognise their personal responsibility for performance and effectiveness of the board, and an organisation should not simply disclose its procedures for assessing performance in a 'boiler plate' fashion.

The chair may also consider the need for changes to the composition of board committees and may ask for the resignation of a committee chair. Some improvements may be achieved by changing board procedures (such as holding meetings more frequently, or changing the dates of meetings to give management more time to prepare the information required).

Although the chair has the primary responsibility for acting on the results of the annual performance review, the FRC guidance *Improving Board Effectiveness* states that: 'The results of a board evaluation should be shared with the board as a whole and fed back, as appropriate, into the board's work on composition, the design of induction and development, and other relevant areas.'

Problems with performance reviews

The performance evaluation of the board and its directors is recognised in the UK as a valuable tool for the assessment of the effectiveness of the board, and stakeholders have shown an interest in obtaining information about the evaluation process. They want to know that an evaluation has taken place, but they also need assurance that the evaluation process is of a suitable quality standard and rigour. This is one reason why the UK Code introduced a requirement for external consultants to be used at least every three years.

Stakeholders would also like to know more about the action that has been taken following an annual performance review, because they want assurance that the review is being used to improve the effectiveness of the board. However, it may be difficult to provide as much information about the performance review, especially the review of individual directors, without compromising the confidentiality of the exercise.

This has encouraged a similar approach in the NHS, as key stakeholders have expressed a similar concern about board performance – hence the development of Monitor's Well-Led Framework.

■ Conflicts of interest

The board of directors of an NHS organisation has a legal obligation to act in the best interests of that organisation, in accordance with the governing document, and to avoid situations where there may be a potential conflict of interest. As such, there are requirements for board members to register personal financial interests that may be perceived as conflicting with that overriding duty.

The NHS Code of Conduct and Accountability is quite clear that NHS boards should act in a way that protects the interest of the NHS in the way they undertake their business. Furthermore, the guidance *Governing the NHS* states: 'NHS boards should conduct themselves and the business of the trust in an open and transparent way that commands public confidence.'

The *Healthy NHS Board* reinforces the importance of NHS boards acting – and being seen to act – with integrity and in the best interests of the organisation:

> 'Probity requires that the board maintains an up-to-date register of board members' interests. Board agendas should include an opportunity for board members to declare conflicts of interests that may relate to specific agenda items so that they can be managed appropriately.'

Under HSCA 2012 section 152, boards in NHS FTs (see Chapter 5) are also required to adopt appropriate standards of conduct, as well as being open and transparent in their decision making and the manner in which conflicts of interest are managed.

It is, therefore, essential that there are clear and robust systems in place for identifying and managing real and potential conflicts of interest of board members to protect the reputation and tangible assets of the NHS trust, as well as the reputation of individual board members.

As the NHS Code of Conduct states: 'Boards have a clear responsibility for corporate standards of conduct and acceptance of the Code (of Conduct) should inform and govern the decisions and conduct of all board directors.'

What are conflicts of interest?

Conflicts arise when the interests of directors, or 'connected persons', are incompatible or in competition with the interests of the trust. Such situations present a risk that directors may make decisions based on these external influences, rather than the best interests of the organisation.

A 'connected person' to a director is defined in section 252 (2) of the Companies Act 2006 as:

a) members of the directors' family (section 253 defines these as spouse or civil partner; any other person with whom the director lives as a partner in an enduring family relationship, the directors' children or step-children, a partners' children or step-children under 18 years of age; and the directors' parents);

b) a body corporate with which the director is connected;

c) a person acting in their capacity as a trustee of a trust – (i) the beneficiaries of which include the director or a person who by virtue of (a) or (b) is connected with them, or (ii) the terms of which confer a power on the trustees that may be exercised for the benefit of the director or any such person, other than a trust for the purposes of an employees' share scheme or pension scheme;

d) a person acting in their capacity as a partner – (i) of the director, or (ii) of a person who by virtue of (a) to (c) is connected with that director;

e) a firm that is a legal person under the law by which it is governed and in which – (i) the director is a partner, (ii) a partner is a person who by virtue of (a) to (c) is connected with the director, or (iii) a partner is a firm in which the director is a partner or in which there is a partner who by virtue of (a), (b) or (c) is connected with the director.

The most common types of conflicts of interest include:

- direct financial interest
- indirect financial interest

- non-financial or personal interests
- conflicts of loyalty.

Direct financial interest

The most easily recognisable form of conflict of interest arises when a director obtains a direct financial benefit over and above the agreed remuneration and terms of service package agreed by the nomination committee. Examples include the award of a contract to a company or other business with which a director is involved, and the sale of assets at below market value to a director.

Indirect financial interest

This arises when a close relative of a director benefits from the trust. Directors will benefit indirectly if their financial affairs are bound with those of the relative in question through the legal concept of 'joint purse', as would be the case if the relative were the spouse, partner, dependent child of the director, or directly connected in some other way.

Non-financial or personal conflicts

These occur where directors receive no financial benefit, but are influenced by external factors. For instance, to gain some other intangible benefit or kudos, or awarding contracts to friends or personal business contacts.

Conflicts of loyalty

Directors may have competing loyalties between the trust to which they owe a primary duty and some other person or entity. Conflicts of interest may present problems in the form of inhibiting free discussion resulting in decisions or actions that are not in the interests of the trust, and risking the impression that the trust has acted improperly.

Decisions made under a conflict of interest may be legally challenged and could result in personal liability for the director. The aim of a conflict of interest policy, therefore, is to protect both the organisation and the individuals involved from any appearance of impropriety.

Declaration of interests

A conflict of interest policy should require the board chair and board members to act impartially and not be influenced by social or business relationships. No one should use their public position to further their private interests. Where there is potential for private interests to be material and relevant to NHS business, the relevant interest should be declared and recorded in the register of interests maintained by the company secretary.

Any interest that arises during the course of a meeting should be declared immediately, and should be recorded in the relevant minutes. When a conflict of interest is established, the person should withdraw and play no part in the relevant discussion or decision. Interests which should be regarded as 'relevant and material' are:

- directorships, including non-executive directorships, held in private companies or PLCs (with the exception of those of dormant companies)
- ownership or part-ownership of private companies, businesses or consultancies likely or possibly seeking to do business with the NHS
- majority or controlling share holdings in organisations likely or possibly seeking to do business with the NHS
- a position of trust in a charity or voluntary organisation in the field of health and social care
- any connection with a voluntary or other organisation contracting for NHS services
- any other commercial interest relating to any relevant decision to be taken by the trust.

Any change in interests should be declared as soon as it is recognised, and should be declared, where appropriate, at the next board meeting following the change occurring.

The register of interests is maintained by the company secretary who formally records the declarations of interests made by members of the board. These details must be kept up-to-date by means of at least an annual review of the register in which any changes to interests declared during the preceding months will be incorporated.

The register is available to the public and to the trust's internal and external auditors and should be published on the trust's website, to ensure compliance with Information Commissioner's Office Publication Scheme. The details of the interests of board members will be published in the trust's annual report.

Hospitality policy and registers

A hospitality policy is intended to assist all employees of an NHS trust (and this includes all board members) in following the various NHS guidance and relevant legislation on the giving and receipt of hospitality or gifts. This covers both the receipt and delivery of hospitality and gifts. Any hospitality, gifts or benefits accepted should be entered on the hospitality register by means of a standardised form. Each employee has a personal responsibility to declare hospitality and gifts in accordance with the policy.

Under the Prevention of Corruption Acts 1906 and 1916, it is an offence for employees corruptly to accept any gifts or consideration as an inducement or reward for; doing, or refraining from doing, anything in their official capacity; or showing favour or disfavour to any person in their official capacity. Under the 1916 Act, any money, gift or consideration received by an employee in public service from a person or organisation holding or seeking to obtain a contract will be deemed to have been received corruptly unless the employee proves to the contrary.

Under NHS Standing Orders and European Commission Directives on Public Purchasing for Works and Supplies, there is a requirement for fair and open competition between prospective contractors or suppliers.

Circular HSG (93) 5, 'Standards of Business Conduct for NHS Staff' (January 1993) provides guidelines for NHS employers and employees. This sets out that NHS employers are responsible for ensuring the guidelines are brought to the attention of all employees, and that machinery is put in place to ensure they are effectively implemented. A hospitality policy is intended to fulfil these requirements by providing clear guidance to employees and by establishing a hospitality register.

The NHS guidance also sets out that it is the responsibility of staff to ensure that they are not placed in a position which risks, or appears to risk, conflict between their private interests and their NHS duties. This applies to both staff who commit resources directly (ordering of goods or services) or indirectly (by policy development).

Examples of hospitality, gifts or benefits where a declaration may be necessary include the following:

- meals and drinks
- crates and bottles of wine or spirits
- tickets for sporting events/theatre, etc.
- events where the cost of accommodation is paid for by a research company
- national and international seminars where the placement has been paid for by the company organising the seminar
- sponsored golf events
- lecture trips (national and international)
- site visits to prospective suppliers of goods and services where hospitality, gifts or benefit is provided or loaned.
- gifts of equipment by drug companies.

The above list is not exhaustive, but it will give an indication of the types of items that may need to be declared. Most trusts set a financial threshold: for example, if an item has a value of more than £50 then it must be declared.

Acceptable hospitality

Hospitality is generally defined as attendance at a social or leisure event or conference (or an occasion that could be perceived as such an event) where the attendance is being funded by a third party. NHS guidance provides that modest hospitality is an accepted courtesy of a business relationship. However, the recipient should not allow themselves to reach a position whereby they might be deemed by others to have been influenced in making a business decision as a consequence of accepting such hospitality. The frequency and scale of hospitality accepted should not be significantly greater than the recipient's employer would be likely to provide in return. Where an employee is offered and receives hospitality from any external body while at work or outside work when they are acting in the capacity of employee of the trust they are required to declare this. Again, most trusts set a financial threshold for the declaration.

As a general principle, all offers of hospitality received from commercial third parties should be refused. Attendance at relevant commercially sponsored conferences and courses is acceptable, but only where acceptance will not, and cannot be seen as compromising purchasing or other decisions in any way. Receipt or provision of such sponsorship should be recorded in the hospitality register.

Employees should pay particular attention to the circumstances in which hospitality is offered: the provision of hospitality by an individual or organisation during a tendering process or where a contract is shortly to end, or where performance of the contract is in question, or in any other circumstance where acceptance might compromise the position of the employee or of the trust, is not acceptable.

Acceptance of gifts

Employees should not accept gifts that may be capable of being construed as being able to influence a purchasing decision or cast doubt on the integrity of such decisions. Casual gifts offered by contractors or others, for example at Christmas time, should be declined except when they are of low intrinsic value, for example small stationery items such as:

- diaries
- calendars
- staplers
- pens.

NHS guidance provides that any gifts of higher value offered or received should be declined.

Where it is not easy to decide whether a gift should be accepted or not, advice should be sought from the line manager. Where an employee is offered and receives gifts or benefits from any external body while they are at work or outside work when they are acting in the capacity of employee of the trust they are required to declare this. Again, most trusts set a financial threshold for the declaration.

The acceptance or giving of monetary gifts, including vouchers, is not acceptable in any circumstances.

The Bribery Act 2010

The Bribery Act 2010 came into force in July 2011 and made it a criminal offence for commercial organisations to fail to prevent bribes being paid on their behalf. NHS organisations are included within the definition of 'commercial'. Therefore, if any NHS organisation fails to take appropriate steps to avoid (or at least minimise) the risk of bribery taking place it could face large fines and even the imprisonment of the individuals involved and those who have turned a blind eye to the problem. The Act makes it a criminal offence to give or offer a bribe, or to request, offer to receive or accept a bribe, whether in the UK or abroad (the measures cover bribery of a foreign public official), and for a director, manager or officer of a business to allow or turn a blind eye to bribery within the organisation.

The Act also introduces a corporate offence of failure to prevent bribery by persons working on behalf of a commercial organisation. However, organisations will have a defence against prosecution if they can show that they have adequate procedures in place to prevent bribery.

Guidance from the Ministry of Justice describes six guiding principles that set out the approach that organisations should take to prevent bribery occurring in their organisation. These are as follows.

- **Proportionate procedures:** designed to prevent bribery by anyone associated with the organisation and should be proportionate to the level of bribery risk to the organisation.
- **Top-level commitment:** senior management teams must show a commitment to preventing bribery, and promote a culture that does not tolerate acts of bribery.
- **Risk assessment:** an assessment of both internal and external risks of bribery to the organisation should be carried out regularly and documented.
- **Due diligence:** there must be effective due diligence procedures in place in respect of those involved in the organisation or carrying services out on behalf of the organisation.
- **Communication:** the organisation's stance on bribery should be clearly communicated to all employees and all those carrying out services on behalf of the organisation. This should include appropriate training.
- **Monitoring and review:** there should be an ongoing review process that regularly monitors the effectiveness of the procedures in place to prevent bribery.

These principles can be implemented by updating existing documentation, for example:

- updating policies and procedures by adding an anti-bribery statement to the organisation's employee handbook/intranet – this should be adequately communicated to all staff;
- amend whistleblowing policies to make specific reference to bribery, and encourage disclosure of bribery offences;
- training/presentations to make employees aware of the strengthened legislation around 'bribery', particularly in relation to corporate hospitality and the organisation's policy on business conduct (or similar);
- updating/adding a clause on bribery to employment contracts;
- ensuring all employees are under an express obligation to report any potential acts of bribery, including where an employee has personally committed an act of bribery;

- ensuring recruitment checks are robust;
- adding bribery to the matters covered by a disciplinary policy; and
- reviewing remuneration structures so that they comply with the new law where applicable.

Governance Checklist

✓ Does the board perform the leadership functions expected of an effective board?

✓ Does it develop strategy, promote behaviours consistent with the culture and values it has defined for the organisation?

✓ Is there an effective process in place to allow the organisation to make well informed and high-quality decisions based on a clear line of sight into the business?

✓ Does the board know what the balance of skills, experience, knowledge and personality it requires currently and in the medium to long term? Does it have that balance?

✓ What consideration has the board given to equality and diversity with regard to its own composition?

✓ Is the nomination committee actively involved in developing the recruitment and appointment process for new board members? Is there a focus on competencies rather than experience?

✓ Is there an open and positive interplay between the nomination and remuneration committees?

✓ Is there a clear and informative report from the nomination committee in the annual report?

✓ Are the terms of reference for the nomination committee available publicly and subject to regular review?

✓ Does the board have a succession plan and is it kept under regular review?

✓ What plans does the board have for annual self-evaluation of itself, its committees and individual directors?

✓ How are external assessors for evaluation appointed so that their independence is assured?

■ Summary

There is a fine balance to be maintained in assessing the effectiveness of a board. There should be quantitative evidence of outcomes achieved and processes followed, yet there must also be a more subjective and qualitative approach which considers the individual skills, experience and personalities that are represented in the board. How do these people work together to make a cohesive unit?

This chapter has sought to demonstrate that there is guidance to outline best practice in processes and procedures though at the same time posing questions or challenges about behaviour and culture which each board and each individual board member must consider in its or their own development.

As John Deffenbaugh says in his 2012 *British Journal of Healthcare Management* article, 'It's the people in the boardroom': 'In a world requiring a high-performing board, the knowledge derived from this insight to behaviour and relationships can enable the individual components to meld into an effective decision-making body.'

7

The chair of the board

Although this chapter explores the role of the chair of the board, it should be also be considered in the light of the next chapter and the role of the CEO. This is because these are the two most powerful roles within the board: there needs to be a clear distinction between the roles and a clear understanding by the individuals fulfilling them how they are meant to complement and work together.

Much of the friction in board relationships is centred upon this key dynamic; effective boards often demonstrate what the dynamic should be and vice versa. Much of what follows here can also be applied to the role of board committee chairs. Obviously, the focus here on the role of the chair must not distract from the underlying principle of the unitary board, with the chair having the same duties and responsibilities of every other board director. However, the role of the chair in creating the right team dynamic for a disparate group of board directors with varied and strongly held views to reach agreement on strategic direction and corporate objectives is absolutely crucial.

As the FRC *Guidance on Board Effectiveness* states: 'good boards are created by good chairs': therefore, the role warrants further examination here.

■ The role of the chair

Whereas the CEO is responsible for the executive management, the chair's responsibilities relate primarily to managing the board of directors, and ensuring that the board functions effectively. To do this, a chair needs to ensure that the board discusses relevant issues in sufficient depth, with all the information needed to reach a decision, and with all the directors contributing to the discussions and decision-making.

The UK Code states that

- 'The chair is responsible for leadership of the board and ensuring its effectiveness on all aspects of its role.'
- 'The chair is responsible for setting the board's agenda and ensuring that adequate time is available for discussion of all agenda items, in particular strategic issues.'
- 'The chair should also promote a culture of openness and debate by facilitating the contribution of non-executives in particular and ensuring constructive relations between executive and NEDs.'
- 'The chair should ensure that communications with shareholders are "effective".'

These principles emphasise the role of the chair in trying to ensure that all directors, in particular NEDs, contribute effectively to board discussions. There is always a risk that individuals who do not work full time for the organisation may have difficulty in challenging the views of full-time EDs. The chair should make sure that this does not happen.

The FRC *Guidance on Board Effectiveness* states that: 'the chair creates the conditions for overall board and individual director effectiveness.' It emphasises that an effective chair is a team-builder, developing a board whose members communicate effectively and enjoy good relationships with each other. They should develop a close relationship of trust with the CEO, giving support and advice while still respecting the CEO's responsibilities for executive matters. They should also ensure the effective implementation of board decisions, provide coherent leadership for the organisation and understand the views of the stakeholders.

The FRC guidance also provides a detailed list of matters for which the chair is responsible, which includes:

- setting the board agenda, which is primarily focused on strategy, performance, value, creation and accountability, and ensuring that issues relevant to these areas are reserved for board decision;
- making certain that the board determines the nature, and extent, of the significant risks the organisation is willing to embrace in the implementation of its strategy, and that there are no 'no go' areas that prevent directors from operating effective oversight in this area;
- making certain that the board has effective decision-making processes and applies sufficient challenge to major proposals;
- encouraging all board members to engage in board and committee meetings by drawing on their skills, experience, knowledge and, where appropriate, independence;
- fostering relationships founded on mutual respect and open communication between the NEDs and the executive team;

- developing productive working relationships with all EDs, and the CEO in particular, providing support and advice while respecting executive responsibility;
- taking the lead on issues of director development, including through induction programmes for new directors and regular reviews with all directors. Acting on the results of board evaluation; and
- ensuring effective communication with all stakeholders and, in particular, that all directors are made aware of the views of those who provide the organisation's capital.

The NHS TDA role description for an NHS trust chair sets out that they are accountable to the Secretary of State through the NHS TDA, for giving leadership to the NHS trust board and delivering value for money for NHS resources in terms of quality of service and financial balance. They will:

- provide leadership to the board, the trust, the other non-executives, the CEO and EDs; and ensure the effectiveness of the board in all aspects of its role and agenda; including directing the organisation towards achieving the government's objective of all trusts achieving FT status;
- ensure the provision of accurate, timely and clear information to the board and directors to meet statutory requirements;
- ensure effective communication with the board, staff, patients and the public in a changing healthcare environment;
- arrange the regular evaluation of the performance of the board, its committees and individual non-executives, directors, and the CEO;
- plan and conduct board meetings with the CEO;
- facilitate the effective contribution of NEDs and ensure constructive relations within the organisation and between executive and NEDs, and
- share and use relevant expertise of all members of the board.

In particular, the chair will:

- proactively direct and manage the development of major board decisions ensuring that 'due process' has been applied at all stages of decision making and full and complete consideration has been given to all options during the process;
- hold the CEO to account for the effective management and delivery of the organisation's strategic aims and objectives;
- ensure the board develops and oversees strategies, which will result in tangible improvements to the health of the population and clinical services;
- ensure the board establishes clear objectives to deliver agreed strategies and regularly review performance against these objectives;
- ensure the board maintains its responsibility for the effective governance of the organisation by making the best use of resources including the development of effective risk and performance management processes;

- ensure the board, and the organisation, observe the Secretary of State's policies and priorities, including the requirements of the Codes of Conduct and Accountability;
- be aware of relevant, regulatory and central government policies;
- play a key role in building strong partnerships with the local authorities, local health economy, and other stakeholders in the community and nationally, including regulators such as Monitor and the CQC. For FTs this includes developing an effective council of governors and promoting harmonious relations with the board;
- ensure that the interests of all stakeholders, and influence of all advisers, are fairly balanced;
- provide the leadership needed by the board to shape the organisation; develop a culture which supports the values of the NHS, and ensure the organisation values diversity in its workforce and demonstrates equality of opportunity in its treatment of staff and patients and in all aspects of its business;
- be an ambassador for the trust with national, regional and local bodies; be knowledgeable and aware of local issues, and recognise the trust's role as a major local employer; and
- where necessary, assist in the appointment of executives and non-executives and ensure systems of support and appraisal.

Independence of the chair

As a general rule, the chair should be independent when first appointed. This is a provision of the UK Code for listed companies and of the Monitor Code for FTs. See Chapter 12 for a discussion about independence in CCG appointments.

It follows that the CEO of an organisation should not subsequently become the chair as a former CEO will not be independent (although the King III Code states that a former CEO should not become chair for at least three years after ceasing to be CEO, believing that this is sufficient time in which to become independent). If, exceptionally, it is proposed that the current CEO should become the chair when the existing chair retires, shareholders should be consulted first. The UK Code also states that the reasons for appointing a former CEO as chair should be explained to shareholders both at the time of the appointment and in the next annual report and accounts.

A governance problem with 'promoting' the CEO to become the chair is that the incoming CEO may find it difficult to run the organisation as they wish because the former CEO is still on the board, monitoring what they are doing. Even so, there have been several cases where a CEO has gone on to become the chair without any serious protest from shareholders or investor groups.

The National Association of Pension Funds (NAPF)'s *Corporate Governance Policy and Voting Guidelines* (2011) also recommend that if the chair is not independent on appointment, the organisation should consult its shareholders and explain why it considers the appointment desirable. The shareholders should then consider the case on its merits.

The chair's commitments

A problem with non-executive chairs – as with NEDs generally – is that the individual may not have enough time to devote to the role because of a large number of other commitments. For example, the chair of a large company may also be the chair of another organisation, without enough time to fulfil either of these roles adequately.

Chairs need to be able to demonstrate that they have sufficient time to perform their role to the standards expected. NAPF's *Corporate Governance Policy and Voting Guidelines* state that where a chair has 'multiple appointments', investors will require a 'compelling explanation' of how they will be able to handle all the various appointments without any detriment to the organisation. The Walker Report suggested that the chairs of large banks would need to spend about two-thirds of their time with the organisation.

The UK Code is less specific on the amount of time that a chair should commit to the organisation. However, a provision of the Code is that, when a chair is appointed, the nomination committee (see also Chapter 6) should prepare a job description including an assessment of the amount of time commitment that should be expected and recognise the need for the chair to make himself available in a time of crisis.

The chair's other commitments should be disclosed to the board before their appointment and included in the next annual report and accounts. If there are changes to the time commitment required from or provided by the chair, these should be disclosed to the board and reported in the next annual report and accounts.

The Monitor Code also sets out that the board of directors should not agree to a full-time ED taking on more than one non-executive directorship of an NHS FT or another organisation of comparable size and complexity, nor the chair of such an organisation.

The criteria for independence are set out in Chapter 6; the same criteria should be applied to the chair (on appointment) as it is to other NEDs. However, circumstances may change, so the independence of NEDs should be kept under review.

Behaviours of an effective chair

The report *What makes an Outstanding Chair* by Directorbank Group set out the following as key characteristics of an effective chair.

1. **Integrating the board's collective thinking.** This is possible when a chair excels at seeking and sharing information; building ideas into concepts; analysing and considering multiple perspectives and different alternatives; and can subvert their individual needs for commitment to a common goal.

2. **Empathy and promoting openness in board members.** The ability to listen at multiple levels is critical to successful chairship and team dynamics. Listening to what is not being said is as critical as listening to the words that are spoken. Only with this ability can a chair engender deep trust and respect.
3. **Facilitating interaction.** This requires that a chair's behaviour move seamlessly depending upon who needs to be in the conversation, rather than 'managing' the process. It requires that skills and expertise (authority) are valued and respected regardless of hierarchy or power dynamics.
4. **Developing others.** Undertaking active coaching, mentoring and development of talent within the board, in particular with new board members.
5. **Communicating complex messages succinctly.** Effective communication, through written and spoken means, reduces the cognitive load on the board freeing more time for analysis, exploration and learning.
6. **Collaborating across boundaries.** The ability to identify boundaries and successfully navigate across and within them is critical to creating a culture of collaboration and efficiency.
7. **Continuous improvement.** Good behavioural objectives include continuous evaluation against internal and external benchmarks. The continual focus on improvement is as much a mindset as a behaviour.

The report goes on to say that outstanding chairs, according to the directors they work with and by their own admission, are good all-round communicators; they listen in a non-judgmental and non-condemnatory way, taking views from all the board members, though remaining impartial and effectively drawing together the differing opinions around the table. Perhaps most importantly of all, they listen.

On the contrary, an 'ineffective chair is marked out by factors such as a tendency to dominate; weakness in keeping the board on course and making decisions; poor communication and listening skills; insufficient interest or involvement in the business; and poor leadership abilities'.

The appointment and evaluation of the chair

In an FT the responsibility for appointing the chair lies with the council of governors and this is set out in more detail in Chapter 11. For CCGs, the appointment of the chair is an appointment from amongst the members of the governing body. More details are provided in Chapter 12. For NHS trusts, the appointment of the chair is carried out by NHS TDA.

The UK Code states that the NEDs, led by the SID, should be responsible for the performance evaluation of the chair, 'taking into account the views of executive directors'. However, for some organisations, the actual performance review of the chair may be conducted for the NEDs by external consultants.

The chair's performance should be assessed by comparing their responsibilities with their achievements, and asking whether they have been successful in providing the board leadership that should be expected of them.

In an FT, the responsibility for the performance evaluation of the chair lies with the council of governors and this is set out in more detail in Chapter 11. For CCGs the evaluation of the chair is carried out by the Lay Members of the governing body. Further details are provided in Chapter 12.

Overall responsibility for the NHS trust chair appraisal process rests with the chair of the NHS TDA. As there are 96 NHS trust chairs to appraise, it is not possible for the NHS TDA chair to conduct all NHS trust chair appraisals personally. Therefore, some of this activity is delegated to directors of the NHS TDA.

The initial assessment for all appraisals will be prepared by the relevant Director of Delivery and Development (DDD) within the NHS TDA. This will inform the appraisal meetings that will be undertaken either by the NHS TDA chair, the DDD or the NHS TDA NED allocated to that region. At the end of the appraisal exercise, when all of the appraisals are complete, the chair of the NHS TDA will review all of the appraisal reports to ensure that the exercise has been conducted in a way that is fair and consistent. The final appraisal form will be copied to the chair and a copy put on their personal record by the NHS TDA. In the event of a disagreement between the chair and the appraiser on any element of the appraisal, including the overall assessment, further discussions will take place between the chair and appraiser. If, however, it is not possible to reach agreement, the appraisal will stand as drafted by the appraiser but the chair will be invited to provide comments that will be held on file with the appraisal.

The level of remuneration for NHS chairs is generally considerably lower than that of chairs in the private sector. For NHS trusts, the Secretary of State sets the level of remuneration. All NHS trusts are allocated to one of three remuneration bands, dependent on their turnover. These bands are available on the NHS TDA website.

■ Separating the role of chair and chief executive officer

The report from Directorbank Group makes it clear that:

'The success of a chair undoubtedly hinges first and foremost on the relationship the chair has with the CEO. This is a relationship which should be centred on honesty, trust and transparency, and the success of this relationship is based on mutual understanding by both parties of the distinction between their two roles. One of the main faults identified in chairs deemed to be ineffective is their failure to comprehend that they are not there to run the business; that their role is instead to coach, support and guide.'

As leader of the management team and leader of the board of directors, the CEO and chair are the most powerful positions on the board of directors. It is important, therefore, for the proper functioning of the organisation that the chair and CEO work well together. Acting in alliance, the chair and CEO can dominate the board and its decision-making, particularly if the chair also has executive responsibilities in the organisation's management.

More specifically, the *NHS Healthy Board* report sets out some pointers for chairs and chief executives. The chair should not:

- be too operational, interfere with details of management
- exceed part-time hours
- take specific strategic decisions alone
- adopt bullying, macho 'hire and fire' culture.

Chief executives should not:

- be too controlling or autocratic towards the chair
- get too involved in NED role (e.g. no consultation on shaping board agendas)
- break the fundamental rule of 'no surprises'
- be too entrenched in the organisation.

Table 7.1 sets out the key distinctions in role for the chair and CEO.

Table 7.1 Distinctions between NHS chair and CEO roles

	Chair	Chief executive
Formulate strategy	Ensures board develops vision, strategies and clear objectives to deliver organisational purpose	Leads strategy development process
Ensure accountability	Holds CEO to account for delivery of strategy	Leads the organisation in the delivery of strategy
	Ensures board committees that support accountability are properly constituted	Establishes effective performance management arrangements and controls
		Acts as accountable officer
Shape culture	Provides visible leadership in developing a positive culture for the organisation, and ensures that this is reflected and modelled in their own and in the board's behaviour and decision making	Provides visible leadership in developing a positive culture for the organisation, and ensures that this is reflected in their own and the executive's behaviour and decision making
	Board culture: leads and supports a constructive dynamic within the board, enabling contributions from all directors	

	Chair	Chief executive
Context	Ensures all board members are well briefed on external context	Ensures all board members are well briefed on external context
Intelligence	Ensures requirements for accurate, timely and clear information to board/directors (and governors for FTs) are clear to executive	Ensures provision of accurate, timely and clear information to board/directors (and governors for FTs)
Engagement	Plays key role as an ambassador, and in building strong partnerships with: • patients and public • members and governors (FTs) • clinicians and staff • key institutional stakeholders • regulators.	Plays key leadership role in effective communication and building strong partnerships with: • patients and public • members and governors (FTs) • clinicians and staff • key institutional stakeholders • regulators.

Source: The NHS Healthy Board

When the same person holds the position of both chair and CEO, there is a possibility that they could become a dominant influence in decision-making in the organisation. As leader of the executive management team, a chair-cum-CEO may be reluctant to encourage challenges from NEDs about the organisation's performance or to question management proposals about future business strategy.

In some countries (including the US), it is common to find organisation leaders who are both chair and CEO, although separation of the roles has become more common there. The UK Code states as a principle that the roles should be separated:

'There should be a clear division of responsibilities at the head of the organisation between the running of the board and the executive responsibility for the running of the organisation's business. No one individual should have unfettered powers of decision.'

The UK Code therefore states that the roles of chair and CEO should not be performed by the same individual. In addition, the division of responsibilities between the chair and CEO should be set out clearly in writing, to prevent one of them from encroaching on the area of responsibility of the other. The Monitor Code makes a similar statement.

When an individual holds the positions of chair and CEO, they could exercise dominant power on the board, unless there are strong individuals on the board, such as a deputy chair or a SID, to act as a counterweight. If the individual also has a domineering or bullying personality, the situation will be even worse, because a chair-cum-CEO who acts in a bullying manner will not listen to advice from any board colleagues, and the board would not function as an effective body.

There is even a risk that the individual will run the organisation for their own personal benefit rather than in the interests of the shareholders/stakeholders. The only way to prevent a chair-cum-CEO from dominating an organisation is to have an influential group of directors capable of making their opinions heard. However, it is important to distinguish between the position of 'unfettered power' that is created when the roles of chair and CEO are combined and given to one individual and the ability to act in a dominant or tyrannical way, possibly out of self-interest.

Combining the two roles increases the risk that the organisation and its board will be dominated by a tyrannical individual, but this does not happen every time.

CASE STUDY: Marks & Spencer

In the UK, Mr Luc Vandevelde was appointed as chair and CEO of Marks & Spencer some years ago, at a time when its business operations were in difficulty and the share price was falling sharply. This appointment attracted some criticism but appears to have been a successful short-term measure. By 2002, the organisation's fortunes had improved to the point where he relinquished the position of CEO and announced his intention to become part-time chair.

When in 2008 the then-CEO, Sir Stuart Rose, was also appointed as organisation chair for a limited period until a successor to the role of CEO could be appointed this, given the previous appointment of Vandevelde, attracted strong criticism from institutional investors. Institutional investor Legal & General publicly criticised the decision by Marks & Spencer to appoint Sir Stuart Rose as executive chair, saying it was an arrangement that made it difficult to appoint a successor to Sir Stuart as CEO.

However, shareholders could not prevent the appointment of the new chair because this was a decision of the board. Shareholders were able, however, to vote on the re-election of Sir Stuart Rose as director at the AGM in 2008, and 22% of shareholders either opposed his re-election or abstained in the vote.

CASE STUDY: Monitor's governance

Dr Bill Moyes was executive chair of Monitor, the independent regulator for NHS FTs, from its establishment January 2004 until January 2010. It was the board's view that the regulator's corporate governance principles, the stature and experience of the members of the board of directors and a culture of open communication were conducive to board effectiveness with a combined chair and CEO position.

The board agreed separate objectives for the chair and chief executive elements of his role and that he would be separately appraised on the chair and chief executive aspects of his role by the deputy chair and the SID.

Following Dr Moyes' departure, the role was separated. Monitor was chaired by Steve Bundred and Dr David Bennett was appointed as an Interim CEO. Following the departure of Mr Bundred in March 2011, Dr Bennett was appointed as chair while continuing as interim CEO. In February 2014 the National Audit Office published its report *Monitor: Regulating NHS foundation trusts*, which reported that Monitor's governance had not been good practice in that the same person acted as both chair and chief executive for nearly three years. It recommended that the DH appoint a permanent chair of Monitor as soon as possible as an independent chair was needed to boost the capacity of Monitor's senior team, hold the executive management to account and strengthen Monitor's accountability to Parliament. Baroness Hanham was appointed in September 2014.

There might occasionally be situations where it is appropriate for the same person to be both chair and CEO. When an organisation gets into business or financial difficulties, for example, there is an argument in favour of appointing a single, all-powerful individual to run the organisation until its fortune has been reversed. The combination of the roles of chair and CEO might have been necessary in the short term to give an organisation strong leadership to get it through its difficulties.

CASE STUDY: Transition from trust to foundation trust

A chair of an NHS trust had served a three-year term of office and was one year into her second three-year term when the trust was authorised as an FT. At the date of authorisation the chair was offered the remaining two years of her term of office which she accepted. At the end of that second term of office the council of governors agreed that while they would be happy to appoint the chair for a further term of three years the appointment had to be subject to open competition. The role was advertised, candidates interviewed, and the chair was reappointed for a further three-year term.

At the end of the third term of three years, the company secretary advised that since the Monitor Code now set out a six-year term of office any further terms of office would be for one year and would have to be subject to open competition. The chair refused to accept this, claiming that her previous term of office before the trust became an FT did not count and that she had only served five years. The trust's lawyers advised the chair similarly and the governor-led nomination committee was advised accordingly. When the position was made clear, the chair refused to stand for a further term of office and resigned.

■ The chair and the company secretary

Though the role of the company secretary is set out more fully in Chapter 10, it is worth highlighting the key dynamics in the relationship between these two roles. The essential criterion is a relationship of mutual trust, with the chair having full confidence in the company secretary and vice versa.

In particular, there are a number of key areas where the two roles will work very closely together. The first is governance. The company secretary should be responsible for advising the board through the chair on all governance matters (UK Code). This should include the evaluation of the board and the periodic review of governance processes, including the effectiveness of board committees.

A second area where the chair and company secretary need to work together is on the development and implementation of training and development programmes for board members, which may include both individual training and board development sessions. Though this remains the chair's responsibility, in practice this is often delegated to the company secretary.

A further area is that of obtaining a good flow of information within the board and its committees, and between senior management and the NEDs. The UK Code sets this out as a responsibility of the company secretary under the direction of the chair. Other areas of work might include agenda planning, quality control of board papers, overseeing the production of accurate minutes, induction programmes for all board members and for FTs, supporting the work of the council of governors.

■ The chair and the senior independent director

In anticipation of the potential for problems arising between shareholders, the chair and CEO, the UK Code requires that the board of directors of large companies should nominate an independent NED as the SID, whom shareholders could approach to discuss problems and issues when the normal communication route through the chair has broken down. In addition, if the chair fails to pass on the views of the institutional shareholders to the NEDs, there should be another channel of communication that could be used instead.

The role of the SID has also been taken up by the Monitor Code for FTs and has been adopted as good practice in NHS trusts. The lay members in a CCG governing body have a similar role in particular, the lay member for governance.

The FT board of directors appoints one of the independent NEDs to be the SID in consultation with the council of governors. The SID is then available to members and governors if they have concerns which contact through the normal channels of chair, CEO or finance director have failed to resolve or for which such contact is inappropriate. Both the UK Code and the Monitor Code state that the SID may also be the deputy chair. In NHS trusts, the board appoints the SID and they are available to all stakeholders where concerns cannot be addressed through the normal channels. In the NHS, the SID often has a key role to play in the organisation's whistleblowing procedures.

Having a SID is a key element of an effective board. The FRC *Guidance on Board Effectiveness* sets this out quite clearly, making a distinction between the role of the SID in 'normal times' and when the board is undergoing 'a period of stress'.

At normal times, the role of the SID is to:

- provide support for the chair
- ensure that the views of other directors, particularly the other NEDs, are conveyed to the chair
- ensure that the views of the shareholders, particularly matters that concern them, are conveyed to the rest of the board
- ensure that the chair is giving sufficient attention to succession planning
- carry out the annual review of the performance of the chair, in conjunction with the other NEDs (see Chapter 5).

At times of stress for the board, the role of the SID should be to take the initiative to resolve the problem, working with the other directors and stakeholders and/or the chair, as appropriate. Examples of problems where intervention by the SID may be appropriate include situations where:

- there is a dispute between the chair and the CEO
- shareholders or the NEDs have expressed serious concerns that are not being addressed by the chair or CEO
- the strategy pursued by the chair or CEO is not supported by the rest of the board
- there is a very close relationship between the chair and the CEO
- decisions are being taken without the approval of the board
- succession planning is being ignored.

Issues where intervention may be required should be considered when defining the responsibilities of the SID and should be set out in writing. The FRC guidance makes it clear that the SID should work alongside the chair and other board directors, but requiring intervention by the SID will also mean at times acting to challenge custom and practice and demonstrating significant people skills to find a solution.

Critics of the SID concept argue that the chair should be able to resolve difficulties between an organisation and its shareholders/stakeholders, and the position of SID should therefore be superfluous. Opening up the possibility of an additional channel of communication for shareholders/stakeholders is perhaps more likely to undermine organisation–stakeholder relationships than improve them.

However, the *ICGN Global Corporate Governance Principles* put forward reasons why a 'lead independent director' or independent deputy chair is necessary:

- If the chair is the CEO or former CEO, or was for another reason not independent when first appointed, the SID should provide independent leadership for the board, and should have a key role in setting the agenda for board meetings and acting as spokesman for the independent members of the board.
- Even when the chair was independent when first appointed, the role inevitably brings them closer than the NEDs over time to the views of the CEO and executive management.
- The SID should provide leadership to the independent members of the board when this situation creates a problem.

The ICGN Principles also recognise the role of the lead independent director as an alternative conduit for communication with the shareholders/stakeholders.

Although not specifically set out in the UK Code, in the event that the chair had to be removed, it would be the SID's job to lead that process. In the NHS, this would also involve Monitor or the NHS TDA for FTs and NHS trusts respectively.

Under the UK Code a further responsibility of the SID is to chair the annual meeting of NEDs, without the chair's presence, and to appraise the chair's performance as well as any other meeting as appropriate. In the NHS, this will happen to some extent but will be bound by the specific appraisal structures for NHS trusts, FTs and CCGs.

The role of the SID is most effective when there is a strong working relationship between the chair and SID, which is often why the SID will also be appointed as the deputy chair.

CASE STUDY: Benefits of an SID

At a board meeting of a well-established FT, which was being held in private session, the chair proposed that a significant donation be made to a local charity that was working alongside one of the healthcare areas delivered by the trust.

The chair was an aggressive person, who bullied and dominated the people working with them; and they often attempted to run the trust regardless of the role of the CEO. The chair was also a trustee of the charity in question. They apparently made no clear distinction between their own private activities and the public sector.

It was only the concerted effort of the senior independent director (SID), in conjunction with the finance director, that enabled the board to turn down the request.

■ The chair and stakeholders

The dissemination of information about the performance of the board and the organisation to stakeholders is important and the chair has a key role to play in that dissemination. This may be through the formal route of publicly available information or more informal meetings to discuss issues with key stakeholders.

The annual report

From a formal perspective, the Preface to the UK Code encourages chairs to report personally in their annual statements how the principles of the Code relating to the role and effectiveness of the board have been applied. This is one way in which the chair is held to account in a very public and personal way for their ability to oversee the role and effectiveness of the board. There is also a requirement for the annual board evaluation to be set out in the annual report, including the evaluation of the board committees and its individual directors. External evaluation should also be declared in the annual report.

From an informal perspective, regular briefing meetings or board to boards with key stakeholders are another useful way of engaging with stakeholders at which the chair will play a vital role. For NHS organisations this is a key role for the chair as such meetings can help to support the development of an active and collaborative local health economy.

The annual meeting

The chair also has a key role to play in the organisation's annual meeting. For companies this will be the annual general meeting with its institutional and individual shareholders in attendance; for NHS trusts this will mean the annual public meeting.

The NHS Trusts (Public Meetings) Regulations 1991 require NHS trusts to present their audited accounts, annual reports and any report on the accounts to a public meeting on or before 30 September in every year. They also provide that an NHS trust shall hold a public meeting to consider an auditor's report other than a report on the audited accounts as soon as practicable, and in any event not later than three months after the date on which the NHS trust received that report.

Governance Checklist

✓ Does the chair have the necessary personal attributes to create the right conditions for the board and its directors to be effective?

✓ What leadership, decision-making and governance skills does the chair possess?

✓ Does the process for appointing and appraising a new chair follow the best practice outlined here?

✓ Does the chair set the board agenda and chair meetings effectively?

✓ Do the chair and the CEO work together effectively? Do they complement each other roles and personalities?

✓ Is the company secretary available to the chair and do they work together effectively? Is there a clear delegation of tasks to the company secretary from the chair?

✓ Is there evidence of high quality, timely information, access to external advice, successful induction programmes and effective annual evaluation?

✓ Has a SID been appointed with a clearly defined role and with the necessary personal attributes to deal with potentially conflicted situations?

✓ Has the chair developed clear lines of communications, both formal and informal, with key stakeholders?

■ Summary

According to the Directorbank Group annual survey *Life in the Boardroom 2013*:

> 'The role of the chair and NED has never been more important nor more challenging and, though the financial rewards are generally not comparable to those for executive roles, the ideal non-executive is one who does not need the position for money and has chosen the company as much as vice versa.'

The survey – which also looks at chair and NED remuneration – commented on the levels of remuneration within the public sector:

> 'The public sector is paying substantially less than listed companies; and for many small public sector organisations no fees are paid. We suspect this is an area for concern – it is difficult to insist on the highest standards of competence, contribution, conduct and performance when directors are not paid a fair reward. If people are paid fairly, then they expect to be held to account. With increasing pressure on costs and value for money in the public sector, this problem can only grow.'

These comments are very perceptive given the current challenges faced by NHS organisations, both financially and reputationally. The NHS organisations with largest challenges and the most fraught relationships with stakeholders will need to be able command the kind of leadership from their chairs set out here as pre-requisites. Consequently, the need for effective selection and appointment processes is hugely important, as is clarity on how the role of the chair complements other key roles within the board.

8

Executive directors

Executive directors combine their role as director with their position within the executive management of the organisation. NEDs perform the functions of director, only without any executive responsibilities. The interests of EDs are therefore likely to differ from those of NEDs.

The focus in this chapter on the role of the CEO and EDs must not distract from the underlying principle of the unitary board. As discussed in Part Two, EDs have the same responsibilities and duties as NEDs; these extend to the entire business of the organisation, not just their own specific portfolio.

■ The role of executive directors

Unlike NEDs, EDs are full-time employees of the organisation, with executive management responsibilities as well their responsibilities as directors. Management is responsible for running the business operations and is accountable to the board of directors and the CEO.

For the EDs, there is a tension between their role as members of the board, 'one step down from the stakeholders' and their role as senior operational directors, 'one step up from management'.

This can manifest in different ways. There will be times when individual EDs and/or the CEO are held to account for their executive performance by fellow EDs, acting alongside NEDs as a unitary board. This can raise tensions – especially if the CEO is being held to account – and highlights the critical role of the chair in maintaining an effective board.

On the other hand, EDs and the CEO may want to present a united front to the rest of the board to justify what the management team has done and achieved, or what it would like to do. However, if the EDs come together with a united opinion, this raises doubts in their ability to provide effective challenge in discussions on strategy. Independent NEDs should not have this problem, which is why they should be more effective in providing effective challenge in board discussions, encouraged by the chair.

The issues for EDs are, therefore, that they may be inclined to support the views of the CEO on all matters, including strategy, and they may mistrust the NEDs as 'outsiders' who do not know much about the organisation and its business.

In recognition of this problem, the FRC *Guidance on Board Effectiveness* suggests that EDs should see themselves as representatives of the shareholders (for NHS, read stakeholders) rather than as executive managers who are responsible and accountable to the CEO. The chair should encourage this attitude among the EDs, partly through ensuring that they receive appropriate induction and training for their role as a board member.

The FRC guidance goes on to say that EDs should have a detailed knowledge of the organisation and its business, and should apply this knowledge when making judgements about organisational strategy. However, they should also recognise that constructive challenge from NEDs is an essential part of good governance, and they should welcome and encourage such challenges. For an effective board, the EDs and NEDs must work constructively together.

The ICSA guidance note *The Governance Challenge for the NHS Executive Director* sets this out quite neatly by suggesting EDs ask 'which hat am I wearing?' to retain an appropriate balance between the varying roles for which they are being paid. These include:

- leadership and management of their particular section or department
- being a member of the senior operational management of the organisation
- wider leadership and management responsibility within the operational environment
- ensuring the organisation remains focused on delivering its core business objectives
- governance and strategic responsibility from the board perspective.

The 'governance role' is different to the 'management role'. An ED's governance role is to:

- ensure that sufficient assets are aligned against the operational objectives being set though also guarding, maintaining and nurturing those same assets;
- debate, determine and set the strategy for the organisation; and
- monitor progress towards its fulfillment.

In contrast, the management role is to utilise the assets of the organisation in the fulfilment of the operational objectives of the organisation and to deliver the strategy determined by the board. The FTN's publication *New Voices, New Accountabilities* states:

> 'Boards of directors will increasingly have to operate as corporate entities, not sounding boards, in a world of contestable service provision ... Executive directors must make the transition from operating as functional heads of service to members of a corporate board, bearing the full weight of the fiduciary responsibility that falls on their shoulders and contributing fully to the strategic decision-making of the trust.'

▪ The appointment of executive directors

The nomination committee and the appointment committee have a key role to play in the appointment of EDs, as discussed in Chapters 4 and 6. The CEO will bring recommendations to the committees on succession planning and appointment, but the board will delegate the responsibility for appointment to these committees (which are essentially composed of NEDs). The key principle about the appointment of EDs is that it is the responsibility of the chair and the NEDs, acting under the remit of these two committees. The exception worth noting relates to the appointment of the CEO, which is covered below.

Induction of an executive manager as an executive director

The induction process for new ED who is already an executive manager of the organisation needs a specific focus. A senior executive of the organisation should already be familiar with many aspects of the organisation's operations (although their induction might include visits to parts of the organisation they have not worked with before).

An executive manager 'promoted' to the board is more likely to lack knowledge and experience about being a director and governance, although some larger organisations try to give their senior executives experience as a director by allowing them to take a position as a NED in another organisation.

An induction programme for an ED may therefore need to focus on matters such as:

- the role of the board, including matters reserved for the board and oversight of management
- the powers and duties of directors, and the rights of shareholders/stakeholders (the new director should be given a copy of the organisation's constitutional documents)
- the role of board committees and their membership
- the role of the board in monitoring risk and internal control (see also Chapter 14)
- membership of the board and its committees, how the board operates and the role of the company secretary
- frequency of board meetings
- what the new director will be expected to contribute
- who the major shareholders/stakeholders are and their relationship with the organisation
- compliance with governance requirements
- the potential liabilities of directors
- directors' liability insurance
- organisation policy on public involvement and sustainability
- arrangements for monitoring the performance of board members.

For listed companies, the law relating to fair dealing by directors (insider dealing) and the Model Code on share dealing by directors should also be set out.

This list is not exhaustive, although in some cases it might be considered too long. The main point is that an executive manager appointed as a director needs to learn about the differences in the roles of manager and director, and that they have not been appointed as a director simply to be a 'high level' executive of the organisation.

■ The role of the chief executive officer

The FRC *Guidance on Board Effectiveness* says the CEO is the most senior ED on the board, with responsibility for proposing strategy to the board and for delivering the strategy as agreed.

Consequently, the CEO's relationship with the chair is a key relationship that can assist board effectiveness. The CEO leads the executive team, is responsible for the executive management of the organisation's operations and is the senior executive to whom all other executive managers report. Other executive managers might also be directors of the organisation, but the CEO is answerable to the board for the way the business is run and its performance.

The CEO has, with the support of the executive team, primary responsibility for setting an example to the organisation's employees and communicating to them the expectations of the board in relation to the organisational culture, values and behaviours. The CEO is also responsible for supporting the chair to make certain that appropriate standards of governance permeate through all parts of the organisation and will make certain that the board is made aware, when appropriate, of the views of employees on issues of relevance to the business.

In order to improve the standard of boardroom discussion, the CEO should also act as a spokesperson for the executive team in board discussions, explain the views of the executive team to the rest of the board and explain in a balanced way any differences of opinion within the executive team.

The UK Code states that the differing responsibilities of the chair and the CEO should be set out in writing and agreed by the board. Particular attention should be paid to areas of potential overlap.

The role of the accountable/accounting officer in the NHS

At a macro level, the DH accounting officer, as principal accounting officer, has overall responsibility in Government for the proper and effective use of resources as voted by Parliament for the health and care system, including the NHS.

The majority of resources are allocated annually to NHS England. Its CEO, as accounting officer, is responsible for the effective use of these resources. There is a robust system in place to allow the accounting officer to discharge their responsibilities by providing assurance about the commissioning of NHS care and the provision and regulation of services. This system entails the appointment of accountable officers (for NHS trusts and CCGs) and accounting officers (for FTs).

For NHS trusts, the accountable officer is the CEO. He or she is accountable to Parliament via the DH accounting officer and the Secretary of State for Health. The NHS TDA accounting officer is responsible for the appointment of account- able officers for each NHS trust.

In CCGs, the accountable officer is either the chief officer or the chief clinical officer. They are accountable to Parliament via NHS England's accounting officer (the CEO, as designated in HSCA 2012) and the Secretary of State. In NHS FTs, accounting officers are directly responsible to parliament.

The accountable officer memorandum for chief executives of NHS trusts sets out the responsibilities as follows:

- ensuring there are effective management systems in place to safeguard public funds and assets and assisting in the implementation of corporate governance;
- ensuring value for money is achieved from the resources available to the trust;
- ensuring the expenditure and income of the trust has been applied to the purposes intended by Parliament and conform to the authorities which govern them;
- ensuring effective and sound financial management systems are in place; and
- ensuring annual statutory accounts are prepared in a format directed by the Secretary of State, with the approval of HM Treasury, to give a true and fair view of the state of affairs as at the end of the financial year. This should include the income and expenditure, recognised gains and losses and cash flows for the year.

The CCG accountable officer is responsible for ensuring that the CCG fulfils its duties to exercise its functions effectively, efficiently and economically – thus ensuring improvement in the quality of services and the health of the local popu-lation though maintaining value for money. They will ensure that the regular-ity and propriety of expenditure is discharged, and that arrangements are put in place to ensure that good practice is embodied (as identified through the head of the National Audit Office, the Comptroller and Auditor General). They will also ensure that funds are safeguarded through effective financial and management systems.

The CCG accountable officer, working closely with the chair of the govern-ing body, will ensure that proper constitutional, governance and development arrangements are put in place to assure the members of the CCG's ongoing capability and capacity to meet its duties and responsibilities. This will include arrangements for the ongoing development of its members and staff. The indi-vidual who takes on the accountable officer role for a CCG will be proposed by the governing body of the CCG and formally appointed to the role by NHS England in accordance with the 2014 guidance *NHS England – Appointing a new accounta-ble officer to a CCG* (2014). In circumstances where the lead clinician undertakes the accountable officer role, they will be known as the chief clinical officer. When a manager undertakes the role, the individual will be known as the chief officer. The accountable officer may not be the chair of the governing body or the chief finance officer.

Each FT has an accounting officer, who has responsibilities for ensuring regularity, propriety and value for money, including signing the trust's accounts, annual governance statement and annual report. The National Health Service Act 2006 designates the CEO of an NHS FT as the accounting officer. *The NHS Foundation Trust Accounting Officer Memorandum* (2008) sets out the role as responsibility for the overall organisation, management and staffing of the NHS FT and for its procedures in financial and other matters, and ensuring:

- there is a high standard of financial management in the NHS FT as a whole;
- financial systems and procedures promote the efficient and economical conduct of business and safeguard financial propriety and regularity throughout the NHS FT; and
- financial considerations are fully taken into account in decisions on NHS FT policy proposals.

The FT accounting officer has a particular responsibility to see that appropriate advice is tendered to the board and to the council of governors on all matters of financial propriety and regularity and, more broadly, as to all considerations of prudent and economical administration, efficiency and effectiveness. The NED-led appointments committee appoints the accounting officer and the appointment approved by the council of governors.

In all three settings, if the board or the chair is contemplating a course of action which the accountable/accounting officer considers would infringe the requirements of propriety and regularity, they should set out their objections (and the reasons for it) in writing to the chair and the board. If the decision is still taken to proceed, a written instruction to take the action in question should be issued. The audit committee, which has specific terms of reference and delegated powers to inquire into matters of propriety and regularity, should receive a copy of the objections.

If the board is contemplating a course of action which affects the responsibility for obtaining value for money from the organisation's resources, then the accountable/accounting officer should draw the relevant factors to the attention of the board. If the accountable/accounting officer is overruled, despite clear advice to the contrary, then the accountable/accounting officer should refer their concerns to their appointing body. In all such cases, the accountable/accounting officer should, as a board member, vote against the course of action rather than merely abstain from voting.

The accountable officer, together with the director of finance, is responsible for ensuring that the accounts of the trust presented to the board for approval are prepared under principles and in a format directed by the Secretary of State with the approval of HM Treasury (as set out in the NHS Finance Manual and in 'The role of the director of finance in the NHS' – EL(94)18). These accounts must disclose a true and fair view of the trust's income and expenditure, cash flows, gains and losses, and of its state of affairs. The accountable officer will sign these accounts, along with the director of finance/chief finance officer, on behalf of the board.

In FTs, the CEO, as the accounting officer, should sign and date the statement of financial position and annual report after adoption by the board as evidence of this. As accounting officer, the CEO should also sign the foreword to the accounts, the annual governance statement and the remuneration report. Once the annual report and accounts have been approved by the external auditors, the accounting officer or director of finance must sign a certificate which states that the FT consolidation schedules (FTCs) are consistent with the annual accounts.

■ The role of the Director of Finance or Chief Finance Officer

NHS trusts and FTs are required to have a director of finance (DoF) on the board and CCGs are required to have a Chief Finance Officer (CFO) on their governing body.

Though financial management is the corporate responsibility of the board, and the individual responsibility of the CEO/CO as the accountable officer, the DoF has both a professional and corporate role as a board member. The DoF ensures that systems are in place so that the organisation is properly governed in terms of financial transactions, financial reporting, financial performance, financial planning and in securing value for money. They also must also maintain assurance processes to ensure that internal controls and checks are working properly (such as engagement with clinical and non-clinical staff holding delegated financial budgets). These systems also include ensuring that 'treasury management' systems are in place to manage cash flow and liquidity.

The key responsibilities for finance directors are to provide business and commercial advice for the board as well as financial governance and assurance, and to fulfil their corporate responsibilities as a board member. A key requirement for NHS organisations is sustainable financial viability; the DoF has to involve and inform the board in assessing all the options in terms of strategic financial risk, including a 'worst case' scenario.

The DoF should be a professional accountant, and as such is required to behave with confidentiality, integrity, objectivity, professional competence and due care as mandated in the International Federation of Accountants (IFAC)'s Code of Ethics. They must also comply with professional quality standards, especially those relating to professional ethics, continuing professional development, and national and international external reporting requirements. The conduct and behaviour of a DoF must be within the law and, as a professional accountant, they also have a 'public interest' role. However, as a board member, the DoF's contribution is not, and should not be, limited to finance as a specialist area.

The National Health Service (Clinical Commissioning Groups) Regulations 2012 require that the CCG's governing body must also include an employee who has a professional qualification in accountancy and the expertise or experience to lead the financial management of the CCG, to be known as the CFO. If the governing body's membership includes two or more individuals of that description, the CCG must designate one of them as the CFO. They should be an individual with a recognised professional accounting qualification, as well as significant experience and skills. The CFO cannot be the chair of the governing body nor may they undertake the accountable officer role. The role may, however, be combined with that of chief operating officer (COO) in circumstances where a CCG has a COO (for instance, in CCGs where the clinical leader is also the accountable officer). In these circumstances, the role is known as 'chief finance and operating officer'.

■ Other executive director roles

There are several other key ED roles that are an important part of an NHS board. The roles of medical director and director of nursing (or chief nurse or executive nurse) are mandatory roles for a legitimately constituted board. Again, as board members, these roles should not be limited to their areas of professional expertise and they are required to contribute across the breadth of the organisation.

In a CCG, the lead clinician is the individual recognised by the CCG as the clinical voice of its members. This individual is either the chair of the governing body or undertakes the role of accountable officer as chief clinical officer. They will also be invited to be the CCG's member of the NHS Commissioning Assembly. In circumstances where a CCG chooses to appoint a clinician to the chair of the governing body and nominate a clinician for the role of the accountable officer, then the CCG should identify one of them to be known as the lead clinician.

■ The remuneration of executive directors

The remuneration of EDs and other senior executives in the corporate sector is a contentious issue, partly because of the amounts paid to top executives in some companies and partly because remuneration for senior executives has generally risen by a much larger percentage than increases in pay for other employees. While remuneration packages should be sufficient to attract and retain executives of a suitable calibre, they should not be excessive. Such packages should also reward executives for successful performance, in both the short term and the longer term, because pay incentives are expected to encourage executives to perform better. A further area of concern to the corporate sector (and to the NHS) is the <u>payment of large 'rewards for failure'</u>. Contracts of employment for senior executives should try to minimise the risk of these severance payments when a senior director fails to perform to a satisfactory standard and is dismissed.

The remuneration committee is the critical mechanism for governing executive remuneration.

Remuneration in the corporate sector

The remuneration of EDs and senior executives was not seen as a major problem of corporate governance until the 1990s in the UK and early 2000s in the USA. A sense that something might be wrong began when the general public, alerted by the media, criticised some top executives for being paid far more money than they were worth, and investment institutions criticised directors for receiving ever-increasing rewards even when their company performed badly.

In many listed companies in the UK during the 1980s and early 1990s, the CEOs and executive chairmen were involved in deciding their own remuneration package. Concern about remuneration has grown in other countries, particularly with regard to the banking crisis in 2007–2009 and the high rewards earned by senior bankers in spite of the large amounts of public funds provided to prevent banks from financial collapse.

Throughout the 2000s in the UK, the remuneration of top corporate sector executives rose rapidly regardless of company performance, the effects of global recession, and at a faster annual rate than the remuneration of other company employees. This seemed counter to the principle of good corporate governance that remuneration should be linked to some extent to company performance, so that a director will earn more if the company does well, but less if it does badly.

In June 2012, the Secretary of State for Business, Innovation and Skills announced a package of measures to address failings in the corporate governance framework for directors' remuneration. This included:

- giving shareholders more power through binding votes, so they can hold companies to account;
- boosting transparency so that what people are paid is clear and easily understood; and
- working with responsible business and investors to promote good practice and ensure reforms have a lasting impact.

The Enterprise and Regulatory Reform Act 2013 (ERRA) contains amendments to the Companies Act 2006 relating to quoted companies' disclosure of directors' remuneration and shareholder approval of quoted company directors' remuneration reports. The key changes made by ERRA are:

- the directors' remuneration report must include a forward-looking remuneration policy report;

- shareholders have been given a new binding ordinary resolution vote on the remuneration policy report (and retain their existing advisory ordinary resolution vote on the implementation report);
- any subsequent changes to the remuneration policy must be agreed by shareholders and, even if no changes are made to the remuneration policy, it must be must be approved by shareholders at least every three years;
- if shareholders did not approve the advisory vote on the implementation report at the company's previous AGM, the remuneration policy must be put to shareholders at the next AGM;
- all remuneration and loss of office payments to directors must be consistent with the approved remuneration policy; and
- unless a payment has been separately approved by shareholders in advance, any unauthorised payment is held on trust by the party that received it (usually this will be the director him or herself). Directors who authorised the payment will be liable for any loss to the company unless they can demonstrate that they acted honestly and reasonably.

A directors' remuneration report in the new format must be put to shareholders in the first financial year to begin on or after 1 October 2013. Though these regulations apply to companies, not to NHS organisations, the principles they contain are applicable and should still be considered by NHS boards.

NHS remuneration

NHS organisations are subject to a greater level of remuneration regulation than the corporate sector, but pay levels for senior management have still come under close public scrutiny – especially as all public sector wage rises have been capped at an average of 1% for two years from April 2013.

This comes after a two-year policy which saw all NHS staff earning more than £21,000 facing a pay freeze, while those earning up to £21,000 received an award of £250 in both years. From April 2014, staff who are on the top point of their pay band receive a 1% non-consolidated payment paid over 12 months from April 2014. This is given as an additional sum, and will not be added on to hourly rates or count for unsocial hours or overtime payments. Staff who are not on the top point will not receive this 1% pay rise, but continue to have access to incremental points – they will move to the next point in the pay band during 2014–15, providing they perform satisfactorily during the year.

In general, CCGs, NHS trusts and NHS FTs are free to determine their own rates of pay for very senior managers (VSMs) – CEOs, EDs and others with board-level responsibility who report directly to the CEO.

VSM pay in DH arm's-length bodies (ALBs) such as NHS England, Monitor, the CQC and the NHS TDA is subject to two national pay frameworks, one set in 2006 and the other in 2012. VSM pay in non-FT ambulance trusts is subject to the 2006 pay framework, including the requirement to seek Treasury approval (via the DH) for all pay in excess of £142,500 p.a. This requirement also applies to non-FT NHS community trusts.

Performance-related pay is available to VSMs within ALBs on either of the two national pay frameworks, although it is currently restricted by the government to the top 25% of performers and to a maximum of 5% of reckonable pay. Table 8.1 compares the average pay of three VSM roles that commonly exist in ALBs, NHS trusts and FTs:

Table 8.1: Average VSM pay

Role	ALBs	All trusts	Largest trusts by income
CEO	£167,600	£163,679	£206,775
Finance director	£142,408	£120,155	£146,839
HR Director	£119,360	£98,603	£122,688

Comparator figures taken from the IDS NHS Boardroom Pay Report 2013.
ALB figures based on current pay.

Pay data for CCGs is not centrally collected so it will not be available until the analysis of the first set of CCG annual reports. CCGs are free to set their own rates of senior pay but are encouraged to follow guidance produced by NHS England for chief officer and CFO pay. The guidance does not apply to chief officer roles where being a clinician has been deemed an essential requirement.

NHS England has proposed three pay ranges for chief officers and chief finance officers, based on the population sizes of CCGs (see Table 8.2).

Table 8.2: CCG pay ranges

CCG level	Population size	Pay range for chief officer	Pay range for CFO
Level 3	At or over 500,000	£120,000–£130,000	£95,000–£110,000
Level 2	150,000 to 499,000	£105,000–£120,000	£85,000–£95,000
Level 1	149,000 or below	£90,000–£105,000	£75,000–£85,000

Source: NHS England

The Electronic Staff Record does not enable the identification of the pay of NHS VSMs. However, the Incomes Data Services (IDS) publishes a comprehensive report every April on boardroom pay in NHS trusts and FTs, based on their published accounts. While the the data may not be completely up-to-date – for instance, the latest available report is based on the year ending 31 March 2013

– the data shows that trusts were exercising considerable restraint over the pay of their VSMs. Points of interest from the most recent report include:

- in 2013, there was zero increase in the average level of executive pay across all board positions and across all types of NHS organisation for the third year running;
- in the year ending March 2013, 60% of NHS board directors received no salary increase;
- where there have been increases, this is in many cases the result of organisational changes such as the merger of several trusts;
- just seven NHS chief executives received bonus payments.

All other posts within the NHS are governed by the Agenda for Change system, which allocates posts to set pay scales using a job evaluation scheme. All FTs have the freedom to use local terms and conditions when setting pay for all employees. However, in practice, all but one (Southend University Hospital NHS Foundation Trust) has continued to be guided by VSM and to operate Agenda for Change for their staff.

CASE STUDY: Southend University Hospital NHS Foundation Trust
Southend University Hospital NHS Foundation Trust took the decision to opt out of the nationally negotiated Agenda for Change agreement, balloting staff in March 2006 to gain their consent.

The vast majority of employees have opted for local terms, agreed annually between management and unions. The trust has set pay levels that are on a par with Agenda for Change, but has also introduced enhancements to other conditions. Retaining local terms has helped the trust to remain competitive as an employer, and has kept its staff both committed and engaged. The trust has also introduced a bonus scheme linked to operational performance.

Moves to greater independence and local accountability offer freedom on remuneration for NHS EDs. In addition, the increasing complexity of NHS organisations calls for the best candidates possible, yet there is pressure on the government to ensure pay levels reflect the current economic climate.

As the financial position of the NHS tightens due to the economic climate, more attention will be paid to the level of ED remuneration within the NHS. The lessons learned from the corporate sector should offer useful insights to health service governance in this area. In addition, the remuneration levels that are on offer in the corporate sector will also influence NHS remuneration levels, as suggested by the response of the NHS Confederation to IDS's 2011 report:

'NHS organisations are large and complex in nature and require the right managerial skills to be led effectively. A large city hospital could have a budget of between £500 million and £1 billion and employ as many as 10,000 staff – comparable to many FTSE 250 companies. Because of the challenging nature of a chief executive's role, NHS boards must consider a range of factors, including pay, to encourage the best candidates in to these positions. The NHS is looking to involve more clinical staff in top management positions. Given that a number of hospital doctors will be paid more than NHS chief executives, this factor must be taken into consideration when making a decision on pay.'

David Stout, Deputy CEO, NHS Confederation

Public attitudes

Public attitudes about remuneration within the NHS are somewhat contradictory – a fact which was recognised, although not specifically, in the Hutton Review of Fair Pay (2011) in the public sector (covered in more detail later):

'Success [of the public sector] would be a fundamental building block in supporting economic growth and social well-being, but it cannot be done without motivated, high calibre public servants, along with managers to lead them. But while the British public is very sympathetic to front line delivery staff, it is hostile to the public sector managers responsible and accountable for the effective deployment of resources – and even more hostile to their pay. In the eyes of some, they are the quintessential "burdens" on the rest of us.'

The review set out that some of this public reaction is quite reasonable, since public sector managers have also benefited from significant earnings growth at the top remuneration levels, particularly in the early 2000s. However, some balance is required. As the Hutton interim report demonstrated, only £1 of every £100 earned by the top 1% of earners in the UK is earned by public sector employees.

Even so, the perception remains that the public sector is no less awash with 'fat cats' than the private sector; indeed, in one poll, a quarter of respondents thought that public sector executives earned more than their private sector counterparts. Regardless, Hutton maintains that: 'the public has the right to know that pay is deserved, fair, under control and designed to drive improving public sector performance'.

Rewards for failure

In the UK, during 2002–2003, there was institutional investor concern, supported by widespread media coverage, about large remuneration packages for senior corporate directors where the size of the reward did not seem sufficiently linked to performance, and large severance payments (payments on dismissal) to outgoing senior executives who had been ousted from their job following poor company performance.

High severance payments to unsuccessful directors were seen as 'rewards for failure'. Following the global banking crisis of 2007–2009, there was also widespread criticism of remuneration in banks, whereby top executives and traders received large bonuses even though their bank may have been close to collapse or in need of government financial support to remain in business.

Similar problems of rewards for failure have been seen in the NHS and raises very clear issues of health service governance.

CASE STUDY: *Gibb v Maidstone and Tunbridge Wells NHS Trust [2010]*

In *Gibb v Maidstone and Tunbridge Wells NHS Trust [2010]*, G was employed as the trust's CEO with a basic annual salary of £150,000 and an entitlement to six months' notice. Following outbreaks of the 'super bug' C. difficile at hospitals managed by her, there were a significant number of deaths and widespread public anger and anxiety.

G left the trust under a compromise agreement that agreed to pay her around £250,000 including around £75,000 pay in lieu of notice and a compensation payment of £175,000. The compensation payment, which had been agreed, was challenged by G's successor as being *ultra vires*, i.e. beyond the powers of the NHS trust to award. G issued proceedings against the trust to recover the £175,000. The High Court found that the £175,000, which had been agreed under the compromise agreement, was irrationally generous and was therefore outside of the Trust's powers to award. It held that G was not therefore entitled to recover the £175,000. The trust had failed to ensure that it did not reward for failure, and the £175,000 was over and above any contractual or statutory entitlement that G may have had.

The Court also held that she was not entitled to any other lesser payment (such as compensation for unfair dismissal). While G could have claimed for unfair dismissal, she had not done so. G therefore failed to recover the £175,000, which had been an agreed payment under the Compromise Agreement. G was out of time to bring a claim for unfair dismissal, but if she had still been within time, she could have issued proceedings against the trust. The NHS trust was a public body so it was clearly of relevance to those involved in the public sector. The trust had failed to follow specific guidance for NHS bodies in assessing compensation and had acted outside its authority.

The problem of inappropriate remuneration policies for senior executives is now well recognised both within the NHS and the corporate sector, but a satisfactory solution has not necessarily been found. However, a distinction should be made between the unethical 'corporate greed' of some senior executives, and a reasonable desire by senior executives to be well remunerated for what they do. Similarly, it is important to make the distinction between high rewards that are justified by performance, and high rewards that are earned in spite of poor performance.

■ Why is remuneration a governance issue?

Remuneration of senior executives is a governance issue for several reasons.

- ■ Excessive remuneration for senior executives that is not clearly linked to good performance breaches the requirement for economy, efficiency and effectiveness which underpins the NHS.
- ■ Executives should not be rewarded for failure.
- ■ Large organisations need to attract and retain talented professionals to provide them with effective leadership. Top executives are attracted and retained by the remuneration packages they are offered.
- ■ Organisations need effective boards and senior executive management. Remuneration incentives can be used to motivate executives to perform better and to achieve better results, however, remuneration incentives should be designed carefully to align the interests of the organisation and executives as much as possible, in both the short term and the longer term.
- ■ The remuneration of senior executives may antagonise employees (and employee representatives), when it appears that senior executives are paid excessive amounts in comparison with their own pay. A sense that benefits or rewards are unfairly distributed could lead to industrial unrest within the organisation.

A further reason relates to the stability and continuity of the board. The 2011 IDS study found that turnover in non-FT boardrooms had increased from 17% to 24% in the year to March 2010, and from 14% to 21% for FTs. Additionally, Will Hutton identified in his 2011 review on fair pay that there were real concerns about director tenure in the NHS, where the average tenure of NHS acute trust chief executives was just two years and four months, compared with the average tenure for FTSE 100 chief executives at 5.9 years. He went on:

> 'Such short tenures not only compare unfavourably with the private sector (average tenure for FTSE 100 chief executives is currently 5.9 years), but are also not conducive to successful management: business management research suggests that most chief executives need an average of 30 months to complete their learning curve upon taking up a new role.'

Accusations that the remuneration packages of senior executives have got 'out of hand' can also be harder to defend if there is no robust framework to justify top levels of pay – although the constraints of the VSM Framework do operate within the NHS. Remember, too, that remuneration as a governance issue can apply to senior executives below board level as well as to directors.

■ Principles of executive director remuneration

Principles of remuneration are now included in the corporate governance codes of many countries. In a system of good governance, the remuneration of directors and key senior executives should be sufficient to attract and retain individuals of a suitable calibre. At the same time, the structure of an individual's remuneration package should motivate the individual towards the achievement of performance that is in the best interests of the organisation and its stakeholders, as well as those of the individual.

The UK Corporate Governance Code states as a principle that:

> 'Levels of remuneration should be sufficient to attract, retain and motivate directors of the quality required to run the company successfully, but a company should avoid paying more than is necessary for this purpose. A significant proportion of executive directors' remuneration should be structured so as to link rewards to corporate and individual performance.'

It is widely accepted that senior executives should be able to earn a high level of remuneration in return for the work they do and the responsibilities they carry. If a company does not offer an attractive package, it will not attract individuals of the required calibre. It is also generally accepted that the level of remuneration should be linked in some way to satisfactory performance. If an executive performs well, he should receive more rewards than if he performs only reasonably well.

That said, it is widely recognised that the top levels of pay in the public sector are running at between 50% and 55% of the salaries at the top of the private sector. There is already a very substantial discount being accepted by senior executives who want to work in the public sector and build a career going to the top. There is also the long-held belief that people should want to do the job and should not want to do it for the money, as long as the salary pays them a reasonable living.

The central issue for good corporate governance is concerned with the link between pay and performance. In the corporate sector the remuneration package should include a performance-related element. If the director successfully achieves predetermined levels of performance, they will be rewarded accordingly. There could be some debate as to how much remuneration should be performance related, but there is a view that a substantial part of a director's total potential remuneration should be linked to performance. Linking remuneration, wholly or in part, to performance is not an easy task, however, as the following shows.

■ Unsuitable measures of performance may be selected, so that although the individual executive succeeds in achieving targets that earn high rewards, the organisation does not obtain a comparable benefit.

■ Many performance measures are based on the short term, possibly linked to annual results. This may not be in the interests of the organisation's longer-term development and performance.

- Remuneration systems are normally designed to provide the reward after the performance has been made. This time delay means that if the organisation has poor results in the current year after having done well in the previous year, an executive may be paid high remuneration (for the previous year) at a time the organisation is doing badly.

The UK Code requires that the responsibility for setting the remuneration of EDs (and possibly other senior executives) should be delegated by the board to a remuneration committee. The remuneration committee is explained in more detail later in this chapter; however, an appendix to the UK Code sets out provisions for the design of the performance-related elements of a remuneration package that the remuneration committee should apply. These provisions offer a useful insight into how incentive schemes may be structured and approved.

If it is not an easy task for corporate governance, then it becomes even more difficult for health service governance. As this handbook has already demonstrated, there is significant diversity and complexity amongst stakeholders and their objectives for NHS organisations. Finding suitable measures of performance is a challenge that was highlighted in the Hutton Review (see below). For health service governance, a key principle relates to the public scrutiny and transparency of the remuneration package and the accountability of the ED.

Hutton Review of fair pay in the public sector

The Hutton Review was published in March 2011 and sets out a new Fair Pay Code for senior pay, to be adopted by all organisations delivering public services, on a 'comply or explain' basis based on the principle of fairness as due desert – namely, reward should be proportional to the weight of each role and each individual's performance. The Code also required pay levels to be set according to a fair process, though recognising that an organisation's success derives from the collective efforts of the whole workforce.

The review also set out 12 recommendations to the government that together form the framework for fairness.

1. **Using pay multiples to track executive pay against that of all employees:** the government should not cap pay across public services, but should require that from 2011–2012 all public service organisations publish their top to median pay multiples each year to allow the public to hold them to account.
2. **Informing the public debate through annual Fair Pay Reports:** to support citizen accountability, the government should commission the Senior Salaries Review Body to publish annual Fair Pay Reports, starting from 2011–2012.
3. **Re-calibrating the pay** of non-departmental public body chief executives. NDPBs
4. **From disclosure to explanation – ensuring complete transparency over executive roles and remuneration:** to enable citizens to understand executive remuneration and the nature of executive responsibilities, from 2011–2012 the government should require that all organisations delivering public

services disclose in precise numbers the full remuneration of all executives, alongside an explanation of the responsibilities of each role and of how executives' pay reflects individual performance.

5. **Enabling citizen analysis of executive pay:** from 2011–2012, the government should require public organisations to submit executive pay data through an online template, and make this data available on data.gov.uk, to allow citizens to access and analyse this data and thus have the information required to hold public service organisations to account.

6. **Abandoning arbitrary benchmarks for public service pay:** once this framework of recommendations is in place, the government should refrain from using the pay of the Prime Minister or other politicians as a benchmark for the remuneration of senior public servants, whose pay should reflect their due desert and be proportional to the weight of their roles and their performance.

7. **Preventing rewards for failure through earn-back pay for senior public servants:** to allow pay to vary down as well as up with performance, all public service executives should have an element of their basic pay that needs to be earned back each year through meeting pre-agreed objectives with excellent performers who go beyond their objectives eligible for additional pay.

8. **Extending earn-back pay** to high performing middle managers.

9. **Sharing the rewards of greater productivity:** to prevent executives monopolising the rewards of productivity increases, and allow all employees who have contributed to share the benefits, government departments should identify ways of offering gainsharing schemes linked to achievement of the efficiency aspects of their business plans.

10. **Opening up opportunities for future generations of public service leaders:** to increase the supply of candidates for top positions and reinforce public service management as a career, the government should facilitate greater opportunities for managers to move across different public services.

11. **A Fair Pay Code:** to embed fairness principles and ensure fair process in executive remuneration, all public service organisations should adopt the Fair Pay Code proposed by this Review. Government departments should by July 2011 bring forward proposals for the application of this code to all bodies and sectors in which they have an interest.

12. **Tracking pay multiples across the economy:** to make tracking pay multiples normal practice across the economy, as part of its commitment to improve corporate reporting, the Government should require listed companies to publish top to median pay multiples in their annual reporting from January 2012.

The Senior Salaries Review Body published its own report in response to this review, which sets out clear benchmarks and evaluation processes for setting the pay of VSMs. This was revised in October 2013.

■ The component elements of executive directors' remuneration

The remuneration package for a senior executive in the corporate sector is likely to consist of a combination of: a fixed-pay element – remuneration received regardless of performance, such as a fixed salary and payments made into a salary related pension scheme – and a variable pay element. This might consist of per- formance-related incentives, which might be tied to short-term performance such as an annual bonus, and longer-term incentives such as share option awards. In addition, executives might enjoy a number of other perks such as free private medical insurance, a company car and the use of a company plane or apartment.

The major issue for the corporate sector in negotiating a remuneration pack- age with an executive is deciding on the balance between the fixed and the variable elements, and to agree on measures of performance as the basis for deciding on how much the performance-related payments should be. Short-term incentives are based on annual performance targets. Long-term incentives may be awarded each year, but are linked to performance over a longer period of time, typically three years (or longer). Another problem in deciding a remuneration package is to find a suitable balance between short-term and longer-term incentives.

Admittedly, this is less of an issue for the NHS, where a senior executive remuneration package usually consists of a fixed salary and a final salary-related pension. The FTN Remuneration Survey of executive pay confirms this, although some FTs are now adding a car allowance or lease car to their remuneration packages.

There is also evidence that some FTs offer a performance related pay scheme in connection with the achievement of trust corporate objectives. These schemes, however, are still in their infancy and small in number.

■ The remuneration committee

It is a well-established principle of 'best practice' in governance that there should be a formal procedure for deciding on remuneration for directors and senior exec- utives, and no individual should be involved in setting their own remuneration. This is made clear in the UK Code. This means that EDs should not be involved in setting their remuneration packages (although they can negotiate with the individuals who make the decision) and NEDs should not decide their fees.

The remuneration of EDs was recognised as an important governance issue in the UK in the 1990s with the work of the Greenbury Committee, whose rec- ommendations were subsequently incorporated into the UK governance code in 1998. Health service governance has adopted these principles, either in the con- stitution of an FT or the founding regulations and statutory instruments of other NHS organisations. It is worth, therefore, considering the provisions of the UK Code as they underpin the provisions of health service governance. Specimen terms of reference for NHS Remuneration Committees can be found on the ICSA website.

The requirement for a remuneration committee

The UK Code states that 'the board should establish a remuneration committee ... [which] should make available its terms of reference, explaining its role and the authority delegated to it by the board'.

The remuneration committee is responsible, therefore, for both developing remuneration policy and for negotiating the remuneration of individual directors. Although these two matters are related, they are different. According to the UK Code the remuneration committee in the corporate sector should consist entirely of independent NEDs. In larger companies, the committee should consist of at least three members, and in smaller companies (i.e. companies below the FTSE 350) at least two members. The company chair may be a member of the committee, but not the committee chair, provided that they were considered to be independent on appointment as company chair. The remuneration committee should have delegated responsibility for setting the remuneration for all EDs and the chair (including pension rights and any compensation payments or severance payments). The remuneration committee should also recommend and monitor the level and structure of remuneration for senior management. The definition of 'senior management' is a matter for the board to decide, but it will normally include the first level of management below board level.

The UK Code also states as a supporting principle that the remuneration committee should consult with the chair and/or the CEO about their proposals for the remuneration of the other EDs. This is to ensure that the remuneration committee receives advice about the performance of EDs from individuals who know about their contributions to the management team and to the work of the board.

The remuneration committee may ask for advice from other sources, including other senior executives and is responsible for deciding whether to appoint remuneration consultants to advise it. If executives or senior managers are involved in giving advice to the remuneration committee, the committee should take care to recognise and avoid any conflicts of interest. The committee should keep the chair well informed about its decisions on remuneration policy and the remuneration of individual directors, because the chair should be the point of contact for shareholders/stakeholders who want to ask questions about remuneration or make their opinions known to the organisation.

The specific requirements for a remuneration (and terms of service) committee for are set out more fully in Chapter 4.

The principal duties of the remuneration committee

A list of duties of the remuneration committee were at one time included as an annex to the UK Corporate Governance Code, and they are now indicated in ICSA's guidance note on the terms of reference for a remuneration committee.

Typically, the <u>duties of a remuneration committee in the corporate sector are as follows</u>.

- The committee should determine and agree with the main board the remuneration policy for the CEO, the chair of the board and any other designated executive managers. This policy should provide for executive managers to be given appropriate incentives for enhanced performance.
- To maintain and assure their independence, the committee should also decide the remuneration of the company secretary.
- The committee should decide the targets for performance for any performance-related pay schemes operated by the organisation.
- It should decide the policy for and scope of pension arrangements for each ED.
- It should ensure that the contractual terms for severance payments on termination of office are fair to both the individual and the organisation, that failure is not rewarded and that the director's duty to mitigate losses is fully recognised.
- Within the framework of the agreed remuneration policy, it should determine the remuneration package of each individual ED, including any bonuses, incentive payments and share options.
- It should be aware of and advise on any major changes in employee benefit structures throughout the organisation or group.
- It should agree the policy for authorising expense claims from the chair and CEO.
- It should ensure compliance by the organisation with the requirements for disclosure of directors' remuneration in the annual report and accounts.
- It should be responsible for appointing any remuneration consultants to advise the committee.
- In the annual report, it should report the frequency of committee meetings and the attendance by members
- It should make available to the public its terms of reference, setting out the committee's delegated responsibilities. Where necessary these should be reviewed and updated each year.

NHS remuneration committees are <u>also required to declare the relationship between the remuneration of the highest-paid director in their organisation and the median remuneration of the organisation's workforce in its annual report in line with the Hutton Fair Pay Review</u>.

Evaluation and appraisal of executive directors

Both the Monitor Code and the UK Code state as a main principle that the board should undertake a formal and rigorous annual evaluation of its own performance and that of its committees and individual directors. This includes the EDs in their board member roles. The performance of individual EDs as executive managers is not dealt with by a governance code, because <u>individual executive</u>

performance is not a governance issue. For governance purposes, the evaluation of performance relates to performance as a director.

Good workforce management would require the EDs to undergo an annual appraisal with the CEO as their line manager in respect of the portfolio of management responsibilities that they undertake. However, this appraisal should also take into account the board level responsibilities that they carry and the chair of the board should be asked to participate in this aspect of their appraisal.

The chair of the board will appraise the CEO and this appraisal will also include both their management and board role responsibilities. The remuneration committee should then consider the appraisals of the EDs in considering any annual pay review decisions.

Use of remuneration consultants

Companies and NHS organisations often use remuneration consultants, who give advice to the remuneration committee on remuneration packages, including basic salary levels for senior executives. Consultants should not be given responsibility for deciding remuneration; this responsibility should remain with the remuneration committee of the board. Consultants may use competitive pay data to recommend a basic package for senior executives. Competitive pay data is simply information about the rewards that are being paid to senior executives in other top companies. It is essential that there is a robust tendering exercise for the appointment of such consultants in order to demonstrate their independence and objectivity.

A supporting principle in the UK Code is that the remuneration committee should benchmark its position on remuneration to comparative organisations, but it should exercise caution in making this judgement 'in view of the risk of an upward ratchet of remuneration levels with no corresponding improvement in performance'. If a UK-listed company does use the services of remuneration consultants, it should make available a statement of whether they have any other connection with the organisation. This statement may help to indicate that the consultants are independent and can provide objective advice.

Practice and process

There is no set requirement for the frequency of meeting of the remuneration committee; however, it needs to meet at least annually to approve the remuneration report for the annual report and accounts. Other meetings are likely in order to consider the remuneration policy required by Enterprise and Regulatory Reform Act 2013, any annual reviews of executive remuneration, and decisions on individual EDs as they are appointed. It is routine practice for non-members to be invited to attend the committee as required by the business of the meeting (e.g. the CEO, director of workforce or employment lawyer). The company secretary (or someone from the company secretary's department) should act as secretary to the remuneration committee, because it is the company secretary's responsibility to ensure that the board and its committees are properly consti-tuted and advised. The company secretary can also play a role as intermediary and coordinator between the committee and the main board.

The FRC *Guidance on Board Effectiveness* makes it clear that while the board may make use of a committee to assist its consideration of remuneration, it still retains responsibility for, and makes the final decisions on, all of these areas. The chair should ensure that sufficient time is allowed at the board for discussion of these issues and for allowing the remuneration committee to report on its activity and decisions. As with all board committees the effectiveness of the committee and its terms of reference should be reviewed annually.

■ Severance payments

Most EDs have employment contracts with their organisation that provide for an annual review of their remuneration and a minimum period of notice in the event of dismissal. When an organisation decides to dismiss a director, it is bound by the terms of the employment contract. There are various reasons why an individual might leave the company – for instance, they might be regarded as having failed to do a good job, and someone else should do the job instead. In this instance a high severance payment would be seen as 'rewarding failure'. Alternately, there may have been a disagreement or falling out between directors, resulting in one or more directors being asked to leave, in this instance any severance payment needs to be fair and not calculated to prevent whistleblowing disclosures or reputational damage.

The employment contract of a director might provide for the payment of com-pensation for loss of office. Alternatively, an organisation might be required to give the individual a minimum period of notice, typically one year or six months in the UK. If an individual is asked to leave, they might be paid for the notice period without having to work out the notice. In addition, the individual may be entitled to further bonus payments under the terms of their remuneration pack-age – in spite of being considered a failure in the job.

Shareholder concerns, and the wider public concern in regard to public sector organisations, arise particularly where the severance payment is paid even though an individual is being dismissed for having performed badly. In the past, sever-ance payments have been high for executives who have been seen to have failed. A large compensation payment can seem annoying, because it seems that the individual is being rewarded for failure. Large severance payments reduce com-pany profits and returns to shareholders and in the public sector are viewed as the improper use of public sector monies.

The UK Code contains two provisions about employment contracts and com-pensation for termination of office.

- When negotiating the terms of appointment of a new director, the remuneration committee should consider what compensation commitments the organisation would have in the event of early termination of office. More specifically, the aim should be to avoid rewarding poor performance. The committee should 'take a robust line' on reducing the amount of compensation to reflect a departing director's obligation to mitigate losses.
- Notice periods in the employment contract of an ED should be set at one year or less. If it is necessary to offer a longer notice period to a director coming into the organisation from outside, the notice period should subsequently be reduced to one year or less 'after the initial period'.

Remuneration committees should consider whether the organisation should retain an entitlement to reclaim bonuses if performance achievements are subsequently found to have been materially mis-stated. Contracts of employment should not provide for compensation payments to senior executives in the event of a change of control over the organisation (a takeover).

Remuneration committees should also ensure that the benefits of mitigation are obtained when an individual is dismissed. This should include a contractual obligation of the dismissed individual to mitigate the loss incurred through severance by looking for other employment. The contract should provide for the severance payment to be reduced in circumstances where the individual finds alternative employment.

NHS Employers published *Guidance for employers within the NHS* in December 2013 to assist NHS employers in handling special severance payments. Originally designed to cover senior managers, the guidance also outlined the process for issuing a special severance payment to any employee. Though it made clear that employers needed to take legal and audit advice in each particular situation, the guidance summarised the considerations employers need to make when considering terminating the employment of an individual with a special severance payment.

HM Treasury define a 'special severance payment' as one paid to employees, contractors and others above normal statutory or contractual requirements when leaving employment in public service whether they resign, are dismissed or reach an agreed termination of contract. The guidance also referred to Chapter 5 of the NHS Financial Manual (losses and special payments), the HM Treasury guidance *Managing Public Money*, the Monitor template for FTs, and the NHS Employers guidance on the use of settlement agreements and confidentiality clauses (December 2013).

The process requires all NHS organisations to obtain agreement from a relevant national body to make a special severance payment before presenting a paper to the HM Treasury for approval (see Table 8.3)

Table 8.3: Bodies that approve special severance payments

Organisation type	National body
NHS trust	NHS Trust Development Authority
NHS FT	Monitor
Clinical commissioning group	NHS England
Arm's-length body/special health authority	Department of Health

The guidance sets out the following questions to help inform NHS organisations in their decision-making. ~~SEVERANCE~~

- Is it appropriate to terminate the individual's employment? Severance should not be used as an option if it is primarily to avoid formal performance management action, disciplinary processes, unwelcome publicity or reputational damage.
- What is the appropriate method of termination? For example, in cases involving performance or misconduct issues, generally the capability or disciplinary procedures are appropriate and should be utilised as appropriate.
- Have all the circumstances of the case been considered, including the scope for potential litigation and the consequences of this?
- Is this arrangement in the public interest? Consider:
  - why the severance payment is in the public interest
  - why it represents value for money
  - how it represents the best use of public funds.
- Have Monitor, the NHS TDA or NHS England been informed? (as applicable) The employer should inform their contact at the relevant body at the earliest opportunity.

The guidance also recommends that any specific process requirements should be clarified with the appropriate national body according to Table 8.3 (Monitor for FTs, the NHS TDA for NHS trusts and NHS England for CCGs).

Once the above steps have been taken and the employer is satisfied that termination of the employee's employment, together with making a severance payment, is in the best interests of the employer and represents value for money, then a proposal for the remuneration committee, as appropriate and in line with its terms of reference, should be prepared containing the business case for the severance payment.

This document should be created in order to take legal effect and should be marked as such. In addition to the preparation of the proposal, the following steps should be taken:

- written advice from the trust's auditors and legal advisers should be taken on the proposed business case and severance payment. Advice should also be sought on the proposal and, if appropriate, a settlement agreement should be drafted; and

■ the legal advice about the draft proposal, together with the audit advice and the proposal itself, should be put before the remuneration committee of the employer for approval.

In the event the remuneration committee approves the business case, further approval should be sought from NHS England, the NHS TDA or Monitor (as applicable). If a settlement agreement is to be used, the approving body and HM Treasury will need to be assured that it does not include a confidentiality clause that prohibits an individual raising a concern covered under the Public Interest Disclosure Act (PIDA). If the appropriate national body approves the business case, it will seek HM Treasury approval on behalf of the employer.

The remuneration committee, operating in accordance with its terms of reference, should satisfy itself that it has the relevant information before it to make a decision and should conscientiously discuss and assess the merits of the business case. It should then consider the payment or payment range being proposed and address whether it is appropriate, taking into account the issues set out under initial considerations. The committee should only approve such sum or range which it considers value for money, the best use of public funds and in the public interest. A written record must be kept summarising its discussions and its decision (remembering that such a document could potentially be subject to public scrutiny in various ways – such as by the Public Accounts Committee (PAC)).

It is only once all of the above steps have been taken, and the necessary approvals received, that the employer should enter into the appropriate agreement to terminate the employee's employment and make the severance payment.

In November 2014, HM Treasury announced new proposals in the Small Business Enterprise and Employment Bill that highly paid public sector executives who receive redundancy payments only to return to work within a year will need to repay the taxpayer. The government states that the regulations setting out the detailed rules will be implemented no later than April 2016.

In brief, the proposals mean that individuals earning more than £100,000 who take a new job in the same part of the public sector within 12 months of being made redundant will have to repay all or some of their redundancy payment. The proposals will mainly affect NHS and local government administrators, many of whom have taken redundancy payments only to go back into the public sector. The precise amount of the repayment will be pro-rated depending on the length of time between exit and re-employment. The legislation will require the old employer to inform the individual of their obligation to repay the exit payment. Any new employer would be unable to engage with the individual until recovery arrangements for the money have been agreed.

HM Treasury has said that it intends to include the following payments related to loss of employment within the scope of this policy:

- redundancy payments, both voluntary and compulsory
- voluntary exit payments
- discretionary payments made to buy out actuarial reductions in pensions
- *ex gratia* payments such as special severance payments
- payments representing the value of fixed-term contracts
- payments made to facilitate a dismissal on the grounds of efficiency.

Disclosure of directors' remuneration details

Directors' remuneration report

Under ERRA, companies are required to publish a remuneration report which includes three sections:

- a statement from the chair of the remuneration committee
- a forward-looking remuneration policy report (not subject to audit)
- an annual report on remuneration (audited) which includes both how the policy has been implemented in the year under review and how it will be implemented in the forthcoming year.

Shareholders have a binding vote on the policy report at least every three years, or whenever any changes are made, in addition to an annual advisory vote on the annual remuneration report. The report must set out the total remuneration of individual executive members disclosed as a single figure in the financial statements (including base pay, bonuses, dividend equivalents, pensions etc). The Act does not, however, make a distinction between executive and NEDs and information about both must be included in the report.

The remuneration report must be approved by the board and signed on its behalf. A copy must be circulated to shareholders in the same way as the annual report and accounts, and it is normal for the remuneration report to be included in the same document. The auditors must state whether in their opinion the report has been prepared properly in their audit report (see Chapter 15). For companies, a signed copy of the report must also be filed with the Registrar of Companies, in the same way as the annual accounts, directors' report and auditors' report.

The remuneration committee should also be available at the annual general meeting to assist in answering any questions put to the board on any aspect of the remuneration report or generally on remuneration principles and practice.

Items to be included in the committee chair's statement include the key messages on remuneration, the context in which decisions were taken and any major changes during the year. This places the chair of the remuneration committee in the spotlight with regard to the organisation's approach to executive remuneration.

The remuneration policy must include an explanatory table, with detailed notes, setting out the approach taken to directors' remuneration in the period covered by the policy. This must be supplemented with a bar chart showing illustrative scenarios. It must also include a section on the approach to remuneration for new directors recruited to the board, as well as details of the policy on payments for loss of office. An explanation of the extent to which the views of employees' and shareholders have taken into account is also required.

The annual report then sets out how the remuneration policy was implemented in the previous financial year. A new requirement in this report is the obligation to include a single total figure for the remuneration of each director. The aim is to provide comprehensive disclosure on all types of remuneration – fixed and variable elements, as well as pension provision – in a consistent format. There is also a focus on including a breakdown of payments for loss of office. Any such payment, in addition to being included in the annual report, will also need to be published on the company's website 'as soon as practicable' after the payment has been agreed. These details will need to be kept available until the next annual report is published.

The NHS FT annual reporting manual (NHS FT ARM) and the NHS Finance Manual both require a similar report to be made in the organisation's annual report. This report should include all exit packages, including those paid to senior managers.

Governance Checklist

✓ Are the EDs aware of their wider role as a board member? Does their induction and on-going development support them in their board role?

✓ Does the CEO or chief officer enhance board effectiveness by ensuring high standards of board/committee reporting?

✓ Is there evidence of the CEO implementing board decisions and lead on delivering best practice in governance across the organisation?

✓ Is the DoF an effective partner with the CEO with the required professional and corporate experience to both support and challenge the CEO?

✓ Does the remuneration committee have the necessary skills for its role and is it sufficiently independent of the EDs?

✓ Is there evidence of the committee eliciting the appropriate professional advice as and when required?

✓ If remuneration consultants are retained, then has there been a robust rendering process to ensure their independence and objectivity?

✓ Has the committee determined a coherent policy on director's remuneration, which is regularly reviewed to ensure it remains 'fit for purpose' and in line with best practice?

✓ Does the committee apply the policy to its decisions, taking account of appropriate benchmarking information?

✓ Do the EDs' employment contracts address issues relating to rewards for failure on termination?

✓ Does the committee fulfil its responsibilities with regard to the reporting requirements on remuneration?

✓ Does the committee make itself available at the annual meeting or on other occasions for scrutiny and challenge by the shareholders/stakeholders?

■ Summary

The matter of executive remuneration will continue to be a contentious issue both in the corporate and public sector. The recent changes brought about by ERRA are now becoming apparent with the 2014 round of AGMs. Time will tell whether the proposals go far enough to address the governance issues that are raised in the corporate sector.

It is clear that the greater degree of regulation in the NHS, combined with the attitude of largely well-motivated public servants – including senior managers – is currently providing control and restraints on NHS ED remuneration. Public perception is unlikely to reflect this, however, and therefore boards and their remuneration committees will continue to have to balance the need to attract high calibre appointments, the morale of the wider workforce and the reputation of their organisation.

9

Non-executive directors

A non-executive director (NED) is a member of the board of directors without executive responsibilities in the organisation. NEDs should be able to bring judgement and experience to the deliberations of the board that the EDs on their own would lack.

To be effective, a NED has to understand the organisation's business, but there appears to be general consensus that the experience and qualities required of a NED can be obtained from working in other industries or in other aspects of commercial and public life. NEDs may therefore include individuals who:

- are EDs in other public companies
- hold NED positions and chair positions in other public companies
- have professional qualifications (e.g. partners in firms of solicitors)
- have experience in government, as politicians or former senior civil servants.

NEDs are expected not only to bring a wide range of skills and experience to the deliberations of the board, particularly in the area of strategy and business development, but also to ensure that there is a suitable balance of power on the board. A powerful chair or CEO might be able to dominate other EDs, but in theory at least, independent NEDs should be able to bring different views and independent thinking to board deliberations. Decisions taken by the board should therefore be better and more in keeping with the aims of good corporate governance.

> **CASE STUDY: The Bristol Royal Infirmary Enquiry**
> The Bristol Royal Infirmary Enquiry, July 2001 stated that:
>
> 'In our view, non-executive directors have a crucial role to play in representing the public interest in the conduct of the Trust's affairs. They must be people with a high level of ability and experience in the leadership and management of organisations ... they should have a commitment to public service.'
>
> Lessons for NEDs that resulted from the Bristol Enquiry were as follows:
>
> - Non-executive directors can be prevented from exerting their authority by 'not being let in on issues' at senior executive level.

- Lack of sound knowledge about trust activity can lead to an inability to challenge chief executives' or EDs' views.
- Role objectives may not be clarified and communicated. There was:
  - a variation in the roles played by non-executives on the board
  - variation in what was expected of non-executives
  - a lack of clarity and direction for the role.

The role and effectiveness of NEDs has been the subject of much scrutiny and challenge since the publication of the Higgs Report in 2003, with doubts being expressed at the level of balance they are able to bring to the board. The role of the NED was also considered as part of the 2009 Walker Review (2009), following the banking crisis. The review found firmly in favour of the NED role, stating that the NED contribution was materially helpful in financial institutions that had weathered the storm better than others.

In broad terms, the role of the NED, under the leadership of the chair is:

- to ensure that there is an effective executive team in place
- to participate actively in the decision-taking process of the board
- to exercise appropriate oversight over execution of the agreed strategy by the executive team.

■ The appointment, induction and evaluation of non-executive directors

The appointment of the chair and NEDs for NHS trusts is now overseen by the NHS TDA as set out in Chapter 6; FT chairs and NEDs are appointed by the council of governors (see Chapter 11). The appointment processes for CCGs are covered in Chapter 12. Even so, the best practice guidance set out below benchmarks best practice for those fulfilling the role of NED in all types of NHS organisation.

Induction for non-executive directors

The FRC *Guidance on Board Effectiveness* provides useful guidance on induction of NEDs.

'A NED should, on appointment, devote time to a comprehensive, formal and tailored induction that should extend beyond the boardroom. Initiatives such as partnering a NED with an executive board member may speed up the process of him or her acquiring an understanding of the main areas of business activity, especially areas involving significant risk. The director should expect to visit, and talk with, senior and middle managers in these areas.'

The chair is responsible for making sure that all NEDs have such a tailored induction programme, although in practice this is often undertaken and overseen by the company secretary. In the NHS, HFMA provides a structured induction for new chairs, NEDs and CCG lay members around key issues. It includes an introduction to NHS board roles, including sessions on structures, roles, patient safety and individual liabilities, and an introduction to their governance responsibilities, including risk assurance, financial obligations and the board role in delivering a safe and high-quality service.

Evaluation of non-executive directors

Both the Monitor Code and the UK Code state as a main principle that the board should undertake a 'formal and rigorous annual evaluation of its own performance and that of its committees and individual directors'.

The UK Code states that: 'Individual evaluation should aim to show whether each director continues to contribute effectively and to demonstrate commitment to the role (including commitment of time for board and committee meetings and any other duties).'

Chairs of NHS trusts are responsible for ensuring that NEDs receive performance appraisals at least annually. Trusts can determine the approach to appraisal that is most relevant to their own circumstances. An NHS TDA good practice guide to appraisal, as well as copies of the chair and non-executive role descriptions and competency frameworks, are also available to support an effective appraisal process.

NHS trusts should retain copies of NED appraisal forms, and share copies with those who have been appraised. This meets the requirement of Office of the Commissioner of Public Appointments that all performance reviews must be formally recorded or in the event of an investigation into a complaint. These copies may be needed to support future re-appointments, as evidence of poor performance The NHS TDA does not intend to collect NED appraisals routinely, but may request them as and when required.

The key board level competencies for a NED set out by the NHS TDA are:

- **Patient and community focus:** a high level of commitment to patients, carers and the community, and to tackling health inequalities in disadvantaged groups
- **Strategic direction:** the ability to think and plan ahead, to develop a clear vision and enthuse others, balancing needs and constraints
- **Holding to account:** the ability to accept accountability for board performance, and probe and challenge constructively
- **Effective influencing and communication:** a high level of ability to gain support and influence, political acumen
- **Team working:** be committed to working as a team member Self belief and drive – the motivation to improve NHS performance and confidence to take on challenges

- **Intellectual flexibility:** the ability think clearly and creatively, make sense of complexity and clarify it for other people
- **Application of standards of public life**: uphold the highest standards of conduct set out in *The Seven Principles of Public Life* (see Chapter 2).

Key questions for independent NED evaluation include the following.

- How many board meetings has the director attended, and how many times have they been absent?
- How well prepared has the individual been for meetings (e.g. have they read the relevant papers in advance)?
- What has been the quality of contributions of the individual to board meetings (e.g. on strategic development and risk management)?
- Has the individual shown independence of character, or have they tended to go along with the opinions of certain other board members?
- How many board committee meetings has the director attended and how many have they missed?
- What has the individual contributed to committee meetings?
- Has the time commitment of the director been sufficient? Has the time commitment been as much as expected, or as much as stated in the director terms of appointment?
- Does the NED continue to show interest in and enthusiasm for the organisation?
- Are there reasons why the director may no longer be considered independent?
- Does the director communicate well with the other directors and with senior executives of the organisation?

The performance evaluation of NEDs in FTs is carried out by the council of governors and is set out in more detail in Chapter 11. The performance evaluation of CCG GP members, lay members, secondary care and nurse members is carried out by the governing body: more details on this can be found in Chapter 12.

Non-executive directors and the UK Corporate Governance Code

The UK Code has largely incorporated the recommendations from the Higgs Report on the role and effectiveness of NEDs. Key among them are:

- NEDs should 'constructively challenge and help develop proposals on strategy'
- NEDs should also scrutinise the performance of management in meeting agreed goals or targets of performance, and they should monitor the reporting of performance (to ensure that this is honest and not misleading)
- NEDs should satisfy themselves about the integrity of the financial information produced by the organisation, and that the financial controls and systems of risk management are 'robust and defensible'

- they should be responsible for deciding the remuneration of EDs
- they should have a significant role in the appointment (and where necessary removal) of EDs and in succession planning for the major positions on the board.

The UK Code recognises there are matters that the NEDs should discuss without EDs being present, and a provision of the UK Code is that the chair should hold meetings with the NEDs without EDs being present. In addition, NEDs should meet at least once a year to discuss the performance of the chair, without the chair and led by the SID (see Chapter 7). They should also meet on other occasions if this is considered necessary or appropriate.

FRC Guidance on Board Effectiveness and the role of NEDs

The FRC *Guidance on Board Effectiveness* makes the following recommendations on the role of NEDs.

- A NED should, on appointment, devote time to a comprehensive, formal and tailored induction and should devote time to developing and refreshing their knowledge and skills.
- NEDs need to make sufficient time available to discharge their responsibilities effectively.
- Their letter of appointment should state the minimum time that the NED will be required to spend on the organisation's business, and indicate the possibility of additional time commitment when the organisation is undergoing a period of particularly increased activity, such as an acquisition or takeover, or as a result of some major difficulty with one or more of its operations.
- NEDs should insist on receiving high-quality information sufficiently in advance so that there can be thorough consideration of the issues prior to, and informed debate and challenge at, board meetings. High-quality information is that which is appropriate for making decisions on the issue at hand – it should be accurate, clear, comprehensive, up-to-date and timely; contain a summary of the contents of any paper; and inform the director of what is expected of them on that issue.

The Walker Report on the role of NEDS in banks

The Walker Report of (2009) suggested that the role of NEDs is crucial to the effectiveness of a board in formulating and implementing business strategy. The report included the following comments.

- Stakeholders have a right to expect that there should be a material input from the NEDs in a unitary board to decisions on strategy and oversight of strategy implementation. It should also be expected that when there is such shared decision-making between EDs and NEDs, the organisation should perform better in general and over time than if strategy were determined exclusively by the executive management. This expectation appeared to have been justified by the banking crisis in the US and Europe.

■ NEDs should provide a 'disciplined but rigorous challenge on substantive issues'. This should be seen as the norm, not an exception, and if any NED has insufficient strength of character to participate in providing a challenge, their continued suitability to remain as a board member should be thrown into question.

The Walker Report did add a note of caution on the extent NEDs should challenge the executive team, however:

'This does not, of course, mean open season for challenge to the executive team. Appropriate balance will only be achieved where the ED expects to be challenged, but where the board debate surrounding such challenge is conducted in a way that leaves the executive team with a sense of having drawn benefit from it.'

The 'inherent tension'

The Cadbury Report – published in 1992 – first raised the issue of the balance for the NED role between monitoring the performance of the executive team against the contribution to the strategic direction of the organisation.

In a heavily regulated sector like the NHS, this can be a particularly challenging balance to achieve. This was covered again in 1998's Hampel Report, which noted that though NEDs are normally appointed to the board primarily for their contribution to the development of the company's strategy, there was also a general acceptance that NEDs should have both a strategic and a monitoring function.

This dual role was supported by the Higgs Report, which recommended that the NED role should not be forced to decide between these two perspectives. For the NED role to be overly concerned with monitoring would be for the NED to take on 'an alien policing influence on the board' whereas being overly concerned with identifying the strategic direction could lead to the NED over-identifying with the executive team.

Keeping these two aspects of the role in 'tension' is what helps NEDs provide a valuable contribution. Though the FRC *Guidance on Board Effectiveness* has overtaken the Hampel and Higgs reports, these reports still offer helpful insights and demonstrate the balance between the role of monitoring and providing strategic direction very clearly. For example, Higgs listed the key elements of the NED role as follows.

■ **Strategy:** NEDs should constructively challenge and contribute to the development of strategy.
■ **Performance:** NEDs should scrutinise the performance of management in meeting agreed goals and objectives and monitor the reporting of performance.

- **Risk:** NEDs should satisfy themselves that financial information is accurate and that financial controls and systems of risk management are robust and defensible.
- **People:** NEDs are responsible for determining appropriate levels of remuneration of EDs and have a prime role in appointing, and where necessary removing, senior management and in succession planning.

Independence of non-executive directors

NEDs are either independent or non-independent. A NED is not independent if their opinions are likely to be influenced, in particular by the senior executive management of the organisation or by a major stakeholder. What follows is an exploration of the importance of independence and the criteria for making that judgment.

Though this applies directly to CCGs, NHS trusts and FTs alike, the implications are somewhat different for CCGs as they are essentially membership organisations. These are explored more fully in Chapter 12.

Independent NEDs are supposed to bring an independent view to the deliberations of the board. However, they are in a difficult position as they are legally liable in the same way as EDs. For example, they owe the same fiduciary duties to the organisation, as well as an obligation to exercise the duty of skill and care. As fellow directors, they might also be reluctant to blow the whistle on their executive colleagues. If they have been selected and appointed by the chair or the CEO, they will be less likely to ask tough questions about the way the organisation is being run.

The UK Code does not suggest that all NEDs should be independent. Non-independent NEDs are permissible, although the majority of the total board should consist of independent NEDs. If there are NEDs on the board who are not considered independent, this could create problems with the size and composition of the board. It may be considered necessary to appoint independent NEDs to act as a counterbalance to the NEDs who are not independent.

The Monitor Code states that:

'The board of directors should identify in the annual report each non-executive director it considers to be independent. The board should determine whether the director is independent in character and judgement and whether there are relationships or circumstances which are likely to affect, or could appear to affect, the director's judgement. The board of directors should state its reasons if it determines that a director is independent notwithstanding the existence of relationships or circumstances which may appear relevant to its determination.'

What is meant by 'independent'? It is easier to answer this question by specifying what is not independent. A NED is not independent if their opinions are likely to be influenced by someone else, in particular by the senior executive management or by a major stakeholder. The independence of an NED could be challenged, for example, if the individual concerned:

- has a family connection with the CEO – a problem in some family controlled public companies
- until recently used to be an ED in the organisation
- until recently used to work for the organisation in a professional capacity (e.g. as its auditor or corporate lawyer)
- receives payments from the organisation in addition to their fees as an NED.

A person cannot be independent if they personally stand to gain, or otherwise benefit, substantially from income from the organisation (in addition to their fee as a NED) or from the organisation's reported profitability and movements in its share price.

A NED cannot be properly independent if, for example, they accept a fee from the organisation for consultancy work. Consultancy involves the individual in the operational aspects of the organisation, and by implication puts them on the side of the executive team. Nor can an individual be independent if they have been awarded a large number of share options by the company. Holding share options gives the individual a direct interest in the share price of the company around the time the options can be exercised. They might therefore favour decisions that improve the reported profitability of the company in the short term, because good financial results are likely to be good for the share price.

Occasionally, NEDs are appointed to represent the opinions of a major stakeholder (e.g. the appointment of a NED from a related university or dental school in NHS teaching hospitals). In such cases, the individual can be expected to voice the wishes of the stakeholder, and so could not be regarded as independent.

To ensure that NEDs should not rely for their tenure in office on one or two individuals, the UK Code recommends that they should be selected through a formal process. Executive directors cannot be independent. Not only are they involved in the running of the organisation's operations and report (and are accountable) to the CEO for this aspect of their work, they also rely on the organisation for most (if not all) of their remuneration.

Criteria for judging independence

The UK Code, and as quoted above, the Monitor Code, both require the board to identify in the annual report each NED it considers to be independent. Although this is a matter for the board's judgement, both codes set out the circumstances in which independence would usually be questionable.

- The director has been an employee of the organisation within the last five years.
- The director has a material business relationship with the organisation (or has had such a relationship within the last three years). This relationship might

be as a partner, shareholder, director or employee in another organisation that has a material business relationship with the organisation.

4 ■ The director receives (or has received) additional remuneration from the organisation other than a director's fee, or is a member of the organisation's pension scheme, or participates in the organisation's share option scheme or a performance-related pay scheme.

5 ■ The director has close family ties with any of the organisation's advisers, directors or senior employees.

6 ■ The director has cross-directorships or has significant links with other directors through involvement in other companies or organisations. A cross-directorship exists when an individual is a NED on the board of Organisation X and an ED on the board of Organisation Y, when another individual is an ED of Organisation X and an NED on the board of Organisation Y.

X ■ The director represents a significant shareholder or stakeholder.

8 ■ The director has served on the board for more than nine years since the date of his first election (six in the case of FTs).

These criteria of independence should be applied to the chair (on appointment) as well as other NEDs. Circumstances may change, and the independence of NEDs should be kept under review.

Independence of serving directors time ——> ↓ independence

There is a general view that the independence of a NED is likely to diminish over time as the NED becomes more familiar with the organisation and executive colleagues. The risk is that the NED will take more of the views of executive colleagues on trust and will be less rigorous in their questioning. This is noted in the UK Code, the King III Code and the Monitor Code.

There will be circumstances where NEDs, having served their full terms, may exceptionally remain on the board. Indeed, the UK Code is pragmatic in its approach to the nine-year rule. If the board considers that a director is still independent even after nine years' service, he may still be considered 'independent' for the purposes of the corporate governance provisions.

The Monitor Code takes a similar approach, although restricting the length of tenure to six years, stating that:

'Any term beyond six years (e.g. two three-year terms) for a NED should be subject to particularly rigorous review, and should take into account the need for progressive refreshing of the board. NEDs may in exceptional circumstances serve longer than six years (e.g. two three-year terms following authorisation of the NHS FT), but subject to annual re-appointment. Serving more than six years could be relevant to the determination of a NED's independence.'

■ Barriers to being an effective NED

There are differing views about the effectiveness of NEDs. The <u>accepted view is</u> <u>that NEDs bring experience and judgement to the deliberations of the board that</u> +
<u>EDs on their own would lack.</u>

An alternative view is that the effectiveness of NEDs can be undermined by —
<u>lack of knowledge about the business operations of the organisation, insufficient</u>
<u>time spent with the organisation, the weight of opinion of the EDs on the board</u>
<u>and that NED involvement leads to delays in decision-making.</u>

(1) Insufficient knowledge

The quality of decision-making depends largely on the quality of information available to the decision-maker. The UK Code states that the board as a whole should be 'supplied in a timely manner with information in a form and of a quality appropriate to enable it to discharge its duties'. However, the senior executives in an organisation control the information systems, and so control the flow of information to the board. It is quite conceivable, for example, that the CEO and other EDs might have access to management information that is withheld from the board as a whole, or that is presented to the board in a distorted manner. Lacking the 'insider knowledge' of EDs about the business operations, and having to rely on the integrity of the information supplied to them by management and the EDs, restricts the scope for NEDs to make a meaningful contribution to board decisions.

(2) Insufficient time

NEDs often have executive positions in other companies and organisations, where most of their working time is spent. As a general rule, NEDs do not have an office at the organisation headquarters and may spend at most two to three days per month on the organisation's business. A further criticism of NEDs is that some individuals hold too many NED positions, with the result that they cannot possibly give sufficient time to any of the organisations concerned. It could be argued, for example, that an individual cannot be an effective NED of an organisation if they are also the CEO of another public organisation and hold four or five other NED positions in other organisations.

The UK Code states that all directors should be able to allocate sufficient time to the organisation to discharge their responsibilities effectively. Although this principle of the code applies to all directors, the main concern is with NEDs (since EDs are usually full-time employees) and in particular the chair. The UK Code requires that when a chair or NED is appointed, the nomination committee should prepare a job specification that includes an assessment of the expected time commitment and in particular for the chair, recognising the need to be available to the organisation in times of crisis. When a NED or a new chair is appointed, the letter of appointment should set out the expected time commitment. In addition the Code requires all new chair or NED appointments to disclose any other significant commitments they already have.

Overriding influence of executive directors

Yet another criticism of NEDs is that if a difference of opinion arises during a meeting of the board, the opinions of the EDs are likely to carry greater weight, because they know more about the organisation. NEDs may be put under pressure to accept the views of their ED colleagues. This potential problem provides an argument for the role of a strong SID, to ensure that the opinions of the independent NEDs are properly considered.

Delays in decision-making

It may be argued that NEDs delay decision-making within an organisation. Major decisions should be reserved for the board; therefore, to implement an important new strategy initiative it may be necessary to call a board meeting. The time required to hold the meeting, giving the NEDs sufficient time to reach a well-informed opinion about the matter, may delay the implementation of the proposed strategy. It has also been argued that NEDs may be conservative in outlook, whereas the board of directors needs to be 'entrepreneurial'.

One counter-argument is that when a major new strategy or initiative is proposed, it should be given full and careful consideration before a decision is made. NEDs, with their range of skills and experience, can contribute positively to this decision-making process.

■ The effectiveness of non-executive directors

The Higgs Report of 2003 is helpful in identifying the behaviours and attitudes that will make for an effective NED.

'Non-executive directors should constantly seek to establish and maintain confidence in the conduct of the company. They should be independent in judgement and have an enquiring mind. To be effective, non-executive directors need to build a recognition by executives of their contribution in order to promote openness and trust. To be effective, non-executive directors need to be well-informed about the company and the external environment in which it operates, with a strong command of issues relevant to the business. A non-executive director should insist on a comprehensive, formal and tailored induction. An effective induction need not be restricted to the boardroom, so consideration should be given to visiting sites and meeting senior and middle management. Once in post, an effective non-executive director should seek continually to develop and refresh their knowledge and skills to ensure that their contribution to the board remains informed and relevant.'

Another aspect to the effectiveness of the NEDs is to ensure that there is a <u>diversity of background and experience</u>. This encourages a diverse range of views to be expressed in consideration of proposals being brought to the board. Being less closely involved in the day-to day running of the organisation enables NEDs to bring a <u>fresh perspective to the discussion</u> – highlighting shareholder/stakeholder concerns is a vital role that NEDs can play. This supports the board in avoiding the 'group-think' tendencies that can develop in any group that works closely together.

The rigour that the NEDs bring to the independent scrutiny and challenge of board decisions is equally important; it is therefore essential that NEDs have the necessary people skills. Exercising influence rather than a 'command and control' role requires very particular interpersonal skills of diplomacy and persuasion.

The Walker Review highlighted that NEDs sitting on the boards of highly complex businesses needed to ensure that they had the right mix of industry-specific experience as well as a diverse range of other backgrounds to ensure there was an external critique of the business being considered. It further recognised that:

> 'Even where the NED composition on the board is well balanced between financial industry experience and deep experience from elsewhere, the effectiveness of the overall NED contribution will be enhanced by a combination of appropriate induction and, thereafter, regular training programmes, adapted to the needs of the individual director; and dependable access for NEDs to support from within the company, for example from a dedicated capability in the company secretariat and greater time commitment.'

■ Non-executive director remuneration

<u>The level of remuneration appropriate for any particular NED role should reflect the likely workload, the scale and complexity of the business and the responsibility involved.</u>

Where a NED has extra responsibilities (such as membership or chairship of board committees), the total remuneration should reflect these. The Higgs Report recommended that NED fees should be clearly built up using an annual fee, meeting attendance fees (to include board committee meetings) and an additional fee for the chairship of committees (typically a multiple of the attendance fee) or role as senior independent director. In addition, organisations should expect to pay <u>additional reasonable expenses in addition to the director's fee to cover related costs incurred by their NEDs</u> (such as travel and administrative costs). Any significant support of this kind should be agreed in advance.

The principle that individuals should not decide their own remuneration applies to NEDs as well as to EDs. This means that a remuneration committee should not decide the fees of the NEDs. In the corporate sector, deciding the remuneration of the NEDs should be the responsibility of the chair and the EDs (or the shareholders if required by the articles of association). Where permitted by the articles, the board may delegate this responsibility to a committee which might include the CEO. A provision in the UK Code is that the level of remuneration for NEDs should reflect the time commitment and responsibilities of the role.

NEDs are not employees. They receive a fee for their services, not a salary. In the UK corporate sector, it is usual for NEDs to receive a fixed annual fee, typically in the region of £20,000 to £60,000 (or possibly more), for attending board meetings, some committee meetings and general meetings of the company. This is substantially less in the health service sector, although the annual NED fees are increasing in larger FTs.

CASE STUDY: Royal Free London NHS Foundation Trust

The Royal Free London NHS Foundation Trust established a set of principles to support the council of governors in setting the remuneration element of non-executive terms and conditions. These were as follows:

- **Competitive:** NED remuneration should be competitive with comparable trusts on a comparative workload basis/the trust should be able to attract at least as good NEDs as other comparable trusts.
- **Value for money:** the total cost of the non-executive team should be demonstrably good value for taxpayers' money in comparison to comparable trusts.
- **Aligned with role:** the remuneration structure should be appropriate to the role of the NEDs in independently holding the executive team to account.
- **Effective team working:** the structure of remuneration for non-executives should encourage behaviour which leads to effective team working.

The 2012 FTN Remuneration Survey of Chairs and NEDs revealed annual NED remuneration in FTs ranging from £6,000 to £18,000. The range for FT chairs was from £15,782 to £64,678. The difference in fees is tied to the size of trust turnover or number of staff in the trust, as these are usually the indicators used to benchmark individual trusts when assessing the level of non-executive fees.

The remuneration for chairs and NEDs in NHS trusts is set by the Secretary of State and overseen by the NHS TDA. In FTs, the council of governors decides their remuneration. This provides the same protection as in the corporate sector, preventing individuals do not set their own remuneration. However, in CCGs the fees for GP members, lay members, secondary care and nurse members are set by the CCG itself. The CCG remuneration committee therefore needs to set clear parameters to ensure that individuals are not allowed to participate in decisions about their own fees. This is explored further in Chapter 12.

In the corporate sector, NEDs may receive other forms of remuneration or reward from the organisation alongside the basic fee (such as payment for additional services); however, this can raise questions about their independence. For example, a NED might be paid additionally as a 'consultant' to the company. No matter how genuine and useful these consultancy services are, they put his independence at risk because executive management decides the size of a consultancy fee. Management also decides whether to extend or renew a consultancy agreement. This kind of arrangement is very unusual in the NHS.

The UK Code makes specific provisions about performance-related rewards for NEDs, including the award of share options to NEDs.

■ As a general rule, the remuneration of NEDs should not include share options or any other performance-related reward.

■ In exceptional cases, share options may be granted. However, the approval of the shareholders should be obtained in advance, and if the NED subsequently exercises options to acquire shares in the company, these shares should be held until at least one year after the NED leaves the board.

■ Holding share options could affect the determination of whether or not the NED is independent.

Resignation

Some of those who responded to the consultation for the Higgs Report described the resignation of a NED as being the ultimate sanction at their disposal. Higgs believed that resignation should be regarded very much as a last resort once other efforts to resolve problems have failed. Indeed, NEDs may be constrained from resigning by their fiduciary duty to act in the organisation's best interests. Where NEDs have real concerns about the way in which an organisation is being run or about a course of action proposed by the board, the first step should be to raise their concerns with the chair and their fellow directors. NEDs should, as a matter of course, ensure that their concerns are recorded in the minutes of the board meeting if they cannot be resolved.

If the NED feels that resignation is the only course of action left, a written statement should be provided to the chair, for circulation to the board, setting out the reasons for resignation. Higgs also recommended that a NED should explain their reasons for resigning when they leave in other circumstances.

Governance Checklist

✓ Do the NEDs contribute to the strategic direction of the organisation, the performance of management, review the risk management system and both appoint and set the remuneration of the EDs?

✓ Are the NEDs provided with timely and sufficient information and resources to fulfil their role?

✓ Do the NEDs have the right attributes, skills and diversity of experience to provide sufficient and credible challenge to board debate and discussion? Do they have the intellectual capacity to test management proposals and the right influencing skills to suggest alternatives where appropriate?

✓ Are at least half of the board members judged to be independent, taking account of the criteria in the UK code?

✓ Do the NEDS have clear terms of appointment in writing, which include independence, time commitment, duties, and fees?

✓ Is there a comprehensive and formal induction programme on appointment tailored to the needs of the individual?

✓ Is there ongoing development for each NED based on the findings of the annual evaluation process?

✓ Do the NEDs give sufficient commitment to such development activities and acknowledge the value of engaging in them?

■ Summary

The role of the NED is a vital link in the chain of governance and a key part of the principle of the unitary board. In balancing the tension between monitoring and setting strategy, the NED acts as an important check and balance to the power and authority of the executive team. It is important for the board to understand the nature of the role and for the chair to develop a good working relationship between the NEDs and the EDs on the board. Clarity as to the independence of each individual NED will provide a robust framework in which to manage any potential conflicts of interest that might arise.

10

The company secretary

'All directors should have access to the advice and services of the company secretary, who is responsible to the board for ensuring that board procedures are complied with.' (UK Code)

With the spotlight firmly fixed on corporate governance issues in the banking sector in recent times, the profile of the company secretary has been increasing. The All Party Parliamentary Corporate Governance Group commissioned research into the role, and their report in May 2012, *Elevating the Role of the Company Secretary*, highlighted the important role that the company secretary can play in ensuring effective corporate governance. The report recognised that *issues* there was a potential for the administrative duties laid on the company secretary to undermine the potential to be seen as a high-level adviser to the board; this was also affected by the use of the term 'secretary' in the title, with a common suggestion that an alternative of corporate governance director be used.

A recurring theme of the review was the unique position of the company secretary as the interface between the board and management. The review considered that this could be developed further, so that the company secretary could coach management to help them understand the expectations of, and value brought by, the board. Interestingly, the review went on to consider that company secretaries might make good NEDs due to their insights from observing and advising a number of boards during their career.

The role of the company secretary is less developed within the NHS. Therefore, this chapter will outline the role within the corporate sector to give a richer and more diverse picture of the role, before looking at its development within the NHS.

■ The skills and knowledge required to be a company secretary   FOR PRIVATE SECTOR

Research by Henley Business School in conjunction with ICSA (November 2014) identified three broad areas of skills and knowledge required by a company secretary:

1 ■ technical expertise
2 ■ commercial and business acumen
3 ■ social skills and emotional intelligence.

Company secretaries need technical expertise in law, governance codes and an understanding of financial issues. They need commercial experience in decision-making, problem-solving, analytical skills, attention to detail and ability to get things done properly. Finally, but just as importantly, they need interpersonal skills and relationship management skills including judgement, diplomacy, tact and discretion – along with adaptability and patience.

Company secretaries also need to be incredibly resilient, as without the authority of a board member position they need to be able to challenge and remain independent of the individual board members while at the same time building good working relationships. Anecdotally, it was once said that the best person to take on the role is someone who has already retired or who is not dependent upon their monthly salary from the organisation, as they can then challenge the chair or CEO when required, without fear of jeopardising their career.

Before setting out specific responsibilities of the company secretary, it is important to note that the most effective company secretary is:

- regarded by the board as its trusted adviser
- can be seen as the board's chief of staff
- who wins the confidence of and acts as a confidential sounding board to the chair and other directors on issues of concern.

They provide, where appropriate, a discreet but challenging voice in relation to board deliberations and decision-making, drawing in particular on their professional experience and historical knowledge of the organisation. They also keep under review legislative, regulatory and governance developments that may impact the organisation and ensures that the board is appropriately briefed on them.

■ The company secretary as an officer of the company

The secretary of a public limited company must be appropriately qualified. Under section 273 of the Companies Act 2006, the board must be satisfied that the secretary has the 'requisite knowledge and experience to discharge the functions of the secretary of the company'. In addition, the Companies Act states they must meet one or more of the following qualifications:

- be a member of any of the following bodies: the Institute of Chartered Secretaries and Administrators; the Institute of Chartered Accountants in England and Wales; the Institute of Chartered Accountants of Scotland; Association of Chartered Certified Accountants; the Institute of Chartered Accountants in Ireland; the Chartered Institute of Management Accountants; or the Chartered Institute of Public Finance and Accounting;
- have held the office of company secretary of a public company for at least three out of the five years immediately before their appointment as secretary;

- be a barrister, advocate or solicitor called or admitted in any part of the UK; or
- be a person who appears to the directors to be capable of carrying out the functions of company secretary, because that person holds or has held a similar position in another body or is or was a member of another body.

This contrasts significantly with the lack of any statutory qualification requirements for a company director. The appointment of a company secretary has to be notified to the registrar of companies, including confirmation of the person's consent to be appointed.

However, like the director, the company secretary is an officer of the company and such owes fiduciary duties to the company and its shareholders. These duties include acting in good faith in the best interests of the company, avoiding conflicts of interest and not making secret profits from dealings for or on behalf of the company.

The Companies Act imposes numerous obligations on companies regarding the conduct of their affairs. Most of these requirements are backed up by criminal sanctions so that, in the event of a breach, the company and every officer of it who is in default is liable to a fine and, in some cases, imprisonment. As an officer of the company, the company secretary can be prosecuted for these offences. For example, if the company becomes insolvent, the company secretary may also become liable under the Insolvency Act 1986, which allows an action in damages against any officer of a company for a misfeasance or breach of trust. Responsibility for ensuring compliance with these matters ultimately rests with the directors. However, by making the company secretary liable as an officer, the Act not only recognises that the directors usually rely on the company secretary in this regard, but also provides a strong indication that they should give the company secretary responsibility for (or an involvement in) these matters.

It is clear that, in view of their potential liabilities, the company secretary should not close their eyes to cases of non-compliance even if the directors have purported to make someone else responsible for those matters. At the very least, the company secretary should draw such cases to the attention of the directors and advise on the company's duties and obligations. The company secretary should be in a position to act independently and not be restricted by their reporting line within the company. The company secretary should also ensure that where certain of their responsibilities have been delegated, such tasks are properly executed, since they can still be held accountable in law for any failure by the company to comply.

■ The responsibilities of the company secretary

Whatever the type of organisation, company secretaries are in a unique position to fulfil an important role in governance. They are not members of the board of directors, and so do not have direct responsibility for governance and accountability to stakeholders. Without being a director, they know about what is taking place at board level in the organisation and can give advice and assistance – not only to the chair, but also to the board as a whole, board committees and individual directors.

Good governance relies on communication and the exchange of information, and the company secretary is able to help ensure that this happens. By attending board meetings and committee meetings, they should ensure that relevant information is passed from board to committee or from one committee to the board or another committee. By acting as a point of communication and contact for NEDs, the company secretary should also be able to contribute to the flows of information between NEDs and senior executive managers in the company. The company secretary should have a full understanding of governance requirements, and should be able to identify governance issues that arise and advise the board accordingly:

'The company secretary should be responsible for advising the board through the chair on all governance matters.' (UK Code)

The specific responsibilities of a company secretary for governance matters should be decided by the organisation. The ICSA guidance note *The Corporate Governance Role of the Company Secretary* (2008) provides a list of responsibilities relating to corporate governance divided into the following areas.

Specific responsibilities derived from the UK Code

Board composition and procedures:

- establishing a formal schedule of matters reserved for decision by the board and a formal division of responsibilities between the chair and CEO
- scheduling board meetings, assisting with the preparation of agendas, providing guidance on board paper content, ensuring good and timely information flows within the board and its committees and between senior management and NEDs; recording board decisions clearly and accurately, pursuing follow-up actions and reporting on matters arising
- ensuring that appropriate insurance cover is arranged in respect of any potential legal action against directors
- ensuring board committees are constituted in compliance with the UK Code and that the committees have the appropriate balance of skills, experience, independence and knowledge of the company
- supporting the board and nominations committee on board succession planning and on the process for the appointment of new directors to the board.

Board information, development and relationships:

- planning and organising director induction programmes which provide a full, formal and tailored introduction to the board and the business
- planning and organising director professional development programmes to refresh the directors' skills and knowledge

- arranging for major shareholders to be offered the opportunity to meet new directors;
- facilitating good information flows between board members, the committees and senior management as well as fostering effective working between executives and NEDs
- establishing and communicating procedures for directors to take independent professional advice at the company's expense if required
- developing a proactive relationship with board members, providing a source of information and advice, and acting as the primary point of contact with NEDs
- supporting the process for the board to undertake formal annual evaluation of its own performance and that of its committees and individual directors.

Financial and business reporting:

- having a detailed knowledge of, and advising on, the board's responsibility to present a fair, balanced and understandable assessment of the company's position and prospects in annual and interim reports plus other price-sensitive public reports and reports to regulators and that information required under statute. The company secretary should also ensure that the requirements of the FCA's Listing, Prospectus, and Disclosure and Transparency Rules (LPDT Rules) are met and be aware of the guidance available on these areas.

Risk management and internal control:

- assisting the board in an annual review of the effectiveness of the company's risk management and internal control systems including financial, operational and compliance controls.

Audit committee and auditors:

- ensuring that the audit committee is fully conversant with the UK Code principles around corporate reporting, risk management and internal control principles. This should include the relationship with the external auditors, in particular as regards audit quality, provisions of non-audit services, recommendations for appointment and renewal of auditors and putting the audit contract out to tender
- ensuring the implementation of and monitoring the effectiveness of the procedure for staff to raise concerns about possible improprieties in matters of financial reporting or other matters.

Remuneration:

- ensuring that the remuneration committee is familiar with the UK Code principles and provisions on remuneration, including the provisions on the design of performance-related remuneration for EDs set out in Schedule A of the UK Code
- ensuring that grants of share options and other long-term incentive awards do not contravene the UK Code

- ensuring that the provisions in the directors' term of appointment in relation to early termination are in accordance with the UK Code
- ensuring that non-executive remuneration is determined in line with UK Code provisions and within the limits set by the articles of association
- ensuring that all new long-term incentive schemes and significant changes to existing schemes are submitted to shareholders for approval, in accordance with the Listing Rules
- ensuring compliance with the legal requirements in relation to directors' remuneration, including any necessary shareholder approvals, contributing to the drafting of the directors' remuneration report and ensuring its compliance with the full range of disclosure requirements.

Relationship with shareholders:
- ensuring the board keeps in touch with shareholder opinion on a continuing basis
- managing relations with institutional investors on corporate governance issues and board procedures in accordance with the principles established in the UK Stewardship Code
- managing the convening and conduct of the AGM in line with statutory and regulatory requirements and the UK Code, and using it as an opportunity to communicate with retail investors.

Disclosure and reporting:
- ensuring that the necessary disclosures on corporate governance and the workings of the board and its committees are included in the annual report. All companies with a premium listing of equity shares in the UK are required under the Listing Rules to report how they have applied the UK Code in the annual report and accounts
- ensuring that the requisite types of governance information are made available, as required (e.g. on the company's website).

The FRC *Guidance on Board Effectiveness* emphasises the role of the company secretary in supporting the board in the areas of director induction and development, as well as the delivery of high-quality information to the board and its committees. It states that the chair, directors and the company secretary who, together, set the agenda for the board's deliberations.

Responsibilities for statutory and regulatory compliance

Compliance with laws and regulations is a requirement of good governance. The company secretary is responsible for implementing procedures to help directors discharge their statutory duties as codified in the Companies Act 2006, in particular their specific duties to promote the success of the company, taking account of a wide range of stakeholder interests and to avoid conflicts of interest. Guidance on these particular duties is available in the ICSA guidance note *Directors' General Duties*.

The company secretary should be responsible for ensuring compliance with all the statutory and regulatory requirements relating to governance. For health service governance, these include the key pieces of NHS legislation and voluntary codes outlined in Chapter 3. For UK corporate governance, these include the requirements of the Companies Act 2006, and the FCA's Listing Rules, Prospectus Rules and Disclosure and Transparency Rules of the

The company secretary should also be responsible for ensuring proper disclosure of information. For example, these include quarterly disclosures to Monitor for FTs. In the case of companies, this includes the dissemination of regulatory news announcements to the stock market, such as trading statements and information about share dealings by directors.

The company secretary should also keep under review all legal and regulatory developments affecting the organisation's operations, and making sure that the directors are properly briefed about them.

In addition, in corporate governance, the Listing Rules require companies to comply with the Model Code, which sets out rules about when directors should not usually be permitted to buy or sell shares in the company. For example, directors should not deal in the company's shares during 'close periods' before an announcement of their financial results. The company secretary is responsible for making sure that directors understand the requirements of the Model Code and comply with them.

Corporate social responsibility (CSR)

The ICSA Guidelines refer to guidelines on CSR published by the ABI and NAPF on how to incorporate environmental, social and governance issues into investment decision-making. The ICSA Guidelines state that:

> '[T]he company secretary should share responsibility with relevant specialist functions for ensuring that the board is aware of current guidelines in this area and that it identifies and takes account of the significance of corporate responsibility issues in its stewardship and oversight of the company.'

The company secretary should therefore try to ensure that the interests of all important stakeholders are remembered when important business decisions are made, particularly those affecting employees.

■ Additional duties of the company secretary

In addition to the core duties above, the duties that the company secretary commonly undertakes in areas such as legal, accounting, financial services, personnel and HR, property, risk management, estates and facilities, pensions and insurance management must also be considered. Though these are not seen as core duties, these duties will frequently take up a substantial proportion of the company secretary's time and their importance should not be underestimated.

The professional background, previous work experience and general personal capabilities of the company secretary will generally dictate the nature and scope of these additional responsibilities as will the nature of the company's business activities. For example, a lawyer is more likely to specialise in litigation and an accountant is more likely to manage a treasury function. A Chartered Secretary, being specifically trained for the role, is more likely to take on additional responsibilities such as property management, pensions and insurance matters.

■ The conscience of the company

In the context of business ethics and governance, the company secretary can be described as the 'conscience of the organisation'. There will often be situations where it is in the best short-term interests of an organisation to ignore best governance practice or even act in an unethical way. For example, the board of directors may want to 'window dress' the financial statements and make the performance of the organisation appear better than it really is, or an organisation may wish to bribe a government official in order to win a major contract.

The company secretary should speak out against bad governance and unethical practice, and remind the board and senior executives of the appropriate course of conduct and the principles of good governance that they should apply.

In order to act in this way, as a 'conscience' for the directors and senior executives, the company secretary must be independent-minded, and should not be under the influence of any other individual, such as the chair or CEO.

The independence of the company secretary

The role of the company secretary in governance is such that it is essential to ensure his or her independence from undue influence and pressure from a senior board member. An ICSA guidance note, *Reporting Lines for the Company Secretary*, comments:

> The company secretary is a key member of the executive team appointed by the board of directors as an officer of the company with specific responsibility to the entity as a whole for its sound corporate governance and for the guidance of the board in its responsible and effective execution of its tasks. Boards of directors have a right to expect the company secretary to give impartial advice and to act in the best interests of the company. However, it is incumbent on boards of directors to ensure that company secretaries are in a position to do so, for example by ensuring that they are not subject to undue influence of one or more of the board of directors. If the board fails to protect the integrity of the company secretary's position, one of the most effective in-built internal controls available to the company is likely to be seriously undermined. The establishment of

appropriate reporting lines for the company secretary will normally be a crucial factor in establishing that protection. It will also be important for NEDs to have access to the advice and services of the company secretary and for them to support the company secretary in his or her role.'

It is neither practical nor desirable in terms of line management for the company secretary to report on a day-to-day basis to all the directors. However, it is important not to lose sight of the ultimate line of authority when establishing these reporting lines. The company secretary is responsible to the board of directors collectively rather than to any individual director. The UK Code reinforces this by stating: 'both the appointment and removal of the company secretary should be a matter for the board as a whole'.

The ICSA *Guidance on the Appointment of the Company Secretary* (November 2014) recommends that the company secretary is responsible to the board, and should be accountable to the board through the chair on all matters relating to corporate governance and their duties as an officer of the company (core duties). As the person elected by the directors to act as their leader, the chair is the person to whom the company secretary should report with respect to responsibilities which concern the whole board.

If, in addition to the core duties mentioned above, the company secretary has other executive or administrative duties, they should report to the chief executive or such other director to whom responsibility for that matter has been delegated by the board. The company secretary should not report to a director (except the chair) on any matter unless responsibility for that matter has been delegated to that director by the board.

A director who is authorised unilaterally to fix the company secretary's remuneration and benefits could gain undue influence. It is therefore recommended (particularly where the company secretary reports to the chair on all matters) that decisions on remuneration and benefits should be taken (or at least noted) by the board as a whole, or by the remuneration committee of the board on the recommendation of the chair or CEO. In this way, the company secretary is not dependent on one individual, or a small group of board members, for their role or remuneration. Where the company secretary has an additional reporting line to the chief executive or other director, the views of that director can be taken into account by the board or board remuneration committee when decisions are taken on the remuneration and benefits of the company secretary.

Similar recommended practice is included in King III, which states that the board should appoint and remove the company secretary and empower the individual to enable them to fulfil their duties properly. It also recommends that the company secretary should have an 'arm's-length relationship' with the board, emphasising the requirement for independence.

Departures from these guidelines will reduce the ability of the company secretary to perform their core duties in accordance with the standards, which boards of directors should expect.

■ The company secretary and the in-house lawyer

Many of the governance duties of a company secretary have a legal aspect or involve compliance with regulations or a voluntary code of governance practice. It could be argued that an in-house lawyer working for the organisation could perform many of these tasks better, since corporate lawyers are specialists in company law and regulations,. However, as stated previously, independence is a critical aspect of the governance role of the company secretary; to perform the task effectively, the company secretary needs to be as independent as it is possible for a full-time employee to be.

In their legal work, an in-house lawyer must at times consider the specific interests of the organisation and individual directors, and may be required to advise them on the most appropriate way of dealing with legal issues that arise. In performing this role, the lawyer will often have to 'take sides' to represent a particular interest. This would be inconsistent with the requirement to be independent when advising on governance issues.

It would therefore be inappropriate for the organisation's in-house lawyers to take on the governance that are usually given to the company secretary. An individual who has trained and qualified as a professional lawyer could be a suitable candidate to act as company secretary or take on governance responsibilities within the organisation, but only if two key conditions are applied:

- the qualified lawyer does no legal work for the organisation, and also
- the independence of the individual can be protected in the same way as for a company secretary, with the board as a whole responsible for appointing and dismissing them and deciding their remuneration.

Appointing a lawyer may increase the company secretary's responsibility and may make them responsible for some of the legal judgments, which is fundamentally not a company secretary role.

■ The development of company secretaries in the NHS

The *Integrated Governance Handbook* attempted to establish an equivalent role within the NHS and the authors had discussions with a number of FTSE 100 companies to look at the role of the company secretary, exploring, more importantly, whether these companies could exist without such an adviser. The evidence clearly pointed to the need for such integrated corporate support.

Foundation trusts began to establish such a role in their corporate structures and guidance was included in the Monitor Code. The significance of the role is to ensure that, for the first time in the history of NHS boards, the board *per se* can confidently assure itself that at the end of the 12-month cycle it has full evidence and is fully appraised before signing off the Annual Governance Statement. The *Integrated Governance Handbook* also clarifies the point by stating that it is not necessary for the company secretary to be either an accountant or a lawyer.

The difficulty in establishing the role within the NHS has been the misapprehension that the role is purely a minute-taking and administrative role which traditionally had been undertaken by the senior personal assistant with the organisation. The other common misapprehension has been that this is a role to be undertaken by the Director of Corporate Affairs, which although they were often responsible for engagement with stakeholders and the annual disclosure and reporting functions, the role did not fully encompass the corporate governance and board advisory role.

There has also been some difficulty with the terminology for the role as the use of the word 'company' in the job title clashes with the public sector NHS. Accordingly, the role is sometimes referred to as board secretary, trust secretary or assistant to the board. There has also been some difficulty with establishing the board-level nature of the role through the AfC job evaluation panels as the use of the word 'secretary' has also imbued the role with too much of an administrative flavour. As a result some posts are advertised on AfC pay bands, while others are advertised as VSM roles.

The creation of the lead governor role in FTs in 2011 demonstrates the limited understanding of the role of the company secretary and also possibly the SID. The lead governor role will be covered in more detail in Chapter 11 but, suffice to say, Monitor already had a direct line of contact with the council of governors through the company secretary and the SID for those situations where it would be inappropriate for Monitor to contact the chair, or vice versa,.

As can be seen by the more extensive and wide-ranging role within the corporate sector that establishes the role as part of the executive team, there is significant scope within NHS organisations to adopt a similar board level role. A number of NHS trusts and FTs have recently established a board level role of director of governance, which has encompassed the role of company secretary. The caveat to this arrangement that the independence of the role must be maintained within a direct line of report to the chair for on all matters relating to corporate governance and their duties as an officer of the company. In addition, the appointment and removal of the company secretary should remain a matter for the board as a whole, not just the CEO as the line manager of the executive function carried out by the director of governance. The Monitor Code departs from this slightly by requiring the appointment and removal of the company secretary to be a joint matter for the chief executive and chair.

The other challenge for NHS organisations is to be clear where the boundaries lie between corporate governance and clinical governance. This too can create tensions for the role of the company secretary. The *Integrated Governance Handbook* helpfully set out the following points to establish the independence of the company secretary.

- The remuneration committee, as opposed to either the chair or the CEO, appoints the company secretary in order to ensure the neutrality of role.

- The company secretary is answerable to the board but will be line managed by the CEO in order to ensure personal development and accountability.
- The company secretary will also work closely with the chair, the CEO and the NEDs.
- The company secretary will be actively involved in or be a member of the executive team to ensure a full understanding of the organisation's business.
- The company secretary will not undertake executive activity in respect of having a specific role, but will be the neutral observer and adviser to the board or executive team.
- An NHS-based company secretary should have sufficient knowledge of the NHS to gain the respect of the doctors in the organisation but need not necessarily be a clinician.
- The company secretary should be appropriately qualified to carry out their role and should ideally be accredited by a professional body such as ICSA.

While current legislation does not specify the need for CCGs to appoint a company secretary, good practice from the corporate sector and experience in FTs suggests that this is also a key role in the governance of an organisation. The company secretary could play a leading role in governance, supporting the chair as well as helping the governing body and committees to function effectively. They could also have a key role in ensuring good communication between the governing body, senior management and committees and helping to ensure compliance with legislation and regulations. It has been interesting to observe the profile of the company secretarial role in the new governing bodies which have been established. In many cases, although a corporate secretary or head of corporate services seems to be in post, further research needs to be carried out to see whether these appointments are in line with the best practice set out here.

ICSA has worked alongside the NHS to produce a sample job description outlining the responsibilities of a FT secretary, set out below.

Core duties of an NHS foundation trust secretary

The following list includes both those duties which are legal obligations as well as those which result from best practice. This is not a comprehensive list and the trust secretary will also need to refer to other pertinent legislation and regulation.

Board meetings – directors and governors:
- facilitating the smooth operation of the FT's formal decision-making and reporting machinery
- organising board of directors and council of governors meetings along with those of their committees (e.g. audit, remuneration, nomination committees etc)
- ensuring that there is proper and appropriate co-ordination of boards and committees and an effective flow of information

- formulating meeting agendas with the chair (and CEO) and advising management on content and organisation of memoranda or presentations for the meeting
- collecting, organising and distributing such information, documents or other papers for meetings
- ensuring that all meetings are minuted and that the minute books are maintained with certified copies of the minutes; and that action is taken on matters arising
- communicating board decisions to those required to implement them and ensure that actions and tasks assigned are managed appropriately and to the required timetable, reporting back as required
- ensuring that the board of directors and council of governors meetings and all board committees are properly constituted and provided with clear reference, and
- managing the FT HQ secretariat ensuring the effective running of the board's support system including the production of board and committee papers.

(2)Annual members' meetings:

- ensuring that an annual members' meeting is held in accordance with the requirements of the National Health Service Act 2006 and the FT's constitution
- preparing and issuing notices of meetings
- obtaining internal agreement to all documentation for circulation to members
- preparing directors and governors for any members' questions and helping them create briefing materials
- formally minuting those aspects of the meeting that are required to be recorded.

(3)Constitution:

- ensuring that the FT complies with its constitution and, drafting and incorporating amendments in accordance with correct procedures
- to lead the process of non-financial compliance with the trust's constitution, including management of the public and staff membership and governance reporting requirements with Monitor
- review, propose and implement approved changes to the trust's constitution.

(4)Monitor requirements:

- establishing and monitoring procedures to ensure that the FT complies with the requirements of the National Health Service Act 2006 and its Monitor licence
- ensuring that the requirements of the compliance framework are fulfilled appropriately and in a timely manner
- submitting the annual risk assessment to Monitor
- ensuring quarterly submissions are accurate and timely
- acting as initial point of contact between the FT, Monitor and other regulators.

⑤ *Statutory registers:*

Maintaining the following statutory registers and responding to appropriate requests concerning the information they contain:

- members, including the constituency they belong to (and class, if relevant)
- members of the council of governors
- governors' interests
- members of the board of directors
- directors' interests.

⑥ *Statutory returns:*

Ensuring that formal documentation is filed with appropriate bodies, as required, and to report certain changes regarding the FT:

- annual report and accounts
- amendments to the constitution
- notices of removal or resignation of the auditors.

⑦ *Annual report and accounts:*

- co-ordinating the preparation, publication, distribution and presentation of the annual report (including annual accounts), in consultation with the FT's internal and external advisers, and ensuring its presentation to Parliament.

⑧ *Membership communications*

- communicating with the members (e.g. through circulars, newsletters); maintaining good general relations with members and other interested parties.
- in liaison with the communications team, co-ordinating communications with the FT's members
- establishing and monitoring the election processes for public and staff governors
- supporting the council of governors in reviewing and suggesting proposals for the membership development strategy
- ensuring that arrangements are made for the election of public and staff governors including:
  - establishing members entitlement to vote
  - obtaining the necessary declarations from candidates
  - arranging the distribution of candidates statements
  - arranging the issue of voting papers
  - arranging for the returning of ballot papers and the counting of votes
  - declaring the results of the elections.

⑨ *Corporate governance:*

- continually reviewing developments in corporate governance
- facilitating the proper induction of directors and governors into their role

- advising and assisting the directors and governors with respect to their duties and responsibilities
- advising and facilitating board performance evaluations and any ongoing development matters resulting from that exercise
- counselling directors and governors when preparing presentations and memoranda
- ensuring the FT has a robust framework for compliance with corporate governance standards, the NHS Foundation Trust Code of Governance and recommended best practice
- maintaining and reviewing procedures for the sound governance of the FT and advising on developments in governance issues
- ensuring the FT has adequate insurance arrangements (if the FT chooses not to be covered via the NHS Litigation Authority schemes), and
- ensuring standing orders, including standing financial instructions, a scheme of delegation, and schedule of matters reserved for the board of directors and associated procedures are reviewed updated and properly discharged.

(10) *Non-executive director and governor development:*
- acting as a channel of communication and information for NEDs and governors
- advising the council of governors on an appropriate approach to reviewing board performance and facilitating an annual board evaluation for NEDs and facilitating any ongoing training highlighted
- management and development of the governors and their appropriate integration and interaction with the FT, including appropriate organisational development
- establishing arrangements for the review of effectiveness of the council of governors and developing ongoing development programme as appropriate, and
- arranging additional training and other support for directors and governors, as required.

(11) *Foundation trust seal:*
- ensuring the safe custody and proper use of any corporate seal(s).

(12) *Trust identity:*
- ensuring that all business letters, notices and other official publications of the FT show the name of the FT and any other information as required by statute.

(13) *General compliance:*
- monitoring and implementing procedures which allow for compliance with relevant regulatory and legal requirements
- providing advice on the impact of FT status on the terms and conditions of contracts with NHS bodies

- ensuring the FT implements the structures associated with the compliance and board assurance frameworks
- co-ordinating and submitting relevant information to other regulatory bodies, as required
- arranging for the FT to access a comprehensive legal service, where appropriate
- monitoring and reporting on compliance with the NHS Constitution
- ensuring any funds held in trust are used and managed appropriately, and
- reporting to the board of directors on any matters of non-compliance.

Subsidiary undertakings

- ensuring that procedures are in place for the correct administration of any subsidiary undertakings and that correct information is given to the holding company
- maintaining a record of the group's structure.

Acquisitions, disposals and mergers

- participating as a key member of the FT's management team established to implement corporate acquisitions, disposals and mergers
- protecting the FT's interests by ensuring the effectiveness of all documentation
- ensuring that due diligence disclosures enable proper commercial evaluation prior to completion of a transaction
- ensuring that the correct authority is in place to allow timely execution of documentation.

Governance Checklist

✓ Are the company secretary's role and reporting lines well defined and in line with best practice?

✓ Does the board understand and promote the role, utilising it to provide support to the board corporately and individual directors?

✓ Does the company secretary have the trust and confidence of the board and possess the necessary qualifications and personal attributes for the role?

✓ If the company secretary's role is combined with another executive role, has the board taken steps to ensure that conflicts of interest are addressed and the independence of the company secretary maintained?

✓ Does the board run efficiently, with high quality and timely information?

✓ Does the company secretary support the chair as leader of the board, supporting them with director induction, professional development, training and evaluation?

✓ Does the company secretary advise the board on all governance matters and in conjunction with the chair, periodically review the board and its committees to ensure they are fit for purpose?

✓ Does the company secretary take responsibility for the co-ordination of the annual report and accounts and provide quality input to the director's report, annual governance statement and other reports required to be published?

✓ Is the organisation's stakeholder management strategy in place and implemented by the company secretary?

✓ Does the company secretary manage and over see the provision of legal services to the organisation?

Summary

There are common issues for the role of the company secretary across both the corporate and public sectors – particularly the recognition of the value added to the organisation if the role is appropriately established at board level. Chairs and CEOs who have worked with high calibre company secretaries are perhaps the best advocates. The understanding of the role of NHS company secretaries still has some way to go in terms of profile and credibility but the increasing recognition of the impact of poor governance on the quality and safety of healthcare is lending an impetus to the discussion and governance practitioners (regardless of job title) are increasingly be look upon to contribute at board level.

The November 2014 research by Henley Business School in conjunction with ICSA concluded that as every organisation is different and leadership teams are unique, there is a need to build discretionary capacity into the role of company secretary. However, it went on to make some broad recommendations for large and medium-sized organisations across all sectors.

■ The company secretary role should be a direct, primary reporting line to the chair and is most effective as a standalone position.

■ The secretariat needs to retain independence to rebalance power as required and demonstrate accountability.

■ The profile of the company secretary role needs to be raised among other board members.

■ Boards need to have more open internal dialogue, so that strategy can fully emerge and be openly understood.

■ Mentoring and succession planning for company secretaries needs to improve to advance junior staff into the top roles.

■ The broader ICSA-qualified professional is best placed to fulfil the needs of effective boards.

PART FOUR

Foundation trusts and clinical commissioning groups

11

Foundation trusts

■ Foundation trusts and the NHS landscape

The introduction of NHS FTs (often referred to as 'foundation hospitals') in 2006 represented a significant change in the way in which hospital services were managed and provided in England. Foundation trusts (FTs) were part of the government's plan for creating a patient-led NHS. The aim of the reforms was to provide high-quality care, with devolved decision making so that they were more responsive to the needs and wishes of patients and local communities. They were also at the leading edge of many of the other reforms and improvements that aim to create a patient-led NHS.

FTs are not subject to direction from the Secretary of State for Health, and as part of their constitution they are required to establish stronger connections with their local communities by encouraging people living locally to become members of the trust. The membership of each FT is therefore made up of local people (including patients and carers) and staff.

Members are able to stand as, and vote to elect, representatives to serve on the council of governors. Governors are responsible for representing the interests of the members and partner organisations in the local health economy in the running of the FT. The intention is that local communities and staff working on the front line can influence the management and provision of NHS services in their area. This allows FTs to direct their services more closely to the needs of their communities, with freedom to develop new ways of working so that hospital services more accurately reflect the needs and expectations of local people.

Governors are unpaid volunteers. Their voluntary role is entirely different to that of a director. Governors are not expected to undertake the above duties or to be ultimately responsible for the performance of the trust. The governor's role does include specific statutory duties, but the board of directors remains ultimately responsible for the trust's operations and performance.

Although run locally, FTs remain fully part of the NHS. They have been set up as public benefit corporations, with a primary purpose to provide NHS services to NHS patients and users according to NHS principles and standards – free care based on need and not ability to pay. This is a unique legal form based on the traditions of mutuality.

Foundation trusts are accountable to:

- their local communities through their members and governors
- their commissioners through contracts
- Parliament (each FT must lay its annual report and accounts before Parliament)
- the CQC (through the legal requirement to register and meet the associated standards for the quality of care provided)
- Monitor (as their regulator).
  NHSI

In a March 2011 memorandum to Parliament in response to HSCA 2012, ICSA has commented as follows:

> 'Regardless of the freedoms proposed in the Bill (i.e. HSCA 2012), FTs still have to operate a governance framework unique within the UK economy and one that presents its own challenges and costs. The additional layer of governance inherent within the dynamic between the council of governors and the board of directors will impact on financial and non-financial resources. The dual nature of the decision-making process on specific areas of business development disadvantages FTs as their governance and accountability framework is more cumbersome operating an almost two-tier board approach.'

Figure 11.1: Foundation trust accountabilities

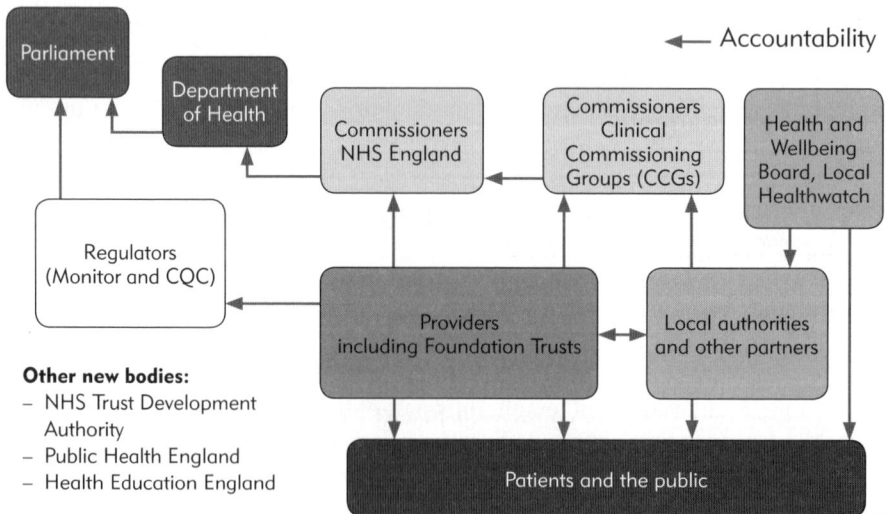

Source: NHS Providers

The two-tier governance structure of FTs referred to above does not refer to the two-tier board structure common in Germany as outlined in Chapter 4. Rather, it refers to the council of governors' oversight role alongside the unitary role of the board of directors, which is unusual in British public services. There is evidence that the structure has led to confusion and conflict, but there has also been a significant amount of development work to clarify the role and powers of the board and the council, and how they relate to one another.

Figure 11.1 outlines the FT accountabilities as set out in the legislation.

■ FTs, the law and the regulatory frameworks

Foundation trusts were established through the Health and Social Care (Community Health and Standards) Act 2003, consolidated into the National Health Service Act 2006. The legislation provided that FTs would not be directed by government and that they would have greater freedom to decide, with their governors and members, their own strategy and the way services are run. Consequently, they have significantly greater freedoms over the way they conduct their finances. Unlike NHS trusts, FTs are able to build up operational surpluses, retain proceeds from asset sales, raise capital in the public and/or private sectors, and manage their organisations and their resources – free from central government control. The other legislation outlined in Chapter 3 also applies to FTs, but should always be considered in the light of these two primary pieces of legislation.

FTs are not required to break even each year, although they must be financially viable. They can borrow money within limits set by the regulator, retain surpluses and decide on service developments and innovations for their local community. The Prudential Borrowing Code, which determined the amount FTs could borrow, was repealed by HSCA 2012 with effect from 1 April 2013.

Becoming a foundation trust

In the Government's July 2010 White Paper *Equity and Excellence: Liberating the NHS'*, it was made clear that all NHS trusts would become or become part of a FT by 2014 and NHS trusts would be abolished. Failure to meet this deadline, or achieve a credible plan for transition, would result in the Secretary of State for Health placing the NHS trust under a special administration regime.

In October 2012, the NHS TDA took over responsibility for the FT pipeline from the outgoing strategic health authorities (SHAs). The NHS TDA was given a fixed term of three years from 1 April 2013 to achieve this work, after which time it is expected that all trusts will have achieved FT status. This informally resets the deadline to achieve FT status to April 2016. However, it is unlikely that this deadline will be met.

The Dalton review, published in December 2014, concluded that many of the 93 trusts that have not yet reached foundation status 'will not reach the required standards in their current organisational form'. It identified a number of organisational forms that have the potential to be adopted across the wider NHS: federations, joint ventures, service level chains, management contracts, integrated care organisations and multi-service chains or Foundation Groups.

Led by the Salford Royal Foundation Trust chief executive Sir David Dalton, the review also identified five key themes for the pace of transformational change that is required within the NHS as follows:

1. One size does not fit all
2. Quicker transformational and transactional change is required
3. Ambitious organisations with a proven track record should be encouraged to expand their reach and have
4. Greater impact
5. Overall sustainability for the provider sector is a priority
6. A dedicated implementation programme is needed to make change happen

In the future, it suggested, organisations are likely to operate more than one organisational form for their service portfolio. It recommends that trust boards consider whether a new organisational form may be most suited to support the delivery of safe, reliable, high quality and economically viable services.

It says that the NHS TDA should publish its assessment of the capacity of each of the 93 organisations capacity to reach FT status, the organisations' plans, and the dates by which they will achieve FT status or another 'suitable organisational form'. It added that the DH should hold the NHS TDA to account for 'meeting the trajectory and milestones for each of the 93 organisations'.

The review also recommends that NHS England require CCGs to set out in their strategic commissioning plans the future service models they wish to support and how they will use allocated funds for service transformation.

The NHS TDA is required to support NHS trusts as they develop and prepare for the NHS FT assessment process. The introduction of the requirement for a full inspection by the Chief Inspector of Hospitals slowed the number of organisations moving through the FT assessment process significantly during 2013, as the new inspection regime was implemented. This was to ensure that quality of care was truly embedded in the assessment process. However, with the inspection regime now up and running, both acute and non-acute organisations are beginning to move through the process once again.

A key part of the formal assessment process is a comprehensive inspection by the Chief Inspector of Hospitals (part of the CQC). Aspirant trusts will be inspected alongside other organisations as part of the Chief Inspector of Hospital's routine programme. An overall rating of 'good' or 'outstanding' from the inspection will be required to pass to the next stage of the assessment process. Trusts that meet the CQC's requirements will move forward in the application process; this culminates in an assessment by the NHS TDA board on the organisation's overall readiness for FT status, including its business plan, FT application and external quality assurance reports. If the NHS TDA board is satisfied that the trust is ready to proceed then it will offer its support, on behalf of the Secretary of State, for the organisation to move to Monitor for assessment. The NHS TDA aims to reach a decision on applications as soon as possible after the CQC's report is published and will aim to give that approval within six weeks of publication.

The process of authorisation as an FT helps equip NHS trust boards more effectively to meet future challenges by testing both clinical quality and financial viability. Not all boards pass these tests. Monitor's assessment was that half of all aspirant NHS trusts whose FT application is deferred during the authorisation process do so due to a failure of governance. More expressly, it means that there have been issues with the capacity and capability of the board. As a result, the DH produced a Board Governance Assurance Framework to assist aspirant FT boards. This consists of a combination of self and independent assessment processes designed to ensure boards are appropriately skilled and prepared to achieve FT authorisation. At the time of writing it is clear that this aspect of the authorisation process is being reconsidered in the light of the introduction of the Well-led Framework (see Chapter 6 and later this chapter).

Organisations already with Monitor for assessment will receive their CQC inspection during the Monitor phase and will not be required to go back to the NHS TDA for approval. Monitor will then undertake its assessment process, as set out in the *Monitor Guide for Applicants*, to determine whether the organisation should be authorised as a FT. Monitor will normally aim to reach a decision on an application within four to six months of receiving a referral from the NHS TDA.

The role of Monitor (NHSI)

The HSCA 2012 also resulted in FTs becoming subject to the provider licence, the new licensing regime for health and adult social care, as set out in Chapter 2. This replaced the earlier system of issuing terms of authorisation. In addition to the new licence conditions for all regulated services, it included an additional four extra conditions for FTs:

- provision of information that Monitor has a duty to maintain on the register of NHS FTs;
- payment to Monitor in respect of any registration and related costs;
- an obligation to provide information requested by the advisory panel established by Monitor; and
- a condition that enables Monitor to continue its oversight of the governance of NHS FTs.

This fourth condition sets out Monitor's expectations that an FT has effective board and committee structures, reporting lines and performance and risk management systems. Foundation trusts do not need to apply for a licence, as Monitor agreed to license existing FTs from 1 April 2013.

Foundation trust Licence Condition 4 allows Monitor to use reasonable evidence, from disclosures made about NHS FTs, to determine if there is a risk of a breach of the licence condition and make a decision regarding intervention. The information Monitor will receive includes:

- a forward-looking disclosure on corporate governance (the corporate governance statement);
- a backward-looking disclosure on corporate governance (statement on compliance with the Monitor Code); and
- a backward-looking statement on internal control, risk and quality governance (the annual governance statement).

In addition, Monitor's Risk Assessment Framework (RAF) describes in detail how each FT's compliance with its licence is monitored. It sets out Monitor's approach to overseeing NHS FTs' compliance with the governance and continuity of services requirements of their provider licence. It replaced the Compliance Framework from 1 October 2013.

Under the RAF, FTs are assigned a quarterly governance risk rating of green if there are no material governance concerns evident. Where potential material concerns have been identified which Monitor is investigating, the trust is described as 'under review'. Trusts currently subject to formal regulatory action are assigned a red rating. The framework also provides for a continuity of services risk rating (CoSRR), where FTs are assigned a rating of one to four, reflecting the degree of financial concern, where four is the lowest level of risk. A low CoSRR does not necessarily imply the trust is in breach of its licence. Rather, it reflects the degree of financial concern Monitor may have in relation to that provider and consequently the frequency of in-year financial monitoring.

The board of directors is the first line of regulation in FTs, and Monitor requires FTs to submit an annual plan and quarterly reports (reporting requirements are covered in more details later). If Monitor considers that problems are developing then it will ensure that the trust has an action plan in place and will monitor progress against that plan. Monitor has powers to intervene in a FT in the event of failings in its healthcare standards, as judged by the CQC, or other aspects of its leadership that result in a significant breach of its licence conditions.

Monitor assesses a breach or a potential breach of the governance and continuity of service licence conditions through a risk-based system of regulation. This determines the intensity of the monitoring undertaken at each FT. Its intervention powers are broad, ranging from closing a specific service – if there are serious concerns about it – and requiring a board to take or not take a specific action(s), to requiring a board to obtain external advice on a particular issue or – in extreme cases – removing any or all of the directors or governors and appointing replacements.

In the most serious cases, where intervention by Monitor cannot resolve the breach, an FT could be dissolved after consultation. If this were to happen, the

Health and Social Care (Community Health and Standards) Act 2003 provides mechanisms to ensure that NHS patients and users continue to receive high-quality treatment.

The Monitor FT Code of Governance (Monitor Code) (KEY)

Though the other health service governance codes and corporate governance codes set out in Chapter 3 set out best practice that FTs should consider, the primary governance code for a FT is the Monitor Code. Key aspects of FT governance emphasised in the Code include:

- the unitary nature of the board of directors and the collective responsibility for all aspects of the performance of the FT, including financial performance, clinical and service quality, management and governance;
- the need for at least 50% of board members to be independent non-executives;
- a recommendation to appoint an SID;
- an emphasis on actively developing the effectiveness of the board of directors through performance evaluation of the board, its committees and individual directors;
- clarification on the committee structure of the board of directors and the council of governors;
- clarification on the roles of the remuneration, audit and nomination committees, including a recommendation for a clear nominations process and for all members of the audit committee to be independent;
- a recommendation for evaluation of the board should be externally facilitated at least every three years. The evaluation needs to be carried out against Monitor's Well-Led Framework;
- clarification of the need for high-quality information tailored to the board's duties and availability of access to external advice;
- a recommendation to appoint a secretary of the board of directors and the council of governors;
- the statutory duty of the council of governors to hold the NEDs individually and collectively to account for the performance of the board of directors;
- the role of a nominated lead governor;
- the duty of the board to take steps to ensure that governors are equipped with the skills and knowledge they need to discharge their duties appropriately;
- board meetings and the annual meeting to be open to the public, with members of the public only to be excluded for special reasons; and
- recommendations to be clear on the purpose and outcomes of the relationships of the FT with other stakeholders including members, patients, the local community, commissioners and other NHS and non-NHS bodies with an interest in the local health economy.

FTs are required to set out a complete set of disclosures in respect of the Monitor Code within their annual report and accounts.

Monitor model core constitution

Every FT has a constitution that has been approved by Monitor upon authorisation. The constitution will set out the governance arrangements for the FT. Although each FT's constitution will be unique, there are legal requirements that apply to all FTs set out in Schedule 7 of the 2006 Act. These requirements are set out in Monitor's model core constitution, on which all NHS FT constitutions must be based. It sets out what Monitor considers 'otherwise appropriate', as set out in the Monitor publication, *Applying for NHS Foundation Trust Status: guide for applicants*. Monitor requires all applicant trusts for FT authorisation to prepare their constitutions on the basis of this model core constitution.

The model core constitution also reflects the legislative changes implemented by the HSC Act 2012. Additions or amendments to the model may be made, however, at authorisation, Monitor requires that any departure be in accordance with Schedule 7, are clearly indicated as a tracked change and are accompanied by an explanation for the intended departure from the model core constutition.

The constitution sets out that the principal purpose of the trust is the provision of goods and services for the purposes of the health service in England and that the trust does not fulfil this purpose unless, in each financial year, its total income from the provision of goods and services for the purposes of the health service in England is greater than its total income from the provision of goods and services for any other purposes. The constitution also covers:

- who may be a member
- the makeup of the council of governors and the board of directors
- how elections of governors will be carried out
- the statutory duties of the governors and directors
- the grounds and procedures for the disqualification and removal of members, governors and directors
- the requirement for open meetings of the council of governors and board of directors
- the management of conflicts of interests
- requirements for the disclosure of public documents and the statutory registers
- the management of mergers and significant transactions.

The constitution also includes a number of annexes as follows:

- the public constituency
- the staff constituency
- the patient constituency (if any)
- composition of the council of governors
- the model election rules
- additional provisions – council of governors
- standing orders – council of governors
- standing orders – board of directors

- further provisions
- annual members meeting.

Any changes to the constitution after authorisation must have the approval of both the board and the council. Where the amendments relates to the powers or responsibilities of the governors, the constitution must also be approved by the members at member meeting. Amendments no longer need to be submitted to Monitor for approval.

◼ FT board structure and its committees

The DH's *Guide to NHS Foundation Trusts* (2002) sets out that the governance of FTs was to be based on experience in other sectors, as the following extracts demonstrate:

> 'The new governance arrangements for NHS FTs have been modelled on cooperative societies and mutual organisations. These combine community ownership with accountability.'

> 'NHS FTs will herald a new form of social ownership where health services are owned by and accountable to local people rather than central Government. In this way, much stronger connections will be established between providers of NHS services and their stakeholder communities ... In a similar way to becoming a member of a co-operative society or mutual organisation, the members of an NHS FT will become its owners, taking on responsibility for their local hospitals from national Government.'

The guidance for FTs establishes that they are to be accountable to their members. This accountability is underpinned by the aforementioned establishment of a council of governors in addition to the board of directors, as shown in Figure 11.2. As previously mentioned, this is not a two-tier board structure, and the Monitor Code reiterates the unitary board principle strongly. This structure is set out in the individual FT's constitution.

The Health and Social Care Act 2012 set out a requirement that all FT board meetings be held in public. Boards need to decide which papers and minutes should be discussed in public session. The ability to meet in closed session is still available for confidential or commercially sensitive matters. Boards should strive to deal with as much business as possible in the public part of the meeting and should be guided by the exemptions in the Freedom of Information Act in deciding where to draw the line with regard to information not in the public domain.

Board composition (KEY)

Under the NHS Act 2006, the FT is to have a board of directors comprising both executive and NEDs. The board must have a non-executive chair, [*] other NEDs; and [*] EDs ([*] denotes a number to be inserted at the trust's discretion). One

Figure 11.2: Foundation trust governance arrangements

FT Governance Arrangements

Operational Services

Day to day running of the Trust

Managing the business

Board of Directors

Made up of:
Non-executives
Chief Executive
Medical Director
Director of Nursing
Finance Director
Director of Operations

Chair

The Chair chairs both the Board and the Council

Council of Governors

Works with the Board of Directors to ensure that the Trust delivers the services that reflect the needs of the local community

Involved in key decisions about future plans

Appoints the Chair

Appoints the Non-executive Directors

Approves Chief Executive appointment

Dialogue to and from community

Membership

Staff

Public

Contribute views & ideas to improve patient care
Receive information
Elect Governors
May stand for election as Governors

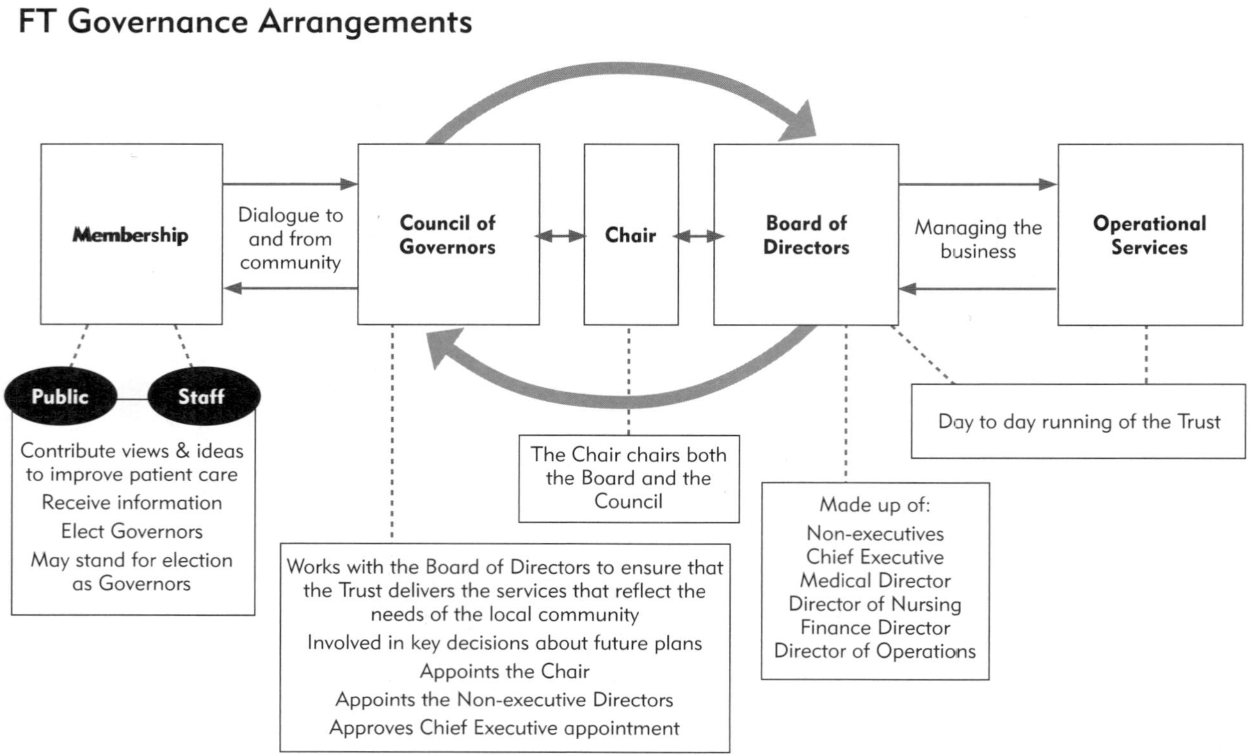

Source: NHS Providers

of the EDs must be the CEO and they must be the accounting officer. One of the EDs must be the finance director. One of the EDs must be a registered medical practitioner or a registered dentist (within the meaning of the Dentists Act 1984). One of the EDs must be a registered nurse or a registered midwife.

The general duty of the board of directors, and of each director individually, is to act with a view to promoting the success of the corporation so as to maximise the benefits for the members of the corporation as a whole and for the public.

A FT board has the same role as that of any other unitary board: to set the strategic direction and to supervise the work of the executive to ensure that corporate objectives and performance targets are achieved. The board is directly accountable through the council of governors to trust membership and the wider community.

The authority of the board is derived from Schedule 7 of the NHS Act 2006, as amended by HSCA 2012. Schedule 7 states that the constitution must provide for all the powers of the corporation (the FT) to be exercisable by the board directors on its behalf. Any of those powers may, however, be delegated to a committee of directors or to an ED.

The Monitor Code recommends that FTs have a schedule of matters reserved for board decision.

Board committees

Under Schedule 7, FT boards may only delegate authority to a committee of directors or to an ED. Committees that have formal memberships which include non-board members cannot have powers delegated to them by the board, and neither can individual NEDs.

FTs are required to establish an audit committee, a nomination committee and a remuneration committee. They may establish other committees as required, such as a quality assurance committee. The board must supervise the work of its committees and keep under review the need for each committee to exist. The committees are there to help the board gain assurance, not to deal with operational matters.

The Monitor Code allows for the establishment of separate NED and governor committees for both nomination and remuneration purposes – dealing with NED appointments and remuneration, and ED appointments and remuneration respectively. Where there is just one nomination and remuneration committee, the membership changes depending upon whether it is considering a NED or ED appointment.

The role of the nomination and remuneration committees for ED appointments/remuneration and the audit committee is in line with the details set out in Chapters 6, 9 and 15 respectively. The role of the nomination and remuneration committees for NED appointments is set out later in this chapter.

The Audit Code for Foundation Trusts (2011) gives the FT audit committee the responsibility for monitoring and ensuring the independence of the external auditors. If the external auditors provide non-audit services to the organisation, the annual report should explain how auditor independence and objectivity are safeguarded.

The auditors of an FT have a primary responsibility to the FT's council of governors. Such auditors may also be responsible to Monitor for the exercise of some functions, and will have responsibilities to the members of the FT, as well as the wider public, in the case of public interest reports.

Auditors of FTs are also required to review the organisation's compliance with the Monitor Code, and to obtain evidence to support the organisation's compliance statement (in the annual report and accounts) of its compliance with the code. In addition, external auditors of FTs are currently required to satisfy themselves that the quality report has been prepared according to the detailed guidance issued by Monitor.

Duties of an FT director

The Health and Social Care Act 2012 introduced into the NHS Act 2006 provisions on duties of NHS FT directors. While some of these duties simply amount to a restatement of the common law in this area, others are new and were intended to address concerns on the need for transparency in the conduct of the business of NHS FT boards. The changes are contained in section. 152 of HSCA 2012 and are as follows.

1. Section 152(1) lays down a general duty of the board, and of each director individually, to act with a view to promoting the success of the corporation so as to maximise the benefits for the members of the corporation as a whole and for the public.

2. Section 152(2) lays down the duties of NHS FT directors to avoid conflicts of interest and duty, and not to accept benefits from third parties in connection with their directorship.

3. Section 152(3) lays down the duty to declare any interest that a director may have in relation a proposed transaction with their FT and provides for exceptions to the duty.

4. Section 152(4) lays down new requirements for an NHS FT board to send a copy of the agenda of its meeting to the council of governors prior to the holding the meeting to which the agenda relates, and send a copy of the minutes of its meeting to the council of governors as soon as practicable after holding of the meeting to which those minutes relate.

5. Section 15(5) lays down the duty of the board to ensure that the constitution of its NHS FT provides for board meetings to be open to members of the public. The provision permits exceptions to be provided for in an NHS FT's constitution in relation to this requirement.

In addition, directors have a role under HSCA 2012 in approving constitutional changes (alongside governors), and a duty to equip governors with the skills they need to do their job.

ICSA welcomed these new duties in its March 2011 memorandum to Parliament 'as it makes explicit the step change from being a senior manager to being an ED, and brings the duties of FT directors in line with the private sector'.

The Monitor Code also specifies that directors on the board of directors, and governors on the council of governors, should meet the 'fit and proper' persons test described in the provider licence and required by the CQC.

FT council structure and its committees

The council of governors is made up of elected governors and appointed governors. Elected governors are those members elected by the membership to represent the staff, patient and public constituencies that make up the membership of a FT. The appointed governors are the representatives from certain key stakeholders, such as local authorities that commission services from the FT. These representatives are appointed to the council of governors to represent those stakeholder groups.

Members

Residents and patients in areas served by an FT with an interest in the wellbeing of their local hospital and health services can register as members of the organisation. Patients who do not live locally, and their carers, may also become members if provided for in the trust's constitution. Members of FTs do not receive any special treatment as NHS patients and users. They have the same access to NHS services as anyone who chooses not to become a member. The eligibility for membership of a FT is open to local residents, patients and carers and staff employed by the trust, in the terms provided in each trust's constitution. All FT members can expect to receive regular information about their local trust and be consulted on plans for future development.

The model constitution sets out that an FT membership will consist of two main groupings, namely staff and public members. In addition, a third grouping of members may be included to represent patient members. These groupings are known as constituencies. Within each constituency there may be a number of classes, which differentiate between geographical areas for public members or between staff categories for staff members. For the public constituency, the constitution must specify the area or areas; each of these areas must be an electoral area for the purposes of local government elections in England and Wales or an area consisting of two or more areas. The constitution may provide for automatic membership of the staff constituency by default.

If an FT decides to have a patient constituency then it may also divide those members into descriptions or classes of individuals. There must, however, be at least three such classes and one must comprise the carers of patients. The constitution may provide for automatic membership of the patients' constituency (if there is one) by default.

If automatic membership for the staff and/or patient constituency is within the constitution, the FT must consider how they will inform staff and/or patients that they are subject to automatic membership.

There is <u>no limit</u> on the number of people who can register as members, providing they meet the eligibility criteria. It is for FTs to ensure they have a representative membership and sufficient members so that they can mount credible election processes. <u>Governance arrangements for FTs need to be reflective of local conditions and proposals that work best for them.</u>

It is <u>this membership body</u> made up of local residents, patients and carers and staff employed by the trust, <u>which are able to vote in the elections to appoint the council of governors of the FT.</u> Each member, if nominated, can stand for election as a governor.

The Monitor Code sets out the key responsibilities of the council and the board in respect to members as follows.

The board should:

- keep in touch with the opinion of members, patients and the local community in whatever ways are most practical and efficient. There must be a members' meeting at least annually;
- ensure governors have the mechanisms in place to secure and report on feedback that will enable them to fulfil their duty to represent the interests of members and the public; and
- monitor how representative the trust's membership is and the level and effectiveness of member engagement and report on this in the annual report. This information should be used to review the trust's membership strategy, taking into account any emerging best practice from the sector.

Governors should:

- seek the views of members and the public on material issues or changes being discussed by the trust; and
- provide information and feedback to members and the public regarding the trust, its vision, performance and material strategic proposals made by the trust board.

Elections

New model council election rules were published in August 2014. These are available on the FTN website.

The <u>new rules allow members to vote for FT governors using e-voting technology (internet, telephone or text), initially in tandem with paper-based voting.</u> They also set out that challenges to the conduct of FT elections will now be determined by the Independent Elections Arbitration Panel, rather than Monitor.

NHS trusts applying to Monitor for FT status after 1 October 2014 must use this version of the rules in their draft constitutions and hold their first elections in line with them. The rules make provision for both first-past-the-post and single transferable voting systems. The model election rules require candidates to declare membership of a political party, and they also set out a clear and strict timetable for the election proceedings. Section 60 of the NHS Act 2006 also requires persons standing for and voting in the elections to make a declaration setting out the particulars of their qualification to vote or stand as a member of the constituency (or class/area) for which the election is being held.

The constitution of each trust sets out a number of criteria for disqualification for standing as a governor. For example, a person cannot be an FT governor if they are bankrupt or have served a prison sentence of three months or more during the last five years. Other grounds include, in the case of an elected governor, ceasing to be a member of the constituency they represent or, in the case of an appointed governor, the sponsoring organisation withdrawing their sponsorship of them.

Governors may not stand for election if they have previously served as a governor of the trust for a total of six years (whether such years were served consecutively or not) or of they have within the preceding two years been dismissed, otherwise than by reason of redundancy or ill health, from any paid employment with a health service body. The following persons are also not eligible to stand:

- a director of the FT itself
- a governor, ED, NED, chair or CEO of another health service body or a body corporate whose business involves the provision of healthcare services, including (for the avoidance of doubt) those who have a commercial interest in the affairs of the trust.

Governors are elected for a maximum of a three-year term of office under Schedule 7 of the NHS Act 2006 but there is some debate about whether they should be allowed two or three terms of office. Some FT constitutions allow for two terms so that the six-year tenure is in line with the terms of office available to NEDs, whereas others allow for nine-year tenures so that they are in line with the UK Code recommendations for independence of NEDS and refreshing of the board.

The latter FTs would argue that the induction and development of governors is a costly exercise and so it is a better use of taxpayers' money. They also argue that the governors are at arm's length from the FT and therefore likely to stay independent of the FT longer. This obviously depends upon the individual governor and the time commitment they make to being a governor.

All elected governors should be submitted for re-election at regular intervals. The Monitor Code states:

Elected governors must be subject to re-election by the members of their constituency at regular intervals not exceeding three years. The names of governors submitted for election or re-election should be accompanied by sufficient biographical details and any other relevant information to enable members to take an informed decision on their election. This should include prior performance information such as attendance records at governor meetings and other relevant events organised by the NHS FT for governors.'

Where a governor stands down mid-term, an election process for a by-election takes place meaning that the newly elected or appointed governor completes the existing term of office. The constitution will often allow for a vacancy to run until the next scheduled election process in order to minimise costs.

Council of governors

The duties of the council of governors are to hold the NEDs individually and collectively to account for the performance of the board of directors and to represent the interests of the members of the corporation as a whole and the interests of the public. The requirement for the council to hold the NEDs to account arises from the fact that they can appoint and remove the NEDs but not the EDs.

The council of governors is responsible for representing the interests of the local community in the management and stewardship of the FT, and for sharing information about key decisions with other FT members. It is not responsible for the day-to-day management of the organisation such as setting budgets, staff pay and other operational matters – the oversight of that management is a matter for the board of directors. However, the council of governors allows local residents, staff and key stakeholders to influence decisions about spending and the development of services.

The council of governors typically meets as a full council four or five times a year. The meetings are held in public and are open to all members and the general public. The council of governors is required to hold an annual members meeting to receive the annual report and accounts and any report of the auditor. This meeting is often used to provide an overview of the year from the CEO.

FTs are allowed some local flexibility over the size and composition of their council of governors. However, every council must have the following.

Public governors

More than half of the members of the council are to be elected by members of the trust other than those who come within the staff constituency. Therefore, there must be a majority of public and patient governors.

Staff governors

At least three governors should represent staff.

Appointed governors

At least one member of the Council of Governors is to be appointed by one or more local authorities which covers the whole or part of an area specified in the constitution as a public constituency. If any of the trust's hospitals includes a medical or dental school provided by a university, at least one member of the council of governors is to be appointed by that university. An FT may also specify other organisations within its constitution as a partnership organisation who may also appoint a member of the council of governors.

The 2012 Act abolished the requirement for a primary care trust (PCT) governor and there is no requirement for a commissioner governor to be appointed in place of former PCT governor/s. Trusts may wish to nominate a specified commissioner as an organisation for the purposes of appointing a governor.

The chair

The chair of the FT is responsible for leadership of both the board of directors and for the council of governors. The Monitor Code sets out that it is the chair's responsibility to ensure that the board and the council work together effectively, but that the governors also have a responsibility to make these arrangements work. The council should take the lead in inviting the CEO or other board members to their meetings, where they may raise questions about the affairs of the trust of the chair or other board members.

The lead governor

Monitor has also recommended that the council of governors appoint a lead governor who would lead the council of governors where it is not considered appropriate for the chair or another one of the NEDs to do so. These occasions are likely to be infrequent, but one example may be a meeting discussing the appointment of the chair. The lead governor could also have a role in certain circumstances where it would not be appropriate for the chair to contact Monitor, or Monitor to contact the chair (e.g. in relation to appointment of the chair). Communication would instead take place between the lead governor and Monitor in such circumstances. Routine communication from Monitor to governors is disseminated through the FT secretary.

The main circumstances where Monitor will contact a lead governor are where Monitor has concerns as to the quality of the board leadership at an FT, which may lead to Monitor's use of its formal powers to remove the chair or NEDs. As the council of governors appoints the chair and NEDs, Monitor would want to consult with the governors as to the capacity and capability of these individuals to lead the trust, to rectify successfully any issues, and also for the governors to understand Monitor's concerns. The other situation where Monitor may wish to contact the lead governor is where it has concerns that the process for the appointment of the chair or other members of the board, or elections for governors, may not have complied with the NHS FT's constitution, or alternatively may be inappropriate.

Monitor suggests: 'The lead governor should take steps to understand Monitor's role, the available guidance and the basis on which Monitor may take regulatory action. The lead governor will then be able to communicate more widely with other governors.'

The existence of a lead governor does not, in itself, prevent any governor from contacting Monitor directly if they feel it is necessary. The term lead governor is used to prevent confusion with the deputy. The council of governors should choose the lead governor, who should not deputise for the deputy chair of the board of directors.

The nomination committee

The council of governors has a similar committee structure to that of the board of directors to fulfil its role of appointing (or removing) the chair and other NEDs. The Monitor Code sets out that:

> The governors are responsible at a general meeting for the appointment, re-appointment and removal of the chair and the other NEDs. They should agree with the nominations committee a clear process for the nomination of a new chair and NEDs. Once suitable candidates have been identified the nominations committee should make recommendations to the council of governors.'

The Monitor Code describes two scenarios for the role of the council of governors in the appointment of NEDs:

> 'In FTs there may be one or two nominations committees. If there are two committees, one will be responsible for considering nominations for EDs and the other for NEDs (including the chair) ... Where a FT has two nominations committees, the nominations committee responsible for the appointment of NEDs should consist of a majority of governors. If only one nominations committee exists, when nominations for non-executives, including the appointment of a chair or a deputy chair, are being discussed, there should be a majority of governors on the committee and also a majority governor representation on the interview panel.'

The chair or an independent NED should chair the nominations committee(s). At the discretion of the committee, a governor can chair the committee in the case of appointments of NEDs or the chair. A person may only be appointed as an NED or chair if they are a member of the public constituency (or the patient constituency, if there is one). Where the trust has a university medical or dental school, a person may be appointed as an NED if they exercise functions for that organisation.

Upon receiving a recommendation to appoint, the council of governors should consider the qualifications, skills and experience required: for the appointment of a chair, they should also consider the time commitment required. The Monitor Code stipulates that 'no individual, simultaneously while being a chair of an NHS FT, should be the substantive chair of another NHS FT'.

In accordance with the FT's constitution, appointment is by a majority of the governors attending the relevant meeting. Removal requires the approval of three-quarters of the members of the council of governors, not just those who attend the meeting.

Remuneration committee

The council of governors is also responsible for setting the remuneration of NEDs and the chair. The council of governors should consult external professional advisers to market-test the remuneration levels of the chair and other NEDs at least once every three years and when they intend to make a material change to the remuneration of a NED. Levels of remuneration for the chair and other NEDs should reflect the time commitment and responsibilities of their roles.

The council of governors may delegate the task of market testing to a remuneration committee consisting solely of governors. Chairing this committee would often be the responsibility of the lead governor if one has been appointed; if not, the council of governors may appoint a chair. The committee then makes its recommendation back to the council of governors for decision.

CASE STUDY: Appointment of an FT chair

The council of governors and board of directors had worked collaboratively in the process of appointing a new chair. The nominations committee, consisting of the deputy chair and other non-executives had considered the make-up of the board and identified the key skills and experience required from the new appointment. They had made their recommendations to the governors nomination committee and these had been accepted.

The governors nomination committee, led by the deputy chair, appointed recruitment consultants to assist them with the search and consulted with executive and NEDs alike on the process for appointment.

The committee – again led by the deputy chair and supported by the company secretary, director of HR and the recruitment advisers – conducted the interviews and offered an opportunity for the candidates to be met by members of the board, the wider council of governors and members of staff.

When it came to a decision to appoint, the committee was divided in its view as to the best candidate for the post. One candidate was very experienced but had demonstrable time constraints on their commitment to the trust, the other was less experienced but much more committed to the organisation. The committee agreed that both candidates were appointable and therefore invited the current CEO to offer her opinion as to which candidate would gain the support of the board. As a result the decision was taken to recommend the less experienced candidate to the council of governors for appointment as the new chair.

The EDs immediately rejected the decision of the committee and refused to support the proposal. The CEO demanded that the committee reconvene and reconsider its decision. The pressure on the committee was such that it subsequently decided not to appoint and to re-advertise the post. The committee complained to Monitor that the EDs had undermined their statutory duty to appoint the chair and Monitor formally reprimanded the EDs. The committee was advised to appoint an independent adviser to work with them on the new recruitment process.

The committee is required to make a report of its activities in the FT's annual report and accounts. This is in line with the reports required of FTs and NHS trusts; likewise, the report must also include the relationship between the remuneration of the highest-paid director in their organisation and the median remuneration of the organisation's workforce, in line with the Hutton Fair Pay Review.

Appointment of auditors

The council of governors should take the lead in agreeing with the audit committee the criteria for appointing, re-appointing and removing external auditors. The council of governors will need to work hard to ensure they have the skills and knowledge to choose the right external auditor and monitor their performance. However, they should be supported in this task by the audit committee, which provides information to the governors on the external auditor's performance as well as overseeing the FT's internal financial reporting and internal auditing.

As part of the appointment process, the FT is required to ensure the appointed auditors meet the criteria set out by Monitor. The auditors must agree the terms of engagement with the FT in a letter of engagement. The auditors must resign if they fail to meet, or have cause to believe that they will not be able to comply with, the criteria set out in the terms of authorisation at any point during their appointment. FTs must provide Monitor with details of their auditors on authorisation and whenever a change to the auditors is made. This information should include the name and address of the organisation. When an auditor's appointment ends, the auditor is required to write to the FT and to Monitor giving notice of resignation and setting out a statement of the circumstances or stating that there are none.

As an important independence point for FT auditors, no member of the audit team may be a member or governor of the FT (Monitor Audit Code 2011). The board of directors' audit committee should make recommendations to the council of governors about the appointment, re-appointment and removal of the external auditor, as well as the approval of the remuneration and terms of engagement of the external auditor. The council of governors may delegate the work involved to an auditor appointments committee, made up of governors and could be chaired by the chair of the audit committee before making its recommendation to the council of governors for decision.

If the council of governors does not accept the recommendation, it should include in the annual report a statement from the audit committee explaining the recommendation and should set out reasons why the council of governors has taken a different position. When the council of governors ends an external auditor's appointment in disputed circumstances, the chair should write to Monitor informing it of the reasons behind the decision

Approval of the appointment of the CEO

It is for the NEDs to appoint and remove the CEO; however, the appointment of a CEO does require the approval of the council of governors. Monitor's guide *Your Statutory Duties: a reference guide for NHS FT governors* sets out a clear process for engaging with the council of governors to reduce the likelihood of the governors not giving their approval. The NEDs should make sure that the governors are kept informed about the appointment process, ensuring that the governors are satisfied with the various stages of the process such as use of advertisements, the criteria for selection and how selection was carried out.

To give their approval, the council of governors needs to be confident that the appointment process has identified a candidate with sufficient experience to fulfil all essential aspects of the job description and that the process has been fair, open and transparent. The council of governors should receive a report setting out that due law and process has been followed, as well as detailing how the proposed candidate's skills and experience meet the agreed role and person specification. The primary responsibility for the appointment lies with the NEDs and the council of governors should only withhold its approval with good cause.

If approval is withheld, the council of governors must set out their reasons to the chair and the other NEDs. The reasons for withholding approval must be justifiable, as there are likely to be financial consequences. The process, the decision and the reasons for the decision should be set out in the FT's annual report, whatever the outcome.

■ Duties, rights and powers of the FT governor

According to ICSA's March 2011 memorandum to Parliament:

> 'Greater clarification is required to inform governors of their role, and potential liability, in those situations where a FT may be heading towards insolvency. Governors will also need to be aware of the powers they have available to prevent a course of action by directors they believe to be financially threatening to the long term existence of the FT, which does not sit within the definition of a 'significant transaction.'

The statutory duties of FT governors are set out in the NHS Act 2006 and HSCA 2012. They are further expanded in the Monitor guidance *Your Statutory Duties: a reference guide for NHS foundation trust governors.* It should be recognised that these publications set out the baseline in terms of duties, rights and powers; how these are fulfilled in practical terms is open to a great deal of local interpretation.

There is also a great deal of helpful guidance on best practice set out in the FTN/ DAC Beachcroft publication *The foundation of good governance – a compendium of good practice*. The following sections set out the statutory duties of governors, which are essential as an introduction to the role of the council of governors.

The NHS Act 2006 set out statutory duties of FT governors as:

- appoint and, if appropriate, remove the chair and NEDs
- decide the remuneration and other allowances of the chair and NEDs
- approve the appointment of the CEO
- appoint and, if appropriate, remove the trust's auditor
- receive the annual accounts, auditor report and annual report.

The Health and Social Care Act 2012 sets out the general duty of the council of governors to hold the NEDs, individually and collectively, to account for the performance of the board of directors. It also has the general duty to represent the interests of the members of the trust as a whole and the interests of the public. HSCA 2012 also gave the council additional rights and powers to:

- require one or more of the directors to attend a governors' meeting for the purpose of obtaining information about the trust's performance of its functions or the directors' performance of their duties (and for deciding whether to propose a vote on the trust's or directors' performance);
- approve 'significant transactions' (i.e. at least half of the governors voting agree with the transaction). The trust may choose to include a description of 'significant transactions' in the trust's constitution;
- approve an application by the trust to enter into a merger, acquisition, separation or dissolution. In this case, approval means at least half of all governors agree with the application;
- to decide whether the trust's private patient work would significantly interfere with the trust's principal purpose (i.e. the provision of goods and services for the health service in England or the performance of its other functions);
- approve any proposed increases in private patient income of 5% or more in any financial year. Approval means at least half of the governors voting agree with the increase; and
- approve any amendments to the trust's constitution. Approval means at least half of the governors voting agree with the amendments.

In addition, HSCA 2012 created the following additional responsibilities.

- Before each board meeting, the board of directors must send a copy of the agenda to the governors. After the meeting, the board of directors must send a copy of the minutes to the governors. The trust must take steps to ensure that governors have the skills and knowledge they require to undertake their role.
- Monitor gains the power to establish a panel of persons to which a governor can refer questions as to whether the trust has failed or is failing to act in

accordance with its constitution. The council must first approve the referral. Approval means at least half of the governors voting agree with the referral.

- The trust must hold annual members' meetings. At least one of the directors must present the trust's annual report and accounts to the members at this meeting.
- Where there has been an amendment to the constitution which relates to the powers, duties or roles of the council, at least one governor must attend the next annual members meeting and present the amendment to the members. Members have the right to vote on and veto these types of constitutional amendments.

The implications of these changes will require additional training and development for governors in their new role and a much more effective working relationship between the board of directors and council of governors. Care will also be required in the definition of 'significant transactions', otherwise FTs will find they regularly have to seek governor approval on more minor or less significant proposals. Judgement will have to be exercised where a number of minor transactions could in fact warrant the attention of the council of governors as collectively they represent a 'significant transaction'.

According to the Monitor Code: 'governors should use their voting rights to hold the NEDs individually and collectively to account and act in the best interest of patients, members and the public. If the council of governors does withhold consent for a major decision, it must justify its reasons to the chair and the other NEDs, bearing in mind that its decision is likely to have a range of consequences for the NHS FT. The council of governors should take care to ensure that reasons are considered, factual and within the spirit of the Nolan principles.'

NHS Providers has a developed a national governor training programme called GovernWell to support FTs in their statutory obligation to ensure that governors have the skills and knowledge they require to carry out their role.

Codes of conduct

The Stewardship Standard for Governors of NHS FTs was developed during 2012 amongst governance practitioners, as part of the North West Company Secretary Network hosted by Hill Dickinson. The standard is not copyrighted and is in free circulation.

This voluntary Stewardship Standard sets out good practice on engagement with FTs and provides an opportunity for the high-quality dialogue needed between councils and boards to underpin good governance. The standard describes actions that councils can take to ensure that they fulfil their statutory duties. For example, at least once every three years the council could seek independent assurance to satisfy themselves, to the extent possible, that the FT board is effective and that NEDs provide adequate oversight of the FT. This is in line with the requirements of the well-led frame work which is set out in more detail later. It also suggests that, governors could use a wide range of activities to listen to the views of their local communities and reflect them back to the FT, ensuring these views are considered by the board in the development of the FT's annual plan. It makes it clear that the principal relationships between governors and the board are via the chair and other NEDs, in relation to the board being held to account. Governors will depend upon the CEO and other EDs for information updates on a regular basis.

Appropriate application of the Stewardship Standard should assist governors to avoid taking on a role in which the council directs management, and therefore it ensures that governors do not unintentionally take on the role of shadow directors.

There are also several other locally determined codes of conduct and published guidance. For example, there is also a sample code of conduct in the aforementioned FTN/Beachcroft publication *The foundation of good governance – a compendium of good practice*.

Liabilities of the council

Monitor has recognised that governors may be concerned about the level of liability they are taking on, particularly when it exercises powers in relation to significant transactions. Governors may be concerned that they will be held responsible if a transaction damages the trust, financially or otherwise.

Though the 2006 Act, as amended, does not make explicit reference to governors' liability in this regard Monitor has made it clear in its guidance on transactions that the governors' duty to 'hold the NEDs, individually and collectively to account for the performance of the board of directors' does not mean that governors are responsible for the decision itself, or the operational detail behind it. Responsibility for a decision remains with the board of directors, acting on behalf of the FT. FTs are not required to provide an indemnity for governors, or insurance to cover their service on the council of governors.

■ Maintaining an effective FT board

The UK Corporate Governance Code states that the evaluation of the board of FTSE companies should be 'externally facilitated' at least every three years; in other words, the company should use specialist external consultants at least once every three years, and where the company uses external consultants, the company should make a statement of whether the consultants have any other connection with the company.

This is echoed in the Monitor Code and has been formalised in the RAF. It has also been published in the Well-Led Framework for governance reviews.

The Well-Led Framework represents a 'core' reference for FTs to structure reviews of their governance. The depth and breadth of these areas for investigation can be shaped through the trust's self-assessment and initial findings of the independent review team at the start of the process. Where trusts choose to exclude core elements of the framework, these must be notified to Monitor in line with a 'comply or explain' approach. Foundation trusts are free to schedule when the reviews take place within the three-year window.

The framework is built along the lines of the pre-existing Quality Governance Framework, with four domains, ten high-level questions, along with a body of 'good practice' outcomes and an evidence base that a FT and its independent reviewers can use to assess governance. The four domains are as follows:

- **Strategy and planning:** how well is the board setting direction for the organisation?
- **Capability and culture:** is the board taking steps to ensure it has the appropriate experience and ability, now and into the future, and can it positively shape the organisation's culture to deliver care in a safe and sustainable way?
- **Process and structures**: do reporting lines and accountabilities support the effective oversight of the organisation?
- **Measurement:** does the board receive appropriate, robust and timely information and does this support the leadership of the trust?

The framework sets out the questions that FTs and reviewers should ask of themselves. Each question has a number of outcomes that the review is seeking to test or investigate. The review is likely to include:

- a desktop review of documents
- board and committee observations
- a board self-assessment
- a board skills inventory
- focus groups with internal and external stakeholders
- one-to-one interviews with board members, the trust secretary, lead governor, clinical leads and local stakeholders
- a peer practice assessment
- stakeholder surveys.

The FT chair is required to write to Monitor within 60 days of the submission of the review to the trust board. The chair should either advise Monitor that the review has been completed and that there are no 'material governance concerns', or advise Monitor of any material governance concerns that have arisen from the review. If there are concerns, the chair should include an action plan (including timings and priorities) in response to those concerns. The framework also includes scoring criteria for the review, which reflects the green/amber-green/amber-red/red approach as used in the Quality Governance Framework.

Monitor does not currently have any plans to accredit suppliers or set up a preferred reviewer list. Therefore, FT boards are required to assure themselves that the provider can carry out a robust and reliable judgment of its governance.

Though the framework does not directly require the engagement of the council of governors, some aspects of the review recognise that clear working arrangements between the council and the board are essential, particularly as there is a requirement for internal and external stakeholder engagement. FT boards may wish to involve their council of governors in designing the review process, and council of governors should have sight of the findings as part of their assurance on board performance.

■ The chair of the board and the council

Under Schedule 7 of the NHS Act 2006, the chair is responsible for leadership of both the board of directors and the council of governors. The governors are also given a responsibility under the Monitor Code to make the arrangements between the board and the council work. The council should take the lead in inviting the CEO to their meetings and inviting attendance by other EDs as appropriate. In these meetings, other members of the council of governors may raise questions of the chair or the deputy chair, or any other relevant director present at the meeting about the affairs of the FT.

Though the council has a statutory duty to appoint the chair and NEDs, they also have a duty to hold the NEDs (including the chair) to account for the performance of the board. This means that there can be a blurring of the role of the chair, who would normally be responsible for appraising and managing the NEDs. Indeed, the appraisal and line management of NEDs has previously been the responsibility of the chair and this presents a potential conflict for the chair in their dual role of chair of both bodies. The council is supported in this role by their power to require directors to attend a meeting to obtain information about their organisation's performance and that of its directors. FT chairs and governors will have to consider how they work together to hold the NEDs to account. There is also a clear role for the SID in supporting the council in holding the chair to account.

Under the existing powers they could, if they were dissatisfied with performance, remove the chair or the NEDs. This, however, must be handled sensitively and in accordance with the law. The council should in the first instance liaise informally with Monitor over its concerns after exhausting all informal and internal mechanisms, before moving to a formal dismissal proposal at a council meeting. The council will require the support of the lead governor, SID and company secretary in these circumstances.

■ The FT company secretary

Most of the conversations around the role of the company secretary (see Chapter 10) is applicable to the FT company secretary. However, there some specific aspects of the company secretary role that are critical for the FT model.

In the Monitor Code, Monitor recommends the 'appointment of a secretary to the board of directors and the board of governors' and states that 'a FT secretary has a significant role to play in the administration of corporate governance'. Ham and Hunt's 2008 report, *Membership Governance in NHS Foundation Trusts: A review for the Department of Health,* also argues that the company secretary has a key role in governance [for the FT].

Specific FT duties include establishing and monitoring procedures to ensure that the trust complies with:

- the requirements of the National Health Service Act 2006
- its licence conditions
- its constitution
- its standing orders.

Duties also include acting as the initial point of contact between the board of directors, the council of governors and the regulator, Monitor as set out above. The role also involves supporting the chair in managing the potential conflicts and tensions created by the duality of their role. FT secretaries provide administrative and governance resources for the effective operation of both the board and the council, including any council committees or working groups.

The role also quite often includes ensuring that arrangements are in place for the board and council to communicate effectively with members through a variety of means, and supporting the governors in communicating and engaging with members. The other distinction for the company secretary role is in overseeing the effective arrangements for the election of public, patient and staff governors including by-elections, as required.

The Monitor Code requires that the appointment and removal of the FT secretary is a joint matter for the CEO and chair.

■ Foundation trust reporting requirements

Foundation trusts are required to follow Monitor's annual planning and reporting cycle. This is based upon Monitor's approach to overseeing an FT's compliance, particularly the the provider licence's governance and continuity of services requirements.

This approach is set out in the RAF, which divides the information Monitor may routinely request into four broad categories:

- annual submissions (plans, statutory reporting requirements of the licence holder, and other annual requirements specified in the licence)
- in-year submissions (financial and other service performance information submitted during the year, generally quarterly)
- exception reports (other information that may have material implications for a licence holder's compliance, but which is not routinely requested by Monitor)
- other information from FTs (such as the Well-led framework reviews of FT governance).

The aim of a Monitor assessment under the RAF is to show:

- when there is a significant risk to the financial sustainability of a provider of key NHS services which endangers the continuity of those services
- poor governance at an FT.

These are assessed separately. Each FT is assigned two risk ratings: the continuity of services risk rating (CoSRR) and the governance risk rating (GRR).

The CoSRR states Monitor's view of the risk facing a provider of key NHS services. The services that were previously referred to as 'mandatory' are now called commissioner requested services (CRS). Each FT will have a list of these services – including activity volumes – and the CoSRR will identify the level of risk to the ongoing availability of key services. There are four rating categories ranging from one, which represents the most serious risk rating, to four, representing the least risk level of risk. A low rating does not necessarily represent a breach of the provider's licence, but reflects the degree of financial concern that Monitor may have about a provider and consequently the frequency with which they will monitor it. The framework describes the detailed methodology for the continuity of services risk calculation.

For the GRR, Monitor uses a combination of existing and new methods to assess governance issues at FTs and to gain assurance of their standards of governance, including:

- using national metrics, including A&E waiting times, referral to treatment targets and rates of C.difficile infection;
- serious concerns about an FT from CQC, which may lead Monitor to consider whether the FT is in breach of its licence and what action is needed to address these concerns;
- information received from third parties (such as relating to patterns of patient complaints or infection outbreaks);
- tracking trends in patient metrics such as satisfaction ratings, staff turnover and absenteeism; and
- reviewing the level of assurance provided in the independent reviews of governance that FTs are recommended to have at least every three years.

There are three GRR categories. A green rating is assigned where there are no grounds for concern. Where no overall rating is assigned, Monitor will have identified a concern but not yet taken action; it will provide a written description stating the issue at hand and the action being considered. A red rating will be assigned when Monitor has already begun enforcement action.

The annual plan

The annual plan review (APR) process is designed to identify short-term risks (quality, financial and operational) and long-term risks to the sustainability of high quality healthcare services. The 2014/15 APR process was aligned with the timetable with NHS England and the NHS TDA for NHS trusts and CCGs, with the annual plan split into two parts. The first part considers the operational plans, while the second looked at the strategic plans.

The operational plan includes a narrative and a supporting two-year financial return describing how the FT board intends to ensure high-quality and cost-effective services for patients over the next two years. Monitor reviews this plan to assess the FT board's understanding of the challenges over the next two years, its level of engagement with stakeholders in the local health economy and how well the commissioner and provider activity and revenue assumptions match up. This enables an assessment of how reasonable the plan's assumptions are and the level of capacity that is planning compared with the likely demand.

The strategic review includes a narrative plan and a supporting five-year financial return which explains how the FT board intends to ensure appropriate, high-quality and cost-effective services for patients on a sustainable basis. Monitor reviews the strategic review and assesses the FT's sustainability by considering the robustness of the strategic planning process, the FT's understanding of its local health economy and any likely financial gap based on its current configuration. It will also consider the strategic options outlined to ensure the sustainability of high-quality services for patients, as well as the schemes and initiatives the FT plans to use to secure its long-term sustainability.

The RAF also requires an FT to complete a corporate governance statement in compliance with the governance conditions of their licence within three months of the end of each financial year. The statement sets out any risks to compliance with the governance condition and actions being taken to maintain future compliance as part of the annual plan. This is a forward-looking statement of expectations regarding corporate governance arrangements over the next 12 months.

The Monitor Code states that governors can 'expect to be consulted on the development of forward plans for the trust and any significant changes to the delivery of the trust's business plan'. The role of the governors is to ensure that the interests of the FT's members are considered when establishing the strategic direction for the FT.

Monitor stress-tested the new five-year plans submitted by FTs, as it was concerned that long-term planning by FTs was not robust enough and that many FTs were making over-optimistic forecasts of the earnings they were likely to reinvest in providing improved patient services in future years. The test found the plans of almost one-third of the sector were potentially exposed to risk in this way. The regulator is working with these trusts to remedy the deficiencies and ensure their plans can deliver sustainability in the long term. Consequently, Monitor has developed a comprehensive strategic development toolkit that will help boards and senior managers devise robust five-year plans. The publication *Developing strategy – What every trust board member should know* was also published in October 2014 to support boards in this area.

In-year reporting

In-year reporting is designed to measure and assess the FT's actual performance against its annual plan. Foundation trusts are monitored depending on their risk ratings; for most FTs, in-year reporting includes a quarterly submission to Monitor and other exception or *ad hoc* reports. High performing trusts may be asked to make six-monthly reports to Monitor, while low-performers may have to report each month. The reports cover the FT's financial performance – including income and expenditure, a statement of financial position and cash flow performance – and its performance against national access and outcomes standards (e.g. waiting times and rates of C.difficile).

Monitor reviews the performance against the FT's annual plan and looks at the FT board's assessment of its compliance with its licence. If there is a significant difference between the in-year submissions and the annual plan, the FT board will have to explain why and what it is doing to address the difference. Each quarter, Monitor publishes an overview of the whole FT sector's performance, using the information the FTs provide.

Exception reports are reports on issues that could affect the FT's ability to comply with its licence. These must be sent to Monitor, even if it is not routinely requested. Examples of these issues are listed in the RAF, and include:

- investigations being opened by other authorities
- patient safety incidents or 'never' events
- any significant reputational issues such as any adverse national press attention
- any change in the board.

Annual report and accounts

Each year, the FT must submit its annual report and accounts to Monitor and lay them before Parliament. These should include:

- the annual report (including the quality report)
- the accounting officer's statement of responsibilities
- the auditor's opinion and certificate
- an annual governance statement (AGS)
- a foreword to the accounts
- four primary financial statements
- notes to the accounts.

The technical guidance for the annual report and accounts is set out each year in the *NHS Foundation Trust Annual Reporting Manual* (FT ARM).

In addition to the forward-looking corporate governance statement submitted in the annual plan, the RAF requires FTs to prepare an AGS as part of their annual report. A model statement is set out in FT ARM. It is a backwards-looking statement that captures information on risk management and internal control, and includes some specific requirements on quality governance. It replaced and expanded upon the former requirement for a statement on internal control and is signed by the FT's CEO. The AGS will continue as it is until such time as the AGS and corporate governance statement may be combined.

Quality report and accounts

Foundation trusts must include a report on the quality of care they provide (the quality report) within their overall annual report as set out by FT ARM for the year under review. The quality report specifically aims to improve public accountability for the quality of care. Foundation trusts must also publish Quality Accounts each year, as required by the NHS Act 2009. The Quality Accounts must be published according to the terms set out in the NHS (Quality Accounts) Regulations 2010, as amended by the NHS (Quality Accounts) Amendments Regulations 2011 and the NHS (Quality Accounts) Amendments Regulations 2012 (collectively the Quality Accounts regulations).

The quality report incorporates all the requirements of the quality account regulations as well as a number of additional reporting requirements set by Monitor. The additional Monitor requirements are as follows.

- A statement which gives a monetary total for the amount of income in the year under review conditional upon achieving quality improvement and innovation goals, and a monetary total for the associated payment in the previous year.
- An explanatory note for clinical coding stating that the results should not be extrapolated further than the actual sample audited and which services were reviewed within the sample.
- An overview of the quality of care offered by the FT based on performance in the year under review against indicators selected by the board in consultation with stakeholders, with an explanation of the underlying reason(s) for selection. The indicator set selected must include at least three indicators each for patient safety, clinical effectiveness and patient experience. Where the quality indicators are the same as those used in the previous year's report, the data reported should be consistent.

The FT board is also required to make a statement of directors' responsibilities that the quality report meets the requirements set out in FT ARM for the year under review, including:

- sustainability/climate change – providing a commentary, summary of performance and an outline of future priorities and targets
- NHS staff survey – a statement of the trust's approach to staff engagement, results from the survey, with action plans to address areas of concern, and future priorities and targets
- their Monitor regulatory ratings.

Monitor also requires FTs to include public interest disclosures on the FT's activities and policies in the following areas set out below in their annual reports, and these are often included in the quality report:

- actions taken by the FT to maintain or develop the provision of information to, and consultation with employees
- the FT's policies in relation to disabled employees and equal opportunities
- information on health and safety performance and occupational health
- information on policies and procedures with respect to countering fraud and corruption
- a statement describing the better payment practice code, or any other policy adopted on payment of suppliers, and performance achieved, together with disclosure of any interest paid under the Late Payment of Commercial Debts (Interest) Act 1998
- details of any consultations completed in the previous year, consultations in progress at the date of the report, or consultations planned for the coming year
- consultation with local groups and organisations, including the OSCs of local authorities covering the membership areas
- any other public and patient involvement activities.

To ensure that the information presented is accurate and fairly interpreted, and that the range of services described and priorities for improvement are representative of the services delivered, assurance is required to ensure accuracy. The commissioners have a legal obligation to review and comment on the Quality Accounts, while local Healthwatch organisations and OSCs will be offered the opportunity to comment on a voluntary basis.

Monitor has also previously required FTs to obtain a limited assurance report from their external auditors on the content of the quality report and to include it in the annual report. The limited assurance report has reported on whether anything has come to the attention of the auditor that leads them to believe that the content of the quality report has not been prepared in line with the requirements set out in FT ARM. This is currently under review, along with an alignment of the quality report, quality account and annual report requirements.

The Quality Governance Framework

Monitor developed the Quality Governance Framework (QGF) as an early response to the lessons developing from the failings at Mid Staffordshire NHS Foundation Trust and tighter public finances. It was embedded it into the assessment process for aspirant FTs from August 2010. Aspirant trusts had to achieve a score of 3.5 or less against the QGF to proceed with an application for FT status.

The QGF was subsequently included in the Compliance Framework for existing FTs from April 2011, and is now incorporated into the RAF. Board statements in the corporate governance statement (annual plan) and the annual governance statement (annual report and accounts) requires the FT to demonstrate that the board has formally assessed itself against the QGF in establishing its own quality processes. Under Monitor's new provider licence, paragraph 6 of licence condition FT4 mirrors those of the QGF.

The framework consists of ten questions, which are used to test the robustness of quality governance.

1. Does quality drive the trust's strategy?
2. Is the board sufficiently aware of potential risks to quality?
3. Does the board have the necessary leadership, skills and knowledge to ensure delivery of the quality agenda?
4. Does the board promote a quality-focused culture throughout the trust?
5. Are there clear roles and accountabilities in relation to quality governance?
6. Are there clearly defined, well-understood processes for escalating and resolving issues and managing quality performance?
7. Does the board actively engage patients, staff and other key stakeholders on quality?
8. Is appropriate quality information being analysed and challenged?
9. Is the board assured of the robustness of the quality information?
10. Is quality information used effectively?

However, Monitor became increasingly aware that not all boards realised the amount of work required to achieve this. As a result they produced supporting guidance for boards of directors on this issue. *Quality Governance: How does a board know that its organisation is working effectively to improve patient care?* was published in April 2013 and it is aimed primarily for members of NHS boards to enable them to perform their role in improving health services for patients. It is designed for use across all types of NHS providers, including existing and aspirant FTs in the acute, specialist, ambulance, community and mental health sectors.

The guidance requires boards to develop an overarching Assurance and Escalation Framework (AEF) that provides an aggregated summary of crucial policy and procedural documents and should describe, as a minimum, the board's requirements for seeking internal and external assurance on quality. The AEF should be available to all staff and it should lay out how to escalate information including:

- how staff can and should raise concerns about the impact of cost improvement plans (CIPs) on the quality of care
- defined and understood processes for exception reporting of incidents to the board
- identification of data quality concerns and the application of a robust programme of data quality review
- identification of early warning triggers in relation to workforce, finance and clinical services.

The guidance supports FTs in formulating their corporate governance statements and can also support aspirant FTs in making their board statement on quality governance. It also covers some practical steps that boards can undertake, such as board walk-arounds with actions to follow up, regular staff surveys and putting in place procedures that enable staff to feel confident that they can raise concerns – and that these will be taken seriously. It concludes with a list of questions boards may want to ask themselves to assess how well they are doing.

■ Foundation trust transactions

An increasing number of FTs may plan transactions (including mergers, acquisitions, significant investments, joint ventures and divestments) as they seek to reorganise or respond to changes in the financial climate or the local health economy.

Foundation trusts contemplating a relevant transaction should therefore engage with Monitor at an early stage. The Competition and Markets Authority (CMA) reviews certain transactions involving one or more FTs (including mergers between an FT and an NHS trust) to determine whether the transaction is likely to have adverse effects on patients by reducing competition between providers. FTs can also approach the CMA for informal advice on whether the transaction is within its jurisdiction (seeking informal advice from the CMA will not automatically trigger a review of the transaction). To be reviewable, a transaction must meet certain thresholds. Broadly, these are:

■ if the UK turnover of the acquired organisation exceeds £70 million or
■ if the merged organisation will supply or acquire at least 25% of particular goods or services in a substantial part of the UK and the merger increases that share.

Monitor's August 2014 guidance *Supporting NHS providers: guidance on transactions for NHS foundation trusts* makes it clear that FTs must satisfy Monitor's requirements before entering into any legally binding commitments related to transactions; these are summarised below.

■ For material transactions, Monitor requires a board certification to be submitted to and agreed.
■ For significant transactions, Monitor requires the opportunity to do a detailed review which will result in a transaction risk rating. FTs should only proceed with the transaction if the risk rating is green or amber.
■ For statutory transactions, in order to grant the formal application Monitor must be satisfied that the FT has undertaken the necessary steps to prepare for the transaction, including approval by the council of governors and gaining a green or amber transaction risk rating from Monitor.

An FT can decide for itself what constitutes a 'significant transaction' and may choose to define this in its constitution. Alternatively, if the governors agree, trusts may choose not to give a definition, but this would need to be stated in the constitution. Examples of a definition include any proposed contract valued over a certain monetary threshold or over a certain percentage of the trust's annual turnover, or alternatively using non-monetary terms. If an FT defines some types of transaction as 'significant' in the terms of their constitution, then the FT will need the consent of more than half of the council of governors to proceed with the transaction. However, the consent of more than half of the governors will always be required for any merger, acquisition or separation of the FT. Unlike 'significant transactions', this is not an optional requirement and this means that, in practice, responsibility for signing off any merger or acquisition moves jointly to the directors and governors. NHSI

Where an FT is seeking to merge with or acquire an NHS trust, NHS TDA will normally have a role as vendor. In this instance, NHS TDA's responsibilities include:

- confirming to the Secretary of State that assurances are in place for various aspects of the transaction (including quality, sustainability and taxpayers' value for money)
- working with the NHS trust to ensure it has the necessary support to navigate the transaction processes
- maintaining quality, operational and financial performance, board focus and risk management.

Directors and governors must agree on a process for the approval of transactions by governors. Such a process might specify:

- the content and timing of information to be provided to governors
- at what point in the process governors will be asked to approve the transaction(s)
- how the views of members will be sought and stakeholders kept informed.

Responsibilities of directors and governors in transactions are shown in Table 11.1

Governors should be provided with as much information as reasonably possible for them to be able to make an informed judgement. To ensure the governors have sufficient information, and are assured that the board has been through a thorough and comprehensive process before voting on the transaction, the governors' formal vote should take place: vote conditions

- after the finalisation of due diligence reports;
- after Monitor's issuance of its amber or green risk rating; and
- soon after the board's approval.

Table 11.1: Responsibilities of directors and governors in transactions

Executive directors	Non-executive directors	Governors
Executive directors should make proposals for the future of the organisation. They should work with governors by providing them with sufficient information on a proposed transaction for the purposes of considering their required approval. They should explain to governors why they believe the transaction is necessary and provide evidence to support their view.	Non-executive directors should challenge the executives to justify their recommendations, deal with the risks involved and seek assurance that the executive directors' decisions are the right ones.	The council of governors must approve any statutory or significant transactions. Governors are responsible for satisfying themselves that the board of directors (that is, executive and NEDs collectively) has been thorough and comprehensive in reaching its proposal (that is, has undertaken proper due diligence) and that it has obtained and considered the interests of trust members and the public as part of the decision-making process. Provided appropriate assurance is obtained, governors should not unreasonably withhold their consent for a proposal to go ahead.

This places the governors' vote shortly before completion in the process, after the full business case stage. The vote should, however, take place before the trust's formal application to Monitor (required for statutory transactions), since governor approval must be obtained before Monitor can grant the application.

Once the governors have approved a transaction and the chair has confirmed that it is not confidential, the council of governors should communicate the result to the FT members and the public. Governors are likely to need the FT's help to do so, for example, through its website or at an advertised drop-in session with the governors. The communication method should be agreed locally.

■ The foundation trust governance challenge

The Health and Social Care Act 2012 significantly extended the role of the council of governors. This raises a number of questions around their capacity and capability; many governors are likely to require significant training to understand and be able to discharge their duties. The increased responsibilities may also reduce or limit the number of people who are willing to fill the role.

ICSA's March 2011 memorandum to Parliament states:

> 'Significant resources will have to be made available to governors in order to hold the board of directors to account and understand the competitive market when asked to vote on significant transactions. The requirements on governors are going to be onerous, and councils of governors will require at least some, if not all, of their number to have the financial and commercial skills to evaluate FT proposals in relation to mergers, acquisitions and other significant transactions ... There is also concern as to how governors can reconcile their role as representatives of the membership and play a significant part in the strategic decision making process.'

To support governors in this role, Monitor has established an independent panel to give 'authoritative' advice to governors in response to concerns about constitutional and governance issues. To limit referrals to material areas of concern, referral of a matter to the panel requires the approval of more than half of the governors' council. This may mean that the FT will need to provide more ongoing support and advice to its council of governors.

In addition, the NHS Leadership Academy, working in partnership with the NHS Providers, has commissioned the Governwell programme as a one-stop national resource for FTs to develop their governors' knowledge and skills.

There are a number of other governance issues that arise for FTs that particularly highlight the challenges that arise in health service governance.

Ultimately, health service governance is concerned with the practices and procedures to ensure that the individual parts of the NHS are run in such a way that they achieve their objectives, as well as being in line with public sector values such as VFM and providing universal and free healthcare benefits to all those in need. This provides an interesting contrast to the objectives of a company in the private sector, where the aim is to maximise the wealth of its owners (the shareholders) subject to various guidelines and constraints and with regard to other groups or individuals with an interest in what the company does.

The question for FTs relates to ownership, and therefore who sets the objectives for the organisation. Who owns the NHS organisation and the healthcare services it provides? The governance structure of FTs has attempted to articulate the answer to this question: the FT is accountable to its members and therefore should be governed according to their interests.

The changes proposed by the HSCA 2012 reinforce this view by further empowering governors (the representatives of the members). This only emphasises the largest health service governance issue for FTs – how to establish an effective relationship between the members and their elected representatives.

It is not appropriate to liken the members of an FT to the shareholders of a listed company, as this does not reflect the complexity and breadth of the diversity of interests that are represented by FT members (although there are limited grounds for viewing the governors as proxy shareholders). In other words, the members authorise governors to speak and act for them in respect of the business of the FT. The challenge for FTs has been how to ensure that governors are aware of, and informed by, the healthcare concerns of their respective constituencies and the members they represent.

In addition, there are a considerable number of other arrangements that already exist to provide patient and public involvement and scrutiny of NHS decision-making, such as HealthWatch and local government overview and scrutiny committees. How do these work alongside the membership and council of governors?

Other governance issues faced by FTs include the following.

- **Accountability:** governors must be accountable to their constituencies. If a governor is not representing the interests of the members who elected him then there must be clear procedures about how such a governor might be removed. The constitution currently sets out grounds for disqualification but these do not include failure to act in the interests of the members.
- **The dual role of the chair:** chairing both the board of directors and the council of governors will expose the chair to ongoing conflicts of interest. With the increasing power of the council of governors, the chair's role will be crucial and it will require high levels of interpersonal and listening skills.
- **The role of the company secretary:** a fundamental support for the chair in this role is the company secretary or FT secretary, who will require 'a sophisticated understanding of the political dynamics at play within the governance structure'. Equally, the secretary will be the senior manager to whom the governors and members relate. They will be a useful player in helping to manage the relationships between stakeholders, and act as an early warning for the chair when issues arise.

The Foundation Trust Network

NHS Providers (now known as NHS Providers) plays a key role in supporting FTs in facing these challenges, as well as representing the views and common interests of FTs and those aspiring to FT status. It has established a track record as the national voice for the FT movement. It has an extensive programme of influencing, networking and learning events for members with a variety of member benefits and opportunities to get involved in their work.

The FTN was originally set up in June 2004 and became NHS Providers in November 2014. It currently has over 200 NHS organisations in membership – including nearly all of the authorised FTs, most of the NHS trusts, mental health and ambulance trusts and, more recently, community services providers. It is led by an elected board of trustees who are chairs and CEO of the member organisations and is an incorporated charity. Membership of the NHS Providers is open to all NHS Provider organisations, including FTs.

In September 2014, the Foundation Trust Governors Association (FTGA) merged with NHS Providers in order to deliver a comprehensive governance support service for members. One of the recommendations of the Francis Report was that the role of FT governors be expanded. The merged organisation aims to support this through targeted support including development days, networking opportunities, enhanced policy support and high quality member communications. This support will complement GovernWell, the national training programme for FT governors.

Governance Checklist

✓ Is the board aware of how the FT's compliance with its licence is assessed by Monitor? In particular, does it understand the requirements of FT licence condition 4?

✓ Does the board review the requirements of the Monitor Code to ensure it is compliant?

✓ Has the FT's constitution been properly approved by the board and council (and members if required)?

✓ Are the board and council confident that the terms of the constitution are in line with HSCA 2012 and that they are followed? How would they become aware of a breach of the constitution?

✓ Are all FT board meetings held in public?

✓ Are the statutory board and council committees properly constituted?

✓ Are the directors aware of their duties under HSCA 2012?

✓ How does the board keep in touch with members, patients and the local community?

✓ How do governors secure and report back on feedback that will enable them to fulfil their duty to represent the interests of members and the public?

✓ How representative is the trust's membership? Is the representation and effectiveness of member engagement report in the annual report?

✓ Have all governors been elected in accordance with the model election rules?

✓ Are the governors actively involved in developing the recruitment and appointment process for new NEDs?

✓ Are the governors aware of the extent of their authority and powers and the purposes for which they have been granted? Is there an induction and development programme for governors in place?

✓ When is the Well-Led Governance Review scheduled?

✓ Does the board and council business programme allow for the FT reporting requirements to be considered in a timely manner?

✓ Has the FT defined a significant transaction?

▪ Summary

The unique governance structure of FTs warrants a complete chapter of its own in this publication as each part of the structure – the membership, the council and the board – has its own specific role to play in an FT's governance arrangements. The reporting requirements of Monitor are also distinct from the arrangements elsewhere with the NHS TDA and NHS England; however, in more recent times there have been demonstrable steps by the agencies to work more closely together.

The original concept for FTs – increased autonomy, freedom from central government and greater local accountability – are still yet to be fully achieved. Neither has the creation of FTs solved the financial or clinical sustainability challenges that the NHS faces. While the private income cap has been lifted, the complexity and immaturity of the new commissioning structures make it hard for FTs to plan and operate strategically despite Monitor's best efforts. In addition, the regulatory burden continues to grow and the response to challenges such as A&E waiting times and financial deficits results in a somewhat hands-on management approach from the Secretary of State and Monitor. Consequently, FTs still continue to look towards their regulator and the DH rather than to the local population and its representatives.

12

Governance of clinical commissioning groups

■ CCGs and the NHS landscape

The Health and Social Care Act 2012 moved responsibility for commissioning care to clinicians by introducing new statutory bodies called clinical commissioning groups (CCGs) which replaced primary care trusts from April 2013.

CCGs are responsible for commissioning secondary and community care services, and they have a legal duty to support quality improvement in primary care. Most of the NHS commissioning budget is now managed by the 211 CCGs. These are groups of general practices which come together in each area to enable GPs, working with other health professionals, to commission services for their local communities. CCGs are different entities from previous NHS arrangements, with each GP practice being a member and clinicians leading commissioning decisions. The CCG is its member practices; the members are the authority and they appoint a governing body to act on their behalf.

The services that CCGs commission include:

- maternity services
- most community health services
- mental health and learning disability services
- planned hospital care
- rehabilitative care
- urgent and emergency care (including out-of-hours and accident and emergency services).

CCGs are accountable to their public and patients, to NHS England (via the local area team) and to their member practices. HSCA 2012 and subsequent regulations require each member of a CCG (each GP practice) to appoint an individual to act on its behalf in dealings with the CCG. The intention is that this person has to be a GP or other healthcare professional. Most CCGs then have some form of member council that comprises either all practice representatives (in smaller CCGs) or locality representatives (in larger CCGs).

All CCGs are required to have a governing body that provides the challenge and assurance that their accountabilities are being effectively met. The NHS England local area teams play a role in holding CCGs to account and providing them with developmental support. CCGs are also supported by commissioning support units (CSUs), which are intended to have a commercial (rather than managerial) relationship with their CCG customers.

CCGs have an important relationship with the new health and wellbeing boards that have been established in local authorities. These boards are intended as a forum for strategic co-ordination and as a means of enhancing the accountability of the health system to the local population. CCGs have a legal obligation to consider the local needs and priorities identified by these boards, as laid out in their health and wellbeing strategies.

Commissioning decisions can impact on numerous services and over wide geographical areas. CCGs need to take this into account and they should seek to work together, developing collaborative commissioning arrangements when such complex decisions are to be made. Clinical senates will exist to help commissioners make the best decisions by considering the strategic impact of proposals. In addition, in order to plan their commissioning decisions, local authorities and CCGs (coming together through health and wellbeing boards) will use Joint Strategic Needs Assessments (JSNAs), and Joint Health and Wellbeing Strategies (JHWSs) to agree local priorities for local health and care commissioning.

The role of NHS England and the local area team

The CCG Assurance Framework published by NHS England describes the very different roles that the NHS England local area teams have with CCGs. These include:

- a developmental role – providing CCGs with support
- an assurance role – holding CCGs to account
- a co-commissioning role – working as a partner in commissioning local services

As co-commissioners of healthcare, CCGs and NHS England have to work together to contribute jointly to improving services for patients. Each organisation has a mutual responsibility to identify areas for improvement. The CCG Assurance Framework identified six domains that underpin the relationship between NHS England and the CCG. These are:

- **Domain 1:** Are patients receiving clinically commissioned, high-quality services?
- **Domain 2:** Are patients and the public actively engaged and involved?
- **Domain 3:** Are CCG plans delivering better outcomes for patients?
- **Domain 4:** Does the CCG have robust governance arrangements?
- **Domain 5:** Are CCGs working in partnership with others?
- **Domain 6:** Does the CCG have strong and robust leadership?

In November 2014, NHS England also published the report *Next steps towards primary care co-commissioning*, which sets out three possible standard models for the co-commissioning of primary care by CCGs and NHS England. The report recognised, however, that such co-commissioning could significantly increase the frequency and range of potential conflicts of interest, especially for delegated arrangements. As a consequence, NHS England established a strengthened approach to managing these conflicts.

■ CCGs, the law and the regulatory frameworks

The CCG's overarching duty to involve patients and the public is outlined in Chapter 3. In addition, HSCA 2012's amendments to the NHS Act 2006 imposes further duties on the establishment of CCGs (in sections 25–28). In summary, these requirements are the duty of the CCG to:

- exercise its functions effectively, efficiently and economically
- obtain appropriate advice
- promote education and training
- promote integration
- promote the NHS Constitution
- promote innovation in the provision of health services (including innovation in the arrangements made for their provision)
- promote patient choice
- promote research on matters relevant to the health service, and the use in the health service of evidence obtained from research
- reduce inequalities in respect of access and outcomes
- secure continuous improvement in the quality of services provided or in the prevention, diagnosis or treatment of illness (quality is defined as the effectiveness and safety of the services, and the quality of the experience undergone by patients).

A CCG also has a general financial duty to:

- ensure its expenditure does not exceed the aggregate of its allotments for the financial year
- ensure its use of resources does not exceed the amount specified by NHS England for the financial year
- take account of any directions issued in respect of specified types of resource used in a financial year to ensure the CCG does not exceed an amount specified by NHS England
- publish an explanation of how the CCG spent any payment in respect of quality made to it by the NHS Commissioning Board.

CCGs are required to have a governing body by HSCA 2012. It is not a committee of the CCG and the constitution must specify the arrangements made by the CCG for the discharge of functions by the group's.

The NHS Commissioning Board and Clinical Commissioning Group (Responsibilities and Standing Rules) Regulations 2012 set out the healthcare services that will be commissioned by NHS England and specifies the categories of people for whom CCGs will commission services. They also set out certain financial matters for the governing body, and the standing rules regulations that detail those people who are disqualified from being a chair or member of a CCG. These include:

- an MP, MEP or London Assembly Member
- a member of a local authority in England, Wales, Scotland or Northern Ireland
- an employee, member, shareholder or partner of an organisation providing commissioning support
- anyone convicted in the prior five years of any UK offence; or offence outside of the UK if deemed illegal at home and convicted to a sentence of three months or more
- anyone subject to (interim) bankruptcy restrictions under insolvency legislation
- anyone dismissed from paid employment (not including redundancy) in the previous five years from any NHS organisation (including Wales, Scotland and Northern Ireland)
- a healthcare professional subject to an investigation or proceedings by a regulatory body resulting in suspension or removal from the register, prevention or conditions on practising from those not removed from the register
- someone subject to an order or undertaking from company directors' disqualification legislation
- a person removed from being a trustee by charities legislation.

Becoming a CCG

NHS England set out the application process for becoming a CCG in the October 2012 publication *Clinical Commissioning Group Authorisation: Guide for applicants*. The requirements to become a CCG were divided into six domains:

1. a strong clinical and multi-professional focus which brings real added value
2. meaningful engagement with patients, carers and their communities
3. clear and credible plans, which continue to deliver the Quality, Innovation, Productivity and Prevention (QIPP) challenge within financial resources, in line with national requirements (including excellent outcomes) and local joint health and wellbeing strategies
4. proper constitutional and governance arrangements, with the capacity and capability to deliver all their duties and responsibilities including financial control, as well as effectively commissioning all the services for which they are responsible
5. collaborative arrangements for commissioning with other CCGs, local authorities and the NHSCB as well as the appropriate commissioning support
6. great leaders who individually and collectively can make a real difference.

In order to be authorised, CCGs have to meet the following requirements:

- they must have a geographical area A
- all of England must be covered without overlaps
- all designated holders of primary care contracts must be members of a CCG
- there must be a governing body, with an accountable officer and a chief finance officer C
- the governing body has to have at least two lay members, who have to take specific responsibility for audit and governance and for public and patient engagement D
- the CCG has to have its constitution authorised by NHS England. E

Each CCG has to complete the authorisation process as laid down by NHS England. There were three possible outcomes of the authorisation process for each CCG.

- **Fully authorised:** the CCG has demonstrated to NHS England that it satisfies all the requirements and criteria for authorisation. A list of the powers and duties that a fully authorised CCG has are set out in the publication *The functions of CCGs* (March 2013)
- **Authorised with conditions:** If the CCG has not fully satisfied NHS England that it meets all the thresholds for authorisation, conditions may be set or directions given as to how it carries out any of its functions. Conditions or directions will be specific to the particular criteria that have not been satisfied, and proportionate to the level of risk associated with the relevant function.
- **Established but not authorised:** legally these 'shadow CCGs' were established 'with conditions' but where the conditions were such that it could not be described as authorised to take on its functions as a CCG. NHS England made alternative arrangements for commissioning for that population until the shadow CCG was ready to move forward to authorisation.

All 211 CCGs were fully authorised by March 2014, meaning they met all 119 criteria for authorisation.

Other NHS England guidance

The NHS England website hosts a substantial amount of guidance on governance in CCGs. Key publications include:

- *Towards establishment: Creating responsive and accountable clinical commissioning groups*
- *Clinical commissioning group governing body members: Role outlines, attributes and skills*
- *The functions of CCGs*
- NHS England directions to CCGs
- CCG annual reporting Guidance

- A best practice resource/practical toolkit for the appointment of lay members to clinical commissioning groups
- *Code of conduct: Managing conflicts of interest*, for situations where GP practices are potential providers of CCG-commissioned services
- Procedures for CCG constitution change, merger or dissolution
- *The Good Governance Standard for Public Services*.

Other than the minimum composition and a model constitution set out in HSCA 2012, there are no specific requirements for CCG governance. NHS England advocates adherence with the *Good Governance Standard for Public Services* as the guidance for best practice. It builds on the Nolan principles for the conduct of individuals in public life, by setting out six core principles of good governance for public service organisations as set out in Chapter 3 and illustrated in Figure 12.1.

Figure 12.1: The six core principles of the Good Governance Standard

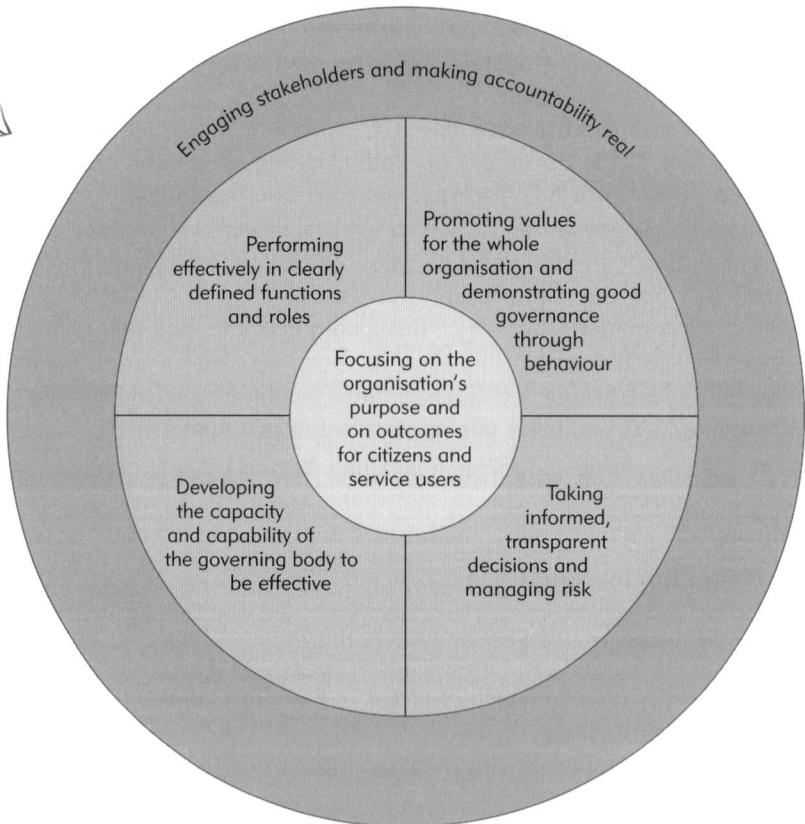

Source: Good Governance Standard for Public Services 2004

It is important to note that the standard presupposes a form of leadership that~~not~~ *unitary* is not based on the principle of a unitary board. This is in stark contrast to most other NHS organisations (such as FTs) for whom the unitary board is a core principle of governance. As such, CCGs are unlikely to operate in a way that is entirely consistent with the major codes of corporate governance practice for the NHS (such as the UK Corporate Governance Code, King III, the Higgs Report and the Monitor Code).

Nevertheless, the Standard states that organisations should be clear about a number of areas that bear a close similarity to the recommendations in the above codes:

- the responsibilities of non-executives and the executive, and that those responsibilities are carried out (Standard 2.2)
- members of the governing body behaving in ways that uphold and exemplify effective governance (Standard 3.2) and
- engaging stakeholders and making accountability real (Standard 6).

The standard also includes a useful appendix, which sets out questions for members of the public and their representatives to ask if they want to assess and challenge standards of governance.

The CCG model constitution

CCG governance and decision-making depends on the form of a CCG's constitution. While every CCG is legally required to have a governing body, audit committee and remuneration committee, there can be some variation between each CCG in the arrangements in place for setting strategy and performing its functions.

The July 2013 King's Fund and Nuffield Trust publication *Clinical commissioning groups: Supporting improvement in general practice?* revealed that:

'In-depth knowledge of the constitution was scarce [within CCGs], both in the governing body and the membership ... many GPs who were, nominally, signatories to the constitution expressed little knowledge of its contents.'

All CCG constitutions should contain the following information:

- the title of the CCG and its geographical area of operation;
- the purpose of the CCG and from where it derives its legal duties and powers;
- its powers – the ways in which the CCG can fulfil its duties, the activities it may or may not undertake;
- amendments and variations to the constitution requiring the permission of NHS England;
- membership criteria, list of members, voting rights and responsibilities and details of any removal procedures. It may also include the requirement for any membership rights to be exercised in the best interests of the CCG;

- functions and general duties and an outline as to how those duties and functions will be fulfilled, including any conditions attached to the CCG by NHS England; and
- governance arrangements – the principles to be followed, how the CCG will be administered and how decisions will be made.

Other details should include information about the governing body, other committees and joint working powers; accountability – how the group will demonstrate and effect accountability to its local health economy; and arrangements for engaging with interested parties in commissioning and service re-configuration.

Further provisions contained in a well-written constitution will include:

- procedures for appointing governing body and committee members
- procedures for appointing the chair
- eligibility conditions for such positions
- re-appointment, tenure, co-option procedures
- procedures for the removal of governing body and committee members
- details of how governing body, committee and member meetings will be run
- the quorum needed to transact business
- frequency of meetings
- a statement and details regarding the management of conflicts of interest
- a clause indemnifying GP member practices and governing body members.

In addition, the model NHS CCG constitution features options to include:

- the mission, values and aims of the CCG
- group committees details
- joint arrangements
- transparency arrangements
- financial policies
- standing orders
- schemes of delegation and reservation
- checklists.

Careful thought should be given as to what material is included within the constitution, as some aspects of administration and strategy are likely to change with time. Such aspects that may be subject to amendment and change and which are not central to the constitution, should not be included in the constitution – such as naming an individual in the constitution as opposed to a role. The constitution forms part of the CCG's authorisation, and any changes to the document must be agreed by NHS England. Any amendments to the constitution will not become valid until that permission has been granted.

A CCG can request an amendment to the constitution twice each year. However any amendments that will impact on the financial allocation for the group have to meet a June deadline. NHS England demands assurance from the accountable officer, on behalf of the CCG, that the constitution will continue to meet legal requirements. There is no appeal process against NHS England's decision to approve proposed changes. As soon as an amended constitution comes into effect, the CCG should make arrangements to ensure the document is available to the public.

ICSA Code of Governance for NHS CCGs

The ICSA published a governance code for CCGs in November 2013. It was developed with the support of an expert panel including NHS leaders and chaired by Lord Hunt of Wirral. There is a commitment to update the code at a future date in an effort to ensure it reflects lessons learned.

The objective of the six principles contained within the code is to:

'support clinicians, and those that work with them, to perform their commissioning activities and help to maintain public trust in clinicians and the NHS. [Moreover] application of the principles...should be proportionate and appropriate for each CCG and its governing body.'

The document outlines some suggestions for how a CCG can achieve each of the six principles and poses a set of questions for consideration (see Table 12.1).

Table 12.1: ICSA Code of Governance for NHS CCGs

Principle	Suggestions
Ensure effective decision-making processes to drive improvements in experience and quality	Member practices and the governing body need a working relationship underpinned by trust, with roles and responsibilities established. Among the suggested mechanisms are: open communication between CCG committees, the governing body and members; transparent approach to resolving any disputes; and clear guidance. The CCG should consider how involved their member practices are involved in its work and whether members understand how to challenge decisions.
Co-operation with 'interested provider parties' to enhance outcomes	This could involve: identification and management of both 'potential and real conflicts of interest'; developing relationships with both 'current and future' providers and keeping them under review; and highlighting outcome improvements in a variety of formats. The CCG also needs to consider how it gathers feedback 'from and about' providers and its processes for responding to concerns from regulators regarding local providers.

Principle	Suggestions
Develop strong relationships with other CCGs and regulators to support local and national health systems and contribute to wider policy debate	The CCG and governing body need to ensure clarity around 'the form, level and scope of co-operation required' with the various actors within the system. This can include: guidance for authorised individuals; provision of appropriate information to other organisations; and clear information requests. CCGs should 'maintain full records of delegated decision-making' and also keep these under regular review.
Combine collective accountability with 'drawing on the strengths and expertise' from individuals	Governing body members hold equal responsibility for the decisions taken and need to ensure that the CCG invariably complies with relevant legislation and regulation. They must also remain fully aware of relationships and responsibilities with others including patients, member practices and committees. All members should have undertaken a comprehensive induction and clear understanding of aspects such as decision-making and collective responsibilities.
The CCG should ensure the views of patients, carers and the public are utilised to inform commissioning and consider consequences of decisions	Among the suggested methods for delivering on this principle are: holding governing body meetings whenever appropriate; effective communication; holding consultations 'on significant changes to services commissioned and policies affecting the wider health economy'; and a system that manages complaints 'constructively, impartially and effectively'. Governing body members need to consider target audience identification, the inclusion of public and patient engagement within CCG annual reports and the publication procedure around learning from complaints.
'Robust and effective processes for decision-making' to provide foundations for 'transparency and accountability at every level'	Governing body members are tasked with ensuring their CCG has strong arrangements in place for governance, which could include: adherence to the Nolan principles; promotion of the NHS Constitution's values; and an updated register of interests. Among the areas for governing body members to consider here are: whether an annual summary of information is publicly available; the regular review of Freedom of Information activity; and feedback in relation to procurement.

■ CCG governance structures, governing bodies and committees

CCGs are clinically led membership organisations accountable to their constituent GP practices. These member practices must decide how the CCG will operate, through developing the CCG constitution within the legislative framework. They must ensure that the CCG is led and governed in an open and transparent way, which allows them to serve their patients and population effectively.

As a membership organisation, it is the CCG members that must ensure the CCG complies with the full range of regulations and legislation to ensure the group is governed appropriately. Whether it is statutory requirements or NHS guidance, CCG members are legally accountable for meeting these obligations though acting in the best interests of the organisation, patients, their carers and the wider CCG community.

Members

All GP practices are required by law to be a member of a CCG. Changes to the General Medical Services (GMS) Contract Regulations in 2013 made it a contractual requirement for all GP practices to be a member of a CCG and for every GP practice to nominate a practice representative to liaise with the CCG.

The legal requirement for a GP practice to be a 'member' of a CCG means:

- that practices must nominate a practice representative to liaise with the CCG
- that practices should be able to demonstrate that they have engaged with the CCG in line with the requirements outlined in the CCG constitution and subject to the reasonableness of the CCG's requests
- that practices should abide by the contents of the CCG constitution
- that, similar to the requirements for practices to work with commissioning decisions of PCTs, practices should work with commissioning decisions of the CCG and NHS England.

The CCG cannot expel a practice as they need to have coherent geographical coverage, therefore there should be no provisions within the constitution that give CCGs the power to expel a practice. The HSCA 2012 does give CCGs the power to apply to NHS England to have a member practice expelled from the group in extreme circumstances. Such circumstances might include refusal to engage or participate with CCG activities, failure to demonstrate active effort to address agreed practice/clinical behaviour, failure to support local plans and/or no commitment to supporting other practices or the CCG by sharing expertise and/or delivery where capacity and resources allow.

The model constitution requires each CCG to define the role of their member practice representatives and to ensure that the arrangements made for the discharge of their functions secure the effective participation by each member of the group in exercising its functions. Practice representatives are individuals

practice rep

appointed by a member practice to act on its behalf in the dealings between it and the group, under regulations made under sections 89 or 94 of the 2006 Act (as amended by section 28 of HSCA 2012) or directions under section 98A of the 2006 Act (as inserted by section 49 of HSCA 2012).

Each CCG may also identify a number of other GPs or primary care health professionals from member practices to support the work of the group and/or represent the group rather than represent their own individual practices. Any such role, which is not required by statute, must be set out in the constitution.

CCGs have a statutory duty to ensure the effective participation of member practices in the exercise of the CCG's functions as set out in HSCA 2012. This means that practices can challenge the CCG if they feel that it is not fulfilling its statutory duty to ensure effective member participation. For example, the constitution will include electoral procedures and how member practices can remove a CCG governing body member. The July 2013 Kings Fund/Nuffield Trust research mentioned earlier recommends that GP practices should ensure that they understand how to hold their CCG to account and to get involved in the decisions of the CCG.

The model constitution establishes that the CCG is accountable for exercising the statutory functions of the group. It may grant authority to act on its behalf to:

- any of its members
- its governing body
- employees
- a committee or sub-committee of the group.

Like FTs and NHS trusts, the governing body is required by statute to have audit and remuneration committees at a minimum. The extent of each party's authority to act depends on the powers delegated to them by the CCG as expressed through its scheme of reservation and delegation (or terms of reference for committees).

The scheme of reservation and delegation sets out those decisions that are reserved for the membership as a whole and those decisions that are the responsibilities of its governing body (and its committees), the group's committees and sub-committees, individual members and employees. The CCG remains accountable for all of its functions, including those that it has delegated. The CCG's standing orders stipulate that ordinary meetings of the CCG shall be held at regular intervals at such times and places as the CCG may determine. They should provide further detail on frequency, notice and authority for calling such meetings.

Many CCGs have interpreted this as some form of 'member council' comprising either representatives from all practices (in smaller CCGs) or locality representatives (in larger CCGs). The precise responsibilities delegated to these members' councils differ, but often include approving the CCG's constitution and proposed changes to the constitution, such as:

- the powers reserved to the membership and those delegated to the governing body, committees, employees or other persons specified in the CCG's constitution
- the overarching scheme of reservation and delegation
- the membership of the CCG's governing body and committees.

Such a council may also be responsible for:

- the arrangements for members joining and leaving the CCG
- the appointment of the chair and chief officer
- ensuring publication of the annual report and accounts by the governing body.

There is no requirement for the members meetings to be held in public, but some CCG councils have voted to do so.

Details as to how practice representatives are selected should be set out in a group's standing orders and must comply with regulations. Many CCGs have local GP groups, which are often known as 'localities'. According to the Kings Fund/Nuffield Trust research, these 'locality' structures have been put in place in approximately 70% of CCGs across England. The locality groups act as an engagement mechanism to pass information between practices and the governing body, as well as a means of identifying local priorities. Some localities may be given a greater degree of autonomy and play a very important role in the organisation. For example, they may be given an annual commissioning budget and allowed to keep a proportion of any underspend for reinvestment in local priorities.

The model constitution requires CCGs that wish to delegate authority to their localities (as a committee of the group) to include in their constitution details of the role of the locality and to whom they are accountable. The locality committee must account to the governing body when it undertakes work which falls within the scope of the functions of the governing body. The CCG is free to determine the scope of the responsibilities delegated to locality committees and to include in the terms of reference for each committee how it will be held to account for its work. Reference should also be made as how the locality committee will relate to the broader membership and the governing body in discharging its functions.

Elections and appointments

The model constitution does not specify exactly how the governing body, officers and committees should be elected and dismissed. Therefore, the accountability structure can vary in the actual details from CCG to CCG.

One version is where the member practices elect a representative to sit on a member council. The member council then appoints the non-officer members of the governing body, and the governing body appoints the specific officers of the CCG (the chair, accountable officer and chief financial officer).

An alternative model sees the member practices directly select and elect or appoint their governing body members and chair. Regardless of the structure used, the governing body is always accountable to the member practices for the running of the CCG in accordance with its constitution.

Appointments are usually made in relation to the executive members, lay members and non-GP clinicians of the governing body – accountable officer, chief financial officer, secondary care clinician and so on. Typically, a process of open competition and advertisement is completed. This may be undertaken by the members council or governing body dependent upon the constitution. These appointments are usually only made on a permanent basis for executive members, with fixed-term appointments for the other roles.

Elections usually take place in relation to GP members and the chair, with nominations will be made by the member practices. An election will then take place if there is more than one candidate,. The election may be overseen and administered by the members council or by the local medical committee. If a CCG has localities, then votes can only be cast for one of the GPs standing in their own locality area. Depending upon the CCG's constitution, votes may be available to all GPs providing primary medical services to a registered list of patients (based on a general medical services, personal medical services or alternative provider medical services contract) and practicing within the geographical area of the CCG (one person, one vote). Alternatively, votes may be allocated to each member practice based on the population it serves.

Some CCG member councils have established members council advisory panels, which is a small panel comprising of three council members and an independent HR adviser. It oversees the process of appointing members to the governing body – including the chair – by assessing prospective candidates to determine their suitability for the role, then inviting suitable candidates to stand for election. The panel then makes recommendations to the members' council on those appointments.

Governing body

The CCG is required by statute and it is not a committee. The constitution must specify the arrangements made by the CCG for the discharge of functions by its governing body. Details concerning the functions and composition of the governing body should be specified in the group's constitution.

The main functions of the governing body are described in section 14L of the 2006 Act (inserted by section 25 of HSCA 2012). The governing body's principal aim is to ensure that the group has made appropriate arrangements for ensuring that it complies with its obligations to exercise its functions effectively, efficiently, economically and in line with relevant generally accepted principles of good governance.

The model constitution framework sets out that the governing body must not have less than six members, consisting of:

- the chair
- representatives of member practices

- other GPs or primary care health professionals
- a minimum of two lay members – one to lead on audit, remuneration and conflict of interest matters and one to lead on patient and public participation matters
- a registered nurse
- a secondary care specialist doctor
- the accountable officer
- the chief finance officer
- any other individuals as required by the CCG.

CCGs may choose to have more than two lay members and other individual roles on the governing body, but this must be specified in their constitution. As with all such structures, the numerical size of the governing body needs to be considered. It should not be so large as to be unwieldy, but not so small as to lack the necessary skills and experience. As the governing body is not a committee, it cannot have terms of reference and, therefore details about its composition must be specified in the CCG's constitution. The standing orders of the CCG should also set out:

- how the group will appoint such members of the governing body (e.g. will they be elected?)
- the tenure of office
- how such a person would resign from their post
- the grounds for removal from office.

Tenure

Terms of office for all elections and appointments to the governing body are as set out in each CCG's constitution. With the exception of executive appointments, which are made on a permanent basis, there is little consistency as to the terms that are offered – some are for two or three years, while others are for five years. There is no mandated limit set on the maximum term of office. The guidance given elsewhere in this handbook may be considered but is only advisory. Even so, it is critical that CCGs consider how to find a balance between continuity of knowledge and renewal of thinking in the governing body.

Section 13 of The National Health Service (Clinical Commissioning Groups) Regulations 2012 states there is nothing to prevent the re-appointment of a chair or a deputy chair whose term of office has come to an end, or a person's appointment as either chair or deputy chair following a term of office as the other (remembering that the deputy chair must be a lay person).

The remuneration committee

The NHS England guidance *Remuneration guidance for chief officers (where the senior manager also undertakes the accountable officer role) and chief finance officers* makes it clear that CCGs must have a remuneration committee drawn from the CCG's governing body, of whom one member should act as its chair.

Section 15 of The National Health Service (Clinical Commissioning Groups) Regulations 2012 stipulates that the committee chair must be appointed by the CCG for a term to be determined by the CCG. It also states that all members of the governing body other than lay persons are disqualified from being the chair.

The committee should not include full-time employees or individuals who claim a significant proportion of their income from the CCG, nor should member practices be in the majority. The committee will make recommendations to the CCG governing body as to the determination of remuneration, fees, pension and allowances payable to the employees of the CCG. No governing body member or senior manager should be present for discussions about their own remuneration (although it is reasonable for the chief officer, the HR lead and other senior managers where appropriate, to attend meetings of the committee during which the remuneration of other staff is discussed). The governing body should approve and keep under review the terms of reference for the remuneration committee, which include information on the membership of the committee and should be available upon request to the public.

In addition, some CCGs have conferred on or delegated to the remuneration committee the authority to make recommendations on remuneration and terms of service for elected governing body members.

The remuneration of CCGs is largely in their own hands. There is minimal national guidance and no control from other bodies. This is very unlike the situation for many other parts of the NHS and other public bodies, and includes the appointment and remuneration of the lay or non-executive members. Therefore, CCGs are at risk of being exposed to reputational challenge from both the public and its membership. To mitigate this, CCGs should ensure that the remuneration process is as transparent as possible, has a credible and carefully considered logic and, where national guidance exists and is not followed, that a clear rationale is in place.

Annex 2 of the NHS England guidance *Clinical commissioning group governing body members: role outlines, attributes and skills* proposes a number of principles that CCGs may wish to take into account as they determine the reimbursement or remuneration rates for individuals on the governing body who undertake their roles on a part-time or sessional basis, since many governing body members will continue in their clinical roles.

The principles recommend that all payments should be evidently in line with the individual's current earnings, commensurate with the average rate for their current employment or the specific role or demonstrably required to provide backfill. The guidance goes on to set out what these principles mean for GPs, other practice staff, lay members, the nurse and the secondary care clinician on the governing body.

In the absence of any specific national guidance, CCGs are therefore able to make their own decisions with regard to remuneration for the CCG chair and GP members. Good practice would suggest that robust benchmarking information be available to support the remuneration committee in this decision-making process – for example, remuneration should be in line with NED payments in other NHS organisations, at a rate commensurate with their salary or as needed for replacement costs, or at a rate commensurate with the average rate for their profession and level of seniority.

National guidance has been published with a set fee for the lay members, secondary care doctor and nurse roles but, where the NHS currently employs these postholders, the guidance recommends their fee is based on their existing NHS salary instead of the set fee. Guidance on salary ranges for executive members based on NHS trust executive pay is provided by NHS England and follows the principles set out in the Hutton Fair Pay Review.

As with all NHS bodies, the actions of the remuneration committee must be publicly defensible. When advising on the pay of the accountable officer, chief finance officer and so on, the remuneration committee should bear in mind the need for properly defensible remuneration packages. These should be linked to clear statements of responsibilities and with rewards linked to the measurable discharge of those responsibilities. One parameter is that the CCG is required to keep within a £25 per head running cost allowance and the remuneration of governing body members must be in line with this allowance.

The remuneration committee is required to make a report of its activities in the CCG's annual report and accounts. This is in line with the reports required of FTs and NHS trusts; likewise, the report must also include the relationship between the remuneration of the highest-paid director in their organisation and the median remuneration of the organisation's workforce in line with the Hutton Fair Pay Review.

The audit committee

Section 15 of The National Health Service (Clinical Commissioning Groups) Regulations 2012 stipulates that the audit committee must have a chair appointed by the CCG (for a term to be determined by the CCG). The chair must be a lay person with such qualifications, expertise or experience as to enable them to express informed views about financial management and audit matters. The chair of the CCG's governing body and the chief finance officer are disqualified from membership of a CCG's audit committee.

The lay member on the governing body, with a lead role in overseeing key elements of governance, is therefore usually the chair of the audit committee. The committee provides assurance and advice to the governing body, and to the accountable officer, on the proper stewardship of resources and assets, including:

- value for money
- financial reporting
- the effectiveness of audit arrangements (internal and external)

- risk management
- control and integrated governance arrangements within the group.

The governing body should approve and keep under review the terms of reference for the audit committee, which include information on the membership of the committee. This should be available upon request to the public. It is recommended that CCGs refer to the HFMA *NHS Audit Committee Handbook* (2014) for further guidance.

Duties, rights and powers of the governing body members

As a member of the CCG's governing body, each individual will share responsibility as part of the team to ensure that the CCG exercises its functions effectively, efficiently, economically, with good governance and in accordance with the terms of the CCG constitution as agreed by its members.

The NHS guidance *Clinical commissioning group governing body members: role outlines, attributes and skills* describes the various roles that make up the governing body. It sets out a core role for all governing body members and then explains the specific nuances of the different roles as follows:

- The GP or other healthcare professionals acting on behalf of member practices will bring the unique understanding of those member practices to the discussion and decision-making of the governing body as their particular contribution.
- The chair is responsible for leading the governing body, ensuring it remains continuously able to discharge its duties and responsibilities as set out in the CCG's constitution. The chair will have a key role in overseeing governance, particularly ensuring that the governing body and the wider CCG behaves with the utmost transparency and responsiveness at all times.
- The lay member on the governing body with a lead role in overseeing key elements of financial management and audit will oversee key elements of governance including audit, remuneration and managing conflicts of interest. They will need to be able to chair the audit committee. Good practice would also suggest that this person would also have a specific role in ensuring that appropriate and effective whistle blowing and anti-fraud systems are in place.
- The lay member on the governing body with a lead role in championing patient and public involvement will help to ensure that the public voice of the local population is heard in all aspects of the CCG's business and that opportunities are created and protected for patient and public empowerment in the work of the CCG. As one of the lay members, they may be asked to fulfil the role of Deputy Chair or Chair of the governing body, if appropriate.
- The secondary care doctor clinical member on the governing body will bring to the governing body an understanding of patient care in the secondary care setting. The registered nurse clinical member on the governing body will bring a broader view, from their perspective as a registered nurse, on health and care

issues to underpin the work of the CCG, especially the contribution of nursing to patient care.

The accountable officer will need to be in the position of understanding the fundamentals in order to take on the responsibility of setting strategic direction and making key decisions, which will come with this role. The chief finance officer will have a professional qualification in accountancy and the expertise or experience to lead the financial management of the CCG.

The Code of Conduct

The NHS Commissioning Board (now NHS England) publication *Code of Conduct: Managing conflicts of interest where GP practices are potential providers of CCG-commissioned services* (October 2012) describes why managing potential conflicts of interest appropriately is needed to protect the integrity of the NHS commissioning system. It is intended to protect clinical commissioning groups (CCGs) and GP practices from any perceptions of wrong-doing.

It sets out additional safeguards that CCGs are advised to use when commissioning services for which GP practices could be potential providers. This is to be incorporated alongside the general safeguards described in *Towards establishment: Creating responsive and accountable CCGs*. These include:

- arrangements for declaring interests
- maintaining a register of interests
- excluding individuals from decision-making where a conflict arises
- engagement with a range of potential providers on service design.

The Code of Conduct provides more specific, additional safeguards that CCGs are advised to have in place when commissioning services that could potentially be provided by GP practices. These safeguards are set out in the form of questions which governing bodies are encouraged to ask themselves.

- How does the proposal deliver good or improved outcomes and value for money – what are the estimated costs and the estimated benefits?
- How does it reflect the CCG's proposed commissioning priorities?
- How have the public been involved in the decision to commission this service?
- What range of health professionals have been involved in designing the proposed service?
- What range of potential providers have been involved in considering the proposals?
- How have the health and wellbeing board(s) been involved?
- How does the proposal support the priorities in the relevant joint health and wellbeing strategy (or strategies)?
- What are the proposals for monitoring the quality of the service?
- What systems will there be to monitor and publish data on referral patterns?

- Have all conflicts and potential conflicts of interests been appropriately declared and entered in registers which are publicly available?
- Why has this procurement route been chosen?
- What additional external involvement will there be in scrutinising the proposed decisions?
- How will the CCG make its final commissioning decision in ways that preserve the integrity of the decision-making process?

Further questions are included for Any Qualified Provider (AQP) or single tender situations.

The ICSA specimen code of conduct for NHS clinical commissioning group governing body members

This guidance reflects current best practice from across economic sectors and the requirements of NHS England. It should be read in conjunction with the Professional Standards Authority's standards for NHS boards and governing bodies. It sets out a specimen code, which covers the following areas:

- appointment and tenure
- ceasing to be a governing body member
- code non-compliance
- conflicts of interest
- confidentiality
- expenses
- mediation
- meetings
- induction and training
- role and function of governing body members
- stakeholder engagement
- standards of conduct (available to ICSA members at www.icsa.org.uk).

Liabilities of governing body members

Guidance issued to the NHS in Health Service Circulars 1998/010 and 1999/104 outlines the extent to which people not employed by an NHS body but taking an active role in decision making may be personally liable for their decisions and action.

In accordance with this guidance, each CCG confers the following indemnity upon its governing body members who are not employees of the group who are undertaking duties on behalf of the Group as part of its governance arrangements.

> 'Such individuals, who have acted honestly and in good faith, will not have to meet out of his or her own personal resources any personal civil liability which is incurred in the execution of his or her governance functions, save where the person has acted recklessly.'

Such individuals need to ensure they act in accordance with the CCG's constitution (including standing orders, prime financial policies and scheme of reservation and delegation), the CCG's policies and procedure, guidance issued by appropriate regulatory bodies and any appropriate statute or regulations.

The position of employees of the CCG is different to that of governing body members, as the CCG is always liable for the actions of its employees in the course of their employment.

Maintaining an effective governing body

The model constitution requires the governing body to have an ongoing role in reviewing the CCG's governance arrangements to ensure that the CCG continues to reflect the principles of good governance.

The research project *Developing CCGs as High Performing Membership Organisations*, in which Calderdale and Greater Huddersfield CCGs worked with Ashridge Business School, established seven areas of competency that demonstrate a high-performing membership organisation. The research was based on the premise that the CCG existed primarily for the benefit of the community, not for the members, but that it was the members who would secure success or otherwise for the CCG. These competencies would make an interesting yardstick for an annual effectiveness review of the governing body and/or members' council. The seven competencies are:

- the membership contract (1)
- encouraging and promoting best practice (2)
- information and advice to members (3)
- the development of member skills (4)
- promoting the CCG to the membership (5)
- policy and decision-making (6)
- engagement with the wider public (7)

Though there are no mandated requirements to annually assess/evaluate their effectiveness, CCGs would be well advised to consider the guidance on evaluation given elsewhere in this handbook. *No effectiveness reg.*

The chair of the governing body

The chair runs governing body meetings and sets the agenda; they are pivotal in creating the conditions for overall committee and individual effectiveness.

The National Health Service (Clinical Commissioning Groups) Regulations 2012 specify that the chair cannot be the accountable officer or chief finance officer, the mandatory secondary care specialist or nurse, or the lay person with a lead role in overseeing key elements of governance.

If the chair is a GP or other healthcare professional, the deputy chair should be a lay member who should take the chair's role for discussions and decisions involving conflict of interest for the chair.

The chair also plays a key role in managing the relationships between member practices, governing body and committee members and staff. The chair's relationship with the accountable officer is particularly critical to the successful functioning of the CCG, its governing body and other committees. This relationship should be clearly defined in writing.

The chair will also have a key role in overseeing governance, particularly ensuring that the governing body and the wider CCG behaves with the utmost transparency and responsiveness at all times. They will ensure that public and patients' views are heard, their expectations understood and, where appropriate, met. The chair will ensure that the organisation is able to account to its local patients, stakeholders and NHS England, as well as ensuring the CCG builds and maintains effective relationships, particularly with the individuals involved in overview and scrutiny from the relevant local authorities.

The chair of the governing body has specific responsibility for:

- leading the governing body, ensuring it remains continuously able to discharge its duties and responsibilities as set out in the CCG's constitution
- building and developing the CCG's governing body and its individual members
- ensuring that the CCG has proper constitutional and governance arrangements in place
- ensuring that, through the appropriate support, information and evidence, the governing body is able to discharge its duties
- supporting the accountable officer in discharging the responsibilities of the organisation
- contributing to the building of a shared vision of the aims, values and culture of the organisation
- leading and influencing clinical and organisational change to enable the CCG to deliver commissioning responsibilities.

■ The accountable officer

The CCG's accountable officer is charged with ensuring that the CCG complies with its:

- duty to exercise its functions effectively, efficiently and economically
- duty to exercise its functions with a view to securing continuous improvement in the quality of services provided to individuals for, or in connection with, the prevention, diagnosis or treatment of illness
- financial obligations, including information requests
- obligations relating to accounting, auditing and the duty to provide information to NHS England following requests from the Secretary of State

- obligations under any other provision of the NHS Act 2006 specified by NHS England for these purposes.

CCGs are responsible for recruiting and selecting their leadership team; NHS England guidance confirms the advice for appointing to senior roles in CCGs (chair, accountable officer and chief finance office) which was established during the transition from the PCT system.

The NHS England guidance *Appointing a new accountable officer to a clinical commissioning group* (January 2014) sets out the procedure which should be followed in appointing a new accountable officer. Only certain people can undertake the accountable officer role. These are:

- an individual who is a member of the CCG (such as a GP)
- a member of any body which is a member of the CCG (such as a partner in a GP practice) an employee of the CCG or of any member of the CCG
- in the case of a joint appointment, an employee or member of any of the CCGs in question or an employee or member of any of the bodies which are members of the CCGs in question.

Though two or more CCGs may choose to share a single person to undertake their accountable officer roles, it is not possible for a single CCG to appoint two individuals to share this role. The accountable officer may not be the chair of the governing body. The CEO of NHS England is legally responsible for confirming accountable officer status on the individual nominated by a CCG, even though they remain an officer, member or employee of the CCG.

CCGs could decide that their accountable officer role will be held by a clinician supported by an expert manager, or undertaken by a manager with expert clinical leadership support. The term chief officer is used to identify senior managers who undertake the accountable officer role, while chief clinical officer is used for senior clinicians who undertake the role. When the accountable officer role is held by a clinician, the CCG's senior manager is called the chief operating officer.

The individual who undertakes the accountable officer role is required to be a member of the governing body. They will therefore need to meet the core requirements as described for governing body members. There are, however, specific responsibilities associated with this role which are highlighted in the January 2014 guidance.

The CCG company secretary

While the current legislation does not specify the need for CCGs to appoint a company secretary, good practice from the corporate sector and experience in FTs would suggests that this is also a key role in the governance of an organisation.

ICSA has issued guidance on the role of a CCG head of governance, which encompasses the company secretary role. The CCG head of governance role covers three main areas:

- the governing body and CCG committees
- the CCG itself
- the member practices.

In brief, the head of governance would be responsible for ensuring that the CCG complies with relevant legislation and its authorisation (including any conditions attached to it) issued by NHS England. They would establish procedures for the sound governance of the CCG and would advise the governing body, committees and member practices on developments in governance issues. The head of governance would also ensure that meetings of the governing body, committees and member practices run efficiently and effectively, are properly recorded and that all relevant participants receive appropriate support to fulfil their legal duties.

CCG reporting requirements

CCGs are subject to an ongoing assurance process overseen by NHS England area teams, which also provide developmental support to CCGs as required. This assurance process consists of quarterly assurance meetings and an annual 'health check' to assess organisational capabilities, delivery and support needs. It might also include measures of quality in primary as well as secondary care.

The CCG Assurance Framework, first published in November 2013, established six broad assurance domains (set out earlier in this chapter) that result in an assessment that meets statutory requirements but also contributes to ongoing CCG ambitions for development. The document *The framework of excellence in clinical commissioning: for CCGs* also sets out in more detail the elements of effective practice in each of these domains.

The framework recognises that, as co-commissioners, CCGs and NHS England need to work together to jointly improve services for patients and to identify areas for improvement. One means of doing this is the assurance conversations instigated by the framework. These provide a supportive and developmental approach for CCGs, building on existing actions to be accountable to their communities, members and stakeholders.

The tone of the framework demonstrates a commitment to development as well as accountability for performance. For example, NHS England published the direct commissioning assurance framework alongside the CCG assurance framework, therefore setting out its own commitment to deliver equal transparency for direct commissioning functions. As a result, direct commissioning assurance will be based around the six assurance domains and will involve quarterly meetings to discuss a set of locally agreed areas for discussion. There is a requirement that lay people are involved in these quarterly assurance meetings, whether that be health and wellbeing board members, CCG lay members or other local patient engagement arrangements. NHS England has committed to publishing detailed guidance on the role of these independent members.

The annual CCG assessment is based on the CCG Assessment Framework. This assumes the CCG and NHS England are engaged in a range of discussions around assurance and development throughout the year, the frequency and nature of which will vary dependent on local circumstances. It describes the formal elements of assurance common for all CCGs and the local area teams. The assurance domains reflect the key elements of an effective clinical commissioner that are integral to CCG authorisation, set out earlier in this chapter. Areas for discussion at the quarterly meetings will be subject to local discretion, but the following will consistently considered across all 211 CCGs:

- any performance concerns identified by the quarterly delivery dashboard
- any evidence to suggest that CCGs are not delivering against their statutory duties
- an annually commissioned 360-degree stakeholder survey providing insight into both CCGs and area teams, this providing another national source of intelligence and insight into the strength of local relationships. The content and core participants for survey is subject to engagement with CCGs and area team representatives.

If the CCG has demonstrated strong performance across the assurance domains, the assurance meetings could be less frequent on the agreement of both the CCG and area team. The minimum legal requirement is for at least one assurance meeting to take place each financial year. Where assurance concerns remain, conversations should continue to take place at a minimum on a quarterly basis. Where evidence emerges that the delivery of statutory duties are at risk, it is expected that these would be raised with the CCG, including the reassessment of the agreed frequency of meetings where necessary. The framework aims to deliver development and support as the default response; only in exceptional circumstances where these are not sufficient would statutory intervention to take place.

The framework outlines a quarterly delivery dashboard aligned to the assurance domains, with a consistent set of national data to inform assurance conversations. The delivery dashboard comprises four sections, each reflecting a specific area of insight set out in the publication *Everyone Counts: Planning for Patients 2014/15 to 2018/19*, as well as key elements of the CCG's statutory duties (namely the NHS Constitution, outcomes and quality, the Better Care Fund, and finance). The dashboard incorporates national performance targets that also apply to provider organisation such as FTs and NHS trusts.

National analysis from policy teams will also inform the assurance assessment through routine information and intelligence, which will be provided to area teams on a regular basis. This will help highlight areas under the planning framework where local performance is presenting a risk to the achievement of the NHS mandate or the continued delivery of statutory duties. Local intelligence will be gathered from internal and external audits, financial and strategic plans, and governing body papers and minutes.

The assurance assessment will result in a quarterly report which the area team should produce and share with the CCG. This contains both a headline assessment and a summary report following quarterly assurance conversations and an annual letter from the area team to the CCG governing body which summarises the annual assessment. NHS England expects CCGs to make these materials available for public review.

The headline assessement sets out whether NHS England is 'assured' or 'not assured' in relation to the CCG, driven by the six assurance domain assessments. There are three categories that can be applied to each assurance domain:

- assured
- assured with support
- not assured – intervention required

Any 'not assured – intervention required' result for any domain would result in a headline assessment of 'not assured'. This would lead to formal statutory powers being exercised. Where NHS England is assured that a CCG can continue to deliver, with or without support, across all six of the individual domains, the headline assessment will be 'assured'.

Intervention represents a significant step for both NHS England and the CCG. Therefore, the framework recognises that this step should only be taken in exceptional circumstances where either the exercise of existing powers over time has been insufficient, or where the quality of patient care was at serious risk. These interventions include:

- directing the CCG as to how it discharges its functions
- directing the CCG or the accountable officer to stop carrying out any functions for a defined period
- terminating the accountable officer 's appointment and appointing a new accountable officer
- varying the CCG's constitution
- carrying out certain functions on behalf of a CCG or arranging for another CCG to do so
- dissolving the CCG.

In addition, CCGs also have a statutory obligation to develop and publish an annual report. In addition to the areas prescribed by statute and details from the CCG Annual Reporting Manual, NHS England expects CCGs to make a formal statement about their delivery against their statutory duties. The publication timescales for the production of annual report runs in parallel with the quarter four annual assurance conversation. It is expected that, at a minimum, the annual report will be used as a key source in generating the areas for discussion at the Q4 meeting.

CCGs' annual planning and delivery cycle

The NHS England publication *Everyone Counts: Planning for patients 2014/15 to 2018/19* sets out the formal planning process that CCGs will take the lead on. CCGs, as the local leaders of health commissioning, will work with all key stakeholders to develop the strategic, operational and financial plans required to achieve the prescribed outcomes. The plans need to demonstrate how the CCG will deliver all the aspects of the government's mandate to the commissioning system, as well as taking account of NHS England's ambitions and steering on the strategic approach. CCGs should also include their own ambitions for what their communities tell them will meet their needs.

The challenge for the CCGs is to plan for the transformation of services on a five-year basis. Each CCG's plan must drive its own decisions to ensure its providers are best placed to deliver high quality and sustainable services for patients. Each five-year plan must include the first two years of operational delivery in detail, based upon the 2014/15 and 2015/16 funding allocations previously set by NHS England. The planning process and timeline has been aligned with Monitor, the NHS TDA, the LGA and Health Education England. The first cycle of this planning process was completed in June 2014.

The assurance framework described above will monitor the achievements of these plans as part of the ongoing assurance process.

Annual report and accounts

NHS England Directions require CCGs to comply with the requirements laid out in the Manual for Accounts issued by the DH. The CCG Annual Reporting Manual brings together the accounting requirements within the DH Manual with the requirements for annual reporting for CCGs, as well as other relevant matters.

The annual report and accounts consists of the annual report, statements by the accountable officer and the annual accounts. The annual report must consist of:

- a governing body report
- an operating and financial review
- a sustainability report
- an equality report
- governing body and senior management profiles
- a remuneration report.

CCGs are also expected to include within their annual report a member practices' introduction, the strategic report and a members' report.

CCGs do not need to present their annual reports and accounts to Parliament, but they must be available on their public website and presented to a public meeting no later than 30 September following the financial year end.

■ The CCG governance challenge

Non-executive members and independence

The independence of the governing body currently rests on the role of the lay members, of which there must be two, both with specified roles to oversee elements of governance and to help champion patient and public engagement. This has the potential to be further strengthened with the appointment of the secondary care specialist and the registered nurse member.

In considering the current makeup of the governing body, the lay members, secondary care specialist and registered nurse member can all be considered non-executive members. They are defined as such in the model CCG Constitution. However, the GP members are also referred to as non-executive members at times.

The Good Governance Standard (following on from the Higgs Report) sets the role of these non-executive members. It says they should:

■ contribute to strategy by bringing a range of perspectives to strategy development and decision-making
■ make sure that effective management arrangements and an effective team are in place at the top level of the organisation
■ delegate which decisions are reserved for the governing body, and then clearly delegate the rest
■ hold the executive to account, by assessing performance in fulfilling their responsibilities, agreeing levels of remuneration and appointment/removal of executives
■ be extremely discriminating about getting involved in matters of operational detail.

As a comparison, the UK Code requires a board and its committees to have the appropriate balance of skills, experience, independence and knowledge to enable them to discharge their duties and responsibilities effectively. This ensures that no individual or group of individuals can dominate the board's decision-making. Non-executive members can be either independent or non-independent. Though non-independent non-executives are permissible, the Code recommends that the majority of the board should consist of independent non-executives. If there are non-executives who are considered to be not independent, the Code suggests that it may be necessary to appoint further independent non-executives to act as a counterbalance. Non-executives are not independent if their opinion is likely to be influenced by the senior executive management of the organisation or by a major stakeholder, or for example, if a person personally stands to gain or otherwise benefit substantially from income from the organisation.

The significant governance issue for CCGs relates to the independence of its non-executive members in carrying out this role of independent scrutiny. The independent non-executives would be identified as the lay members and clinical members. GP members would be classed as non-independent non-executives;

good practice would suggest their number needs to be balanced with an equivalent number of NEDs to ensure good governance.

The boundaries in CCGs can sometimes become further blurred, however. In a number of CCGs, GP members on the governing body take on clinical project leads or operational roles within the CCG. These roles support the CCG in developing robust clinical pathways and models of care in order to deliver the strategic priorities of the CCG. The GPs who undertake these roles will usually have a specific knowledge and expertise in the field in question.

Conflicts of interest

As mentioned in the opening remarks of this chapter, managing conflicts of interest is a critical factor in the success of CCGs. Conflicts can arise in the work of CCGs in a variety of ways: for example, if members of the practice became involved in the process of deciding to commission or awarding a service to a GP provider in their locality or to their own practice, they would be potentially conflicted. It would not be clear that they favoured the decision because of the needs of patients rather than their own financial gain.

For a GP or other clinical commissioner, a conflict of interest may also arise when their own judgment as an NHS commissioner could be, or be perceived to be, influenced and impaired by their own concerns and obligations as a healthcare provider, as a member of a particular peer, professional or special interest group, or those of a close family member. Commissioning decisions that are in the overall best interests of taxpayers and the local population may not always be in the best interest of individual patients for whom GPs are required to advocate, or for the companies and partnerships which they own, manage or work for.

Individual behaviour is a major factor in the effectiveness of the governing body, and also has an influence on the reputation of the organisation, the confidence and trust members of the public have in it and the working relationships and morale within it. Conflicts, real or perceived, can arise between the organisation's interests and those of individual governors; public trust can then be damaged unless the organisation implements clear procedures to deal with these conflicts.

The guidance *Next steps towards primary care co-commissioning* (2014) included a strengthened approach to managing such conflicts in co-commissioning decisions. These requirements related to the make-up of the decision-making committee, where the committee must have a lay and executive majority and have a lay chair.

NHS England also committed to national training for CCG lay members to support and strengthen their role. Local Health Watch and a local authority member of the local health and wellbeing board will also have the right to serve as observers on the decision-making committee in order to secure the external involvement of local stakeholders. The public register of conflicts of interest will include information on the nature of the conflict and details of the conflicted parties. The register will form an obligatory part of the annual accounts and be signed off by external auditors. CCGs will also be required to maintain and publish, on a regular basis, a register of all key procurement decisions.

If the governing body is considering a decision in which a member is conflicted, it is good practice for that member must play no part in that decision – normally leaving the room during the discussion of that agenda item. In making the decision as to whether to exclude the member from the discussion the chair and/or lay member for governance will consider the expertise or insight of the member in relation to the item under discussion. If more than 50% of the members are conflicted then the chair (or deputy) should have the authority to decide whether the discussion can proceed. Where a quorum cannot be achieved, the chair of the meeting could invite other individuals on a temporary basis to make up the quorum. Such an individual may be a member of a relevant health and wellbeing board or a member of another clinical commissioning group.

The lay member for governance should provide oversight of the management of conflicts of interest and impartial, unconflicted advice and judgment to the governing body in cases where it is not obvious whether a material conflict exists or how best to manage it. They should define a reasonable balance to avoid conflicts, though enabling the CCG to harness the knowledge of clinicians and other staff for commissioning in order to improve care to patients and value for money to the taxpayer. The deputy chair of the governing body should deputise for the chair of the governing body where the chair has a conflict of interest.

Being a membership organisation

The Kings Fund and Nuffield Trust report *Clinical commissioning groups: Supporting improvement in general practice?* states:

> 'there are significant disparities between the views of those involved in leading CCGs and member GPs, with the latter being less likely to say that their CCG is 'owned' by its members, that its decisions reflect their views or that it has had a positive impact to date. There is also significant variation in views from one CCG to another, with levels of member ownership and involvement much higher in some areas than others. Larger CCGs may face a particular challenge in engaging member practices and creating a culture of collective ownership.'

There is a significant challenge here to ensure that the member practices are able to play an influential role in setting the direction of the CCG. The balance of power between the members council and the governing body needs to be carefully handled by the chair and the accountable officer.

Procurement

The National Health Service (Procurement, Patient Choice and Competition) Regulations 2013 (No 2) replace the existing administrative rules governing the procurement of NHS-funded services previously set out in the Principles and Rules for Cooperation and Competition and the Procurement Guide for Commissioners of NHS Funded Services.

The substance of many of these principles and rules is still preserved in the regulations. The regulations require commissioners to ensure good practice in relation to the procurement of NHS health care services and to protect patients' rights to make choices regarding their NHS treatment. They also prohibit commissioners from engaging in anti-competitive behaviour unless this is in the interests of health care service users.

It is for commissioners to decide what services to procure and how best to secure them in the interests of health care service users. The regulations adopt a principles-based approach that is intended to give commissioners flexibility. Monitor's role is limited to ensuring that commissioners have operated within the legal framework established by the regulations.

CCGs will need to decide, subject to the National Health Service (Procurement, Patient Choice and Competition) (No 2) Regulations 2013 and current procurement rules set out in the Public Contracts Regulations 2006 where it is appropriate to commission community-based services through competitive tender, through an AQP approach or through single tender. In general, commissioning through competitive tender or AQP will introduce greater transparency and help reduce the scope for conflicts.

On-going developments

In 2014, The Good Governance Institute (GGI), with its partner Capsticks, was commissioned by NHS England to carry out a major work programme to assist the on-going development of CCGs. The work was designed and overseen by a 'task and finish' group of the NHS Commissioning Assembly CCG Development Working Group, made up of CCGs from around the country.

In particular, GGI have developed:

- A consistent language to describe governance that is engaging for clinicians and the public.
- A proposed set of outcomes of good governance that can be described and measured.
- A series of diagnostic tools with which CCGs can measure the outcomes of their governance arrangements supported by a process that CCGs can employ.

Eleven outcomes for good governance were identified by GGI, CCGs and other relevant stakeholders, and are:

Clarity of purpose, including setting tone at the top, leading by example, living the values etc.

Leadership and strategic direction, including understanding of market and context, balance between operational demands and strategic goals and creating a pipeline of clinical leaders for the future

Effectiveness of relationships, including co-operative behaviours

Membership and unity, including member ownership of CCG

Public and community engagement, including openness and transparency

Quality and safety structures and systems, including mechanisms to gather patients and carer experience data, adoption of best practice, commitment to research, investment in development, holding each other to account professionally etc.

Focus on outcomes, including understanding what matters to improve health of population, driving quality and safety, co-design with service users, co-ordination of care

Better decision-making, including development of KPIs, use of information, data integrity, and ongoing audit etc. used to support sound decisions, mature management of conflict of interest

Control systems, including clarity of external authority and expectation, risk appetite, internal assurance on resources and quality, effectiveness of governance structures, quality of challenge etc.

Legal and regulator compliance, including fulfilling statutory and other duties such as the duty of candour

Organisational effectiveness, including resource management, effective procurement, best use of commissioning support, fewer diversions arising from governance failures, etc.

GGI have also now developed a suite of tools that have been tested by more than 40 volunteer CCGs. The tools allow CCGs to self-evaluate the degree to which their governance arrangements deliver on the outcomes of good governance, and include a maturity matrix, a peer review guide, a standards and evidence tool, a board observation guide and a survey that can be administered both online and in hard copy. They are all available for CCGs to use free of charge and can be found at www.ccggovernance.org.

Governance Checklist

✓ How clear is the vision and aims of the CCG to the member practices and the governing body? Do they understand the constitution and their role as set out there?

✓ Do the member practices and governing body understand the statutory duties prescribed for a CCG? To what extent does the information that they receive help them to make rigorous decisions in line with those duties?

✓ What does the size and complexity of the CCG mean for the ways in which they approach each of the main functions of governance set out by the Good Governance Standard for Public Services?

✓ How clearly defined are the respective roles and responsibilities of the member practices, the governing body and the individual members?

✓ Do all members of the governing body take collective responsibility for the governing body's decisions?

✓ How well does the CCG understand the views of the public and service users?

✓ How does the behaviour of members, both individually and collectively as a governing body, show that their responsibilities to the CCG and its stakeholders are taken very seriously?

✓ Are there any ways in which member behaviour might weaken the CCG's aims and values?

✓ Are there formal agreements on the types of decisions that are delegated to the executive and those that are reserved for the governing body and/or the member practices? Is this set out in a clear and up-to-date statement?

✓ Is there clarity on the election/appointment processes for the members' representatives and the governing body members? What approach will be taken to finding a balance between continuity of knowledge and renewal of thinking in the governing body?

✓ How well does the role of the lay members support independent scrutiny and challenge? What further measures might be considered to strengthen this if required?

✓ Is there a process for regularly reviewing the CCG's governance arrangements and practice? Is this independently assessed at any point?

Summary

The governance of CCGs is still maturing, as can be seen from the number of individual CCG variations described in this chapter. However, there are clear signs of consistency developing around the principles, if not around the actual governance processes. CCGs were specifically developed as membership organisations; to expect a rigidity of governance more closely aligned to a publicly listed company may not have been appropriate.

It is clear that there is a requirement for robust governance arrangements within the accountability structure envisaged by NHS England, allowing CCGs the flexibility to develop those arrangements. As CCGs seek to integrate and work more closely with their stakeholders, the opportunity to deliver their statutory duties more effectively may present itself.

PART FIVE

Risk management, assurance and audit

13

Risk management

The responsibility of boards for effective risk management came under close scrutiny following the 2007–2009 banking crisis. Many banks were criticised for getting into financial difficulty because of reckless business strategies and failing to recognise the business risks that they were taking. Within NHS organisations, the scrutiny of risk management is also the responsibility of the board; however, there tends to be rigorous external scrutiny as well.

The leaders of NHS organisations are responsible for deciding risk strategies and risk policies, and for ensuring that the systems to support the management of those risks are effective. There are some similarities between a risk management system and an internal control system, but each has a different purpose. It is important to distinguish between them: in essence, the risk management system is the overarching system that is then underpinned and supported by the internal control system.

The boards of publicly quoted companies currently face a step change in their approach to risk management with the introduction of the new FRC *Guidance on risk management, internal control and related and business reporting* (2014). This new guidance revises, integrates and replaces the current editions of the FRC guidance *Internal Control: Revised Guidance for Directors on the Combined Code* (formerly known as the Turnbull Guidance) and the *Going Concern and Liquidity Risk: Guidance for Directors of UK Companies*. It also reflects the changes made to the UK Code in 2014.

The guidance sets out its aims as 'bring[ing] together elements of best practice for risk management; prompt[ing] boards to consider how to discharge their responsibilities in relation to the existing and emerging principal risks faced by the company; reflect[ing] sound business practice, whereby risk management and internal control are embedded in the business process by which a company pursues its objectives; and highlight[ing] related reporting responsibilities'.

The new FRC risk management guidance has resulted from the economic recession and high-profile failures of risk management in the corporate sector. Many boards outside of the financial sector have delegated most risk matters to the audit committee and then only in a limited fashion – this is now an outdated and untenable model. As seen in Chapter 14, the introduction of the strategic report now requires boards to report annually on their principal risks and why they are important to the organisation. This new guidance states that board responsibilities for risk include:

> 'financial, operational, reputational, behavioural, organisational, third party, or external risks, such as market or regulatory risk, over which the board may have little or no direct control'.

Consequently, the challenge is to include behavioural and organisational risk into their risk management systems. The FRC's rationale behind this has been the recognition that the root causes of most crises lie in human behaviour and in the way that organisations are led, structured and managed. The guidance recommends that boards should evaluate their skills as to understanding risk as part of the annual board evaluation process so ignorance of risk will cease to be an excuse. Boards therefore need to understand:

- the nature of their principal risks
- the responsibility of the board to decide how much risk the organisation should be prepared to accept in order to achieve hoped-for financial or performance returns
- how much risk the organisation should be able to tolerate.

Exposures to business risk should not exceed the levels determined by the board. The business risk management system should be effective in ensuring that board strategies and policies are implemented and also reviewed.

Risk has a higher profile within NHS organisations with the active involvement of the audit committee in the board assurance framework (BAF) and the regular scrutiny of principal risks, or the existence of specific committees, which consider risk as part of the quality and/or governance agenda. Even so, this new FRC guidance provides a new benchmark for consideration.

■ The regulatory framework for risk management and internal control

Though not required to follow the UK Code, NHS organisations and health service governance can benchmark best practice against the provisions in the Code in recognition of the connection between good corporate governance and risk management. It is therefore worth setting out these provisions in more detail.

The Turnbull Guidance on internal control

When principles and provisions relating to internal control and risk management were first introduced into the UK (then the Combined Code) in 1998, a working party known as the Turnbull Committee published guidelines to listed companies on how to apply them. This was referred to as the Turnbull Guidance, and was the responsibility of the FRC.

This guidance has now been replaced by the FRC Guidance on *Risk Management, Internal Control and Related Financial and Business Reporting*, which revises, integrates and replaces the Turnbull Guidance and reflects changes made to the UK Code in 2014. The new guidance also links the traditional Turnbull Guidance on internal control with emerging good practice for risk management. However, the Turnbull Guidance still offers helpful insights on the effective working of an internal controls system.

The guidance applied to the entire system of internal control, including operational and compliance controls as well as financial controls. The Turnbull Guidance defined an internal control system as 'the policies, processes, tasks, behaviours and other aspects of an organisation' that, taken together:

- help it to operate effectively and efficiently so that the organisation can respond in an appropriate way to principal risks to achieving the organisation's objectives
- help it to ensure the quality of external and internal reporting
- help to ensure compliance with applicable laws and regulations, and also with internal policies for the conduct of business.

According to the guidance, internal control should be embedded in the business and its operating systems. Controls should not be applied occasionally or from an external source, and they should be applied regularly and automatically as part of established procedures. Controls also have to remain relevant over time. As circumstances change, controls should be altered or adapted to meet the new requirements as controls that are appropriate to an organisation should take account of its particular circumstances.

The Turnbull Guidance also suggested that a system of internal control includes control activities, information and communications processes and process for monitoring the effectiveness of the system. The system of internal control should be embedded in the operations of the organisation and form part of its culture; be capable of responding quickly to evolving risks to the business arising from factors within the organisation and to changes in the business environment; and include procedures for reporting immediately to appropriate levels of management any significant control failings or weaknesses that are identified together with details of corrective action being undertaken.

FRC Guidance on Risk Management, Internal Control and Related Financial and Business Reporting

The new guidance aims to bring together elements of best practice for risk management; prompt boards to consider how to discharge their responsibilities in relation to the existing and emerging principal risks faced by the organisation; reflect sound business practice, whereby risk management and internal control are embedded in the business process by which an organisation pursues its objectives; and highlight related reporting responsibilities.

The guidance is primarily aimed at companies subject to the UK Code but provides useful best practice benchmarking for NHS organisations and will referenced throughout this chapter.

UK Corporate Governance Code requirements

A core principle of the UK Code is that: 'the board should maintain sound risk management and internal control systems.' The board has overall responsibility for the system of internal control, but the responsibility for designing and implementing the system, and for operating it, is delegated to management.

The UK Code also includes the following principle: 'the board is responsible for determining the nature and extent of the significant risks it is willing to take in achieving its strategic objectives.' This is elaborated upon in the following provision: 'the board is required to conduct a review of the effectiveness of the organisation's system of internal controls at least annually, and should report to the stakeholders that they have done so. The review should cover all material controls, including financial, operational and compliance controls.' In other words, the board's responsibility for reviewing internal controls (and risk management) extends beyond financial matters to business operations and regulatory compliance.

Within the NHS, this review is known as the annual governance statement (AGS, previously known as the statement on internal control). It is covered in more detail in Chapter 14.

■ The nature of risk

Risk refers to the possibility that something unexpected or unplanned for will happen. In many cases, risk is seen as the possibility that something bad might happen. In everyday life, there is a risk of becoming seriously ill, being involved in a road accident, having a house burgled or flooded, having a motorcar breakdown, and so on. This can be described as downside risk, because it is a risk that something will happen that would not normally be expected.

There is also upside risk – the possibility that events might turn out better than expected. In a health service context, an example is the possibility that activity levels will be higher than planned or that working days lost through industrial action will be lower than anticipated. Another example is investment decisions. Every investment is risky, and actual returns could be lower or higher than expected. In deciding whether to undertake an investment, the risks as well as the potential returns should be considered. Some risks are easy to recognise because they are always present and an NHS organisation may have had many years of experience in dealing with them. For example, financial risks include the risk that tariff will be set at a substantially lower level or that the costs of pharmaceutical supplies will increase. Other risks, however, are more difficult to identify and anticipate.

The 2014 FRC guidance describes the board's responsibilities for an organisation's overall approach to risk management and internal control as follows:

- ensuring the design and implementation of appropriate risk management and internal control systems that identify the risks facing the company and enable the board to make a robust assessment of the principal risks;
- determining the nature and extent of the principal risks faced and those risks which the organisation is willing to take in achieving its strategic objectives (determining its 'risk appetite');
- ensuring that appropriate culture and reward systems have been embedded throughout the organisation;
- agreeing how the principal risks should be managed or mitigated to reduce the likelihood of their incidence or their impact;
- monitoring and reviewing the risk management and internal control systems, and the management's process of monitoring and reviewing, and satisfying itself that they are functioning effectively and that corrective action is being taken where necessary; and
- ensuring sound internal and external information and communication processes and taking responsibility for external communication on risk management and internal control.

That said, it is still management's role to implement and take day-to-day responsibility for board policies on risk management and internal control. The board needs to satisfy itself that management has understood the risks, implemented and monitored appropriate policies and controls, and are providing the board with timely information so that it can discharge its own responsibilities.

Risk appetite and risk tolerance

The board has overall responsibility for risk management and for deciding the organisation's risk appetite. Risk appetite is the level of risk that an organisation is willing to take in the pursuit of its objectives. Risk appetite can be defined as the combination of the desire to take on risk to obtain a specific return (financial or quality), risk capacity and risk tolerance. The 'desire to take on risk' refers to the amount and type of risk that the board of directors would like the organisation to have exposure to. Risk capacity is the maximum risk exposures that the organisation can accept without threatening its financial stability. Risk tolerance is the amount of risk that the organisation is prepared to accept to achieve its financial objectives. Risk tolerance is therefore the amount of risk that an organisation's board of directors allows the organisation to accept.

Risk appetite and risk tolerance are closely related. One is the amount of business risk (and types of business risk) the board would like the organisation to have and the other is the amount of risk that the board is prepared to tolerate. Although the Walker Report made recommendations for corporate boards, which has been picked up by the 2014 FRC guidance, these should also be considered by NHS organisations. The Walker Report recommended that the board should consider risk appetite and risk tolerance, and that much more attention should be given to these issues:

> 'Board-level engagement in risk oversight should be materially increased, with particular attention to the monitoring of risk and discussion leading to decisions on the entity's risk appetite and tolerance.'

The 2014 FRC guidance confirms that the board has ultimate responsibility determining its risk appetite. The board should review risk appetite regularly, and decisions should be taken about the scale of risk that is desired or acceptable. Risk tolerance could be expressed in numerical terms, such as the maximum loss that the board would be willing to accept on a particular venture if events turn out adversely or in terms of the quality of the service that is provided. Alternatively, risk tolerance could be expressed in terms of a total ban on certain types of business activity or behaviour.

The relevance of risk for health service governance

NHS organisations must take risks in order to deliver healthcare. How much risk should they be prepared to tolerate, and would they be able to withstand 'shocks' in the business environment if an unexpected event or development were to occur? The board has the responsibility for strategic decisions on risk, and an important aspect of health service governance is for the board to recognise its responsibilities and ensure that the risk management system in the organisation is effective.

The board has a responsibility to govern the organisation in the interests of the stakeholders. A part of this responsibility is to decide the objectives and strategic direction for the organisation, to approve detailed strategic plans put forward by management, and to monitor and review the implementation of those plans. An important objective of NHS organisations is to make economic, efficient and effective use of public resources in its provision of healthcare, and the organisation's strategies should be directed towards this. However, any business strategy involves taking risks and actual results may be better or worse than expected.

Bad health service governance can result in the collapse of an organisation, and excessive risk-taking is one aspect of poor governance. The board should consider risk when it makes strategic business decisions. It should choose policies that are expected to deliver the key objectives, but should limit the risks to a level that it considers acceptable. For example, when the board takes major investment decisions or decides on a new corporate strategy such as a clinical services strategy, risks as well as expected returns must be properly assessed. The board should also be satisfied that managers take risk as well as expected outcomes into account in their decision-making. The Cadbury Report (1992) described risk management as:

'the process by which executive management, under board supervision, identifies the risk arising from business .... and establishes the priorities for control and particular objectives.'

The significance of risk management for corporate governance was demonstrated forcibly by the global banking crisis in 2007–2009. In the UK, the government-initiated Walker Report into the failures in the banking industry commented that while there were failures in the regulation of the banking industry, much of the blame for the crisis was attributable to poor governance, and in particular inadequate attention to risk management. The significance of risk management for health service governance has already been well documented in case studies throughout this publication.

Types of risks

A distinction can be made between business risk and internal control risk (sometimes called governance risk). Business risks are risks that occur and arise in the business environment in which an organisation operates. Business risks may also be referred to as strategic risks, as they are determined by the strategies that the organisation pursues. Risks will differ between organisations but may include financial, operational, reputational, behavioural, third party, or external risks, such as market or regulatory risk, over which the board may have little or no direct control. In the NHS, business risks could be risks to patient safety and financial security that arise from factors in their external environment, including competition or government policy, over which management has no direct control.

Categories of business risk

The nature and severity of business risks varies from one organisation to another. Risks change over time: some become less significant, and new risks emerge. Business risks are risks that the actual performance of the business could be much worse (or better) than expected due to unexpected developments in the business environment. For example, when an organisation develops a new service, it will have an expectation of the likely activity level. Actual levels could be higher or lower than expected. With some new services, the risk that activity levels will differ from expectation could be much more severe than with other new services. There are various reasons why activity levels may be less than expected, or may fall unexpectedly. Competitors may take away some of the organisation's market share; an organisation may suffer from bad publicity; there may be new regulations making the provision of a particular service more difficult.

Business risks can be categorised or identified in different ways, but it may help to understand the variety of risks by considering the following sources of risk.

- **Financial risk:** these are risks that financial conditions may change, with adverse changes in tariff or interest rates, higher losses from bad debts or changes in prices from major suppliers.
- **Operational risk:** the risk of losses resulting from inadequate or failed internal processes, people and systems, or external events.
- **Reputational risk:** the risk of loss in customer loyalty or customer support following an event that damages the organisation's reputation.
- **Behavioural risk:** these are risks connected with the workplace and lifestyle behaviors of employees and organisations that have a negative impact on its productivity.
- **Third-party or competition risk:** the risk that business performance will differ from expected performance because of actions taken (or not taken) by other organisations.
- **External risks:** these are risks of significant changes in the business environment from political and regulatory factors, economic factors, social and environmental factors and technology factors (the so-called 'PEST' factors). For example, business performance may be affected by the introduction of new regulations, a change of government, economic decline or growth, environmental issues, unexpected changes in social habits or technological change.

Each industry and each organisation within an industry faces different risks. The questions that management should ask are 'What risks does this organisation face?' and 'How can these risks be measured?' It has to be possible to assess the risk in a business, even one with unpredictable variations in key factors such as activity levels or market prices. High volatility is associated with high business risk.

CASE STUDY: Heart of England NHS Foundation Trust

Heart of England NHS Foundation Trust was the first FT to acquire another NHS trust, Good Hope Hospital, in 2007. The board realised that making an acquisition was a complex process – especially in the NHS – and had to establish clear governance structures to manage the inherent risk in the project. Key areas for consideration were:

- understanding the strategic imperative to acquire
- appraising options
- how to value a trust
- how to negotiate terms
- handling the actual transaction process and interacting with key stakeholders
- planning for post-merger integration
- organisational development post merger to enhance staff morale.

Large-scale mergers and acquisitions have inherent risks and Monitor's role in this area was to ensure that the trust did not jeopardise its quality of services or financial stability. It did this by providing indicative risk ratings of major transactions, leaving the board to put in place strategies and mechanisms to mitigate any material risks.

- For each of these risks, how would the organisation be affected if the worst outcome came about, or if a fairly bad outcome happened?
- What is the likelihood of a bad outcome for that risk item?
- What is the organisation's risk appetite or risk tolerance?
- What should the organisation be doing to manage the risk, either by avoiding it altogether or planning to deal with the problems that will arise in the event of a bad outcome?

Though all manner of principal risks in the business environment may cause an organisation to fail to achieve its objectives, further principal risks are failures or weaknesses within its own internal systems and operating procedures or human error. These failures and weaknesses could be avoided, or the consequences of failures could be limited, by means of internal controls. Internal controls are measures or arrangements that are intended to prevent failures from happening, limiting their potential effect, or identifying when a failure has occurred so that corrective measures can be taken. The failure or weakness of these controls is classified as an internal control risk.

Internal control is also an aspect of governance, because the board of directors has a responsibility to ensure that the assets of the organisation are not threatened, and that the interests of the stakeholders are not damaged, by making sure that an effective system of internal control is in place.

Internal control risks

An internal control system is the system that an organisation has for identifying internal control risks, applying controls to reduce the risk of losses from these risks and taking corrective action when losses occur. There should be controls to ensure that the organisation, its systems and procedures operate in the way that is intended, without disruption or disturbance. In addition, there should be controls to ensure that assets are safeguarded, such as controls to ensure that money received is banked and is not stolen, and that operating assets such as items of equipment and computers are not damaged or lost. Such controls should include measures to reduce the risk of fraud and financial controls that should ensure the completeness and accuracy of accounting records, and the timely preparation of financial information. Controls should also be in place to ensure compliance with key regulations, such as CQC regulations, Monitor regulations or health and safety regulations.

However, just like risk management, the board needs to be clear on its strategy and corporate objectives in order to assess what internal risks exist and therefore what controls are needed. The Auditing Practices Board says:

> 'Clear business objectives need to be identified before an effective system of internal control can be established. Without clear objectives, management will be unable to identify and evaluate the risks that threaten the achievement of their objectives and design and operate a system of internal control to manage those risks.'

Internal control risks are risks that arise within an organisation because of weaknesses in its systems, procedures, management or personnel. Unless there are controls to deal with them, internal control risks can lead to losses because of operational failures, errors or fraud. The controls for these risks are 'internal controls' and internal controls are applied within an internal control system. It is the responsibility of the board of directors of an organisation to ensure that the internal control system (and the internal controls within this system) is effective in preventing losses from internal control risks, or identifying losses and taking corrective action when they occur.

CASE STUDY: Internal controls weaknesses

A hospital operated from three separate locations in the same city. At one of these locations, a considerable amount of cash had built up following donations from grateful patients. This was kept in a safe in the manager's office. One day, two uniformed individuals came to the building and said that they had instructions to take the safe to the organisation's head office, which was in a different building. They were allowed to take the safe and the security guard actually helped them to put it into their vehicle, parked outside the front door of the building. The two individuals drove off with the safe, containing over £30,000, and were not seen again.

It should be apparent that the organisation lost £30,000 because of basic mistakes, which point to weaknesses in internal controls:

- Why was there was a lot of money in the safe? Why had most of it not been taken to the bank?
- Why were the two individuals allowed to take the safe without checking their authorisation to take it?
- How did they gain access to the building so easily?

There were weaknesses in the procedures for managing donations, banking cash, building security and authorisation of actions. If suitable internal controls had been in place, the loss of the money would not have occurred.

Categories of internal control risks

A useful definition of internal control was given by the US Committee of Sponsoring Organizations of the Treadway Commission (COSO). The COSO Framework defines internal control as 'a process, effected by an entity's board of directors, management and other personnel, designed to provide reasonable assurance regarding the achievement of objectives' in the areas of effectiveness and efficiency of operations (through operational controls), the reliability of financial reporting (through financial controls) and compliance with relevant laws and regulations (through compliance controls).

It follows then that internal control risks can be categorised into three broad types, namely, financial, operational and compliance.

- **Financial risks**: these are risks of errors or fraud in accounting systems and accounting and finance activities. Errors or fraud could lead to losses for the organisation, or to incorrect financial statements. Weak controls may also mean that financial assets are not properly protected. Examples of financial risks include the risk of failure to record transactions in the bookkeeping system, failure to collect money owed by customers, failure to protect cash and misreporting (deliberate or unintentional) in the financial statements.
- **Operational risks:** the Basel Committee for banking supervision gives a helpful definition of 'operational risk'. Although this definition applies to risks in the banking industry, it has a wider application. Operational risk is 'the risk of losses resulting from inadequate or failed internal processes, people and systems, or external events'. Operational risks include the risks of a breakdown in a system due to machine failures or software errors, the risk of losing information from computer files or having confidential information stolen, the risk of a terrorist attack, and losses arising from mistakes or omissions by staff.
- **Compliance risks:** these are risks that important laws or regulations will not be complied with properly. Failure to comply with the law could result in legal action against the organisation and/or fines.

■ Responsibilities for risk management and internal control

The organisation's risk management strategy should set out how the authority, responsibility and accountability for risk management and internal control is defined, co-ordinated and documented throughout the organisation from individual employees through to board members. This strategy should be reviewed and approved by the board.

The board

The board is responsible for risk at a high level, but responsibilities for the management of risk are delegated to executive management. The board should decide the level of risks that are acceptable at a strategic level, and should ensure that the management team consider risk in the decisions that they make.

The 2014 FRC guidance explains:

'The board should define the processes to be adopted for its on-going monitoring and review [of risk management and internal control systems], including specifying the requirements, scope and frequency for reporting and assurance. Regular reports to the board should provide a balanced assessment of the risks and the effectiveness of the systems of risk management and internal control in managing those risks. The board should form its own view on effectiveness, based on the evidence it obtains, exercising the standard of care generally applicable to directors in the exercise of their duties.'

The 2014 FRC guidance goes on to recommend questions that the board should consider throughout the year.

- How effectively have the risks been assessed and the principal risks determined?
- How have they been managed or mitigated?
- Have the necessary actions been taken promptly to remedy any significant failings or weaknesses?
- Do the causes of the failing or weakness indicate poor decision-taking, a need for more extensive monitoring or a reassessment of the effectiveness of management's on-going processes?

In addition to the board's ongoing monitoring and review role, the 2014 FRC guidance recommends that it should undertake an annual review of the effectiveness of the systems to ensure that it has considered all significant aspects of risk management and internal control for the year under review, up to the date of approval of the annual report and accounts. An effectiveness review of should consider:

- the organisation's willingness to take on risk (its risk appetite), the desired culture within the organisation and whether this culture has been embedded;
- the operation of the risk management and internal control systems, covering the design, implementation, monitoring and review and identification of risks and determination of those which are principal to the organisation;
- the integration of risk management and internal controls with considerations of strategy and business model, and with business planning processes;
- the changes in the nature, likelihood and impact of principal risks, and the organisation's ability to respond to changes in its business and the external environment;
- the extent, frequency and quality of the communication of the results of management's monitoring to the board which enables it to build up a cumulative assessment of the state of control in the organisation and the effectiveness with which risk is being managed or mitigated;
- issues dealt with in reports reviewed by the board during the year, in particular the incidence of significant control failings or weaknesses that have been

identified at any time during the period and the extent to which they have, or could have, resulted in unforeseen impact; and

■ the effectiveness of the organisation's public reporting processes.

At board level, responsibility for reviewing the effectiveness of the risk management system may be delegated by the board to the audit committee, which is also likely to have responsibility for reviewing the internal control system. Alternatively, the board may prefer to establish a separate risk committee. Where delegation does occur, the 2014 FRC guidance makes it clear that:

'The board should be satisfied that the arrangements for the work carried out, for the co-ordination of their work (if more than one committee is involved), and for reporting to the board are appropriate and operating effectively. The board retains ultimate responsibility for the risk management and internal control systems and should reach its own conclusions regarding the recommendations it receives.'

The board should also ensure that the remuneration committee takes appropriate account of risk when determining remuneration policies and awards, and should also ensure that the links between the remuneration committee and the risk and/ or audit committee are operating effectively.

Risk committees

The advantages of having a separate risk committee are as follows.

■ It can focus on risk issues and reviewing the organisation's risk management system, without having to concern itself with other issues (such as the external auditors). It would give advice to the board on matters such as risk appetite and risk strategy.

■ The composition of the board is not restricted by statutory requirements. A risk committee should ideally consist mainly of NEDs but should also have the finance director as a member. If the audit committee had responsibility for the oversight of risk management, the finance director could not be a committee member (although they could be invited to meetings of the audit committee to give their views).

However, a separate risk committee is probably more useful for a large public organisation than for a smaller listed organisation. The Walker Report recommended that another risk committee could be established, consisting of senior executives and chaired by the CEO. This committee would be responsible for risk management at an operational level. The responsibilities of this committee and the board risk committee would be very different as:

'The role of the board risk committee is to advise the board on all high-level risk matters and should not extend into operational matters which are for the executive within the overall risk framework determined by the

board. The NEDs on the committee cannot be expected to be able to repli-
cate the industry expertise of the executive team nor will their capacity to
contribute be enhanced by information overload. The materials presented
to them should be in succinct format, highlighting major issues.'

This provides an interesting consideration for larger NHS organisations, where a
similar structure may be helpful.

Risk officers

In common with larger companies, some larger NHS organisations may also
appoint specialist executive managers with responsibility for risk – a chief risk
officer (CRO). The Walker Report recommended that the CRO should report
directly to the finance director or CEO, but also have direct access to the board.
They should also be able to provide advice to the board on all risk issues affecting
the organisation. The Walker Report added:

> 'Alongside an internal reporting line to the chief executive officer or [CFO],
> the CRO should report to the board risk committee, with explicit, and
> what is clearly understood to be, direct access to the chair of the committee
> in the event of need, for example, if there is a difference of view with the
> chief executive officer or CFO.'

The report emphasises the need to protect the independence of the CRO from
the influence of the CEO or finance director. It also recommends that (like the
company secretary) only the board should be able to appoint or dismiss the CRO,
and the remuneration of the CRO should be decided by the organisation chair or
the remuneration committee.

Again, this provides an interesting consideration for larger NHS organisations
where a similar role may be helpful or the function may be appended to the role
of the company secretary.

■ Risk management systems and procedures

To enable the board of directors to carry out its responsibilities for risk management effectively, there are two essential requirements. Firstly, board members
should have an understanding of risks and risk management. Secondly, there
should be a risk management system in place that the board as a whole or the
appropriate board committee can review.

Risk registers

An organisation might use a risk register for recording identified risks, the evaluation of the risks, and the measures that have been taken to deal with them. Executive
management maintains the risk register, but it can be used by the risk committee
of the board (or the audit committee) as a way of reviewing the effectiveness of

the risk management system. At board level, there should be regular programmed scrutiny of the register of principal risks, including:

- the risk score
- mitigation/action being taken
- escalation or de-escalation of risks.

Individual areas or divisions within the organisations should have processes in which the same risk management system operates with the responsibility of escalating risks, which are outside of their resources or authority to manage.

Interestingly, the King III Code is much more explicit about risk management than the Monitor Code and UK Code. Provisions in the King III Code relating to risk management include the following.

- The board's risk strategy should be executed by management by means of risk management systems and processes.
- The board should ensure that effective and ongoing risk assessments are performed by management.
- Risks should be prioritised and ranked, in order to focus on areas where action is most needed.
- The board should regularly receive and review a register of the organisation's key risks.
- Key risks should be quantified where practicable (e.g. in terms of maximum potential loss or expected loss).
- The board should ensure that processes are in place for anticipating unpredictable risks.
- Management should identify and note in the risk register the responses that have been decided upon and taken.
- Management should provide assurances to the board that the risk management plan is integrated into the daily activities of the business.

Stress testing

Stress testing is widely used by major organisations to assess their ability to withstand extreme 'shocks' or unexpected events in the business environment. This can be done by taking the normal business planning or forecasting model used by the organisation and altering a key variable, such as the rate of growth (or decline) in economic growth, a very large increase in a major resource such as staff costs, loss of access to a key market for service provision, and so on. The purpose of stress testing is to assess whether the organisation could survive the shock. If there are doubts about this ability, the organisation should consider measures to reduce the risk, perhaps by developing contingency plans, or taking measures to improve their capital or liquidity.

This is not widely used in individual NHS organisations, although Monitor does make extensive use of downside scenario planning in its FT application process to assess the financial resilience of the applicant NHS trust.

Elements of the risk assessment process

The 2014 FRC guidance does not set out in detail the procedure by which a company designs and implements its risk management and internal control systems. Defining a single approach to achieving best practice would be misguided, as it would lead boards to underestimate the crucial importance to high-quality risk management of the culture and behaviour they promote. However, it still possible to identify some basic elements to a risk management system. These elements are:

- risk identification
- risk evaluation
- risk management measures
- risk control and review.

A further element that might be considered is that of risk training. Risk identification involves an organisation having a procedure in place for reviewing and identifying the risks it faces. Risks change over time, and risk reviews should therefore be undertaken regularly.

Risk evaluation calls for procedures to assess the potential size of the risk. The expected losses that could occur from adverse events or developments depend on the probability that an adverse outcome will occur and size of the loss in the event of an adverse outcome. Where a risk is unlikely to materialise into an adverse outcome, and the loss would in any case be small, no management action might be necessary. Where the risk is higher, measures should be taken to protect the organisation so that the remaining exposure to risk is within the organisation's tolerance level and consistent with its risk appetite.

The 2008 NHS National Patient Safety Agency publication *A risk matrix for risk managers* was developed to assist NHS risk managers in implementing an integrated system of risk assessment. The guidance sets out a matrix for NHS organisations to score both the probability and the size of the loss. The matrix covers risks associated with:

- adverse publicity/reputation
- business objectives/projects
- environmental impact
- finance, including claims
- human resources/organisational development/staffing/competence
- impact on the safety of patients, staff or public (physical/psychological harm)
- quality/complaints/audit
- service/business interruption
- statutory duty/ inspections.

Management should decide the measures taken to deal with each risk and is accountable to the board for these measures. In broad terms, risks can be dealt with by avoiding them or by taking steps to limit the exposure. Some risks can be avoided but many risks have to be accepted as an inevitable feature of business. For principal risks, an organisation should decide what measures might be necessary to reduce the risk to acceptable proportions. Risks may be reduced through measures such as stakeholder management and collaborative ventures. From a health service governance perspective, it should be a responsibility of the board to make sure that risks are reviewed regularly and that management takes suitable measures to deal with them.

Executive management should establish control systems to monitor risks that include identifying situations that are getting out of control, or where significant events have developed or are developing.

A further consideration for NHS organisations is the requirement of the 2014 FRC guidance that:

> 'the board should consider whether it, and any committee or management group to which it delegates activities, has the necessary skills, knowledge, experience, authority and support to enable it to assess the risks the organisation faces and exercise its responsibilities effectively. Boards should consider specifically assessing this as part of their regular evaluations of their effectiveness.'

This should ensure that they are capable of contributing proactively to board discussions on risk strategy. Training in risk management should be particularly important for members of the board committee (audit committee or risk committee) with responsibility for reviewing the risk management system.

■ Internal control systems and procedures

The board of directors is responsible for maintaining a sound system of risk management and internal control, as shown earlier in the UK Code and FRC Guidance 2014. They require the board of directors to set appropriate policies on internal control, to seek regular assurance to satisfy itself that the system is operating effectively and to ensure that the system of internal control is effective in managing risks in the way that it has approved.

In deciding its policies for internal control and assessing what constitutes an effective system of internal control, the board should consider:

- the nature and extent of the risks facing the organisation
- the amount of risk and types of risk that it regards as acceptable for the organisation to bear
- the likelihood that the risks will materialise
- the organisation's ability to reduce the impact on the business of the risks that do materialise
- the costs of operating particular controls relative to the benefits to be obtained from managing the risks they control. Controls are not worth having if they cost more than the expected benefits or savings they will provide.

Having identified the responsibilities of the board for maintaining a sound system of internal control, the 2014 FRC guidance adds that it is the job of management to implement the board's policies on control. Management must have procedures for identifying and evaluating the risks faced by the organisation, as well as designing, implementing and monitoring a control system to deal with these risks in a way that is consistent with the board's policies. In addition, all employees have some responsibility for internal control, for example to avoid making mistakes in their work and also to ensure that the control procedures for which they are responsible are properly performed.

The board needs to have assurance that there is a robust and resilient internal control system for managing internal control risks that feeds into and underpins the risk management system. Having established the internal control risks to the organisation's strategic objectives, management needs to identify the internal controls to limit or manage those risks. The controls are an essential part of an internal control system; their nature and extent will depend to a large extent on the organisation's size, what controls it can afford and whether the benefits obtained from any particular control measure are sufficient to justify its cost. The internal control system should be sufficiently robust and effective to minimise the risk of serious losses through error or fraud. In a large organisation, there would be thousands of different financial operational and compliance controls, each designed to prevent particular financial, operational or compliance failures, or to detect them if they occur.

An important aspect of health service governance is to ensure that the system of internal control (and the internal controls within that system) is adequate and effective in preventing or detecting failures in the system. For example, if the system is ineffective, an organisation may be exposed to a high risk of fraud and also to a high risk that its annual financial statements will not be accurate or reliable.

A sound system of internal control should be embedded in the operations of the organisation and form part of its culture. It should be capable of responding quickly to risks to the business as they emerge and develop, should include procedures for reporting immediately to the management responsible and control failings that have been identified and any corrective action that has been undertaken.

The Turnbull Guidance emphasises that a sound system of internal control cannot provide certain protection against an organisation suffering losses or breaches of laws or regulations or failing to meet its business objectives. The possibility will always exist of 'poor judgement in decision-making, human error, control processes being deliberately circumvented by employees and others, management overriding controls and the occurrence of unforeseen circumstances'. A sound system of internal control provides reasonable assurance that risks will be suitably controlled, but cannot provide absolute assurance that there will not be any material losses, fraud, errors or breaches of laws and regulations.

In addition to the internal controls themselves, an internal control system should also have other elements to be effective and achieve its objectives. The

COSO Framework identifies five elements to a system of internal control (also recognised in the Turnbull Report).

- A control environment that describes the awareness of (and attitude to) internal controls in the organisation, shown by the directors, management and employees generally. It therefore encompasses corporate culture, management style and employee attitudes to control procedures.
- There should be a system or procedures for identifying the risks facing the organisation (and how these are changing) and assessing their significance. Controls or management initiatives should be devised to deal with significant risks.
- Controls should be devised and implemented to eliminate, reduce or control risks.
- All employees who are responsible for the management of risks should receive information that enables them to fulfil this task.
- The effectiveness of internal controls and the internal control system generally should be monitored regularly. Internal audit is one method of monitoring the internal control system. Internal controls are also monitored by executive management and (as part of their annual audit) by the external auditors. The board of directors also has a responsibility to review the effectiveness of the system.

Types of internal controls

Financial controls are internal accounting controls that are sufficient to provide reasonable assurance that:

- transactions are made only according to the general or specific authorisation of management
- transactions are recorded so that financial statements can be prepared according to accounting standards and generally accepted accounting principles
- transactions are recorded so that assets can be accounted for
- access to assets is only allowed according to the general or specific authorisation of management
- the accounting records for assets are compared with actual assets at reasonable intervals of time
- appropriate action is taken whenever there are found to be differences.

The maintenance of proper accounting records is an important element of internal control. Effective financial controls should ensure the quality of external and internal financial reporting, so that there are no material errors in the accounting records and financial statements. They should ensure that no fraud is committed (or that fraud is detected when it occurs) and that the financial assets of the organisation are not stolen, lost or needlessly damaged, or that these risks are reduced.

A useful method of categorising internal financial controls was used in an old guideline issued by the UK Auditing Practices Board, using the mnemonic SPAMSOAP. In this guideline (no longer in issue) internal financial controls are categorised as follows.

S: **Segregation of duties:** where possible, duties should be split between two or more people, so that the work done by one person acts as a check on the work done by another. With segregation of duties, it is more difficult for fraud to take place, because several individuals would have to collude in the fraud. It is also more difficult for accidental errors to occur, because when several people are involved in a task, they act as a check on each other.

P: **Physical controls:** measures to ensure the physical safety of assets, such as putting cash in a safe, banking cash receipts immediately, and preventing unauthorised access to computer systems through the use of passwords and internet firewalls.

A: **Authorisation and approval:** all financial transactions should require the authorisation or approval of an appropriate responsible person, and there should be an authorisation limit to how much spending each responsible person can approve.

M: **Management controls:** management should exercise control over financial systems, for example by preparing a budget and then monitoring actual performance by comparing it with the budget. Management controls can also be exercised by reviewing other financial statements, such as a balance sheet, profit and loss account and cash flow statement.

S: **Supervision:** the day-to-day work of employees should be properly supervised. Good supervision will reduce the likelihood of errors or fraud.

O: **Organisation:** everyone should be fully aware of his responsibilities, and lines of authority, lines of reporting and levels of responsibility should be clear. Errors and fraud are much more likely where it is uncertain who is responsible for what and who should be reporting to whom.

A: **Arithmetical and accounting controls:** these are procedures in an accounts office to check the accuracy of the records and the numbers. They include the use of control totals and reconciliations.

P: **Personnel:** the quality of internal controls is dependent on the quality of the individuals working in the organisation. Personnel selected to do a job should have the right personal qualities and be properly trained and/or qualified.

This list of different types of control is provided as a guide to the nature of financial controls. Health service governance is concerned with the adequacy of internal controls and the effectiveness of the internal control system; designing and implementing controls is a responsibility of management.

Operational controls are controls that help to reduce operational risks, or identify failures in operational systems when these occur. They are designed to prevent failures in operational procedures, or to detect and correct operational failures if they do occur. Operational failures may be caused by machine breakdowns, human error, failures in the performance of systems (possibly due to human error), weaknesses in procedures and poor management. Operational controls are measures designed to prevent these failures from happening, or identifying and correcting problems that do occur. Regular equipment maintenance, better training of staff, automation of standard procedures, and reporting systems that make managers accountable for their actions are all examples of operational controls.

Compliance controls are concerned with making sure that an entity complies with all the requirements of relevant legislation and regulations. It can be difficult to understand the nature of internal control risks and internal controls to deal with them. There are many different risks and many controls that are applied. The following are simple examples:

CASE STUDY: Risk reporting in an FT applicant trust

A trust had a cumulative deficit of £20 million at 31 March 2012. However, the trust's sights were set firmly on achieving FT status, which meant that the trust's ongoing financial performance had to improve and the cumulative deficit had to be recovered.

Over the past three years the trust had recovered the deficit and was forecasting a £12 million surplus for 2014/2015. The trust achieved this in a number of ways, notably with significant improvements in its arrangements to manage performance against budgets.

The trust reorganised its management structure, moving from 13 clinical directorates to five clinical divisions, plus a sixth division covering corporate services. Key to this restructuring was the decision to have a clinician as the head of division, who is then accountable to the chief executive. The head of division is paid to manage the division (four sessions per week) as well as undertake clinical activities.

Another key part of the trust's strategy was to minimise its reliance on non-recurrent measures. The financial strategy allows for non-recurrent measures to account for no more than 1% of turnover. If this limit is exceeded, the director of finance works with divisions to replace non-recurrent with recurrent.

The trust has also improved reporting to the board so that key risks are more readily apparent. A new format of finance report to the trust board has been introduced, which includes traffic light risk indicators for the high level summary and includes commentary on high level details of the main risks in relation to each division's financial performance.

As a result the trust's budgetary control arrangements have improved considerably over the past three years, which has resulted in the trust being well-placed to deliver significant surpluses in the short to medium term and embark on an investment programme to replace all of the trust's facilities that are currently unfit for purpose.

> **CASE STUDY: Prescribing practice in CCGs**
>
> Delivering healthcare to satisfy the local population and providing clinically effective treatment requires the extensive use of medicines. External benchmarking suggested that through improved generic prescribing alone, GPs could save at least £350,000 each year. A CCG's medicines management team worked closely with GPs in trying to improve prescribing practice both in terms of clinical effectiveness and the assurance of best value. Education, incentive schemes, practice profiling and local drug formularies all helped to improve prescribing habits, but the decision over which drug to prescribe ultimately rested with the GP during their consultation with the patient.
>
> The CCG completed a business case for the use of a new software package that tied into the GP's electronic prescribing system. Under the control of the medicines management team, a series of protocols were programmed into the system that automatically raised a flag in response to the GP's drug selection. Alternative drug choices were offered, giving the GP an option to accept the recommended alternative(s).
>
> After eight months of full implementation, the CCG reported actual savings in excess of £400,000. In addition to financial savings, the implementation of the software had been a successful means of getting important information to GPs at the moment that they made their prescribing decision. The system provides the CCG with an opportunity to realise financial savings in drug prescribing while at the same time influencing good prescribing practice and supporting clinical effectiveness.

■ Reviewing the effectiveness of risk management and internal control

The UK Code states that the board of directors (or the audit committee) should carry out a review of the effectiveness of the system of risk management and internal control at least annually. NHS bodies, as part of the DH's NHS Controls Assurance project, were required to include a statement on internal controls (SIC) in its annual report and accounts. This has now been replaced by the AGS (see Chapter 14).

In order to review the effectiveness of the system, there must be procedures for monitoring and review. The board or audit committee needs to form its own view about the effectiveness of the system, based on the information and assurances it receives. The sources of information about risk management and internal control are management, the internal auditors (if the organisation has an internal audit function) and the external auditors, who notify management and the audit committee about weaknesses in internal controls that they have discovered in their audit. Their roles are set out in more detail in Chapter 15.

The board of directors and the audit committee do not have the time to carry out a detailed review themselves, and they must therefore rely on information provided to them by management and internal auditors. The most regular source of information for the board or audit committee about internal control should be management reports. Additional reporting may be provided, however, by the internal auditors, or by a firm of external accountants or auditors hired to perform a specific internal audit investigation.

In its *Guidance on Audit Committees* (revised 2010), the FRC states that except where the responsibility is retained by the entire board, or delegated to a risk committee:

'The audit committee should receive reports from management on the effectiveness of the systems they have established and the conclusions of any testing carried out by internal and external auditors.'

■ Emergency preparedness and business continuity

Emergency preparedness is a plan of what to do if a disaster that is unconnected with the organisation's business and outside the control of management occurs. Disaster recovery planning goes beyond procedures that should be taken in an emergency, such as a fire or explosion in a building. It is intended to establish what should be done if an extreme disaster threatens the ability of the organisation to maintain its operations. Examples of disasters are natural disasters, such as major fires or flooding or storm damage to key installations or offices, major terrorist attacks and pandemics.

Emergency preparedness plans are vital for NHS organisations, as lengthy or widespread overwhelming demand or shutdown of operations could be catastrophic. While the training of appropriate NHS staff regarding such arrangements in the UK is the responsibility of NHS organisations, the DH fund an extensive training programme delivered by the HPA to support the NHS in England in planning and preparing for major incidents.

Guidance is given in *The NHS Emergency Planning Guidance 2005*, which sets out general principles to guide all NHS organisations in developing their ability to respond to a major incident (or incidents) and to manage recovery whether the incident or incidents has effects locally, regionally, or nationally, within the context of the requirements of the Civil Contingencies Act 2004 (the CCA). The guidance contains strategic national guidance for all NHS organisations in England and equivalent guidance is provided by Health Departments in devolved administrations. The CCA defines an emergency as:

'An event or a situation which threatens serious damage to human welfare in a place in the UK, the environment of a place in the UK, or war or terrorism which threatens serious damage to the security of the UK.'

The definition is concerned with consequences rather than the cause or source. For the NHS, major incident is the term in general use and is defined as:

'Any occurrence that presents serious threat to the health of the community, disruption to the service or causes (or is likely to cause) such numbers or types of casualties as to require special arrangements to be implemented by hospitals, ambulance trusts or primary care organisations.'

The levels of incident for which NHS organisations are required to develop emergency preparedness arrangements are as follows.

- **Major:** individual ambulance trusts and acute trusts are well versed in handling incidents such as multi-vehicle motorway crashes within the long-established major incident plans. More patients will be dealt with, probably faster and with fewer resources, than usual but it is possible to maintain the usual levels of service.
- **Mass:** much larger-scale events affecting potentially hundreds rather than tens of people, possibly also involving the closure or evacuation of a major facility (e.g. because of fire or contamination) or persistent disruption over many days. These will require a collective response by several or many neighbouring trusts.
- **Catastrophic:** events of potentially catastrophic proportions that severely disrupt health and social care and other functions (e.g. mass casualties, power, water, etc.) and that exceed even collective local capability within the NHS.

Although not formally described, there may be events occurring on a national scale, such as fuel strikes, pandemics or multiple events that require the collective capability of the NHS nationally. In each NHS organisation, the CEO is responsible for ensuring that their organisation has a Major Incident Plan in place that will be built on the principles of risk assessment, cooperation with partners, emergency planning, communicating with the public and information sharing. The plan will link into the organisation's arrangements for ensuring business continuity as required by the CCA.

The CEO will ensure that the board receives regular reports, at least annually, regarding emergency preparedness, including reports on exercises, training and testing undertaken by the organisation, and that adequate resources are made available to allow discharge of these responsibilities. As a minimum requirement, NHS organisations will be required to undertake a live exercise every three years; a tabletop exercise every year and a test of communications cascades every six months. A review of emergency preparedness plans may therefore be a part of the annual review of the effectiveness of internal control by the board or audit committee.

To support this arrangement, the guidance suggests that an executive board director be designated to take responsibility for emergency preparedness on behalf of the organisation. It is further suggested that a NED be nominated to support the ED lead in this role. In some cases this may be best achieved through the linkage of emergency planning and business continuity to the organisation's risk management committee (or equivalent). It is considered good practice for NHS organisations to designate an adequately resourced officer, usually referred to as the emergency planning liaison officer (EPLO), to support the executive in the discharge of their duties for emergency preparedness.

Business continuity management also forms an important part of risk management arrangements and is a further requirement of the CCA. The aim of business continuity management is to ensure that NHS organisations are able to maintain the highest level of service possible whatever might happen to the infrastructure. There is a range of problems that might affect NHS organisations and services at any time, for example, loss of water or power, flooding, or criminal action. The aim of business continuity planning is to enable planning and reaction in a coordinated manner. While business continuity and major incident planning are usually separate processes within an organisation, a major incident may occur at the same time as a business continuity issue, or be triggered by it.

Business continuity management, including processes for recovery and restoration, should be considered by NHS organisations as part of its everyday business processes. Business continuity should be seen as embedded in the culture of the NHS as principles of health and safety, and there must be demonstrable commitment to the process from the boards of NHS organisations. The skills to develop business continuity plans are complementary to those involved in emergency planning and may therefore need to be undertaken by separate officers. It is critical though that both plans are integrated and complementary to each other.

■ High reliability organisations

There has been some interesting work carried out in recent years with regard to major hazard organisations such as airlines and oil refineries, who have been attempting to influence the organisational and safety culture at their sites to transform them into high reliability organisations (HROs) with a positive safety culture. These are organisations that are able to manage and sustain almost error-free performance despite operating in hazardous conditions where the consequences of errors could be catastrophic.

Descriptions of HROs usually include organisations where failure may have far-reaching, potentially catastrophic consequences. Such organisations will be typically characterised by a high level of interactive complexity: for example, interaction among system components is unpredictable and/or invisible, and there is a high level of interdependence amongst a system's component parts (including people, equipment and procedures). Much like many HROs, the healthcare industry does complex, high-stakes work where mistakes can equal great harm.

A review of the literature published by the Health and Safety Executive (HSE) in 2011 identified key features and characteristics that could be adopted by organisations to achieve ongoing high reliability and safety objectives.

Successful containment of unexpected events by:

- having in place back-up systems in the event of failures and cross-checking of important decisions (redundancy);
- allowing people with expertise, irrespective of rank, to make important safety-related decisions in emergencies, though maintaining a clear hierarchical structure and an understanding of who is responsible for what during routine operations (deference to expertise in emergencies; oscillation between hierarchical and flat organisational structures), investment in training and technical competence; and
- well-defined procedures for all possible unexpected events.

Effective anticipation of potential failures through:

- engagement with front line staff in order to obtain 'the bigger picture' of operations (sensitivity to operations);
- attentiveness to minor, or what may appear as trivial, signals that may indicate potential problem areas within the organisation; using incidents and near misses as indicators of a system's 'health' (preoccupation with failure); and
- systematic collection and analysis of all warning signals, no matter how trivial they may appear to be, and avoiding assumptions regarding the nature of failures. Explanations regarding the causes of incidents tend to be systemic rather than focusing on individual, 'blame the operator' justifications (reluctance to simplify).

Just culture, characterised by:

- open reporting systems for near misses and accidents without fear of punishment;
- follow-up of accident investigation outcomes by implementing corrective actions;
- empowering staff to abandon work on safety grounds; and
- fostering a sense of personal accountability for safety.

Learning orientation, characterised by:

- continuous technical training;
- systematic analysis of incidents to identify their root causes and accident types or trends within the organisation;
- open communication of accident investigation outcomes; and
- updating procedures in line with the organisational knowledge base.

5. *Mindful leadership, characterised by:*

- proactive commissions of audits to identify problems in the system (often in response to incidents that occur in other similar industries);
- 'bottom-up' communication of 'bad news';
- engagement with front line staff through site visits; and
- investment of resources in safety management and the ability to balance profits with safety.

In addition to this review, further research into the applicability of the characteristics and systems of HROs for the healthcare sector has been carried out to further the safety culture in healthcare services. The most commonly applied resulting principles include:

- attempts to improve safety culture
- checklists and other tools
- initiatives to build teamwork using crew resource management and human factors approaches
- standardised processes using care bundles.

It will be interesting to see how developments in this area can be built into NHS risk management processes.

Governance Checklist

✓ How has the board agreed the organisation's risk appetite? With whom has it conferred?

✓ How has the board assessed the organisation's culture? In what way does the board satisfy itself that the organisation has a 'speak-up' culture and that it systematically learns from past mistakes?

✓ How do the organisation's culture, code of conduct, and human resource policies support the business objectives, risk management and internal control systems?

✓ How has the board considered whether senior management promotes and communicates the desired culture and demonstrates the necessary commitment to risk management and internal control?

✓ How is inappropriate behaviour dealt with? Does this present consequential risks?

✓ How does the board ensure that it has sufficient time to consider risk, and how is that integrated with discussion on other matters for which the board is responsible?

✓ To what extent do the risk management and internal control systems underpin and relate to the organisation's business model?

✓ How is the risk management strategy communicated through out the organisation? How does the board determine whether this is clear, appropriate and effective?

✓ How effectively is the organisation able to withstand risks, and risk combinations, which do materialise? How effective is the board's approach to risks with 'low probability' but a very severe impact if they materialise?

✓ What are the channels of communication that enable individuals, including third parties, to report concerns, suspected breaches of law or regulations, other improprieties or challenging perspectives?

✓ What are the responsibilities of the board and senior management for crisis management? How effectively have the organisation's crisis management planning and systems been tested?

✓ To what extent has the organisation identified risks from joint ventures, third parties and from the way the organisation's business is organised? How are these managed?

✓ How effectively does the organisation capture new and emerging risks and opportunities? How and when does the board consider risk when discussing changes in strategy or approving new transactions, projects, products or other significant commitments?

✓ To what extent has the board considered the cost-benefit aspects of different control options?

✓ How does the board ensure it understands the organisation's exposure to each principal risk before and after the application of mitigations and controls, what those mitigations and controls are and whether they are operating as expected?

✓ What are the processes by which senior management monitor the effective application of the systems of risk management and internal control?

✓ In what way do the monitoring and review processes take into account the organisation's ability to re-evaluate the risks and adjust controls effectively in response to changes in its objectives, its business, and its external environment?

✓ How are processes or controls adjusted to reflect new or changing risks, or operational deficiencies? To what extent does the board engage in horizon scanning for emerging risks?

✓ How has the board satisfied itself that the disclosures on risk management and internal control contribute to the annual report being fair, balanced and understandable, and provide shareholders with the information they need?

✓ How has the board satisfied itself that its reporting on going concern and the longer-term viability statement gives a fair, balanced and understandable overview of the organisation's position and prospects?

Adapted from Appendix C of the 2014 FRC guidance

■ Summary

The FRC Guidance 2014 is very clear that good stewardship by the board should not inhibit the sensible risk-taking that is critical to growth. However, the assessment of risks as part of the normal business planning process should support better decision-making, ensure that the board and management respond promptly to risks when they arise, and ensure that stakeholders are well informed about the principal risks and prospects of the organisation.

The addition of behavioural and organisational risk into the risk management system highlights the challenge that is embedding risk management processes into an organisation. This seems to be a critical area for boards to consider as part of their ongoing training and development.

14

Assurance

In corporate governance, the annual report and accounts is seen as the most important communication between a company and its stakeholders. This is not the case in health service governance. Although significant, the annual report and accounts is not the sole means of communication for NHS organisations. Instead, there are a wide variety of reporting requirements. These primarily focus on reporting to the regulators, as well as providing information to key NHS stakeholders.

These complex reporting requirements seek to provide assurance to the board, regulators and a much wider public audience. Assurance can be understood as the provision of accurate and current information about the efficiency and effectiveness of an organisation's policies and operations, and the status of its compliance with statutory obligations. Assurance is the process of establishing the integrity and validity of disclosures, including statements and reports. Good assurance is confidence backed by sufficient evidence: the board should obtain assurance that performance and quality are as they should be, that risks are properly controlled and that strategy is being implemented successfully and sustainably. Board members, regulators and others need to have information from more than one source in order to be able to validate this evidence.

Regulators are primarily required to provide assurance on the stewardship of public money, as well as the corporate governance and performance of the NHS organisation. By contrast, inspection (by bodies such as CQC) provides assurance that services satisfy service users and are achieving levels of quality consistent with national standards. Trustworthy reporting and auditing is probably the most significant issue for health service governance. Good health service governance should ensure that quality, performance and financial reporting is reliable and honest, and that the opinion of the external auditors is objective and unbiased.

■ Performance reporting

Frameworks for the NHS in England are published each year. They describe the national priorities, system levers and enablers needed for NHS organisations to maintain and improve the quality of services provided, while delivering transformational change and maintaining financial stability.

Foundation trusts follow an annual planning and reporting cycle based upon Monitor's approach to overseeing an FT's compliance with the governance and continuity of services requirements of their provider licence. This is set out in the Risk Assessment Framework, which replaced the Compliance Framework from 1 October 2013. CCGs are subject to an ongoing assurance process overseen by NHS England area teams, which consists of quarterly assurance meetings and an annual 'health check' assessing organisational capabilities, delivery and support needs. It might also include measures of quality in primary as well as secondary care under the CCG Assurance Framework, which was first published in November 2013. Both of these frameworks were covered in Chapters 11 and 12 respectively.

NHS trusts are subject to the framework imposed by the *Delivering for Patients: the 2014/15 Accountability Framework for NHS trust boards*, published by the NHS TDA. The oversight approach for measuring and tracking NHS trust performance is focused on three areas:

- quality performance
- financial performance
- sustainability performance.

Quality performance is measured against five domains (aligned to the five CQC domains of caring, effective, responsive, safe and well led). Financial performance is measured against two domains: in-year financial delivery and the Monitor continuity of service rating. Each of these domains has an associated set of indicators, and performance against all of these indicators determines a score for each domain. These domain scores in turn contribute towards an overall escalation score for each NHS trust.

During 2014, NHS trusts have been required to submit a two-year operational plan, a five-year strategic plan and a development support plan. The sustainability assessment rests on considering five broad strategic areas in the NHS trust's five-year plan in:

- Clinical and workforce
- Financial and business
- Future commissioning and service strategy
- Securing a sustainable organisational form
- Leadership capability and capacity.

The NHS TDA intend to develop a score for the sustainability domain following the assessment of the five-year plans. This will, in turn, feed through to the overall escalation level.

The measurement and monitoring process described above results in each NHS trust being placed in one of five oversight categories, based on how they score against the various oversight domains, relevant views of third parties such as the CQC, and the judgement of the TDA. The measurement and monitoring process described above will continue to place each NHS trust in one of five oversight categories:

- **Special measures:** significant delivery issues and limited confidence in board capacity
- **Intervention:** significant delivery issues and concerns on board capacity
- **Intervention:** some delivery issues and confidence in board capacity
- **Standard oversight:** limited or no delivery issues and confidence in board capacity
- **Standard oversight:** sound FT application, 'Good' or 'Outstanding' CQC and confidence in board capacity.

For 2014/15, NHS trusts will be scored using escalation levels one to five, with escalation level one being the highest risk rating and level five the lowest. This is to ensure consistency with the CQC's approach to assessing risk through its Intelligent Monitoring system.

All of this performance information is publicly available through publications from the regulators and on the UK's biggest health website NHS Choices, which provides a comprehensive health information service.

The performance indicators in this oversight approach form the basis of most quality, financial and sustainability reporting to the NHS trust board and its committees. The NHS TDA *Delivering for patients framework* includes proposed indicators for monthly oversight and escalation that are relevant to the different services provided – for example, ambulance service and community health. The indicators are quality assured by the Health and Social Care Information Centre. This is an ENDPB established by the regulations underpinning HSCA 2012 to 'establish procedures for the assessment of a quality indicator; establish, maintain and publish a database of quality indicators; and arrange for each quality indicator published in the library to be periodically reviewed'.

■ Quality governance

The growing political agenda for assurance on the delivery of quality services, as well as quality outcomes for patients, has led to the growth of quality governance as a specialised area of governance. While not strictly part of health service governance, many NHS company secretaries will find themselves involved in the quality agenda purely because the board is required by its regulators to give regular and specific assurance on the delivery of quality within their organisation.

Quality has been part of government strategy for modernising the NHS for many years. *A First Class Service: quality in the new NHS*, published in July 1998, set out the agenda for quality improvement in the NHS. The framework established:

- clear quality standards, through the establishment of NICE to provide clear advice on clinical and cost-effectiveness and the development of National

Service Frameworks (NSFs) to help raise standards of care and reduce unacceptable variations
- effective local delivery of these standards through a system of clinical governance
- strong monitoring mechanisms, including the NHS Performance Assessment Framework, together with a new statutory Commission for Health Improvement (CHI) and a programme of national patient and user surveys.

The publication of Lord Darzi's 2008 report *High quality care for all* revived and reinforced this strategy. He highlighted four key areas that would demonstrate improving quality of care:

- patient safety
- effectiveness, including clinical outcomes and patient reported outcome measures (PROMs)
- user experience
- innovation.

As a result, greater clarity on quality standards was required; metrics had to be developed to measure quality; Quality Accounts were to be published; the delivery of quality was to be rewarded via Commissioning for Quality Improvement (CQUINs); and standards were to be raised with the creation of the National Quality Board.

Since, ultimately, the board of an NHS organisation is responsible for the quality of care delivered across all services that it provides, this has to be achieved through governance arrangements which delegate responsibility down to the operating levels in the organisation. In the case of quality, this means that, although individuals and clinical teams are at the frontline and responsible for delivering quality care, it is the responsibility of the board to create a culture within the organisation that enables clinicians and clinical teams to work at their best. In addition, the board must have in place arrangements for measuring and monitoring quality and for escalating issues, including, where needed, to the board. Boards should encourage a culture where services are improved by learning from mistakes, where staff and patients are encouraged to identify areas for improvement, and where they are not afraid to speak out.

The term quality governance is used to refer to the values and behaviours and the structures and processes that need to be in place to enable the board to discharge its responsibilities for quality. The board's responsibilities for quality are threefold:

- to ensure that the essential standards of quality and safety (as determined by CQC's registration requirements) are at a minimum being met by every service that the organisation delivers
- to ensure that the organisation is striving for continuous quality improvement and outcomes in every service

■ to ensure that every member of staff that has contact with patients, or whose actions directly impact on patient care, is motivated and enabled to deliver effective, safe and person-centred care.

The arrangements for quality governance should complement and be fully integrated with the governance arrangements for other aspects of the board's responsibilities, such as finance governance and research governance. The National Quality Board sets out the definition of quality governance in terms of its four component parts in its 2011 guidance *Quality Governance in the NHS – A guide for provider boards*. These are:

■ strategy
■ capabilities and culture
■ processes and structures
■ measurement.

Monitor also established the Quality Governance Framework (QGF) in 2010, which FTs and NHS trusts are required to assess themselves against as part of their annual reporting cycle.

The Quality Governance Framework
The QGF applies to FTs and NHS trusts. It requires self-assessment and independent assessment with any improvement actions specified with clear timescales. See Chapter 11 for more on the QGF.

Quality accounts
The significant report relating to quality is the annual quality account, which reports on the quality of services provided by an NHS healthcare service. Quality accounts are not intended as marketing documents, but as an opportunity for NHS providers to enter into an open and honest dialogue with the public regarding the quality of care in the organisation. The details surrounding the form and content of Quality Accounts were designed in partnership between the DH, Monitor, the CQC and NHS East of England. It involved a wide range of people from the NHS, patient organisations and the public, representatives of professional organisations and of the independent and voluntary sector. A consultation ran between September and December 2009 and the responses shaped the framework for the regulations and guidance in 2010.

According to the *DH Quality Accounts Toolkit* (2010), Quality Accounts aim to improve organisational accountability to the public and engage boards in the quality improvement agenda. They should enable providers to review services, decide and show where they are doing well, but also where improvement is required demonstrate what improvements are planned. They provide information on the quality of services to patients and the public, though explain how providers respond to feedback from patients and the public, as well as other stakeholders.

The quality account is published annually by each NHS healthcare provider and is available to the public. Quality accounts aim to <u>enhance accountability</u> to the public and <u>engage the leaders of an organisation in the quality improvement agenda</u>. All providers of NHS services are required to produce a quality account as set out in the Health Act 2009 and supporting regulations.

CASE STUDY: University College London Hospital NHS Foundation Trust

University College London Hospital NHS Foundation Trust has published Quality Accounts for a number of years and has developed a format for establishing the quality priorities.

First of all a long list of contenders are drawn up. Three of the trust's top ten objectives are around improving patient safety, experience and clinical outcomes so the long list contains contenders across all these domains. Possible priorities are derived from three sources: the trust's performance over the past year against its quality and safety indicators; national or regional priorities and finally, from horizon scanning. The list of contenders has to be in areas that fulfilled most or all of the following criteria:

- where the trust genuinely had a desire or need to drive improvement
- known improvement strategies; so that the Trust could hit the ground running in delivering tangible improvement in a defined timeline
- have measures either in place or in development
- capable of historic or benchmark comparison.

The long list plus the rationale for selection was then discussed and consulted on extensively with groups of internal and external stakeholders to develop a shortlist. The trust also asks if there is a good reason to carry forward any of the quality priorities from the previous year. The trust found that the shortlist and final selection became virtually self-selecting following this process in that there was wide consensus on what should be the final priorities.

Once established, the trust has put delivery strategies in place for all the quality priorities. It has also tracked performance against improvement trajectories at all levels from ward to board on a monthly basis using the quality scorecard and priority specific improvement charts.

Recommendations for Quality Accounts preparation for 2014/15 are as follows.

- Healthwatch to consider producing guidance that will enable them to effectively challenge Quality Accounts locally. This recommendation came directly from a number of Healthwatch organisations and the thinking is that NHS England would ask Healthwatch to produce this guidance.

- NHS Choices website functionality reviewed from a patients and provider perspective.
- Presentational guidance, which will focus on the use of plain English and simplifying/standardising the presentation of data.

Financial reporting

As previously mentioned, NHS trusts provide regular financial reporting to comply with the oversight approach of the NHS TDA *Delivering for Patients Framework.* However, the other key financial reporting tool for NHS organisations is the annual report and accounts.

NHS organisations are obliged to comply with the determination and directions given by the Secretary of State for Health in the preparation of their annual report and annual accounts. These directions are set out in the *NHS Finance Manual*, published by the DH. In addition, the government publishes the *Financial Reporting Manual* (FReM), which is the technical accounting guide to the preparation of financial statements. Foundation trusts are required to follow the guidance given by Monitor in the FT ARM; CCGs should follow the guidance in the *CCG Annual Reporting Manual* (CCG ARM).

NHS organisations must publish an annual report and (full) audited accounts as one document and present it at a public meeting, whether or not summary financial statements are also produced. Where an NHS body has dissolved, or taken FT status, an annual report and audited accounts for its final accounting period must still be published and presented at a public meeting by a successor organisation. NHS organisations still have the option to prepare and distribute an annual report and summary financial statements, however, this is additional to the annual report and accounts described above which must be available if requested.

For NHS trusts that become FTs part way through the year, part-year financial monitoring and accounts forms must be prepared and submitted to DH in accordance with the timetable in the *NHS Finance Manual.* Separate accounts and an annual report will be prepared for the FT as specified by Monitor. Each set of accounts and annual report must formally be presented at separate public meetings, although these can take place on the same day and at the same venue.

The year-end for all NHS organisations is 31 March and the timetable for the production of the annual accounts is quite constrained. For 2013/2014, the deadline for sending unaudited accounts to the external auditors was 22 April 2014 and the deadline for submitting audited accounts to DH was 9 June 2014. The annual accounts of each NHS organisation are summarised as part of the NHS Annual Accounts and laid before Parliament in July of each year. The annual report and accounts are made up of:

- the annual report (including the directors' report, remuneration report and other public sector disclosures mandated by the FReM)

- a statement of the accountable officer's responsibilities
- a governance statement
- foreword to the accounts, referencing the relevant accounts direction
- the four primary financial statements (statement of comprehensive income; statement of financial position; statement of changes in taxpayers' equity; and statement of cash flows)
- notes to the accounts
- the audit opinion and report.

The guidance sets out the minimum content of the annual report. Beyond this, however, the entity must take ownership of the annual report. It should ensure that additional information is included where necessary to reflect the position of the NHS body within the community and give sufficient information to meet the requirements of public accountability.

The financial statements report on the financial performance of the organisation over the previous financial year and the financial position of the organisation as at the end of that year. The directors' report and other statements published in the same document provide supporting information, much of it in narrative rather than in numerical form. Stakeholders use the information in the annual report and accounts to assess the stewardship of the directors and the financial health of the organisation.

Accountability and transparency

The annual report and accounts is an important document for health service governance because it is a means by which the directors are made accountable to the stakeholders, and it provides a channel of communication from directors to stakeholders. The report and accounts enable the stakeholders to assess how well the organisation has been governed and managed. It should therefore be clear and understandable to a reader with reasonable financial awareness, and reliable and 'believable'.

The reliability of the annual report and accounts depends on several factors, including those that follow.

- The honesty of the organisation in preparing them: if allowed to do so by accounting regulations, organisations might indulge in window dressing their financial performance or financial position through the use of accounting policies (methods) that hide the true position.
- The care used by directors to satisfy themselves that the financial statements do give a 'true and fair view' and that everything of relevance has been properly reported.
- The opinion of the external auditors, which the stakeholders should be able to rely on as an objective and professional opinion.

If financial statements are produced in a way that is intended deliberately to mislead stakeholders, the persons responsible would be guilty of fraud, which is a crime. Misleading financial statements, however, could only be issued if the audit committee is satisfied with their preparation, external auditors provide a 'clean' audit report, and the board of directors approves the financial statements. In most organisations, this would require deception by a small group of executives, such as the CEO and finance director.

The diverse requirements for reporting in health service governance highlight a number of ways in which the organisation's directors are held accountable to stakeholders. The information given can be used to assess the success of the organisation and the effectiveness of its board. It is therefore essential that the reporting should give a clear presentation of the position and performance of the organisation. In other words, there should be 'transparency' in reporting by organisation, so that the recipients of the reports can see what the organisation has achieved and assess what is likely to happen in the future.

The UK Code states as a main principle that: 'the board should present a balanced and understandable assessment of the company's position and prospects' in its report and accounts, as well as in its interim reports and other public statements. This principle applies to narrative reporting in the annual report as well as to the financial statements. These principles are mirrored in the *NHS Finance Manual*, FReM, the FT ARM and the CCG ARM.

The Companies Act 2006 (Strategic Report and Directors' Report) Regulations 2013 requires directors to prepare a strategic report that is separate to the directors' report. It must therefore be separately approved by the board of directors and signed on behalf of the board by a director or secretary of the company. The strategic report has replaced the business review previously required by section 417 of the Companies Act 2006. In support of these regulations, the FRC *Guidance on the Strategic Report* was issued in June 2014 to set out best practice principles.

The overriding purpose of the strategic report is to inform members of the company and to help them assess how the directors have performed their duty to promote the success of the company. The strategic report should include the business model, strategy, objectives and principal risks, a review of the year and future outlook. It should provide context to the financial statements and insight into the main objectives, strategies, and risks and how these might impact future performance. The rules will also require quoted companies to make new disclosures about human rights, gender diversity and greenhouse gas emissions.

The 'principal risks' reference is important as it ties into the 2014 FRC guidance on *Risk Management, Internal Control and Related Financial and Business Reporting*, which is considered more fully in Chapter 13. Principal risks that are included in the strategic report should be limited to those considered by the organisation's management to be material to the development, performance, position or future prospects of the organisation. They will generally be matters that the directors regularly monitor and discuss because of their likelihood or the magnitude of their potential effect on the organisation or a combination of the two.

Under section 496 of the Companies Act 2006 the auditor is required to state whether, in their opinion, the information in the strategic report is consistent with the accounts. The FReM, FT ARM and CCG ARM have adopted these changes and the previous directors' report (including an operating and financial review) has now been split into a strategic report and a directors' report.

■ Directors' duties and responsibilities for financial reporting

An organisation's directors are responsible for the preparation and content of the financial statements. The UK Code states that the directors should explain in the annual report their responsibility for preparing the annual report and financial statements. There should also be a supporting statement by the auditors (in their report) about their reporting responsibilities. The UK Code also requires that the directors should include in their annual report an explanation of the basis on which the company generates or preserves value over the longer term (its 'business model'), and strategy for delivering the objectives of the company.

Responsibilities of the directors for financial reporting

There is sometimes confusion and misunderstanding about responsibilities for financial reporting, and a mistaken belief that the external auditors are responsible for the 'true and fair view' in the financial statements. If misleading and incorrect financial statements are produced, it may therefore be supposed that the auditors have been negligent and must be to blame. This view is incorrect. The directors are responsible for the financial statements: they prepare the financial statements and have the primary responsibility for the reliability of the information they provide. Management and the directors are therefore responsible for identifying and correcting any errors or misrepresentations in the financial statements.

The responsibility of the external auditors is to obtain reasonable assurance, in their professional opinion, that the financial statements are free from material error or misstatement. They present a professional opinion to the stakeholders, not to the directors of the organisation, and the directors should not rely on the opinion of the external auditors in reaching their own view.

In UK law, the directors are also potentially liable for any errors or misleading information in the annual report and accounts. Any person (e.g. an investor) suffering a loss because of an error or misstatement in an organisation's report and accounts may sue the organisation, and the organisation may then take legal action against the directors to recover any losses it has occurred from the legal action.

Going concern statement

A key accounting concept is the 'going concern' concept. This is the view that the organisation will continue to trade for the foreseeable future (at least the next 12 months). This is different to an understanding of an organisation's viability.

In the UK Code, the board is required to make an explicit statement in the financial statements about whether the going concern basis of accounting has been adopted and whether there are any material uncertainties about the company's ability to continue to do so in future. It is also required to make a broader statement about the board's reasonable expectation as to the company's viability based on a robust assessment of the company's principal risks and the company's current position. This is developed in the latest FRC guidance on *Risk Management, Internal Control and Related Financial and Business Reporting* which states:

> 'A company that is able to adopt the going concern basis of accounting and does not have related material uncertainties to report, for the purposes of the financial statements, is not necessarily free of risks that would threaten the company's business model, future performance, solvency or liquidity were they to materialise. The board is responsible for ensuring this distinction is understood internally and communicated externally.'

The financial statements are therefore prepared on the going concern basis, and assets are valued differently from what their value might be if the organisation went into liquidation. The statement of going concern should also give reasons why the directors have reached their view, and also indicate any doubts there might be. Where there is fundamental uncertainty over the going concern basis (for instance, continuing operational stability depends on finance or income that has not yet been approved), or where the going concern basis is not appropriate, the directors will need to disclose the relevant circumstances and should discuss the basis of accounting and the disclosures to be made with their auditors. Similarly, the UK Listing Rules require the directors to make a statement in the report and accounts that the company is a going concern, together with supporting assumptions and qualifications as necessary. These requirements are mirrored in the NHS Finance Manual, FReM, NHS FT ARM and CCG ARM.

The auditor's responsibility is to consider the appropriateness of the use of the going concern assumption in preparing the financial statements. They should also consider if there are material uncertainties about the organisation's ability to continue as a going concern that need to be disclosed in the financial statements

A typical going concern statement within an annual report might be as follows:

> 'After making enquiries, the directors have a reasonable expectation that the NHS foundation trust has adequate resources to continue in operational existence for the foreseeable future. For this reason, they continue to adopt the going concern basis in preparing the accounts.'

In the UK, disclosures about the assumptions or qualifications about going concern status are becoming more extensive. The directors may be personally liable if they make a statement that the organisation is a going concern without giving the matter careful consideration. Liability could arise if the organisation subsequently goes into liquidation within the next 12 months and stakeholders claim that they relied on the going concern statement when making their investment decisions.

In the strict accounting sense, NHS bodies cannot prepare accounts on any other basis than as a going concern. Various Acts of Parliament prevent NHS organisations from becoming insolvent in the strict accounting sense, as the DH bears the ultimate liability for any debts. Even so, NHS annual reporting requirements still require NHS organisations to include a statement on whether or not the financial statements have been prepared on a going concern basis and the reasons for this decision, with supporting assumptions or qualifications as necessary. The distinction between going concern and viability make for interesting audit committee discussions, particularly for small district general hospitals.

■ The corporate governance statement

In 2006, the EU adopted a Company Reporting Directive that required quoted companies to produce a corporate governance statement in their annual reports. The statement must refer to the corporate governance code applied by the company (e.g. the UK Code) and explain whether, and to what extent, the company complies with that code. The statement must also include a description of the main features of the company's internal control and risk management systems in relation to the financial reporting process, and provide a description of the composition and operation of the board and its committees.

In the UK, listed companies were already required to report much of the corporate governance information required by the Company Reporting Directive. The UK Listing Rules require companies to include in their annual report a statement of how they have applied the principles of the UK Code, for example disclosures about the composition of board committees and their work.

However, the Company Reporting Directive required the information to be presented in a separate 'corporate governance statement' and that the statement should include a description of the main features of the company's internal control and risk management systems relating to the financial reporting process, neither of which were contained in the UK Code.

The parallel arrangement for FTs is that they are required to include a statement of compliance with the Monitor Code.

■ The annual governance statement

The statement on internal controls (SIC) was originally developed as part of the DH's NHS controls assurance project and was subsequently introduced across the wider public sector by HM Treasury. This requirement is in line with the UK Code, which states that the board should report to shareholders each year that it has conducted the annual review of the effectiveness of the systems of internal control and risk management. The FSA's Disclosure and Transparency Rules for listed companies also requires companies to report on the main features of their internal control and risk management systems in relation to financial reporting.

All public bodies (including NHS organisations) must provide assurance that they are appropriately managing and controlling the resources for which they are responsible. The SIC was a mandatory disclosure for all central government entities that comply with the FReM. It was a primary accountability document. The external auditors did not provide an explicit audit opinion on the content, but it was subject to external audit review to ensure that it had been prepared according to government guidance and that it was consistent with the auditors' knowledge of the entity. The SIC was an important accountability document in communicating these assurances to parliament and the wider public audience.

The SIC has since been superseded by the annual governance statement. FTs were required to produce an AGS, with enhanced reporting on quality governance, in place of the SIC for reporting periods commencing on or after 1 April 2011. Monitor's NHS FT ARM 2011/2012 set out a model AGS, but required each FT to adapt the model to reflect their own particular circumstance. The AGS also included reference to quality governance. The requirement for an AGS rather than the SIC has now been rolled out across all NHS organisations and a template for guidance issued for NHS trusts, FTs and CCGs.

The annual guidance from the DH continues to set out the key elements that need to be considered when producing the AGS. While NHS organisations will have risk management, control and review processes in place, the detail of these processes vary from one organisation to another depending on circumstances such as size and the complexity of the risks faced. The annual guidance, therefore, offers a summary of characteristics under six high-level elements to help with consideration of the completeness of the processes that have been put in place in a particular body.

NHS organisations are required to ensure that they have sufficient evidence to demonstrate that they have implemented processes appropriate to their circumstances under the following seven high level elements:

- scope of responsibility
- the governance framework of the organisation
- risk assessment
- the risk and control framework
- review of the effectiveness of risk management and internal control
- significant issues.

The guidance also requires full disclosure of any significant control issues or weaknesses. This is to deliver assurance that significant internal control issues have been, or are being, addressed and that the AGS is a balanced reflection of the actual control position. Although not required, it may help the disclosure in relation to a significant internal control issue if the description of the weakness and its impact is given to provide context for the actions taken. NHS bodies may exercise discretion in such disclosure to avoid further adverse impacts or exploitation of the weakness.

A single definition of a significant internal control issue is not possible and NHS organisations are required to exercise their judgement in deciding whether or not a particular issue should be regarded as falling into this category. The guidance sets out factors that may be helpful in exercising that judgement, including:

- the issue seriously prejudiced or prevented achievement of a principal objective
- the issue has had significant one-off financial implications or concerns general financial standing (e.g. deficits)
- the external auditor regards it as having a material impact on the accounts
- the audit committee advises it should be considered significant for this purpose
- the head of internal audit reports on it as significant, for this purpose, in their annual opinion on the whole of risk, control and governance
- the issue, or its impact has attracted significant public interest or has seriously damaged the reputation of the organisation (e.g. an external auditor's public interest report)
- non compliance with CQC core standards
- underachievement against World Class Commissioning assurance
- serious untoward data security incidents
- non-compliance with equality and human rights legislation.

The audit committee plays a key role in the production of the AGS. It supports the board and AO by reviewing the comprehensiveness of assurances in meeting the board and AO's assurance needs, and reviewing the reliability and integrity of the assurances. The audit committee also advises the board and AO of any control issues that could be considered significant and are therefore appropriate for disclosure in the AGS.

■ The Board Assurance Framework

In order to sign off the AGS, NHS boards need to be assured that the systems, policies and people they have put in place are operating in a way that is effective, is focused on key risks and is driving the delivery of objectives. There is, however, the potential for a lack of clarity within the board (and beyond) to what is meant by the term 'assurance'. This can extend to uncertainty over the level of assurance required, where that assurance comes from and how the reporting of assurance is managed in a coordinated manner.

Although the process of securing assurance has always been a fundamental principle of good management and accountability, the requirement for all NHS AO's to sign the AGS has focused attention on the level of assurance that boards receive. To provide this statement, boards need to be able to demonstrate that they have been properly informed through assurances about the totality of their risks, not just financial, and have arrived at their conclusions based on all the evidence presented to them.

The Board Assurance Framework (BAF) is a framework that NHS organisations are required to put in place to identify the key risks to the trust's achievement of its strategic objectives and how these risks are being managed. It provides an organisation with a method for the effective and focused management of the principal risks to meeting its objectives. It also provides a structure for the evidence to support the AGS. It identifies which of the organisation's objectives are at risk because of inadequacies in the operation of controls or where the organisation has insufficient assurance about them. At the same time it provides structured assurances about where risks are being managed effectively and objectives are being delivered. This allows the board to determine where to make efficient use of resources and to address the issues identified to improve the quality and safety of care. In documented form, a BAF would include:

- the trust's strategic objectives
- the key risks to achieving the objectives
- the controls in place to manage the risks
- the assurances that the trust used to provide evidence that the controls were operating effectively
- any gaps in the assurances
- an action plan to address the gaps.

Every NHS organisation must design its own framework, which will relate to the delivery of its own objectives within the context of an understanding of the principal risks that the organisation faces. The BAF should enable the board to:

- establish principal objectives (strategic and directorate)
- identify the principal risks that may threaten the achievement of these objectives – typically in the range of 75–200 depending on the complexity of the organisation
- identify and evaluate the design of key controls intended to manage these principal risks, underpinned by core controls assurance standards
- set out the arrangements for obtaining assurance on the effectiveness of key controls across all areas of principal risk
- evaluate the assurance across all areas of principal risk
- identify positive assurances and areas where there are gaps in controls and/or assurances
- put in place plans to take corrective action where gaps have been identified in relation to principal risks
- maintain dynamic risk management arrangements including, crucially, a well-founded risk register.

The audit committee should not be responsible for creating the BAF; instead, it should satisfy itself that line management is carrying it out appropriately and that the processes and format are valid, relevant and effective. The committee needs to be satisfied that it contains the high-risk areas pertinent to the organisation.

The publications *Building the Assurance Framework: a practical guide for NHS Boards* by the DH and *Taking it on Trust* by the Audit Commission contributed significantly to the development of the BAF.

CASE STUDY: areas of concern within a trust

In 2011, the Care Quality Commission inspected a service area within a trust and found a number of areas of concern resulting in a series of recommendations for improvement. A year later the trust had failed to make the required level of progress against two of the three recommendations, with some of the recommendations still requiring significant steps in order to be implemented. Two specific problems related to the failure to appoint a consultant and to recruit sufficient staff to ensure the trust operated a service that was safe and effective.

The trust had put in place an action plan to deal with service delivery problems in by the end of 2012. However the board devoted insufficient effort to ensuring that action plan was delivered in a timely manner and there was insufficient evidence of the board driving improvement forward.

In particular the effectiveness of board assurance processes, leadership by the board and clinical leadership within the trust was a cause for concern. The trust remained under enhanced monitoring.

Integrated reporting

A reporting initiative from the International Integrated Reporting Council (IIRC) may provide a benchmark for further developments in NHS reporting requirements. The IIRC is a global body established to promote the worldwide adoption of integrated reporting as the main annual report by companies.

The IIRC aims to 'promote a more cohesive and efficient approach to corporate reporting that draws on different reporting strands and communicates the full range of factors that materially affect the ability of the organisation to create value over time'. The IIRC has been working to achieve consensus among governments, listing authorities, standard setters, companies and investors about the use of integrated reporting by listed companies. As its name suggests, an integrated report should bring together into a single report different aspects of a company's activities, which contribute, to the creation of (or destruction of) value. Value is accumulated in the form of six different types of capital:

- financial capital
- human capital
- intellectual capital
- manufactured capital
- natural capital
- social capital.

It is therefore argued that an integrated report should provide information about the company's policies and performance with regard to each of these aspects of capital. It is sufficient at this stage to note that 'capital', as defined for the purpose of integrated reporting, includes aspects of the company's policies and performance with regard to employees, the environment and society. These are issues that quoted companies may be expected to include in their strategic report.

IIRC guidance published in 2013 states that an integrated report should contain eight elements:

1. an overview of the organisation and its external environment
2. how the governance structure supports the company's ability to create value
3. a description of the company's business model
4. risks and opportunities that affect the organisation's ability to create value, and how the organisation is dealing with them
5. material on strategy and resource allocation, outlining the company's strategies and strategic objectives, and how it intends to achieve these
6. performance information covering whether the company achieved its strategic objectives for the period in terms of effects on the 'six capitals'
7. an outlook based on challenges and uncertainties
8. information on the basis of presentation, detailing how the organisation decides what to include in the integrated report and how are these matters are quantified and measured.

Changes in the required contents of the annual report from October 2013 may be a first step towards integrated reporting by UK quoted companies.

Governance Checklist

✓ Has the board signed off the operational plan, a five-year strategic plan and a development support plan?

✓ Does the board have a good understanding of the requirements imposed by the relevant framework for performance reporting? Is the board clear about how this aligns to its overall strategy and corporate objectives for the organisation?

✓ Is the board confident that the performance and quality dashboard it reviews is supported by robust and viable data?

✓ Has the board signed off the operational plan, a five-year strategic plan and a development support plan?

✓ Does the board have a good understanding of the requirements imposed by the relevant framework for performance reporting? Is the board clear about how this aligns to its overall strategy and corporate objectives for the organisation?

✓ Is the board confident that the performance and quality dashboard it reviews is supported by robust and viable data?

✓ Is the board confident that the annual report and accounts present a balanced and understandable assessment of the organisation's position and prospects?

✓ Does the annual report meet the appropriate reporting requirements, including the addition of a strategic report?

✓ Was the annual governance statement signed by the accountable officer?

✓ How regularly does the board consider the BAF? Is it a live, dynamic, document that changes as the organisation changes?

Summary

Assurance can sometimes be hard to find in the NHS, not because of the lack of information but because there is so much information. In addition, the validity and robustness of some of the information can also create difficulties, such as problems with coding. There is clearly a large and complex reporting structure for NHS organisations with NHS England, the NHS TDA, Monitor and the CQC responsible for the design of much of its content. Since the publication of the Francis Inquiry findings, there has been a growing commitment for these agencies to work together and align their reporting requirements. This alignment can already be seen; for example, in the use of the CQC domains in the NHS TDA oversight model, and the commitment to develop the well-led framework for FTs and NHS trusts.

There is, however, a significant amount of information in the public domain, allowing key stakeholders and the general public to assess whether, indeed, the board is fulfilling its statutory duties. In the context of this highly regulated sector, the work of internal and external audit and the role of the audit committee is a significant contribution to the assurance evidence required by the NHS board to fulfil its statutory duties. This is considered in the next chapter.

15

Audit

The role of audit is important in ensuring accurate reporting, which is one of the foundations for health service governance. Given the range and diversity of reporting requirements that are imposed on NHS organisations, the role of audit clearly becomes a crucial tool in the reliability and robustness of those reports and provides vital independent assurance to NHS boards.

■ The role of audit

All stakeholders rely on the quality, performance and financial information that is published by the organisation. It is important, therefore, that the information is objective and robust. As a result, the work of both internal and external audit are vital in making sure that, as far as is reasonably possible, the information is objective and can be relied on. Within NHS organisations the remit of internal and external audit includes the review of quality, performance and financial information. Part of the audit committee's role is to monitor the work of both internal and external auditors and to ensure that the external auditors can place full reliance on the work of internal audit in these three areas of information.

Audit Commission and the National Audit Office

The Audit Commission used to play a significant role in the provision of audit services to the NHS. However, in August 2010 the Department for Communities and Local Government (DCLG) announced plans to put in place new arrangements for auditing England's local public bodies. The Local Audit and Accountability Act 2014 makes it possible for the Audit Commission to close on 31 March 2015 in line with Government expectations, 30 years after it was established.

In the place of the Audit Commission, there will be a new framework for local public audit, due to start after the Commission's current contracts with audit suppliers end in 2016/17 or in 2019/20 if all the contracts are extended. A transitional body will oversee the contracts in the intervening period. The transitional body will be an independent, private company to be created by the LGA.

The Local Audit and Accountability Act 2014 gave the Comptroller and Auditor General (C&AG) a duty to prepare and issue Codes of Audit Practice and guidance to auditors, as well as the power to carry out examinations into the economy, efficiency and effectiveness with which relevant authorities have used their resources. The Act also provided for the Commission's data matching powers, and therefore the National Fraud Initiative, to transfer to the Cabinet Office. The Commission's counter-fraud function will transfer to a new public sector Counter Fraud Centre to be established by the Chartered Institute of Public Finance and Accountancy (CIPFA).

The Commission's in-house Audit Practice was the successor to the District Audit Service, which was first established in 1844 and was absorbed into the Audit Commission when it was set up in 1983. It kept its separate brand name until 2002. The Audit Practice used to undertake the majority of audits for local public bodies. In July 2011, DCLG ministers confirmed their preference for transferring this work to the private sector by outsourcing contracts.

In March 2012, the Commission announced the results of a procurement exercise awarding five-year contracts to four private firms and on 1 November 2012 around 700 auditors transferred to new private sector employers and the Commission's Audit Practice closed. The result of these changes is that Grant Thornton, KPMG, Ernst & Young or the DA Partnership currently audit all NHS trusts and CCGs. Foundation trusts were not required to be audited by the Audit Commission and were free to make external audit appointments from the wider market of audit firms. They are currently subject to Monitor's Audit Code for Foundation Trusts (2011).

The DH is currently consulting on The Local Audit (Health Service Bodies Auditor Panel and Independence) Regulations 2015 to ensure the audit committees of NHS trusts and CCGs are appropriately constituted to advise on the selection, appointment and maintenance of independent relationships with external auditors for their future audit contracts.

The C&AG of the National Audit Office is also consulting on a revised Code of Audit Practice. It will prescribe the framework within which local auditors are to carry out their statutory responsibilities. The new code will be considered by parliament in 2015 and will take effect from 1 April 2015 for audit work relating to the 2015-16 financial year onwards. The code covers the audits of all local NHS bodies including CCGs and will supersede the Code of Audit Practice 2010 for local NHS bodies, and the 2011 Audit Code for NHS Foundation Trusts.

Function and scope of external audit

External audit traditionally has been the process by which the annual accounts of public and private sector bodies are subject to external scrutiny to provide independent assurance that they have been prepared in accordance with relevant legal and professional standards and give a 'true and fair' view of the financial performance and financial position of the audited body. More recently, however, external audit has comprised quality, performance and financial audits. According to the Public Audit Forum:

'It is one of the basic principles of audit in the public sector, that the scope of the audit should be understood to go beyond giving assurance on the accounts, to include examination of aspects of corporate governance and the use of resources.'

External audit in the public sector is characterised by three distinct features:

- auditors are appointed independently from the bodies being audited
- the scope of auditors' work is extended to cover not only the financial statements, but also aspects of corporate governance and arrangements to secure the economic, efficient and effective use of resources
- auditors may report aspects of their work to the public and other key stakeholders.

The statutory responsibilities and powers of appointed auditors for public bodies including NHS organisations are set out in the Local Audit and Accountability Act 2014. In discharging these specific statutory responsibilities and powers, auditors will be required to carry out their work according to the proposed National Audit Office's Code of Audit Practice. The Code will be supplemented by detailed guidance to auditors provided by the National Audit Office (NAO) on the C&AG's behalf. Auditors are required to have regard to this guidance under the Act. Key components of the guidance package will include:

- planning local NHS audits
- planning local government audits
- the auditor's work on value-for-money arrangements
- limited assurance engagements at smaller authorities
- the auditor's additional duties and powers
- auditor reporting
- dealing with technical queries.

Schedule 7 of the NHS Act 2006 provides the C&AG with access rights to FTs that allow his representatives to inspect the accounts and any records relating to them, including the auditor's report. Although the C&AG is not the appointed auditor of individual FTs, he may wish to examine financial aspects of one or more FTs in the context of his wider roles in providing assurance to parliament over the proper use of public monies.

After completing their annual audit, auditors are required to prepare a report to the stakeholders of the organisation, which is included in the published report and accounts. The audit report has two main purposes:

- to give an expert and independent opinion on whether the financial statements give a true and fair view of the financial position of the organisation as at the end of the financial year covered by the report, and of its financial performance during the year to give an expert and independent opinion on whether the financial statements comply with the relevant laws.

However, in carrying out their audit, external audit must also have regard to aspects of corporate governance and securing economy, efficiency and effectiveness in its use of resources.

Auditors must be appointed by 31 December of the year prior to the relevant financial year. Any public body that fails to do so must notify the Secretary of State, who will have reserve powers to make, or direct the body to make, an appointment.

Function and scope of internal audit

Internal audit is defined by the Chartered Institute of Management Accountants (CIMA) as 'an independent appraisal activity established within an organisation as a service to it. It is a control that functions by examining and evaluating the adequacy and effectiveness of other controls'.

The Chartered Institute of Internal Auditors (IIA) describes the role as follows:

The role of internal audit is to provide independent assurance that an organisation's risk management, governance and internal control processes are operating effectively. Internal auditors deal with issues that are fundamentally important to the survival and prosperity of any organisation. Unlike external auditors, they look beyond financial risks and statements to consider wider issues such as the organisation's reputation, growth, its impact on the environment and the way it treats its employees.'

The NHS Accounting Officer Memorandum requires all NHS trusts to have an internal audit function. An organisation might have an internal audit unit or section, which carries out investigative work. An internal audit function should act independently of executive managers, but normally reports to a senior executive manager such as the finance director.

In the corporate sector, the FRC *Guidance on Audit Committees* (2012) suggests that the audit committee should ensure that the internal auditor has direct access to the board chair and the audit committee, and is also responsible to the audit committee. This means that the internal auditors maybe in an unusual position within the organisation. For operational reasons they may have a line reporting responsibility to a senior executive manager such as the finance director. Executive managers may also ask the internal auditors to carry out audits or reviews of the systems or procedures (and internal controls) for which they are responsible. However, the senior internal auditor should have some control over deciding what aspects of the organisation's systems should be investigated or audited, and also has a responsibility for reporting to the audit committee and the chair of the board.

The work done by any internal audit unit is not prescribed by regulation, but is decided by management or by the board (or audit committee). The possible tasks of internal audit include the following.

■ **Reviewing the internal control system**: traditionally, an internal audit department has carried out independent checks on the financial controls in an organisation, however, this has now extended to include quality and performance controls as well. The checks would be to establish whether suitable quality, performance and financial controls exist and if so, whether they are applied properly and are effective. It is not the function of internal auditors to manage risks, only to monitor and report them, and to check that risk controls are efficient and cost-effective.

■ **Special investigations:** internal auditors might conduct special investigations into particular aspects of the organisation's operations (systems and procedures), to check the effectiveness of operational controls.

■ **Examination of financial and operating information:** internal auditors might be asked to investigate the timeliness of reporting and the accuracy of the information in reports.

■ **VFM audits:** this is an investigation into an operation or activity to establish whether it is economical, efficient and effective.

■ **Reviewing compliance by the organisation with particular laws or regulations:** this is an investigation into the effectiveness of compliance controls.

■ **Risk assessment:** internal auditors might be asked to investigate aspects of risk management, and in particular the adequacy of the mechanisms for identifying, assessing and controlling significant risks to the organisation, from both internal and external sources.

Reliance on the work of internal audit

It is expected that the external auditors will liaise with the internal audit function to obtain a sufficient understanding of internal audit activities to assist in planning the audit and developing an effective audit approach. The auditors may also wish to place reliance upon certain aspects of the work of internal audit in satisfying their statutory responsibilities as set out in the National Health Service Act 2006 and in the Monitor Audit Code. In particular the auditors may wish to consider the work of internal audit when undertaking their procedures in relation to the AGS.

The Audit Commission's Code of Audit Practice (2010) requires external audit to establish effective coordination arrangements with internal audit. External audit should seek to place maximum reliance on the work of internal audit whenever possible.

This all demonstrates the key relationship between internal and external audit as it is vital for the external auditors to be able to rely on the work undertaken by internal audit, not just on financial controls but on quality and performance controls as well.

The role of external audit

Audit report

The audit report is contained in the organisation's annual report and accounts, and is addressed by the auditors to the stakeholders of the organisation. The main purpose of the audit report is to give the users of an organisation's financial statements (and in particular the stakeholders) some reassurance that the information in the statements is believable and that the financial statements present a 'true and fair view' of the organisation's financial position and performance. The opinion of the auditors should be the opinion of independent professional experts, based on an investigation of the organisation's control systems, accounting systems and financial/ business transactions. The audit report itself provides only limited information to stakeholders, even though stakeholders often assume that an unqualified audit report means that the financial statements of the organisation are accurate and reliable.

An unmodified audit report (sometimes called an 'unqualified opinion') is given when the auditor believes that the accounts give a true and fair view of the organisation's financial position and performance. The wording of an unmodified audit report is usually fairly standard, although reports are longer for public companies (where the auditors might also report on some corporate governance statements) and differ between countries. Such a report may include an 'emphasis of matter' paragraph. Although the audit report is unmodified, and the auditors consider that the financial statements present a true and fair view, there is an item that the auditor wants to bring to the attention of users because it is of some importance for an understanding of the statements.

Auditors may present a modified audit report, although this is unusual. If it happens, there is a potentially serious problem with the financial statements and, by implication, the financial condition of the organisation. It also means that the auditors have been unable to agree with the directors of the organisation about what information the financial statements should contain. Because the directors and the auditors cannot agree, the auditors have considered it necessary to give a statement to stakeholders to this effect. There are three types of modified audit opinion, namely, a qualified opinion, an adverse opinion, and a disclaimer of opinion.

A qualified audit opinion is sometimes called an 'except for' opinion. It is given when, in the opinion of the auditor, the financial statements would give a true and fair view except for a particular matter, which the auditor explains.

An adverse opinion is given when the auditor considers that there are material misstatements in the accounts and that these are 'pervasive'. In effect, the auditor is stating that the figures in the accounts are seriously wrong.

A disclaimer of opinion is given in cases where the auditor has been unable to obtain the information that he needs to give an audit opinion. The lack of information means that the auditor is unable to state that the financial statements give a true and fair view, and that there may possibly be serious misstatements that the auditor has been unable to check.

In the rare circumstances that the auditors give a modified audit report to the stakeholders, a situation has arisen where professional accountants have given an opinion that the stakeholders cannot trust the information that has been given to them by the directors. If the stakeholders cannot trust the directors, the quality of corporate governance could hardly be lower.

CASE STUDY: An audit report

Here is a simplified example of a typical unmodified audit report.

Report on the financial statements

We have audited the accompanying financial statements of XYZ Organisation, which comprise the statement of financial position as at 31 December 20XX, and the statement of comprehensive income, statement of changes in equity, and cash flows for the year then ended, and a summary of significant accounting policies and other explanatory notes.

Management's responsibility for the financial statements

Management is responsible for the preparation and fair presentation of these financial statements in accordance with International Financial Reporting Standards. This responsibility includes: designing, implementing and maintaining internal control relevant to the preparation and fair presentation of financial statements that are free from material misstatement, whether due to fraud or error; selecting and applying appropriate accounting policies; and making accounting estimates that are reasonable in the circumstances.

Auditor's responsibility

Our responsibility is to express an opinion on these financial statements based on our audit. We conducted our audit in accordance with International Standards on Auditing. Those standards require that we comply with ethical requirements and plan and perform the audit to obtain reasonable assurance whether the financial statements are free from material misstatement.

An audit involves performing procedures to obtain audit evidence about the amounts and disclosures in the financial statements. The procedures selected depend on the auditor's judgement, including the assessment of the risks of material misstatement of the financial statements, whether due to fraud or error. In making those risk assessments, the auditor considers internal control relevant to the entity's preparation and fair presentation of the financial statements in order to design audit procedures that are appropriate in the circumstances, but not for the purpose of expressing an opinion on the

---

effectiveness of the entity's internal control. An audit also includes evaluating the appropriateness of accounting policies used and the reasonableness of accounting estimates made by management, as well as evaluating the overall presentation of the financial statements.

We believe that the audit evidence that we have obtained is sufficient and appropriate to provide a basis for our audit opinion.

Opinion

In our opinion, the financial statements give a true and fair view (or present fairly, in all material respects) of the financial position of XYZ Organisation as of 31 December 20XX, and of its financial performance and its cash flows for the year then ended in accordance with International Financial Reporting Standards.

Report on other legal and regulatory requirements

[Form and content of this section of the report will vary depending on the nature of the auditor's other reporting responsibilities.]

Signed: (Auditor) _____

Date: _____

Responsibility for detecting errors and fraud

Stakeholders would probably like to assume that if the auditors provide a favourable audit report, the financial statements must be 'correct', and there has not been any fraud or error that has resulted in incorrect use of accounting policies, omissions of fact or misinterpretation of fact. This view is based on the belief that if professional accountants have checked the figures, they must be correct – unless the accountants have been negligent and have failed to do their job properly. However, it is a popular misconception that the auditor is responsible for detecting fraud or error in an organisation's financial statements. This is not the case.

The board of directors is responsible for preventing fraud in their organisation, or detecting fraud if it occurs. The organisation's system of internal control, described in Chapter 14, should be designed to limit the risk of fraud and error, and the board is responsible for monitoring the effectiveness of the internal control system. The responsibility of the board (with delegated responsibility of management) for the prevention and detection of fraud and error is a core principle of corporate governance. The directors are fully accountable to the stakeholders and so are fully responsible for the information presented in the annual report and accounts.

It is not the primary responsibility of the external auditors to detect fraud. The auditors will assess the risk or possibility that fraud or error might have caused the financial statements to be materially misleading. The auditors should therefore design audit procedures that will provide reasonable reassurance that material fraud or error has not occurred, and that the financial statements give a true and fair view of the organisation's financial position and performance. The external audit might also act as a deterrent to fraud, because the auditors will carry out checks of control procedures, documents and transactions in the course of their audit work. They might discover fraud during the course of their audit work, in which case it would be their responsibility to report the matter to the directors (unless the fraud is carried out by the directors themselves).

No matter how well an audit is planned and carried out, there will always be some risk that fraud or error has occurred but not been detected. Given the nature of auditing, for which there is only a limited amount of time and resources, and which is carried out through a process of sampling and testing, it would be impossible to ensure that all errors are detected. Accounting systems and internal control procedures are also vulnerable to fraud and error, arising, for example, from criminal collusion between employees or decisions by management to override the system of controls.

An area for dispute, however, is whether the auditors ought to be able to identify fraud or a significant error during the course of their audit work, whenever a fraud or error occurs. Although they are not responsible for the financial statements, it can be argued that a failure by the auditors to discover a major fraud or material error might be the result of professional negligence. If they are negligent, they should be held liable to the organisation and its stakeholders. In the UK, the Companies Act 2006 introduced new rules on auditors' liability for negligence, breach of duty or breach of trust regarding the conduct of the audit. Shareholders of both public and private companies can vote by ordinary resolution to limit the potential liability of the external auditors, by means of a liability limitation agreement (LLA). Such an agreement can limit the liability to the company by the auditor in respect of negligence, default, breach of duty or breach of trust occurring in the course of the audit of accounts. The Act states that in considering what is fair and reasonable in the circumstances, the court should have no regard to the possibility or otherwise of recovering compensation from other persons who are jointly or partly responsible for the loss that has been incurred. Although the Act provides the possibility of some protection for auditors against liability for negligence or breach of duty with LLAs, it also introduced two new criminal offences for auditors in connection with the auditors' report (i.e. it is a criminal offence, punishable by a fine, to knowingly or recklessly cause an audit report to 'include any matter that is misleading, false or deceptive in any material particular', or knowingly or recklessly cause an audit report to omit a statement that is required by certain specified sections of the Act).

Auditors' liability to third parties

The auditors have a legal duty of care to the organisation and its stakeholders. There is some doubt as to whether they might also have a duty of care to other parties. In the UK, the extent of auditor liability to external parties has been tested in two legal cases: *Caparo Industries plc v Dickman [1990]* and *Royal Bank of Scotland v Bannerman Johnstone Maclay [2002]*. In response to these cases PricewaterhouseCoopers decided to include a disclaimer of liability to third parties using its audit reports. In January 2003, the Institute of Chartered Accountants in England and Wales (ICAEW) recommended the inclusion of this disclaimer in audit reports. A disclaimer within the audit report might be worded as follows:

> 'This report, including the opinion, has been prepared for and only for the organisation's members as a body in accordance with the Companies Act 2006 and for no other purpose. We do not, in giving this opinion, accept or assume responsibility for any other purpose or to any other person to whom this report is shown or into whose hands it may come save where expressly agreed by our prior consent in writing.'

Independence of external audit

The external auditor should be independent of the client organisation so that the audit opinion will not be influenced by the relationship between the auditor and the organisation. The auditors are expected to give an unbiased and honest professional opinion to the stakeholders about the financial statements.

An unmodified audit report is often seen by investors as a 'clean bill of health' for the organisation. However, doubts are sometimes expressed about the independence of the external auditors. It could be argued that unless suitable governance measures are in place, a firm of auditors may reach audit opinions and judgements that are heavily influenced by their wish to maintain good relations with the management of a client organisation. If this happens, the auditors are no longer independent and the stakeholders cannot rely on their opinion. For example, in the corporate sector, an official 2010 report on the collapse of Lehman Brothers in 2008 criticised the external auditors Ernst & Young for allowing the company to account for certain transactions (repo 105 transactions) in a way that misleadingly improved the look of the end-of-quarter balance sheets during 2007 and 2008, in the months before the bank eventually collapsed.

Perhaps the most significant threat to auditor independence is that the audit firm relies on the organisation's management to secure its appointment and re-appointment as the organisation's auditor. Although companies may give their audit committee responsibility for recommending the appointment of the auditors, the opinions of senior management are often decisive in the matter of auditor selection. The auditor is therefore reliant for future audit work from the organisation on the views of the management whose financial statements it is their job to audit. In addition, the audit firm has to rely extensively on management for the information and explanations needed to enable them to carry out their audit work. A UK Ethical Standards Board has commented on this situation, saying:

> 'Any reasonable and informed third party – for example, a shareholder – is likely to regard this as a significant threat to the auditor's objectivity.'

Professional guidelines are given to auditors by national and international accountancy bodies, notably the International Federation of Accountants (IFAC). The IFAC Code of Ethics for Professional Accountants identifies certain ways in which the integrity, objectivity and independence of the auditors might be put at risk. An audit firm should not have to rely on a single organisation for a large proportion of its total fee income, because undue dependence on a single audit client could impair objectivity. IFAC does not specify what amounts to 'undue dependence' on a single client. However, in the UK, the rules of the Association of Chartered Certified Accountants (ACCA) state that the fee income from a single audit client should not exceed 15% of the gross annual income of the audit practice. A risk to objectivity and independence arises when the audit firm or anyone closely associated with it (such as an audit partner) has a mutual business interest with the organisation or any of its officers. Similarly, objectivity could be threatened when there is a close personal relationship between a member of the audit firm and an employee of the organisation. The audit firm should not have a client organisation in which a partner holds a significant number of stakes. The IFAC Code does not have any objection in principle to an audit firm providing non-audit services (such as consultancy services) to a client, although the auditor should not perform any management functions in an organisation nor take any management decisions.

The audit profession has identified five categories of potential threats to auditor independence.

- **Self-interest threats:** if the audit firm earns a large proportion of its revenue from a client organisation, it may be unwilling to annoy that client by challenging the figures and assumptions used by management to prepare the organisation's financial statements.
- **Self-review threat:** this can arise when the audit firm does non-audit work for the organisation, and the annual audit involves checking the work done by the firm's own employees. The auditors may not be as critical of the work, or prepared to challenge it, because this would raise questions about the professional competence of the audit firm.
- **Advocacy threat:** this can arise if the audit form is asked to give its formal support to the organisation by providing public statements on particular issues or supporting the organisation in a legal case. Acting as advocate for an organisation means taking sides, and this implies a loss of independence.

- **Familiarity threat:** a threat to independence occurs when an auditor is familiar with an organisation or one of its directors or senior managers, or becomes familiar with them through a working association over time. Familiarity leads to trust and a willingness to believe what the other person says. The auditor will also be unwilling to think that the other person is capable of making a serious error or committing fraud. A familiarity threat arises through personal association (for example, family connections) and through long association with the organisation and its management.

- **Intimidation threat:** an auditor may feel threatened by the directors or senior management of an organisation. Both real and imagined threats can affect the auditor's independence. Intimidation may result from a domineering and bullying personality on the organisation's board of directors (for example the CEO). An organisation may also threaten to take away the audit or stop giving the firm non-audit work unless the auditor accepts the opinions of management.

Threats to auditor independence must be identified, and measures should be taken to limit the threat to an acceptable level of risk. Two areas of debate about how to ensure auditor independence have been whether auditors should be prevented from carrying out non-audit work for clients, or whether the amount of non-audit work they do should be restricted, and whether there should be a regular rotation of either the audit firm or the audit partner and other senior members of the audit team.

Non-audit work for a client by an audit firm

The codes of conduct of national professional accountancy bodies are similar to the IFAC Code and lack any clear restrictions on the performance of non-audit work for an audit client. Suggestions for regulatory measures to ensure auditor independence have included proposals to restrict the amount of non-audit work, or the type of non-audit work, that the firm of auditors is permitted to carry out for a client organisation. Non-audit work might include:

- consultancy on taxation issues, for example helping an organisation to minimise tax liabilities
- investigating targets for a potential takeover bid
- helping an organisation to construct a bid for a major government contract
- providing advice and expert assistance on IT systems
- internal audit services
- valuation and actuarial services
- services relating to litigation
- services relating to recruitment and remuneration.

The main problem with auditors doing non-audit work is that when the firm audits transactions recommended by its consultancy arm, it is unlikely to take an independent view.

The risk to auditor objectivity and independence from carrying out non-audit work became apparent in the wake of the Enron collapse. Arthur Andersen were the auditors of Enron, and in the financial year before the company's collapse in 2001, Andersen earned more fee income from Enron for non-audit work than from audit work. The audit firm was suspected of failing to carry out a proper audit of the company. It was claimed that the audit firm would have been reluctant to question the accounts of Enron because it would risk losing not just the audit work but also the substantial non-audit fee income. In addition, it was suggested that since the information in the company's financial statements reflected the non-audit consultancy advice given by the audit firm, the firm's auditors would be unlikely to challenge the fairness and accuracy of the statements. In other words, Andersen's auditors would not challenge the opinions of Andersen's consultants.

Audit firms have denied that fees from non-audit work will affect their independence, arguing that the individuals who work as consultants for a client organisation (such as on IT projects) are not the same individuals who work on the audit. Even so, activist shareholder groups continue to challenge this assertion. In the UK, a well-reported attempt was made in 2002 by some institutional stakeholders to vote against the re-appointment of Deloitte as auditors to Vodafone at the AGM of the company. The 'dissidents' argued their case because the audit firm did too much non-audit work for the company and so could not be considered sufficiently independent.

There are three broad approaches to the regulation of non-audit work by audit firms:

- there should be no restrictions at all on non-audit work by the audit firm.
- there should be a total prohibition on non-audit work for a corporate client by the audit firm.
- there should be a partial prohibition on non-audit work for a corporate client by the audit firm.

A partial restriction could take either of two forms. There could be a prohibition on audit firms from taking on certain types of consultancy work where their independence as auditors could be put at risk, such as tax planning advice work. However, audit firms would be free to carry out other types of non-audit work. The second approach to restricting non-audit work would be to set a limit on the amount of fees an audit firm could earn from non-audit work, expressed perhaps as a proportion of the fees it earns from the audit. For example, a limit might be imposed restricting non-audit fees to, say, 50% of the fees from the audit work.

The difficulty with a partial restriction on non-audit work is that rules have to be devised and agreed as to what permissible and non-permissible non-audit work should be, or what the maximum amount of non-audit fee income should be. In the UK, the audit profession is governed by ethical principles rather than rules and regulations about non-audit work for audit clients. The ICAEW has made the following statements about non-audit work:

'The most effective way to ensure the reality of independence is to provide guidance centred around a framework of principles rather than a detailed set of rules that can be complied with to the letter but circumvented in substance.'

'A blanket prohibition on the provision of non-audit services to audit clients can be inefficient for the client and is neither necessary to ensure independence, nor helpful in contributing to the knowledge necessary to ensure the quality of the audit.'

The need for auditor independence when the audit firm does non-audit work is recognised in the UK Code. The code includes a provision that 'the annual report should explain to stakeholders how, if the auditor provides non-audit services, auditor objectivity and independence is safeguarded.'

Another suggestion for protecting auditor independence is that there should be 'rotation' of auditors. There is an important distinction, however, between the rotation of an audit firm, whereby a firm is required to give up the audit for an organisation after a maximum number of years, and the organisation must appoint different auditors; and rotation of audit personnel, whereby the audit engagement partner and other key individuals involved in the annual audit should be removed from the audit after a certain number of years, and new individuals assigned to the work.

Rotation of audit firm

Rotation of the audit firm would enhance auditor independence because a firm of auditors would have little to gain by agreeing with the wishes of the client organisation, and carrying out a less than rigorous audit, if it knows that it will soon lose the audit work anyway. The work of outgoing auditors would also be subject to review – and criticism – by the firm of auditors taking their place.

In 2013 the Competition Commission published a report on the statutory audit services market. The report reached the following conclusions about the restricted nature of competition in the market for audit services.

- Companies are reluctant to switch auditors, partly because it is difficult for them to compare the services of different auditors and partly because the costs of switching would be high.
- Too often auditors focus on the needs of senior management, who are the key decision takers on whether to retain their services.
- Companies and audit firms invest in a relationship of mutual trust and confidence 'from which neither will lightly walk away'.

The report concluded that the Competition Commission would be investigating the following possible combinations of remedies including:

- mandatory tendering for audits (which is already a UK Code requirement)
- mandatory rotation of audit firms

- prohibition of 'Big-Four-only' clauses in loans to companies by banks
- greater accountability of the auditors to the audit committee.

On 1 April 2014, the functions of the Competition Commission transferred to the CMA which made the Statutory Audit Services for Large Companies Market Investigation (Mandatory Use of Competitive Tender Processes and Audit Committee Responsibilities) Order 2014. This Order comes into force on 1 January 2015 and applies to FTSE 350 companies. As a consequence of the Order all such companies must put their statutory audit services engagement out to tender every ten years or earlier. This means that an auditor may not conduct more than ten consecutive statutory audits of a FTSE 350 company without a competitive tender process having taken place. In addition, it required that the terms of the statutory audit services agreement must have been negotiated and agreed between the audit committee and the auditor.

The UK Code already recommends that 'FTSE 350 companies should put the external audit out to tender at least every ten years' and this is reinforced in the FRC *Guidance on Audit Committees*, which adds the explanation that the purpose of the tendering process should be to enable the audit committee (acting on behalf of the board) to compare the quality and effectiveness of the services provided by the incumbent auditor with those of other firms. Monitor's 2011 Audit Code recommends that FTs undertake a market-testing exercise at least once every five years.

Audit partner rotation

An argument put forward by the major accountancy firms is that the requirement for rotation should apply, not to the firm of auditors, but to the individual partner of a firm in charge of the audit. For example, it might be acceptable for ABC Corporation to retain the services of Ernst & Young indefinitely, provided that the partner in charge of the audit is replaced every, say, five or seven years. Supporters of this argument claim that the independence of the audit is threatened by the personal relationship an audit partner builds up with the client organisation, not the length of association of the audit firm with the organisation.

In the case of large organisations, there is also an argument for a regular rotation of other senior audit managers, as well as the lead partner.

Peter Wyman, former president of the ICAEW, stressed the distinction between audit partner and audit firm rotation. Writing in the *Financial Times* on 25 July 2002, he commented:

'Improvements could be made in the area of audit partner and audit firm rotation, although it is vital not to confuse the two. Audit firm rotation achieves the appearance of greater auditor independence but research shows it is likely to produce a reduction in audit quality, particularly in the first two years after the new firm is appointed. Because people rather than organisations are likely to get "cosy" with one another, greater audit independence could be achieved by rotating the audit partner. This approach avoids quality loss which arises when the entire cumulative knowledge of the audit firm is cast aside when a new firm is appointed.'

A counter-argument, however, is that audit partner rotation would not have prevented the problem that arose between Andersen and its clients Enron and WorldCom. Although Andersen as a whole was not over-dependent on Enron, the company was a vital client for the firm's Houston office, which carried out the audit. Similarly, the Andersen office in Jackson, Mississippi was heavily dependent on the work that it did for WorldCom. To prevent loss of audit independence, audit partner rotation would almost certainly have been ineffective, whereas audit firm rotation might have been much more effective.

Currently, regulations in most countries favour audit partner rotation rather than audit firm rotation. In the UK, for example, the ICAEW's ethical standards require the rotation of various members of an audit team, including the rotation of the audit engagement partner at least every five years.

■ The role of internal audit

The NHS Accounting Officer Memorandum requires all NHS trusts to have an internal audit function. The NHS Internal Audit Standards (or Government Internal Audit standards for Foundation Trusts for FTs) set out the requirements for internal audit and how to assess the service that is delivered.

Internal audit is the 'independent appraisal activity established within an organisation as a service to it. It is a control which functions by examining and evaluating the adequacy and effectiveness of other controls', according to CIMA official terminology. The Chartered Institute of Internal Auditors describes the role as being to 'provide independent assurance that an organisation's risk management, governance and internal control processes are operating effectively. Internal auditors deal with issues that are fundamentally important to the survival and prosperity of any organisation'.

The work done by any internal audit unit is not prescribed by regulation, but is decided by management or by the board (or audit committee). The possible tasks of internal audit include the following.

■ **Reviewing the internal control system:** traditionally, an internal audit department has carried out independent checks on the financial controls in an organisation; however, this has now extended to include quality and performance controls as well. The checks would be to establish whether suitable quality, performance and financial controls exist and if so, whether they are applied properly and are effective. It is not the function of internal auditors to manage risks, only to monitor and report them, and to check that risk controls are efficient and cost-effective.

■ **Special investigations:** internal auditors might conduct special investigations into particular aspects of the organisation's operations (systems and procedures), to check the effectiveness of operational controls.

■ **Examination of financial and operating information:** internal auditors might be asked to investigate the timeliness of reporting and the accuracy of the information in reports.

■ **VFM audits:** this is an investigation into an operation or activity to establish whether it is economical, efficient and effective.

■ **Reviewing compliance by the organisation with particular laws or regulations:** this is an investigation into the effectiveness of compliance controls.

■ **Risk assessment:** internal auditors might be asked to investigate aspects of risk management, and in particular the adequacy of the mechanisms for identifying, assessing and controlling significant risks to the organisation, from both internal and external sources.

Investigation of internal financial controls

Internal auditors are commonly required to check the soundness of internal financial controls. In assessing the effectiveness of individual controls, and of an internal control system generally, the following factors should be considered.

■ **Whether the controls are manual or automated:** automated controls are by no means error-proof or fraud-proof, but may be more reliable than similar manual controls.

■ **Whether controls are discretionary or non-discretionary:** non-discretionary controls are checks and procedures that must be carried out. Discretionary controls are those that do not have to be applied, either because they are voluntary or because an individual can choose to disapply them. Risks can infiltrate a system, for example, when senior management chooses to disapply controls and allow unauthorised or unchecked procedures to occur.

■ **Whether the control can be circumvented easily:** an activity can be carried out in a different way where similar controls do not apply.

■ **Whether the controls are effective in achieving their purpose:** are they extensive enough or carried out frequently enough? Are the controls applied rigorously? For example, is a supervisor doing his job properly?

Reports by internal auditors can provide reassurance that internal controls are sound and effective, or might recommend changes and improvements where weaknesses are uncovered.

The objectivity and independence of internal auditors

The manager of a directorate or department should monitor the internal controls within the operation and try to identify and correct weaknesses. They should also report on reviews of the effectiveness of internal control. However, a line manager cannot be properly objective, because they could face 'blame' for control failures in the system or operation for which they are responsible.

In contrast, internal auditors ought to be objective, because they investigate the control systems of other directorates and departments. However, they are also employees within the organisation and report to someone on the organisation structure. If the internal auditors report to the finance director, they will find it difficult to be critical of the finance director. Similarly, if the internal auditors report to the CEO, they will be reluctant to criticise the CEO. In this respect, their independence could be compromised.

In its *Guidance for Audit Committees*, the ICAEW comments that the internal auditors should be separate and independent from line management, but that 'independence' for internal auditors does not have the same meaning as independence for external auditors. To protect the independence of the internal audit function, the FRC's *Guidance on Audit Committees* suggests that the audit committee should have the responsibility for the appointment of the head of internal audit, and his removal from office.

Review of the effectiveness of the internal audit function

The board or audit committee should review the effectiveness of the internal audit function each year. As part of this review, the 2014 *HFMA NHS Audit Committee Handbook* (HFMA Handbook) suggests that the audit committee should make sure that the head of internal audit has direct access to the chair of the board and the audit committee, and is accountable to the audit committee.

There should also be a review and assessment of the annual internal audit work plan along with regular reports on the results of work done by the internal auditors. The review should consider and monitor the responses of management to the recommendations made to them by the internal auditors. The audit committee should also meet with the head of internal audit at least once a year without executive management being present. The *HFMA Handbook* states that the audit committee should actively review the plans of both internal and external audit and assess the quality of the services that are provided.

■ The audit committee

The UK Code requires that a board of directors should establish formal and transparent arrangements for considering how they should apply the corporate reporting and risk management and internal control principles, and maintaining an appropriate relationship with the organisation's auditors. These arrangements should be met by establishing an audit committee, which should be given certain responsibilities by the board. This does not detract from the unitary board principle and despite of the work of the audit committee, the board remains responsible for making the final decision.

There is a formal requirement for every NHS board to establish an audit committee. The role of the audit committee in applying the principles of risk management and internal controls is described in Chapters 13 and 14; this chapter concentrates on the role of the audit committee is applying corporate reporting principles and maintaining an appropriate relationship with the external auditors.

Role and responsibilities of the audit committee

The *HFMA Handbook* describes the role of the audit committee as 'critically reviewing and reporting on the relevance and robustness of the governance and assurance processes on which the governing body places reliance'. This is a wider role than the traditional role of financial scrutiny, as envisaged by the UK Code, and has resulted from the broad range of stakeholder requirements that exist in the NHS. The two key areas that the audit committee should provide assurance to the board on are the BAF and documents that are to be publicly disclosed (the AGS, registration evidence for the CQC, the annual report and accounts and Quality Accounts).

The role of internal audit is addressed earlier in this chapter. However, the role of the audit committee is to review the adequacy of the organisation's internal control system, and in the absence of a separate risk committee to review the organisation's capacity to manage its risk management systems. In NHS organisations there is usually an overlap between the work of the audit committee and the quality committee. Clarity on how these areas will be addressed by the two committees is vital to ensure that duplication of work is avoided and no gaps of assurance arise. The committee should challenge and test the effectiveness of the internal audit function and should promote its role within the organisation ensuring that it has adequate resources.

With regard to public disclosure statements the audit committee has an essential role in reviewing these prior to approval by the board. It should be satisfied with the strength of the processes and the quality of data that has been relied upon to produce the statements.

In addition the UK Code lists the role and responsibilities of an audit committee (excluding those concerned with risk management and internal control set out in Chapter 14) as follows:

- to monitor the integrity of the organisation's financial statements and any formal announcements relating to the organisation's financial performance. In doing so, it should review 'significant financial judgements' that these statements and announcements contain;
- to make recommendations to the board in relation to the appointment, re-appointment or removal of the organisation's external auditors, and for putting these recommendations to the stakeholders for approval at a general meeting of the organisation;
- to approve the remuneration and terms of engagement of the external auditors (after they have been negotiated with the auditors by management);
- to review and monitor the independence and objectivity of the external auditors, and also the effectiveness of the audit process, taking into account relevant UK professional and regulatory requirements;

- to develop and implement the organisation's policy on using the external auditors to provide non-audit services. This should take into account any relevant external ethical guidance on the subject. The committee should report to the board, identifying actions or improvements that are needed and recommending the steps to be taken;
- to provide advice on whether the annual report and accounts, taken as a whole, is fair, balanced and understandable and provides the information necessary for shareholders to assess the company's position and performance, business model and strategy;
- to review arrangements by which staff of the company may, in confidence, raise concerns about possible improprieties in matters of financial reporting or other matters. The audit committee's objective should be to ensure that arrangements are in place for the proportionate and independent investigation of such matters and for appropriate follow-up action; and
- to report to the board on how it has discharged its responsibilities.

The board should decide just what the role of the audit committee should be, and the terms of reference should be tailored to the organisation's particular circumstances. A separate section of the annual report should describe the work of the committee. The audit committee should review its terms of reference and effectiveness annually, and recommend any necessary changes to the board. The board should also review the effectiveness of the audit committee annually.

The core functions of the audit committee are concerned with oversight, assessment and review of other functions and systems in the organisation. It is not the committee's duty to carry out those functions – for example, management remains responsible for preparing the financial statements and the auditors remain responsible for preparing the audit plan and carrying out the audit.

However, the high-level oversight function can sometimes lead to more detailed work. For example, in a recent case of a FT where there were concerns over payroll, the audit committee requested a full-scale independent review of payroll services and the Director of HR was required to attend to give a full response to the recommendations made.

Composition of the audit committee

The specific requirements in respect of composition are set out in Chapter 4. However, the distinctive characteristic of the audit committee is that it comprises only NEDs.

The FRC *Guidance on Audit Committees* suggests that appointments to the committee should be made by the board on the recommendation of the nomination committee, in consultation with the audit committee chair. Appointments should be made for a period of up to three years, extendable by no more than two additional three-year periods and so long as the director remains independent.

The UK Code states that a separate section of the company's annual report should describe the work of the audit committee. 'This deliberately puts the spotlight on the audit committee and gives it an authority it might otherwise lack.' Similar recommendations are contained in the DH's model standing orders for NHS trusts and in the Monitor Code.

The organisation's management is under an obligation to make sure that the audit committee is kept properly informed and should take the initiative in providing the committee with information instead of waiting to be asked. The EDs should also have regard to their common law duty to provide all directors, including the audit committee members, with all the information they need to discharge their duties as directors of the organisation. This point is crucial: the audit committee can only do its work properly if it is kept properly informed by the executive management.

Remuneration, induction and training of committee members

Because audit committees carry out wide-ranging and time-consuming work, organisations must make the necessary resources available. This includes making suitable payments to the members of the audit committee in view of the responsibilities they have and the time they must commit to the work. The amount of remuneration paid to the audit committee members should take account of the remuneration paid to other members of the board. The committee chair's responsibilities and time commitments will normally be greater than those of the other committee members, and this should be reflected in their remuneration.

The committee should have the support of the company secretary and should have access to the services of the organisation's secretariat. Audit committee members must also be given suitable induction and training. Ongoing training should include keeping the committee members up to date on developments in quality, performance and financial reporting and related NHS guidance or legislation. It may include:

- understanding financial statements
- the application of particular accounting standards
- the regulatory framework for the organisation's business
- the role of internal and external auditing
- risk management.

Induction and training can take various forms, including attendance at formal courses and conferences, internal organisation talks and seminars and briefings by external advisers.

Audit committee meetings

The audit committee chair should decide the timing and frequency of committee meetings, in consultation with the company secretary. There should be as many meetings as the role and responsibilities of the committee require. The

FRC *Guidance on Audit Committees* suggests that there should be no fewer than three committee meetings each year, timed to coincide with key dates in the financial reporting and audit calendar. For example, meetings might be held when the audit plans are available for review and when interim statements, preliminary announcements and the full annual report are near completion. Most audit committee chairs will probably want to call meetings more frequently. In practice most NHS audit committees meet quarterly, if not bi-monthly, to manage the significant workload carried by the committee. This is reflected in the HFMA Handbook.

Sufficient time should be allowed between audit committee meetings and meetings of the main board to allow any work arising out of the committee meeting to be carried out and reported to the board as appropriate. This is reflected in the NHS Audit Committee Handbook. Only the audit committee chair and members are entitled to attend meetings of the committee. It is for the committee to decide whether other individuals should be invited to attend for a particular meeting or a particular agenda item. It is expected that the external and internal audit lead partners and the organisation's finance director will be invited regularly to attend meetings.

At least once a year, the audit committee should meet the external and internal auditors, without management being present, to discuss matters relating to its responsibilities and issues arising from the audit.

The audit committee's role in quality, performance and financial reporting

It is the responsibility of management, not the audit committee, to prepare complete and accurate quality, performance and financial statements. It is the responsibility of the audit committee to review the significant reporting issues and judgements that are made in connection with these statements. For example, the audit committee should consider significant accounting policies used to prepare the financial statements, any changes to them, and any significant estimates or judgements on which the statements have been based. Management should inform the committee about the methods they have used to account for significant or unusual transactions, particularly where the accounting treatment is open to different approaches. Taking the external auditors' views into consideration, the committee should consider whether the organisation has adopted appropriate accounting policies and made appropriate estimates and judgements.

The committee should also consider the clarity and completeness of the disclosures in the quality, performance and financial statements. If the committee is not satisfied with any aspect of the proposed reporting by the organisation, it should report its views to the board. The committee should also review related information presented with the quality, performance and financial statements, including the business review and the corporate governance statements relating to audit and risk management.

Appointment and removal of external auditors

Under the UK Code, the audit committee has the primary responsibility for making a recommendation to the board on the appointment, reappointment or removal of the external auditors. FRC guidance recommends that the audit committee should 'oversee' the selection process if it recommends to the board that new external auditors should be selected. The committee's recommendation should be based on the qualification and expertise of the auditors, the resources of the auditors and the independence of the auditors.

In FTs, while the audit committee may make recommendations as to appointment, re-appointment or removal of the external auditors, it is the council of governors who make the decision.

For NHS trusts and CCGs, auditors have been appointed based upon the procurement exercise which took place in March 2012 (see earlier this chapter). Future appointments will be made by the organisation's audit committee under the Local Audit (Health Service Bodies Auditor Panel And Independence) Regulations 2015.

Under the FRC guidance, if the audit committee recommends that new external auditors should be selected, the committee should 'oversee' the selection process and its recommendation should be based on the qualification and expertise of the auditors, the resources of the auditors, the independence of the auditors and the effectiveness of the audit process. The assessment should cover all aspects of the audit service provided by the audit firm. In carrying out the assessment the committee should obtain from the audit firm a report on its own internal quality control procedures. If the external auditors resign, the audit committee should investigate the issues that led to the resignation, and consider whether any action is needed.

The audit committee should consider the terms of engagement of the external auditors and the remuneration to be paid to the auditors for their audit services. It should satisfy itself that the fee payable for the audit services is appropriate, and that an effective audit can be carried out for such a fee. The fee should not be too large, but neither should it be too low. A low audit fee creates a risk that the audit might be of an inadequate scope or quality. The audit committee should then make a recommendation to the board of directors (or council of governors in the case of FTs). The committee is not required to negotiate terms and remuneration.

The FRC guidance also recommends that the committee should review and agree the engagement letter issued by the external auditors at the start of each audit, to make sure that it has been updated to reflect any changes in circumstances since the previous year. In addition, the committee should review the scope of the audit with the auditor. If it is not satisfied that the proposed scope is adequate, the committee should arrange for additional audit work to be undertaken.

Audit committee responsibilities and auditor independence

The Local Audit (Health Service Bodies Auditor Panel and Independence) Regulations 2015 and resulting National Audit Office Code of Practice gives the audit committee the responsibility for monitoring and ensuring the independence of the external auditors. If the external auditors provide non-audit services to the organisation, the annual report should explain how auditor independence and objectivity are safeguarded. The audit committee should have procedures for ensuring the independence and objectivity of the external auditors annually. The FRC guidance recommends that the committee should:

- seek reassurance that the auditors and their staff have no family, financial, employment, investment or business relationship with the organisation that could adversely affect their independence or objectivity. The committee should seek from the audit firm, annually, information about the firm's policies and processes for maintaining independence and monitoring compliance with relevant requirements, such as those regarding the rotation of audit partners and staff;
- agree with the board the organisation's policy on employing former employees of the external auditor. Particular attention should be given to the organisation's policy on former employees of the auditor who were members of the audit team and then moved directly to the organisation. This policy should be drafted, and the audit committee should monitor its application. The committee should monitor the number of former employees of the external auditor who now hold senior positions within the organisation, and consider whether there may be some impairment (or appearance of impairment) in the auditors' judgement and independence with regard to the audit;
- monitor the audit firm's compliance with ethical guidance in the UK about the rotation of audit partners, and the fees the organisation pays as a proportion of the overall fee income of (1) the firm; (2) the office of the firm responsible for the audit; and (3) the audit partner;
- develop and recommend to the board the organisation's policy relating to the provision of non-audit services by the external auditors. The committee's objective should be to ensure that the provision of such services does not impair the independence or objectivity of the auditors.

Provision of non-audit services

The audit committee should ensure that the provision of non-audit services by the organisation's audit firm will not impair the objectivity and independence of the auditors. The committee should consider:

- whether the skills and experience of the audit firm make it a suitable supplier of the non-audit services

- whether there are safeguards in place for ensuring that there would be no threat to the objectivity and independence of the auditors arising from the provision of these services
- the nature of the non-audit services and the fees for these services
- the level of fees for individual non-audit services and the fees in aggregate for these services, relative to the size of the audit fee
- the criteria governing the compensation of the individuals who perform the audit.

The audit committee should set and apply a formal policy specifying the types of non-audit work from which the external auditors are excluded and for which the external auditors can be engaged without referral to the audit committee. It should be established on a case-by-case basis and in these cases, it may be appropriate to give a general pre-approval for certain classes of work, subject to a fee limit decided by the audit committee and ratified by the board. If the external auditor subsequently provides any of these services, the engagement of the auditors should then be ratified at the next audit committee meeting. The policy may also set fee limits generally or for particular classes of non-audit work.

In deciding its policy on the provision of non-audit work by the external auditors, the committee should take into account relevant ethical guidance. The FRC guidance recommends that the external auditor should not be engaged for non-audit work if the result is that the external auditor would audit work done by its own employees or make management decisions for the organisation or create a mutuality of interest or where the external auditor is put in the role of advocate for the organisation.

The Monitor Code states that, if the external auditors do provide non-financial services, the annual report should explain to stakeholders how auditor independence and objectivity is safeguarded.

The audit committee and the annual audit cycle

The FRC Guidance on Audit Committees goes into some detail on the annual audit cycle, and the relationship between the audit committee and the external auditors during this process. At the start of each annual audit, the audit committee should ensure that appropriate plans are in place for the audit. The committee should consider whether the auditors' overall work plan (including the planned levels of materiality and the proposed resources to carry out the audit) seems consistent with the scope of the audit engagement. This assessment should have regard to the seniority, expertise and experience of the audit team.

The audit committee should review, with the external auditors, the findings of their work. As a part of this review, the committee should:

- discuss with the auditors any major issues that arose during the audit (and whether these have been resolved)
- review key accounting or audit judgements

■ review levels of errors identified during the audit and obtain explanations as to why certain errors might remain unadjusted.

The FRC guidance states that the audit committee should review the audit representation letters from management before they are signed, and consider whether the information provided is complete and appropriate based on the knowledge the committee has. It should also review the management letter from the auditors, and the responsiveness of the organisation's management to the auditors' findings and recommendations.

Representation letters from the organisation's management are a part of the audit evidence collected and considered by the auditors. They contain information from management to the auditors. These deal with matters for which other audit evidence does not exist; therefore, the auditors are relying on what management tell them. Representations are required from the directors, acknowledging their collective responsibility for the financial statements and confirming that they have approved them. These should have regard to matters where knowledge of the facts is confined to management (e.g. management's intention to sell off a division of the business) or where there is a matter of judgement and opinion (for example, with regard to the trading position of a major customer and debtor, or the likely outcome of litigation in progress).

The audit committee should review these representations from management and assess whether (on the basis of the knowledge of the committee members) the information provided seems complete and appropriate. At the end of the audit cycle, the audit committee should assess the effectiveness of the audit process. As a part of this assessment, the committee should:

■ review whether the auditors have met the agreed audit plan and consider the reasons for any changes
■ consider the 'robustness and perceptiveness' of the auditors, in their handling of key accounting and audit judgements, and in their commentary on the appropriateness of the organisation's internal controls
■ obtain feedback about the conduct of the auditors from key people within the organisation, such as the finance director and the head of internal audit
■ review the auditor's management letter, to assess whether it is based on a good understanding of the business and to establish whether the auditors' recommendations have been acted on (and if not, why not).

Management reports to the audit committee

Management is accountable to the board (or the audit committee) for monitoring the system of internal control and for providing assurances that it has done so. To be effective, monitoring should be on a regular basis, and management should also provide regular reports to the audit committee (or the board). These regular reports should each deal with a specific aspect of operations and provide an assessment of the significance of the risks and the effectiveness of the system of internal control for dealing with them. They should also report any significant control weaknesses or failings that have been identified, the impact these have had (or may have) on the organisation and the action that has been taken to deal with the problem.

The board or audit committee may also receive independent reports from the internal auditors. In addition to receiving regular reports from management on internal control, the board (or audit committee) should carry out an annual review of the effectiveness of the internal control system. The annual review should consider the following in particular:

- the changes that have occurred since the previous annual review – in what ways have the significant risks for the organisation changed, and how successful has the organisation been in responding to those changes
- the scope and quality of monitoring of the control system by management
- the scope and quality of the investigations by the internal audit function, the weaknesses in the system identified by the internal auditors and the measures taken to implement recommendations of the internal auditors.

■ Whistleblowing procedures

The UK Code states that the audit committee should 'review arrangements by which staff of the organisation may, in confidence, raise concerns about possible improprieties in matters of financial reporting or other matters'.

In other words, the audit committee should be responsible for the review of the provisions and procedures for whistleblowing within the organisation. The UK Code specifies that the objective of the audit committee should be to ensure that there are satisfactory arrangements in place for the 'proportionate and independent investigation' of allegations by whistleblowers, and appropriate follow-up action. The code is referring to the adequacy of what the NHS understand to be whistleblowing procedures within the organisation.

The *HFMA Handbook* sets out a similar provision in its recommended terms of reference for an NHS audit committee. Chapter 3 sets out the details of the specific legislation, namely, the Public Interest Disclosure Act 1998 and the Employment Rights Act 1996.

The Francis Report

In March 2013, the Government gave an announcement in response to the Francis Report, which is designed to create a culture of 'zero harm' and compassionate care. The announcement included a number of items which related to whistleblowing:

- the creation of a new post of Chief Inspector of Hospitals and Care Homes, which will be a 'chief whistleblower' with the power to name and shame poorly performing trusts

- the introduction of a statutory duty to be honest about mistakes which harm patients, known as a duty of candour
- the barring of hospital managers who manipulate statistics or who try and cover up cases of poor care from any future role in healthcare
- the banning of clauses gagging ex-NHS staff from raising concerns publicly about patient safety.

The NHS Constitution

As part of a series of measures intended to highlight the importance of whistle-blowing in the NHS, and in response to the Francis Report, the 2013 Constitution includes:

- an expectation that staff should raise concerns at the earliest opportunity
- a pledge that NHS organisations should support staff when raising concerns by ensuring their concerns are fully investigated, and that there is someone independent to speak to outside of their team
- clarity around the existing legal right for staff to raise concerns about safety, malpractice or other wrong doing without suffering any detriment.

The need for whistleblowing

There is a strong connection between health service governance and whistleblow-ing. An employee may honestly believe that there is (or has been or could soon be) serious malpractice by someone within the organisation, but feel unable to report his concerns in the normal way. This could be because the individual to whom he normally reports is involved in the suspected malpractice. Serious malpractice or a misdemeanour could be damaging to the organisation, such as:

- it might suffer financial loss if some employees are acting fraudulently
- it might incur severe penalties as a consequence of employees breaking the law or regulations
- there could be damage to the organisation's reputation if the misdemeanour is made public.

The need for whistleblowing arises when normal procedures and internal controls will not reveal the illicit activity because the individuals responsible for the activity are somehow able to ignore or 'get around' the normal controls.

However, although whistleblowing procedures are an internal control, they are not an embedded control within the organisation's regular procedures. Their effectiveness relies on the willingness of genuine whistleblowers to come forward with their allegations. The incidence of illicit or illegal behaviour should be uncommon; therefore whistleblowing should be an occasional event. Extensive inquiries into the baby heart unit at Bristol Royal Infirmary and into the extraordinary behaviour of the GP Dr Harold Shipman have raised questions about the protection provided to whistleblowers within the health service.

Sir Robert Francis QC is currently leading an independent review into creating the open and honest reporting culture in the NHS. The Freedom to Speak Up Review will gather information through inviting anyone with an interest to share experiences and ideas; conducting research projects and holding a number of seminars with individuals and relevant organisations to discuss issues and emerging themes. Using the evidence gathered, Sir Robert will make recommendations to the Secretary of State for Health in early 2015. As part of the review, NHS employees are being asked to complete a survey on whistleblowing procedures and practices in the NHS.

Whistleblowing: best practice

'Health and social care professionals have a responsibility to raise concerns if they believe that patients or people who use services are being put at risk. The first course of action should be to raise these concerns within your organisation – but if you feel unable to, or if your voice is not being heard, it's important to know that there are other options open to you.'

Cynthia Bower, ex-CEO of the CQC

If an employee has a genuine, honest concern about something happening within the organisation which they believe to be unsafe or improper, there should be a way for the employee's concerns to be brought to the attention of management and dealt with in a constructive way. Having a system for listening to employees' concerns should be a part of an effective risk management system within the organisation, because diligent employees can act as an early warning system of problems.

However, there are several problems with whistleblowing procedures and policies. For example, experience in many organisations appears to show that an individual who reports concerns about illegal or unethical conduct is often victimised by colleagues and management. If the allegations by the whistleblower are rejected, he might not receive the same salary increases as colleagues, or could be overlooked for promotion. The attitude of colleagues and managers might also be hostile, making it difficult for the individual to continue in the job.

On the other hand, employees may deliberately make false claims about their colleagues or bosses, out of spite or a desire for revenge for some actual or perceived 'wrong'. It would be inappropriate to provide protection for individuals making malicious and intentionally false allegations.

Organisations therefore need to establish a whistleblowing system that encourages employees to report of illegal or unethical behaviour, but discourages malicious and unfounded allegations. The DH consultation paper *The NHS Constitution and Whistleblowing* states:

'There are two distinct issues in relation to whistleblowing and the legislation relating to it (the Public Interest Disclosure Act 1998 (PIDA)). The first issue is around whether there are sufficient protections under PIDA for those who wish to raise concerns. The second is about creating and encouraging a culture of openness, where individuals who wish to raise concerns, feel confident enough to speak out and employers act upon these concerns as part of good governance.'

An organisation might state its policy on whistleblowing in the following terms.

- An employee is acting correctly if, in good faith, he or she seeks advice about improper behaviour or reports improper behaviour, where it is not possible to resolve the individual's concerns through discussions with colleagues or line management. Whistleblowing is appropriate if the employee does it in good faith and is not being malicious, and there is no other way to resolve the problem.
- The organisation will not tolerate any discrimination by employees or management in the organisation against an individual who has reported in good faith their concerns about illegal or unethical behaviour. This is a policy statement that whistleblowers will be protected if they have made their report in good faith.
- Disciplinary action will be taken against any employee who knowingly makes a false report of illegal or improper behaviour by someone else. Malicious reporting should not be tolerated.

In practice, employees may feel obliged to take their concerns (possibly anonymously) to someone outside the organisation, risking the anger of the employer for breach of proper procedures if he is identified. An employee can be disciplined for making groundless complaints and allegations in bad faith about his employer. On the other hand, there is an 'official' whistleblowing channel that provides a way of reporting concerns to someone outside the employer organisation provided by the government-funded whistleblowing helpline, which changed to a freephone service in January 2012.

CASE STUDY: Whistleblowing at Queen Elizabeth Hospital Trust
At Queen Elizabeth Hospital Trust, consultant Ramon Neikrash was suspended in 2008 after writing a series of letters to management warning about the impact of cost cutting. An employment tribunal ruled the suspension was unlawful and that Mr Neikrash had been acting as a whistleblower.

Internal procedures for whistleblowers' allegations
An organisation should have a fair system for dealing internally with accusations from whistle-blowers so that an honest individual does not feel under threat. Employees ought to know what those procedures are. Since whistleblowing is

not a regular event, an organisation may simply try to deal with each case on its merits when it arises, without any formal procedures or channels of complaint being established. The employee will therefore not know whom to complain to, and will probably go to the most senior manager available – possibly the CEO.

A problem with dealing with whistleblowing incidents on an *ad hoc* basis is that the accusations may relate to senior members of staff or the EDs themselves. An employee who believes the CEO or finance director to be guilty of wrong-doing will have no option other than to resign or take the complaint to an external authority.

It is, therefore, more appropriate to establish a formal internal channel for dealing with whistleblowers. All NHS organisations will have an established whistleblowing policy. This policy will provide:

- documented internal whistleblowing procedures available to all employees
- the procedures by which an allegation will be investigated
- a named person to whom employees should report their suspicions or concerns
- an independent means of investigation
- a statement that the employer takes malpractice or misconduct seriously, and is committed to a culture of openness in which employees can report legitimate concerns without fear of penalty or punishment
- examples of the type of misconduct for which employees should use the procedure and set out the level of proof that there should be in an allegation (although positive proof might not be required, a whistleblower should be able to provide good reasons for his concern)
- that false or malicious allegations will result in disciplinary action against the individual making them
- that no employee will be victimised for raising a genuine concern. Victimisation for raising a qualified disclosure is a disciplinary offence
- an external whistleblowing route, as well as an internal reporting procedure
- that, as far as possible, whistleblowers will be informed about the outcome of their allegations and the action that has been taken
- that whistleblowers will be promised confidentiality, as far as this is possible.

Whistleblowing procedures and the Bribery Act 2010

In the UK, the Bribery Act 2010 introduced a new offence of 'failure of commercial organisations to prevent bribery' by a person associated with them (such as an employee or agent). However, an organisation could avoid conviction if it can show that, although bribery may have occurred, it has in place 'adequate processes' to prevent bribery. Having suitable whistleblowing procedures is likely to be a sufficient defence against a criminal charge, provided that the organisation can demonstrate that the procedures work well in practice. It would not be sufficient simply to have a whistleblowing policy in existence that no one uses.

The majority of trusts should already have an anti-fraud and corruption policy or equivalent policy; the reporting of potential acts of bribery should follow the same procedure. It is important that NHS organisations update their whistle-blowing policies to cover potential acts of bribery, so employees are aware of what behaviour is unacceptable.

Governance Checklist

✓ Does the audit committee have the requisite skills, financial experience, resources, time commitment and robust independence to undertake its tasks?

✓ Does the audit committee review all financial statements, the Quality Accounts and any supporting audit assurance prior to their release?

✓ Does the audit committee control (or, in the case of FTs, support) the process of appointing and assessing the external auditors and is it satisfied as to their independence and effectiveness?

✓ Has account been taken of the ten-yearly audit tender requirements (five-yearly for FTs) and is the audit committee involved in the tender process?

✓ Is the external audit plan in place? Does the audit committee review and monitor the auditors' performance against that plan?

✓ Does the audit committee meet at least annual with the external and internal auditors without management being present?

✓ Is the internal audit team effectively and adequately resourced?

✓ Does the audit committee regularly challenge and review the effectiveness of the internal audit function?

✓ Is the internal audit function used effectively to provide objective assurance to the board on the key risks?

✓ Is the head of internal audit appointed by and accountable to the audit committee, and do they have unrestricted access to the audit committee and board chair? Is the management team responsive to their findings and recommendations?

✓ What action has the audit committee taken to review the whistleblowing policy and procedures in the last twelve months.

■ Summary

Audit plays a key role in providing assurance to the board and wider NHS stake-holders. This critical role means that ensuring the independence of those functions is high on the agenda of the board and its audit committee. This, however, is only part of the role of the audit committee, which has a broad and extensive role that is not restricted to considering just the financial aspects of the organisation.

Glossary

accountability: the requirement for a person in a position of responsibility to justify, explain or account for the exercise of his/her authority and his/her performance or actions. Accountability is to the person or persons from whom the authority is derived.

accountable officer: the primary authority for providing financial management and accountability for NHS property and services.

annual governance statement: the AGS is a mandatory disclosure for all central government entities that comply with the FReM. All public bodies (including NHS organisations) must provide assurance that they are appropriately managing and controlling the resources for which they are responsible. The AGS replaces the statement on internal control.

apply or explain rule: similar to the comply or explain rule. Companies should apply the principles of a code or explain why they have not done so.

audit committee: committee of the board, consisting entirely of independent non-executive directors, with responsibility (among other things) for monitoring the reliability of the financial statements, the quality of the external audit and the organisation's relationship with its external auditors.

audit firm rotation: changing the firm of external auditors on a regular basis, say every seven years. Not common in practice.

audit partner rotation: changing the lead partner (and possibly other partners) involved with an organisation's audit on a regular basis, typically every five or seven years.

audit report: report for stakeholders produced by the external auditors on completion of the annual audit, and included in the organisation's published annual report and accounts. The report gives the opinion of the auditors on whether the financial statements present a true and fair view of the organisation's financial performance and position.

balance of power: a situation in which power is shared out more or less evenly between a number of different individuals or groups, so that no single individual or group is in a position to dominate.

board committee: a committee established by the board of directors, with delegated responsibility for a particular aspect of the board's affairs. For example, audit committee, remuneration/ compensation committee and nominations committee.

board succession: the replacement of a senior director (typically the chair or CEO) when he or she retires or resigns.

box-ticking approach: an approach to compliance based on following all the specific rules or provisions in a code, and not considering the principles that should be applied and circumstances where the principles are best applied by not following the detailed provisions.

Bribery Act 2010: UK Act of Parliament making it a criminal offence to give or receive bribes, to bribe a foreign public official for business benefit or to fail to prevent the payment of bribes by employees or agents.

business ethics: standards of business behaviour, sometimes set out by companies in a code of corporate ethics.

business risk: the risk from unexpected events or developments in a business or in the business environment, which are outside the control of management. In the NHS, business risks are to patient safety and financial security.

business risk management: the management of business risks within a strategy based on risk appetite and risk tolerance. The board is responsible for business risk strategy and management is responsible for implementing the strategy within a business risk management system. The board is also responsible for monitoring the effectiveness of the business risk management system, at least annually according to the UK Corporate Governance Code.

Cadbury Code: a code of corporate governance, published by the Cadbury Committee in the UK in 1992 (and since superseded).

Care Quality Commission (CQC): the safety and quality regulator for all health services, which is also responsible for the regulation of adult social care services.

chair: leader of the board of directors. Often referred to as the 'company chair' in companies and 'chair' in public bodies and voluntary organisations.

chief executive officer: the executive director who is head of the executive management team in an organisation.

clinical commissioning groups (CCGs): groups of GPs and other health professionals responsible under the Health and Social Care Act 2012 for commissioning most healthcare.

Combined Code: the UK code on corporate governance for listed companies from 1998 to 2010. It was revised in 2010 and re-named the UK Corporate Governance Code.

comply or explain rule: requirement (e.g. in the UK, a requirement of the Listing Rules) for a company to comply with a voluntary code of corporate governance (in the UK, the UK Corporate Governance Code) or explain any non-compliance.

connected person: a person with whom a director has an enduring and direct relationship, such as a family member, including a spouse, civil partner, children and step children (and equivalent relationships arising through civil partnerships) and companies in which the director has an interest of 20% or more.

corporate governance: the system by which a company is directed, so as to achieve its overall objectives. It is concerned with relationships, structures, processes, information flows, controls, decision-making and accountability at the highest level in a company.

council of governors: a council of governors is a several member group that oversees or manages the running of an institution. In the context of an NHS FT it is an elected body of members who hold the board of directors to account.

Davies Review: a government-sponsored report (published February 2011) recommending greater diversity on the boards of companies and in particular a greater proportion of women on the boards of FTSE350 companies.

directors' report: the 'report' in the annual report and accounts of a company or organisation. A report by the board of directors to the stakeholders, contained in the annual report and accounts and containing a variety of reports and information disclosures, such as the business review and remuneration report.

Disclosure and Transparency Rules: in the UK, rules on disclosures that listed companies are required to comply with. The rules (like the Listing Rules) are issued and enforced by the UK financial markets regulator.

downside risk: a risk that actual events will turn out worse than expected. Downside risk can be measure in terms of the amount by which profits could be worse than expected. The expected outcome is the forecast or budget expectation.

duty of skill and care: a duty owed by a director to the company or organisation. In the UK, this has been a common law duty, but became a statutory duty under the provisions of the Companies Act 2006. A question can be raised, however, about what level of skill and care should be expected from a director.

elective care: planned specialist medical care.

emergency preparedness: emergency preparedness is a plan of what to do if a disaster that is unconnected with the organisation's business and outside the control of management occurs.

EU Directive: an instruction, devised by the European Commission and approved by the European Council and European Parliament. The contents of a Directive must be introduced into national law or regulations by all members states of the EU. Some Directives, such as the Shareholder Rights Directive, deal wholly or partly with corporate governance issues.

European Commission: the managing and administrative body of the EU.

executive director: a director who also has executive responsibilities in the management structure. Usually a full-time employee with a contract of employment.

external audit: statutory annual audit of an organisation by independent external auditors.

fairness: impartiality, a lack of bias. In a corporate governance context, the quality of fairness refers to things that are done or decided in a reasonable manner, and with sense of justice, avoiding bias.

fiduciary duty: a duty of a trustee. The directors of a company or organisation are given their powers in trust, and have fiduciary duties towards the company or organisation.

financial risk: a risk of a failure or error, deliberate (fraud) or otherwise, in the systems or procedures for recording financial transactions and reporting financial performance and position, or the risk of a failure to safeguard financial assets such as cash and accounts receivable.

fixed pay: the elements in a remuneration package that are a fixed amount each year, such as basic salary.

going concern statement: a requirement of some corporate governance codes, such as the UK Corporate Governance Code. A statement by the board of directors that in their view the organisation will remain as a going concern for the next financial year.

Greenbury Report: report in the UK in 1995 by the Greenbury Committee, focusing mainly on corporate governance issues related to directors' remuneration.

Hampel Committee: committee set up in the UK to continue the review of corporate governance practices in the UK, following the Cadbury and Greenbury Committee Reports. The Hampel Committee suggested that the recommendations of all three committees should be integrated into a single code of corporate governance, which was published in 1998 as the Combined Code.

health service governance: the system, practices and procedures by which power is shared and exercised by the board of directors (and the council of governors in foundation trusts) and how the holders of that power are held accountable for ensuring that the individual parts of the NHS achieve their objectives and are in line with public sector values such as value for money and providing universal and free healthcare benefits to all those in need.

Higgs Report: the 2003 UK government commissioned review into the role and effectiveness of non-executive directors.

induction: process of introducing a newly-appointed director into his or her role, by providing appropriate information, site visits, meetings with management and (where necessary) training.

internal audit: investigations and checks carried out by internal auditors of an organisation. Internal audit is a function rather than a specific activity. However, the work programme of the internal audit team might reduce the amount of work the external auditors need to carry out in their annual audit, provided the internal and external auditors collaborate properly.

internal control: a procedure or arrangement that is implemented to prevent an internal control risk, reduce the potential impact of such a risk, or detect a failure of internal control when it occurs (and initiate remedial action).

internal control risk: a risk of failure in a system or procedure due to causes that are within the control of management. They can be categorised as financial risks, operational risk and compliance risks.

internal control system: a system of internal controls within an organisation. The system should have a suitable control environment, and should provide for the identification and assessment of internal control risks, the design and implementation of internal controls, communication and information and monitoring. In the UK, the board of directors of a listed company has responsibility for the system of internal control.

International Corporate Governance Network (ICGN): a voluntary association of institutional investors that has the objective of raising standards of corporate governance globally, to meet the requirements and expectations of global investors.

King Code: also called the King Report and King III (because it is the third version of the Code/Report, issued in 2009). The corporate governance code for listed companies in South Africa.

lead governor: the lead governor's role is to facilitate direct communication between Monitor and the NHS foundation trust's board of governors in a limited number of circumstances and in particular where it may not be appropriate to communicate through the normal channels.

management board: a board of executive managers, chaired by the CEO, within a two-tier board structure. The chair of the management board reports to the chair of the supervisory board. The management board has responsibility for the operational performance of the business.

modified audit report: audit report in which the auditors express some reservations about the financial statements of the organisation, because of insufficient information to reach an opinion or disagreement with the figures in the statements.

money laundering: the process of transferring or using money obtained from criminal activity, so as to make it seem to have come from legitimate (non-criminal) sources. Companies are often used as a cover for money laundering.

Monitor: the regulator of foundation trusts. Under the Health and Social Care Act its role will be extended to become the sector regulator for health making it responsible for licensing providers of NHS- funded services.

mutual society: a mutual, mutual organisation, or mutual society is an organisation (which is often, but not always, a company or business) based on the principle of mutuality. A mutual is therefore owned by, and run for the benefit of, its members – it has no external shareholders to pay in the form of dividends, and as such does not usually seek to maximise and make large profits or capital gains.

nomination committee: a committee of the board of directors (or council of governors in foundation trusts), with responsibility for identifying potential new members for the board of directors. Suitable candidates are recommended to the main board (or to the council of governors), which then makes a decision about their appointment.

non-audit work: work done by a firm of auditors for a client organisation, other than work on the annual audit, such as consultancy services and tax advice. In the context of corporate governance, the independence of the auditors might be questionable when they earn high fees for non-audit work.

non-executive director (NED): a director who is not an employee of the company and who does not have any responsibilities for executive management in the company.

OECD Principles of Corporate Governance: general principles of corporate governance issued by the Organisation for European Cooperation and Development, which all countries are encouraged to adopt.

policy governance theory: policy governance theory is an integrated set of concepts and principles that describes the job of any governing board. It outlines the manner in which boards can be successful in their servant-leadership role, as well as in their all-important relationship with management.

postcode lottery: a situation where local budgets and decision-making can lead to different levels of public services in different places especially with regard to health and social services, e.g. access to cancer drugs or quality of education.

primary care: the first point of healthcare such as GPs, dentists, pharmacists and optometrists.

public benefit corporation: a public benefit corporation is usually a corporation created by the government that performs a specific function for the benefit of the public, such as a hospital or public library.

Quality Account: a Quality Account is a report about the quality of services provided by an NHS healthcare service. The report is published annually by each NHS healthcare provider, including the independent sector and made available to the public.

quality governance: the combination of structures and processes at and below board level to lead on trust-wide quality performance including:

- ensuring required standards are achieved
- investigating and taking action on sub-standard performance
- planning and driving continuous improvement
- identifying, sharing and ensuring delivery of best-practice
- identifying and managing risks to quality of care.

remuneration committee: a committee of the board of directors (or council of governors in foundation trusts), with responsibility for deciding remuneration policy for top executives and the individual remuneration packages of certain senior executives, for example, all the executive directors (or non-executive directors in foundation trusts).

reputation risk: risk to the reputation of a company or other organisation in the mind of the public (including customers and suppliers) when a particular matter becomes public knowledge

responsibility: having power and authority over something. A person in a position of responsibility should be held accountable for the exercise of that authority.

risk appetite: the amount and type of business risk that the board of directors would like their organisation to have exposure to. Identifying risk appetite should be a part of strategic planning.

risk assessment: an assessment of risks faced by an organisation, Typically risks are assessed according to how probably or how frequent an adverse outcome is likely to be in the planning period and the potential size of the losses if an adverse outcome occurs. The greatest risks are those with a high probability of an adverse outcome combined with the likelihood of a large loss if this were to happen.

risk capacity: the maximum risk exposures that the organisation can accept without threatening its financial stability.

risk committee: a committee of the board that an organisation may establish, with the responsibility of monitoring the risk management system within the organisation, instead of the audit committee. A risk committee may be established when the audit committee has too many other responsibilities to handle.

risk management: a function of the administration of the NHS body directed toward identification, evaluation, and correction of potential risks that could lead to injury to patients, staff members, or visitors and result in loss or damage.

risk management committee: a committee of senior executive managers and risk managers, whose responsibility is to implement the risk management strategy of the board.

risk tolerance: the amount of business risk that the board is willing to let their organisation be exposed to. Alternatively, the amount of risk that the organisation is able to accept without serious threat to its stability.

Sarbanes-Oxley Act: legislation, largely on corporate governance issues, introduced in the USA in 2002 following a series of corporate scandals such as Enron and WorldCom.

secondary care: acute healthcare, either elective or emergency.

secret profit: a profit that is not revealed. In the context of corporate governance, a director should not make a secret profit for his/her personal benefit and at the expense of the company or organisation.

senior independent director: a non-executive director who is the nominal head of all the non-executive directors on the board. The SID may act as a channel of communication between the NEDs and the chair, or (in some situations) between major stakeholders and the board.

severance payment: payment to a director (or other employee) on being required to resign (or otherwise leave the company).

shareholder value approach: approach to corporate governance based on the view that the objective of its directors should be to maximise benefits for shareholders.

Smith Report: a report concerned with the independence of auditors in the wake of the collapse of Arthur Andersen and the Enron scandal in the US in 2002. It raised the important point that an auditor himself should look at whether a company's corporate governance structure provides safeguards to preserve his own independence.

stakeholder: a stakeholder group is an identifiable group of individuals or organisations with a vested interest. Stakeholder groups in a company include the shareholders, the directors, senior executive management and other employees, customers, suppliers. In the NHS stakeholders will also include patients, employees, the regulators, the general public and the government.

Statement on Internal Control: the SIC is a mandatory disclosure for all central government entities that comply with the FReM. All public bodies (including NHS organisations) must provide assurance that they are appropriately managing and controlling the resources for which they are responsible. This has now been replaced by the AGS.

statutory duties: duties imposed by statute law.

strategic risk: the risks of taking decisions on strategy that will result in exposures to excessive business risk and so could lead to losses or even business collapse.

stress testing: testing the ability of a business to withstand the effects of extreme adverse events or developments in the business environment.

succession planning: planning for the eventual replacement of a senior member of the board (chair, CEO and possibly finance director) by his or her successor.

supervisory board: a board of non-executive directors, found in an organisation with a two-tier board structure. The supervisory board reserves some responsibilities to itself. These include oversight of the management board.

sustainability: conducting business operations in a way that can be continued into the foreseeable future, without using natural resources at such a rate or creating such environmental damage that the continuation of the business will eventually become impossible.

sustainability report: report on the economic, social and environmental performance of a company or organisation.

transparency: openness. Being clear about historical performance and future intentions, and not trying to hide information.

Turnbull Guidance: initially a report of the Turnbull Committee in the UK, giving listed companies guidance on how the directors should carry out their responsibility for the internal control system, as required by the UK corporate governance code. Now the responsibility of the FRC.

two-tier board: board structure in which the responsibilities are divided between a supervisory board of non-executive directors led by the chair, and a management board of executives led by the CEO.

UK Corporate Governance Code: the code of corporate governance issued by the FRC in the UK, which is applied to UK listed companies. Formerly (until 2010) called the Combined Code.

UK Listing Rules: rules that apply to all listed companies in the UK. They include the 'comply or explain' rule on compliance with the UK Corporate Governance Code.

ultra vires: in corporate law, ultra vires describes acts attempted by a corporation that are beyond the scope of powers granted by the corporation's objects clause, articles of incorporation or in a clause in its bylaws, in the laws authorising a corporation's formation, or similar founding documents.

unitary board: board structure in which decisions are taken by a single group of executive and non-executive directors, led by the company chair.

upside risk: a risk that actual events will turn out better than expected and will provide unexpected profits. Some risks, such as the risk of a change in foreign exchange rates, or a change in interest rates, or a change in consumer buying patterns could be 'two-way' with both upside and downside potential.

variable pay: the elements in a remuneration package that vary each year according to the individual's performance, such as annual bonuses, and the grant of shares or share options

voluntary code of governance: a code of governance that is not enforced by law or regulation. However, as in the UK and South Africa, listed companies may be encouraged to adopt a voluntary code by means of a 'comply or explain' or 'apply or explain' regulation.

Walker Report: a report published in the UK in 2009 about corporate governance in banks and other financial services organisations, following the banking crisis of 2007–2009.

whistleblowing: the disclosure by a person, usually an employee in a government agency or private enterprise, to the public or to those in authority, of mismanagement, corruption, illegality, or some other wrongdoing.

window dressing of accounts: applying accounting policies that are just within the limits of permissible accounting practice, but which have the effect of making the company's performance or financial position seem better than it would if more conservative accounting policies were used. For example, accounting policies might be used that recognise income at an early stage in a transaction process, or defer the recognition of expenses.

Women on Boards Report: a report highlighting the poor representation of women on boards, relative to their male counterparts, and raised questions about whether board recruitment is in practice based on skills, experience and performance. This report presents practical recommendations to address this imbalance.

wrongful trading: wrongful trading occurs when a company continues to trade when the directors are aware that the company had gone into (or would soon go into) insolvent liquidation.

Directory

■ Further reading, codes of practice and guidance

A First Class Service: Quality in the new NHS, Department of Health, 1998.

Audit Code for NHS Foundation Trusts, Monitor, 2011.

Board Governance Assurance Framework, Department of Health, 2011.

Carver, J. *Boards that Make a Difference: a New Design for Leadership in Nonprofit and Public Organisations*, Jossey-Bass, 2006.

Chait R, Ryan W, and Taylor B. *Governance as Leadership: Reframing the Work of Nonprofit Boards*, Wiley, 2005.

Code and Report on Governance for South Africa (King III), Institute of Directors South Africa, 2009 (see www.iodsa.co.za).

Code of Ethics for Professional Accountants, International Federation of Accountants, 2006.

Code of Governance for Foundation Trusts, Monitor, 2010. See Appendix 2.

Corporate Governance Policy and Voting Guidelines, National Association of Pension Funds, 2011.

Davies Review into Women on Boards, Department of Business, Innovation and Skills, 2011.

Effective Boards in the NHS, NHS Confederation, 2005.

Equity and Excellence: Liberating the NHS, Department of Health, 2010.

The Foundations of Good Governance, Foundation Trust Network, 2010.

Good Governance: a Code for the Voluntary Sector, NCVO, 2010. See: www.ncvo-vol.org.uk/codeofgovernance

Government Financial Reporting Manual (FReM), HM Treasury, annual.

Guidance on Audit Committees, FRC, 2010 (see Appendix 5).

Guidance on Board Effectiveness, FRC, 2011 (see Appendix 4).

Guidance on Risk Management, Internal Control and Related Financial and Business Reporting, FRC, 2005 (see Appendix 6).

The Healthy NHS Board: Principles for Good Governance, NHS Leadership Council, 2010 (see Appendix 3).

High Quality Care for All (Darzi Report), Department of Health, 2008.

Hutton Review of Fair Pay in the Public Sector, HM Treasury, 2011.

ICGN Global Corporate Governance Principles, ICGN, 2009.

The Integrated Governance Handbook, Department of Health, 2006

New Voices, New Accountabilities: A guide to Wider Governance in Foundation Trusts, Foundation Trust Network, 2005.

NHS Audit Committee Handbook, Department of Health, 2005.

The NHS Emergency Planning Guidance, Department of Health, 2005.

The Nolan Principles of Standards in Public Life, Committee on Standards in Public Life, 1995

Plurality, Stewardship and Engagement, The Ownership Commission, 2012.

Quality Governance Framework, Monitor, 2010.

Quality Governance in the NHS: A Guide for Provider Boards, Department of Health, 2011.

Sonnenfeld, J.A. 'What Makes Boards Great', *Harvard Business Review*, September 2002.

Taking it on Trust, Audit Commission, 2009

The UK Corporate Governance Code, FRC, 2010 (see Appendix 1).

Walker Review of Corporate Governance of UK Banking Industry, HM Treasury, 2009.

Your Statutory Duties: A Reference Guide for NHS Foundation Trust Governors, Monitor, 2009.

■ Useful websites

Association of British Insurers (ABI)
www.abi.org.uk

Audit Commission
www.audit-commission.gov.uk

Care Quality Commission
www.cqc.org.uk

Chartered Institute of Internal Auditors
www.iia.org.uk

The Chartered Institute of Public Finance and Accountancy
www.cipfa.org.uk

Department for Business, Innovation and Skills (BIS)
www.bis.gov.uk

Department of Health
www.dh.gov.uk

European Corporate Governance Institute
www.ecgi.org/codes/all_codes.php.

Financial Reporting Council (FRC)
www.frc.org.uk

Foundation Trust Governors Association
www.ftga.org.uk

Foundation Trust Network
www.foundationtrustnetwork.org

HM Treasury
www.hm-treasury.gov.uk

The Institute of Chartered Secretaries and Administrators (ICSA)
www.icsa.org.uk

The Intelligent Board series
www.drfosterintelligence.co.uk/thought-leadership/intelligent-board

International Corporate Governance Network (ICGN)
www.icgn.org

The International Federation of Accountants (IFAC)
www.ifac.org

National Association of Pension Funds (NAPF)
www.napf.co.uk

Monitor
www.monitor-nhsft.gov.uk

NHS Confederation
www.nhsconfed.org

OECD
www.oecd.org

The Ownership Commission
www.ownershipcomm.org

Appendix 1

The UK Corporate Governance Code

Governance and the Code

1. The purpose of corporate governance is to facilitate effective, entrepreneurial and prudent management that can deliver the long-term success of the company.
2. The first version of the UK Corporate Governance Code (the Code) was produced in 1992 by the Cadbury Committee. Its paragraph 2.5 is still the classic definition of the context of the Code:
    Corporate governance is the system by which companies are directed and controlled. Boards of directors are responsible for the governance of their companies. The shareholders' role in governance is to appoint the directors and the auditors and to satisfy themselves that an appropriate governance structure is in place. The responsibilities of the board include setting the company's strategic aims, providing the leadership to put them into effect, supervising the management of the business and reporting to shareholders on their stewardship. The board's actions are subject to laws, regulations and the shareholders in general meeting.
3. Corporate governance is therefore about what the board of a company does and how it sets the values of the company. It is to be distinguished from the day to day operational management of the company by full-time executives.
4. The Code is a guide to a number of key components of effective board practice. It is based on the underlying principles of all good governance: accountability, transparency, probity and focus on the sustainable success of an entity over the longer term.
5. The Code has been enduring, but it is not immutable. Its fitness for purpose in a permanently changing economic and social business environment requires its evaluation at appropriate intervals.
6. The new Code applies to accounting periods beginning on or after 1 October 2014 and applies to all companies with a Premium listing of equity shares regardless of whether they are incorporated in the UK or elsewhere.

Preface

1. Over two decades of constructive usage of the Code have contributed to improved corporate governance in the UK. The Code is part of a framework of legislation, regulation and best practice standards which aims to deliver high quality corporate governance with in-built flexibility for companies to adapt their practices to take into account their particular circumstances. Similarly, investors must take the opportunity to consider carefully how companies have decided to implement the Code. There is

      always scope for improvement, both in terms of making sure that the Code remains relevant and improving the quality of reporting.

2.   Boards must continue to think comprehensively about their overall tasks and the implications of these for the roles of their individual members. Absolutely key in these endeavours are the leadership of the chair of a board, the support given to and by the CEO, and the frankness and openness of mind with which issues are discussed and tackled by all directors.

3.   Essential to the effective functioning of any board is dialogue which is both constructive and challenging. The problems arising from "groupthink" have been exposed in particular as a result of the financial crisis. One of the ways in which constructive debate can be encouraged is through having sufficient diversity on the board. This includes, but is not limited to, gender and race. Diverse board composition in these respects is not on its own a guarantee. Diversity is as much about differences of approach and experience, and it is very important in ensuring effective engagement with key stakeholders and in order to deliver the business strategy.

4.   One of the key roles for the board includes establishing the culture, values and ethics of the company. It is important that the board sets the correct 'tone from the top'. The directors should lead by example and ensure that good standards of behaviour permeate throughout all levels of the organisation. This will help prevent misconduct, unethical practices and support the delivery of long-term success.

5.   In this update of the Code the FRC has focused on the provision by companies of information about the risks which affect longer term viability. In doing so the information needs of investors has been balanced against setting appropriate reporting requirements. Companies will now need to present information to give a clearer and broader view of solvency, liquidity, risk management and viability. For their part, investors will need to assess these statements thoroughly and engage accordingly. In addition, boards of listed companies will need to ensure that executive remuneration is aligned to the long-term success of the company and demonstrate this more clearly to shareholders.

6.   To run a corporate board successfully should not be underrated. Constraints on time and knowledge combine with the need to maintain mutual respect and openness between a cast of strong, able and busy directors dealing with each other across the different demands of executive and non-executive roles. To achieve good governance requires continuing and high quality effort.

7.   Chairmen are encouraged to report personally in their annual statements how the principles relating to the role and effectiveness of the board (in Sections A and B of the Code) have been applied. Not only will this give investors a clearer picture of the steps taken by boards to operate effectively but also, by providing fuller context, it may make investors more willing to accept explanations when a company chooses to explain rather than to comply with one or more provisions.

8.   While in law the company is primarily accountable to its shareholders, and the relationship between the company and its shareholders is also the main focus of the Code, companies are encouraged to recognise the contribution made by other providers of capital and to confirm the board's interest in listening to the views of such providers insofar as these are relevant to the company's overall approach to governance.

Comply or Explain

1. The "comply or explain" approach is the trademark of corporate governance in the UK. It has been in operation since the Code's beginnings and is the foundation of its flexibility. It is strongly supported by both companies and shareholders and has been widely admired and imitated internationally.

2. The Code is not a rigid set of rules. It consists of principles (main and supporting) and provisions. The Listing Rules require companies to apply the Main Principles and report to shareholders on how they have done so. The principles are the core of the Code and the way in which they are applied should be the central question for a board as it determines how it is to operate according to the Code.

3. It is recognised that an alternative to following a provision may be justified in particular circumstances if good governance can be achieved by other means. A condition of doing so is that the reasons for it should be explained clearly and carefully to shareholders,[1] who may wish to discuss the position with the company and whose voting intentions may be influenced as a result. In providing an explanation, the company should aim to illustrate how its actual practices are consistent with the principle to which the particular provision relates, contribute to good governance and promote delivery of business objectives. It should set out the background, provide a clear rationale for the action it is taking, and describe any mitigating actions taken to address any additional risk and maintain conformity with the relevant principle. Where deviation from a particular provision is intended to be limited in time, the explanation should indicate when the company expects to conform with the provision.

4. In their responses to explanations, shareholders should pay due regard to companies' individual circumstances and bear in mind in particular the size and complexity of the company and the nature of the risks and challenges it faces. Though shareholders have every right to challenge companies' explanations if they are unconvincing, they should not be evaluated in a mechanistic way and departures from the Code should not be automatically treated as breaches. Shareholders should be careful to respond to the statements from companies in a manner that supports the "comply or explain" process and bearing in mind the purpose of good corporate governance. They should put their views to the company and both parties should be prepared to discuss the position.

5. Smaller listed companies, in particular those new to listing, may judge that some of the provisions are disproportionate or less relevant in their case. Some of the provisions do not apply to companies below the FTSE 350. Such companies may nonetheless consider that it would be appropriate to adopt the approach in the Code and they are encouraged to do so. Externally managed investment companies typically have a different board structure which may affect the relevance of particular provisions; the Association of Investment Companies' Corporate Governance Code and Guide can assist them in meeting their obligations under the Code.

6. Satisfactory engagement between company boards and investors is crucial to the health of the UK's corporate governance regime. Companies and shareholders both have responsibility for ensuring that "comply or explain" remains an effective alternative to a rules-based system. There are practical and administrative obstacles to improved interaction between boards and shareholders. But certainly there is also scope for an increase in trust which could generate a virtuous upward spiral in attitudes to the Code and in its constructive use.

The Main Principles of the Code

Section A: Leadership

Every company should be headed by an effective board which is collectively responsible for the long-term success of the company.

There should be a clear division of responsibilities at the head of the company between the running of the board and the executive responsibility for the running of the company's business. No one individual should have unfettered powers of decision.

The chair is responsible for leadership of the board and ensuring its effectiveness on all aspects of its role.

As part of their role as members of a unitary board, non-executive directors should constructively challenge and help develop proposals on strategy.

Section B: Effectiveness

The board and its committees should have the appropriate balance of skills, experience, independence and knowledge of the company to enable them to discharge their respective duties and responsibilities effectively.

There should be a formal, rigorous and transparent procedure for the appointment of new directors to the board.

All directors should be able to allocate sufficient time to the company to discharge their responsibilities effectively.

All directors should receive induction on joining the board and should regularly update and refresh their skills and knowledge.

The board should be supplied in a timely manner with information in a form and of a quality appropriate to enable it to discharge its duties.

The board should undertake a formal and rigorous annual evaluation of its own performance and that of its committees and individual directors.

All directors should be submitted for re-election at regular intervals, subject to continued satisfactory performance.

Section C: Accountability

The board should present a fair, balanced and understandable assessment of the company's position and prospects.

The board is responsible for determining the nature and extent of the principal risks it is willing to take in achieving its strategic objectives. The board should maintain sound risk management and internal control systems.

The board should establish formal and transparent arrangements for considering how they should apply the corporate reporting, risk management and internal control principles and for maintaining an appropriate relationship with the company's auditors.

Section D: Remuneration

Executive directors' remuneration should be designed to promote the long-term success of the company. Performance-related elements should be transparent, stretching and rigorously applied.

There should be a formal and transparent procedure for developing policy on executive remuneration and for fixing the remuneration packages of individual directors. No director should be involved in deciding his or her own remuneration.

Section E: Relations with shareholders

There should be a dialogue with shareholders based on the mutual understanding of objectives. The board as a whole has responsibility for ensuring that a satisfactory dialogue with shareholders takes place.

The board should use general meetings to communicate with investors and to encourage their participation

Section A: Leadership

A.1: The Role of the Board

Main Principle

Every company should be headed by an effective board which is collectively responsible for the long-term success of the company.

Supporting Principles

The board's role is to provide entrepreneurial leadership of the company within a framework of prudent and effective controls which enables risk to be assessed and managed. The board should set the company's strategic aims, ensure that the necessary financial and human resources are in place for the company to meet its objectives and review management performance. The board should set the company's values and standards and ensure that its obligations to its shareholders and others are understood and met.

All directors must act in what they consider to be the best interests of the company, consistent with their statutory duties.[2]

Code Provisions

A.1.1. The board should meet sufficiently regularly to discharge its duties effectively. There should be a formal schedule of matters specifically reserved for its decision. The annual report should include a statement of how the board operates, including a high level statement of which types of decisions are to be taken by the board and which are to be delegated to management.

A.1.2. The annual report should identify the chair, the deputy chair (where there is one), the chief executive, the senior independent director and the chairmen and members of the board committees.[3] It should also set out the number of meetings of the board and those committees and individual attendance by directors.

A.1.3. The company should arrange appropriate insurance cover in respect of legal action against its directors.

A.2: Division of Responsibilities

Main Principle

There should be a clear division of responsibilities at the head of the company between the running of the board and the executive responsibility for the running of the company's business. No one individual should have unfettered powers of decision.

Code Provision

A.2.1   The roles of chair and chief executive should not be exercised by the same individual. The division of responsibilities between the chair and chief executive should be clearly established, set out in writing and agreed by the board.

A.3: The Chair

Main Principle

The chair is responsible for leadership of the board and ensuring its effectiveness on all aspects of its role.

Supporting Principles

The chair is responsible for setting the board's agenda and ensuring that adequate time is available for discussion of all agenda items, in particular strategic issues. The chair should also promote a culture of openness and debate by facilitating the effective contribution of non-executive directors in particular and ensuring constructive relations between executive and non-executive directors.

The chair is responsible for ensuring that the directors receive accurate, timely and clear information. The chair should ensure effective communication with shareholders.

Code Provision

A.3.1.   The chair should on appointment meet the independence criteria set out in B.1.1 below. A chief executive should not go on to be chair of the same company. If exceptionally a board decides that a chief executive should become chair, the board should consult major shareholders in advance and should set out its reasons to shareholders at the time of the appointment and in the next annual report.[4]

A.4: Non-Executive Directors

Main Principle

As part of their role as members of a unitary board, non-executive directors should constructively challenge and help develop proposals on strategy.

Supporting Principle

Non-executive directors should scrutinise the performance of management in meeting agreed goals and objectives and monitor the reporting of performance. They should satisfy themselves on the integrity of financial information and that financial controls and systems of risk management are robust and defensible. They are responsible for determining appropriate levels of remuneration of executive directors and have a prime role in appointing and, where necessary, removing executive directors, and in succession planning.

Code Provisions

A.4.1. The board should appoint one of the independent non-executive directors to be the senior independent director to provide a sounding board for the chair and to serve as an intermediary for the other directors when necessary. The senior independent director should be available to shareholders if they have concerns which contact through the normal channels of chair, chief executive or other executive directors has failed to resolve or for which such contact is inappropriate.

A.4.2. The chair should hold meetings with the non-executive directors without the executives present. Led by the senior independent director, the non-executive directors should meet without the chair present at least annually to appraise the chair's performance and on such other occasions as are deemed appropriate.

A.4.3. Where directors have concerns which cannot be resolved about the running of the company or a proposed action, they should ensure that their concerns are recorded in the board minutes. On resignation, a non-executive director should provide a written statement to the chair, for circulation to the board, if they have any such concerns.

Section B: Effectiveness

B.1:The Composition of the Board

Main Principle

The board and its committees should have the appropriate balance of skills, experience, independence and knowledge of the company to enable them to discharge their respective duties and responsibilities effectively.

Supporting Principles

The board should be of sufficient size that the requirements of the business can be met and that changes to the board's composition and that of its committees can be managed without undue disruption, and should not be so large as to be unwieldy.

The board should include an appropriate combination of executive and non-executive directors (and, in particular, independent non-executive directors) such that no individual or small group of individuals can dominate the board's decision taking.

The value of ensuring that committee membership is refreshed and that undue reliance is not placed on particular individuals should be taken into account in deciding chair and membership of committees.

No one other than the committee chair and members is entitled to be present at a meeting of the nomination, audit or remuneration committee, but others may attend at the invitation of the committee.

Code Provisions

B.1.1. The board should identify in the annual report each non-executive director it considers to be independent.[5] The board should determine whether the director is independent in character and judgement and whether there are relationships or circumstances which are likely to affect, or could appear to affect, the director's judgement. The board should state its reasons if it determines that a director is independent notwithstanding the existence of relationships or circumstances which may appear relevant to its determination, including if the director:

- has been an employee of the company or group within the last five years;
- has, or has had within the last three years, a material business relationship with the company either directly, or as a partner, shareholder, director or senior employee of a body that has such a relationship with the company;
- has received or receives additional remuneration from the company apart from a director's fee, participates in the company's share option or a performance-related pay scheme, or is a member of the company's pension scheme;
- has close family ties with any of the company's advisers, directors or senior employees;
- holds cross-directorships or has significant links with other directors through involvement in other companies or bodies;
- represents a significant shareholder; or
- has served on the board for more than nine years from the date of their first election.

B.1.2. Except for smaller companies,[6] at least half the board, excluding the chair, should comprise non-executive directors determined by the board to be independent. A smaller company should have at least two independent non-executive directors.

B.2: Appointments to the Board

Main Principle

There should be a formal, rigorous and transparent procedure for the appointment of new directors to the board.

Supporting Principles

The search for board candidates should be conducted, and appointments made, on merit, against objective criteria and with due regard for the benefits of diversity on the board, including gender.

The board should satisfy itself that plans are in place for orderly succession for appointments to the board and to senior management, so as to maintain an appropriate balance of skills and experience within the company and on the board and to ensure progressive refreshing of the board.

Code Provisions

B.2.1. There should be a nomination committee which should lead the process for board appointments and make recommendations to the board. A majority of members of the nomination committee should be independent non-executive directors. The chair or an independent non-executive director should chair the committee, but the chair should not chair the nomination committee when it is dealing with the appointment of a successor to the chair. The nomination committee should make available its terms of reference, explaining its role and the authority delegated to it by the board.[7]

B.2.2. The nomination committee should evaluate the balance of skills, experience, independence and knowledge on the board and, in the light of this evaluation, prepare a description of the role and capabilities required for a particular appointment.

B.2.3. Non-executive directors should be appointed for specified terms subject to re-election and to statutory provisions relating to the removal of a director. Any term beyond six years for a non-executive director should be subject to particularly rigorous review, and should take into account the need for progressive refreshing of the board.

B.2.4. A separate section of the annual report should describe the work of the nomination committee,[8] including the process it has used in relation to board appointments. This section should include a description of the board's policy on diversity, including gender, any measurable objectives that it has set for implementing the policy, and progress on achieving the objectives. An explanation should be given if neither an external search consultancy nor open advertising has been used in the appointment of a chair or a non-executive director. Where an external search consultancy has been used, it should be identified in the annual report and a statement made as to whether it has any other connection with the company.

B.3: Commitment

Main Principle

All directors should be able to allocate sufficient time to the company to discharge their responsibilities effectively.

Code Provisions

B.3.1. For the appointment of a chair, the nomination committee should prepare a job specification, including an assessment of the time commitment expected, recognising the need for availability in the event of crises. A chair's other significant commitments should be disclosed to the board before appointment and included in the annual report. Changes to such commitments should be reported to the board as they arise, and their impact explained in the next annual report.

B.3.2. The terms and conditions of appointment of non-executive directors should be made available for inspection.[9] The letter of appointment should set out the expected time commitment. Non-executive directors should undertake that they will have sufficient time to meet what is expected of them. Their other significant commitments should be disclosed to the board before appointment, with a broad indication of the time involved and the board should be informed of subsequent changes.

B.3.3. The board should not agree to a full time executive director taking on more than one non-executive directorship in a FTSE 100 company nor the chair of such a company.

B.4: Development

Main Principle

All directors should receive induction on joining the board and should regularly update and refresh their skills and knowledge.

Supporting Principles

The chair should ensure that the directors continually update their skills and the knowledge and familiarity with the company required to fulfil their role both on the board and on board committees. The company should provide the necessary resources for developing and updating its directors' knowledge and capabilities.

To function effectively all directors need appropriate knowledge of the company and access to its operations and staff.

Code Provisions

B.4.1. The chair should ensure that new directors receive a full, formal and tailored induction on joining the board. As part of this, directors should avail themselves of opportunities to meet major shareholders.

B.4.2. The chair should regularly review and agree with each director their training and development needs.

B.5: Information and Support

Main Principle

The board should be supplied in a timely manner with information in a form and of a quality appropriate to enable it to discharge its duties.

Supporting Principles

The chair is responsible for ensuring that the directors receive accurate, timely and clear information. Management has an obligation to provide such information but directors should seek clarification or amplification where necessary.

Under the direction of the chair, the company secretary's responsibilities include ensuring good information flows within the board and its committees and between senior management and non-executive directors, as well as facilitating induction and assisting with professional development as required.

The company secretary should be responsible for advising the board through the chair on all governance matters.

Code Provisions

B.5.1. The board should ensure that directors, especially non-executive directors, have access to independent professional advice at the company's expense where they judge it necessary to discharge their responsibilities as directors. Committees should be provided with sufficient resources to undertake their duties.

B.5.2. All directors should have access to the advice and services of the company secretary, who is responsible to the board for ensuring that board procedures are complied with. Both the appointment and removal of the company secretary should be a matter for the board as a whole.

B.6: Evaluation

Main Principle

The board should undertake a formal and rigorous annual evaluation of its own performance and that of its committees and individual directors.

Supporting Principles

Evaluation of the board should consider the balance of skills, experience, independence and knowledge of the company on the board, its diversity, including gender, how the board works together as a unit, and other factors relevant to its effectiveness.

The chair should act on the results of the performance evaluation by recognising the strengths and addressing the weaknesses of the board and, where appropriate, proposing new members be appointed to the board or seeking the resignation of directors.

Individual evaluation should aim to show whether each director continues to contribute effectively and to demonstrate commitment to the role (including commitment of time for board and committee meetings and any other duties).

Code Provisions

B.6.1. The board should state in the annual report how performance evaluation of the board, its committees and its individual directors has been conducted.

B.6.2. Evaluation of the board of FTSE 350 companies should be externally facilitated at least every three years. The external facilitator should be identified in the annual report and a statement made as to whether they have any other connection with the company.

B.6.3. The non-executive directors, led by the senior independent director, should be responsible for performance evaluation of the chair, taking into account the views of executive directors.

B.7: Re-election

Main Principle

All directors should be submitted for re-election at regular intervals, subject to continued satisfactory performance.

Code Provisions

B.7.1. All directors of FTSE 350 companies should be subject to annual election by shareholders. All other directors should be subject to election by shareholders at the first annual general meeting after their appointment, and to re-election thereafter at intervals of no more than three years. Non-executive directors who have served longer than nine years should be subject to annual re-election. The names of directors submitted for election or re-election should be accompanied by sufficient biographical details and any other relevant information to enable shareholders to take an informed decision on their election.

B.7.2. The board should set out to shareholders in the papers accompanying a resolution to elect a non-executive director why they believe an individual should be elected. The chair should confirm to shareholders when proposing re-election that, following formal performance evaluation, the individual's performance continues to be effective and to demonstrate commitment to the role.

Section C: Accountability

C.1: Financial and Business Reporting

Main Principle

The board should present a fair, balanced and understandable assessment of the company's position and prospects.

Supporting Principles

The board's responsibility to present a fair, balanced and understandable assessment extends to interim and other price-sensitive public reports and reports to regulators as well as to information required to be presented by statutory requirements.

The board should establish arrangements that will enable it to ensure that the information presented is fair, balanced and understandable.

Code Provisions

C.1.1. The directors should explain in the annual report their responsibility for preparing the annual report and accounts, and state that they consider the annual report and accounts, taken as a whole, is fair, balanced and understandable and provides the information necessary for shareholders to assess the company's position and performance, business model and strategy. There should be a statement by the auditor about their reporting responsibilities.[10]

C.1.2. The directors should include in the annual report an explanation of the basis on which the company generates or preserves value over the longer term (the business model) and the strategy for delivering the objectives of the company.[11]

C.1.3. In annual and half-yearly financial statements, the directors should state whether they considered it appropriate to adopt the going concern basis of accounting in preparing them, and identify any material uncertainties to the company's ability to continue to do so over a period of at least twelve months from the date of approval of the financial statements.[12]

C.2: Risk Management and Internal Control

Main Principle

The board is responsible for determining the nature and extent of the principal risks it is willing to take in achieving its strategic objectives. The board should maintain sound risk management and internal control systems.

Code Provisions

C.2.1. The directors should confirm in the annual report that they have carried out a robust assessment of the principal risks facing the company, including those that would threaten its business model, future performance, solvency or liquidity. The directors should describe those risks and explain how they are being managed or mitigated.

C.2.2. Taking account of the company's current position and principal risks, the directors should explain in the annual report how they have assessed the prospects of the company, over what period they have done so and why they consider that period to be appropriate. The directors should state whether they have a reasonable expectation that the company will be able to continue in operation and meet its liabilities as they fall due over the period of their assessment, drawing attention to any qualifications or assumptions as necessary.

C.2.3. The board should monitor the company's risk management and internal control systems and, at least annually, carry out a review of their effectiveness, and report on that review in the annual report.[13] The monitoring and review should cover all material controls, including financial, operational and compliance controls.

C.3: Audit Committee and Auditors[14]

Main Principle

The board should establish formal and transparent arrangements for considering how they should apply the corporate reporting and risk management and internal control principles and for maintaining an appropriate relationship with the company's auditors.

Code Provisions

C.3.1. The board should establish an audit committee of at least three, or in the case of smaller companies[15] two, independent non-executive directors. In smaller companies the company chair may be a member of, but not chair, the committee in addition to the independent non-executive directors, provided he or she was considered independent on appointment as chair. The board should satisfy itself that at least one member of the audit committee has recent and relevant financial experience.[16]

C.3.2. The main role and responsibilities of the audit committee should be set out in written terms of reference[17] and should include:

– to monitor the integrity of the financial statements of the company and any formal announcements relating to the company's financial performance, reviewing significant financial reporting judgements contained in them;

– to review the company's internal financial controls and, unless expressly addressed by a separate board risk committee composed of independent directors, or by the board itself, to review the company's internal control and risk management systems;

– to monitor and review the effectiveness of the company's internal audit function;

– to make recommendations to the board, for it to put to the shareholders for their approval in general meeting, in relation to the appointment, re-appointment and removal of the external auditor and to approve the remuneration and terms of engagement of the external auditor;

- to review and monitor the external auditor's independence and objectivity and the effectiveness of the audit process, taking into consideration relevant UK professional and regulatory requirements;
- to develop and implement policy on the engagement of the external auditor to supply non-audit services, taking into account relevant ethical guidance regarding the provision of non-audit services by the external audit firm; and to report to the board, identifying any matters in respect of which it considers that action or improvement is needed and making recommendations as to the steps to be taken; and
- to report to the board on how it has discharged its responsibilities.

C.3.3. The terms of reference of the audit committee, including its role and the authority delegated to it by the board, should be made available.[18]

C.3.4. Where requested by the board, the audit committee should provide advice on whether the annual report and accounts, taken as a whole, is fair, balanced and understandable and provides the information necessary for shareholders to assess the company's position and performance, business model and strategy.

C.3.5. The audit committee should review arrangements by which staff of the company may, in confidence, raise concerns about possible improprieties in matters of financial reporting or other matters. The audit committee's objective should be to ensure that arrangements are in place for the proportionate and independent investigation of such matters and for appropriate follow-up action.

C.3.6. The audit committee should monitor and review the effectiveness of the internal audit activities. Where there is no internal audit function, the audit committee should consider annually whether there is a need for an internal audit function and make a recommendation to the board, and the reasons for the absence of such a function should be explained in the relevant section of the annual report.

C.3.7. The audit committee should have primary responsibility for making a recommendation on the appointment, reappointment and removal of the external auditors. FTSE 350 companies should put the external audit contract out to tender at least every ten years. If the board does not accept the audit committee's recommendation, it should include in the annual report, and in any papers recommending appointment or re-appointment, a statement from the audit committee explaining the recommendation and should set out reasons why the board has taken a different position.

C.3.8. A separate section of the annual report should describe the work of the committee in discharging its responsibilities.[19] The report should include:

- the significant issues that the committee considered in relation to the financial statements, and how these issues were addressed;
- an explanation of how it has assessed the effectiveness of the external audit process and the approach taken to the appointment or reappointment of the external auditor, and information on the length of tenure of the current audit firm and when a tender was last conducted; and
- if the external auditor provides non-audit services, an explanation of how auditor objectivity and independence are safeguarded.

Section D: Remuneration

D.1: The Level and Components of Remuneration

Main Principle

Executive directors' remuneration should be designed to promote the long-term success of the company. Performance-related elements should be transparent, stretching and rigorously applied.

Supporting Principles

The remuneration committee should judge where to position their company relative to other companies. But they should use such comparisons with caution, in view of the risk of an upward ratchet of remuneration levels with no corresponding improvement in corporate and individual performance, and should avoid paying more than is necessary.

They should also be sensitive to pay and employment conditions elsewhere in the group, especially when determining annual salary increases.

Code Provisions

D.1.1. In designing schemes of performance-related remuneration for executive directors, the remuneration committee should follow the provisions in Schedule A to this Code. Schemes should include provisions that would enable the company to recover sums paid or withhold the payment of any sum, and specify the circumstances in which it would be appropriate to do so.

D.1.2. Where a company releases an executive director to serve as a non-executive director elsewhere, the remuneration report[20] should include a statement as to whether or not the director will retain such earnings and, if so, what the remuneration is.

D.1.3. Levels of remuneration for non-executive directors should reflect the time commitment and responsibilities of the role. Remuneration for non-executive directors should not include share options or other performance-related elements. If, exceptionally, options are granted, shareholder approval should be sought in advance and any shares acquired by exercise of the options should be held until at least one year after the non-executive director leaves the board. Holding of share options could be relevant to the determination of a non-executive director's independence (as set out in provision B.1.1).

D.1.4. The remuneration committee should carefully consider what compensation commitments (including pension contributions and all other elements) their directors' terms of appointment would entail in the event of early termination. The aim should be to avoid rewarding poor performance. They should take a robust line on reducing compensation to reflect departing directors' obligations to mitigate loss.

D.1.5. Notice or contract periods should be set at one year or less. If it is necessary to offer longer notice or contract periods to new directors recruited from outside, such periods should reduce to one year or less after the initial period.

D.2: Procedure

Main Principle

There should be a formal and transparent procedure for developing policy on executive remuneration and for fixing the remuneration packages of individual directors. No director should be involved in deciding his or her own remuneration.

Supporting Principles

The remuneration committee should take care to recognise and manage conflicts of interest when receiving views from executive directors or senior management, or consulting the chief executive about its proposals. The remuneration committee should also be responsible for appointing any consultants in respect of executive director remuneration.

The chair of the board should ensure that the committee chair maintains contact as required with its principal shareholders about remuneration.

Code Provisions

D.2.1. The board should establish a remuneration committee of at least three, or in the case of smaller companies[21] two, independent non-executive directors. In addition the company chair may also be a member of, but not chair, the committee if he or she was considered independent on appointment as chair. The remuneration committee should make available its terms of reference, explaining its role and the authority delegated to it by the board.[22] Where remuneration consultants are appointed, they should be identified in the annual report and a statement made as to whether they have any other connection with the company.

D.2.2. The remuneration committee should have delegated responsibility for setting remuneration for all executive directors and the chair, including pension rights and any compensation payments. The committee should also recommend and monitor the level and structure of remuneration for senior management. The definition of 'senior management' for this purpose should be determined by the board but should normally include the first layer of management below board level.

D.2.3. The board itself or, where required by the Articles of Association, the shareholders should determine the remuneration of the non-executive directors within the limits set in the Articles of Association. Where permitted by the Articles, the board may however delegate this responsibility to a committee, which might include the chief executive.

D.2.4. Shareholders should be invited specifically to approve all new long-term incentive schemes (as defined in the Listing Rules[23]) and significant changes to existing schemes, save in the circumstances permitted by the Listing Rules.

Section E: Relations with shareholders

E.1: Dialogue with Shareholders

Main Principle

There should be a dialogue with shareholders based on the mutual understanding of objectives. The board as a whole has responsibility for ensuring that a satisfactory dialogue with shareholders takes place.[24]

Supporting Principles

Though recognising that most shareholder contact is with the chief executive and finance director, the chair should ensure that all directors are made aware of their major shareholders' issues and concerns.

The board should keep in touch with shareholder opinion in whatever ways are most practical and efficient.

Code Provisions

E.1.1. The chair should ensure that the views of shareholders are communicated to the board as a whole. The chair should discuss governance and strategy with major shareholders. Non-executive directors should be offered the opportunity to attend scheduled meetings with major shareholders and should expect to attend meetings if requested by major shareholders. The senior independent director should attend sufficient meetings with a range of major shareholders to listen to their views in order to help develop a balanced understanding of the issues and concerns of major shareholders.

E.1.2. The board should state in the annual report the steps they have taken to ensure that the members of the board, and in particular the non-executive directors, develop an understanding of the views of major shareholders about the company, for example through direct face-to-face contact, analysts' or brokers' briefings and surveys of shareholder opinion.

E.2: Constructive Use of General Meetings

Main Principle

The board should use general meetings to communicate with investors and to encourage their participation.

Code Provisions

E.2.1. At any general meeting, the company should propose a separate resolution on each substantially separate issue, and should in particular propose a resolution at the AGM relating to the report and accounts. For each resolution, proxy appointment forms should provide shareholders with the option to direct their proxy to vote either for or against the resolution or to withhold their vote. The proxy form and any announcement of the results of a vote should make it clear that a 'vote withheld' is not a vote in law and will not be counted in the calculation of the proportion of the votes for and against the resolution.

E.2.2. The company should ensure that all valid proxy appointments received for general meetings are properly recorded and counted. For each resolution, where a vote has been taken on a show of hands, the company should ensure that the following information is given at the meeting and made available as soon as reasonably practicable on a website which is maintained by or on behalf of the company:

- the number of shares in respect of which proxy appointments have been validly made;
- the number of votes for the resolution;

- the number of votes against the resolution; and
- the number of shares in respect of which the vote was directed to be withheld. When, in the opinion of the board, a significant proportion of votes have been cast against a resolution at any general meeting, the company should explain when announcing the results of voting what actions it intends to take to understand the reasons behind the vote result.

E.2.3.   The chair should arrange for the chairmen of the audit, remuneration and nomination committees to be available to answer questions at the AGM and for all directors to attend.

E.2.4.   The company should arrange for the Notice of the AGM and related papers to be sent to shareholders at least 20 working days before the meeting. For other general meetings this should be at least 14 working days in advance.

Schedule A: The design of performance-related remuneration for executive directors

Balance

The remuneration committee should determine an appropriate balance between fixed and performance-related, immediate and deferred remuneration. Performance conditions, including non-financial metrics where appropriate, should be relevant, stretching and designed to promote the long-term success of the company. Remuneration incentives should be compatible with risk policies and systems. Upper limits should be set and disclosed.

The remuneration committee should consider whether the directors should be eligible for annual bonuses and/or benefits under long-term incentive schemes.

Share-based remuneration

Traditional share option schemes should be weighed against other kinds of long-term incentive scheme. Executive share options should not be offered at a discount save as permitted by the relevant provisions of the Listing Rules.

Any new long-term incentive schemes which are proposed should be approved by shareholders and should preferably replace any existing schemes or, at least, form part of a well-considered overall plan incorporating existing schemes. The total rewards potentially available should not be excessive.

For share-based remuneration the remuneration committee should consider requiring directors to hold a minimum number of shares and to hold shares for a further period after vesting or exercise, including for a period after leaving the company, subject to the need to finance any costs of acquisition and associated tax liabilities. In normal circumstances, shares granted or other forms of deferred remuneration should not vest or be paid, and options should not be exercisable, in less than three years. Longer periods may be appropriate. Grants under executive share option and other long-term incentive schemes should normally be phased rather than awarded in one large block.

Pensions

In general, only basic salary should be pensionable. The remuneration committee should consider the pension consequences and associated costs to the company of basic salary increases and any other changes in pensionable remuneration, especially for directors close to retirement.

Schedule B: Disclosure of corporate governance arrangements

Corporate governance disclosure requirements are set out in three places:

- FCA Disclosure and Transparency Rules ("DTR") sub-chapters 7.1 and 7.2, which set out certain mandatory disclosures;
- FCA Listing Rules ("LR") 9.8.6 R, 9.8.7 R, and 9.8.7A R, which includes the "comply or explain" requirement; and
- The UK Corporate Governance Code ("the Code") – in addition to providing an explanation where they choose not to comply with a provision, companies must disclose specified information in order to comply with certain provisions.

These requirements are summarised below, with the full text contained in the relevant chapters of the FCA Handbook.

The DTR sub-chapters 7.1 and 7.2 apply to issuers whose securities are admitted to trading on a regulated market (this includes all issuers with a Premium or Standard listing). The LR 9.8.6 R, 9.8.7 R and 9.8.7A R and the Code apply to issuers of Premium listed equity shares only.

There is some overlap between the mandatory disclosures required under the DTR and those expected under the Code. Areas of overlap are summarised in the Appendix to this Schedule. In respect of disclosures relating to the audit committee and the composition and operation of the board and its committees, compliance with the relevant provisions of the Code will result in compliance with the relevant Rules.

Disclosure and Transparency Rules

DTR sub-chapter 7.1 concerns audit committees or bodies carrying out equivalent functions.

DTR 7.1.1 R and 7.1.3 R set out requirements relating to the composition and functions of the committee or equivalent body:

- DTR 7.1.1 R states than an issuer must have a body which is responsible for performing the functions set out in DTR 7.1.3 R, and that at least one member of that body must be independent and at least one member must have competence in accounting and/or auditing.
- DTR 7.1.2 G states that the requirements for independence and competence in accounting and/or auditing may be satisfied by the same member or by different members of the relevant body.
- DTR 7.1.3 R states that an issuer must ensure that, as a minimum, the relevant body must:

1. monitor the financial reporting process;
2. monitor the effectiveness of the issuer's internal control, internal audit where applicable, and risk management systems;
3. monitor the statutory audit of the annual and consolidated accounts;
4. review and monitor the independence of the statutory auditor, and in particular the provision of additional services to the issuer.

DTR 7.1.5 R sets out what disclosure is required. Specifically:

- DTR 7.1.5 R states that the issuer must make a statement available to the public disclosing which body carries out the functions required by DTR 7.1.3 R and how it is composed.
- DTR 7.1.6 G states that this can be included in the corporate governance statement required under sub-chapter DTR 7.2 (see below).
- DTR 7.1.7 G states that compliance with the relevant provisions of the Code (as set out in the Appendix to this Schedule) will result in compliance with DTR 7.1.1 R to 7.1.5 R.

Sub-chapter 7.2 concerns corporate governance statements. Issuers are required to produce a corporate governance statement that must be either included in the directors' report (DTR 7.2.1 R); or in a separate report published together with the annual report; or on the issuer's website, in which case there must be a cross-reference in the directors' report (DTR 7.2.9 R).

DTR 7.2.2 R requires that the corporate governance statements must contain a reference to the corporate governance code to which the company is subject (for companies with a Premium listing this is the Code). DTR 7.2.3 R requires that, to the extent that it departs from that code, the company must explain which parts of the code it departs from and the reasons for doing so. DTR 7.2.4 G states that compliance with LR 9.8.6 R (6) (the "comply or explain" rule in relation to the Code) will also satisfy these requirements.

DTR 7.2.5 R, DTR 7.2.6 R, DTR 7.2.7 R and DTR 7.2.10 R set out certain information that must be disclosed in the corporate governance statement:

- DTR 7.2.5 R states that the corporate governance statement must contain a description of the main features of the company's internal control and risk management systems in relation to the financial reporting process. DTR 7.2.10 R states that an issuer which is required to prepare a group directors' report within the meaning of Section 415(2) of the Companies Act 2006 must include in that report a description of the main features of the group's internal control and risk management systems in relation to the process for preparing consolidated accounts.
- DTR 7.2.6 R states that the corporate governance statement must contain the information required by paragraph 13(2)(c), (d), (f), (h) and (i) of Schedule 7 to the Large and Medium-sized Companies and Groups (Accounts and Reports) Regulations 2008 (SI 2008/410) where the issuer is subject to the requirements of that paragraph.
- DTR 7.2.7 R states that the corporate governance statement must contain a description of the composition and operation of the issuer's administrative, management and supervisory bodies and their committees. DTR 7.2.8 G states that compliance with the relevant provisions of the Code (as set out in the Appendix to this Schedule) will satisfy these requirements.

Listing Rules

LR 9.8.6 R (for UK incorporated companies) and LR 9.8.7 R (for overseas incorporated companies) state that in the case of a company that has a Premium listing of equity shares, the following items must be included in its annual report and accounts:

- a statement of how the listed company has applied the Main Principles set out in the Code, in a manner that would enable shareholders to evaluate how the principles have been applied;
- a statement as to whether the listed company has:
  - complied throughout the accounting period with all relevant provisions set out in the Code; or
  - not complied throughout the accounting period with all relevant provisions set out in the Code, and if so, setting out:
    (i)   those provisions, if any, it has not complied with;
    (ii) in the case of provisions whose requirements are of a continuing nature, the period within which, if any, it did not comply with some or all of those provisions; and
    (iii) the company's reasons for non-compliance.

The UK Corporate Governance Code

In addition to the "comply or explain" requirement in the LR, the Code includes specific requirements for disclosure which must be provided in order to comply. These are summarised below.

The annual report should include:

- a statement of how the board operates, including a high level statement of which types of decisions are to be taken by the board and which are to be delegated to management (A.1.1);
- the names of the chair, the deputy chair (where there is one), the chief executive, the senior independent director and the chairmen and members of the board committees (A.1.2);
- the number of meetings of the board and those committees and individual attendance by directors (A.1.2);
- where a chief executive is appointed chair, the reasons for their appointment (this only needs to be done in the annual report following the appointment) (A.3.1);
- the names of the non-executive directors whom the board determines to be independent, with reasons where necessary (B.1.1);
- a separate section describing the work of the nomination committee, including the process it has used in relation to board appointments; a description of the board's policy on diversity, including gender; any measurable objectives that it has set for implementing the policy, and progress on achieving the objectives. An explanation should be given if neither external search consultancy nor open advertising has been used in the appointment of a chair or a non-executive director. Where an external search consultancy has been used it should be identified and a statement made as to whether it has any other connection with the company (B.2.4);

- the impact of any changes to the other significant commitments of the chair during the year should explained (B.3.1);
- a statement of how performance evaluation of the board, its committees and its directors has been conducted (B.6.1). Where an external facilitator has been used, they should be identified and a statement made as to whether they have any other connection to the company (B.6.2);
- an explanation from the directors of their responsibility for preparing the accounts and a statement that they consider that the annual report and accounts, taken as a whole, is fair, balanced and understandable and provides the information necessary for shareholders to assess the company's position and performance, business model and strategy. There should also be a statement by the auditor about their reporting responsibilities (C.1.1);
- an explanation from the directors of the basis on which the company generates or preserves value over the longer term (the business model) and the strategy for delivering the objectives of the company (C.1.2);
- a statement from the directors whether they considered it appropriate to adopt the going concern basis of accounting in preparing them, and identify any material uncertainties to the company's ability to continue to do so over a period of at least twelve months from the date of approval of the financial statements (C.1.3);
- confirmation by the directors that they have carried out a robust assessment of the principal risks facing the company, including those that would threaten its business model, future performance, solvency or liquidity. The directors should describe the risks and explain how they are being managed or mitigated (C.2.1);
- a statement from the directors explaining how they have assessed the prospects of the company (taking account of the company's current position and principal risks), over what period they have done so and why they consider that period to be appropriate. The directors should state whether they have a reasonable expectation that the company will be able to continue in operation and meet its liabilities as they fall due over the period of their assessment, drawing attention to any qualifications or assumptions as necessary (C.2.2);
- a report on the board's review of the effectiveness of the company's risk management and internal controls systems (C.2.3);
- where there is no internal audit function, the reasons for the absence of such a function (C.3.6);
- where the board does not accept the audit committee's recommendation on the appointment, reappointment or removal of an external auditor, a statement from the audit committee explaining the recommendation and the reasons why the board has taken a different position (C.3.7);
- a separate section describing the work of the audit committee in discharging its responsibilities, including: the significant issues that it considered in relation to the financial statements, and how these issues were addressed; an explanation of how it has assessed the effectiveness of the external audit process and the approach taken to the appointment or reappointment of the external auditor, including the length of tenure of the current audit firm and when a tender was last conducted; and, if the external auditor provides non-audit services, an explanation of how auditor objectivity and independence is safeguarded (C.3.8);

- a description of the work of the remuneration committee as required under the Large and Medium-Sized Companies and Groups (Accounts and Reports) Regulations 2013, including, where an executive director serves as a non- executive director elsewhere, whether or not the director will retain such earnings and, if so, what the remuneration is (D.1.2);
- where remuneration consultants are appointed they should be identified and a statement made as to whether they have any other connection with the company (D.2.1); and
- the steps the board has taken to ensure that members of the board, and in particular the non-executive directors, develop an understanding of the views of major shareholders about their company (E.1.2).

The following information should be made available (which may be met by placing the information on a website that is maintained by or on behalf of the company):

- the terms of reference of the nomination, audit and remuneration committees, explaining their role and the authority delegated to them by the board (B.2.1, C.3.3 and D.2.1); and
- the terms and conditions of appointment of non-executive directors (B.3.2) (see footnote 9).

The board should set out to shareholders in the papers accompanying a resolution to elect or re-elect directors:

- sufficient biographical details to enable shareholders to take an informed decision on their election or re-election (B.7.1);
- why they believe an individual should be elected to a non-executive role (B.7.2); and
- on re-election of a non-executive director, confirmation from the chair that, following formal performance evaluation, the individual's performance continues to be effective and to demonstrate commitment to the role (B.7.2).

The board should set out to shareholders in the papers recommending appointment or reappointment of an external auditor:

- if the board does not accept the audit committee's recommendation, a statement from the audit committee explaining the recommendation and from the board setting out reasons why they have taken a different position (C.3.7).

Additional guidance

The FRC publishes guidance on the strategic report, risk management, internal control, business and financial reporting and audit committees, which relate to Section C of the Code. These guidance notes are available on the FRC website.

Notes:

1 References to shareholders in this section also apply to intermediaries and agents employed to assist shareholders in scrutinising governance arrangements.
2 For directors of UK incorporated companies, these duties are set out in the Sections 170 to 177 of the Companies Act 2006.

3   Provisions A.1.1 and A.1.2 overlap with FCA Rule DTR 7.2.7 R; Provision A.1.2 also overlaps with DTR 7.1.5 R (see Schedule B).

4   Compliance or otherwise with this provision need only be reported for the year in which the appointment is made.

5   A.3.1 states that the chair should, on appointment, meet the independence criteria set out in this provision, but thereafter the test of independence is not appropriate in relation to the chair.

6   A smaller company is one that is below the FTSE 350 throughout the year immediately prior to the reporting year.

7   The requirement to make the information available would be met by including the information on a website that is maintained by or on behalf of the company.

8   This provision overlaps with FCA Rule DTR 7.2.7 R (see Schedule B).

9   The terms and conditions of appointment of non-executive directors should be made available for inspection by any person at the company's registered office during normal business hours and at the AGM (for 15 minutes prior to the meeting and during the meeting).

10   This requirement may be met by the disclosures about the audit scope and responsibilities of the auditor included, or referred to, in the auditor's report pursuant to the requirements of ISA (UK and Ireland) 700, "The Independent Auditor's Report on Financial Statements". Copies are available from the FRC website.

11   Section 414C(8) (a) and (b) of the Companies Act 2006 requires a description of a company's business model and strategy as part of the Strategic Report that forms part of the annual report. Guidance as to the matters that should be considered in an explanation of the business model and strategy is provided in the FRC's "Guidance on the Strategic Report". Copies are available from the FRC website.

12   Additional information relating to C.1.3 and C.2 can be found in "Guidance on Risk Management, Internal Control and Related Financial and Business Reporting". Copies are available from the FRC website.

13   In addition FCA Rule DTR 7.2.5 R requires companies to describe the main features of the internal control and risk management systems in relation to the financial reporting process.

14   "Guidance on Audit Committees" suggests means of applying this part of the Code. Copies are available from the FRC website.

15   See footnote 6.

16   This provision overlaps with FCA Rule DTR 7.1.1 R (see Schedule B).

17   This provision overlaps with FCA Rule DTR 7.1.3 R (see Schedule B).

18   See footnote 7.

19   This provision overlaps with FSA Rules DTR 7.1.5 R and 7.2.7 R (see Schedule B).

20   As required for UK incorporated companies under the Large and Medium-Sized Companies and Groups (Accounts and Reports) Regulations 2013.

21   See footnote 6.

22   This provision overlaps with FCA Rule DTR 7.2.7 R (see Schedule B).

23   Listing Rules LR 9.4. Copies are available from the FCA website.

24   Nothing in these principles or provisions should be taken to override the general requirements of law to treat shareholders equally in access to information.

Appendix 2

The King Code of Governance Principles (KING III)

September 2009

1. Ethical leadership and corporate citizenship

Responsible leadership

1.1. The board should provide effective leadership based on an ethical foundation
Ethical leaders should:

1.1.1. direct the strategy and operations to build a sustainable business;

1.1.2. consider the short- and long-term impacts of the strategy on the economy, society and the environment;

1.1.3. do business ethically;

1.1.4. do not compromise the natural environment; and

1.1.5. take account of the company's impact on internal and external stakeholders.

The board's responsibilities

The board should:

1.1.6. be responsible for the strategic direction of the company and for the control of the company;

1.1.7. set the values to which the company will adhere formulated in its code of conduct;

1.1.8. ensure that its conduct and that of management aligns to the values and is adhered to in all aspects of its business; and

1.1.9. promote the stakeholder-inclusive approach of governance.

Ethical foundation

The board should:

1.1.10. ensure that all deliberations, decisions and actions are based on the four values underpinning good governance; and

1.1.11. ensure that each director adheres to the duties of a director.

1.2. The board should ensure that the company is and is seen to be a responsible corporate citizen

The board should:

    1.2.1. consider not only on financial performance but also the impact of the company's operations on society and the environment;

    1.2.2. protect, enhance and invest in the wellbeing of the economy, society and the environment;

    1.2.3. ensure that the company's performance and interaction with its stakeholders is guided by the Constitution and the Bill of Rights;

    1.2.4. ensure that collaborative efforts with stakeholders are embarked upon to promote ethical conduct and good corporate citizenship;

    1.2.5. ensure that measurable corporate citizenship programmes are implemented; and

    1.2.6. ensure that management develops corporate citizenship policies.

1.3. The board should ensure that the company's ethics are managed effectively

The board should ensure that:

    1.3.1. it builds and sustains an ethical corporate culture in the company;

    1.3.2. it determines the ethical standards which should be clearly articulated and ensures that the company takes measures to achieve adherence to them in all aspects of the business;

    1.3.3. adherence to ethical standards is measured;

    1.3.4. internal and external ethics performance is aligned around the same ethical standards;

    1.3.5. ethical risks and opportunities are incorporated in the risk management process;

    1.3.6. a code of conduct and ethics-related policies are implemented;

    1.3.7. compliance with the code of conduct is integrated in the operations of the company; and

    1.3.8. the company's ethics performance should be assessed, monitored, reported and disclosed.

2. Boards and directors

Role and function of the board

2.1. The board should act as the focal point for and custodian of corporate governance

The board should:

    2.1.1. have a charter setting out its responsibilities;

    2.1.2. meet at least four times per year;

    2.1.3. monitor the relationship between management and the stakeholders of the company; and

    2.1.4. ensure that the company survives and thrives.

2.2. The board should appreciate that strategy, risk, performance and sustainability are inseparable.

The board should:

    2.2.1. inform and approve the strategy;

    2.2.2. ensure that the strategy is aligned with the purpose of the company, the value drivers of its business and the legitimate interests and expectations of its stakeholders;

2.2.3.   satisfy itself that the strategy and business plans are not encumbered by risks that have not been thoroughly examined by management; and

2.2.4.   ensure that the strategy will result in sustainable outcomes taking account of people, planet and profit.

2.3.   The board should provide effective leadership based on an ethical foundation
Refer to principle 1.1

2.4.   The board should ensure that the company is and is seen to be a responsible corporate citizen
Refer to principle 1.2

2.5.   The board should ensure that the company's ethics are managed effectively
Refer to principle 1.3

2.6.   The board should ensure that the company has an effective and independent audit committee
Refer to chapter 3

2.7.   The board should be responsible for the governance of risk
Refer to chapter 4

2.8.   The board should be responsible for information technology (IT) governance
Refer to chapter 5

2.9.   The board should ensure that the company complies with applicable laws and considers adherence to non-binding rules, codes and standards
Refer to chapter 6

2.10.   The board should ensure that there is an effective risk-based internal audit
Refer to chapter 7

2.11.   The board should appreciate that stakeholders' perceptions affect the company's reputation
Refer to chapter 8

2.12.   The board should ensure the integrity of the company's integrated report
Refer to chapter 9

2.13.   The board should report on the effectiveness of the company's system of internal controls
Refer to chapters 7 and 9

2.14.   The board and its directors should act in the best interests of the company

       2.14.1. The board must act in the best interests of the company.

       2.14.2. Directors must adhere to the legal standards of conduct.

       2.14.3. Directors or the board should be permitted to take independent advice in connection with their duties following an agreed procedure.

       2.14.4. Real or perceived conflicts should be disclosed to the board and managed.

       2.14.5. Listed companies should have a policy regarding dealing in securities by directors, officers and selected employees.

2.15.   The board should consider business rescue proceedings or other turnaround mechanisms as soon as the company is financially distressed as defined in the Act The board should ensure that:

       2.15.1. the solvency and liquidity of the company is continuously monitored;

       2.15.2. its consideration is fair to save a financially distressed company either by way of workouts, sale, merger, amalgamation, compromise with creditors or business rescue;

2.15.3. a suitable practitioner is appointed if business rescue is adopted; and

2.15.4. the practitioner furnishes security for the value of the assets of the company.

2.16. The board should elect a chair of the board who is an independent non-executive director. The CEO of the company should not also fulfil the role of chair of the board

2.16.1. The members of the board should elect a chair on an annual basis.

2.16.2. The chair should be independent and free of conflict upon appointment.

2.16.3. A lead independent director should be appointed in the case where an executive chair is appointed or where the chair is not independent or conflicted.

2.16.4. The appointment of a chair, who is not independent, should be justified in the integrated report.

2.16.5. The role of the chair should be formalised.

2.16.6. The chair's ability to add value, and his performance against what is expected of his role and function, should be assessed every year.

2.16.7. The CEO should not become the chair until three years have lapsed.

2.16.8. The chair together with the board, should consider the number of outside chairs held.

2.16.9. The board should ensure a succession plan for the role of the chair.

2.17. The board should appoint the chief executive officer and establish a framework for the delegation of authority

The board should:

2.17.1. appoint the CEO;

2.17.2. provide input regarding senior management appointments;

2.17.3. define its own level of materiality and approve a delegation of authority framework;

2.17.4. ensure that the role and function of the CEO is formalised and the performance of the CEO is evaluated against the criteria specified; and

2.17.5. ensure succession planning for the CEO and other senior executives and officers is in place.

Composition of the board

2.18. The board should comprise a balance of power, with a majority of non-executive directors. The majority of non-executive directors should be independent

2.18.1. The majority of board members should be non-executive directors.

2.18.2. The majority of the non-executive directors should be independent.

2.18.3. When determining the number of directors serving on the board, the knowledge, skills and resources required for conducting the business of the board should be considered.

2.18.4. Every board should consider whether its size, diversity and demographics make it effective.

2.18.5. Every board should have a minimum of two executive directors of which one should be the CEO and the other the director responsible for finance.

2.18.6. At least one third of the non-executive directors should rotate every year.

2.18.7. The board, through its nomination committee, should recommend the eligibility of prospective directors.

2.18.8. Any independent non-executive directors serving more than nine years should be subjected to a rigorous review of his independence and performance by the board.

2.18.9. The board should include a statement in the integrated report regarding the assessment of the independence of the independent non-executive directors.

2.18.10. The board should be permitted to remove any director without shareholder approval.

Board appointment process

2.19. Directors should be appointed through a formal process

2.19.1. A nomination committee should assist with the process of identifying suitable members of the board.

2.19.2. Background and reference checks should be performed before the nomination and appointment of directors.

2.19.3. The appointment of non-executive directors should be formalised through a letter of appointment.

2.19.4. The board should make full disclosure regarding individual directors to enable shareholders to make their own assessment of directors.

Director development

2.20. The induction of and ongoing training and development of directors should be conducted through formal processes

The board should ensure that:

2.20.1. a formal induction programme is established for new directors;

2.20.2. inexperienced directors are developed through mentorship programmes;

2.20.3. continuing professional development programmes are implemented; and

2.20.4. directors receive regular briefings on changes in risks, laws and the environment.

Company secretary

2.21. The board should be assisted by a competent, suitably qualified and experienced company secretary

2.21.1. The board should appoint and remove the company secretary.

2.21.2. The board should empower the individual to enable him to properly fulfil his duties. The company secretary should:

2.21.3. have an arm's-length relationship with the board;

2.21.4. not be a director of the company;

2.21.5. assist the nominations committee with the appointment of directors;

2.21.6. assist with the director induction and training programmes;

2.21.7. provide guidance to the board on the duties of the directors and good governance;

2.21.8. ensure board and committee charters are kept up to date;

2.21.9. prepare and circulate board papers;

2.21.10. elicit responses, input, feedback for board and board committee meetings;

2.21.11. assist in drafting yearly work plans;

2.21.12. ensure preparation and circulation of minutes of board and committee meetings; and

2.21.13. assist with the evaluation of the board, committees and individual directors.

Performance assessment

2.22 The evaluation of the board, its committees and the individual directors should be performed every year

2.22.1. The board should determine its own role, functions, duties and performance criteria as well as that for directors on the board and board committees to serve as a benchmark for the performance appraisal.

2.22.2. Yearly evaluations should be performed by the chair or an independent provider.

2.22.3. The results of performance evaluations should identify training needs for directors.

2.22.4. An overview of the appraisal process, results and action plans should be disclosed in the integrated report.

2.22.5. The nomination for the re-appointment of a director should only occur after the evaluation of the performance and attendance of the director.

Board committees

2.23. The board should delegate certain functions to well-structured committees but without abdicating its own responsibilities

2.23.1. Formal terms of reference should be established and approved for each committee of the board.

2.23.2. The committees' terms of reference should be reviewed yearly.

2.23.3. The committees should be appropriately constituted and the composition and the terms of reference should be disclosed in the integrated report.

2.23.4. Public and state-owned companies must appoint an audit committee.

2.23.5. All other companies should establish an audit committee and define its composition, purpose and duties in the memorandum of incorporation.

2.23.6. Companies should establish risk, nomination and remuneration committees.

2.23.7. Committees, other than the risk committee, should comprise a majority of nonexecutive directors of which the majority should be independent.

2.23.8. External advisers and executive directors should attend committee meetings by invitation.

2.23.9. Committees should be free to take independent outside professional advice at the cost of the company subject to an approved process being followed.

Group boards

2.24. A governance framework should be agreed between the group and its subsidiary boards

2.24.1. Listed subsidiaries must comply with the rules of the relevant stock exchange in respect of insider trading.

2.24.2. The holding company must respect the fiduciary duties of the director serving in a representative capacity on the board of the subsidiary.

2.24.3. The implementation and adoption of policies, processes or procedures of the holding company should be considered and approved by the subsidiary company.

2.24.4. Disclosure should be made on the adoption of the holding company's policies in the integrated report of the subsidiary company.

Remuneration of directors and senior executives

2.25. Companies should remunerate directors and executives fairly and responsibly

2.25.1. Companies should adopt remuneration policies aligned with the strategy of the company and linked to individual performance.

2.25.2. The remuneration committee should assist the board in setting and administering remuneration policies.

2.25.3. The remuneration policy should address base pay and bonuses, employee contracts, severance and retirement benefits and share-based and other long-term incentive schemes.

2.25.4. Non-executive fees should comprise a base fee as well as an attendance fee per meeting.

2.26. Companies should disclose the remuneration of each individual director and certain senior executives

The remuneration report, included in the integrated report, should include:

2.26.1. all benefits paid to directors;

2.26.2. the salaries of the three most highly-paid employees who are not directors;

2.26.3. the policy on base pay;

2.26.4. participation in share incentive schemes;

2.26.5. the use of benchmarks;

2.26.6. incentive schemes to encourage retention;

2.26.7. justification of salaries above the median;

2.26.8. material payments that are ex-gratia in nature;

2.26.9. policies regarding executive employment; and

2.26.10. the maximum expected potential dilution as a result of incentive awards.

2.27. Shareholders should approve the company's remuneration policy

2.27.1. Shareholders should pass a non-binding advisory vote on the company's yearly remuneration policy.

2.27.2. The board should determine the remuneration of executive directors in accordance with the remuneration policy put to shareholder's vote.

3. Audit Committes

3.1. The board should ensure that the company has an effective and independent audit committee

3.1.1. Listed and state-owned companies must establish an audit committee.

3.1.2. All other companies should establish an audit committee and define its composition, purpose and duties in the memorandum of incorporation.

3.1.3. The board should approve the terms of reference of the audit committee.

3.1.4. The audit committee should meet as often as is necessary to fulfil its functions but at least twice a year.

    3.1.5. The audit committee should meet with internal and external auditors at least once a year without management being present.

Membership and resources of the audit committee

3.2. Audit committee members should be suitably skilled and experienced independent non-executive directors

    3.2.1. All members of the audit committee should be independent non-executive directors.

    3.2.2. The audit committee should consist of at least three members.

    3.2.3. The chair of the board should not be the chair or member of the audit committee.

    3.2.4. The committee collectively should have sufficient qualifications and experience to fulfil its duties.

    3.2.5. The audit committee members should keep up-to-date with developments affecting the required skill-set.

    3.2.6. The committee should be permitted to consult with specialists or consultants subject to a board-approved process.

    3.2.7. The board must fill any vacancies on the audit committee.

3.3. The audit committee should be chaired by an independent non-executive director

    3.3.1. The board should elect the chair of the audit committee.

    3.3.2. The chair of the audit committee should participate in setting and agreeing the agenda of the committee.

    3.3.3. The chair of the audit committee should be present at the AGM.

Responsibilities of the audit committee

3.4. The audit committee should oversee integrated reporting

    3.4.1. The audit committee should have regard to all factors and risks that may impact on the integrity of the integrated report.

    3.4.2. The audit committee should review and comment on the financial statements included in the integrated report.

    3.4.3. The audit committee should review the disclosure of sustainability issues in the integrated report to ensure that it is reliable and does not conflict with the financial information.

    3.4.4. The audit committee should recommend to the board to engage an external assurance provider on material sustainability issues.

    3.4.5. The audit committee should consider the need to issue interim results.

    3.4.6. The audit committee should review the content of the summarised information.

    3.4.7. The audit committee should engage the external auditors to provide assurance on the summarised financial information.

3.5. The audit committee should ensure that a combined assurance model is applied to provide a coordinated approach to all assurance activities

3.5.1. The audit committee should ensure that the combined assurance is received is appropriate to address all the significant risks facing the company.

3.5.2. The relationship between the external assurance providers and the company should be monitored by the audit committee.

Internal assurance providers

3.6. The audit committee should satisfy itself of the expertise, resources and experience of the company's finance function

3.6.1. Every year a review of the finance function should be performed by the audit committee.

3.6.2. The results of the review should be disclosed in the integrated report.

3.7. The audit committee should be responsible for overseeing of internal audit

3.7.1. The audit committee should be responsible for the appointment, performance assessment and/or dismissal of the CAE.

3.7.2. The audit committee should approve the internal audit plan.

3.7.3. The audit committee should ensure that the internal audit function is subject to an independent quality review as and when the committee determines it appropriate.

3.8. The audit committee should be an integral component of the risk management process

3.8.1. The charter of the audit committee should set out its responsibilities regarding risk management.

3.8.2. The audit committee should specifically have oversight of:

3.8.2.1. financial reporting risks;

3.8.2.2. internal financial controls;

3.8.2.3. fraud risks as it relates to financial reporting; and

3.8.2.4. IT risks as it relates to financial reporting.

External assurance providers

3.9. The audit committee is responsible for recommending the appointment of the external auditor and overseeing the external audit process

The audit committee:

3.9.1. must nominate the external auditor for appointment;

3.9.2. must approve the terms of engagement and remuneration for the external audit engagement;

3.9.3. must monitor and report on the independence of the external auditor;

3.9.4. must define a policy for non-audit services provided by the external auditor and must approve the contracts for non-audit services;

3.9.5. should be informed of any Reportable Irregularities identified and reported by the external auditor; and

3.9.6. should review the quality and effectiveness of the external audit process.

Reporting

3.10. The audit committee should report to the board and shareholders on how it has discharged its duties

3.10.1.   The audit committee should report internally to the board on its statutory duties and duties assigned to it by the board.

3.10.2.   The audit committee must report to the shareholders on its statutory duties:

    3.10.2.1.   how its duties were carried out;

    3.10.2.2.   if the committee is satisfied with the independence of the external auditor;

    3.10.2.3.   the committee's view on the financial statements and the accounting practices; and

    3.10.2.4.   whether the internal financial controls are effective.

3.10.3.   The audit committee should provide a summary of its role and details of its composition, number of meetings and activities, in the integrated report.

3.10.4.   The audit committee should recommend the integrated report for approval by the board.

4. The Governance of risk

The board's responsibility for risk governance

4.1.   The board should be responsible for the governance of risk

    4.1.1.   A policy and plan for a system and process of risk management should be developed.

    4.1.2.   The board should comment in the integrated report on the effectiveness of the system and process of risk management.

    4.1.3.   The board's responsibility for risk governance should be expressed in the board charter.

    4.1.4.   The induction and ongoing training programmes of the board should incorporate risk governance.

    4.1.5.   The board's responsibility for risk governance should manifest in a documented risk management policy and plan.

    4.1.6.   The board should approve the risk management policy and plan.

    4.1.7.   The risk management policy should be widely distributed throughout the company.

    4.1.8.   The board should review the implementation of the risk management plan at least once a year.

    4.1.9.   The board should ensure that the implementation of the risk management plan is monitored continually.

4.2.   The board should determine the levels of risk tolerance

    4.2.1.   The board should set the levels of risk tolerance once a year.

    4.2.2.   The board may set limits for the risk appetite.

    4.2.3.   The board should monitor that risks taken are within the tolerance and appetite levels.

4.3.   The risk committee or audit committee should assist the board in carrying out its risk responsibilities

    4.3.1.   The board should appoint a committee responsible for risk.

4.3.2. The risk committee should:

    4.3.2.1. consider the risk management policy and plan and monitor the risk management process;

    4.3.2.2. have as its members executive and non-executive directors, members of senior management and independent risk management experts to be invited, if necessary;

    4.3.2.3. have a minimum of three members; and

    4.3.2.4. convene at least twice per year.

4.3.3. The performance of the committee should be evaluated once a year by the board.

Management's responsibility for risk management

4.4. The board should delegate to management the responsibility to design, implement and monitor the risk management plan

    4.4.1. The board's risk strategy should be executed by management by means of risk management systems and processes.

    4.4.2. Management is accountable for integrating risk in the day-to-day activities of the company.

    4.4.3. The CRO should be a suitably experienced person who should have access and interact regularly on strategic matters with the board and/or appropriate board committee and executive management.

Risk assessment

4.5. The board should ensure that risk assessments are performed on a continual basis

    4.5.1. The board should ensure effective and ongoing risk assessments are performed.

    4.5.2. A systematic, documented, formal risk assessment should be conducted at least once a year.

    4.5.3. Risks should be prioritised and ranked to focus responses and interventions.

    4.5.4. The risk assessment process should involve the risks affecting the various income streams of the company, the critical dependencies of the business, the sustainability and the legitimate interests and expectations of stakeholders.

    4.5.5. Risk assessments should adopt a top-down approach.

    4.5.6. The board should regularly receive and review a register of the company's key risks.

    4.5.7. The board should ensure that key risks are quantified where practicable.

4.6. The board should ensure that frameworks and methodologies are implemented to increase the probability of anticipating unpredictable risks

    4.6.1. The board should ensure that a framework and processes are in place to anticipate unpredictable risks.

Risk response

4.7. The board should ensure that management considers and implements appropriate risk responses

      4.7.1.   Management should identify and note in the risk register the risk responses decided upon.

      4.7.2.   Management should demonstrate to the board that the risk response provides for the identification and exploitation of opportunities to improve the performance of the company.

Risk monitoring

4.8.   The board should ensure continual risk monitoring by management

      4.8.1.   The board should ensure that effective and continual monitoring of risk management takes place.

      4.8.2.   The responsibility for monitoring should be defined in the risk management plan.

Risk assurance

4.9.   The board should receive assurance regarding the effectiveness of the risk management process

      4.9.1.   Management should provide assurance to the board that the risk management plan is integrated in the daily activities of the company.

      4.9.2.   Internal audit should provide a written assessment of the effectiveness of the system of internal controls and risk management to the board.

Risk disclosure

4.10. The board should ensure that there are processes in place enabling complete, timely, relevant, accurate and accessible risk disclosure to stakeholders

      4.10.1. Undue, unexpected or unusual risks should be disclosed in the integrated report.

      4.10.2. The board should disclose its view on the effectiveness of the risk management process in the integrated report.

5. The governance of information technology

5.1.   The board should be responsible for information technology (IT) governance

      5.1.1.   The board should assume the responsibility for the governance of IT and place it on the board agenda.

      5.1.2.   The board should ensure that an IT charter and policies are established and implemented.

      5.1.3.   The board should ensure promotion of an ethical IT governance culture and awareness and of a common IT language.

      5.1.4.   The board should ensure that an IT internal control framework is adopted and implemented.

      5.1.5.   The board should receive independent assurance on the effectiveness of the IT internal controls.

5.2.   IT should be aligned with the performance and sustainability objectives of the company

5.2.1. The board should ensure that the IT strategy is integrated with the company's strategic and business processes.

5.2.2. The board should ensure that there is a process in place to identity and exploit opportunities to improve the performance and sustainability of the company through the use of IT.

5.3. The board should delegate to management the responsibility for the implementation of an IT governance framework

5.3.1. Management should be responsible for the implementation of the structures, processes and mechanisms for the IT governance framework.

5.3.2. The board may appoint an IT steering committee of similar function to assist with its governance of IT.

5.3.3. The CEO should appoint a Chief Information Officer responsible for the management of IT.

5.3.4. The CIO should be a suitably qualified and experienced person who should have access and interact regularly on strategic IT matters with the board and/or appropriate board committee and executive management.

5.4. The board should monitor and evaluate significant IT investments and expenditure

5.4.1. The board should oversee the value delivery of IT and monitor the return on investment from significant IT projects.

5.4.2. The board should ensure that intellectual property contained in information systems are protected.

5.4.3. The board should obtain independent assurance on the IT governance and controls supporting outsourced IT services.

5.5. IT should form an integral part of the company's risk management

5.5.1. Management should regularly demonstrate to the board that the company has adequate business resilience arrangements in place for disaster recovery.

5.5.2. The board should ensure that the company complies with IT laws and that IT related rules, codes and standards are considered.

5.6. The board should ensure that information assets are managed effectively

5.6.1. The board should ensure that there are systems in place for the management of information which should include information security, information management and information privacy.

5.6.2. The board should ensure that all personal information is treated by the company as an important business asset and is identified.

5.6.3. The board should ensure that an Information Security Management System is developed and implemented.

5.6.4. The board should approve the information security strategy and delegate and empower management to implement the strategy.

5.7. A risk committee and audit committee should assist the board in carrying out its IT responsibilities

5.7.1. The risk committee should ensure that IT risks are adequately addressed.

5.7.2. The risk committee should obtain appropriate assurance that controls are in place and effective in addressing IT risks.

5.7.3. The audit committee should consider IT as it relates to financial reporting and the going concern of the company.

> 5.7.4. The audit committee should consider the use of technology to improve audit coverage and efficiency.

6. Compliance withs laws rules codes and standards

6.1. The board should ensure that the company complies with applicable laws and considers adherence to nonbinding rules, codes and standards
> 6.1.1. Companies must comply with all applicable laws.
> 6.1.2. Exceptions permitted in law, shortcomings and proposed changes expected should be handled ethically.
> 6.1.3. Compliance should be an ethical imperative.
> 6.1.4. Compliance with applicable laws should be understood not only in terms of the obligations that they create, but also for the rights and protection that they afford.
> 6.1.5. The board should understand the context of the law, and how other applicable laws interact with it.
> 6.1.6. The board should monitor the company's compliance with applicable laws, rules, codes and standards.
> 6.1.7. Compliance should be a regular item on the agenda of the board.
> 6.1.8. The board should disclose details in the integrated report on how it discharged its responsibility to establish an effective compliance framework and processes.

6.2. The board and each individual director should have a working understanding of the effect of the applicable laws, rules, codes and standards on the company and its business
> 6.2.1. The induction and ongoing training programmes of directors should incorporate an overview of and any changes to applicable laws, rules, codes and standards.
> 6.2.2. Directors should sufficiently familiarise themselves with the general content of applicable laws, rules, codes and standards to discharge their legal duties.

6.3. Compliance risk should form an integral part of the company's risk management process
> 6.3.1. The risk of non-compliance should be identified, assessed and responded to through the risk management processes.
> 6.3.2. Companies should consider establishing a compliance function.

6.4. The board should delegate to management the implementation of an effective compliance framework and processes
> 6.4.1. The board should ensure that a legal compliance policy, approved by the board, has been implemented by management.
> 6.4.2. The board should receive assurance on the effectiveness of the controls around compliance with laws, rules, codes and standards.
> 6.4.3. Compliance with laws, rules, codes and standards should be incorporated in the code of conduct of the company.
> 6.4.4. Management should establish the appropriate structures, educate and train, and communicate and measure key performance indicators relevant to compliance.

6.4.5. The integrated report should include details of material or often repeated instances of non-compliance by either the company or its directors in their capacity as such.

6.4.6. An independent, suitably skilled compliance officer may be appointed.

6.4.7. The compliance officer should be a suitably skilled and experienced person who should have access and interact regularly on strategic compliance matters with the board and/or appropriate board committee and executive management.

6.4.8. The structuring of the compliance function, its role and its position in terms of reporting lines should be a reflection of the company's decision on how compliance is to be integrated with its ethics and risk management.

6.4.9. The compliance function should have adequate resources to fulfil its function.

7. Internal audit

The need for and role of internal audit

7.1. The board should ensure that there is an effective risk based internal audit

    7.1.1. Companies should establish an internal audit function.

    7.1.2. Internal audit should perform the following functions:

        7.1.2.1. evaluate the company's governance processes;

        7.1.2.2. perform an objective assessment of the effectiveness of risk management and the internal control framework;

        7.1.2.3. systematically analyse and evaluating business processes and associated controls; and

        7.1.2.4. provide a source of information as appropriate, regarding instances of fraud, corruption, unethical behaviour and irregularities.

    7.1.3. An internal audit charter should be defined and approved by the board.

    7.1.4. The internal audit function should adhere to the IIA Standards and code of ethics.

Internal audit's approach and plan

7.2. Internal audit should follow a risk-based approach to its plan

    7.2.1. The internal audit plan and approach should be informed by the strategy and risks of the company.

    7.2.2. Internal audit should be independent from management.

    7.2.3. Internal audit should be an objective provider of assurance that considers:

        7.2.3.1. the risks that may prevent or slow down the realisation of strategic goals;

        7.2.3.2. whether controls are in place and functioning effectively to mitigate these; and

        7.2.3.3. the opportunities that will promote the realisation of strategic goals that are identified, assessed and effectively managed by the company's management team.

7.3.   Internal audit should provide a written assessment of the effectiveness of the company's system of internal controls and risk management

7.3.1.   Internal audit should form an integral part of the combined assurance model as internal assurance provider.

7.3.2.   Internal controls should be established not only over financial matters, but also operational, compliance and sustainability issues.

7.3.3.   Companies should maintain an effective governance, risk management and internal control framework.

7.3.4.   Management should specify the elements of the control framework.

7.3.5.   Internal audit should provide a written assessment of the system of internal controls and risk management to the board.

7.3.6.   Internal audit should provide a written assessment of internal financial controls to the audit committee.

7.4.   The audit committee should be responsible for overseeing internal audit

7.4.1.   The internal audit plan should be agreed and approved by the audit committee.

7.4.2.   The audit committee should evaluate the performance of the internal audit function.

7.4.3.   The audit committee should ensure that the internal audit function is subjected to an independent quality review.

7.4.4.   The CAE should report functionally to the audit committee chair.

7.4.5.   The audit committee should be responsible for the appointment, performance assessment and dismissal of the CAE.

7.4.6.   The audit committee should ensure that the internal audit function is appropriately resourced and has appropriate budget allocated to the function.

7.4.7.   Internal audit should report at all audit committee meetings.

Internal audit's status in the company

7.5.   Internal audit should be strategically positioned to achieve its objectives

7.5.1.   The internal audit function should be independent and objective.

7.5.2.   The internal audit function should report functionally to the audit committee.

7.5.3.   The CAE should have a standing invitation to attend executive committee meetings.

7.5.4.   The internal audit function should be skilled and resourced as is appropriate for the complexity and volume of risk and assurance needs.

7.5.5.   The CAE should develop and maintain a quality assurance and improvement programme.

8. Governing stakeholder relationships

Code of governance principles

8.1.   The board should appreciate that stakeholders' perceptions affect a company's reputation

8.1.1. The gap between stakeholder perceptions and the performance of the company should be managed and measured to enhance or protect the company's reputation.

8.1.2. The company's reputation and its linkage with stakeholder relationships should be a regular board agenda item.

8.1.3. The board should identify important stakeholder groupings.

8.2. The board should delegate to management to proactively deal with stakeholder relationships

8.2.1. Management should develop a strategy and formulate policies for the management of relationships with each stakeholder grouping.

8.2.2. The board should consider whether it is appropriate to publish its stakeholder policies.

8.2.3. The board should oversee the establishment of mechanisms and processes that support stakeholders in constructive engagement with the company.

8.2.4. The board should encourage shareholders to attend AGMs.

8.2.5. The board should consider not only formal, but also informal, processes for interaction with the company's stakeholders.

8.2.6. The board should disclose in its integrated report the nature of the company's dealings with stakeholders and the outcomes of these dealings.

8.3. The board should strive to achieve the appropriate balance between its various stakeholder groupings, in the best interests of the company

8.3.1. The board should take account of the legitimate interests and expectations of its stakeholders in its decision-making in the best interests of the company.

8.4. Companies should ensure the equitable treatment of shareholders

8.4.1. There must be equitable treatment of all holders of the same class of shares issued.

8.4.2. The board should ensure that minority shareholders are protected.

8.5. Transparent and effective communication with stakeholders is essential for building and maintaining their trust and confidence

8.5.1. Complete, timely, relevant, accurate, honest and accessible information should be provided by the company to its stakeholders though having regard to legal and strategic considerations.

8.5.2. Communication with stakeholders should be in clear and understandable language.

8.5.3. The board should adopt communication guidelines that support a responsible communication programme.

8.5.4. The board should consider disclosing in the integrated report the number and reasons for refusals of requests of information that were lodged with the company in terms of the Promotion of Access to Information Act, 2000.

Dispute resolution

8.6. The board should ensure that disputes are resolved as effectively, efficiently and expeditiously as possible

8.6.1. The board should adopt formal dispute resolution processes for internal and external disputes.

8.6.2. The board should select the appropriate individuals to represent the company in ADR.

9. Integrated reporting and disclosure

Transparency and accountability

9.1. The board should ensure the integrity of the company's integrated report

9.1.1. A company should have controls to enable it to verify and safeguard the integrity of its integrated report.

9.1.2. The board should delegate to the audit committee to evaluate sustainability disclosures.

9.2. Sustainability reporting and disclosure should be integrated with the company's financial reporting

9.2.1. The board should include commentary on the company's financial results.

9.2.2. The board must disclose if the company is a going concern.

9.2.3. The integrated report should describe how the company has made its money.

9.2.4. The board should ensure that the positive and negative impacts of the company's operations and plans to improve the positives and eradicate or ameliorate the negatives in the financial year ahead are conveyed in the integrated report.

9.3. Sustainability reporting and disclosure should be independently assured

9.3.1. General oversight and reporting of sustainability should be delegated by the board to the audit committee.

9.3.2. The audit committee should assist the board by reviewing the integrated report to ensure that the information contained in it is reliable and that it does not contradict the financial aspects of the report.

9.3.3. The audit committee should over see the provision of assurance over sustainability issues

Appendix 3

The NHS Foundation Trust Code of Governance

Updated July 2014

Foreword

One of Monitor's objectives is to make sure that public providers are well led. To this end, the *NHS Foundation Trust Code of Governance* (the Code) is our way of providing guidance to NHS foundation trusts to help them deliver effective corporate governance, contribute to better organisational performance and ultimately discharge their duties in the best interests of patients.

We last updated the Code in 2010, and a great deal has changed since then. In addition to setting out new duties for Monitor, the 2012 Health and Social Care Act (the 2012 Act) established a range of new duties for governors and boards of NHS foundation trusts. As a result, we have also developed new regulatory tools – *the provider licence* and the *Risk Assessment Framework* – which have implications for how trusts establish and report on corporate governance arrangements. The UK Corporate Governance Code (formerly the Combined Code), on which the Code is based, has also been significantly updated a number of times since 2010.

As well as making changes to reflect the new regulatory and policy landscape, we also wanted to make sure that the updated Code was a useful, practical tool for trusts to use. We therefore asked for feedback from across the sector on a draft of the revised Code. The draft which we published in November 2013 included a number of significant changes including a new introduction, a new structure, greater clarity regarding disclosure requirements and a section which explains how the Code fits alongside Monitor's other governance tools.

We have received over 40 responses to our request for feedback and we are grateful to the sector for responding in short timescales in so much detail. We hope it is clear from the changes we have made to the final version of the Code that we have sought to take on as much of the feedback as was appropriate. In particular:

- **You told us that reporting on all of the principles was too burdensome**. We are therefore now only asking for a report on how the principles are applied in cases of non-compliance. This reflects the reporting requirements of the UK Corporate Governance Code.
- **You told us that including all of the information in a separate disclosure created duplication and unnecessary effort**. As a result, where information is already included in the annual report, you need only clearly reference the location of that information in the disclosure rather than duplicating the content.

- **You told us that the combination of statutory, mandatory and comply or explain requirements was confusing.** We have therefore clearly identified statutory provisions separately throughout the Code.

The feedback exercise also raised a number of questions which we have been unable or chosen not to address in the Code. These include:

- **Questions about the format, scope and resources required for the tri-annual governance reviews.** Monitor will be consulting separately on guidance for these reviews in January 2014.
- **Questions about the expectations on, and knowledge and capacity of, governors in undertaking their statutory duties.** We would strongly recommend referring to the detailed governance on these questions, which is available elsewhere. In particular *Your statutory duties: A reference guide for NHS foundation trust governors* and *Director-governor interaction in NHS foundation trusts: A best practice guide for boards of directors*.

There are two other changes that we would like to highlight since the draft was published:

- We stated in our consultation a desire to maintain the current requirement for three independent members of the audit committee. Feedback from the professional bodies that responded to the consultation (including the authors of the UK Corporate Governance Code on which the *NHS Foundation Trust Code of Governance* is based) suggested that this was not best practice. **We have therefore revised the Code to require all members of the audit committee to be independent. The option to 'explain' non-compliance is available for trusts that have valid reasons for failing to meet this standard.**
- We stated in the draft Code that it would apply from 1 April 2014. Feedback from the sector highlighted that because the 2010 edition of the Code does not reflect the 2012 Act or other regulatory developments including the licence it would be more practical to report against the revised Code. **We have therefore revised the Code to apply from 1 January 2014. This means that trusts should report on the revised code for 2013/14. The option to 'explain' non-compliance is available in the case of provisions that are new and cannot be applied retrospectively.**

It is our intention to continue to improve the Code to ensure that it reflects best practice in the private and public sectors, and remains a valuable tool for trusts to use in maintaining good corporate governance. We would therefore welcome any further feedback on the revised Code for us to consider in the future.

Stephen Hay
Managing Director, Provider Regulation

Introduction

1.1 Why is there a code of governance for NHS foundation trusts?

The principal purpose of NHS foundation trusts is to provide health care services in England. Together, they deliver care to a huge number of patients each year. To make sure the care that NHS foundation trusts provide is safe, effective, caring and responsive for patients, trust boards must be founded on and supported by a strong governance structure. Monitor, as sector regulator, seeks to protect patients and promote their interests, and ultimately good governance enables the kind of decision-making and processes that are essential to achieving these goals.

NHS foundation trusts are created as legal entities in the form of public benefit corporations by the National Health Service Act 2006 (the 2006 Act). This legislation provided NHS foundation trusts with a governance regime that is fundamentally different from NHS trusts and so requires its own guidance. The boards of directors of NHS foundation trusts have more autonomy to make financial and strategic decisions than NHS trusts; these are to be taken with the goal of maximising the benefit to patients. The Health and Social Care Act 2012 (the 2012 Act) provided further changes to the governance regime for NHS foundation trusts.

The board of directors is a unitary board. This means that within the board of directors, the non-executive directors and executive directors make decisions as a single group and share the same responsibility and liability. All directors, executive and non-executive, have responsibility to constructively challenge during board discussions and help develop proposals on priorities, risk mitigation, values, standards and strategy.

The board of directors also has a framework of local accountability through members and a council of governors, which replaced central control from the Secretary of State for Health. NHS foundation trust governors are responsible as a council for holding the non-executive directors, individually and collectively, responsible for the performance of this unitary board. In turn, NHS foundation trust governors are accountable to the members who elect or appoint them and must represent their interests and those of the public.

In this code of governance we bring together the best practices of the public and private sector in order to help NHS foundation trust boards maintain good quality corporate governance. We believe this is necessary if the needs of patients are to be met. In this document, we set out a common overarching framework for the corporate governance of NHS foundation trusts that complements the statutory and regulatory obligations they have (which are referenced throughout this document).

1.2 What is corporate governance?

An NHS foundation trust's board has a duty to promote the success of the organisation so as to maximise the benefits for the members of the trust as a whole and for the public who will be treated by the trust. Therefore, a board needs to be able to deliver prudent and effective leadership and effective oversight of the trust's operations to ensure it is operating in the best interests of patients.

Corporate governance is the means by which boards lead and direct their organisations so that decision-making is effective and the right outcomes are delivered. In the NHS this means delivering safe, effective services in a caring and compassionate environment in a way that is responsive to the changing needs of patients and service users. Robust governance structures that encourage proper engagement with stakeholders and strong local accountability will help NHS foundation trusts to maintain the trust and confidence of the people and communities that they service. Good corporate governance is dynamic. Governing bodies should be committed to improving governance on a continuing basis through a process of evaluation and review.

Good corporate governance is the means by which quality governance is overseen. Robust corporate and quality governance arrangements complement and reinforce one another. Individuals working in clinical teams providing NHS services are at the front line of ensuring quality of care to patients. However, it is the board of directors that takes final and definitive responsibility for improvements, successful delivery, and equally failures, in the quality of care. Effective governance therefore requires that boards pay as much attention to quality of care and quality governance as they do to the financial health of their organisation. More information on the role of boards in quality governance can be found in *Quality Governance in the NHS – a guide for provider boards* from the National Quality Board.

1.3 About the Code

The *NHS Foundation Trust Code of Governance* (the Code) was first published in 2006 and was revised in 2010. Following significant regulatory change as a result of the 2012 Act and taking account of developments in our regulatory toolkit since then, we have updated the Code. **This updated version will apply from 1 January 2014.**

As with the 2010 version of the Code, our approach has been to bring best practice from the private sector to the NHS foundation trust sector, with the ultimate goal of ensuring a strong governance structure is in place to enable high-quality patient care. The Code therefore builds on the significant update to the *UK Corporate Governance Code* which was issued in 2012.

1.4 Application of the Code

1.4.1 What do NHS foundation trusts need to do to fulfil the Code's requirements?

This Code is best practice advice. It is not our role to prescribe in detail what governance systems and processes should look like or set rigid rules; instead we seek to support good governance by offering sound guidance. We are keen that NHS foundation trusts should have the autonomy and flexibility to ensure their structures and processes work well for their individual organisations now and in the future, while making sure they meet our overall requirements which are dictated by patient interest.

There are a number of advantages to the "comply or explain" approach on which the Code is based. Its inherent flexibility means that it is possible for us to set more demanding standards than can be done through hard rules. Experience has shown that the vast majority of private companies are able to meet these standards, which can easily be translated to suit the NHS foundation trust model. In addition, requiring NHS foundation trusts to report to members and patients means that the decision on whether a trust's governance is adequate is taken by those in whose interest the board is required to act.

Comply or explain

The provisions of the Code, as best practice advice, do not represent mandatory guidance and accordingly non-compliance is not in itself a breach of NHS Foundation Trust Condition 4 of the NHS provider licence (also known as the Governance condition). However, trusts should note the relevant statutory requirements that we have highlighted within the Code.

Good governance is an important tool for ensuring the quality of care. Some trusts may decide that the provisions are disproportionate or less relevant in their case. Such trusts may still consider that it would be appropriate to adopt the approach in the Code, and it is recognised that departure from the specific provisions of the Code may be justified in particular circumstances. All NHS foundation trusts are encouraged to take account of the best practice provisions described in this Code.

Reasons for non-compliance with the Code should be explained. This "comply or explain" approach has been in successful operation for at least the last 15 years in the private sector and is not new to the NHS foundation trust sector. In providing an explanation for non-compliance, the NHS foundation trust should aim to illustrate how its actual practices are consistent with the principle to which the particular provision relates. It should set out the background, provide a clear rationale, and describe any mitigating actions it is taking to address any risks and maintain conformity with the relevant principle. Where deviation from a particular provision is intended to be limited in time, the explanation should indicate when the NHS foundation trust expects to conform to the provision.

Satisfactory engagement between the board of directors, the council of governors, members and patients is crucial to the effectiveness of NHS foundation trusts' corporate governance approach. Directors and governors both have a responsibility for ensuring that "comply or explain" remains an effective alternative to a rules-based system and a key aspect of this is ensuring improved interaction between directors, governors, members and – crucially – patients, communities and the public.

Behaviours

In this NHS Foundation Trust *Code of Governance*, we set out best practice principles and structures and processes (through the Code's provisions), but ultimately only directors and governors can demonstrate and promote the effective board *behaviour* that is needed to guarantee good corporate governance in practice. The achievement of good governance requires continuing and determined effort and boards have opportunities within the framework of the Code to decide themselves how they should act. It is therefore incumbent on boards to think deeply, thoroughly and on an ongoing basis about their overall tasks and the implications of this for the roles of their individual members.

NHS foundation trust governors should also be mindful of the principles of the Code and the disclosures that the board is making as part of their role in holding the non-executives to account.

Disclosure requirements

To meet the requirements of "comply or explain" each trust must comply with each of the provisions of the code (which in some cases will require a statement or information to be required in the annual report) or, where appropriate, explain in each case why the trust has departed from the Code.

In addition, to help us verify that the right behaviours and approach are in place where a trust opts not to comply with a provision, the trust must explain how its approach still reflects the principles of the Code relating to that provision. The form and content of this part of the statement are not prescribed, the intention being that trusts should have a free hand to explain their governance policies in the light of the principles, including any special circumstances applying to them which have led to a particular approach.

It is important to note that:

- a comprehensive list of the provisions to which "comply or explain" applies, are clearly stated in Schedule A to this document;
- we have clearly noted throughout the document and in Schedule A where a provision may be statutory as a result of other legislation and therefore where compliance is mandatory;
- although in some cases disclosures may be contained elsewhere in the annual reporting documentation, a statement for the Code is required which includes everything listed in Schedule A. Where information would be duplicated, trusts need only provide a clear reference to the location of the information within the annual report; and
- a completed set of disclosures as per Schedule A should be included within a trust's annual report.

1.4.2 How does the Code fit with other Monitor requirements?

Although compliance with the provisions in this Code is on a "comply or explain" basis, we have included and clearly identified any relevant statutory requirements that fit closely with the Code. In the first instance, boards, directors and governors should ensure they are meeting the specific governance requirements described in the Health and Social Care Act 2012 and subsequently set out in *The new NHS provider licence* and *Risk assessment framework*. These are concerned with issues such as continuity of services, which is vital for effective patient care. In the list of disclosure requirements in Schedule A, we have clearly highlighted any provisions which are required as a result of legislation or other regulatory obligations.

It is important to note that as a result of NHS Foundation Trust Condition 4 of the NHS provider licence, trusts must also now provide a "forward looking governance statement" in the form of the corporate governance statement submitted during the annual planning round. Any issues that are raised at this forward plan stage can then be discussed to identify how they can be mitigated in advance of any breach taking place. However, any issues not identified and subsequently arising can be used as evidence of self-certification failure.

In addition to the corporate governance statement mentioned above, this Code sits alongside a number of other Monitor reporting requirements which relate to governance but do not conflict or connect with the Code. The Code also includes references to other Monitor publications, which focus on audit and on internal control:

- NHS Foundation Trust Annual Reporting Manual;[1]
- *Audit Code for NHS Foundation Trusts*.

For clarity, we have provided a detailed explanation of how the different requirements sit together and the purpose of each in Appendix C.

1.4.3 How will Monitor use the Code?

We will continue to oversee the effectiveness and applicability of the Code and develop it, in consultation with NHS foundation trusts where appropriate, as best practice both in the sector and outside of the sector evolves. We will also continue to ensure that any relevant changes or recommendations in the wider regulatory framework are reflected in updates to the Code and vice versa. Regarding disclosures made by trusts in respect of the Code, we will monitor widespread areas of non-compliance in more detail to assess whether there is evidence of systemic variation from the Code so that we can understand the reasons for that variation. In all cases, our activity will be dictated by our primary duty to patients.

As we noted above, NHS foundation trusts should also take note of the new *Risk assessment framework* (which came into effect on 1 October 2013), which sets out in detail our approach to overseeing NHS foundation trusts' compliance with the governance requirement of their provider licence. This includes important information about the board leadership and governance framework (which are also referenced in B.6.2. of this document).

1.4.4 Further information

NHS foundation trusts may also find it useful to consult other available guidance and sources of best practice about governance of public bodies and the NHS. In particular, the following publications are likely to be of use when considered alongside the Code:

- Your statutory duties: A reference guide for NHS foundation trust governors
- Director-governor interaction in NHS foundation trusts: A best practice guide for boards of directors
- The Healthy NHS Board 2013 – Principles for Good Governance

In addition, leadership and governance in the public sector, and specifically in the NHS, is the subject of several reports, which might also be of interest:

- *Healthcare Leadership Model* is the result of recent work by the NHS Leadership Academy to set out the nine dimensions of leadership behaviour.
- *The Nolan Principles* covers in detail the standards of behaviour and principles in public life with particular focus on appointment on merit, with an independent element on all selection panels recommended as the way forward for public bodies.
- *Board Governance Essentials: A Guide for Chairs and Boards of Public Bodies* developed by CIPFA (the Chartered Institute of Public Finance Accountants), this guide provides chairs and board members advice on the roles that they perform.

The main principles of the Code

Section A: Leadership

Every NHS foundation trust should be headed by an effective board of directors. The board is collectively responsible for the performance of the NHS foundation trust.

The general duty of the board of directors, and of each director individually, is to act with a view to promoting the success of the organisation so as to maximise the benefits for the members of the trust as a whole and for the public.

There should be a clear division of responsibilities at the head of the NHS foundation trust between the chairing of the boards of directors and the council of governors, and the executive responsibility for the running of the NHS foundation trust's affairs. No one individual should have unfettered powers of decision.

The chair is responsible for leadership of the board of directors and the council of governors, ensuring their effectiveness on all aspects of their role and leading on setting the agenda for meetings.

As part of their role as members of a unitary board, non-executive directors should constructively challenge and help develop proposals on strategy. Non-executive directors should also promote the functioning of the board as a unitary board.

The council of governors has a statutory duty to hold the non-executive directors individually and collectively to account for the performance of the board of directors. This includes ensuring the board of directors acts so that the foundation trust does not breach the conditions of its licence. It remains the responsibility of the board of directors to design and then implement agreed priorities, objectives and the overall strategy of the NHS foundation trust.

The council of governors is responsible for representing the interests of NHS foundation trust members and the public in the governance of the NHS foundation trust. Governors must act in the best interests of the NHS foundation trust and should adhere to its values and code of conduct.

Governors are responsible for regularly feeding back information about the trust, its vision and its performance to members and the public and the stakeholder organisations that either elected or appointed them. The trust should ensure governors have appropriate support to help them discharge this duty.

Section B: Effectiveness

The board of directors and its committees should have the appropriate balance of skills, experience, independence and knowledge of the NHS foundation trust to enable them to discharge their respective duties and responsibilities effectively.

There should be a formal, rigorous and transparent procedure for the appointment of new directors to the board. Directors of NHS foundation trusts must be "fit and proper" to meet the requirements of the general conditions of the provider licence.

All directors should be able to allocate sufficient time to the NHS foundation trust to discharge their responsibilities effectively.

All directors and governors should receive appropriate induction on joining the board of directors or the council of governors and should regularly update and refresh their skills and knowledge. Both directors and governors should make every effort to participate in training that is offered.

The board of directors and the council of governors should be supplied in a timely manner with relevant information in a form and of a quality appropriate to enable them to discharge their respective duties. Statutory requirements on the provision of information from the board of directors to the council of governors are provided in *Your statutory duties: A reference guide for NHS foundation trust governors.*

The board of directors should undertake a formal and rigorous annual evaluation of its own performance and that of its committees and individual directors.

The outcomes of the evaluation of the executive directors should be reported to the board of directors. The chair should take the lead on the evaluation of the executive directors.

The council of governors, which is responsible for the appointment and re-appointment of non-executive directors, should take the lead on agreeing a process for the evaluation of the chair and the non-executives, with the chair and the non-executives. The outcomes of the evaluation of the non-executive directors should be agreed with them by the chair. The outcomes of the evaluation of the chair should be agreed by him or her with the senior independent director. The outcomes of the evaluation of the non-executive directors and the chair should be reported to the governors. The governors should bear in mind that it may be desirable to use the senior independent director to lead the evaluation of the chair.

The council of governors should assess its own collective performance and its impact on the NHS foundation trust.

All non-executive directors and elected governors should be submitted for re-appointment or re-election at regular intervals. The performance of executive directors of the board should be subject to regular appraisal and review. The council of governors should ensure planned and progressive refreshing of the non-executive directors.

The board of directors is responsible for ensuring ongoing compliance by the NHS foundation trust with its licence, its constitution, mandatory guidance issued by Monitor, relevant statutory requirements and contractual obligations. In so doing, it should ensure it retains the necessary skills within its board and directors, and works with the council of governors to ensure there is appropriate succession planning.

Section C: Accountability

The board of directors should present a fair, balanced and understandable assessment of the NHS foundation trust's position and prospects.

The board of directors is responsible for determining the nature and extent of the significant risks it is willing to take in achieving its strategic objectives. The board should maintain sound risk management systems.

The board of directors should maintain a sound system of internal control to safeguard patient safety, public and private investment, the NHS foundation trust's assets, and service quality. The board should report on internal control through the Annual Governance Statement (formerly the Statement on Internal Control) in the annual report.

The board of directors should establish formal and transparent arrangements for considering how they should apply the corporate reporting and risk management and internal control principles and for maintaining an appropriate relationship with the NHS foundation trust's auditors.

Section D: Director remuneration

Levels of remuneration should be sufficient to attract, retain and motivate directors of quality, and with the skills and experience required to lead the NHS foundation trust successfully, but an NHS foundation trust should avoid paying more than is necessary for this purpose and should consider all relevant and current directions relating to contractual benefits such as pay and redundancy entitlements.

There should be a formal and transparent procedure for developing policy on executive remuneration and for fixing the remuneration packages of individual directors. No director should be involved in deciding his or her own remuneration.

Section E: Relations with stakeholders

The board of directors should appropriately consult and involve members, patients and the local community.

The council of governors must represent the interests of trust members and the public.

Notwithstanding the complementary role of the governors in this consultation, the board of directors as a whole has responsibility for ensuring that regular and open dialogue with its stakeholders takes place.

The board of directors is responsible for ensuring that the NHS foundation trust co-operates with other NHS bodies, local authorities and other relevant organisations with an interest in the local health economy.

Section A: Leadership

A.1 The role of the board of directors

Main principles

A.1.a. Every NHS foundation trust should be headed by an effective board of directors. The board is collectively responsible for the performance of the NHS foundation trust.

A.1.b. The general duty of the board of directors, and of each director individually, is to act with a view to promoting the success of the organisation so as to maximise the benefits for the members of the trust as a whole and for the public.

Supporting principles

A.1.c. The role of the board of directors is to provide entrepreneurial leadership of the NHS foundation trust within a framework of prudent and effective controls, which enables risk to be assessed and managed.

A.1.d. The board of directors is responsible for ensuring compliance by the NHS foundation trust with its licence, its constitution, mandatory guidance issued by Monitor, relevant statutory requirements and contractual obligations.

A.1.e. The board of directors should develop and articulate a clear "vision" for the trust. This should be a formally agreed statement of the organisation's purpose and intended outcomes which can be used as a basis for the organisation's overall strategy, planning and other decisions.

A.1.f. The board of directors should set the NHS foundation trust's strategic aims at least annually taking into consideration the views of the council of governors, ensuring that the necessary financial and human resources are in place for the NHS foundation trust to meet its priorities and objectives and, then, periodically reviewing progress and management performance.

A.1.g. The board of directors as a whole is responsible for ensuring the quality and safety of health care services, education, training and research delivered by the NHS foundation trust and applying the principles and standards of clinical governance set out by the Department of Health (DH), NHS England, the Care Quality Commission (CQC) and other relevant NHS bodies.

A.1.h. The board of directors should also ensure that the NHS foundation trust functions effectively, efficiently and economically.

A.1.i. The board of directors should set the NHS foundation trust's vision, values and standards of conduct and ensure that its obligations to its members are understood, clearly communicated and met.

A.1.j. All directors must take decisions objectively in the best interests of the NHS foundation trust and avoid conflicts of interest.

A.1.k. All members of the board of directors have joint responsibility for every decision of the board regardless of their individual skills or status. This does not impact upon the particular responsibilities of the chief executive as the accounting officer.

A.1.l. All directors, executive and non-executive, have a responsibility to constructively challenge during board discussions and help develop proposals on priorities, risk mitigation, values, standards and strategy.

A.1.m. As part of their role as members of a unitary board, all directors have a duty to ensure appropriate challenge is made. In particular, non-executive directors should scrutinise the performance of the executive management in meeting agreed goals and objectives, receive adequate information and monitor the reporting of performance. They should satisfy themselves as to the integrity of financial, clinical and other information, and make sure that financial and clinical quality controls, and systems of risk management and governance, are robust and implemented. Non-executive directors are responsible for determining appropriate levels of remuneration of executive directors and have a prime role in appointing and, where necessary, removing executive directors, and in succession planning.

Code provisions

A.1.1. The board of directors should meet sufficiently regularly to discharge its duties effectively. There should be a schedule of matters specifically reserved for its decision. The schedule of matters reserved for the board of directors should include a clear statement detailing the roles and responsibilities of the council of governors (as described in A.5). This statement should also describe how any disagreements between the council of governors and the board of directors will be resolved. The annual report should include this schedule of matters or a summary statement of how the board of directors and the council of governors operate, including a summary of the types of decisions to be taken by each of the boards and which are delegated to the executive management of the board of directors. These arrangements should be kept under review at least annually.

A.1.2. The annual report should identify the chair, the deputy chair (where there is one), the chief executive, the senior independent director (see A.4.1) and the chair and members of the nominations, audit and remuneration committees. It should also set out the number of meetings of the board and those committees and individual attendance by directors.

A.1.3. The board of directors should make available a statement of the objectives of the NHS foundation trust showing how it intends to balance the interests of patients, the local community and other stakeholders, and use this as the basis for its decision-making and forward planning.

A.1.4. The board of directors should ensure that adequate systems and processes are maintained to measure and monitor the NHS foundation trust's effectiveness, efficiency and economy as well as the quality of its health care delivery. The board should regularly review the performance of the NHS foundation trust in these areas against regulatory and contractual obligations, and approved plans and objectives.

A.1.5. The board of directors should ensure that relevant metrics, measures, milestones and accountabilities are developed and agreed so as to understand and assess progress and delivery of performance. Where appropriate and, in particular, in high risk or complex areas, independent advice, for example, from the internal audit function, should be commissioned by the board of directors to provide an adequate and reliable level of assurance.

A.1.6. The board of directors should report on its approach to clinical governance and its plan for the improvement of clinical quality in accordance with guidance set out by the DH, NHS England, the CQC and Monitor. The board should record where, within the structure of the organisation, consideration of clinical governance matters occurs.

A.1.7. The chief executive as the accounting officer should follow the procedure set out by Monitor for advising the board of directors and the council of governors and for recording and submitting objections to decisions considered or taken by the board of directors in matters of propriety or regularity, and on issues relating to the wider responsibilities of the accounting officer for economy, efficiency and effectiveness.

A.1.8. The board of directors should establish the constitution and standards of conduct for the NHS foundation trust and its staff in accordance with NHS values and accepted standards of behaviour in public life, which includes the principles of selflessness, integrity, objectivity, accountability, openness, honesty and leadership *(The Nolan Principles)*.

A.1.9. The board of directors should operate a code of conduct that builds on the values of the NHS foundation trust and reflect high standards of probity and responsibility. The board of directors should follow a policy of openness and transparency in its proceedings and decision-making unless this is in conflict with a need to protect the wider interests of the public or the NHS foundation trust (including commercial-in-confidence matters) and make clear how potential conflicts of interest are dealt with.

A.1.10. The NHS foundation trust should arrange appropriate insurance to cover the risk of legal action against its directors. Assuming the governors have acted in good faith and in accordance with their duties, and proper process has been followed, the potential for liability for the council should be negligible. Governors may have the benefit of an indemnity and/or insurance from the trust. While there is no legal requirement for trusts to provide an indemnity or insurance for governors to cover their service on the council of governors, where an indemnity or insurance policy is given, this can be detailed in the trust's constitution.

A.2 Division of responsibilities

Main principle

A.2.a. There should be a clear division of responsibilities at the head of the NHS foundation trust between the chairing of the boards of directors and the council of governors, and the executive responsibility for the running of the NHS foundation trust's affairs. No one individual should have unfettered powers of decision.

Code provisions

A.2.1. The division of responsibilities between the chair and chief executive should be clearly established, set out in writing and agreed by the board of directors.

Relevant statutory requirements

A.2.2. The roles of chair and chief executive must not be undertaken by the same individual.

1.3 The chair

Main principle

A.3.a. The chair is responsible for leadership of the board of directors and the council of governors, ensuring their effectiveness on all aspects of their role and leading on setting the agenda for meetings.

Supporting principles

A.3.b. The chair is responsible for leading on setting the agenda for the board of directors and the council of governors and ensuring that adequate time is available for discussion of all agenda items, in particular strategic issues.

A.3.c. The chair is responsible for ensuring that the board and council work together effectively.

A.3.d. The chair is also responsible for ensuring that directors and governors receive accurate, timely and clear information which enables them to perform their duties effectively. The chair should take steps to ensure that governors have the skills and knowledge they require to undertake their role.

A.3.e. The chair should promote effective and open communication with patients, service users, members, staff, the public and other stakeholders.

A.3.f. The chair should also promote a culture of openness and debate by facilitating the effective contribution of non-executive directors, in particular and ensuring constructive relations between executive and non-executive directors.

Code provision

A.3.1. The chair should, on appointment by the council of governors, meet the independence criteria set out in B.1.1. A chief executive should not go on to be the chair of the same NHS foundation trust.

A.4 Non-executive directors

Main principle

A.4.a. As part of their role as members of a unitary board, non-executive directors should constructively challenge and help develop proposals on strategy. Non- executive directors should also promote the functioning of the board as a unitary board.

Supporting principles

A.4.b. Non-executive directors should scrutinise the performance of management in meeting agreed goals and objectives, and monitor the reporting of performance. They should satisfy themselves on the integrity of financial information and that financial controls and systems of risk management are robust and defensible. They are responsible for determining appropriate levels of remuneration of executive directors and have a prime role in appointing, and where necessary, removing executive directors, and in succession planning.

Code provisions

A.4.1. In consultation with the council of governors, the board should appoint one of the independent non-executive directors to be the senior independent director to provide a sounding board for the chair and to serve as an intermediary for the other directors when necessary. The senior independent director should be available to governors if they have concerns that contact through the normal channels of chair, chief executive, finance director or trust secretary has failed to resolve, or for which such contact is inappropriate. The senior independent director could be the deputy chair.

A.4.2. The chair should hold meetings with the non-executive directors without the executives present. Led by the senior independent director, the non- executive directors should meet without the chair present, at least annually, to appraise the chair's performance, and on other such occasions as are deemed appropriate.

A.4.3. Where directors have concerns that cannot be resolved about the running of the NHS foundation trust or a proposed action, they should ensure that their concerns are recorded in the board minutes. On resignation, a director should provide a written statement to the chair for circulation to the board, if they have any such concerns.

A.5 Governors

The 2012 Act made significant changes to the powers of, and obligations upon, governors of NHS foundation trusts. Monitor has described in this section of the Code those areas of the governors' role that are relevant and which NHS foundation trusts may find helpful.

In addition, in August 2013, Monitor published a separate document which examines how governors can deliver their duties: *Your statutory duties: A reference guide for NHS foundation trust governors*.

Main principles

A.5.a. The council of governors has a duty to hold the non-executive directors individually and collectively to account for the performance of the board of directors. This includes ensuring the board of directors acts so that the foundation trust does not breach the conditions of its licence. It remains the responsibility of the board of directors to design and then implement agreed priorities, objectives and the overall strategy of the NHS foundation trust.

A.5.b. The council of governors is responsible for representing the interests of NHS foundation trust members and the public and staff in the governance of the NHS foundation trust. Governors must act in the best interests of the NHS foundation trust and should adhere to its values and code of conduct.

A.5.c. Governors are responsible for regularly feeding back information about the trust, its vision and its performance to members and the public and the stakeholder organisations that either elected or appointed them. The trust should ensure governors have appropriate support to help them discharge this duty.

Supporting principles

A.5.d. Governors should discuss and agree with the board of directors how they will undertake these and any other additional roles, giving due consideration to the circumstances of the NHS foundation trust and the needs of the local community and emerging best practice.

A.5.e. Governors should work closely with the board of directors and must be presented with, for consideration, the annual report and accounts and the annual plan at a general meeting. The governors must be consulted on the development of forward plans for the trust and any significant changes to the delivery of the trust's business plan.

A.5.f. Governors should use their voting rights (including those described in A.5.14 and A.5.15) to hold the non-executive directors individually and collectively to account and act in the best interest of patients, members and the public. If the council of governors does withhold consent for a major decision, it must justify its reasons to the chair and the other non-executive directors, bearing in mind that its decision is likely to have a range of consequences for the NHS foundation trust. The council of governors should take care to ensure that reasons are considered, factual and within the spirit of the Nolan principles.

Code provisions

A.5.1. The council of governors should meet sufficiently regularly to discharge its duties. Typically the council of governors would be expected to meet as a full council at least four times a year. Governors should, where practicable, make every effort to attend the meetings of the council of governors. The NHS foundation trust should take appropriate steps to facilitate attendance.

A.5.2. The council of governors should not be so large as to be unwieldy. The council of governors should be of sufficient size for the requirements of its duties. The roles, structure, composition, and procedures of the council of governors should be reviewed regularly as described in provision B.6.5.

A.5.3. The annual report should identify the members of the council of governors, including a description of the constituency or organisation that they represent, whether they were elected or appointed, and the duration of their appointments. The annual report should also identify the nominated lead governor. A record should be kept of the number of meetings of the council and the attendance of individual governors and it should be made available to members on request.

A.5.4. The roles and responsibilities of the council of governors should be set out in a written document. This statement should include a clear explanation of the responsibilities of the council of governors towards members and other stakeholders and how governors will seek their views and keep them informed.

A.5.5. The chair is responsible for leadership of both the board of directors and the council of governors (see A.3) but the governors also have a responsibility to make the arrangements work and should take the lead in inviting the chief executive to their meetings and inviting attendance by other executives and non-executives, as appropriate. In these meetings other members of the council of governors may raise questions of the chair or his/her deputy, or any other relevant director present at the meeting about the affairs of the NHS foundation trust.

A.5.6. The council of governors should establish a policy for engagement with the board of directors for those circumstances when they have concerns about the performance of the board of directors, compliance with the *new provider licence* or other matters related to the overall wellbeing of the NHS foundation trust. The council of governors should input into the board's appointment of a senior independent director (see A.4.1).

A.5.7. The council of governors should ensure its interaction and relationship with the board of directors is appropriate and effective. In particular, by agreeing the availability and timely communication of relevant information, discussion and the setting in advance of meeting agendas and, where possible, using clear, unambiguous language.

A.5.8. The council of governors should only exercise its power to remove the chair or any non-executive directors after exhausting all means of engagement with the board of directors. The council should raise any issues with the chair with the senior independent director in the first instance.

A.5.9. The council of governors should receive and consider other appropriate information required to enable it to discharge its duties, for example clinical statistical data and operational data.

Relevant statutory requirements

A.5.10 The council of governors has a statutory duty to hold the non-executive directors individually and collectively to account for the performance of the board of directors.

A.5.11. The 2006 Act, as amended, gives the council of governors a statutory requirement to receive the following documents. These documents should be provided in the annual report as per the *NHS Foundation Trust Annual Reporting Manual*:
a) the annual accounts;
b) any report of the auditor on them; and
c) the annual report.

A.5.12. The directors must provide governors with an agenda prior to any meeting of the board, and a copy of the approved minutes as soon as is practicable afterwards. There is no legal basis on which the minutes of private sessions of board meetings should be exempted from being shared with the governors. In practice, it may be necessary to redact some information, for example, for data protection or commercial reasons. Governors should respect the confidentiality of these documents.

A.5.13. The council of governors may require one or more of the directors to attend a meeting to obtain information about performance of the trust's functions or the directors' performance of their duties, and to help the council of governors to decide whether to propose a vote on the trust's or directors' performance.

A.5.14. Governors have the right to refer a question to the independent panel for advising governors. More than 50% of governors who vote must approve this referral. The council should ensure dialogue with the board of directors takes place before considering such a referral, as it may be possible to resolve questions in this way.

A.5.15. Governors should use their new rights and voting powers from the 2012 Act to represent the interests of members and the public on major decisions taken by the board of directors. These new voting powers require:
- More than half of the members of the board of directors who vote and more than half of the members of the council of governors who vote to approve a change to the constitution of the NHS foundation trust.
- More than half of governors who vote to approve a significant transaction.
- More than half of all governors to approve an application by a trust for a merger, acquisition, separation or dissolution.
- More than half of governors who vote, to approve any proposal to increase the proportion of the trust's income earned from non-NHS work by 5% a year or more. For example, governors will be required to vote where an NHS foundation trust plans to increase its non-NHS income from 2% to 7% or more of the trust's total income.
- Governors to determine together whether the trust's non-NHS work will significantly interfere with the trust's principal purpose, which is to provide goods and services for the health service in England, or its ability to perform its other functions.

NHS foundation trusts are permitted to decide themselves what constitutes a "significant transaction" and may choose to set out the definition(s) in the trust's constitution. Alternatively, with the agreement of the governors, trusts may choose not to give a definition, but this would need to be stated in the constitution.

Section B: Effectiveness

B.1 The composition of the board

Main principle

B.1.a. The board of directors and its committees should have the appropriate balance of skills, experience, independence and knowledge of the NHS foundation trust to enable them to discharge their respective duties and responsibilities effectively.

Supporting principles

B.1.b. The board of directors should be of sufficient size that the requirements of the organisation can be met and that changes to the board's composition and that of its committees can be managed without undue disruption, and should not be so large as to be unwieldy.

B.1.c. The board of directors should include an appropriate combination of executive and non-executive directors (and in particular, independent non-executive directors) such that no individual or small group of individuals can dominate the board's decision taking.

B.1.d. All directors should be able to exercise one full vote, with the chair having a second or casting vote on occasions where voting is tied.

B.1.e. The value of ensuring that committee membership is refreshed and that undue reliance is not placed on particular individuals should be taken into account in deciding chair and the membership of committees. The value of appointing a non-executive director with a clinical background to the board of directors should be taken into account by the council of governors.

B.1.f. Only the committee chair and committee members are entitled to be present at meetings of the nominations, audit or remuneration committees, but others may attend by invitation of the particular committee.

Code provisions

B.1.1. The board of directors should identify in the annual report each non-executive director it considers to be independent. The board should determine whether the director is independent in character and judgement and whether there are relationships or circumstances which are likely to affect, or could appear to affect, the director's judgement. The board of directors should state its reasons if it determines that a director is independent despite the existence of relationships or circumstances which may appear relevant to its determination, including if the director:

- has been an employee of the NHS foundation trust within the last five years;
- has, or has had within the last three years, a material business relationship with the NHS foundation trust either directly, or as a partner, shareholder, director or senior employee of a body that has such a relationship with the NHS foundation trust;
- has received or receives additional remuneration from the NHS foundation trust apart from a director's fee, participates in the NHS foundation trust's performance-related pay scheme, or is a member of the NHS foundation trust's pension scheme;
- has close family ties with any of the NHS foundation trust's advisers, directors or senior employees;
- holds cross-directorships or has significant links with other directors through involvement in other companies or bodies;
- has served on the board of the NHS foundation trust for more than six years from the date of their first appointment; or
- is an appointed representative of the NHS foundation trust's university medical or dental school.

B.1.2. least half the board of directors, excluding the chair, should comprise non-executive directors determined by the board to be independent.

B.1.3. No individual should hold, at the same time, positions of director and governor of any NHS foundation trust.

B.1.4. The board of directors should include in its annual report a description of each director's skills, expertise and experience. Alongside this, in the annual report, the board should make a clear statement about its own balance, completeness and appropriateness to the requirements of the NHS foundation trust. Both statements should also be available on the NHS foundation trust's website.

B.2 Appointments to the board

Main principle

B.2.a. There should be a formal, rigorous and transparent procedure for the appointment of new directors to the board. Directors of NHS foundation trusts must be "fit and proper" to meet the requirements of the general conditions of the provider licence.

Supporting principles

B.2.b. The search for candidates for the board of directors should be conducted, and appointments made, on merit, against objective criteria and with due regard for the benefits of diversity on the board and the requirements of the trust.

B.2.c. The board of directors and the council of governors should also satisfy themselves that plans are in place for orderly succession for appointments to the board, so as to maintain an appropriate balance of skills and experience within the NHS foundation trust and on the board.

Code provisions

B.2.1. The nominations committee or committees, with external advice as appropriate, are responsible for the identification and nomination of executive and non-executive directors. The nominations committee should give full consideration to succession planning, taking into account the future challenges, risks and opportunities facing the NHS foundation trust and the skills and expertise required within the board of directors to meet them.

B.2.2. Directors on the board of directors and governors on the council of governors should meet the "fit and proper" persons test described in the provider licence. For the purpose of the licence and application criteria, "fit and proper" persons are defined as those without certain recent criminal convictions and director disqualifications, and those who are not bankrupt (undischarged). Trusts should also abide by the updated guidance from the CQC regarding appointments to senior positions in organisations subject to CQC regulations.

B.2.3. There may be one or two nominations committees. If there are two committees, one will be responsible for considering nominations for executive directors and the other for non-executive directors (including the chair). The nominations committee(s) should regularly review the structure, size and composition of the board of directors and make recommendations for changes where appropriate. In particular, the nominations committee(s) should evaluate, at least annually, the balance of skills, knowledge and experience on the board of directors and, in the light of this evaluation, prepare a description of the role and capabilities required for appointment of both executive and non-executive directors, including the chair.

B.2.4. The chair or an independent non-executive director should chair the nominations committee(s). At the discretion of the committee, a governor can chair the committee in the case of appointments of non-executive directors or the chair.

B.2.5. The governors should agree with the nominations committee a clear process for the nomination of a new chair and non-executive directors. Once suitable candidates have been identified the nominations committee should make recommendations to the council of governors.

B.2.6. Where an NHS foundation trust has two nominations committees, the nominations committee responsible for the appointment of non-executive directors should consist of a majority of governors. If only one nominations committee exists, when nominations for non-executives, including the appointment of a chair or a deputy chair, are being discussed, there should be a majority of governors on the committee and also a majority governor representation on the interview panel.

B.2.7. When considering the appointment of non-executive directors, the council of governors should take into account the views of the board of directors and the nominations committee on the qualifications, skills and experience required for each position.

B.2.8. The annual report should describe the process followed by the council of governors in relation to appointments of the chair and non-executive directors.

B.2.9. An independent external adviser should not be a member of or have a vote on the nominations committee(s).

B.2.10. A separate section of the annual report should describe the work of the nominations committee(s), including the process it has used in relation to board appointments. The main role and responsibilities of the nominations committee should be set out in publicly available, written terms of reference.

Relevant statutory requirements

B.2.11. It is a requirement of the 2006 Act that the chair, the other non-executive directors and – except in the case of the appointment of a chief executive – the chief executive, are responsible for deciding the appointment of executive directors. The nominations committee with responsibility for executive director nominations should identify suitable candidates to fill executive director vacancies as they arise and make recommendations to the chair, the other non-executives directors and, except in the case of the appointment of a chief executive, the chief executive.

B.2.12. It is for the non-executive directors to appoint and remove the chief executive. The appointment of a chief executive requires the approval of the council of governors.

B.2.13 The governors are responsible at a general meeting for the appointment, re-appointment and removal of the chair and the other non-executive directors.

B.3 Commitment

Main principle

B.3.a. All directors should be able to allocate sufficient time to the NHS foundation trust to discharge their responsibilities effectively.

Code provisions

B.3.1. The appointment of a chair, the nominations committee should prepare a job specification defining the role and capabilities required including an assessment of the time commitment expected, recognising the need for availability in the event of emergencies. A chair's other significant commitments should be disclosed to the council of governors before appointment and included in the annual report. Changes to such commitments should be reported to the council of governors as they arise, and included in the next annual report. No individual, simultaneously though being a chair of an NHS foundation trust, should be the substantive chair of another NHS foundation trust.

B.3.2. The terms and conditions of appointment of non-executive directors should be made available to the council of governors. The letter of appointment should set out the expected time commitment. Non-executive directors should undertake that they will have sufficient time to meet what is expected of them. Their other significant commitments should be disclosed to the council of governors before appointment, with a broad indication of the time involved and the council of governors should be informed of subsequent changes.

B.3.3. The board of directors should not agree to a full-time executive director taking on more than one non-executive directorship of an NHS foundation trust or another organisation of comparable size and complexity, nor the chair of such an organisation.

B.4 Development

Main principle

B.4.a. All directors and governors should receive appropriate induction on joining the board of directors or the council of governors and should regularly update and refresh their skills and knowledge. Both directors and governors should make every effort to participate in training that is offered.

Supporting principles

B.4.b. The chair should ensure that directors and governors continually update their skills, knowledge and familiarity with the NHS foundation trust and its obligations to fulfil their role both on the board, the council of governors and on committees. The NHS foundation trust should provide the necessary resources for developing and updating its directors' and governors' skills, knowledge and capabilities.

B.4.c. To function effectively, all directors need appropriate knowledge of the NHS foundation trust and access to its operations and staff.

Code provisions

B.4.1. The chair should ensure that new directors and governors receive a full and tailored induction on joining the board or the council of governors. As part of this, directors should seek out opportunities to engage with stakeholders, including patients, clinicians and other staff. Directors should also have access, at the NHS foundation trust's expense, to training courses and/or materials that are consistent with their individual and collective development programme.

B.4.2. The chair should regularly review and agree with each director their training and development needs as they relate to their role on the board.

Relevant statutory requirements

B.4.3 The board has a duty to take steps to ensure that governors are equipped with the skills and knowledge they need to discharge their duties appropriately.

B.5 Information and support

Main principle

B.5.a. The board of directors and the council of governors should be supplied in a timely manner with relevant information in a form and of a quality appropriate to enable them to discharge their respective duties. Statutory requirements on the provision of information from the board of directors to the council of governors are provided in *Your statutory duties: A reference guide for NHS foundation trust governors.*

Supporting principles

B.5.b. The chair is responsible for ensuring that directors and governors receive accurate, timely and clear information. Management has an obligation to provide such information but directors and governors should seek clarification or detail where necessary.

B.5.c. The responsibilities of the chair include ensuring good information flows across the board, the council of governors and their committees, between directors and governors, and between senior management and non-executive directors, as well as facilitating appropriate induction and assisting with professional development as required.

Code provisions

B.5.1. The board of directors and the council of governors should be provided with high-quality information appropriate to their respective functions and relevant to the decisions they have to make. The board of directors and the council of governors should agree their respective information needs with the executive directors through the chair. The information for the boards should be concise, objective, accurate and timely, and it should be accompanied by clear explanations of complex issues. The board of directors should have complete access to any information about the NHS foundation trust that it deems necessary to discharge its duties, including access to senior management and other employees.

B.5.2. The board of directors and in particular non-executive directors, may reasonably wish to challenge assurances received from the executive management. They need not seek to appoint a relevant adviser for each and every subject area that comes before the board of directors, although they should, wherever possible, ensure that they have sufficient information and understanding to enable challenge and to take decisions on an informed basis. When complex or high-risk issues arise, the first course of action should normally be to encourage further and deeper analysis to be carried out in a timely manner, within the NHS foundation trust. On occasion, non-executives may reasonably decide that external assurance is appropriate.

B.5.3. The board should ensure that directors, especially non-executive directors, have access to the independent professional advice, at the NHS foundation trust's expense, where they judge it necessary to discharge their responsibilities as directors. Decisions to appoint an external adviser should be the collective decision of the majority of non-executive directors. The availability of independent external sources of advice should be made clear at the time of appointment.

B.5.4 Committees should be provided with sufficient resources to undertake their duties. The board of directors should also ensure that the council of governors is provided with sufficient resources to undertake its duties with such arrangements agreed in advance.

B.5.5. Non-executive directors should consider whether they are receiving the necessary information in a timely manner and feel able to raise appropriate challenge of recommendations of the board, in particular making full use of their skills and experience gained both as a director of the trust and also in other leadership roles. They should expect and apply similar standards of care and quality in their role as a non-executive director of an NHS foundation trust as they would in other similar roles.

B.5.6. Governors should canvass the opinion of the trust's members and the public, and for appointed governors the body they represent, on the NHS foundation trust's forward plan, including its objectives, priorities and strategy, and their views shouldbe communicated to the board of directors. The annual report should contain a statement as to how this requirement has been undertaken and satisfied.

B.5.7. Where appropriate, the board of directors should take account of the views of the council of governors on the forward plan in a timely manner and communicate to the council of governors where their views have been incorporated in the NHS foundation trust's plans, and, if not, the reasons for this.

Relevant statutory requirements

B.5.8 The board of directors must have regard for the views of the council of governors on the NHS foundation trust's forward plan.

B.6 Evaluation

Main principles

B.6.a. The board of directors should undertake a formal and rigorous annual evaluation of its own performance and that of its committees and individual directors.

B.6.b. The outcomes of the evaluation of the executive directors should be reported to the board of directors. The chief executive should take the lead on the evaluation of the executive directors.

B.6.c. The council of governors, which is responsible for the appointment and re-appointment of non-executive directors, should take the lead on agreeing a process for the evaluation of the chair and the non-executives, with the chair and the non-executives. The outcomes of the evaluation of the non-executive directors should be agreed with them by the chair. The outcomes of the evaluation of the chair should be agreed by him or her with the senior independent director. The outcomes of the evaluation of the non-executive directors and the chair should be reported to the governors. The governors should bear in mind that it may be desirable to use the senior independent director to lead the evaluation of the chair.

B.6.d. The council of governors should assess its own collective performance and its impact on the NHS foundation trust.

Supporting principles

B.6.e. Evaluation of the board of directors should consider the balance of skills, experience, independence and knowledge of the NHS foundation trust on the board, its diversity, including gender, how the board works together as a unit, and other factors relevant to its effectiveness. This should be reported to the council of governors with a specific focus on what changes are needed for improvement.

B.6.f. Individual evaluation of directors should aim to show whether each director continues to contribute effectively and to demonstrate commitment and has the relevant skills for the role (including commitment of time for board and committee meetings and any other duties) going forwards.

B.6.g. The chair should act on the results of the performance evaluation by recognising the strengths and addressing the weaknesses of the board, identifying individual and collective development needs, and, where appropriate, proposing new members be appointed to the board or seeking the resignation of directors.

B.6.h. The focus of the chair's appraisal will be his/her performance as leader of the board of directors and the council of governors. The appraisal should carefully consider that performance against pre-defined objectives that support the design and delivery of the NHS foundation trust's priorities and strategy described in its forward plan.

Code provisions

B.6.1. The board of directors should state in the annual report how performance evaluation of the board, its committees, and its directors, including the chair, has been conducted, bearing in mind the desirability for independent assessment, and the reason why the NHS foundation trust adopted a particular method of performance evaluation.

B.6.2. valuation of the boards of NHS foundations trusts should be externally facilitated at least every three years. The evaluation needs to be carried out against the board leadership and governance framework set out by Monitor. The external facilitator should be identified in the annual report and a statement made as to whether they have any other connection to the trust.

B.6.3. The senior independent director should lead the performance evaluation of the chair, within a framework agreed by the council of governors and taking into account the views of directors and governors.

B.6.4. The chair, with assistance of the board secretary, if applicable, should use the performance evaluations as the basis for determining individual and collective professional development programmes for non-executive directors relevant to their duties as board members.

B.6.5. Led by the chair, the council of governors should periodically assess their collective performance and they should regularly communicate to members and the public details on how they have discharged their responsibilities, including their impact and effectiveness on:

■ holding the non-executive directors individually and collectively to account for the performance of the board of directors;

■ communicating with their member constituencies and the public and transmitting their views to the board of directors; and

■ contributing to the development of forward plans of NHS foundation trusts.

The council of governors should use this process to review its roles, structure, composition and procedures, taking into account emerging best practice. Further information can be found in Monitor's publication: *Your statutory duties: A reference guide for NHS foundation trust governors.*

B.6.6. There should be a clear policy and a fair process, agreed and adopted by the council of governors, for the removal from the council of any governor who consistently and unjustifiably fails to attend the meetings of the council of governors or has an actual or potential conflict of interest which prevents the proper exercise of their duties. This should be shared with governors. In addition, it may be appropriate for the process to provide for removal from the council of governors where behaviours or actions of a governor or group of governors may be incompatible with the values and behaviours of the NHS foundation trust. Where there is any disagreement as to whether the proposal for removal is justified, an independent assessor agreeable to both parties should be requested to consider the evidence and determine whether the proposed removal is reasonable or otherwise.

B.7 Re-appointment of directors and re-election of governors

Main principle

B.7.a. All non-executive directors and elected governors should be submitted for re-appointment or re-election at regular intervals. The performance of executive directors of the board should be subject to regular appraisal and review. The council of governors should ensure planned and progressive refreshing of the non-executive directors.

Code provisions

B.7.1. In the case of re-appointment of non-executive directors, the chair should confirm to the governors that following formal performance evaluation, the performance of the individual proposed for re-appointment continues to be effective and to demonstrate commitment to the role. Any term beyond six years (eg, two three-year terms) for a non-executive director should be subject to particularly rigorous review, and should take into account the need for progressive refreshing of the board. Non-executive directors may, in exceptional circumstances, serve longer than six years (eg, two three-year terms following authorisation of the NHS foundation trust) but this should be subject to annual re-appointment. Serving more than six years could be relevant to the determination of a non-executive's independence.

B.7.2. Elected governors must be subject to re-election by the members of their constituency at regular intervals not exceeding three years. The names of governors submitted for election or re-election should be accompanied by sufficient biographical details and any other relevant information to enable members to take an informed decision on their election. This should include prior performance information.

Relevant statutory requirements

B.7.3. Approval by the council of governors of the appointment of a chief executive should be a subject of the first general meeting after the appointment by a committee of the chair and non-executive directors. All other executive directors should be appointed by a committee of the chief executive, the chair and non- executive directors.

B.7.4. Non-executive directors, including the chair should be appointed by the council of governors for the specified terms subject to re-appointment thereafter at intervals of no more than three years and subject to the 2006 Act provisions relating to removal of a director.

B.7.5. Elected governors must be subject to re-election by the members of their constituency at regular intervals not exceeding three years.

B.8 Resignation of directors

Main principle

B.8.a. The board of directors is responsible for ensuring ongoing compliance by the NHS foundation trust with its licence, its constitution, mandatory guidance issued by Monitor, relevant statutory requirements and contractual obligations. In so doing, it should ensure it retains the necessary skills within its board and directors and works with the council of governors to ensure there is appropriate succession planning.

Code provision

B.8.1 The remuneration committee should not agree to an executive member of the board leaving the employment of an NHS foundation trust, except in accordance with the terms of their contract of employment, including but not limited to service of their full notice period and/or material reductions in their time commitment to the role, without the board first having completed and approved a full risk assessment.

Section C. Accountability

C.1 Financial, quality and operational reporting

Main principle

C.1.a. The board of directors should present a fair, balanced and understandable assessment of the NHS foundation trust's position and prospects.

Supporting principle

C.1.b. The responsibility of the board of directors to present a fair, balanced and understandable assessment extends to all public statements and reports to regulators and inspectors, as well as information required to be presented by statutory requirements.

C.1.c. The board of directors should establish arrangements that will enable it to ensure that the information presented is fair, balanced and understandable.

Code provisions

C.1.1. The directors should explain in the annual report their responsibility for preparing the annual report and accounts, and state that they consider the annual report and accounts, taken as a whole, are fair, balanced and understandable and provide the information necessary for patients, regulators and other stakeholders to assess the NHS foundation trust's performance, business model and strategy. There should be a statement by the external auditor about their reporting responsibilities. Directors should also explain their approach to quality governance in the Annual Governance Statement (within the annual report).

C.1.2. The directors should report that the NHS foundation trust is a going concern with supporting assumptions or qualifications as necessary.

C.1.3. At least annually and in a timely manner, the board of directors should set out clearly its financial, quality and operating objectives for the NHS foundation trust and disclose sufficient information, both quantitative and qualitative, of the NHS foundation trust's business and operation, including clinical outcome data, to allow members and governors to evaluate its performance. Further requirements are included in the *NHS Foundation Trust Annual Reporting Manual*.

C.1.4. a) The board of directors must notify Monitor and the council of governors without delay and should consider whether it is in the public's interest to bring to the public attention, any major new developments in the NHS foundation trust's sphere of activity which are not public knowledge, which it is able to disclose and which may lead by virtue of their effect on its assets and liabilities, or financial position or on the general course of its business, to a substantial change to the financial wellbeing, health care delivery performance or reputation and standing of the NHS foundation trust.

b) The board of directors must notify Monitor and the council of governors without delay and should consider whether it is in the public interest to bring to public attention all relevant information which is not public knowledge concerning a material change in:

- the NHS foundation trust's financial condition;
- the performance of its business; and/or
- the NHS foundation trust's expectations as to its performance which, if made public, would be likely to lead to a substantial change to the financial wellbeing, health care delivery performance or reputation and standing of the NHS foundation trust.

C.2 Risk management and internal control

Main principles

C.2.a. The board of directors is responsible for determining the nature and extent of the significant risks it is willing to take in achieving its strategic objectives. The board should maintain sound risk management systems.

C.2.b. The board of directors should maintain a sound system of internal control to safeguard patient safety, public and private investment, the NHS foundation trust's assets, and service quality. The board should report on internal control through the Annual Governance Statement (formerly the Statement on Internal Control) in the annual report.

Supporting principles

C.2.c. An internal audit function can assist a trust to accomplish its objectives by bringing a systematic, disciplined approach to evaluating and continually improving the effectiveness of its risk management and internal control processes.

C.2.d. If a trust has an internal audit function, the head of that function should have a direct reporting line to the board or to the audit committee to bring the requisite degree of independence and objectivity to the role.

Code provision

C.2.1. The board of directors should maintain continuous oversight of the effectiveness of the NHS foundation trust's risk management and internal control systems and should report to members and governors that they have done so in the annual report. A regular review should cover all material controls, including financial, operational and compliance controls.

C.2.2. A trust should disclose in the annual report:
   a) if it has an internal audit function, how the function is structured and what role it performs; or
   b) if it does not have an internal audit function, that fact and the processes it employs for evaluating and continually improving the effectiveness of its risk management and internal control processes.

C.3 Audit committee and auditors

Main principle

C.3.a. The board of directors should establish formal and transparent arrangements for considering how they should apply the corporate reporting and risk management and internal control principles and for maintaining an appropriate relationship with the NHS foundation trust's auditors.

Monitor's publications, *Audit Code for NHS Foundation Trusts and Your statutory duties: A reference guide for NHS foundation trust governors,* provide further guidance.

Code provision

C.3.1 The board of directors should establish an audit committee composed of at least three members who are all independent non-executive directors. The board should satisfy itself that the membership of the audit committee has sufficient skills to discharge its responsibilities effectively, including ensuring that at least one member of the audit committee has recent and relevant financial experience. The chair of the trust should not chair or be a member of the audit committee. He can, however, attend meetings by invitation as appropriate.

C.3.1 The main role and responsibilities of the audit committee should be set out in publicly available, written terms of reference. The council of governors should be consulted on the terms of reference, which should be reviewed and refreshed regularly. It should include details of how it will:

- Monitor the integrity of the financial statements of the NHS foundation trust, and any formal announcements relating to the trust's financial performance, reviewing significant financial reporting judgements contained in them;
- Review the NHS foundation trust's internal financial controls and, unless expressly addressed by a separate board risk committee composed of independent directors, or by the board itself, review the trust's internal control and risk management systems;
- Monitor and review the effectiveness of the NHS foundation trust's internal audit function, taking into consideration relevant UK professional and regulatory requirements;
- Review and monitor the external auditor's independence and objectivity and the effectiveness of the audit process, taking into consideration relevant UK professional and regulatory requirements;
- Develop and implement policy on the engagement of the external auditor to supply non-audit services, taking into account relevant ethical guidance regarding the provision of non-audit services by the external audit firm; and
- Report to the council of governors, identifying any matters in respect of which it considers that action or improvement is needed and making recommendations as to the steps to be taken.

C.3.3. The council of governors should take the lead in agreeing with the audit committee the criteria for appointing, re-appointing and removing external auditors. The council of governors will need to work hard to ensure they have the skills and knowledge to choose the right external auditor and monitor their performance. However, they should be supported in this task by the audit committee, which provides information to the governors on the external auditor's performance as well as overseeing the NHS foundation trust's internal financial reporting and internal auditing.

C.3.4. The audit committee should make a report to the council of governors in relation to the performance of the external auditor, including details such as the quality and value of the work and the timeliness of reporting and fees, to enable to council of governors to consider whether or not to re-appoint them. The audit committee should also make recommendation to the council of governors about the appointment, re-appointment and removal of the external auditor and approve the remuneration and terms of engagement of the external auditor.

C.3.5. If the council of governors does not accept the audit committee's recommendation, the board of directors should include in the annual report a statement from the audit committee explaining the recommendation and should set out reasons why the council of governors has taken a different position.

C.3.6. The NHS foundation trust should appoint an external auditor for a period of time which allows the auditor to develop a strong understanding of the finances, operations and forward plans of the NHS foundation trust. The current best practice is for a three- to five-year period of appointment.

C.3.7. When the council of governors ends an external auditor's appointment in disputed circumstances, the chair should write to Monitor informing it of the reasons behind the decision.

C.3.4. The audit committee should review arrangements that allow staff of the NHS foundation trust and other individuals where relevant, to raise, in confidence, concerns about possible improprieties in matters of financial reporting and control, clinical quality, patient safety or other matters. The audit committee's objective should be to ensure that arrangements are in place for the proportionate and independent investigation of such matters and for appropriate follow-up action. This should include ensuring safeguards for those who raise concerns are in place and operating effectively. Such processes should enable individuals or groups to draw formal attention to practices that are unethical or violate internal or external policies, rules or regulations and to ensure that valid concerns are promptly addressed. These processes should also reassure individuals raising concerns that they will be protected from potential negative repercussions.

C.3.9. A separate section of the annual report should describe the work of the committee in discharging its responsibilities. The report should include:

- the significant issues that the committee considered in relation to financial statements, operations and compliance, and how these issues were addressed;
- an explanation of how it has assessed the effectiveness of the external audit process and the approach taken to the appointment or re-appointment of the external auditor, the value of external audit services and information on the length of tenure of the current audit firm and when a tender was last conducted; and
- if the external auditor provides non-audit services, the value of the non-audit services provided and an explanation of how auditor objectivity and independence are safeguarded.

Section D. Remuneration

D.1 The level and components of remuneration

Main principle

D.1.a. Levels of remuneration should be sufficient to attract, retain and motivate directors of quality, and with the skills and experience required to lead the NHS foundation trust successfully, but an NHS foundation trust should avoid paying more than is necessary for this purpose and should consider all relevant and current directions relating to contractual benefits such as pay and redundancy entitlements.

Supporting principles

D.1.b. Any performance-related elements of executive directors' remuneration should be stretching and designed to promote the long-term sustainability of the NHS foundation trust. They should also take as a baseline for performance any competencies required and specified within the job description for the post.

D.1.c. The remuneration committee should decide if a proportion of executive director's remuneration should be structured so as to link reward to corporate and individual performance. The remuneration committee should judge where to position its NHS foundation trust relative to other NHS foundation trusts and comparable organisations. Such comparisons should be used with caution to avoid any risk of an increase in remuneration levels with no corresponding improvement in performance.

D.1.d. The remuneration committee should also be sensitive to pay and employment conditions elsewhere in the NHS foundation trust, especially when determining annual salary increases.

Code provisions

D.1.1. Any performance-related elements of the remuneration of executive directors should be designed to align their interests with those of patients, service users and taxpayers and to give these directors keen incentives to perform at the highest levels. In designing schemes of performance-related remuneration, the remuneration committee should consider the following provisions:

    i) The remuneration committee should consider whether the directors should be eligible for annual bonuses in line with local procedures. If so, performance conditions should be relevant, stretching and designed to match the long-term interests of the public and patients.

    ii) Payouts or grants under all incentive schemes should be subject to challenging performance criteria reflecting the objectives of the NHS foundation trust. Consideration should be given to criteria which reflect the performance of the NHS foundation trust relative to a group of comparator trusts in some key indicators, and the taking of independent and expert advice where appropriate.

    iii) Performance criteria and any upper limits for annual bonuses and incentive schemes should be set and disclosed.

iv) The remuneration committee should consider the pension consequences and associated costs to the NHS foundation trust of basic salary increases and any other changes in pensionable remuneration, especially for directors close to retirement.

D.1.2. Levels of remuneration for the chair and other non-executive directors should reflect the time commitment and responsibilities of their roles.

D.1.3. Where an NHS foundation trust releases an executive director, for example to serve as a non-executive director elsewhere, the remuneration disclosures of the annual report should include a statement of whether or not the director will retain such earnings.

D.1.4. The remuneration committee should carefully consider what compensation commitments (including pension contributions and all other elements) their directors' terms of appointments would give rise to in the event of early termination. The aim should be to avoid rewarding poor performance. Contracts should allow for compensation to be reduced to reflect a departing director's obligation to mitigate loss. Appropriate claw-back provisions should be considered in case of a director returning to the NHS within the period of any putative notice.

D.2 Procedure

Main principle

D.2.a There should be a formal and transparent procedure for developing policy on executive remuneration and for fixing the remuneration packages of individual directors. No director should be involved in deciding his or her own remuneration.

Supporting principle

D.2.b The remuneration committee should consult the chair and/or chief executive about its proposals relating to the remuneration of other executive directors.

D.2.c The remuneration committee should also be responsible for appointing any independent consultants in respect of executive director remuneration.

D.2.d Where executive directors or senior management are involved in advising or supporting the remuneration committee, care should be taken to recognise and avoid conflicts of interest.

Code provisions

D.2.1 The board of directors should establish a remuneration committee composed of non-executive directors which should include at least three independent non-executive directors. The remuneration committee should make available its terms of reference, explaining its role and the authority delegated to it by the board of directors. Where remuneration consultants are appointed, a statement should be made available as to whether they have any other connection with the NHS foundation trust.

D.2.2 The remuneration committee should have delegated responsibility for setting remuneration for all executive directors, including pension rights and any compensation payments. The committee should also recommend and monitor the level and structure of remuneration for senior management. The definition of senior management for this purpose should be determined by the board, but should normally include the first layer of management below board level.

D.2.3. The council of governors should consult external professional advisers to market-test the remuneration levels of the chair and other non-executives at least once every three years and when they intend to make a material change to the remuneration of a non-executive.

Relevant statutory requirements

D.2.4. The council of governors is responsible for setting the remuneration of non- executive directors and the chair.

Section E. Relations with stakeholders

E.1 Dialogue with members, patients and the local community

Main principle

E.1 a. The board of directors should appropriately consult and involve members, patients and the local community.

E.1.b The council of governors must represent the interests of trust members and the public.

E.1.c. Notwithstanding the complementary role of the governors in this consultation, the board of directors as a whole has responsibility for ensuring that regular and open dialogue with its stakeholders takes place.

Supporting principles

E.1.d. The board of directors should keep in touch with the opinion of members, patients and the local community in whatever ways are most practical and efficient. There must be a members' meeting at least annually.

E.1.e. The chair (and the senior independent director and other directors as appropriate) should maintain regular contact with governors to understand their issues and concerns.

E.1.f. NHS foundation trusts should use an open annual meeting and open board meetings, both of which trusts are required to hold, to encourage stakeholder engagement.

E.1.g. Governors should seek the views of members and the public on material issues or changes being discussed by the trust. Governors should provide information and feedback to members and the public regarding the trust, its vision, performance and material strategic proposals made by the trust board.

E.1.h. It is also incumbent on the board of directors to ensure governors have the mechanisms in place to secure and report on feedback that will enable them to fulfil their duty to represent the interests of members and the public

Code provisions

E.1.1. The board of directors should make available a public document that sets out its policy on the involvement of members, patients and the local community at large, including a description of the kind of issues it will consult on.

E.1.2. The board of directors should clarify in writing how the public interests of patients and the local community will be represented, including its approach for addressing the overlap and interface between governors and any local consultative forums (eg, Local Healthwatch, the Overview and Scrutiny Committee, the local League of Friends, and staff groups).

E.1.3. The chair should ensure that the views of governors and members are communicated to the board as a whole. The chair should discuss the affairs of the NHS foundation trust with governors. Non-executive directors should be offered the opportunity to attend meetings with governors and should expect to attend them if requested by governors. The senior independent director should attend sufficient meetings with governors to listen to their views in order to help develop a balanced understanding of the issues and concerns of governors.

E.1.4. The board of directors should ensure that the NHS foundation trust provides effective mechanisms for communication between governors and members from its constituencies. Contact procedures for members who wish to communicate with governors and/or directors should be made clearly available to members on the NHS foundation trust's website and in the annual report.

E.1.5. The board of directors should state in the annual report the steps they have taken to ensure that the members of the board, and in particular the non-executive directors, develop an understanding of the views of governors and members about the NHS foundation trust, for example through attendance at meetings of the council of governors, direct face-to-face contact, surveys of members' opinions and consultations.

E.1.6. The board of directors should monitor how representative the NHS foundation trust's membership is and the level and effectiveness of member engagement and report on this in the annual report. This information should be used to review the trust's membership strategy, taking into account any emerging best practice from the sector.

Relevant statutory requirements

E.1.7. The board of directors must make board meetings and the annual meeting open to the public. The trust's constitution may provide for members of the public to be excluded from a meeting for special reasons.

E.1.8 The trust must hold annual members' meetings. At least one of the directors must present the trust's annual report and accounts, and any report of the auditor on the accounts, to members at this meeting.

E.2 Co-operation with third parties with roles in relation to NHS foundation trusts

Main principle

E.2.a. The board of directors is responsible for ensuring that the NHS foundation trust co-operates with other NHS bodies, local authorities and other relevant organisations with an interest in the local health economy.

Supporting principle

E.2.b. The board of directors should enter a dialogue at an appropriate level with a range of third party stakeholders and other interested organisations with roles in relation to NHS foundation trusts based on the mutual understanding of objectives.

Code provisions

E.2.1. The board of directors should be clear as to the specific third party bodies in relation to which the NHS foundation trust has a duty to co-operate. The board of directors should be clear of the form and scope of the co-operation required with each of these third party bodies in order to discharge their statutory duties.
E.2.2. The board of directors should ensure that effective mechanisms are in place to co-operate with relevant third party bodies and that collaborative and productive relationships are maintained with relevant stakeholders at appropriate levels of seniority in each. The board of directors should review the effectiveness of these processes and relationships annually and, where necessary, take proactive steps to improve them.

Schedule A: Disclosure of corporate governance arrangements

NHS foundation trusts are required to provide a specific set of disclosures to meet the requirements of the *NHS Foundation Trust Code of Governance*, which should be submitted as part of the Annual Report (as referenced in the *NHS Foundation Trust Annual Reporting Manual*). The following list specifies everything that is required within this separate disclosure.

1. Below are the statutory requirements that we have highlighted in the Code. This supersedes the "comply or explain" requirements of the Code. **However, there is no need to report on these provisions in the Code disclosure.**

Reference	Statutory requirement:
A.2.2	The roles of chair and chief executive must not be undertaken by the same individual.
A.5.10	The council of governors has a statutory duty to hold the non-executive directors individually and collectively to account for the performance of the board of directors.
A.5.11	The 2006 Act, as amended, gives the council of governors a statutory requirement to receive the following documents. These documents should be provided in the annual report as per the *NHS Foundation Trust Annual Reporting Manual*: a) the annual accounts; b) any report of the auditor on them; and c) the annual report.

Reference	Statutory requirement:
A.5.12	The directors must provide governors with an agenda prior to any meeting of the board, and a copy of the approved minutes as soon as is practicable afterwards. There is no legal basis on which the minutes of private sessions of board meetings should be exempted from being shared with the governors. In practice, it may be necessary to redact some information, for example, for data protection or commercial reasons. Governors should respect the confidentiality of these documents.
A.5.13	The council of governors may require one or more of the directors to attend a meeting to obtain information about performance of the trust's functions or the directors' performance of their duties, and to help the council of governors to decide whether to propose a vote on the trust's or directors' performance.
A.5.14	Governors have the right to refer a question to the independent panel for advising governors. More than 50% of governors who vote must approve this referral. The council should ensure dialogue with the board of directors takes place before considering such a referral, as it may be possible to resolve questions in this way.
A.5.15	Governors should use their new rights and voting powers from the 2012 Act to represent the interests of members and the public on major decisions taken by the board of directors. These are outlined in full at A.5.15.
B.2.11	It is a requirement of the 2006 Act that the chair, the other non-executive directors and – except in the case of the appointment of a chief executive – the chief executive, are responsible for deciding the appointment of executive directors. The nominations committee with responsibility for executive director nominations should identify suitable candidates to fill executive director vacancies as they arise and make recommendations to the chair, the other non-executives directors and, except in the case of the appointment of a chief executive, the chief executive.
B.2.12	It is for the non-executive directors to appoint and remove the chief executive. The appointment of a chief executive requires the approval of the council of governors.
B.2.13	The governors are responsible at a general meeting for the appointment, re-appointment and removal of the chair and the other non-executive directors.
B.4.3	The board has a duty to take steps to ensure that governors are equipped with the skills and knowledge they need to discharge their duties appropriately.
B.5.8	The board of directors must have regard for the views of the council of governors on the NHS foundation trust's forward plan.

Reference	Statutory requirement:
B.7.3	Approval by the council of governors of the appointment of a chief executive should be a subject of the first general meeting after the appointment by a committee of the chair and non-executive directors. All other executive directors should be appointed by a committee of the chief executive, the chair and non-executive directors.
B.7.4	Non-executive directors, including the chair should be appointed by the council of governors for the specified terms subject to re- appointment thereafter at intervals of no more than three years and subject to the 2006 Act provisions relating to removal of a director.
B.7.5	Elected governors must be subject to re-election by the members of their constituency at regular intervals not exceeding three years.
D.2.4	The council of governors is responsible for setting the remuneration of non-executive directors and the chair.
E.1.7.	The board of directors must make board meetings and the annual meeting open to the public. The trust's constitution may provide for members of the public to be excluded from a meeting for special reasons.
E.1.8	The trust must hold annual members' meetings. At least one of the directors must present the trust's annual report and accounts, and any report of the auditor on the accounts, to members at this meeting.

2. The provisions listed below require a supporting explanation, even in the case that the NHS foundation trust is compliant with the provision. **Where the information is already contained within the annual report, a reference to its location is sufficient to avoid unnecessary duplication.**

Provision	Requirement
A.1.1	This statement should also describe how any disagreements between the council of governors and the board of directors will be resolved. The annual report should include this schedule of matters or a summary statement of how the board of directors and the council of governors operate, including a summary of the types of decisions to be taken by each of the boards and which are delegated to the executive management of the board of directors.
A.1.2	The annual report should identify the chair, the deputy chair (where there is one), the chief executive, the senior independent director (see A.4.1) and the chair and members of the nominations, audit and remuneration committees. It should also set out the number of meetings of the board and those committees and individual attendance by directors.

Provision	Requirement
A.5.3	The annual report should identify the members of the council of governors, including a description of the constituency or organisation that they represent, whether they were elected or appointed, and the duration of their appointments. The annual report should also identify the nominated lead governor.
B.1.1	The board of directors should identify in the annual report each non-executive director it considers to be independent, with reasons where necessary.
B.1.4	The board of directors should include in its annual report a description of each director's skills, expertise and experience. Alongside this, in the annual report, the board should make a clear statement about its own balance, completeness and appropriateness to the requirements of the NHS foundation trust.
B.2.10	A separate section of the annual report should describe the work of the nominations committee(s), including the process it has used in relation to board appointments.
B.3.1	A chair's other significant commitments should be disclosed to the council of governors before appointment and included in the annual report. Changes to such commitments should be reported to the council of governors as they arise, and included in the next annual report.
B.5.6	Governors should canvass the opinion of the trust's members and the public, and for appointed governors the body they represent, on the NHS foundation trust's forward plan, including its objectives, priorities and strategy, and their views should be communicated to the board of directors. The annual report should contain a statement as to how this requirement has been undertaken and satisfied.
B.6.1	The board of directors should state in the annual report how performance evaluation of the board, its committees, and its directors, including the chair, has been conducted.
B.6.2	Where there has been external evaluation of the board and/or governance of the trust, the external facilitator should be identified in the annual report and a statement made as to whether they have any other connection to the trust.

Provision	Requirement
C.1.1	The directors should explain in the annual report their responsibility for preparing the annual report and accounts, and state that they consider the annual report and accounts, taken as a whole, are fair, balanced and understandable and provide the information necessary for patients, regulators and other stakeholders to assess the NHS foundation trust's performance, business model and strategy. There should be a statement by the external auditor about their reporting responsibilities. Directors should also explain their approach to quality governance in the Annual Governance Statement (within the annual report).
C.2.1	The annual report should contain a statement that the board has conducted a review of the effectiveness of its system of internal controls.
C.2.2	A trust should disclose in the annual report: a) if it has an internal audit function, how the function is structured and what role it performs; or b) if it does not have an internal audit function, that fact and the processes it employs for evaluating and continually improving the effectiveness of its risk management and internal control processes.
C.3.5	If the council of governors does not accept the audit committee's recommendation on the appointment, reappointment or removal of an external auditor, the board of directors should include in the annual report a statement from the audit committee explaining the recommendation and should set out reasons why the council of governors has taken a different position.
C.3.9	A separate section of the annual report should describe the work of the audit committee in discharging its responsibilities. The report should include: ■ the significant issues that the committee considered in relation to financial statements, operations and compliance, and how these issues were addressed; ■ an explanation of how it has assessed the effectiveness of the external audit process and the approach taken to the appointment or re-appointment of the external auditor, the value of external audit services and information on the length of tenure of the current audit firm and when a tender was last conducted; and ■ if the external auditor provides non-audit services, the value of the non-audit services provided and an explanation of how auditor objectivity and independence are safeguarded.
D.1.3	Where an NHS foundation trust releases an executive director, for example to serve as a non-executive director elsewhere, the remuneration disclosures of the annual report should include a statement of whether or not the director will retain such earnings.

Provision	Requirement
E.1.4	Contact procedures for members who wish to communicate with governors and/or directors should be made clearly available to members on the NHS foundation trust's website.
E.1.5	The board of directors should state in the annual report the steps they have taken to ensure that the members of the board, and in particular the non-executive directors, develop an understanding of the views of governors and members about the NHS foundation trust, for example through attendance at meetings of the council of governors, direct face-to-face contact, surveys of members' opinions and consultations.
E.1.6	The board of directors should monitor how representative the NHS foundation trust's membership is and the level and effectiveness of member engagement and report on this in the annual report.

3. The provisions listed below require supporting information to be made **publicly available** even in the case that the NHS foundation trust is compliant with the provision. This requirement can be met by making supporting information available on request and on the NHS foundation trust's website.

Provision	Information required on website:
A.1.3	The board of directors should make available a statement of the objectives of the NHS foundation trust showing how it intends to balance the interests of patients, the local community and other stakeholders, and use this as the basis for its decision-making and forward planning.
B.1.4	A description of each director's expertise and experience, with a clear statement about the board of director's balance, completeness and appropriateness.
B.2.10	The main role and responsibilities of the nominations committee should be set out in publicly available, written terms of reference.
B.3.2	The terms and conditions of appointment of non-executive directors.
C.3.2	The main role and responsibilities of the audit committee should be set out in publicly available, written terms of reference.
D.2.1	The remuneration committee should make available its terms of reference, explaining its role and the authority delegated to it by the board of directors. Where remuneration consultants are appointed, a statement should be made available as to whether they have any other connection with the NHS foundation trust.

Provision	Information required on website:
E.1.1	The board of directors should make available a public document that sets out its policy on the involvement of members, patients and the local community at large, including a description of the kind of issues it will consult on.
E.1.4	Contact procedures for members who wish to communicate with governors and/or directors should be made clearly available to members on the NHS foundation trust's website.

The provisions listed below require supporting information to be made **available to governors**, even in the case that the NHS foundation trust is compliant with the provision. This information should be set out in papers accompanying a resolution to re-appoint a non-executive director.

Provision	Information required:
B.7.1	In the case of re-appointment of non-executive directors, the chair should confirm to the governors that following formal performance evaluation, the performance of the individual proposed for re-appointment continues to be effective and to demonstrate commitment to the role.

4. The provisions listed below require supporting information to be made **available to members**, even in the case that the NHS foundation trust is compliant with the provision. This information should be set out in papers accompanying a resolution to elect or re-elect a governor.

Provision	Information required:
B.7.2	The names of governors submitted for election or re-election should be accompanied by sufficient biographical details and any other relevant information to enable members to take an informed decision on their election. This should include prior performance information.

5. For all provisions listed below there are no special requirements as per 1–6 above. For these provisions, the basic "comply or explain" requirement stands. The disclosure should therefore contain **an explanation in each case where the trust has departed from the Code, explaining the reasons for the departure and how the alternative arrangements continue to reflect the main principles of the Code (page 13–16).**

A disclosure is only required for **departures** from the Code for the provisions listed in this section. NHS foundation trusts are welcome but not required to provide a simple statement of compliance with each individual provision. This may be useful in ensuring the disclosure is comprehensive and may help to ensure that each provision has been considered in turn.

In providing an explanation for any variation from the *NHS Foundation Trust Code of Governance*, the NHS foundation trust should aim to illustrate how its actual practices are consistent with the principle to which the particular provision relates. It should set out the background, provide a clear rationale, and describe any mitigating actions it is taking to address any risks and maintain conformity with the relevant principle. Where deviation from a particular provision is intended to be limited in time, the explanation should indicate when the NHS foundation trust expects to conform to the provision.

The table below provides a summary of the provisions – the full provisions as listed in the document should be used for reference. In this summary '"the board" refers to the board of directors, "the council" to the council of governors, and "trust" refers to the NHS foundation trust.

Provision	Summary:
A.1.4	The board should ensure that adequate systems and processes are maintained to measure and monitor the NHS foundation trust's effectiveness, efficiency and economy as well as the quality of its health care delivery.
A.1.5	The board should ensure that relevant metrics, measures, milestones and accountabilities are developed and agreed so as to understand and assess progress and delivery of performance.
A.1.6	The board should report on its approach to clinical governance.
A.1.7	The chief executive as the accounting officer should follow the procedure set out by Monitor for advising the board and the council and for recording and submitting objections to decisions.
A.1.8	The board should establish the constitution and standards of conduct for the NHS foundation trust and its staff in accordance with NHS values and accepted standards of behaviour in public life.
A.1.9	The board should operate a code of conduct that builds on the values of the NHS foundation trust and reflect high standards of probity and responsibility.
A.1.10	The NHS foundation trust should arrange appropriate insurance to cover the risk of legal action against its directors.
A.3.1	The chair should, on appointment by the council, meet the independence criteria set out in B.1.1. A chief executive should not go on to be the chair of the same NHS foundation trust.
A.4.1	In consultation with the council, the board should appoint one of the independent non-executive directors to be the senior independent director.
A.4.2	The chair should hold meetings with the non-executive directors without the executives present.

Provision	Summary:
A.4.3	Where directors have concerns that cannot be resolved about the running of the NHS foundation trust or a proposed action, they should ensure that their concerns are recorded in the board minutes.
A.5.1	The council of governors should meet sufficiently regularly to discharge its duties.
A.5.2	The council of governors should not be so large as to be unwieldy.
A.5.4	The roles and responsibilities of the council of governors should be set out in a written document.
A.5.5	The chair is responsible for leadership of both the board and the council but the governors also have a responsibility to make the arrangements work and should take the lead in inviting the chief executive to their meetings and inviting attendance by other executives and non-executives, as appropriate.
A.5.6	The council should establish a policy for engagement with the board of directors for those circumstances when they have concerns.
A.5.7	The council should ensure its interaction and relationship with the board of directors is appropriate and effective.
A.5.8	The council should only exercise its power to remove the chair or any non-executive directors after exhausting all means of engagement with the board.
A.5.9	The council should receive and consider other appropriate information required to enable it to discharge its duties.
B.1.2	At least half the board, excluding the chair, should comprise non-executive directors determined by the board to be independent.
B.1.3	No individual should hold, at the same time, positions of director and governor of any NHS foundation trust.
B.2.1	The nominations committee or committees, with external advice as appropriate, are responsible for the identification and nomination of executive and non-executive directors.
B.2.2	Directors on the board of directors and governors on the council should meet the "fit and proper" persons test described in the provider licence.
B.2.3	The nominations committee(s) should regularly review the structure, size and composition of the board and make recommendations for changes where appropriate.
B.2.4	The chair or an independent non-executive director should chair the nominations committee(s).

Provision	Summary:
B.2.5	The governors should agree with the nominations committee a clear process for the nomination of a new chair and non-executive directors.
B.2.6	Where an NHS foundation trust has two nominations committees, the nominations committee responsible for the appointment of non-executive directors should consist of a majority of governors.
B.2.7	When considering the appointment of non-executive directors, the council should take into account the views of the board and the nominations committee on the qualifications, skills and experience required for each position.
B.2.8	The annual report should describe the process followed by the council in relation to appointments of the chair and non-executive directors.
B.2.9	An independent external adviser should not be a member of or have a vote on the nominations committee(s).
B.3.3	The board should not agree to a full-time executive director taking on more than one non-executive directorship of an NHS foundation trust or another organisation of comparable size and complexity.
B.5.1	The board and the council governors should be provided with high-quality information appropriate to their respective functions and relevant to the decisions they have to make.
B.5.2	The board and in particular non-executive directors, may reasonably wish to challenge assurances received from the executive management. They need not seek to appoint a relevant adviser for each and every subject area that comes before the board, although they should, wherever possible, ensure that they have sufficient information and understanding to enable challenge and to take decisions on an informed basis.
B.5.3	The board should ensure that directors, especially non-executive directors, have access to the independent professional advice, at the NHS foundation trust's expense, where they judge it necessary to discharge their responsibilities as directors.
B.5.4	Committees should be provided with sufficient resources to undertake their duties.
B.6.3	The senior independent director should lead the performance evaluation of the chair.
B.6.4	The chair, with assistance of the board secretary, if applicable, should use the performance evaluations as the basis for determining individual and collective professional development programmes for non-executive directors relevant to their duties as board members.

Provision	Summary:
B.6.5	Led by the chair, the council should periodically assess their collective performance and they should regularly communicate to members and the public details on how they have discharged their responsibilities.
B.6.6	There should be a clear policy and a fair process, agreed and adopted by the council, for the removal from the council of any governor who consistently and unjustifiability fails to attend the meetings of the council or has an actual or potential conflict of interest which prevents the proper exercise of their duties.
B.8.1	The remuneration committee should not agree to an executive member of the board leaving the employment of an NHS foundation trust, except in accordance with the terms of their contract of employment, including but not limited to service of their full notice period and/or material reductions in their time commitment to the role, without the board first having completed and approved a full risk assessment.
C.1.2	The directors should report that the NHS foundation trust is a going concern with supporting assumptions or qualifications as necessary.
C.1.3	At least annually and in a timely manner, the board should set out clearly its financial, quality and operating objectives for the NHS foundation trust and disclose sufficient information, both quantitative and qualitative, of the NHS foundation trust's business and operation, including clinical outcome data, to allow members and governors to evaluate its performance.
C.1.4.	a) The board of directors must notify Monitor and the council of governors without delay and should consider whether it is in the public's interest to bring to the public attention, any major new developments in the NHS foundation trust's sphere of activity which are not public knowledge, which it is able to disclose and which may lead by virtue of their effect on its assets and liabilities, or financial position or on the general course of its business, to a substantial change to the financial wellbeing, health care delivery performance or reputation and standing of the NHS foundation trust. b) The board of directors must notify Monitor and the council of governors without delay and should consider whether it is in the public interest to bring to public attention all relevant information which is not public knowledge concerning a material change in: ■ the NHS foundation trust's financial condition; ■ the performance of its business; and/or ■ the NHS foundation trust's expectations as to its performance which, if made public, would be likely to lead to a substantial change to the financial wellbeing, health care delivery performance or reputation and standing of the NHS foundation trust.

Provision	Summary:
C.3.1	The board should establish an audit committee composed of at least three members who are all independent non-executive directors.
C.3.3	The council should take the lead in agreeing with the audit committee the criteria for appointing, re-appointing and removing external auditors.
C.3.6	The NHS foundation trust should appoint an external auditor for a period of time which allows the auditor to develop a strong understanding of the finances, operations and forward plans of the NHS foundation trust.
C.3.7	When the council ends an external auditor's appointment in disputed circumstances, the chair should write to Monitor informing it of the reasons behind the decision.
C.3.8	The audit committee should review arrangements that allow staff of the NHS foundation trust and other individuals where relevant, to raise, in confidence, concerns about possible improprieties in matters of financial reporting and control, clinical quality, patient safety or other matters.
D.1.1	Any performance-related elements of the remuneration of executive directors should be designed to align their interests with those of patients, service users and taxpayers and to give these directors keen incentives to perform at the highest levels.
D.1.2	Levels of remuneration for the chair and other non-executive directors should reflect the time commitment and responsibilities of their roles.
D.1.4	The remuneration committee should carefully consider what compensation commitments (including pension contributions and all other elements) their directors' terms of appointments would give rise to in the event of early termination.
D.2.2	The remuneration committee should have delegated responsibility for setting remuneration for all executive directors, including pension rights and any compensation payments.
D.2.3	The council should consult external professional advisers to market-test the remuneration levels of the chair and other non-executives at least once every three years and when they intend to make a material change to the remuneration of a non-executive.
E.1.2	The board should clarify in writing how the public interests of patients and the local community will be represented, including its approach for addressing the overlap and interface between governors and any local consultative forums.
E.1.3	The chair should ensure that the views of governors and members are communicated to the board as a whole.

Provision	Summary:
E.2.1	The board should be clear as to the specific third party bodies in relation to which the NHS foundation trust has a duty to co-operate.
E.2.2	The board should ensure that effective mechanisms are in place to co-operate with relevant third party bodies and that collaborative and productive relationships are maintained with relevant stakeholders at appropriate levels of seniority in each.

Appendix A: The role of the NHS foundation trust secretary

The NHS foundation trust secretary has a significant role to play in the administration of corporate governance. In particular, the trust secretary would normally be expected to:

- ensure good information flows within the board of directors and its committees and between senior management, non-executive directors and the governors;
- ensure that board procedures of both the board of directors and the council of governors are complied with;
- advise the board of directors and the council of governors (through the chair) on all governance matters; and
- be available to give advice and support to individual directors, particularly in relation to the induction of new directors and assistance with professional development.

Accordingly, the NHS foundation trust should give careful consideration to the appointment of a trust secretary in view of the clear benefits of the role. A trust secretary is normally employed by the NHS foundation trust. All directors and governors would have access to the advice and services of the trust secretary. Both the appointment and removal of the trust secretary would be a matter for the chief executive and chair jointly.

Appendix B: The role of the nominated lead governor

The lead governor has a role to play in facilitating direct communication between Monitor and the NHS foundation trust's council of governors. This will be in a limited number of circumstances and, in particular, where it may not be appropriate to communicate through the normal channels, which in most cases will be via the chair or the trust secretary, if one is appointed.

It is not anticipated that there will be regular direct contact between Monitor and the council of governors in the ordinary course of business. Where this is necessary, it is important that it happens quickly and in an effective manner. To this end, a lead governor should be nominated and contact details provided to Monitor, and then updated as required. The lead governor may be any of the governors.

The main circumstances where Monitor will contact a lead governor are where Monitor has concerns as to board leadership provided to an NHS foundation trust, and those concerns may in time lead to the use by Monitor's board of its formal powers to remove the chair or non-executive directors. The council of governors appoints the chair and non-executive directors, and it will usually be the case that Monitor will wish to understand the views of the governors as to the capacity and capability of these individuals to lead the trust, and to rectify successfully any issues, and also for the governors to understand Monitor's concerns.

Monitor does not, however, envisage direct communication with the governors until such time as there is a real risk that an NHS foundation trust may be in significant breach of its licence. Once there is a risk that this may be the case, and the likely issue is one of board leadership, Monitor will often wish to have direct contact with the NHS foundation trust's governors, but at speed and through one established point of contact, the trust's nominated lead governor. The lead governor should take steps to understand Monitor's role, the available guidance and the basis on which Monitor may take regulatory action. The lead governor will then be able to communicate more widely with other governors.

Similarly, where individual governors wish to contact Monitor, this would be expected to be through the lead governor.

The other circumstance where Monitor may wish to contact a lead governor is where, as the regulator, we have been made aware that the process for the appointment of the chair or other members of the board, or elections for governors, or other material decisions, may not have complied with the NHS foundation trust's constitution, or alternatively, though complying with the trust's constitution, may be inappropriate.

In such circumstances, where the chair, other members of the board of directors or the trust secretary may have been involved in the process by which these appointments or other decisions were made, a lead governor may provide a point of contact for Monitor.

Accordingly, the NHS foundation trust should nominate a lead governor, and to continue to update Monitor with their contact details as and when these change.

Appendix C: The *NHS Foundation Trust* Code of Governance and other regulatory requirements

Although compliance with the provisions in this guide is not necessarily mandatory, some of the provisions in this document are statutory requirements because they are enshrined elsewhere in legislation. In the first instance, boards, directors and governors should ensure they are meeting the governance requirements for NHS foundation trusts as set out in the 2006 Act (as amended by the 2012 Act) and reflected in the new provider licence and *Risk assessment framework*. This Code sits alongside a number of other Monitor reporting requirements which relate to governance.

Foundation Trust Condition 4: Governance in the new NHS foundation trust provider licence allows Monitor to use reasonable evidence, from disclosures made to us by NHS foundation trusts, to determine if there is a risk of a breach of the licence condition and make a decision regarding intervention. The information we receive includes: a **forward looking** disclosure on corporate governance (the Corporate Governance Statement); a **backward looking** disclosure on corporate governance (the *NHS Foundation Trust Code of Governance*); and **a backward looking statement on internal control**, **risk** and **quality governance** (the Annual Governance Statement).

For clarity, here, we have provided a brief explanation of how the different requirements sit together and the purpose of each.

- **The Corporate Governance Statement – in the Annual Plan**
  In order to comply with both the new provider licence and the *Risk assessment framework*, the Annual Plan also includes a requirement for a Corporate Governance

Statement. This is a **mandatory requirement**. This is a forward looking statement of expectations regarding corporate governance arrangements over the next 12 months and trusts should be aware that "**issues not identified and subsequently arising can be used as evidence of self-certification failure**". The requirement for the completion of the Corporate Governance Statement is separate to the disclosure requirements of this Code.

■ **The Code disclosure requirements – listed in this document and the** *NHS Foundation Trust Annual Reporting Manual*
This document is designed to set out **standards of best practice for corporate govern-ance** – that is the behaviours and systems governing directors, and governors, and their role in ensuring adequate standards of audit and stakeholder engagement.
It is not mandatory to comply with this guidance, however, Section 7 of the *Annual Reporting Manual* **does require trusts to make some specific disclosures on a "comply or explain" basis** regarding the provisions listed in this document. (A detailed list of the disclosures required is provided in Schedule A of this document and duplicated in the *Annual Reporting Manual*, for ease of reference.) This is a backward looking statement which should be submitted with the Annual Report.

■ **The Annual Governance Statement – in the** *NHS Foundation Trust Annual Reporting Manual*
In addition to listing the Code disclosure requirements, the *Annual Reporting Manual* also requires an Annual Governance Statement. The Annual Governance Statement is a backward looking statement which captures information on risk management and internal control, and includes some specific requirements on quality governance. It replaced and expanded on the former requirement for a Statement on Internal Control. Completion of the Annual Governance Statement is a **mandatory requirement**. The Annual Governance statement does not relate to this Code.

Notes

1 This is updated on a yearly basis and made available on the Monitor website.

The Healthy NHS Board 2013

Principles for Good Governance

1 Introduction

This chapter explains the purpose of the Healthy NHS Board guidance and provides a visual summary to help readers navigate through the document.

The NHS Leadership Academy recognises the crucial importance of effective, engaged, accountable board leadership and is therefore very pleased to have commissioned this refreshed edition of 'The Healthy NHS Board 2013 – Principles for Good Governance'.

This guidance supports the NHS Leadership Academy's mission to develop outstanding leadership in health in order to improve people's health and their experience of the NHS.

The strong relationship between leadership capability and performance is well demonstrated in the evidence. Good leadership leads to a good organisational climate and good organisational climates lead, via improved staff satisfaction and loyalty, to sustainable, high performing organisations.

The updated guide has been enormously enriched by the insights of experienced, thoughtful leaders of NHS, regulatory and patient advocacy organisations who have generously responded to our call to contribute their time and their wisdom.

We are also very grateful to our partners – Monitor, the NHS Trust Development Authority, the Care Quality Commission, the Foundation Trust Network and the NHS Confederation – all of whom fielded senior leaders to join us as part of a steering group to provide advice and oversight to the process.

The guide will serve as a cornerstone of the Academy's wider programme of work to support and enable board and governance development. We hope that boards of NHS organisations will find that it can also serve as a cornerstone for your board development.

Karen Lynas
Deputy Managing Director, NHS Leadership Academy

Purpose of this guidance

This document sets out the guiding principles that will allow NHS board members to understand the:

- Collective role of the board including effective governance in relation to the wider health and social care system

- Activities and approaches that are most likely to improve board effectiveness in governing well
- Contribution expected of them as individual board members.

It is hoped that NHS board members will continue to find this good practice guidance valuable and will focus effort in ways that the evidence suggestsshould be most productive. 'The Healthy NHS Board' (February 2010) was underpinned by a comprehensive review of governance literature and an extensive process of engagement with the NHS. In all, some 1,000 NHS staff and board members took part in this consultation, and the shape and content of the guide reflect their contributions. The first literature review, entitled 'The Healthy NHS Board: a review of guidance and research evidence[42], considered over 140 sources. This second edition has again been supported by a process of engagement with leaders across the NHS. It is informed by a further review of governance research evidence and good practice guidance[42] available since the initial publication, both the original and updated reviews are available for download together at www.leadershipacademy.nhs.uk/healthyboard.

This guidance is primarily intended for boards of NHS Trusts and Foundation Trusts. With some interpretation it will be relevant for organisations operating at a national level. Clinical Commissioning Groups, as membership organisations, have developed very specific governance architecture and are not therefore the primary focus of this guidance, although the general principles outlined are relevant to them. It offers a framework that will help them to place reliance on the effective governance of provider organisations.

The guidance will also be of interest to those aspiring to be NHS board members, to governors of Foundation Trusts who have a role in ensuring that the board operates effectively and to those who support and work with NHS boards.

This document aims to describe the enduring principles of high quality governance, that transcend immediate policy imperatives and the more pressing features of the current health care environment. It can be used by board members as an introduction to the subject of governance in the NHS. Since it is designed to be enduring, it can be kept as a reference – a first place to turn – in the future.

2 Purpose and role of NHS boards

The purpose and role of NHS boards is set out in this chapter, helping board members to navigate through the wide range of guidance available.
The purpose of NHS boards is to govern effectively and in doing so build patient, public and stakeholder confidence that their health and healthcare is in safe hands. This fundamental accountability to the public and stakeholders is delivered by building confidence:

- In the quality and safety of health services.
- That resources are invested in a way that delivers optimal health outcomes.
- In the accessibility and responsiveness of health services.
- That patients and the public can help to shape health services to meet their needs.
- That public money is spent in a way that is fair, efficient, effective and economic.

This guide aims to provide board members with an overarching and durable framework that will allow them to make sense, and effective use, of the wide range of available advice and guidance both in the United Kingdom and internationally. It draws on established good practice in governance and a wide- ranging review of more recent literature, from all sectors.

The role of NHS boards is described below and is illustrated in Figure 2.

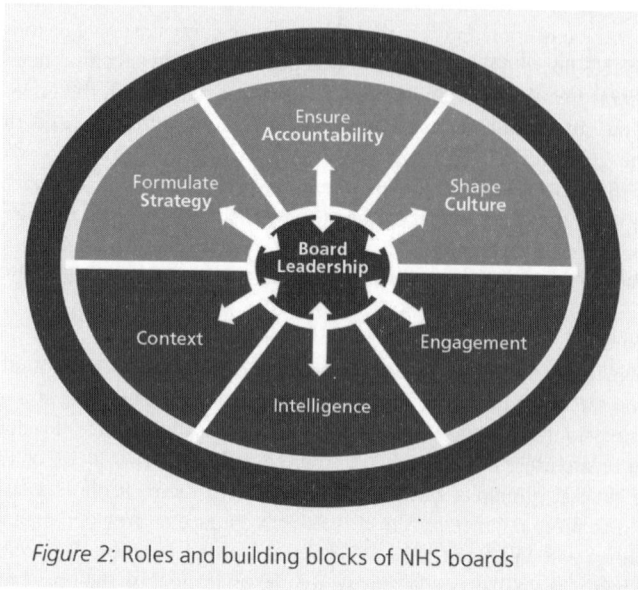

Figure 2: Roles and building blocks of NHS boards

Effective NHS boards demonstrate leadership by undertaking three key roles:

- Formulating strategy for the organisation.
- Ensuring accountability by: holding the organisation to account for the delivery of the strategy; by being accountable for ensuring the organisation operates effectively and with openness, transparency and candour and by seeking assurance that systems of control are robust and reliable.
- Shaping a healthy culture for the board and the organisation.

Underpinning these three roles are three building blocks that allow boards to exercise their role. Effective boards:

- Are informed by the external context within which they must operate.
- Are informed by, and shape, the intelligence which provides an understanding of local people's needs, trend and comparative information on how the organisation is performing together with market and stakeholder analyses.
- Give priority to engagement with stakeholders and opinion formers within and beyond the organisation; the emphasis here is on building a healthy dialogue with, and being accountable to, patients, the public, and staff, governors and members, commissioners and regulators.

The three roles of the board and the three building blocks all interconnect and influence one another. This is shown in Figure 2. They are examined in more detail in the next sections.

Roles of the board

1. Formulate Strategy

The first of the three roles of the board is formulating strategy. There are three main elements to consider:

- The **process** of developing strategy
- The **hallmarks** of an effective strategy
- The approach to strategic **decision-making**

Strategic Process

In general, an effective strategic **process**:

- Ensures that the strategy, including identification of strategic options, is demonstrably shaped and owned by the board
- Provides for the active involvement of and influence by staff
- Ensures that there have been open, transparent, accountable consultation and involvement processes with patients, the community, governors and through them members (in the case of Foundation Trusts)
- Ensures that there has been collaborative engagement with partners to shape strategy in the interests of patients
- Ensures that these consultation and involvement processes help to identify strategic choices, risks and proposed ways forward
- Is underpinned by regular strategic discourse in the board, throughout the year. Strategy needs to be dynamic in responding to changes in the external environment

Hallmarks of an effective strategy

Some of the **hallmarks** of an effective strategy include:

- Vision and purpose: putting patients first
- A compelling organisational vision for the future that puts quality of care and the safety of its patients at its heart
- A clear statement of the organisation's purpose
- Well-developed values and behaviours, owned by the organisation and supporting the desired culture to deliver the vision
- A vision that is underpinned with clear strategic objectives that are reflected in an explicit statement of desired outcomes and key performance indicators, including a balance of locally and nationally relevant indicators
- Explicit attention paid to the ability of the organisation to implement the strategy successfully
- Demonstrable influence of the needs and preferences of users, patients and communities served
- Inclusion at its heart so that services that are delivered produce accessible, fair and equitable services and outcomes for all sections of the population served
- Commitment to treating patients, service users and staff with equity
- Inspires and enables innovation
- An integrated approach to prevention and health promotion

Takes account of external context and drivers

- An approach that takes appropriate account of the external context and related risk environment in which the organisation is operating, including the organisation's responsibility as part of the wider health economy, and provides evidence of doing so
- A perspective which balances the priority given to national and local performance indicators and targets

Based on well-informed intelligence

- Evidence that the strategy has been shaped by the intelligence made available to the board (both hard and soft data)

Takes a longer term view

- A longer term view, with at least a 3 to 5 year planning horizon
- A long-term financial model and risk analysis
- A long-term people strategy (see Building Effectiveness for more information)

Strategic Decision Making

Strategic **decision-making** is an integral part of the board's role in formulating strategy. Good practice here includes:

- Strategic decisions which are aligned to overall strategic direction, and are expressly identified as such
- Testing strategic decisions to ensure that they balance excellence in the safety and quality of care together with long term financial sustainability and value for money
- A formal statement that specifies the types of strategic decisions, including levels of investment and those representing significant service changes that are expressly reserved for the board, and those that are delegated to committees or the executive
- Early involvement of board members in debating and shaping strategic decisions and appropriate consultation with internal and external stakeholders
- For significant strategic decisions: consideration by the board of options and analyses of those options and the board's appetite/tolerance for the major risks involved
- Criteria and rationale for decision making that are transparent, objective and evidence based
- Clarity about which key strategic decisions also require approval of 12 governors (for Foundation Trusts), such as: mergers, acquisitions, separations or dissolutions; significant increases in private patient income and amendments to the Trust's constitution
- Clarity about which strategic decisions require approval of other external organisations or bodies

Roles of the board
2. Ensure Accountability

The second core role of NHS boards is **ensuring accountability**. This has three main aspects:

- Holding the organisation to account for the delivery of the strategy
- Being accountable for ensuring the organisation operates effectively and with openness, transparency and candour
- Seeking assurance that the systems of control are robust and reliable

Holding the organisation to account for its performance in the delivery of strategy

In unitary NHS boards, all directors are collectively and corporately accountable for organisational performance.

This aspect is, therefore, a fundamental part of the board's role in pursuing high performance for its organisation, ensuring that the best interests of patients are central to all it does. It is important that boards are assured rather than too readily reassured. Where issues arise they need to be addressed – swiftly, decisively, knowledgeably and with humanity – by the whole unitary board. A robust but fair approach is important, particularly where there are problems of underperformance. Effective boards recognise that 'the buck stops with the board'.

Assurance: being assured because the board has reviewed reliable sources of information and is satisfied with the course of action.

Reassurance: being told by the executive or staff that performance or actions are satisfactory.

Monitor: Quality Governance Guidance [4]

A key observation from a review[5] of how boards get their assurance is 'that there has been no lack of guidance ... the challenge for boards is therefore not finding out what to do, but instead translating the theory into an approach that works in their Trust and then following through with appropriate rigour'.

The fundamentals for the board in holding the organisation to account for performance include:

- Drawing on timely board intelligence – to monitor the performance of the organisation in an effective way and satisfy itself that performance is continually improving and that appropriate action is taken to remedy problems as they arise
- Looking beyond written intelligence to develop an understanding of the daily reality for patients and staff, to make data more meaningful
- Seeking assurance that staff are clear about their responsibilities and accountabilities and how these fit with the organisation's vision and purpose
- Triangulation[4] which ensures that board members are able to 'test' the intelligence and seek assurance by looking at more than one source and type of information, including through direct engagement with the services
- Seeking assurance of sustained improvement where remedial action has been required to address performance concerns
- Offering appreciation and encouragement where performance is excellent or improving
- Taking account of, and positively encouraging, independent scrutiny of performance, including from governors (for Foundation Trusts), regulators and overview and scrutiny committees

- Rigorous but constructive challenge from all board members, executive and non-executive as corporate board members

Being accountable for ensuring the organisation operates with openness, transparency and candour

The board has an overarching responsibility, through its leadership and oversight, to ensure and be assured that the organisation operates with openness, transparency, and candour, particularly in relation to its dealings with patients and the public.

The board, itself, will be held to account by a wide range of stakeholders, for the overall effectiveness and performance of the organisation that it oversees, and the extent to which the board and the organisation operates with openness, transparency and candour. The approach to engagement of key stakeholders is described in the Engagement section.

One key part of this accountability includes the need for the board to ensure that published figures on all aspects of the quality of care are accurate and provide an honest and fair account to commissioners, regulators, patients and the public (see section on Intelligence for more information).

Boards of health and care providers will also need to be assured that the organisation is complying with the contractual duty of candour,[7] which requires providers to inform people if they believe treatment or care has caused death or serious injury.

Boards have a role in creating the culture which supports open dialogue. This should include directors personally listening to complaints, concerns and suggestions from patients and staff, and being seen to act on them fairly.

To complement this, boards need to be assured that there is a clear 'Assurance and Escalation Framework'[4] which lays out how to escalate issues and risks. Are staff clear about what they can escalate and how they should raise their concerns? Is this included in induction and training for staff? A good framework will provide clarity about how staff can raise concerns about:

- The impact of cost improvement plans on the quality of care
- Exception reporting of incidents to the board
- Identification of data quality concerns
- Early warning triggers in relation to workforce, finance and clinical services

A key element is ensuring that there is a clear whistle blowing policy, with support and protection for bona fide whistle blowers. The right to raise concerns should be reflected in staff contracts. Boards, through their remuneration committees, must be assured that any compromise agreements do not stop staff speaking out on matters of public interest.[8]

These responsibilities permeate all aspects of the leadership role of the board, including the approach taken to ensuring accountability and to shaping culture (see Culture section).

Seeking assurance that the systems of control are robust and reliable

This third aspect of accountability has eight elements:

- Quality governance
- Financial stewardship
- Risk management

- Legality
- Decision-making
- Probity
- Information governance
- Corporate Trustee

Quality governance

NHS organisations (providers and commissioners) have a statutory duty to secure continuous improvement of quality[11] and in practice this will be the responsibility of the board. If the board is effectively to deliver its ultimate accountability for safeguarding the quality of care received by patients it needs to give robust, systematic and consistent attention to the three key facets of quality: effectiveness and outcomes; patient safety and patient experience.

The board needs to become both a nurturing and driving force for continuous quality improvement across the full range of services both within the organisation and in an effective partnership with commissioners and providers along the whole patient journey.

It is the responsibility of the board to set and monitor fundamental standards of care. Boards are accountable to external inspectors and regulators for the quality and safety of the care provided, and are required to endorse and sign off declarations to regulators. However the board's own assurance needs to be drawn from robust internal monitoring rather than relying on reports to or from external regulators and inspectors.

There needs to be a clear chain of delegation that cascades accountability for delivering quality performance from the board to the point of care, ensuring that robust quality intelligence then flows back to the board.

Quality should be a core part of main board meetings both as a standing agenda item and as an integrated element of all major discussions and decisions.

The board needs to consider quality, finance and performance decisions in the round, including a full understanding of the quality impacts of initiatives or significant service changes.

Boards should regularly review a quality report, including a dashboard which provides both quantitative and qualitative data at the right level of detail. The quality report should provide information in all three facets of quality. Information provided in quality reports should be clear, comparative, accurate and recent enough to be relevant. The research finding cited in the box to the left, emphasises the importance of boards being realistic about the quality performance of their organisation.

Boards will wish to ensure that clinical leaders are properly empowered to lead on issues relating to clinical quality. Boards benefit from regular opportunities both to take advice from clinical leaders and to reflect on ways they encourage innovative practice in relation to quality improvement. This includes encouraging managers within the organisation to respond positively to suggestions for improvement from those in clinical roles.

Quality performance (including monitoring of actions to maintain and improve performance) and current risks to quality of care (including controls and mitigations) should be systematically identified in the first instance by frontline clinical leaders. These are then escalated for regular, more detailed review by a quality-focused board committee with a stable, regularly attending membership that includes key clinical leaders (see section on board committees).

Boards should hold the organisation to account for timely, effective and compassionate complaints handling. Complaints are considered an important source of quality information. Boards also need to ensure that they understand trends and patterns in the substance of complaints.

Critically however, boards need to recognise that ensuring accountability in relation to quality is facilitated by more than regular board and committee scrutiny of information on quality – however exemplary. Research[42] suggests that effective quality governance demands that board members actively seek opportunities directly to hear the voice and experience of staff, patients and the public. This means that board members need regularly to step outside of the boardroom to engage directly with the reality on the ground to gain first-hand knowledge of the staff and patient experience in giving and receiving care. For Foundation Trusts, Governors can also offer boards a useful perspective and this should be actively and regularly sought. (See section on engagement).

Financial stewardship

The exercise of effective financial stewardship requires that the board assures itself that the organisation is operating effectively, efficiently, economically and with probity in the use of resources. It is also required to ensure that financial reporting and internal control principles are applied, and appropriate relationships with the Trust's internal and external auditors are maintained.

In exercising this role, it is important that financial stewardship is seen as underpinning and facilitating the delivery of quality care. This includes a careful assessment and understanding of the quality and patient care consequences of financial decisions.

The challenge of balancing effective financial stewardship and effective quality governance is a significant one for boards operating in a financially constrained context. Boards are encouraged to work with staff, patients and commissioners to identify opportunities for reshaping services and improving quality of care which also delivers value for money.

Risk management

The role of the board in risk management is twofold.

- Firstly, within the board itself an informed consideration of risk and risk tolerance should underpin organisational strategy, decision-making and the allocation of resources
- Secondly, the board is responsible for ensuring that the organisation has appropriate risk identification and risk management processes in place to deliver the annual business plan and comply with the registration and licensing requirements of key regulators. This includes systematically assessing and managing its risks.
  - These include clinical, financial and corporate risks. For Foundation Trusts, this also includes risks to compliance with the terms of its licence

Oversight of effective risk management by the board is underpinned by four interlocking systems of control:

The Board Assurance Framework: This is a document that sets out strategic objectives, identifies risks in relation to each strategic objective along with controls in place and assurances available on their operation. The most effective boards use this as a dynamic tool to drive the board agenda. Formats vary but the framework generally includes:

- Objective
- Principal risk and risk owner
- Key controls
- Sources of assurance
- Gaps in control/assurance
- Action plans for addressing gaps

Organisational Risk Management: Strategic risks are reflected in the Board Assurance Framework. A more detailed operational risk register will be in use within the organisation. The board needs to be assured that an effective risk management approach is working within the organisation, and that the operational and strategic registers do join up. This involves both the design of appropriate processes and ensuring that they are properly embedded into the operations and culture of the organisation

Audit: External and internal auditors play an important independent role in board assurance on internal controls, and form part of the board's second and third lines of defence, providing assurance that Executive systems of control are sufficiently comprehensive and operating effectively. There needs to be a clear line of sight from the Board Assurance Framework and the operational risk register to the programme of internal audit and a demonstrable link to the overall programme of clinical audit. Clinical audit serves as a significant source of assurance of clinical quality

The annual governance statement: This is signed by the chief executive as Accountable Officer and comprehensively sets out the overall organisational approach to internal control. It should be scrutinised by the board to ensure that the assertions within it are supported by a robust body of evidence.

The approach to risk management and related processes within the organisation need to be systematic and rigorous with risks understood and owned at the right levels. The board's risk oversight work needs to combine assurance over executive risk management processes particularly through the Audit Committee, with attention to hard and soft evidence stemming from other areas of the board's work, and identifying leading indicators that may point to escalating problems. It is crucial that boards stay alert to the reality of what is happening within the organisation. What matters substantively is recognition of, and reaction to, real risks – not unthinking pursuance of bureaucratic processes.

Legality

The board seeks assurance that the organisation is operating within the law and in accordance with its statutory duties. This will include seeking assurance that the organisation's contractual and commercial relationships are honest, legal and regularly monitored.

Decision making

The board seeks assurance that processes for operational decision making are robust and are in accordance with agreed schemes of delegation.

Probity

The board and its members adheres to the seven principles of public life[13] and to the Standards for NHS Board members.[14] This includes implementing a transparent and explicit approach to the declaration and handling of conflicts of interest. Good practice here includes the maintenance and publication of a register of interest for all board members. Board meeting agendas include an opportunity to declare any conflict at the beginning.

Another key area in relation to probity relates to the effective oversight of top level remuneration. Boards are expected to adhere to HM Treasury guidance and to document and explain all decisions made.

Information Governance

Practising information governance means applying principles of good management and appropriate use to information. It covers all information in the organisation, including personal information (relating to patients/service users, employees and others) and corporate information (e.g. financial and accounting records).

Boards have a responsibility to assure themselves that the organisation has implemented adequate policies and procedures, and is addressing the responsibilities and key actions required for effective information governance. Each organisation must have a Senior Information Risk Owner (SIRO) who is effectively supported, and who updates the board regularly on information risk issues.

Corporate trustee

If the organisation holds NHS charitable funds as sole corporate trustee, it is jointly responsible for the management and control of those charitable funds and is accountable to the Charity Commission.

Some NHS organisations have a separate trustee body which manages the charitable funds linked to the work of the NHS body. Where this applies the NHS organisation does not have responsibility for charitable funds.

Committees of the board that support accountability

In order to enable accountability, boards are required to establish committees responsible for **audit** and **remuneration**.[15] Current good practice also recommends a quality-focused committee of the board. Over time NHS organisations have configured board committees in a variety of ways to discharge these functions. For ease of reference, these are described as three core committees which are:

Audit Committee: This committee's focus is to seek assurance that financial reporting and internal control principles are applied, and to maintain an appropriate relationship with the organisation's auditors, both internal and external. The Audit Committee offers advice to the board about the reliability and robustness of the processes of internal control. This includes the power to review any other committees' work, including in relation to quality, and to provide assurance to the board with regard to internal controls. The Audit Committee may also have responsibility for the oversight of risk management, although some Trusts have established a separate Risk Committee. The committee should be positioned as an independent source of assurance to the board and guard its independence. Ultimately however the responsibility for effective stewardship of the organisation belongs to the board as a whole.

Remuneration Committee: The duties of this committee are to determine the remuneration and terms of service for the chief executive and other executive directors, as delegated to the committee by the board; to monitor and evaluate the performance of the executive directors and to oversee contractual arrangements, including proper calculation and scrutiny of termination payments and terms. The remuneration committee should take into account relevant nationally determined parameters on pay, pensions and compensation payments. No director should be involved in deciding his/ her own remuneration. The committee may additionally have a role in succession planning for executive level roles.

Quality Committee: The ultimate accountability for quality rests with the board. However recent good practice recommends the establishment of a quality-focused board committee as a means of enhancing board oversight of quality performance and risk by ensuring input from people with particular quality expertise and responsibility for frontline clinical leadership.

This committee offers scrutiny to ensure that required standards are achieved and that action is taken where sub-standard performance is identified. It seeks assurance that the organisational systems and processes in relation to quality are robust and well-embedded so that priority is given, at the appropriate level within the organisation, to identifying and managing risks to the quality of care.

All board committees normally have a non-executive chair. Audit Committee members are all non-executive directors with executives in attendance as appropriate for the work being done. At least one member of the Audit Committee must have a recent and relevant financial background. Checks and balances need to be maintained in committee membership. So, for example, the board chair cannot be a member of the Audit Committee (and should not regularly attend it), nor can the Audit Committee chair be the senior independent director.

Good practice suggests that the vice chair of the organisation should not chair the Audit Committee in order to avoid potential conflicts of interest.

Effective boards minimise the number of standing board committees. However, boards may establish other committees. Examples include finance and investment committees, risk committees,[16] people strategy committees and charitable funds committees. Some FTs have also extended the remit of remuneration committees to become nomination and remuneration committees.

Roles of the board
3. Shape culture

The third core role of the board is shaping a healthy culture for the board and the organisation. This recognises that good governance flows from a shared ethos or culture, as well as from systems and structures. The board also takes the lead in establishing, modelling and promoting values and standards of conduct for the organisation and its staff.

There is now widespread recognition that the board does indeed have a key role in shaping the culture of a healthcare organisation.

It is important for boards to develop a good understanding of the current values, behaviours and attitudes operating within the organisation, and to work with the staff to shape the desired values, behaviours and attitudes. The challenge then is how to achieve change.

What we do know is that the 'how' is less about exhorting the adoption of a culture, and more about leaders of organisations being mindful of the cultural messages that they send, intentionally or passively. For example: by the board's agenda; by the nature of the debate in the board; by the relative emphasis given to different performance criteria; by how visible board members are in the organisation; by where leaders choose to invest time and resource. All of these things are culture-shaping activities.

We also know that how to achieve change includes an active process of dialogue and engagement with staff and service users. These ideas are developed further below.

The extent to which common aspects of 'culture' can be defined, identified and then deliberately changed is hotly contested within the literature on organisational culture. There is however some consensus about the value of encouraging explicit and open exploration of 'culture' at every level and in every corner of organisations. Boards have a key role in prioritising, valuing and supporting this work within the organisation.

Shaping organisational culture

Effective boards shape a culture for the organisation which is caring, ambitious, self-directed, nimble, responsive, inclusive and encourages innovation. A commitment to openness, transparency and candour means that boards are more likely to give priority to the organisation's relationship and reputation with patients, the public and partners as the primary means by which it meets policy and/or regulatory requirements. As such it holds the interest of patients and communities at its heart.

- **Openness:** enabling concerns to be raised and disclosed freely without fear and for questions to be answered
- **Transparency:** allowing true information about performance and outcomes to be shared with staff, patients and the public
- **Candour:** ensuring that patients harmed by a healthcare service are informed of the fact and that an appropriate remedy is offered, whether or not a complaint has been made or a question asked about it

Source: Second Francis Inquiry Report[3]

Boards need to recognise the importance of ensuring that the culture of their organisation reflects the NHS values, as defined in the NHS Constitution. These are:

- Working together for patients
- Respect and dignity
- Commitment to quality of care
- Compassion
- Improving lives
- Everyone counts

If shaping the culture of the organisation is a vital role for boards, then embedding the culture, so that it becomes a lived reality, is equally important and arguably the most challenging part of the role.

Embedding a healthy culture across an organisation requires sustained effort and consistency of approach, often over a number of years. International research provides some helpful points on how boards can play a role in achieving desired culture change in a health context.

An approach to shaping culture

Boards should consider adopting a culture shaping process that involves active but focused dialogue and engagement with staff and service users. This approach has a great deal to offer NHS boards as they seek to shape organisational culture and, in turn, use their learning from staff and user experience to set strategy and ensure accountability.

As boards undertake their strategy development role, this approach could involve interactive engagement with key stakeholders, staff, members and patients, at key stages in the strategy development process.

It ensures that the board as a whole is listening, learning and shaping, rather than just receiving draft strategies for approval. It is more likely to achieve a viable and responsive direction, build commitment and buy in, enrich board discussion and challenge board 'group think'.

Similarly, when ensuring accountability, a more interactive style of governance could move beyond paper reporting. Examples could include patient safety walk rounds, hearing patient stories at the board and staff focus groups.

While the importance of board visibility in the organisation has long been recognised, a more interactive process allows board members, staff and users to shape organisational values and culture through direct engagement. It also ensures that board members take back to the boardroom an enriched understanding of the lived reality for staff, users and partners.

Board's role in exemplifying and modelling culture

An outward looking board leadership culture that actively embraces change, fosters innovation, encourages learning and maintains an unswerving commitment to quality and safety of patients offers the best prospect of navigating effectively through a demanding and rapidly changing environment.

The board needs to be seen as champions of these values in the way the board itself operates and behaves. There are a number of facets to this. Effective boards and their members:

- Prioritise quality and patient safety
- Behave consistently in line with the seven principles of public life
- Model an open approach to learning
- Invest time to develop constructive relationships around the board table
- Reflect a drive to challenge discrimination, promote equality, diversity, equity of access and quality of services. They respect and protect human rights in the treatment of staff, patients, their families and carers, and the wider community
- Ensure that their approach to strategy, accountability and engagement are consistent with the values they seek to promote for the organisation

3 Building blocks

Context

The first building block requires that boards have a comprehensive and up to date understanding of the changing external national and regional context in which they operate.

While many of the fundamental principles of good governance are common across a range of different types of organisations (both private and public sector), the complexity of the statutory, accountability and organisational context in which NHS boards operate is a key difference that must be fully understood by all board members. Boards operate in a demanding and changing environment. Some of these challenges are illustrated here Figure 3.

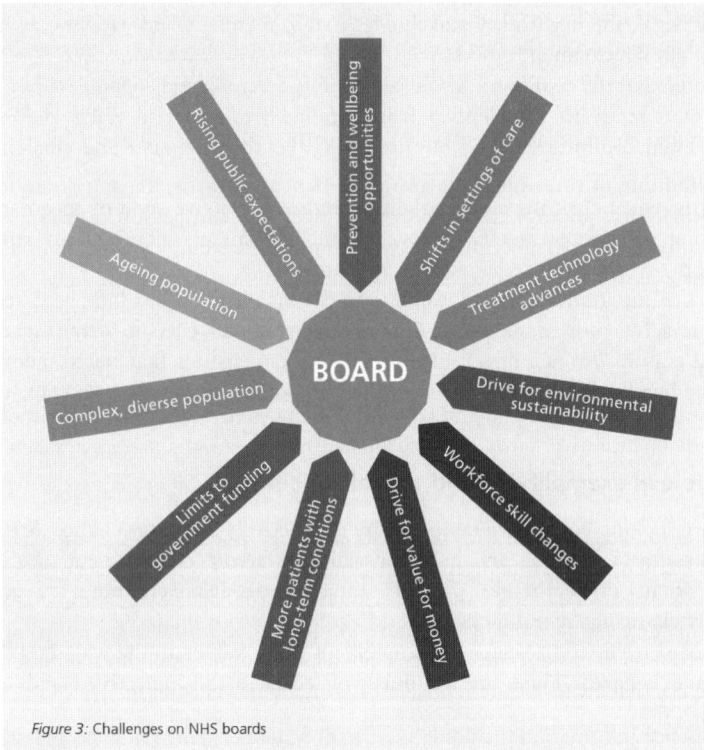

Figure 3: Challenges on NHS boards

The areas that boards will need to consider when developing an understanding of context are set out below:

Policy: It is important for boards to have a good understanding of the current and emerging policy direction, and the strategies for the NHS and its key partners.

Economy: Boards need to be aware of information on the economic environment for public services, and the wider economy. This assists boards in understanding the implications for future funding as well as the potential impact of economic changes on the health of the public, and the demand for health services.

Legislation: NHS bodies are subject to a wide range of legislation, from central government and from the European Union. This includes statutes, regulations and a variety of directives and Secretary of State directions.

Institutional landscape: An understanding of the structures and institutions of the NHS and those with whom the NHS does business is essential for boards to undertake their role effectively. This includes central and local government and other public and voluntary services which contribute to health and well-being.

Regulation: NHS bodies are subject to oversight from several regulators. Developing a good understanding of the most significant regulators and their requirements and expectations of NHS bodies will greatly assist boards as they steer the organisation.

Public expectations: Expectations of all public services are rising; arguably this is most pronounced in relation to the NHS. Even the most stretching national targets and standards have struggled to keep pace with mounting public expectations. The most effective NHS boards energetically develop their own understanding of trends in public and patient expectation and ensure that this actively informs their strategic choices.

An understanding of the wider determinants of health status: It is important for boards to develop an understanding of the wide range of factors that impact on health status. These include poor housing, neighbourhood deprivation, limited employment and educational opportunities, as well as the effects of affluence. This understanding helps inform the board's strategic response and shapes its whole system and partnership working.

Intelligence

Intelligence is the second key building block. It includes performance information, which can be both quantitative (such as performance metrics) and qualitative (such as staff, patient and stakeholder perspectives). It also includes information on the external local environment.

Boards need to be provided with information that is timely, reliable, comprehensive and suitable for board use. The Intelligent Board series[21,22,23,24,25,26] continues to offer excellent guidance to boards, and some of the key elements of this advice are summarised below. However, guidance can never be a substitute for discussion in the board aimed at evaluating the usefulness of current intelligence and shaping future intelligence requirements.

Intelligence that boards need to consider falls under two headings:

- Performance information including information about quality, finance and staffing
- Intelligence on the external local environment

Performance information

This describes how the organisation is performing both strategically and operationally. The key requirement here is that the intelligence:

- Allows the board to arrive at sound judgments about organisational performance in the delivery of strategy
- Allows the board to scrutinise operational performance 'in the round' – bringing together its appraisal of organisational performance in relation to operational activity, quality, finance and the workforce

Intelligence about **strategic performance** needs to:

■ Be structured around an explicit set of strategic goals
■ Show trends in performance in terms of quality, including treatment outcomes and the experience and satisfaction of patients; business development; and finance
■ Provide forecasts and anticipate future performance issues
■ Encourage an external focus
■ Enable comparison with the performance of similar organisations, including internationally, for example through benchmarking

Intelligence about **operational performance** needs to:

■ Provide an accurate, timely and balanced picture of current and recent performance – including patient, clinical, regulatory, staffing and financial perspectives
■ Focus on the most important measures of performance, and highlight exceptions
■ Be appropriately standardised in order to take account of known factors that affect outcomes, such as the age and deprivation profile of patients and communities served
■ Integrate informal sources of intelligence from staff and patients
■ Include consideration of assessments from key regulators including comparator information
■ Enable comparisons with the performance of similar organisations
■ Include key indicators in relation to a People Strategy, including:
■ workforce capacity and capability to deliver future strategy
■ intelligence on values, behaviours and attitudes
■ key HR health indicators, including information in equality and diversity
■ performance appraisal, training and development
■ leadership and management development, including talent mapping

Focus on Quality

Quality is the organising principle of the NHS and needs to be at the front of the board's mind in everything the board does.

While significant progress has been made in shaping and sharpening the finance and activity information generally available to boards, progress has been slower in relation to information that will allow boards to scrutinise the 'quality' of services. Quality accounts should become at least as important as financial statements for boards and be seen as a key opportunity for the board to provide the public with an open and comprehensive account of the quality of care. As such they should include a balanced account both of achievements and instances where compliance with commissioned/expected standards has not been achieved and what is being done to expedite improvement.

Quality comprises three dimensions:

■ Clinical effectiveness or patient outcomes
■ Patient safety
■ Quality of the patient experience

As with other organisational priorities, boards should receive this information in an easily digested summary. The closer the data is to 'real time' the greater its value.

Intelligence on the external local environment

In the previous section on context, the emphasis was on ensuring that boards have a good grasp of the national context for health and social care. Intelligence on the **local** environment is also critical and should be as important to boards as performance information. It includes:

- **Stakeholder mapping:** One of the key challenges facing NHS boards is the complex stakeholder and accountability landscape. Boards need to have a clear grasp of the entire system within which they operate. This includes an understanding of who the key local stakeholders are, their agendas, priorities and perspectives. For Foundation Trust boards, this includes developing a good understanding of governor and member perspectives
- **Market analysis:** Likewise it is important for boards to build their understanding of the local market and the place that the organisation wishes to occupy within it. In an increasingly competitive market, boards need to keep abreast of their competitors (other NHS organisations, independent providers and the voluntary sector), including an understanding of their relative strengths and weaknesses. Considering comparative benchmarks about performance, especially on quality measures, is of strategic importance. Market analysis can also inform potential integrated care pathways.
- **Health need and demography including diversity and equality issues.** Although these aspects are generally considered to be particularly important for commissioners, this understanding is critical in informing strategic processes for providers and in ensuring that provider boards are able to forge constructive collaborative relationships in the local health and social care economy. It includes intelligence to assist boards to understand the local population, its demographic and health profile, particularly health status, healthcare needs, behaviours and aspirations; and the key equality gaps experienced by different groups within the community, both in relation to each other and compared to similar groups in other localities. This aspect of intelligence should be based on shared analysis and monitoring with local government as well as commissioners

Board members have a key role to play in actively shaping and designing the sort of intelligence they wish to receive.

The research evidence supports the view that the provision of too much or too little information can be a significant risk to a board functioning effectively, so the key is to strike a balance between providing sufficient and meaningful information in an easily digestible format without overloading board members.

A final, and important, thought on intelligence: There is an increasing recognition that paper-based (or even tablet-based) intelligence can only take the board so far. The Board needs to ensure that it operates on the basis of a sophisticated blend between soft and hard intelligence. Direct interaction between the board and key stakeholders, including staff, provides this soft intelligence and underpins the development of strategy, it gives 'texture' to ensuring accountability and shapes a culture of openness and dialogue within the organisation. This brings us to the third key building block: engagement

Engagement

The effective board gives priority to engaging with key stakeholders and opinion formers within and beyond the organisation. Engaging effectively is vital for the board and the organisation to demonstrate its openness, transparency and accountability. There are also some circumstances where involving the public is underpinned by a legal obligation.[28]

Engagement informs and supports the board in creatively formulating strategy, shaping culture, and in key aspects of ensuring accountability. The range of internal and external stakeholders with which boards engage includes:

- Patients and the public.
- Members and governors (for Foundation Trusts).
- Staff from all disciplines across the organisation.
- Key partners in the wider health and social care system.

Engagement with staff, patients, the public and stakeholders is not new, and has long been a priority of senior leaders in NHS organisations. Boards as a whole generally receive and consider the results of these processes in the form of reports and papers.

Research has identified the role that direct interaction between the board and staff, patients, the public and key partners plays in effective governance.

Patient and public engagement

A wide range of guidance is available for boards on patient and public engagement. There are three main aspects for boards to consider:

- Empowering **people:** Patients and the public want to be able to influence the priorities of the organisations that provide healthcare. They also have the right to play a full and active part in decisions regarding their own care. Boards play an important role in setting an organisational expectation that clinical staff will actively engage patients in shared decision-making
- **Putting patient experience centre stage:** Organisations need to ensure the routine, systematic collection and analysis of feedback from people who use services, including real-time patient feedback and an understanding of the perspectives of minority and hard to reach groups. Crucially, boards need to demonstrate that this feedback, alongside intelligence on effectiveness and patient safety, actively informs board priority setting, resource allocation and decision-making.
- Boards benefit most from an approach that blends direct engagement with patients and their carers, the views reflected by HealthWatch and consideration of reports and papers
- **Accountability to local communities:** The organisation, and therefore the board, has a statutory 'duty to involve'.[28] In addition, the organisation exercises its local accountability through overview and scrutiny arrangements led by local government.

Members and governors (for Foundation Trusts)

Boards of Foundation Trusts need to recognise that the autonomy and freedoms granted to them in this model rest, in large part, on effective accountability to patients and the public. This is delivered by maintaining an open and accountable relationship with governors who, in turn, engage effectively with an active membership reflective of the patients and public served by the organisation and the staff who serve them.

If governors are to exercise this aspect of their role effectively, they require regular and meaningful engagement with the board. Governors need to be trained and supported to work effectively with directors and to engage with the members and the wider public so that they can contribute these wider perspectives and expectations in their discussions with the board. Indeed, the provision of sufficient training to governors is now a statutory duty.

This demands effort and commitment from directors, who need to demonstrate that they value the governors' contribution to the Trust. The chair is integral to developing this professional, engaged and constructive mind-set, and ensuring that directors also receive development to work effectively with governors.

Staff

Engagement with staff, is a vital means by which the organisation's leaders shape organisational culture. It can help boards drive culture change, for example in encouraging staff to feed into the risk management system and actively engage in quality improvement. Boards should be alert to possible differences in culture between shifts, wards and departments and what that might indicate.

A review[29] of how best to engage staff suggests that use of established approaches, such as surveys seeking staff opinion, are an important but not sufficient approach as they can leave engagement as an 'add-on'. Ideally, boards should aim to achieve 'transformational engagement', staff are given space to reflect and discuss improvements and see themselves as integral to developing and delivering departmental and organisational strategy. Boards can project a 'human face of leadership', fostering trust and respect, through direct engagement including holding 'Question Time' style events and participating in web-chats. For Foundation Trusts, staff governors are an important conduit for staff engagement.

Clinicians might be engaged to lead improvement and innovation work as 'change agents'; to provide input and leadership on quality committees; and as a key source of 'wisdom' in an engaging approach to governance.

Key Partners

NHS boards exist within a crowded organisational landscape that includes a range of public, private and community organisations all serving broadly the same citizens. To deliver their core purpose of building public and stakeholder confidence in health and healthcare, NHS boards need to see beyond the boundaries of their individual organisations. This delicate balance involves operating within a 'community of governance' while simultaneously respecting divergent interests in a vibrant market.

In a financially constrained environment this as boards consider options for strategic partnerships, joint management arrangements, outsourcing, major service reconfigurations, and potential mergers. But whatever the economic environment, the need to develop an effective community of governance is important because:

- Patients and users travel across organizational boundaries to receive services and tend to see the NHS as one organisation

- Approaches to health improvement and prevention, as well as tackling health inequalities can only be addressed by taking a holistic health and social care economy
  perspective
- Health and social care organisations at the local level share responsibility for ensuring
  that patients and the public get the very best value for the taxpayer resources invested
- NHS organisations and other public bodies have a legal duty to co-operate on improving local health outcomes

The health and social care system in England relies on a complex interplay between collaboration and competition. Boards need to reach finely balanced judgments about how
they engage with this complexity.

The public interest is best served when all the main actors in the system reach agreement about:

- Local health need
- A shared vision for health and healthcare including health outcomes
- The 'rules of the compact' – how players within the system will work together, includ-
  ing the development of a culture of co-operative transparency
- Mutual understanding of, and respect for, individual organisational interests and
  constraints

This shared understanding and agreement can only be reached through regular and ongoing
processes of formal and informal dialogue and relationship building. Both chair and chief
executive play an important role in shaping the climate for inter-organisational engagement and in keeping lines of communication open – especially at times when negotiations
may have strained relationships within their organisations. A regular cycle of whole 'board
to board' processes has proved valuable in many health economies. The joint production of
an annual health system development plan could also be valuable.

Boards are therefore advised to develop a coherent strategy for engagement with key
partners. These include commissioners, NHS providers, local government, universities and
further education, the voluntary sector, independent sector and of course regulators.

Although this stakeholder engagement is most often led by the chair and chief executive, it must form part of a systematic and agreed approach that encourages other directors and a wide range of other leaders in the organisation to be empowered to engage
across organisational boundaries, informed by a shared vision and clear messages.

A number of boards choose to hold 'board to board' meetings with key partners.
Properly focused, this can be an important part of building understanding of, and relationships with, stakeholders.

Ultimately however, public and stakeholder perceptions can be very significantly shaped
by media messaging. The Board's engagement strategy will need to include attention to
effective media management, particularly in relation to the local press.

4 Improving board effectiveness

This chapter sets out the approaches to improving board effectiveness.

This chapter sets out five important clusters of activity that enable boards to improve their
effectiveness, shown in figure 4:

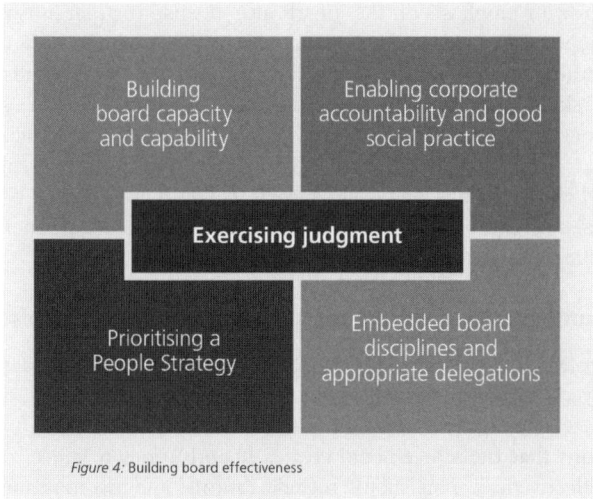

Figure 4: Building board effectiveness

Building board capacity and capability

This involves activity in the four areas shown in the table below:

Board composition, knowledge and skills
Whole board and individual board member performance appraisal
Systematic attention to board learning and development
Appointment and remuneration of board members

Board composition, knowledge and skills

NHS boards should not be so large as to be unwieldy, but must be large enough to provide the balance of skills and experience that is appropriate for the organisation. The number of directors is defined in the Trust's establishment order, or in an Foundation Trust's constitution. The composition of the board should achieve a balance between continuity and renewal. Chairs and non-executive directors (NEDs) of NHS Trusts serve a maximum of 10 years in the same NHS post (or two 3 year terms for Foundation Trusts) to ensure this balance. Within this period, any second reappointment must be through open competition.

In most NHS organisations, governance is the responsibility of a unitary board, with at least half the board, excluding the chair, made up of independent NEDs.

The time commitment required of non-executive directors continues to be a focus of debate. Non-executive directors should be encouraged to look at their time requirements over an annual cycle. There will be a number of situations where more time is required than on average. This includes the first year after appointment, through the Foundation Trust application process and when the organisation is considering major strategic changes. All directors must be appropriately qualified to discharge their roles effectively, including setting strategy, monitoring and managing performance and nurturing continuous quality improvement.

There is a growing emphasis on the importance of ensuring that prospective directors bring both the appropriate skills and a demonstrable commitment to NHS values – and the behaviours that these imply. Over time the strategic challenges facing boards give rise to the need for specific skills, and this requirement must be kept under review in a systematic way. In order to ensure an effective balance of knowledge, skills and backgrounds boards should undertake regular skills audits of current board members. Good practice suggests that this account of board member skills and experience as well as a clear annual board statement about its own balance, completeness and appropriateness to the requirements of it, should be available on the organisation's website.

Whole board and individual board member performance appraisal

Guidance and research suggests that organisations are best served by boards drawn from a wide diversity of backgrounds and sectors. This includes the expectation that board composition reflects the diverse communities they serve.

It is important that the whole board creates opportunities to reflect on its own performance and effectiveness. This should include a formal and rigorous annual evaluation of its own performance and that of its committees. Some boards choose to supplement self-assessment periodically with views obtained from a range of internal and external stakeholders who do not sit on the board but nonetheless experience its impact. This could include leading clinicians, senior managers who are not board members and external partners and stakeholders including patient groups and partner organisations both within and outside of the NHS.

It is important for boards to develop a framework of knowledge, skills and competencies that fit their organisational requirements and context and that can serve as the basis for whole board and board member appraisal.

Alongside whole board performance evaluation, board members should undergo an annual appraisal of their individual contribution and performance. This appraisal should focus on the director's contribution as a member of the corporate board; in the case of executive directors (EDs) this is distinct from their functional leadership role. The appraisal of the chief executive (CE) by the chair is particularly important because the effective performance management of the CE is critical to the success of the organisation and sets the benchmark for other senior NHS managers. In a unitary board setting this is particularly necessary. Responsibilities for carrying out these appraisals are:

Role	Is appraised by
Chair (non-Foundation Trusts)	NHS Trust Development Agency (NTDA)
Chair (in Foundation Trusts)	Senior independent director, drawing on the views and perspectives of governors, fellow directors, and key partners
Chief executive	Chair
NEDs	Chair
EDs	Chief executive with input from the chair on their contribution as a member of the board

A growing number of NHS boards are choosing to support the development of individual board members by undertaking a '360 degree review'. This offers board members feedback on their approach, performance and contribution from a wide range of colleagues with whom they have regular contact. This can be very helpful, though experience shows that it requires time and commitment from all board members. It must also be undertaken in a manner that respects and protects confidentiality and trust within the board. The whole process – especially individual feedback- needs to be handled independently and pro-fessionally. 360 degree review approaches are intended to support individual development rather than to inform re-appointment.

All appraisal processes should culminate in a personal development plan, the delivery of which is actively supported by the organisation.

Systematic attention to board learning and development

Effective boards use the performance appraisal processes outlined above as the basis for focused board development action plans. The plan should include:

- A **structured process for induction of new board members.** This is an opportunity to attend to board members' understanding of local and – especially if they are new to the NHS – national context. Mentoring by more experienced board members can also be helpful and build relationships quickly
- **Individual board member opportunities to refresh and update skills and knowl-edge.** Conferences and similar events are likely to be very helpful. Organisations should ensure that board members are aware of relevant development opportunities and that new policy and contextual knowledge is systematically shared with board members, including through informal briefings between board meetings
- **Opportunities for the board to learn together.** Board development should not be limited to externally provided development events and conferences. These are valu-able events, especially for the transmission of knowledge and information, but carving out time for the whole board to learn together is valuable. This is particularly true when exploring the applicability of new or innovative ways of working in the board, or when developing new skills and capabilities, for example new developments in quality improvement
- **Opportunities to learn good practice from peers.** Board are encouraged to identify opportunities to network with and learn from peers within and beyond the health and social care system.

Foundation Trust boards should give particular attention to supporting the develop-ment of governors. Careful and comprehensive induction is critical. Foundation Trusts have a responsibility to ensure that governors have the skills and capability to deliver their core statutory functions.[1,33] Governors also need to be supported to build their skills and capacity to engage with their 'constituencies' in order to deliver and be accountable for their role.

Support for chairs, chief executives and directors in challenging roles needs particu-lar attention. It should be clear to board members during the appointment process, if the posts are deemed challenging. Experienced directors should be appointed to these roles, and additional development support clearly agreed and put in place from an early stage.

Appointment and remuneration of board members

Formal, rigorous and transparent procedures for both the appointment and the remuneration of directors must be in place.

The appointments process must ensure that all appointments are made on merit and against objective criteria. Appointments panels for executives should always include an independent external assessor. Responsibilities for these appointments are summarised in the following table.

Role	In FTs is appointed by	In other organisations is appointed by
Chair	Governors, at a general meeting, informed by the nominations committee and/or governors working group, after taking account of advice of the board of directors	NHS Trust Development Authority ('NHS TDA') on behalf of the Secretary of State ('SoS')
Chief executive	Committee of the chair and NEDs, approved by the governors	Committee of the chair and NEDs with the NHS TDA and an independent external assessor, approved by the board
NEDs	Governors, at a general meeting, informed by the nominations committee and/or governors working group, after taking account of advice of the board of directors	NHS TDA on behalf of the SoS
EDs	Committee of the chair, chief executive and NEDs	Committee of the chair, chief executive and NEDs with the NHS TDA and an independent external assessor

Likewise, the responsibilities for setting remuneration are shown in the following table

Role	In FTs remuneration is decided by	In other organisations remuneration is decided by
Chair	Governors' at a general meeting, informed by the Nominations/ Remuneration Committee or a governors working group	SoS with advice from the NHS TDA

Role	In FTs remuneration is decided by	In other organisations remuneration is decided by
Chief executive	Remuneration committee of at least three independent non-executive directors	Remuneration Committee of at least three non-executive directors
NEDs	Governors' at a general meeting, informed by the Nominations/ Remuneration Committee or a governors working group	SoS with advice from the NHS TDA
EDs	Remuneration Committee of at least three independent non-executive directors	Remuneration Committee of at least three non-executive directors

The Remuneration Committee remit will be determined by its specific terms of reference, however, in general, it has delegated responsibility for setting not only remuneration for the chief executive and all executive directors, but also including pension rights and compensation payments. This committee also recommends and monitors the level and structure of remuneration for senior management.

Remuneration Committees are expected to consult with external professionals to market test such remuneration levels at least every 3 years.

Enabling corporate accountability and good social processes

In unitary NHS boards, all directors are collectively and corporately accountable for organisational performance.

A key strength of unitary boards is the opportunity provided for the exchange of views between executives and NEDs, drawing on and pooling their experience and capabilities.

Boards are 'social systems'. The most effective boards invest time and energy in the development of mature relationships and ways of working.

Some techniques and practices that support and hinder the effectiveness of these social systems are summarised in the following table.

Ways of working that support good social processes	Ways of working that obstruct good social processes
Building and publishing a crystal clear understanding of the roles of the board and individual board members	Board members behaving in a way that suggests a 'master-servant' relationship between non-executive and executive
Actively working to develop and protect a climate of trust and candour	Executive directors only contributing in their functional leadership area rather than actively participating across the breadth of the board agenda

Ways of working that support good social processes	Ways of working that obstruct good social processes
Building cohesion by taking steps to know and understand each other's backgrounds, skills and perspectives	Demonstrating an unwillingness to consider points of view that are different from individual directors' starting positions or being disinterested in others
Encouraging all board members to raise issues of concern and offer constructive challenges	Challenge primarily coming from non-executive directors, rather than all directors feeling empowered to challenge one another in board meetings
Sharing corporate responsibility and collective decision- making	Challenging in a way that is unnecessarily antagonistic and not appropriately balanced with appreciation, encouragement and support
Ensuring that neither chair nor chief executive power and dominance act to stifle appropriate participation in board debate	Working in ways that don't demonstrate overall confidence in the executive and that feed individual anxiety and insecurity about capability

Embedding board disciplines and appropriate delegation

Competent, systematic board disciplines form the bedrock of good board functioning. These disciplines include:

- **Giving thoughtful attention to board agenda planning and management:** The chair is central in this process, as well as seeking contributions of other board members in agenda planning. The chair needs to be vigilant in ensuring that board agendas maintain a complex range of 'balances':
  - between strategy and performance management
  - between quality, activity and finance
  - between organisational priorities and the demands of regulators
  - between information sharing (presentation) by executives and whole board discussion
  - between formal meeting time and less structured 'away' time
  - Chairs face the challenge of attending to the full breadth of the board's role while ensuring that board meetings do not descend into a gruelling test of board member endurance
- **Board and committee year planners and annual programmes of work:** The board and its committees should be supported by an annual plan that sets out a coherent overall programme for formal board meetings, board seminars and away-days and committee meetings. It needs to take account of the organisational and system-wide planning cycle including key 'watershed events' such as contract negotiations, budget setting, regulatory returns and so on. It is good practice for the work of every committee of the board to be shaped by an annual plan

- **Board papers:** The effectiveness of the board is predicated on the timely availability of board papers. Increasingly boards are receiving their papers electronically, for example on tablets.

Whether they are sent electronically or on paper, the core disciplines for board papers include:

- **Timeliness:** papers provided ideally a week ahead of meetings
- **Cover sheets:** including, for each paper, the name of the author, a brief summary of the issue, the organisational forums where the paper has been considered, the strategic objective or regulatory requirement to which it relates, and an explicit indication of what is required of the board
- **Executive summaries:** Succinct executive summaries that direct the readers' attention to the most important aspects
- **Action logs:** Boards and committees can be helped to keep track of actions agreed by maintaining and monitoring a log. The log should show all actions agreed by the board, and for each action the 'ownership', due dates, and status
- **Declaration and resolution of conflicts of interest:**[14] Probity requires that the board maintains an up-to-date register of board members' interests. Increasingly, board agendas include an opportunity for board members to declare conflicts of interest that may relate to specific agenda items so that these can be managed appropriately
- **Transparency and openness:** There is an important obligation on public services to ensure that they operate in an open and transparent manner. For NHS organisations this is partially achieved by holding formal board meetings in public and the publication of papers. The default position ought to be that business is conducted in the public board meeting. However, when a compelling case can be made for an item to be considered in private (for example a matter that involves individual confidentiality or commercial sensitivity), there is provision for attending to it in private. Some boards follow the principles in *The Freedom of Information Act*[35] in deciding which items are considered in private.

Foundation Trust boards are now required to hold board meetings in public, with a caveat that members of the public may be excluded from a meeting for special reasons. Foundation Trusts remain a part of the public service and thus retain the obligation to ensure openness and transparency to the public. Foundation Trust governors are required to meet in public, and also have the right to receive the agenda and minutes of board meetings.

Public board meetings alone are not a guarantee of transparency, and boards need to ensure that there is a wide range of ways for the public to access information about the way in which public resources are deployed. These include clear, informative, jargon-free annual reports, regular updating of an easily navigable website, the availability of key information in a range of appropriate languages and in forms that are accessible to those with disabilities.

Delegating Appropriately:

The formal powers of an NHS organisation are vested in the board but the NHS Code of Accountability[36] allows the board to delegate some of its business to board committees and to the executive. The board approach to delegation should be consistently set out in:

- Standing Orders which specify how the organisation conducts its business
- Standing financial instructions which detail the financial responsibilities, policies and procedures adopted
- The scheme of reservation and delegation.
- This sets out which responsibilities and accountabilities remain at board level and which have been delegated to committees and to
- the executive, together with the appropriate reporting arrangements that ensure the board has oversight

Approaches and schemes of delegation must be subject to regular board review to ensure that the distribution of functions and accountabilities is accurately and appropriately described, and remains appropriate despite changes in the organisation.

The following table lists some tests that a board should take into account when considering its committee structure.

Boards may wish to apply the following tests before establishing a new committee:
Are the proposed functions of the committee really board functions or are they executive functions?
Is a standing committee really required – or can the task be undertaken by a short life working group?
Are there good reasons why the proposed functions cannot be carried out by the whole board?
Is the committee being established because of one major incident or issue – is it a proportionate response?
Does the creation of the committee reduce clarity of role or create lack of alignment between other committees of the board and the board itself?

Prioritising a People Strategy

In each domain, the board needs to build its understanding of:

- The current baseline position
- The position to which the board and organisation aspire to meet its strategic goals
- The focused and connected network of HR approaches and developmental interventions that will support moving the organisation and its people towards its aspiration

NHS Boards are increasingly recognising that an effective board gives priority to the development of a 'people strategy' as a key enabler in meeting organisational strategic goals. Such a strategy straddles the following domains (see figure 5 below).

Within each of the domains, there are key questions that a robust 'people strategy' should answer. These include:

Domain	Baseline	Future
Workforce model	What is the shape of our current workforce? How have we designed our organisation in terms of structure and roles, job design? How sophisticated is our understanding of workforce costs? How diverse is our workforce?	How do we need to shape our workforce, our roles and our organisation to meet our strategic goals? What does this mean in order to develop effective multi-disciplinary working? What approach is needed to develop a diverse, inclusive workforce?
Values, behaviours and attitudes	What do we know about current values, behaviours and attitudes? What sources of information are we drawing on: • Staff survey • Patient survey • Patient feedback • Complaints and compliments • How do we currently engage with all of our people • Board • Executive	What are the values, behaviours and attitudes to which we aspire, that will safeguard dignified and compassionate care for patients and that will underpin the delivery of our strategy? What will this mean in terms of approaches to staff engagement?
HR health indicators	What does our current performance across the range of HR indicators tell us about how effectively we are managing our staff? Which are the important leading indicators? • Turnover • Sickness • Recruitment • Vacancies and time to fill • Staff complaints and whistle blowing • Disciplinary actions	Are these the right indicators? What level of performance would give us confidence that we are supporting our staff to perform reliably in their roles?

Domain	Baseline	Future
Training and professional development	How effectively are we equipping our people with the right skills to undertake their roles to a high standard? What professional training and development is being offered to all staff, including through other training and education bodies – and how effectively?	What would a 'fit for purpose' approach to training and professional development look like for all staff? What approach to personal development and performance appraisal is required?
Training and professional development	• What are performance appraisal ratcs, and what do we know about the quality of appraisals? • How are we performing in the uptake of mandatory training? • How are we approaching specific initiatives e.g. customer care or quality improvement? • Costs and value for money	
Leadership and management model	How explicit is the board about the leadership culture that it seeks to promote? How do we invest in leadership and management development? What is our approach to talent management? How do we evaluate its effectiveness? How well supported is team working?	What is the leadership model and culture that we need to promote? How do we give effect to this across all five domains? How do we describe the management model that we operate and build management competency accordingly? What is the approach to supporting team working across the organisation?

A good people strategy will set out the range of focused and connected organisational development interventions and HR approaches that will support moving the organisation and its people from the baseline position towards its aspiration. The key is one of 'fit', i.e. that the people strategies must fit with each other and with the overall organisational strategies for maximum impact.[37]

Exercising judgment

This document draws the principles of effective governance from the available evidence and good practice. It is however important to recognise that at the heart of good governance is healthy debate about a spectrum of dilemmas that are not amenable to uniform guidance. Resolution of these dilemmas requires a willingness to reflect and learn good judgment and acumen on the part of the board.

Some of the dilemmas that present themselves to boards are set out in the appendix. They are an illustrative, not an exhaustive list. The optimal board responses to these issues cannot sensibly be mandated in guidance. Rather, boards are encouraged to set aside the necessary time to debate and explore these issues as part of their developmental journey.

5 Roles of board members

The distinct roles of members of NHS boards are outlined in this section.

All board members share corporate responsibility for formulating strategy, ensuring accountability and shaping culture. They also share responsibility for ensuring that the board operates as effectively as possible.

The chair and chief executive have complementary roles in board leadership. These are set out in more detail at the end of this section, but it is helpful to identify the essence of these two roles, which are:

- The chair leads the board and ensures the effectiveness of the board
- For Foundation Trusts, the chair also chairs the council of governors
- The chief executive leads the executive and the organisation

However there are also distinct roles for different members of the board, and indeed there are distinct roles depending on the type of NHS organisation.

These distinct roles are set out in the table overleaf, showing how they are aligned to the role of the board. The following abbreviations are used:

- **CE:** chief executive
- **NED:** non-executive director
- **ED:** executive director
- **FT:** Foundation Trust

Roles of board members

	Chair	Chief Executive	Non-executive Director	Executive Director
Formulate Strategy	Ensures board develops vision, strategies and clear objectives to deliver organisational purpose	Leads strategy development process	Brings independence, external perspectives, skills, and challenge to strategy development	Takes lead role in developing strategic proposals – drawing on professional and clinical expertise (where relevant)

	Chair	Chief Executive	Non-executive Director	Executive Director
Ensure accountability	Makes sure the board understands its own accountability for governing the organisation Ensures board committees that support accountability are properly constituted Holds CE to account for delivery of strategy Leads the board in being accountable to governors and leads the council in holding the board to account	Leads the organisation in the delivery of strategy Establishes effective performance management arrangements and controls Acts as Accountable Officer	Holds the executive to account for the delivery of strategy Offers purposeful, constructive scrutiny and challenge Chairs or participates as member of key committees that support accountability Account individually and collectively to Governors for the effectiveness of the board	Leads implementation of strategy within functional areas Manages performance within their area and deals effectively with suboptimal outcomes
Shape culture	Provides visible leadership in developing a healthy culture for the organisation, and ensures that this is reflected and modelled in their own and in the board's behaviour and decision-making Board culture: Leads and supports a constructive dynamic within the board, enabling grounded debate with contributions from all directors	Provides visible leadership in developing a healthy culture for the organisation, and ensures that this is reflected in their own and the executive's behaviour and decision-making	Actively supports and promotes a healthy culture for the organisation and reflects this in their own behaviour Provides visible leadership in developing a healthy culture so that staff believe NEDs provide a safe point of access to the board for raising concerns	Actively supports and promotes a positive culture for the organisation and reflects this in their own behaviour Nurtures good leadership at all levels, actively addressing problems impacting staff's ability to do a good job

	Chair	Chief Executive	Non-executive Director	Executive Director
Context	Ensures all board members are well briefed on external context	Ensures all board members are well briefed on external context	Mentors less experienced NEDs where relevant	
Intelligence	Ensures requirements for accurate, timely and clear information to board/directors (and governors for FTs) are clear to executive	Ensures provision of accurate, timely and clear information to board/directors (and governors for FTs)	Satisfies themselves of the integrity of financial and quality intelligence including getting out and about, observing and talking to patients and staff	Takes principal responsibility for providing accurate, timely and clear information to the board
Engagement	Plays key role as an ambassador, and in building strong partnerships with: • Patients and public • Members and governors (FT) • All staff • Key partners • Regulators	Plays key leadership role in effective communication and building strong partnerships with: • Patients and public • Member and governors (FT) • All staff • Key partners • Regulators	Ensures board acts in best interests of patients and the public Senior independent director is available to members and governors if there are unresolved concerns (FTs) Shows commitment to supporting the work of the Council of Governors (FTs)	Leads on engagement with specific internal or external stakeholder groups Shows commitment to supporting the work of the Council of Governors (FTs)

Board members' roles in building capacity and capability

The preceding table described roles of board members that are related to the role of the board as a whole. Some members have, in addition, specific responsibilities to support board effectiveness.

These specific responsibilities relate in particular to building the capacity and capability of the board. They are summarised in the following table, and explained below.

Chair	Chief Executive	Non-executive Director
Ensures that the board sees itself as a team, has the right balance and diversity of skills, knowledge and perspective, both NED and ED, and the confidence to challenge on clinical as well as other intelligence and service plans	Ensures that the executive team has the right balance and diversity of skills, knowledge and perspectives	Senior independent director assists the chair to recognise his/ her own development needs via appraisal and discussion
For FTs, supports the Governors' Nomination committee to undertake its role of appointing and appraising NEDs effectively		
With NEDs, appoints and removes the CE		NEDs including the chair, appoint and remove the chief executive
Advises the Remuneration Committee on the appropriate remuneration for EDs		For members of the Remuneration Committee: determine appropriate remuneration for EDs
Has a prime role in appointing, and where necessary removing, executive directors, and in succession planning	With the chair, has a prime role in appointing and where necessary removing executive directors, and in succession planning	As for chair, but a particular responsibility for members of the Remuneration Committee, which supports the chair
Ensures that directors (and governors) have a full induction and continually update their skills, knowledge and familiarity with the organisation	Supports the chair in ensuring that development programmes are in place for board members (and governors for FTs)	

Chair	Chief Executive	Non-executive Director
Arranges regular evaluation of performance of the board, and its committees and the governors (for FTs), externally run at least every 2–3 years. Conducts regular performance reviews of the NEDs, the CE and executive directors in relation to their board contribution. Acts on the results of these evaluations, including supporting personal development planning	Uses the (board) performance evaluations as the basis for determining individual and collective professional development programmes for executive directors relevant to their duties as board members	For FTs: senior independent director (SID) and NEDs meet annually without the chair present to review the chair's performance. The SID also takes soundings from governors

Chair and chief executive roles and relationship

Clarity of role and an effective working relationship between chair and chief executive are crucial to the effectiveness of the board.

In essence the chair leads the board and non-executive directors, and the chief executive leads the executive and the organisation. In Foundation Trusts, the chair also chairs the council of governors.

The table below shows a number of helpful tips and cautionary pointers for chairs and chief executives to support the development of their relationship.[39]

Tips for maintaining a good relationship

Being honest and open
Communicating well
Agreeing and reviewing clearly defined working styles and roles
Establishing trust
Building a personal relationship
Developing shared values
Promoting a 'no surprises' culture

Pointers for chairs and chief executives

Chairs should NOT...	Chief Executives should NOT...
Be too operational, interfere with details of management	Be too controlling or autocratic towards the chair
Be remote from the organisation and unknown by the majority of staff	Obstruct the Chair's access to observing services being delivered in any part of the organisation at any time
Exceed part-time hours	Get too involved in NED or Chair role – e.g. no consultation on board agendas, or personally shaping them
Take specific strategic decisions alone	Break the fundamental rule of 'no surprises'
Adopt bullying, macho 'hire and fire' culture	Be too entrenched in the organisation

Non-executive directors' time commitment

This guidance does not specify the time expected of non-executive directors, but does set out some principles that may help:

- Chairs, in their board leadership role, have a key responsibility to plan and manage the time commitment required of non-executive directors in line with their role on the board in relation to strategy, accountability and culture
- Some tasks that non-executive directors are asked to do can be undertaken by other, appropriately selected and trained lay people (for example chairing appeals panels)
- Experience has shown that the higher the time commitment expected of non-executive directors, the less likely boards are to attract and retain candidates with a diverse background (such as people who are younger, of black and minority ethnic origin, women)
- There is a balance to be struck between developing a good understanding of the organisation and how it is functioning in its health economy, and getting too involved in operational matters. It is important for non- executive directors to maintain the ability for objectivity and independent scrutiny
- Newly appointed non-executive directors may find that they need and want to spend more time initially as they learn about the organisation, its people and its context
- In times of significant organisational or service change, or in the preparation for a Foundation Trust application more time is likely to be required of non-executive directors for a limited period

Role of the company secretary

The role of company secretary is well established in Foundation Trusts, and is becoming increasingly prominent in other NHS organisations.

The company secretary:

- Is accountable to the chair
- Ensures good information flows within the board and its committees between senior management and non-executive directors
- Facilitates induction and assists with professional development[40]
- Is responsible for advising the board through the chair on all governance matters, including ensuring that the organisation complies with the relevant legislation and regulations (and in Foundation Trusts the terms of authorisation)
- Is responsible to the board for ensuring compliance with board probity and procedures and should be accessible to all directors

For Foundation Trusts, the company secretary has additional responsibilities to support the council of governors.

Appendix 1

Judgment and dilemmas

Exercising judgment has already been identified as key to building an effective board. This appendix sets out a spectrum of dilemmas that many boards are grappling with, and yet are not amenable to uniform guidance. They are provided here to encourage boards to set aside the time to debate and explore them as part of their developmental journey.

How to ensure clarity of respective roles of governors and directors?

The Foundation Trust model rests to a very significant degree on robust local account-ability. The council of governors plays a crucial role in ensuring that the board of directors operates in a way that is effective and accountable.

But the need to develop clear roles, constructive relationships and ways of working between governors and directors gives rise to a range of dilemmas including:

- How to arrive at the best balance in the governor role between the internally facing role to deliver on their formal statutory duties (including ensuring that the board of directors is performing effectively) and the externally facing role in hearing and amplify-ing the voice of members, patients and the public?
- How governors are supported to develop sufficient understanding of the organisation and its challenges to feel they are on a firm footing to make a constructive contribution?
- How to ensure that there is clarity in the respective roles of governors and directors?
- How governors have appropriate influence over strategic direction though retaining the independent voice that they need to hold the board of directors to account – how can governors avoid 'marking their own homework'?
- How much information about the board's business is shared with governors – includ-ing risk registers, and if they are what confidentiality safeguards need to be put in place?

The experience seems to be that responding to these dilemmas lies less in seeking 'hard and fast' rules and more in the creation of well designed, thoughtful processes to:

- Give early attention to building and maintaining a clear and shared understanding between governors and directors of the core purpose and priorities of the council of governors
- Facilitation to develop an explicit 'compact' between governors and directors about how they want to work together
- Use of the shared sense of purpose, priorities and ways of working as the basis for directors and the organisation to embrace the role and contribution of governors and proactively identify opportunities for governors to make their best contribution

Paying attention to culture: beyond exhorting a person-centred culture

The emerging consensus about the critical importance of organisational culture in delivering compassionate, high quality care is to be welcomed; but also prompts a range of questions for boards:

- Healthcare organisations are complex and multi- faceted and rarely have a single culture. How does the board really 'know' what the culture is – especially in the light of the lively academic debate about the extent to which culture can be 'measured'?
- To what extent can the board really shape culture in a deliberate and purposeful way?
- What sorts of approaches will help the board to move beyond exhorting the culture that it aims to shape?

The lessons from both success and failure seem to be:

- Boards can learn a great deal about culture by hearing about the lived daily experience of staff, patients and carers. Boards need to ensure that priority is given to hearing this experience – systematically and directly
- Attending to culture starts with shining a light on it. Which specific tool or framework is used seems less important than the permission, space and priority that is given to having the conversation – whether this is in the board, the executive, within teams at the frontline or in the feedback given and received in individual appraisal
- There are examples from both inside and outside of healthcare where culture has been successfully changed over a period of time. Learning the leadership and governance lessons from these case studies may provide important pointers for boards

Building trust with local people in a financially constrained environment

Most boards would wish to support an approach which suggests that 'if organisations concentrate on quality – the resources will follow' but evidence of the extent to which this is the case in practice seems inconsistent.

Although there are some salutary examples (notably infection control), boards are often called upon to balance competing priorities where the 'high quality care can be more cost effective' mantra is more difficult to see.

In the financially constrained environment within which NHS boards are operating, the challenge is for organisations to work with patients, the local community, and across the health and social care divide to identify opportunities for service integration and redesign, across patient pathways to deliver better outcomes for patients in a more cost effective way in the longer term.

More often than not, delivering these longer term improvements will require significant service change and these can trigger anxiety, opposition and concern in the community. It is important that boards are able to work with partners, commissioners, local people and local political leaders to help to build understanding of the choices and 'trade-offs' and thereby build public trust and confidence. Difficult service decisions may never be welcome or palatable for local people but the motivation and basis for making them can be more transparent.

Boards may want to anticipate and explore which approaches to working with patients and local people are likely to garner their support and enable positive service change to be made. Some approaches include:

- Early and open communication with the local community on the issues and challenges facing health services – a regular process of dialogue based on the evidence
- A track record of being consistently open and transparent
- Engaging patients, the community and key staff in early stages of shaping possible solutions, and at key stages throughout the decision-making process
- Potentially using socio technological approaches to decision making which combine value for money with patient involvement[41]
- Visibility of clinicians in discussions with the community about service change

Maintaining the balance between holding to account and being accountable

Boards and organisations devote a great deal of time and resource responding to the demands and expectations of external regulators. This brings the risk that 'accountability' comes to mean accounting for what the organisation has done rather than taking meaningful responsibility for the performance of the organisation and its adherence to standards.

Flowing from the findings of both Francis Reviews, there is a growing understanding that robust assurance processes begin with the intrinsic motivation of the board to set, exemplify and monitor organisational values and fundamental standards and support staff to deliver them. External regulation should be seen as a 'failsafe' rather than a primary source of assurance.

Few boards would now disagree with this perspective, however the capacity of the organisation to provide robust assurance is finite. The requirements of external regulators seldom seem to begin with an assessment of the information and assurance that the organisation routinely generates.

These competing demands are extremely difficult to reconcile. However, it is important that boards model and encourage an approach that makes it clear that adherence to external standards is not enough. Rather, staff are expected to give robust and thoughtful attention to the standards of quality, service and conduct that matter most to them, to their patients and to carers – and that this thinking is reflected in the broader suite of standards that are set and monitored in the organisation.

Achieving a balance between managing risk and encouraging innovation

A systematic approach to the management of risk is one way that boards build public confidence.

However, it is also clear that the future sustainability of the NHS and its founding values will require creative and innovative solutions. Some of the questions boards may wish to debate include:

- How do we ensure that risk and innovation aren't seen as mutually exclusive?
- How do boards ensure that individuals and teams within the organisation take full and active responsibility for the management of risk without creating a straightjacket of anxiety that stifles creativity?
- How does your board know about and act on good practice emerging from the literature on encouraging innovation?
- How does your board engage with the Academic Health Science Networks as well as tapping into other networks as sources of innovative practice?

Zero tolerance of poor care... in a learning organisation

The appropriate board response to flagrantly poor care is, hopefully now, beyond debate and prevarication.

Arguably more challenging are questions about care that is simply sub-optimal – the services that are persistently mediocre. The dilemma for boards is to identify the point at which they need to move from working collaboratively to gain improvement on an issue to the 'zero tolerance' point – and, having made that judgment, what that means the board does in practice.

There is a broad consensus that an open culture that encourages transparency and learning in response to adverse events is a key pre-requisite for reliably high quality, safe, compassionate care. How do boards ensure that in pursuing a policy of 'zero avoidable harm' they do not, inadvertently, drive a climate of fear and reduce the likelihood that staff will be open about mistakes so that the learning can be surfaced and disseminated?

If organisations are both to respond to resource constraints and encourage innovation, there will be a need for experimentation with new models of care – how do boards maintain a commitment to 'zero harm' though allowing space for innovation and experimentation?

To what extent are staff rewarded for bringing forward and/or implementing innovative ideas which improve quality?

Notes

1   *Your statutory duties: A draft reference guide for NHS foundation trust governors.* Monitor December 2012.
2   *Health and Social Care Act 2012* – sections 161,164(3) (3D), 167, 168, 169, 170 and 171
3   *The Mid Staffordshire NHS Foundation Trust Public Inquiry*, Chaired by Sir Robert Francis, February 2013
4   *Quality Governance: How does a board know its organisation is working effectively to improve patient care?* Guidance for boards of NHS Provider Organisations. Monitor. April 2013
5   *Taking it on trust*, Audit Commission, 2009
6   Deffenbaugh J, *It's the people in the boardroom.* British Journal of Healthcare Management, 2012; 18:364–72

7   NHS Standard Contract for 2012/14 at Service Condition 35

8   *Compromise agreements guide* and *severance payments guidance*, NHS Employers, April 19, 2013

9   Jha AK and Epstein AM, *A Survey of Board Chairs of English Hospitals Shows Greater Attention to Quality of Care than among their US Counterparts: Quality and Governance Health Affairs*, April, 2013

10   Jha AK, Epstein AM, *Boards and Governance in U.S. Hospitals and the Relationship to Quality of Care. Health Affairs*. November, 2009

11   Section 18 of the Health Act 1999. Later repealed and replaced by Section 45 of the Health and Social Care (Community Health Standards) Act 2003. Note: CCGs have a duty to improve the quality of services in section 14R of the Healthy and Social Care Act 2012

12   *Corporate governance and the financial crisis*. Organisation for Economic Co-operation and Development, Paris. OECD, 2009

13   *Standards matter: A review of best practice in promoting good behaviour in public life*. Committee on the Standards of Public Life, January, 2013

14   Professional Standards Authority, *Standards for NHS Board Members*, November, 2012

15   Monitor's Code of Governance E2.1 and F3.1; For CCGs Schedule 2, paragraph 7(2) of the Health and Social Care Act 2012, Codes of Conduct and Accountability 2004

16   There are interesting lessons on the need for risk committees emerging from the banking crises of 2008. See Walker D. *A review of corporate governance in UK banks and other financial industry entities*, London, 2009

17   Davies HTO, Mannion R, *Will Prescriptions for cultural change improve the NHS?* BMJ, 1 March, 2013

18   *Patients First and Foremost, Initial Government Response to the Report of the Mid Staffordshire NHS Foundation Trust Public Inquiry*, March, 2013

19   *Schwartz Centre Rounds – Evaluation of the UK Pilots*, King's Fund, June, 2011

20   Welbourn D, Warwick R, Carnall C, Fathers D, *Leadership of Whole Systems*, Kings Fund 2012

21   *The Intelligent Board*, Dr Foster Intelligence, 2006

22   *The Intelligent Commissioning Board*, London, Dr Foster Intelligence, 2006

23   *The Intelligent Board 2009: Commissioning to reduce inequalities*, Dr Foster Intelligence, 2009

24   *The Intelligent Mental Health Board*, Dr Foster Intelligence, 2007

25   *The Intelligent Ambulance Board*, Dr Foster Intelligence, 2006

26   *The Intelligent Board – Patient Experience*, 2010

27   Mannion R, Davies HTO, Marshall MN. *Cultures for Performance in Healthcare*, Open University Press, 2004

28   See Section 242 of the NHS Act 2006 as amended. For CCGs Section 14 2 of the Health and Social Care Act 2012

29   MacLeod D, Clarke N. *Engaging for success: Enhancing performance through employee engagement*, London: Crown, 2009

30   West M, Dawson J, Admasachew L, Topakas A, *NHS Staff Management and Health Service Quality: Results from the NHS Staff Survey and Related Data*, Department of Health (2011)

31 Chambers N, Harvey G, Mannion M, Bond, J, Marshall J, *Towards a Framework for Enhancing the Performance of NHS Boards: A synthesis of the evidence about board governance, board effectiveness and board development*. In press 2013

32 Storey et al, *The intended and unintended outcomes of new governance arrangements within the NHS*, March 2010

33 Section 151 (5) Health and Social Care Act 2012 – (Public Benefit corporations must take steps to secure that governors are equipped with the skills and knowledge they require in their capacity as such)

34 Sonnenfeld, Professor Jeffrey. *What Makes Great Boards Great*, Harvard Business Review, 2002

35 The Freedom of Information Act 2000

36 *Code of Conduct. Code of Accountability in the NHS*, Department of Health, July, 2004

37 *Strategic Human Resources Management* factsheet, CIPD, July, 2012

38 *Director-Governor interaction in NHS Foundation Trusts*, Monitor, June, 2012

39 *Leading Together: Co-action and counteraction in Chair-Chief Executive relationships*, NHS Institute, August, 2009

40 *Role of Company Secretary*. Institute of Chartered Secretaries and Administrators. www.icsa.org.uk

41 *STAR: Socio Technological Allocation of Resources*, Health Foundation website

42 *The Healthy NHS Board: A review of guidance and research evidence*, Ramsey, Fulop, Fresko and Rubenstein Feb 2010 and Addendum May 2013

Appendix 5

FRC Guidance on Board Effectiveness

1. The Role of the Board and Directors

An Effective Board

1.1. The board's role is to provide entrepreneurial leadership of the company within a framework of prudent and effective controls which enables risk to be assessed and managed.

1.2. An effective board develops and promotes its collective vision of the company's purpose, its culture, its values and the behaviours it wishes to promote in conducting its business. In particular it:
- provides direction for management;
- demonstrates ethical leadership, displaying – and promoting throughout the company – behaviours consistent with the culture and values it has defined for the organisation;
- creates a performance culture that drives value creation without exposing the company to excessive risk of value destruction;
- makes well-informed and high-quality decisions based on a clear line of sight into the business;
- creates the right framework for helping directors meet their statutory duties under the Companies Act 2006, and/or other relevant statutory and regulatory regimes;
- is accountable, particularly to those that provide the company's capital; and
- thinks carefully about its governance arrangements and embraces evaluation of their effectiveness.

1.3. An effective board should not necessarily be a comfortable place. Challenge, as well as teamwork, is an essential feature. Diversity in board composition is an important driver of a board's effectiveness – creating a breadth of perspective among directors, and breaking down a tendency towards 'group think'.

The Role of the Chair

1.4. Good boards are created by good chairmen. The chair creates the conditions for overall board and individual director effectiveness.

1.5. The chair should demonstrate the highest standards of integrity and probity, and set clear expectations concerning the company's culture, values and behaviours, and the style and tone of board discussions.

1.6. The chair, with the help of the executive directors and the company secretary, sets the agenda for the board's deliberations.

1.7. The chair's role includes:
- demonstrating ethical leadership;
- setting a board agenda which is primarily focused on strategy, performance, value creation and accountability, and ensuring that issues relevant to these areas are reserved for board decision;
- ensuring a timely flow of high-quality supporting information;
- making certain that the board determines the nature, and extent, of the significant risks the company is willing to embrace in the implementation of its strategy, and that there are no 'no go' areas which prevent directors from operating effective oversight in this area;
- regularly considering succession planning and the composition of the board;
- making certain that the board has effective decision-making processes and applies sufficient challenge to major proposals;
- ensuring the board's committees are properly structured with appropriate terms of reference;
- encouraging all board members to engage in board and committee meetings by drawing on their skills, experience, knowledge and, where appropriate, independence;
- fostering relationships founded on mutual respect and open communication – both in and outside the boardroom – between the non-executive directors and the executive team;
- developing productive working relationships with all executive directors, and the CEO in particular, providing support and advice while respecting executive responsibility;
- consulting the senior independent director on board matters in accordance with the Code;
- taking the lead on issues of director development, including through induction programmes for new directors and regular reviews with all directors;
- acting on the results of board evaluation;
- being aware of, and responding to, his or her own development needs, including people and other skills, especially when taking on the role for the first time; and
- ensuring effective communication with shareholders and other stakeholders and, in particular, that all directors are made aware of the views of those who provide the company's capital.

1.8. The chair of each board committee fulfils an important leadership role similar to that of the chair of the board, particularly in creating the conditions for overall committee and individual director effectiveness.

The Role of the Senior Independent Director

1.9. In normal times the senior independent director should act as a sounding board for the chair, providing support for the chair in the delivery of his or her objectives, and leading the evaluation of the chair on behalf of the other directors, as set out in the Code. The senior independent director might also take responsibility for an orderly succession process for the chair.

1.10. When the board is undergoing a period of stress, however, the senior independent director's role becomes critically important. He or she is expected to work with the chair and other directors, and/or shareholders, to resolve significant issues. Boards should ensure they have a clear understanding of when the senior independent director might intervene in order to maintain board and company stability. Examples might include where:

- there is a dispute between the chair and CEO;
- shareholders or non-executive directors have expressed concerns that are not being addressed by the chair or CEO;
- the strategy being followed by the chair and CEO is not supported by the entire board;
- the relationship between the chair and CEO is particularly close, and decisions are being made without the approval of the full board; or
- succession planning is being ignored.

1.11. These issues should be considered when defining the role of the senior independent director, which should be set out in writing.

The Role of Executive Directors

1.12. Executive directors have the same duties as other members of a unitary board. These duties extend to the whole of the business, and not just that part of it covered by their individual executive roles. Nor should executive directors see themselves only as members of the CEO's executive team when engaged in board business. Taking the wider view can help achieve the advantage of a unitary system: greater knowledge, involvement and commitment at the point of decision. The chair should make certain that executives are aware of their wider responsibilities when joining the board, and ensure they receive appropriate induction, and regular training, to enable them to fulfil the role. Executive directors are also likely to be able to broaden their understanding of their board responsibilities if they take up a non-executive director position on another board.

1.13. The CEO is the most senior executive director on the board with responsibility for proposing strategy to the board, and for delivering the strategy as agreed. The CEO's relationship with the chair is a key relationship that can help the board be more effective. The Code states that the differing responsibilities of the chair and the CEO should be set out in writing and agreed by the board. Particular attention should be paid to areas of potential overlap.

1.14. The CEO has, with the support of the executive team, primary responsibility for setting an example to the company's employees, and communicating to them the expectations of the board in relation to the company's culture, values and behaviours. The CEO is responsible for supporting the chair to make certain that appropriate standards of governance permeate through all parts of the organisation. The CEO will make certain that the board is made aware, when appropriate, of the views of employees on issues of relevance to the business.

1.15. The CEO will ensure the board knows the executive directors' views on business issues in order to improve the standard of discussion in the boardroom and, prior to final decision on an issue, explain in a balanced way any divergence of view in the executive team.

1.16. The CFO has a particular responsibility to deliver high-quality information to the board on the financial position of the company.

1.17. Executive directors have the most intimate knowledge of the company and its capabilities when developing and presenting proposals, and when exercising judgement, particularly on matters of strategy. They should appreciate that constructive challenge from non-executive directors is an essential aspect of good governance, and should encourage their non-executive colleagues to test their proposals in the light of the non-executives' wider experience outside the company. The chair and the CEO should ensure that this process is properly followed.

The Role of Non-Executive Directors

1.18. A non-executive director should, on appointment, devote time to a comprehensive, formal and tailored induction which should extend beyond the boardroom. Initiatives such as partnering a non-executive director with an executive board member may speed up the process of him or her acquiring an understanding of the main areas of business activity, especially areas involving significant risk. The director should expect to visit, and talk with, senior and middle managers in these areas.

1.19. Non-executive directors should devote time to developing and refreshing their knowledge and skills, including those of communication, to ensure that they continue to make a positive contribution to the board. Being well-informed about the company, and having a strong command of the issues relevant to the business, will generate the respect of the other directors.

1.20. Non-executive directors need to make sufficient time available to discharge their responsibilities effectively. The letter of appointment should state the minimum time that the non-executive director will be required to spend on the company's business, and seek the individual's confirmation that he or she can devote that amount of time to the role, consistent with other commitments. The letter should also indicate the possibility of additional time commitment when the company is undergoing a period of particularly increased activity, such as an acquisition or takeover, or as a result of some major difficulty with one or more of its operations.

1.21. Non-executive directors have a responsibility to uphold high standards of integrity and probity. They should support the chair and executive directors in instilling the appropriate culture, values and behaviours in the boardroom and beyond.

1.22. Non-executive directors should insist on receiving high-quality information sufficiently in advance so that there can be thorough consideration of the issues prior to, and informed debate and challenge at, board meetings. High-quality information is that which is appropriate for making decisions on the issue at hand – it should be accurate, clear, comprehensive, up-to-date and timely; contain a summary of the contents of any paper; and inform the director of what is expected of him or her on that issue.

1.23. Non-executive directors should take into account the views of shareholders and other stakeholders, because these views may provide different perspectives on the company and its performance.

2. Board Support and the Role of the Company Secretary

2.1. The requirement for a company secretary of a public company is specified in section 271 of the Companies Act 2006. The obligations and responsibilities of the company secretary outlined in the Act, and also in the Code, necessitate him or her playing a leading role in the good governance of the company by supporting the chair and helping the board and its committees to function efficiently.

2.2. The company secretary should report to the chair on all board governance matters. This does not preclude the company secretary also reporting to the CEO in relation to his or her other executive management responsibilities. The appointment and removal of the company secretary should be a matter for the board as a whole, and the remuneration of the company secretary might be determined by the remuneration committee.

2.3. The company secretary should ensure the presentation of high-quality information to the board and its committees. The company secretary can also add value by fulfilling, or procuring the fulfilment of, other requirements of the Code on behalf of the chair, in particular director induction and development. This should be in a manner that is appropriate to the particular director, and which has the objective of enhancing that director's effectiveness in the board or board committees, consistent with the results of the board's evaluation processes. The chair and the company secretary should periodically review whether the board and the company's other governance processes, for example board and committee evaluation, are fit for purpose, and consider any improvements or initiatives that could strengthen the governance of the company.

2.4. The company secretary's effectiveness can be enhanced by his or her ability to build relationships of mutual trust with the chair, the senior independent director and the non-executive directors, while maintaining the confidence of executive director colleagues.

3. Decision making

3.1. Well-informed and high-quality decision making is a critical requirement for a board to be effective and does not happen by accident. Flawed decisions can be made with the best of intentions, with competent individuals believing passionately that they are making a sound judgment, when they are not. Many of the factors which lead to poor decision making are predictable and preventable. Boards can minimise the risk of poor decisions by investing time in the design of their decision-making policies and processes, including the contribution of committees.

3.2. Good decision-making capability can be facilitated by:
- high-quality board documentation;
- obtaining expert opinions when necessary;
- allowing time for debate and challenge, especially for complex, contentious or business-critical issues;
- achieving timely closure; and
- providing clarity on the actions required, and timescales and responsibilities.

3.3.   Boards should be aware of factors which can limit effective decision making, such as:

- a dominant personality or group of directors on the board, which can inhibit contribution from other directors;

- insufficient attention to risk, and treating risk as a compliance issue rather than as part of the decision-making process – especially cases where the level of risk involved in a project could endanger the stability and sustainability of the business itself;

- failure to recognise the value implications of running the business on the basis of self-interest and other poor ethical standards;

- a reluctance to involve non-executive directors, or of matters being brought to the board for sign-off rather than debate;

- complacent or intransigent attitudes;

- a weak organisational culture; or

- inadequate information or analysis.

3.4.   Most complex decisions depend on judgment, but the judgment of even the most well intentioned and experienced leaders can, in certain circumstances, be distorted. Some factors known to distort judgment in decision making are conflicts of interest, emotional attachments, and inappropriate reliance on previous experience and previous decisions. For significant decisions, therefore, a board may wish to consider extra steps, for example:

- describing in board papers the process that has been used to arrive at and challenge the proposal prior to presenting it to the board, thereby allowing directors not involved in the project to assess the appropriateness of the process as a precursor to assessing the merits of the project itself; or

- where appropriate, putting in place additional safeguards to reduce the risk of distorted judgements by, for example, commissioning an independent report, seeking advice from an expert, introducing a devil's advocate to provide challenge, establishing a sole purpose sub-committee, or convening additional meetings. Some chairmen favour separate discussions for important decisions; for example, concept, proposal for discussion, proposal for decision. This gives executive directors more opportunity to put the case at the earlier stages, and all directors the opportunity to share concerns or challenge assumptions well in advance of the point of decision.

3.5.   Boards can benefit from reviewing past decisions, particularly ones with poor outcomes. A review should not focus just on the merits of the decision itself but also on the decision-making process.

4. Board Composition and Succession Planning

4.1.   Appointing directors who are able to make a positive contribution is one of the key elements of board effectiveness. Directors will be more likely to make good decisions and maximise the opportunities for the company's success in the longer term if the right skill-sets are present in the boardroom. This includes the appropriate range and balance of skills, experience, knowledge and independence. Non-executive directors should possess critical skills of value to the board and relevant to the challenges facing the company.

4.2. The nomination committee, usually led by the chair, should be responsible for board recruitment. The process should be continuous and proactive, and should take into account the company's agreed strategic priorities. The aim should be to secure a boardroom which achieves the right balance between challenge and teamwork, and fresh input and thinking, while maintaining a cohesive board.

4.3. It is important to consider a diversity of personal attributes among board candidates, including: intellect, critical assessment and judgement, courage, openness, honesty and tact; and the ability to listen, forge relationships and develop trust. Diversity of psychological type, background and gender is important to ensure that a board is not composed solely of like-minded individuals. A board requires directors who have the intellectual capability to suggest change to a proposed strategy, and to promulgate alternatives.

4.4. Given the importance of committees in many companies' decision-making structures, it will be important to recruit non-executives with the necessary technical skills and knowledge relating to the committees' subject matter, as well as the potential to assume the role of committee chair.

4.5. The chair's vision for achieving the optimal board composition will help the nomination committee review the skills required, identify the gaps, develop transparent appointment criteria and inform succession planning. The nomination committee should periodically assess whether the desired outcome has been achieved, and propose changes to the process as necessary.

4.6. Executive directors may be recruited from external sources, but companies should also develop internal talent and capability. Initiatives might include middle management development programmes, facilitating engagement from time to time with non-executive directors, and partnering and mentoring schemes.

4.7. Good board appointments do not depend only on the nomination committee. A prospective director should carry out sufficient due diligence to understand the company, appreciate the time commitment involved, and assess the likelihood that he or she will be able to make a positive contribution.

5. Evaluating the Performance of the Board and Directors

5.1. Boards continually need to monitor and improve their performance. This can be achieved through board evaluation, which provides a powerful and valuable feedback mechanism for improving board effectiveness, maximising strengths and highlighting areas for further development. The evaluation process should aim to be objective and rigorous.

5.2. Like induction and board development, evaluation should be bespoke in its formulation and delivery. The chair has overall responsibility for the process, and should select an appropriate approach and act on its outcome. The senior independent director should lead the process which evaluates the performance of the chair. Chairs of board committees should also be responsible for the evaluation of their committees.

5.3. The outcome of a board evaluation should be shared with the whole board and fed back, as appropriate, into the board's work on composition, the design of induction and development programmes, and other relevant areas. It may be useful for a company to have a review loop to consider how effective the board evaluation process has been.

5.4. The Code recommends that FTSE350 companies have externally-facilitated board evaluations at least every three years. External facilitation can add value by introducing a fresh perspective and new ways of thinking. It may also be useful in particular circumstances, such as when there has been a change of chair, there is a known problem around the board table requiring tactful handling, or there is an external perception that the board is, or has been, ineffective.

5.5. Whether facilitated externally or internally, evaluations should explore how effective the board is as a unit, as well as the effectiveness of the contributions made by individual directors. Some areas which may be considered, although they are neither prescriptive nor exhaustive, include:

- the mix of skills, experience, knowledge and diversity on the board, in the context of the challenges facing the company;
- clarity of, and leadership given to, the purpose, direction and values of the company;
- succession and development plans;
- how the board works together as a unit, and the tone set by the chair and the CEO;
- key board relationships, particularly chair/CEO, chair/senior independent director, chair/company secretary and executive/non-executive;
- effectiveness of individual non-executive and executive directors;
- clarity of the senior independent director's role;
- effectiveness of board committees, and how they are connected with the main board;
- quality of the general information provided on the company and its performance;
- quality of papers and presentations to the board;
- quality of discussions around individual proposals;
- process the chair uses to ensure sufficient debate for major decisions or contentious issues;
- effectiveness of the secretariat;
- clarity of the decision processes and authorities;
- processes for identifying and reviewing risks; and
- how the board communicates with, and listens and responds to, shareholders and other stakeholders.

6. AUDIT, RISK AND REMUNERATION

6.1. While the board may make use of committees to assist its consideration of audit, risk and remuneration, it retains responsibility for, and makes the final decisions on, all of these areas. The chair should ensure that sufficient time is allowed at the board for discussion of these issues. All directors should familiarise themselves with the associated provisions of the UK Corporate Governance Code and its related guidance, and any relevant regulatory requirements.

6.2. Sufficient time should be allowed after committee meetings for them to report to the board on the nature and content of discussion, on recommendations, and on actions to be taken. The minutes of committee meetings should be circulated to all board members, unless it would be inappropriate to do so, and to the company secretary (if he or she is not secretary to the committee). The remit of each committee, and the processes of interaction between committees and between each committee and the board, should be reviewed regularly.

7. Relations with Shareholders

7.1. Communication of a company's governance presents an opportunity for the company to improve the quality of the dialogue with its shareholders and other stakeholders, generating greater levels of trust and confidence.

7.2. The Annual Report and Accounts is an important means of communicating with shareholders. It can also be used to provide well thought-out disclosures on the company's governance arrangements and the board evaluation exercise. Thinking about such disclosures can prompt the board to reflect on the quality of its governance, and what actions it might take to improve its structures, processes and systems.

7.3. The Code emphasises the importance of continual communication with major shareholders, and of the AGM, as two aspects of a company's wider communications strategy. The chair has a key role to play in representing the company to its principal audiences, and is encouraged to report personally about board leadership and effectiveness in the corporate governance statement in the annual report.

Appendix 6

Guidance on Risk Management, Internal Control and Related Financial and Business Reporting

September 2014

Section 1 Introduction Applicability

1. This guidance revises, integrates and replaces the current editions of the Financial Reporting Council's ("FRC") 'Internal Control: Revised Guidance for Directors on the Combined Code' and 'Going Concern and Liquidity Risk: Guidance for Directors of UK Companies', and reflects changes made to the UK Corporate Governance Code ("the Code").

2. It aims to bring together elements of best practice for risk management; prompt boards to consider how to discharge their responsibilities in relation to the existing and emerging principal risks faced by the company; reflect sound business practice, whereby risk management and internal control are embedded in the business process by which a company pursues its objectives; and highlight related reporting responsibilities.

3. While it is hoped that this guidance will be useful to other entities, it is primarily directed to companies subject to the Code.[1] It applies to such companies for accounting periods beginning on or after 1 October 2014.

Background

4. The Code defines the role of the board as being "to provide entrepreneurial leadership of the company within a framework of prudent and effective controls which enables risk to be assessed and managed". Effective development and delivery of a company's strategic objectives, its ability to seize new opportunities and to ensure its longer term survival depend upon its identification, understanding of, and response to, the risks it faces.

5. Economic developments and some high profile failures of risk management in recent years have reminded boards of the need to ensure that the company's approach to risk has been properly considered in setting the company's strategy and managing its risks. There may be significant consequences if the company does not do so effectively.

6. Good stewardship by the board should not inhibit sensible risk taking that is critical to growth. However, the assessment of risks as part of the normal business planning process should support better decision-taking, ensure that the board and management respond promptly to risks when they arise, and ensure that shareholders and

other stakeholders are well informed about the principal risks and prospects of the company.[2] The board's responsibility for the organisation's culture is essential to the way in which risk is considered and addressed within the organisation and with external stakeholders.

7. The Code was updated in 2010 to make it clear that, in addition to being responsible for ensuring sound risk management and internal control systems, boards should explain the company's business model and should determine the nature and extent of the principal risks they were willing to take to achieve the company's strategic objectives.

8. The Code was further updated in 2012 to improve financial and business reporting by making it clear that the board should:

    ■ confirm that the annual report and accounts taken as a whole is fair, balanced and understandable and provides the information necessary for shareholders to assess the company's position and performance, business model and strategy; and

    ■ establish arrangements that will enable it to make this assessment.

9. In 2011 the FRC published the 'Boards and Risk' report, which reflected the views of directors, investors and risk professionals and highlighted that the board's responsibilities for risk management and internal control are not limited to the oversight of the internal control system.

10. In 2012 the Sharman Inquiry into going concern and liquidity risk concluded that the board's declaration of whether the company remained a going concern should be more broadly based than is required to determine the accounting approach to be taken.

11. Taken together, the conclusions of the two reports can be summarised as:

    ■ the board must determine its willingness to take on risk, and the desired culture within the company;

    ■ risk management and internal control should be incorporated within the company's normal management and governance processes, not treated as a separate compliance exercise;

    ■ the board must make a robust assessment of the principal risks to the company's business model and ability to deliver its strategy, including solvency and liquidity risks. In making that assessment the board should consider the likelihood and impact of these risks materialising in the short and longer term;

    ■ once those risks have been identified, the board should agree how they will be managed and mitigated, and keep the company's risk profile under review. It should satisfy itself that management's systems include appropriate controls, and that it has adequate sources of assurance;

    ■ the assessment and management of the principal risks, and monitoring and review of the associated systems, should be carried out as an on-going process, not seen as an annual one-off exercise; and

    ■ this process should inform a number of different disclosures in the annual report: the description of the principal risks and uncertainties facing the company; the disclosures on the going concern basis of accounting and material uncertainties thereto; and the report on the review of the risk management and internal control systems.

12.   In April 2014 the FRC also published its 'Guidance on the Strategic Report' as best practice.[3] It encourages companies to make the information in annual reports more relevant to shareholders. Recognising that an annual report comprises a number of components, it aims to promote cohesiveness amongst these components, with related information appropriately linked together.

Risk Management and Internal Control

13.   The board has ultimate responsibility for risk management and internal control, including for the determination of the nature and extent of the principal risks it is willing to take to achieve its strategic objectives and for ensuring that an appropriate culture has been embedded throughout the organisation. This guidance provides a high-level overview of some of the factors boards should consider in relation to the design, implementation, monitoring and review of the risk management and internal control systems. Such systems cannot eliminate all risks, but it is the role of the board to ensure that they are robust and effective and take account of such risks.

14.   Consistent with the amendment to Principle C.2 in the 2014 edition of the Code, this guidance asks boards to determine their "principal" risks, rather than "significant" risks as in earlier Code editions. This decision was taken to align the terminology with the new Strategic Report requirements. The term "principal risk" is defined in the FRC's "Guidance on the Strategic Report". The FRC considers that in this context the words "principal" and "significant" are interchangeable and that the amendment should not be seen as implying a change in the nature of the risks referred to in Principle C.2.

15.   The guidance does not set out in detail the procedure by which a company designs and implements its risk management and internal control systems. Attempting to define a single approach to achieving best practice would be misguided if it led boards to underestimate the crucial importance to high quality risk management of the culture and behaviour they promote.

The Board's Statements on Longer Term Viability and on the Going Concern Basis of Accounting

16.   The Sharman Inquiry concluded that the board's assessment as to whether a company remains a "going concern" should be more broadly based than is required to determine whether to adopt the going concern basis of accounting in the current financial statements and identify any material uncertainties about the company's ability to continue to do so in future.

17.   The revised Code and this guidance use the term "going concern" only in the context of referring to the going concern basis of accounting for the preparation of financial statements, as defined in accounting standards. This usage is well-established but is different from the ordinary English usage of the term "going concern" to describe an entity that has a viable future.

18.   In the 2014 edition of the Code, Provision C.1.3 has been revised to require an explicit statement in the financial statements about whether: the going concern basis of accounting has been adopted; and there are any material uncertainties

about the company's ability to continue to do so in future. A new provision (C.2.2) requires a broader statement about the board's reasonable expectation as to the company's viability based on a robust assessment of the company's principal risks and the company's current position. This guidance addresses each of these statements.

How this Guidance is Structured

19. Sections 2 and 3 of this guidance summarise the board's responsibilities for risk management and internal control and identify some of the factors boards should consider in order to exercise those responsibilities effectively. Section 4 addresses the establishment of the risk management and internal control systems, Section 5 discusses the monitoring and review of those systems and Section 6 addresses the board's related financial and business reporting responsibilities.

20. Sections 4, 5 and 6 incorporate the core of the previous 'Internal Control: Guidance for Directors'. Sections 2 and 3 are new, and are intended to align the scope of the guidance with Principle C.2 on Risk Management and Internal Control and Provision C.1.3 on the going concern basis of accounting, by addressing the full range of the board's responsibilities for these matters and their inter-relationships.

21. Appendices A and B provide further guidance on adopting the going concern basis of accounting and related disclosures and on the longer term viability statement. In addition, the FRC has issued a separate Supplement for Banks on going concern, which addresses considerations specific to the banking sector, and which should be read in conjunction with this Guidance.

22. Appendix C contains questions that may assist boards in assessing how they are carrying out their responsibilities, the culture of the company, and the effectiveness of the risk management and internal control systems.

23. Appendix D contains an overview of a company's reporting requirements relating to risk and going concern.

Section 2

Board Responsibilities for Risk Management and Internal Control

24. The board has responsibility for an organisation's overall approach to risk management and internal control. The board's responsibilities are:
   - ensuring the design and implementation of appropriate risk management and internal control systems that identify the risks facing the company and enable the board to make a robust assessment of the principal risks;
   - determining the nature and extent of the principal risks faced and those risks which the organisation is willing to take in achieving its strategic objectives (determining its "risk appetite");
   - ensuring that appropriate culture and reward systems have been embedded throughout the organisation;
   - agreeing how the principal risks should be managed or mitigated to reduce the likelihood of their incidence or their impact;

- monitoring and reviewing the risk management and internal control systems, and the management's process of monitoring and reviewing, and satisfying itself that they are functioning effectively and that corrective action is being taken where necessary; and
- ensuring sound internal and external information and communication processes and taking responsibility for external communication on risk management and internal control.

25. The board's specific responsibility for determining whether to adopt the going concern basis of accounting and related disclosures of material uncertainties in the financial statements is a sub set of these broader responsibilities. A company that is able to adopt the going concern basis of accounting and does not have related material uncertainties to report, for the purposes of the financial statements, is not necessarily free of risks that would threaten the company's business model, future performance, solvency or liquidity were they to materialise. The board is responsible for ensuring this distinction is understood internally and communicated externally.

26. It is the role of management to implement and take day-to-day responsibility for board policies on risk management and internal control. But the board needs to satisfy itself that management has understood the risks, implemented and monitored appropriate policies and controls, and are providing the board with timely information so that it can discharge its own responsibilities. In turn, management should ensure internal responsibilities and accountabilities are clearly established, understood and embedded at all levels of the organisation. Employees should understand their responsibility for behaving according to the culture.

Section 3

Exercising Responsibilities

27. The board should establish the tone for risk management and internal control and put in place appropriate systems to enable it to meet its responsibilities effectively. These will depend upon factors such as the size and composition of the board; the scale, diversity and complexity of the company's operations; and the nature of the principal risks the company faces. But in deciding what arrangements are appropriate the board should consider, amongst other things:
- The culture it wishes to embed in the company, and whether this has been achieved.

  As with all aspects of good governance, the effectiveness of risk management and internal control ultimately depend on the individuals responsible for operating the systems that are put in place. In order to ensure the appropriate culture is in place it is not sufficient for the board simply to set the desired values. It also needs to ensure they are communicated by management, incentivise the desired behaviours and sanction inappropriate behaviour, and assess whether the desired values and behaviours have become embedded at all levels.

  This should include consideration of whether the company's leadership style and management structures, human resource policies and reward systems support or undermine the risk management and internal control systems.

- How to ensure there is adequate discussion at the board.

  The board should agree the frequency and scope of its discussions on strategy, business model and risk; how its assessment of risk is integrated with other matters considered by the board; and how to assess the impact on the company's risk profile of decisions on changes in strategy, major new projects and other significant commitments. The board needs to ensure that it engages in informed debate and constructive challenge and keeps under review the effectiveness of its decision-making processes.

- The skills, knowledge and experience of the board and management.

  The board should consider whether it, and any committee or management group to which it delegates activities, has the necessary skills, knowledge, experience, authority and support to enable it to assess the risks the company faces and exercise its responsibilities effectively. Boards should consider specifically assessing this as part of their regular evaluations of their effectiveness.

- The flow of information to and from the board, and the quality of that information.

  The board should specify the nature, source, format and frequency of the information that it requires. It should ensure that the assumptions and models underlying this information are clear so that they can be understood and if necessary challenged. Risks can crystallise quickly and the board should ensure that there are clear processes for bringing significant issues to its attention more rapidly when required, and agreed triggers for doing so.

  The board should monitor the quality of the information it receives and ensure that it is of a sufficient quality to allow effective decision-making.

- The use, if any, made of delegation.

  The board should determine to what extent it wishes to delegate some activity to, or obtain advice from, committees or the management group and the appropriate division of responsibilities and accountabilities.

  To the extent that designated committees or the management group carry out, on behalf of the board, activities that this guidance attributes to the board, the board should be satisfied that the arrangements for the work carried out, for the co- ordination of their work (if more than one is involved), and for reporting to the board are appropriate and operating effectively. The board retains ultimate responsibility for the risk management and internal control systems and should reach its own conclusions regarding the recommendations it receives.

  The board should ensure that the remuneration committee takes appropriate account of risk when determining remuneration policies and awards, and whether the links between the remuneration committee and the risk and/or audit committee are operating effectively.

- What assurance the board requires, and how this is to be obtained.

  The board should identify what assurance it requires and, where there are gaps, how these should be addressed. In addition to the board, committee and management's own monitoring activities, sources of assurance might include reports on relevant matters from any compliance, risk management, internal control and internal audit functions within the company, the external auditor's communications to the audit committee about matters it considers relevant in fulfilling its responsibilities, and other internal and external sources of information or assurance.

The board should satisfy itself that these sources of assurance have sufficient authority, independence and expertise to enable them to provide objective advice and information to the board.

Section 4

Establishing the Risk Management and Internal Control Systems

28. The risk management and internal control systems encompass the policies, culture, organisation, behaviours, processes, systems and other aspects of a company that, taken together:
    - facilitate its effective and efficient operation by enabling it to assess current and emerging risks, respond appropriately to risks and significant control failures and to safeguard its assets;
    - help to reduce the likelihood and impact of poor judgement in decision-making; risk-taking that exceeds the levels agreed by the board; human error; or control processes being deliberately circumvented;
    - help ensure the quality of internal and external reporting; and
    - help ensure compliance with applicable laws and regulations, and also with internal policies with respect to the conduct of business.

29. A company's systems of risk management and internal control will include: risk assessment; management or mitigation of risks, including the use of control processes; information and communication systems; and processes for monitoring and reviewing their continuing effectiveness.

30. The risk management and internal control systems should be embedded in the operations of the company and be capable of responding quickly to evolving business risks, whether they arise from factors within the company or from changes in the business environment. These systems should not be seen as a periodic compliance exercise, but instead as an integral part of the company's day to day business processes.

31. The board should ensure that sound risk management and internal control systems are in place to identify the risks facing the company and to consider their likelihood and impact if they were to materialise.

32. When determining the principal risks, the board should focus on those risks that, given the company's current position, could threaten the company's business model, future performance, solvency or liquidity, irrespective of how they are classified or from where they arise. The board should treat such risks as principal risks and establish clearly the extent to which they are to be managed or mitigated.

33. Risks will differ between companies but may include financial, operational, reputational, behavioural, organisational, third party, or external risks, such as market or regulatory risk, over which the board may have little or no direct control.

34. The design of a robust assessment process to determine the principal risks and consider their implications for the company should be appropriate to the complexity, size and circumstances of the company and is a matter for the judgement of the

board, with the support of management. Circumstances may vary over time with changes in the business model, performance, strategy, operational processes and the stage of development the company has reached in its own business cycles, as well as with changes in the external environment.

35. When considering risk the board should consider the following aspects:
    - the nature and extent of the risks, including principal risks, facing, or being taken by, the company which it regards as desirable or acceptable for the company to bear;
    - the likelihood of the risks concerned materialising, and the impact of related risks materialising as a result or at the same time;
    - the company's ability to reduce the likelihood of the risks materialising, and of the impact on the business of risks that do materialise;
    - the exposure to risks before and after risks are managed or mitigated, as appropriate;
    - the operation of the relevant controls and control processes;
    - the effectiveness and relative costs and benefits of particular controls; and
    - the impact of the values and culture of the company, and the way that teams and individuals are incentivised, on the effectiveness of the systems.

36. Training and communication assist in embedding the desired culture and behaviours in the company. To build a company culture that recognises and deals with risk, it is important that the risk management and internal control systems consider how the expectations of the board are to be communicated to staff and what training may be required. In considering communication systems, the board should also consider the company's whistle-blowing procedures.

37. Effective controls are an important element of the systems of risk management and internal control and can cover many aspects of a business, including strategic, financial, operational and compliance.

38. The board should agree how the principal risks will be managed or mitigated and which controls will be put in place. In agreeing the controls the board should determine what constitutes a significant control failing.

Section 5

Monitoring and Review of the Risk Management and Internal Control Systems

39. The existence of risk management and internal control systems does not, on its own, signal the effective management of risk. Effective and on-going monitoring and review are essential components of sound systems of risk management and internal control. The process of monitoring and review is intended to allow the board to conclude whether the systems are properly aligned with strategic objectives; and satisfy itself that the systems address the company's risks and are being developed, applied and maintained appropriately.

40. The board should define the processes to be adopted for its on-going monitoring and review, including specifying the requirements, scope and frequency for reporting and assurance. Regular reports to the board should provide a balanced assessment

of the risks and the effectiveness of the systems of risk management and internal control in managing those risks. The board should form its own view on effectiveness, based on the evidence it obtains, exercising the standard of care generally applicable to directors in the exercise of their duties.

41. When reviewing reports during the year, the board should consider: how effectively the risks have been assessed and the principal risks determined; how they have been managed or mitigated; whether necessary actions are being taken promptly to remedy any significant failings or weaknesses; and whether the causes of the failing or weakness indicate poor decision-taking, a need for more extensive monitoring or a reassessment of the effectiveness of management's on-going processes.

42. In addition to its on-going monitoring and review, the board should undertake an annual review of the effectiveness of the systems to ensure that it has considered all significant aspects of risk management and internal control for the company for the year under review and up to the date of approval of the annual report and accounts. The board should define the processes to be adopted for this review, including drawing on the results of the board's on-going process such that it will obtain sound, appropriately documented, evidence to support its statement in the company's annual report and accounts.

43. The annual review of effectiveness should, in particular, consider:
   - the company's willingness to take on risk (its "risk appetite"), the desired culture within the company and whether this culture has been embedded;
   - the operation of the risk management and internal control systems, covering the design, implementation, monitoring and review and identification of risks and determination of those which are principal to the company;
   - the integration of risk management and internal controls with considerations of strategy and business model, and with business planning processes;
   - the changes in the nature, likelihood and impact of principal risks, and the company's ability to respond to changes in its business and the external environment;
   - the extent, frequency and quality of the communication of the results of management's monitoring to the board which enables it to build up a cumulative assessment of the state of control in the company and the effectiveness with which risk is being managed or mitigated;
   - issues dealt with in reports reviewed by the board during the year, in particular the incidence of significant control failings or weaknesses that have been identified at any time during the period and the extent to which they have, or could have, resulted in unforeseen impact; and
   - the effectiveness of the company's public reporting processes.

Section 6

Related Financial and Business Reporting

44. The assessment and processes set out in this guidance should be used coherently to inform a number of distinct but related disclosures in the annual report and accounts. These are:

- reporting on the principal risks facing the company and how they are managed or mitigated (as required by the Companies Act 2006 (the "Companies Act") and the Code);
- reporting on whether the directors have a reasonable expectation that the company will be able to continue in operation and meet its liabilities as they fall due (as required by the Code);
- reporting on the going concern basis of accounting (as required by accounting standards and the Code); and
- reporting on the review of the risk management and internal control system (as required by the Code), and the main features of the company's risk management and internal control system in relation to the financial reporting process (as required under the UK Listing Authority's Disclosure and Transparency Rules).

45. The purpose of such reporting is to provide information about the company's current position and prospects and the principal risks it faces. It helps to demonstrate the board's stewardship and governance, and encourages shareholders to perform their own stewardship role by engaging in appropriate dialogue with the board and holding the directors to account as necessary.

46. As with all parts of the annual report and accounts, the board should provide clear and concise information that is tailored to the specific circumstances material to the company, and should avoid using standardised language which may be long on detail but short on insight. In considering how to meet the different disclosures summarised below, the board should bear in mind the need for the annual report and accounts as a whole to be fair, balanced and understandable.

47. For groups of companies, all reporting should be from the perspective of the group as a whole. An explanation should be given of how the board assesses and manages the risks faced in relation to investments in material joint ventures and associates. Where the board does not have access to, and oversight of, detailed information concerning those entities' business planning, risk management and internal controls, this fact should also be disclosed.

Principal risks

48. The Companies Act requires companies to publish a Strategic Report that must include "a fair review of the company's business, and a description of the principal risks and uncertainties facing the company". The Code states that the board should confirm that it has carried out a robust assessment of the principal risks and that the board should describe those risks and explain how they are being managed or mitigated (Provision C.2.1).

49. A risk or uncertainty may be unique to the company, a matter that is relevant to the market in which it operates or something that applies to the business environment more generally. Where the risk or uncertainty is more generic, the description should make clear how it might affect the company specifically.

50. The descriptions of the principal risks and uncertainties should be sufficiently specific that a shareholder can understand why they are important to the company. The report might include a description of the likelihood of the risk, an indication of the circumstances under which the risk might be most relevant to the company and

its possible impacts. Significant changes in principal risks such as a change in the likelihood or possible impact, or the inclusion of new risks, should be highlighted and explained. A high-level explanation of how the principal risks and uncertainties are being managed or mitigated should also be included.

Reasonable expectation that the company can continue in operation

51.   Provision C.2.2 of the Code requires that the directors should explain in the annual report – taking account of the company's current position and principal risks – how they have assessed the prospects of the company, over what period they have done so and why they consider that period to be appropriate. They should also state whether they have a reasonable expectation that the company will be able to continue in operation and meet its liabilities as they fall due over the period of their assessment, drawing attention to any qualifications or assumptions as necessary. Further guidance is provided in Appendix B.

52.   There is likely to be a degree of overlap with the disclosures on principal risks and any material uncertainties relating to the going concern basis of accounting, and companies should consider how best to link them.

Going concern basis of accounting and related disclosures

53.   Accounting standards require companies to adopt the going concern basis of accounting, except in circumstances where management intends to liquidate the entity or to cease trading, or has no realistic alternative to liquidation or cessation of operations.

54.   Provision C.1.3 of the Code states that the directors should make an explicit statement of whether they considered it appropriate to adopt the going concern basis of accounting in preparing the annual and half-yearly financial statements.

55.   Accounting standards also require companies to make an assessment of their ability to continue to adopt the going concern basis of accounting and to disclose any material uncertainties identified. In performing this assessment, the directors should consider all available information about the future, the possible outcomes of events and changes in conditions and the realistically possible responses to such events and conditions that would be available to the directors.

56.   The Code states that the directors should identify in the financial statements any such material uncertainties over a period of at least twelve months from the date of approval of those financial statements. Further guidance on adopting and reporting on the going concern basis of accounting and disclosures on material uncertainties to be included in the financial statements is provided in Appendix A.

Statement on risk management and internal control

57.   Provision C.2.3 of the Code states that the board should report in the annual report and accounts on its review of the effectiveness of the company's risk management and internal control systems. In its statement the board should, as a minimum, acknowledge: that it is responsible for those systems and for reviewing their effectiveness and disclose:

- that there is an on-going process for identifying, evaluating and managing the principal risks faced by the company;
- that the systems have been in place for the year under review and up to the date of approval of the annual report and accounts;
- that they are regularly reviewed by the board; and
- the extent to which the systems accord with the guidance in this document.

58.   The board should summarise the process it has applied in reviewing the effectiveness of the system of risk management and internal control. The board should explain what actions have been or are being taken to remedy any significant failings or weaknesses. Where this information has been disclosed elsewhere in the annual report and accounts, for example in the audit committee report, a cross-reference to where that information can be found would suffice. In reporting on these actions, the board would not be expected to disclose information which, in its opinion, would be prejudicial to its interests.

59.   The statement should incorporate, or be linked to, a description of the main features of the company's risk management and internal control system in relation to the financial reporting process, as required under the Disclosure and Transparency Rules.

60.   The report on the review of the risk management and internal control systems is normally included in the corporate governance section of the annual report and accounts, but this reflects common practice rather than any mandatory requirement and companies can choose where to position it in their report. In any event, companies should consider whether and how to link reporting on the review of the risk management and internal control systems to the information on principal risks in the Strategic Report and material uncertainties relating to the going concern basis of accounting in the financial statements.

Safe Harbour Provision in relation to the Strategic Report, Directors' Report and the Directors' Remuneration Report

61.   In considering where and how to report, the board is likely to find it helpful to be mindful of its legal duties and the so-called safe harbour afforded it.

62.   Section 463 of the Companies Act provides that directors are liable to compensate the company if the company suffers any loss as the result of any untrue or misleading statement in (or any omission from) the Strategic Report, the Directors' Remuneration Report or the Directors' Report. The extent of the liability is limited: directors are only liable to the company. Further, directors are only liable to the company if they knew that the statements were untrue or misleading or if they knew that the omission was a dishonest concealment of a material fact. This protection is sometimes known as 'safe harbour'.

63.   Accordingly, provided directors do not issue a deliberately or recklessly untrue or misleading statement or dishonestly conceal a material fact by way of an omission, they will not be liable to compensate the company for any loss incurred by it in reliance on the report.

64.   In order to benefit from this protection, it is generally accepted that directors should ensure that information required in one of the three specified reports is included in those reports, either directly or via a specific cross-reference.

65.   The exact scope and extent of the protection (including whether it extends to information included in a report on a voluntary basis) has not been tested in court and hence the legal position in relation to the inclusion of such information remains uncertain.

Appendix A

Going Concern Basis of Accounting and Material Uncertainties

Determining whether to adopt the going concern basis of accounting

1.   Companies are required to adopt the going concern basis of accounting, except in circumstances where management intends to liquidate the entity or to cease trading, or has no realistic alternative to liquidation or cessation of operations.

2.   Accordingly, the threshold for departing from the going concern basis of accounting is a very high hurdle, as there are often realistic alternatives to liquidation or cessation of trading even when material uncertainties related to events or conditions that may cast significant doubt upon the entity's ability to continue as a going concern have been identified.

3.   Provision C.1.3 of the Code requires that the directors make an explicit statement in annual and half-yearly financial statements whether they considered it appropriate to adopt the going concern basis of accounting in preparing the financial statements, and in identifying any material uncertainties to its ability to continue to do so.

Determining whether there are material uncertainties

4.   Accounting standards also require an assessment to be made of the entity's ability to continue to adopt the going concern basis of accounting.[4] In performing this assessment, the directors should consider all available information about the future, the possible outcomes of events and changes in conditions and the realistically possible responses to such events and conditions that would be available to the directors.

5.   Events or conditions might result in the use of the going concern basis of accounting being inappropriate in future reporting periods. As part of their assessment, the directors should determine if there are any material uncertainties relating to events or conditions that might cast significant doubt upon the continuing use of the going concern basis of accounting in future periods. Uncertainties relating to such events or conditions should be considered material, and therefore disclosed, if their disclosure could reasonably be expected to affect the economic decisions of shareholders and other users of the financial statements. This is a matter of judgement. In making this judgement, the directors should consider the uncertainties arising from their assessment, both individually and in combination with others.

6.   In determining whether there are material uncertainties, the directors should consider:
    ■ the magnitude of the potential impacts of the uncertain future events or changes in conditions on the company and the likelihood of their occurrence;

- the realistic availability and likely effectiveness of actions that the directors would consider undertaking to avoid, or reduce the impact or likelihood of occurrence, of the uncertain future events or changes in conditions; and
- whether the uncertain future events or changes in conditions are unusual, rather than occurring with sufficient regularity to make predictions about them with a high degree of confidence.

7. Uncertainties should not usually be considered material if the likelihood that the company will not be able to continue to use the going concern basis of accounting is assessed to be remote, however significant the assessed potential impact.

Reporting on the going concern basis of accounting and material uncertainties

8. To be useful the disclosures of material uncertainties must explicitly identify that they are material uncertainties that may cast significant doubt upon the entity's ability to continue to apply the going concern basis of accounting.[5] Provision C.1.3 of the Code requires that the directors identify in the financial statements any such material uncertainties over a period of at least twelve months from the date of approval of the financial statements.[6]

9. In the annual financial statements, three reporting scenarios follow from the directors' assessment of whether to adopt the going concern basis of accounting and whether there are material uncertainties:
- the going concern basis of accounting is appropriate and there are no material uncertainties. The directors should adopt the going concern basis of accounting as part of the company's financial statements, make an explicit statement that the adoption of the going concern basis of accounting is considered appropriate and make any disclosures necessary to give a true and fair view; or
- the going concern basis of accounting is appropriate but there are material uncertainties. The directors should adopt the going concern basis of accounting in preparing the financial statements, make an explicit statement that the adoption of the going concern basis of accounting is considered appropriate, disclose and identify any material uncertainties and make any other disclosures necessary to give a true and fair view; or
- the going concern basis of accounting is not appropriate. Such a conclusion is likely to be rare. The directors should make an explicit statement that the adoption of the going concern basis of accounting is not considered appropriate, disclose the basis of accounting adopted and make any other disclosures necessary to give a true and fair view.

Half-yearly financial statements

10. Where an entity is required to prepare half-yearly financial statements,[7] the same considerations should apply as for the annual financial statements in relation to disclosures about the going concern basis of accounting and material uncertainties. Directors should therefore build on their understanding of these matters since the completion of the last annual report, update their conclusions on the basis of

accounting and the existence of material uncertainties and revise their disclosures as necessary.

Appendix B
Longer Term Viability Statement

1.   Provision C.2.2 of the Code requires that the directors should explain in the annual report – taking account of the company's current position and principal risks – how they have assessed the prospects of the company, over what period they have done so and why they consider that period to be appropriate. They should also state whether they have a reasonable expectation that the company will be able to continue in operation and meet its liabilities as they fall due over the period of their assessment, drawing attention to any qualifications or assumptions as necessary. This statement is intended to express the directors' view about the longer term viability of the company over an appropriate period of time selected by them.

Reasonable expectation and period covered

2.   Reasonable expectation does not mean certainty. It does mean that the assessment can be justified. The longer the period considered, the more the degree of certainty can be expected to reduce.

3.   That does not mean that the period chosen should be short. Except in rare circumstance it should be significantly longer than 12 months from the approval of the financial statements. The length of the period should be determined, taking account of a number of factors, including without limitation: the board's stewardship responsibilities; previous statements they have made, especially in raising capital; the nature of the business and its stage of development; and its investment and planning periods.

4.   The statement should be based on a robust assessment of those risks that would threaten the business model, future performance, solvency or liquidity of the company, including its resilience to the threats to its viability posed by those risks in severe but plausible scenarios. Such an assessment should include sufficient qualitative and quantitative analysis, and be as thorough as is judged necessary to make a soundly based statement. Stress and sensitivity analysis will often assist the directors in making their statement. These simulation techniques may help in assessing both the company's overall resilience to stress and its adaptability and the significance of particular variables to the projected outcome.

5.   The directors should consider the individual circumstances of the company in tailoring appropriate analysis best suited to its position and performance, business model, strategy and principal risks. These should be undertaken with an appropriate level of prudence, i.e. weighting downside risks more heavily than upside opportunities. This may include analysis of reverse stress, starting from a presumption of failure and seeking to identify the circumstances in which this could occur.

Ability to continue in operation and meet liabilities as they fall due

6. Directors are encouraged to think broadly as to relevant matters which may threaten the company's future performance and so its ability to continue in operation and remain viable. Directors should consider risks to solvency (the company's ability to meet its financial liabilities in full), as well as liquidity (the ability to meet such liabilities as they fall due) – which may be a timing issue even if the entity appears to be solvent over time – and other threats to the company's viability.

7. The board's consideration of whether a risk or combination of risks could lead to an inability to continue in operation should take full account of the availability and likely effectiveness of actions that they would consider undertaking to avoid or reduce the impact or occurrence of the underlying risks and that realistically would be open to them in the circumstances. In considering the likely effectiveness of such actions, the conclusions of the board's regular monitoring and review of risk and internal control systems should be taken into account.

Qualifications or assumptions

8. Any qualifications or assumptions to which the directors consider it necessary to draw attention in their statement should be specific to the company's circumstances, rather than so generic that they could apply to any predictions about the future. They should be relevant to an understanding of the directors' rationale for making the statement. They should only include matters that are significant to the company's prospects and should not include matters that are highly unlikely either to arise or to have a significant impact on the company. Where relevant, they should cross-refer to, rather than repeat, disclosures given elsewhere.

Appendix C
Questions for the Board to Consider

Questions which the board may wish to consider and discuss with management and others such as the risk or internal audit functions are set out below. If the answers to the questions pose concern for the board it may wish to consider whether action is needed to address possible failings. The questions are not intended to be exhaustive and not all will be appropriate in all circumstances, but should be tailored to the company.

This Appendix should be read in conjunction with the guidance set out in this document.

Risk appetite and culture

- How has the board agreed the company's risk appetite? With whom has it conferred?
- How has the board assessed the company's culture? In what way does the board satisfy itself that the company has a 'speak-up' culture and that it systematically learns from past mistakes?
- How do the company's culture, code of conduct, human resource policies and performance reward systems support the business objectives and risk management and internal control systems?

- How has the board considered whether senior management promotes and communicates the desired culture and demonstrates the necessary commitment to risk management and internal control?
- How is inappropriate behaviour dealt with? Does this present consequential risks?
- How does the board ensure that it has sufficient time to consider risk, and how is that integrated with discussion on other matters for which the board is responsible?

Risk management and internal control systems

- To what extent do the risk management and internal control systems underpin and relate to the company's business model?
- How are authority, responsibility and accountability for risk management and internal control defined, co-ordinated and documented throughout the organisation? How does the board determine whether this is clear, appropriate and effective?
- How effectively is the company able to withstand risks, and risk combinations, which do materialise? How effective is the board's approach to risks with 'low probability' but a very severe impact if they materialise?
- How has the board assessed whether employees have the knowledge, skills and tools to manage risks effectively?
- What are the channels of communication that enable individuals, including third parties, to report concerns, suspected breaches of law or regulations, other improprieties or challenging perspectives?
- How does the board satisfy itself that the information it receives is timely, of good quality, reflects numerous information sources and is fit for purpose?
- What are the responsibilities of the board and senior management for crisis management? How effectively have the company's crisis management planning and systems been tested?
- To what extent has the company identified risks from joint ventures, third parties and from the way the company's business is organised? How are these managed?
- How effectively does the company capture new and emerging risks and opportunities?
- How and when does the board consider risk when discussing changes in strategy or approving new transactions, projects, products or other significant commitments?
- To what extent has the board considered the cost-benefit aspects of different control options?
- How does the board ensure it understands the company's exposure to each principal risk before and after the application of mitigations and controls, what those mitigations and controls are and whether they are operating as expected?

Monitoring and Review

- What are the processes by which senior management monitor the effective application of the systems of risk management and internal control?
- In what way do the monitoring and review processes take into account the company's ability to re-evaluate the risks and adjust controls effectively in response to changes in its objectives, its business, and its external environment?
- How are processes or controls adjusted to reflect new or changing risks, or operational deficiencies? To what extent does the board engage in horizon scanning for emerging risks?

Public reporting

- How has the board satisfied itself that the disclosures on risk management and internal control contribute to the annual report being fair, balanced and understandable, and provide shareholders with the information they need?
- How has the board satisfied itself that its reporting on going concern and the longer term viability statement gives a fair, balanced and understandable overview of the company's position and prospects?

Appendix D
UK Corporate Governance Code and Other Regulatory Requirements

UK Corporate Governance Code (2014 edition)

Section C: Accountability

Principle C.1: Financial and Business Reporting: *The board should present a fair, balanced and understandable assessment of the company's position and prospects.*

Provision C.1.3: *In annual and half-yearly financial statements, the directors should state whether they considered it appropriate to adopt the going concern basis of accounting in preparing them, and identify any material uncertainties to the company's ability to continue to do so over a period of at least twelve months from the date of approval of the financial statements.*

Principle C.2: Risk Management and Internal Control: *The board is responsible for determining the nature and extent of the principal risks it is willing to take in achieving its strategic objectives. The board should maintain sound risk management and internal control systems.*

Provision C.2.1: *The directors should confirm in the annual report that they have carried out a robust assessment of the principal risks facing the company, including those that would threaten its business model, future performance, solvency or liquidity. The directors should describe those risks and explain how they are being managed or mitigated.*

Provision C.2.2: *Taking account of the company's current position and principal risks, the directors should explain in the annual report how they have assessed the prospects of the company, over what period they have done so and why they consider that period to be appropriate. The directors should state whether they have a reasonable expectation that the company will be able to continue in operation and meet its liabilities as they fall due over the period of their assessment, drawing attention to any qualifications or assumptions as necessary.*

Provision C.2.3: *The board should monitor the company's risk management and internal control systems and, at least annually, carry out a review of their effectiveness, and report on that review in the annual report. The monitoring and review should cover all material controls, including financial, operational and compliance controls.*

Provision C.3.2 states that it is the responsibility of the audit committee *"to review the company's internal financial controls and, unless expressly addressed by a separate board risk committee composed of independent directors, or by the board itself, to review the company's internal control and risk management systems"*. Further guidance on the audit committee's responsibilities is set out in the FRC's *Guidance on Audit Committees*.

Other Code provisions are also relevant to the board's consideration of, and reporting on, risk. For example, Provision C.1.1 states that the board must make a statement that "the annual report and accounts, taken as a whole, is fair, balanced and understandable and provides the information necessary for shareholders to assess the company's performance, business model and strategy". Provision C.1.2 states that "the directors should include in the annual report an explanation of the basis on which the company generates or preserves value over the longer term (the business model) and the strategy for delivering the objectives of the company".

Companies Act 2006
Section 414A of the Companies Act 2006 requires all UK incorporated companies that are not small to prepare a strategic report for each financial year of the company. This report must include, amongst other things, "a fair review of the company's business, and a description of the principal risks and uncertainties facing the company". The review should be a balanced and comprehensive analysis of "the development and performance of the company's business during the financial year, and the position of the company's business at the end of the year".

The purpose of the Strategic Report is to help "members of the company" (shareholders) assess how the board has performed its duty under Section 172 of the Companies Act, which requires that "a director of a company must act in the way he considers, in good faith, would be most likely to promote the success of the company for the benefit of its members as a whole".[8]

Disclosure and Transparency Rules
Section 7.2.5R of the UK Listing Authority's Disclosure and Transparency Rules states that companies whose securities are admitted to trading on a regulated market (which includes all companies with Premium or Standard listings in the UK) are required to include in the corporate governance statement contained in their annual report and accounts "a description of the main features of the company's internal control and risk management systems in relation to the financial reporting process".

Separately, the Disclosure and Transparency Rules also require companies to include in their half-yearly financial reports a description of the principal risks and uncertainties for the remaining six months of the year (DTR 4.2.7) and, where accounting policies are to be changed in the subsequent annual financial statements, to follow the new policies and disclose the changes and the reasons for the changes (DTR 4.2.6).

UK Listing Rules
Under the UK Listing Authority's Listing Rules all companies with a Premium listing of equity shares in the UK, irrespective of their country of incorporation, are required to include in the annual report and accounts a statement of how they have applied the Main

Principles of the Code and whether they have complied with its provisions. Where they have not complied with a provision, they are required to explain the reason.

Under Listing Rule LR 9.8.6R (3), the annual report for a premium listed company must include "A statement made by the directors that the business is a going concern, together with supporting assumptions or qualifications as necessary, that has been prepared in accordance with Going Concern and Liquidity Risk: Guidance for Directors of UK Companies 2009, published by the Financial Reporting Council in October 2009". The FRC has contacted the Financial Conduct Authority and companies should use this guidance for reporting years starting on or after 1 October 2014 though the reference to out of date guidance is being updated.

Accounting Standards

Paragraph 25 of International Accounting Standard 1 (IAS 1)[9] states that: "When preparing financial statements, management shall make an assessment of an entity's ability to continue as a going concern. An entity shall prepare financial statements on a going concern basis unless management either intends to liquidate the entity or to cease trading, or has no realistic alternative but to do so. When management is aware, in making its assessment, of material uncertainties related to events or conditions that may cast significant doubt upon the entity's ability to continue as a going concern, the entity shall disclose those uncertainties. When an entity does not prepare financial statements on a going concern basis, it shall disclose that fact, together with the basis on which it prepared the financial statements and the reason why the entity is not regarded as a going concern".

Other regulatory requirements

Some companies may be subject to other relevant regulatory requirements, for example because they operate within a regulated sector or because they are registered or listed in more than one jurisdiction. Companies will need to bear any such requirements in mind when considering how to apply this guidance.

Notes

1   The UK Corporate Governance Code applies to all companies with a Premium listing of equity shares on the London Stock Exchange regardless of whether they are incorporated in the UK or elsewhere.

2   Principal risks are defined in the Guidance on the Strategic Report (2014) – see: https://www.frc.org.uk/Our-Work/Publications/Accounting-and-Reporting-Policy/Guidance-on-the-Strategic-Report.pdf. A principal risk is a risk or combination of risks that can seriously affect the performance, future prospects or reputation of the entity. These should include those risks that would threaten its business model, future performance, solvency or liquidity.

3   The Companies Act 2006 requires companies to provide a Strategic Report.

4   IAS 1 paragraphs 25 and 26.

5   IFRIC Update July 2010.

6   IAS 1 paragraph 26 requires that the minimum period considered be at least, but not limited to, twelve months from the reporting date. FRS 102 paragraph 3.8 requires that the minimum period considered be at least, but not limited to, twelve months from the date the financial statements are authorised for issue.

7   Companies listed on a regulated market are required under the Disclosure and Transparency Rules to produce half-yearly financial reports.

8   FRC Guidance on the Strategic Report: https://www.frc.org.uk/Our-Work/Publications/ Accounting-and- Reporting-Policy/Guidance-on-the-Strategic-Report.pdf.

9   The equivalent requirement under UK GAAP is in paragraphs 3.8 – 3.9 of FRS 102.

Index